A Genealogical History

of

The Montgomerys
and
Their Descendants

by
David B. Montgomery

Originally Published 1903
By J.P. Cox
Owensville, Indiana

THIS SPECIAL EDITION OF

A GENEALOGICAL HISTORY OF
THE MONTGOMERYS
AND THEIR DESCENDANTS

ORIGINALLY PUBLISHED IN 1903

WAS ESPECIALLY CREATED FOR

ROBERTA DECKERD

AND DEDICATED TO HER LOVING FAMILY

ISBN: **978-0615567488**
0615567487

BADGLEY PUBLISHING COMPANY
2011

ALL RIGHTS RESERVED

And Their Descendants

INTRODUCTION

About 1878 an aged, but neat and intelligent man, with gentlemanly appearance, and an entertaining conversationalist, appeared at my door and asked if a tramp could have the privilege of using his own material and take a shave and change clothes. The request was granted, and when redressed he presented a remarkably fine appearance; and on learning my name he began quoting poems from the works of Captain Alexander Montgomery's works. He was quite an elocutionist, and after reciting several pieces politely left us by bidding us adieu by a wave of the hand and passed on. I had been interested in these poems before, but this increased my desire to know more of the man who wrote them. This was really the first beginning of my researches into the history of the Montgomery family.

About this time Hon. J. W. Montgomery, an uncle of mine, dictated to me a partial genealogy of the Montgomerys in south-western Indiana, who had settled here in 1806-11-14.

Also a Mr. Al. Barclay, of Evansville, Ind., and Mr. Marshall Mauck, a school-teacher in the neighborhood, called on me about this time. Mr. Barclay, in our conversation, referred to the honorable record the Montgomery family had made in the world's history. He mentioned the history of Normandy, which work I soon consulted, which gave much information of which I had known little before.

Later on, about 1892, Mr. Arthur Hudelson, an educated and very brilliant young man of Owensville, Ind., but at that time a reporter on one of the great daily papers of Chicago, Ill., while in the Cook County Library of Chicago, saw the history of the Montgomery family published in 1863 by Thomas H. Montgomery, of Philadelphia, and very thoughtfully notified me of his find. It is proper to state here that it is probable that this work is in all the libraries of most of the large cities in the United States. There are many libraries in which it is not found, and as genealogical history has been so much neglected during the last two hundred years, but few people were interested sufficiently to look after such works to any great extent.

After learning of this work, I set about trying to find a copy *to* purchase. In the meantime, Jessie, daughter of Dr. T. J. Montgomery of Owensville, Ind., and wife of Hon. Woodfin D. Robinson, Judge of the Appellate Court, Indianapolis, Ind., had become interested in family genealogies and sought information from the writer on this question. He told her of the work at Chicago and of the two copies in the National Library at Washington, D. C.

Not long after this, or about 1898, Mr. and Mrs. Robinson made a visit to Washington, and consulted the work of Thomas H. Montgomery in the National Library, and were so much interested that they sought, found and purchased a copy from a dealer in secondhand books, and tried to find a copy for the writer, but did not succeed. While there are quite a number of these books in existence, they are not easily found. In reply to my inquiries parties said that they had not seen a copy for ten years, notwithstanding they had had many calls for them.

Finally, in 1900, through the kindness of Mr. Dransfield, Secretary of the New Harmony Library, New Harmony, Ind., I obtained a copy. Since then I have seen other copies; one in the library of Cincinnati, Ohio, and one in the library of Judge H. P. Montgomery, of Georgetown, Ky. By December of the year 1900 I secured a copy of the Montgomery Manuscript from the Robert Clark Co., Cincinnati, Ohio, by William Montgomery, published in Belfast. 1830, and is a book of 472 pages, with copious notes.

PREVIOUS HISTORIES

The histories principally devoted to the Montgomery family are as follows: Note 5, page 2, Montgomery's MS., says—"It is supposed that there had existed at Eglinton Castle a MS. account of the Montgomery family in Scotland, which was destroyed when that old pile was burnt by the Cunninghams in 1528." Therefore the work of William Montgomery, written between 1698 and 1704, is the earliest existing attempt to illustrate the family history, and it is especially valuable because treating of persons who came within the reach of his personal knowledge and events that had occurred during the period of his own life. Since these memoirs were written the following compilations have been made, intended by their authors chiefly to illustrate the genealogical history of the Montgomerys:

1. Hugh Montgomery, of Broomslands, in the parish of Irvin, compiled, prior to the year 1760 what is known as the Broomslands Manuscript, containing records of the Montgomery family from an early period. The author of this work, which is still in manuscript, died in 1766, aged eighty years.

2. John Hamilton Montgomery of Barnahill, in the County of Ayr, who was a captain in the 76th Regiment, wrote a genealogy of the family of the Montgomerys compiled from various authorities, which also remains in manuscript. Patterson's account of the parishes and families of Ayrshire, Vol. 11, page 225, note 3. Mrs. E. G. S. Reilly printed for private circulation in 1842 a genealogical history of the family of Montgomerys comprising the lines of Eglinton and Braidstane in Scotland, and Mt. Alexander and Grey-Abbey in Ireland. This lady was the daughter of the Rev. Hugh Montgomery of Rosemount, who died in 1815, and a descendant through John of Gransheogh, in common with the author of the Montgomery Manuscript in the Braidstane line.

4. William Anderson printed at Edinburgh, in 1858, a genealogical account of the family of Montgomerie, formerly of Brigend of Doon Ayrshire, lineal representative of the ancient and noble families of Eglinton and Lyle. This account commences only with the beginning of the sixteenth century.

5. James Fraser published at Edinburgh, in 1859, two volumes, quarto, entitled Memorials of the Montgomeries, Earls of Eglinton. This is a most valuable work, principally because in it are printed many original letters, charters and marriage contracts. The letters contain much important information on public as well as family affairs between the years 1170 and 1728.

6. Thomas Harrison Montgomery published at Philadelphia, in 1863, a genealogical history of the Montgomerys, including Montgomery pedigree—a work which contains much information respecting the families of the surname who immigrated to the United States.

In his preface the author says, "Many years ago my attention was drawn to the examination of records and doings of the generations of Montgomerys immediately preceding that one which came to America. This was due chiefly to the perusal of documents and papers brought from Scotland to this country by the first one of the family who crossed the ocean. William Montgomery, of Brigend, now more than one hundred and sixty years ago, or in 1702, came with his wife and children and settled in the province of East New Jersey, on the lands of his father-in-law, who was one of its largest proprietors. He brought with much care many valuable manuscripts relating to his ancestry, the majority of which are preserved by his representatives at this day; many are undoubtedly missing, as no special attention seemed to be paid to their preservation by his descendants until within the last thirty years." This author is in error when he supposes that William Montgomery of Brigend, who settled in East New Jersey in 1702, to have been the first to cross the ocean, as will be seen later on in this work, pointed out by Judge H. P. Montgomery, and elsewhere. Others were here as early as 1666.

The last mentioned author. Thomas Harrison Montgomery was born in Philadelphia, Penn., Feb. 23. 1830, and is now (1902) living in that city. I have had considerable correspondence with him, and have found him to be an obliging and willing helper in this work. So far as the author treats of the Montgomery's in America his remarks relate principally to those in and east of Pennsylvania. However, he mentions others in several of the western states; mentions those in Noddaway and Andrews counties, Missouri, and those in Macoupin County, Illinois, and some in Virginia; but of that vast number that settled in Missouri, North Carolina, Kentucky, Ohio, Indiana, South Carolina. Georgia, Tennessee, Mississippi, and other states, he knew absolutely nothing. But I have understood that his sons contemplate re-publishing his valuable work with much valuable additional information. We shall anxiously await this important work.

Then Professor Frank Montgomery, of Granville, Ohio, now of Davenport, Iowa, has given us an admirable account of the Montgomerys and Somervilles "who emigrated to America from Ireland in the opening years of the 19th century" and settled in Virginia, subsequently moving to Ohio. That part of the above work which refers to the Montgomerys will appear in this work and will prove interesting to all its readers.

Then one among the most important documents of traditional information, nearly all of which has been substantiated by historical facts, is the Notes taken by Mrs. Clara Montgomery White, of Chicago, Ill., given out by her father, Commodore J. Ed. Montgomery. Mrs. White jotted down these notes for her own satisfaction as they were repeatedly told her by her father, who had received them from his grandfather, Samuel Montgomery, who was also the grandfather of Judge H. P. Montgomery, of Georgetown, Ky. These notes were put on a printed sheet for the satisfaction of the immediate family of Commodore Montgomery, and they have proved of inestimable value to that host of relatives in the South and West. Clearly established, as will be seen in this work, a chain of relationship runs back to at least 1666 in America. The relatives have all vied with each other to see who could do the most favors in furnishing the necessary material for this work, for which I am truly grateful, and without which the work could not have been accomplished.

I must not fail to mention others who have rendered especial services in this work, and without whose services the work would have been much less interesting than it is. Judge H. P. Montgomery, of Georgetown, Ky., whose picture and a sketch of his busy life appear on page (see index), has proven himself a worker indeed, as his sketch furnished with 1620 names will abundantly show.

Then W. G. Montgomery, of Birmingham, Ala., of whom I learned through Judge Montgomery, by the loan of books and personal work, has done much to advance the work. He is connected with the Montgomery-Houston family.

Then Frank S. Montgomery, whose sketch and picture appear on page (see index), is unexcelled in finding and obtaining material from the isolated branches of Montgomerys scattered all over the United States, Canada and elsewhere, as this work will show.

Then Bishop Montgomery, of Los Angeles, California, and many others, as their letters will show, have rendered valuable services.

Then comes Honorable Sylvester Benson, of Owensville, Ind., the ex-County commissioner of Gibson County, and large land owner of Montgomery Township, born July 10, 1823 and raised among the older Montgomerys and lives among the younger ones, and who knows more of the Montgomerys hero than we know of ourselves. Therefore he has enabled us to do what could not possibly have otherwise been done. With his assistance and the little manuscript left by Hon. J. W. Montgomery and one left by John D. Mounts are the bases from which the work here in south-western Indiana have been compiled.

Then Dr. Belton Landrum of Campobello, South Carolina, gives an excellent account of the Montgomerys in South Carolina. The Doctor is a descendant of the Montgomerys and an author of note.

Col. Win. Cockrum, of Oakland City, Intl., has assisted me very materially in lending me books and with personal recollections.

Then I received much valuable information by consulting authorities in the city library of Cincinnati, Ohio, in November, 1900, for which credit is given by mentioned authors consulted as such material is quoted in this work.

Honorable James A. Hemenway, Congressman from the first congressional district, in Indiana, rendered me valuable service in the way of looking up the records concerning the revolutionary services of the Montgomerys.

William H. Montgomery and daughter, Clara Nicholson, of Orleans, Ind., also the history of Gibson County, published in 1889, helped me considerably.

G. S. Montgomery wrote a history of the Montgomery family, but I do not know when or where. It is mentioned in some of the genealogical references, I believe in Munsel & Son, of Albany, N.Y., who make a specialty of genealogical work.

Col. F. O. Montgomery and Brig. Gen. George Montgomery, both wrote manuscript histories of the Montgomerys in the nineteenth century, but I have not seen them.

I also wish to call your attention to that part of this work furnished by Mrs. Jasper Cobb, of Greensburg, Ind., and Mrs. Welch, of Jonesville, Va., also to that by Miss M. L. Montgomery, of Meridian, Miss., Col. Win. Montgomery of Edwardsville, Miss., and the Hon. M. A. Montgomery of Oxford, Miss. And to all others who have furnished sketches.

With all these helps I feel my inability for the work before me, and the main inducement for continuing in it is to at least place on record material that has been collected at much sacrifice of time, labor and expense, that if not recorded now may be entirely lost. It would be a great satisfaction to many of those writing to me to be able to find just a few statements concerning their ancestors who first came to America. In many cases this cannot be done. However, a work of this kind will preserve much of interest for our descendants.

Further, I refer the reader to The "Dictionary of National Biography," Vol. 38, pages 299-326, inclusive. Letters M. I. L., and M. O. R. Published by McMillin & Co., New York. This gives a remarkably fine account of the Scotch-Irish branch of Montgomerys.

The following other works have been consulted: Chambers Cyclopedia, Wheeler, N. C., Collins, Ky. Green's Historic Families of Kentucky, Heraldic Review, Boston, Mass., History of Augusta County, Va., Houston-Montgomery Family of Virginia and Other States. Munsel & Son Genealogy, Hatton's Genealogy, Military Annals of U. S. History Va. History Indiana, History Texas, History Tennessee, by Haywood & Ramsey, Foots, Va. History of Montgomerys and Summerville in Ohio. Leonard's Genealogy loaned me by Mr. Chas. Leonard of Owensville, Ind.

I have also made liberal quotations from a work published by W. W. Smith of Owensville in 1891, entitled "Marriages and Deaths." Mr. Smith informs me that this work is now undergoing a revision for a second edition.

And Their Descendants

CHAPTER I

ORIGIN OF THE NAME MONTGOMERY

We cannot learn definitely the origin of the name Montgomery. Nor do we know certainly in what country the name originated. It was a prominent and well-known name in French Normandy, in the ninth century, but there are strong evidences that the name and family were in existence many centuries before this, and probably may have originated in Danemark or Swedland. See the Montgomery Manuscripts, page 447, note 20.

Mr. Thomas Montgomery, of Philadelphia, in his history of the family of Montgomerys, gives quite an exhaustive account of this matter on pages 10 and 11 of his work, which we here insert for the benefit of those who are interested in this matter:

"The derivation of the name Montgomery can be but a matter of conjecture. It is suggested, however, by a writer who has made the derivation of proper names a study, to be a corruption of the Latin— 'Mons Gomeris'—Gomer's Mount, Gomer, the son of Japhet, being the hereditary name of the Gauls. There was more than one locality in Europe bearing this designation. Eustice, in his 'Classical Tour,' mentions that not far from Loretto in Italy is a lofty hill called "Monte Gomero,' which was the ancient 'cumerium promontorium'; and it is quite possible that a locality bearing a similar designation in Menstro, embraced within the hereditary estates of one family, should have conferred its name on its lords. This view of its derivation is confirmed by the name 'Mons Gomerici,' being equally with 'Montgomery' applied by the English to the town in Wales, subsequently named after Roger-De-Montgomerie, whose property it has become. The spelling of the name has been various. 'Moutgomeri' and 'Mundgumbrie' were the most frequently used by the earlier generations, but later 'Montgomerie' was employed altogether, until within a century, when many of the branches substituted 'Montgomery' for that having the terminal 'ie.'"

The Montgomery Manuscript, speaking more fully on this question, says:

"Other instances of other diverse ways, to the purpose aforesaid (that of keeping up surnames) I willingly pass over; because the premises are foreign to my intended design, which is not general, but special. And it being without my reach to ascertain whence the origin of the Montgomerys in the province of Normandy, is deduced as being a stranger to the records of the Count of that surname may have, and to what the French Histories, except Du-serres, de Girard and others as heralds, may mention thereof, viz: Whether the family are native Gauls and homologized in their style, with the Normans; or come in with them into that country, now called Normandy, from the Colony, who, transmigrating from the north part, perchance, of Denmark or Swedland, seated themselves there. I must lay this matter aside and not debate nor determine it: being totally ignorant thereof. But what I have read of the surname in France shall be remembered after mention hath been made of the Montgomery Famines in England, Scotland and Ireland. However, for the honor of the nation in general, let it be known to all men that there is at this day the title of a Count or Earl—the dignity is all one, though the words be of divers languages—in Latin called 'Comes'—in all his matters four kingdoms, viz: Count de Montgomery in France, Earl of Montgomery in England, Earl of Eglinton in Scotland, and Earl of Mount Alexander in Ireland. The like whereof cannot be truly said, as I believe, of any other surname in the entire world."

As to whether the Montgomeries were originally French or Northmen: "Count Roger Montgomery, who came to England in the year 1068 and not in 1066 as is generally supposed, had a son also named Roger who spoke of himself and his father in the act of foundation for the Abby of Troarn as follows: 'Ago Rogerus ex Normaviuis Normannus Magui autem Rogerii filius.'"

See Fraser's Memorials, vol. 1, page 1.

In these words Montgomery undoubtedly claimed for himself a Scandinavian descent, although Sir Francis Palgrave on the Authority of the Monk of Jumieges stoutly contests this point in his history of Normandy and England, Chapter 5, page 28, as follows: He, Roger, designated himself as Northmounus Northmonrium; but for all practical purposes he was a Frenchman of the Frenchmen, though he might not like to own it. This ancestral reminiscence must have resulted from peculiar fancy. No Montgomery possessed or transmitted any memorials of his Norman progenitors. But thus to set aside Count Roger's distinct assertion of his Norman descent some evidence would be necessary.

"The old Scottish minstrels or rhymes were expected to recite poems in connection with the surnames of the leading nobility who were praised especially for martial exploits."

"Very few, if indeed any, of the minstrels' chantings on this theme now remain. There was published in Glasgow in 1770 a ballad of the seventeenth century entitled 'Memrables of the Montgomeries,' which appears to have been manufactured from some earlier productions, and may thus be regarded as a representation of what was sung by the minstrels respecting certain martini exploits performed by members of the family. This poem was printed from the only copy known to remain, which has been preserved above sixty years by the care of Hugh Montgomery, Sr. at Eglinton, long one of the factors of the family of Eglinton."

'It was reprinted in 1822; the author represents the founder of the family to have been a noble Roman and the family name to have been derived from 'Gomericus,' a mountain in Italy. From this original seat a descendant came to France, where another branch was founded, which flourished for the long space of six centuries. The representatives of this branch came to England with William the Conqueror, and so mightily distinguished himself at the battle of Hastings that" this rhyme was recited in his honor:

> "Earl Roger—then the greatest man
> Next to the King, was thought;
> And nothing that he could desire
> But it to him was brought.
> Montgomery town, Montgomery shire,
> And Earl of Shrewsberie,
> Arundale do show this man
> Of grandeur full to be."

A grandson of Earl Roger, named Philip, settled and was the founder of the Scottish house—

> "Where many ages they did live,
> By king and country loved,
> As men of valor and renown,
> Who were with honor moved,
> To shun no hazard when they could,

*To either service do.
Thus did they live, thus did they spend,
Their blood and money too."'*

Now this Earl Roger came into England with William the Conqueror in 1068, and Philip was born 1101.

Although the family was not known in Normandy before the conquest of that province by Ralo of Hrolf, the Granger, it may have come there in some previous invasion from the North, a supposition rendered highly probable by the readiness even the delight, with which the Montgomerys evidently welcomed the coming of Hrolf. The facts, too, of the Montgomerys having retained their landed possessions undisturbed by the northern conquerors, and of their soon having formed marriage alliances with the family of Hrolf, lead to the same conclusion.

Professor Lee-Hericher, of the College of Avranches, referring to Roger Montgomery's statement, above mentioned, remarks that from it *"we can see that if the language of the Scandinavians was then forgotten in Normandy the pride of the race was not."*—See Ulster Journal of Archaeology, vol. 9, page 293. The reader can examine these evidences and decide for himself whether the Montgomerys were of French, Italian or Scandinavian descent. The above evidence is recorded in the Montgomery Manuscripts, note 20, pages 447-8; note 111, pages 148-9.

The Montgomery Manuscript, page 446, speaking of surnames that have passed into oblivion forever, and changes of one kind or another, says that the name of Montgomery is among the exceptions and still remains and exists in an unbroken connection. We here insert a brief account bearing on this subject, written by Frank S. Montgomery, of Shepard, Ohio, of whom we will speak further hereafter:

THE MONTGOMERY FAMILY

Yves de Bellesme, Count of Alencou in Normandy, who died in 944, is the first person of whom there is historical trace who bore the name of Montgomery. The family was, next to the King's, the most powerful in Normandy. (See page 543 of Vol. XVII, Encyclopedia Britannica.) All of the Montgomery families, throughout the earth, are without doubt descended from this source. Roger de Montgomery, who belonged to this Norman family, commanded the vanguard of King William's army at Hastings, Oct. 14, 1068, when he conquered England, was made an Earl, and settled there, his descendants afterwards spreading into Scotland and Ireland. The Irish branch was very prolific, and most Americans who bear the name are descended from some poor relation of Sir Hugh of Newtown, County Down. Here is my theory of the meaning of the name. 'Mont' is a French word meaning mountain, while 'gom' is Swedish or Danish for the word man: hence we have 'mountain man' or man of the mountain. As the family had an ancestry of Northmen or Scandinavians, and as the Norman language became mingled with the French, as it afterward did with the English and finally ceased to be spoken at all, such an origin of the name becomes plausible, although I do not claim that there is any proof of the correctness of this theory."

The Montgomery Manuscript, pages 356-7, quotes from Fraser's Memorials, vol. 2, pages 366-7. In speaking of the carelessness in spelling the name Montgomery it says:

"It appears that it has been spelled forty-four different ways during the interval between the commencement of the eleventh and the close of the seventeenth century, as the following list will show:

And Their Descendants

1.	Montgomerie,	1000
2.	Mundegumbri,	1170
3.	Mundegumeri,	1170
4.	Mundegumry,	1362
5.	Mundgumry	1362
6.	Mungumbry,	1362
7.	Moungumry,	1368
8.	Montegomorri.	1392
9.	Montgomery,	1407
10.	Montegomerie,	1413
11.	Montegomery,	1421
12.	Montegomorry	1421
13.	Mungumry,	1425
14.	Mongomry,	1438
15.	Montgumry,	1448
16.	Montgummery,	1466
17.	Muntgumry,	1468
18.	Montegomori,	1471
19.	Muntgumri,	1483
20.	Montgumury,	1488
21.	Mungumbre,	1489
22.	Montgumery,	1501
23.	Montgomerye,	1502
24.	Montgumerye,	1502
25.	Mongumry,	1505
26.	Mungumre,	1506
27.	Montgumre,	1506
28.	Muntogumbery,	1509
29.	Montgumiry,	1523
30.	Mungumbrie.	1524
31.	Mungumbri,	1527
32.	Montgumrie,	1546
33.	Montgumrye,	1546
34.	Mongomery,	1548
35.	Munghmry.	1562
36.	Mungumrie,	1562
37.	Montgomrie,	1563
38.	Mungomery,	1565
39.	Montgumerie,	1567
40.	Montgomeri,	1570
41.	Montgummerie,	1582
42.	Montgomerie,	1632
43.	Mungumrie,	1640
44.	Mountgomery	1674."

Notwithstanding all these changes and this carelessness, you can clearly understand that the name is intended for Montgomery.

The Montgomerys

Thomas H. Montgomery of Philadelphia, on page 9, says:

"The earliest records we have of the family of Montgomery place its origin in the north of France in the ninth century. Its history leads us up from the present through an unbroken succession of ten centuries in length to the first known of the name, Roger de Moutgomerie, who was Count of Montgomerie before the coming of Rollo in 912. A native of Neustrio himself, his ancestors were probably for many generations back natives of that province which, when conquered by the Northmen, was afterwards known as Normandy."

Mr. Montgomery, above quoted, follows up this statement with the succession of the male line with appropriate remarks of history and biography in a very condensed and interesting manner. It was our object in the outset to have this work of Mr. Montgomery appear in full in connection with this book; but after some correspondence with him along this line it was decided otherwise—for the reason that Mr. Montgomery and his sons have collected much valuable additional material and contemplate sometime in the future to re-publish his work.

Therefore we will quote quite freely from this work, but the work itself must be read to be fully appreciated.

The first Roger was succeeded by his son—
Roger de Montgomery, Count of Montgomerie, the second of the name, whose son—
Roger de Montgomery, Count of Montgomerie, the third of the name, was father of—
1—William
2—Hugh

These two brothers are represented as being restless and turbulent during the minority of Duke William—

William de Montgomery, the fourth Count of Montgomerie; He was accused of murdering the High Steward of Normandy and was speedily punished for it.

Hugh de Montgomery, the son of William, was the fifth Count of Montgomerie. He married into a very distinguished Norman family. They had four children—

1—Roger
2—Robert
3—William
4—Gilbert, who was poisoned by drinking a cup prepared for another person.

Roger, first son of Hugh de Montgomerie, became the sixth Count of Montgomerie. Thos. H. Montgomery says on page 14—

"But little is known of this Roger's history prior to the year 1048, the date of his first marriage. We gather the story of his Norman life chiefly from the pages of the Monk of St. Evrault Ordericus Vitalis." He says of him that *"he was a very prudent and moderate man, pious, a great lover of equity, and of discrete and modest person."*

"For a long time he had near him three scholars full of prudence — Gadebould, Ordelieins and Herbert—whose counsels he followed with great advantage."

It was this Roger de Montgomerie, the sixth Count of Montgomerie that successfully led the cavalry charge at Hastings on Oct. 14, 1068 (Actually 1066) which gained England for William, who placed great confidence in Montgomerie and gave him personal instructions just as they started into the battle.

Robert Wace, in his Roman de Ron, relates the following incident of Roger's boldness and skill:

"The Normans were playing their part well when an English knight came rushing up having in his company one hundred men furnished with various arms. He wielded a northern hatchet with the blade a full foot long, and was well armed after his manner; being tall, bold and of noble carriage. In the front of the battle, where the Normans thronged most, he came bounding on swifter than the stag, many Normans falling before him and his company. He rushed straight upon a Norman who was armed and riding a war horse, and tried with his hatchet of steel to cleave his helmet; but the blow miscarried and the sharp blade glanced down before the saddle-bow, driving

through the horse's neck down to the ground, so that both horse and master fell together to the earth. I know not whether the Englishman struck another blow; but the Normans who saw the blow were astonished and about to abandon the assault when Roger de Montgomerie came galloping up with his lance set and, heeding not the long-handled ax which the Englishman wielded aloof, struck him down and left him stretched upon the ground. Then Roger cried out: 'Frenchmen, strike! The day is ours!'" —Thomas Montgomery History, pages 15 and 16.

The Battle of Hastings
October 14, 1066

Roger was well remembered by the king for this hazardous service, and his already large possessions were greatly enlarged; and Roger did much after this to strengthen the king's cause. This is the Roger referred to in poetry on page 15.

Roger, the sixth Count of Montgomerie, had by his first wife— Mabel— five sons and four daughters: 1—Robert, Count of Belesame and Alecon; 2—

Hugh de Montgomery, Earl of Shrewsbury; 3— Roger of Lancaster; 4—Philip the Grammarian, who died at the siege of Antioch in the first crusade; 5— Arnulph de Montgomery, keeper of Pembroke Castle. His daughters were Emma, Abbess of Almenesches, who died on the 4th of March, 1113; 2nd— Matilda, wife of Robert, earl of Morton, half brother of the Conqueror; 3rd—Mabel, who married Hugh, lord of Chateaunenf and was alive in 1131; 4th—Sybil, wife of Robert Fitz Hamon, lord of Tewkesbury. On the death of Mabel, his first wife, Count Roger married Adeliza, daughter of Everhard Puiset, by whom he left one son, Everhard, who became one of the royal chaplains.—Montgomery Manuscript, page 449, note 22.

This Roger de Montgomerie, the sixth in succession, is said to have been *"one of the most powerful and influential nobles at William's court."*

He married into a *very "violent and turbulent family, which brought him into some serious family feuds,"* and Robert, his son, the seventh in succession, seems to have inherited the good qualities of his father and the dangerous qualities of his mother, as his life will show. Robert and his brothers, instead of following after his father's prudent course, *"boldly supported Robert, Duke of Normandy, in his claims to the throne of England, against Henry."* Henry's vengeance against the brothers drove every member of the family out of the kingdom, and since then no descendant of the name has ever had a foot of the large territories in England or Wales over which Roger or his sons exercised lordship. Honor was not lost, however, for they lost their estates and titles only in resistance to usurpation; for Henry's claim to the throne of England rested but on possession and not on right."

After this, however, he rebelled against Henry and came near overthrowing his kingdom, but was captured and died in prison.

At the death of Roger the sixth Count of Montgomerie, Robert and Hugh seem to have come into possession of the larger part of a very large estate left by Roger.

Hugh died four years later unmarried, and Robert obtained possession of his estate.

Roger, who had followed his brothers in their attempt to dethrone Henry I of England, from this cause finally (in 1094) lost all his possessions in

England, Wales and Normandy, most of which he had obtained by marriage. Philip, the grammarian, so called on account of having more than an average education, died at the siege of Antioch in 1097.

While Roger and Arnulph had little or no part in their father's estate, they ranked high among their countrymen as knights and men of worth, by their father's advice they married noble wives, procured for them by him, and both were made earls and for some time were distinguished for their power and wealth; but before their death they forfeited for their treason the honors and estates they had acquired. Their forfeiture was incurred by their having in common with their eldest brother, Robert, espoused the cause of Robert Curt-Hase in 1102. These possessions were in the most pleasant County of all Wales.

This Robert de Montgomerie had a brother named Arnulph who engaged with him in most of his ill-fated enterprises, and in several others on his own account, in Ireland and other places, and died in Ireland in 1120. He had an only son, Philip de, born 1101, who was the first of that name who settled in Scotland in 1102, and who finally married Lady Margaret Dunbar, in 1120, by whom he came into possession of au estate about six miles east and west, and seven north and south, and was confirmed to his successors by the middle of the 12th century.

This estate, which was the first of an extent and for two centuries the chief possession of the Scottish family of Montgomery, has remained their property, undiminished, for the long period of seven hundred years. This is known as the estate of Eaglesham, which signifies the church hamlet.

The reader will observe that I am following this line of succession only by way of reference, in order to give an idea of the origin and a few of the vicissitudes through which the early families of Montgomery passed, which brings us up from France, through England, Wales, Scotland and Ireland. Still, as the work proceeds we shall mention many prominent characters in all of these countries, also in Holland and the United States.

Thomas H. Montgomery, in his history, follows up this succession with clear and interesting remarks, as before stated, with William de Montgomery, the eighth Count, John de Montgomery, the ninth Count, William de Montgomery, the tenth Count, who had an only child, a daughter, thus bringing to an end the succession of the male line of what is called the First House of Montgomery, when the representation of the family devolved on Sir Robert de Montgomerie, Knight of Eaglesham, in Scotland, descended from Arnulph de Moutgomerie. Sir Robert was a son of Philip de Montgomery, who was a son of Arnulph de Montgomery.

Thus the eleventh in the line of succession starts out in Scotland. Sir Robert de Montgomery died before 1261.

This line of succession is followed up to the thirty-third in number and finally came to America, and the claim is made and believed to have been clearly established, that the representative of the male line is now 1865, carried by a lawyer in Philadelphia, Pa. —James T. Montgomery.

We give place to an account of this genealogy, taken from the Heraldic Journal, published in 1855 by Z. H. Wiggins, Boston Mass.:

"This very interesting volume has attracted much attention in England as well as here, from the well substantiated claim put forth therein, that the representative of the ancient family of the Montmogerys is to be found in the branch existing in America.

"The family is of Norman origin, the first of the name being Roger 1, Count of Moutgomerie, in A. D. 912. The sixth Count, Roger 6, concerning whom the historians narrate many particulars, joined the army of William the Conqueror and received great rewards for his services in England. He was created Earl of Shrewsbury, and died in 1094. His sons were Robert 7, Count of Moutgomerie, whose grandson, Guy, Count of Pauthien had a grandson, William, the last male of this oldest branch, (William's granddaughter married Ferdinand III., King of Castile.), Robert 7, Count of Morche, whose line became extinct in 1181, and Arnulph 7, Earl of Pembroke, ancestor of the present family.

"This Arnulph had a son Philip de Moutgomerie, who settled in Scotland and there had a son Robert 9, of Eaglesham and Thourntoun. From him (through Zulm 10, Alen 11, John 12, Zulm 13, and Alexander 14), was descended Sir John 15 de Montgomery, who married in 1361 the heiress of Hugh Eglinton.

"His son, Sir John 16, was the father of Alexander 17, Lord Moutgomerie, so created about 1448. His great-grandson, Hugh 20, third

The Montgomerys

Lord Moutgomerie, was created Earl of Eglinton in 1508. The third son of this earl was Sir Neil 21 Moutgomerie of Lainshaw.

"In the main line, Hugh, the 5th Earl of Eglinton, died in 1612, when the title went, by reason of a new charter, which he had obtained, to his cousin, Sir Alexander Seaton, son of his Aunt Margaret, Countess of Winton.

"The representation of the family now devolved upon the Lainshaw branch. Neil's son, Neil 22, married the heiress of Lord Lyle, and had Neil 23, who died before 1621. This last Neil 23 married Elizabeth, daughter of John Cunningham, and had:

"Neil 24 of Lainshaw
"William 25 of Brigand
"James 24 of Dunlap
"John 24 of Cockilbie

"Of these, Neil and his son John in 1654, sold their estates at Lainshaw to his brother John of Cockilbie, and this younger branch thus usurped the place which belonged to the Brigend branch as representatives of the family.

"William 24 Montgomerie married a lady of the same family name, though of what branch is unknown, viz: daughter of James Montgomerie, of Brigend, in Ayrshire. He had four sons, of whom the second and third died without issue, and the youngest, Hugh 5, became ultimately the owner of Brigend.

"John 25 Montgomerie, oldest son of William of Brigend, had a son Hugh 26, styled in the deeds as of Brigend, in 1654, who married Katherine, daughter of Sir William Scott, of Clerkington, and had two sons and two daughters. He died 6th of May, 1710, aged over 80 years. In 1692 he had joined his son William 27 in sale of Brigend to their cousin John. His other son, James 27, had a family, but none of his sons left issue.

"The oldest son and representative of the family was William 27, who married 8th of January, 1684, Isabel, daughter of Robert Burnett, of Lethintie County, Aberdeen and in 1702 he removed to East Jersey, where his father-in-law had a large estate. There he settled on an estate which he named Eglinton, and from this time the family is to be considered American.

"The volume under notice has a very full account of the descendants of William the emigrant, but we will confine our extracts to the line of representation.

"William's oldest son, Robert 28, married Sarah Stacy in February, 1709 or 10, and his heir was James 29, who married Esther Wood in 1746. Their son, Robert 30, of Eglinton, married Margaret Leonard in 1771, and was succeeded by Austin 31 Montgomery, son of John 30. This Austin 31 died s. p. in 1855. His brother, the Rev. James 31 Montgomery, rector of Grace church, New York, and St. Stephen's Philadelphia, had a son James 32. T. Montgomery, a lawyer of Philadelphia, who is the present representative (1865) of the family.

"In reviewing the vicissitudes of the family we notice two salient points. In the first place, the title passed from the Lainshaw branch in consequence of a family feud, carried even to the murder of the fourth Earl of Eglinton by the family of the wife of his nearest male heir, Sir Neil Montgomerie of Lainshaw, in 1586. Thus this line was shorn of its honors and estates.

"Again, Hugh of Brigend, father of the emigrant, seems to have inherited a valuable property, but be lost it all, as letters remain to show, by a lack of business ability, and very possibly by adopting the losing side in religious matters.

"Thus, though quite a number of family papers were brought here to America, the knowledge of the rights of this branch was forgotten and ignored in Scotland, and various junior branches have from time to time claimed the representation.

"After a careful examination of the evidence here presented it seems plain that the case has been made out by the claimants here, and so far as it is a matter of interest to the family, they may be congratulated on their undoubted right to be considered the main line and representatives of a very ancient and distinguished family."

CHAPTER II

We have seen that the Montgomerys have been prominent in France, England, Holland and Scotland, and we will now take some notice of them in Ireland. At just what time they first made settlements in Ireland as individual settlers we are not prepared to say. Arnulph de Montgomery was in Ireland on some of his warring expeditious in the latter part of the eleventh century. And other Montgomerys doubtless had settled there as well as in other countries. But the first prominent settlement seems to have been made by Sir Hugh Montgomery of Scotland, who was the sixth Laird of Braidstane and grandfather of the author of the Montgomery Manuscript. This Hugh afterward became the first Viscount of Montgomery of the Great Ards. This section of country in Ireland is so called because of the great number of hares or rabbits that were found along the banks of the watercourses that traversed its territory.

This Hugh Montgomery was descended from the earls of Eglintoune, and some of the families were very prominent—viz, Col James and Major, General Robert. Hugh also had three brothers who became men of note—viz, George, who was "for his worth and learning by the late Queen Elizabeth preferred to the parsonage of Chedchec and finally became chaplain to the court of King James I, and afterwards made bishop of a large diocese. His brother Patrick also, who, by his prowess and conduct, going from Scotland a captain of foot into France, did arise to great credit and a colonel's post under King Henry IV, and was killed in a fight where he had commanded five hundred horse. He had no wife; neither had John, his youngest brother, who was graduated Doctor of Physics in a French university or college. He, returning homewards, came to London, where, having practiced his art with good repute, he died of that sweating, immoveable disease which raged in Queen Elizabeth's reign; 17,800 persons died of this disease in London. All persons attacked by this disease either died or recovered inside of 24 hours. The only remedy found was for the person attacked to immediately retire to bed with their clothes on or, if attacked while in bed, to remain there, without sleeping, for 24 hours."

This Hugh Montgomery, after leaving the college at Glasgow, traveled in France and attended the court there for some months. Then he settled in Holland and became a captain of foot in a Scotch regiment under the Prince of Orange, great-grandfather of William III of England. Hearing of the death of his mother and father, which took place about 1587, and also learning that his sisters were married and that his business affairs needed attention, he disposed of his commission and returned to Scotland, and visited the court of Edenborough. He was favorably received *"as an accomplished gentleman."* and by many noblemen introduced to King James the 6th, and allowed to kiss his hand. The King paid him special attention, which continued to increase on account of a regular correspondence which he had kept up with his brother "George, who was then Dean of Norwich in the Church of England."

The information given in that correspondence was of vast importance to the King. Hugh Montgomery married about this time, and lived in peace with his neighbors and friends until he was insulted by one Mr. Cunningham. Montgomery sought satisfaction, but Cunningham refused to meet him and went to Loudon. Montgomery followed him. Then Cunningham went to Holland. Montgomery found him there and forced him into a combat with swords. A powerful thrust from the sword of Montgomery hit the buckle on Cunningham's belt which threw him on his back. Montgomery, supposing that he had killed Cunningham, put up his sword and started to leave, when he was arrested and placed in prison, from which he escaped by strategy and again reached Scotland; and through the intervention of friends and the King, concessions seem to have been made on both sides and a temporary reconciliation effected. The insult referred to above seems to have had some reference to an old feud that had existed between the Montgomerys and Cunninghams for a long period of time, which in boldness, desperation and results equaled anything that ever took place between feudalists.

We will here insert an account of this affair, taken from the Montgomery Manuscript, page 17. Note 2:

"The author truly describes this feud as 'old,' for it had its origin as early as the year 1366, when Sir Hugh Montgomery, of Eglinton, obtained a grant from the Crown of the offices of Bailhe, in the Barony of Cunningham and Chamberlain Irvine. This grant was renewed and enlarged from time to time, the Cunninghams, however, claiming the offices now mentioned as belonging from ancient and established right to the representatives of their family or clan. In 1448 James the II renewed the grant to Lord Montgomery, and from that date the feud continued without much interruption for upward of two centuries. In 1488 the strong castle of Kerrielow, a residence of the Cunninghams in the parish of Stevenston, was sacked and destroyed by the Montgomerys under the command of that warlike Hugh, afterwards created first Earl of Eglinton. In the year 1528 the fall of Kerrielow was avenged by the burning of Eglinton Castle, together with all the important family records therein. During the interval between 1488 and 1528 many terrible collisions had occurred, especially in the years 1505, 1507, 1517, 1523 and 1526. Although an arbitration held by the earls of Angus, Argyle, Cassilis, assisted by the bishop of Maray, had decided in 1509 in favor of Eglinton's claims, and although in 1523 the first Earl of Eglinton had been honorably acquitted of the charge of murdering Edward Cunningham, of Auchin-Harrie, the feud continued with increasing fury until the Cunninghams assassinated the fourth Earl at the Ford of Annoch. From that date, 1586, the strife began gradually to subside, but had not entirely ceased until the close of the seventeenth century."—Paterson's Parishes and Families, Vol. I., pages 51, 53, 54. Fraser's Memorials, Vol. I., pages 27-31.

About 1602, when James VI was proclaimed king, and political affairs seemed somewhat improved—and much of Ireland being at the disposal of the King, men who were in favor with him began to cast about to in some way take advantage of those opportunities. Hugh Montgomery began looking toward Ireland for his future, and it has been supposed by some that he sought an opportunity to take advantage of Con Oneil in his distressed situation, in order to obtain the larger part of his large estate in Ireland. We will here give a detailed account of this whole affair.

Con Oneil was of a prominent family and in possession of a very large estate, but it was taken from him once before this, and then restored to him. He is represented as being a very rebellious and a drunken, sluggish man. The trouble out of which Montgomery delivered him was brought on by forcing his servants into an open conflict with the Queen's soldiers, in which one of the soldiers was mortally wounded. The penalty for this offense was imprisonment and death. On page 37—and note 19—of Montgomery's Manuscript we find the following concerning this affair:

His life and estate: Among Con's enemies, the most formidable was supposed to be Sir Arthur Chichester.

"The author of the Stewart Manuscript mentions the peril with which Con was threatened from this quarter as follows: This man Con being rebellious, and his land falling to the King, was apprehended by the then deputy Chichester and was laid up in the King's castle at Carrickfergus, a drunken, sluggish man; but he had a sharp, nimble woman to his wife. The deputy thought to have him suffer according to law and to be chief sharer in his lands. But divine Providence had otherwise appointed. For the woman, his wife, in the greatness of her spirit, taking in high indignation that her husband was not only captive but appointed to an ignominious death, soon resolved that the saving of his life with a part of his estate was better than to lose all. Therefore this she strongly intends and diligently endeavors. But in a throng of thoughts how to accomplish her desire she lights on this expedient, viz: To pass secretly to the next Scottish shore and there light if she could on some good instrument for making good her design. And God leading her to Mr. Hugh Montgomery of Braidstane in Scotland, a man sober, kind, humane and trusty, to whom she revealed her husband's case and her own desire, saying if Mr. Montgomery would be on pains, and charge to purchase from the King her husband's life and liberty with a third part of the estate for him and her to live on, the said Montgomery should with their great good will have the other two parts to be purchased by the King's grant. Montgomery, considering the matter wisely and maturely, entertains the gentle woman with all kindness till he was ripe to give her answer, which in short was this: that if she should find the way to deliver her husband Con out of the deputy's hands and let him have the secure keeping of his person, with such assurance as he could give that the articles should be performed which she had proposed in her husband's name, then would he make adventure and labor for the paid Con's life and liberty."— Stewart's MS., quoted in Dr. Reid's Hist. First Presbyterian Church, Vol. I. pages 82 and 83.

"The conduct of Hugh Montgomery is very different from that of others who profited also by the confiscation of Con Oniel's estates. Had it not been for his prompt and able interposition, Con would no doubt have met the inevitable doom of land owners at that period that could in any way be found guilty of treason. Con had no means and no friends, and when Montgomery began to expend money on his behalf the prospect of recompense must have been but very faint, seeing that Chichester was all-powerful in Ulster."

Accordingly Con made his escape by the assistance of his wife and others, and in due time arrived in Scotland and placed himself in the hands of Mr. Montgomery, who endeavored to carry out his part of the contract to the letter. He secured his pardon and liberty, and saw that he was again established in the rights of one-third of his estate"

The Montgomerys

But other parties interfered and secured to themselves one-half of the estate that Con and his wife had given to Mr. Montgomery, and still Montgomery was faithful to Con as long as he lived. Mr. Montgomery was made secure in the title of one-third of Con's estate in 1605.

Immediately he set about to place a desirable class of emigrants from Scotland on the large possessions he had secured. We find the statement made that in an incredibly short time—five years—after he had obtained possession he reported 1000 men at the service of the King, and it has been supposed by some that these were all Montgomerys; but that was not the case, for we find in the Montgomery Manuscript that of the first 51 families that emigrated from Scotland to Ireland and settled on that Montgomery land only six appear among them by the name of Montgomery. But all of those families were of that sturdy, industrious, honest class that so much improved the society of Ireland, and afterwards their descendants did much to develop and establish a permanent form of government in the United States. The Irish at this time —1603-5, were in a deplorable condition, having been almost continuously engaged in war for more than four hundred years and were treacherously dealt with by King James VI. But, notwithstanding this, it is evident that the Irish as a people were much improved by coming in contact with the settled and industrious habits of the thousands of emigrants that were brought into their country by Hugh Montgomery and other Scotch knights; and out of this amalgamation came the Scotch-Irish family, a large number of whom emigrated to America and largely settled in Virginia and subsequently in every state in the Union.

While Sir Hugh Montgomery succeeded in securing pardon for Con Oneil and getting one-third of his estate restored to him, the stipulations seemed very severe. The Montgomery Manuscript, page 21), note 36, says in regard to this matter that the other Irish, or such of the Irish as had no free or English blood in them, were forbidden by law to purchase land. And Englishmen could not even give or sell to the Irish. This law was modified to some extent from time to time, but finally, in 1703, the Irish were declared by the English Parliament to be incapable of purchasing at auction or of taking a lease of more than two acres. Shortly afterward another act disqualified them forever from purchasing or acquiring any lands in Ireland and declared the purchase void. Is it any wonder that the Irish have been a turbulent, dissatisfied, rebellious people?

Sir Hugh Montgomery himself had to obtain "a grant of denization from the Crown by which he was made free of the yoke of servitude of the Scotch-Irish, or any other nation, and made capable of holding and enjoying all the rights and privileges of an English subject."

Sir Hugh seems to have been very fortunate in his selections of families to settle his large possessions in Ireland. He not only encouraged farmers, but mechanics, artificers and chaplains, and soon prepared a place for worship. The farms yielded abundantly, and not only supplied their own wants but soon furnished a good foreign demand.

In 1613 Hugh Montgomery's province was organized into a corporation, with privileges of representing in Parliament and conducting a court. Hon. Hugh Montgomery was the first Provost of this corporation.

In 1610 a grand-nephew of Sir Thomas Smith set up a claim to the estate of Sir Hugh. The first Sir Thomas Smith was a most remarkable man, both as a statesman and in classical attainments. This litigation continued for two years, when Smith's claim was lost, chiefly for failing to keep the contract upon which his claim rested. Hugh Montgomery soon became involved again in litigation with Sir James Hamilton, and again the decision of the court was in his favor, in 1618. Later on the Smiths renewed their suits and some other litigation which also involved Hugh Montgomery the second Viscount, who succeeded his father, which was not settled until the breaking out of the rebellion in 1641. This was a period of almost continued law-suits for thirty-six years, which all together made Sir Hugh Montgomery's lands obtained from Con Oniel's estate a pretty costly affair. In 1634 Hugh Montgomery, second cousin to Viscount Hugh, represented the corporation of Newton Town in the English Parliament, and subsequently by Hugh, Jr., George, and William Montgomery.

The first Viscount, Hugh, died in 1636, at the age of 76 years. He married the second time, which proved to be a very unfortunate affair. She refused to live in Ireland and returned to Scotland, notwithstanding many additional improvements had been made for her especial benefit. This was a great annoyance to Sir Hugh, for his first wife had been a great stay to him; took an interest in all his affairs and in the developing of their country.

A funeral of Hugh Montgomery, the first Viscount of the Great Ards of Ireland, was conducted according to the custom of that day, with considerable display as well as with great solemnity.

The history of the second Viscount Hugh having been lost, but little is said of his reign, which was from 1636 to 1642. There were turbulent times in this reign, as it was in 1641 that the Irish rebellion came, and in less than one week a very large part of Ireland was in possession of the rebels. The Ards, however, did not suffer materially during that week. Montgomery Manuscript, page 153, note 4, says: "The second Viscount died suddenly on the 15th day of November, 1642, in the 45th year of his age. In 1637, the year after his father's death, he was appointed a member of the Privy Council. On the breaking out of the rebellion ... he received a commission from the Irish government and soon afterward from the King, to be colonel of 1000 foot and five troops of horse, the greater part of which he raised, equipped, and for one year supported at an expense of 1000 pounds. With these forces he joined Colonel Chichester at Lisbon and continued to take an active and successful part in suppressing the rebellion until the time of his death. His oldest son Hugh succeeded him. His second son, Henry, died young. His third son, James, was born at Dunskey in 1639 and died at Rosemount in 1689. . . . His only daughter, Elizabeth, married her cousin, William Montgomery, author of the Montgomery Manuscript."

This third Viscount Hugh Montgomery had received a severe fall, by which a fracture in his left side made an opening that never healed, and exposed the heart to that extent the beating or pulsations were plainly visible; and when he came into the presence of the King, preparatory to entering upon his official duties in Ireland, his old physician was present and informed the King of this peculiar matter. After the King had closely examined it, he said: "I wish I could perceive the thoughts of some of my nobility's hearts as I have seen your heart." To this Mr. Montgomery readily replied: "I assure your Majesty before God here present, and this company, it shall never entertain any thought against your concerns, but be always full of dutiful affection and steadfast resolution to serve your Majesty."

Just here, as we have mentioned several titles of honor which from time to time have been bestowed upon the Montgomerys from the earliest period of their recorded history to the present time, we will explain that a duke stood first, next to the king, sometimes governing a country without the title of king. Earl or count stood second in prestige and influence, and viscount stood third.

In the Irish rebellion, from 1641 to 1652, Sir James Montgomery was the oldest colonel, and Hugh Montgomery was the youngest at the beginning of the war. Hugh the third Viscount was given chief command of all the forces in Ulster, in Ireland, in 1649 and took part in all those terrible struggles with Oliver Cromwell's forces, and was the last of the generals to surrender, and finally, in 1650, made his way to Cromwell's headquarters and gave himself up. Cromwell treated him respectfully and made capitulations for their coming home and peaceably living there without deserting the realm or acting against the Parliament, and for being admitted their estates upon composition money to be paid by them as Parliament should think fit: which done, Oliver Cromwell went to England in winter of 1649, leaving Ireton to attend the blockade of Limerick, to which the Irish had retired for their last refuge to obtain conditions of peace.

Soon after this, however, they dealt harshly with him, as he seemed to be a veritable Napoleon Bonaparte. They compelled him to leave his family, relatives, friends, and go to London by way of Dublin, and not through any part of Scotland, and appear before a committee of *Parliament "to wit, the Rump,"* which banished him into Holland. He was forbidden to have any correspondence with Chas, Stewart or to come back to England or Ireland without the council of state license.

"The Rump," so the remnant of the long Parliament was nicknamed after 1648, when the Presbyterian members were expelled by the process known as "Pride's Purge." The Rump Parliament was one of the most distinguished legislative assemblies ever witnessed In England. Among its leading men were Sir Henry Vane, the most practical of statesmen; Thomas Scott, whose speeches are described as among the most eloquent in the English language; Algernon Sidney, a descendant by his mother's side from Hotspur, and as impatient as Hotspur himself of all courtly arts or kingly arrogance, and Thomas Harrison, who carried his daring as a soldier to the most chivalrous extent. The great practical error of this Parliament was its reluctance and delay in dissolving itself, thus giving Cromwell a pretext violently to put an end to its sittings in 1653 after an existence of thirteen years.

While the third Viscount Hugh Montgomery was thus banished, he passed the time by visiting in disguise many important cities in Holland, among which was the university town of Holland, where the author of the Montgomery Manuscript was studying. In all these travels he hoped that his disguise would shield him, but his noble visage would betray him and hotels would charge him as a nobleman. In 1653 he was permitted to return home, according to the stipulations made between him and Oliver Cromwell at the time of his surrender. But the hardship placed upon him by the authorities, which kept him passing to and from Ireland, was very expensive and trying on his health; so much so that life was scarcely worth living. But he endured it all and lived to see the Royalist fully restored, on the accession of Charles the second (1660) to the throne of England, and was made one of the commissioners to adjust landed estates after this date. And be it said to his honor that he was just and merciful in these adjustments.

The third Viscount was created Earl of Mt. Alexander June 20, and received the patent July 18, 1661, and died Sept. 15, 1663.

The author of the Montgomery Manuscript says that in obtaining favors and positions of trust the Montgomerys can never be accused of bartering or paying a money consideration for them.

The most of the Montgomerys in England, Scotland and Ireland were staunch loyalists.

We will here give place to a part of the will of Hugh Montgomery, the third Viscount, or first Earl of Mt. Alexander.

May, 1660. This will, which is preserved in the court of probate, Henrietta Street, Dublin, was drawn up before his leaving England and intended to confirm a prior arrangement of his affairs. His oldest son, Hugh Montgomery, succeeded to the family estates, his son Henry is liberally provided for, and to his only daughter, Jane, or Jean, he bequeathed only 100 pounds yearly. This lady died unmarried at Chester in the year 1663.

Following is the introductory sentence of this document: "I, Hugh, Lord Viscount of the Ards, being in my full strength and memory, but being now upon a journey into England and desirous to settle my estate, do make my last will and testament. First, I bequeath my soul to the holy and undivided Trinity, trusting in the alone merits of Christ Jesus my Lord, who came into the world to save sinners, whereof I acknowledge myself to be the greatest; and my body to be decently interred as my executors and overseers, or the greater part of them, shall think most fitting my degree and present condition."

The author of the Montgomery Manuscript says: "The elegy which is inserted in my opera virilio being too long to be herein placed. I have therefore only given the reader the epitaph which I made on his Lordship, as followeth:

>"'Here lies the much-lamented, much-beloved,
>One greatly hoped of and one much approved.
>Kind to the good he was; to all men just;
>Most careful in discharging of a trust;
>Compassionate to the poor, devout towards God,
>A cheerful sufferer of the common rod
>Which scourged thousands; not proud when he was high,
>Nor yet dejected in adversity;
>Unalterably loyal to his King,
>He truly noble was in everything,
>Yet died thus in his prime.
>But do not pity him who blessed is.'"

Montgomery Manuscript, page 254, in speaking of the most excellent qualities of Hugh Montgomery, first Earl of Mt. Alexander, in Ireland, refers to his reddish curly hair, which denotes vigor of brain to give counsel according to the proverbial advice—namely, "At a red man read thy reed." Note 56 on same page says, "In other words, learn counsel; take advice from a red-haired man, who is supposed to possess peculiar clearness and vigor of intellect." To read in this sense means to learn from. This word is sometimes superseded by "reck," signifying to care for, to take note of. For "read," meaning advice or counsel, some authors have "reade," and others have "rede." The poet Burns uses the proverbial phrase happily as follows:

>"In plowman's phrase, God send you speed
>Still daily to grow wiser;
>And may you better reck the read
>Than ever did th' adviser."

"Another proverbial phrase, not so complimentary to persons having hair of this color, was, when you meet a red-haired man, say your prayers, for he is not to be trusted."

This expression may have arisen from two causes: First, the Danes were a red-haired race and their atrocities had rendered them hateful to the Irish; or, second, it was a general opinion during the Middle Ages that Judas Iscariot had red hair, and in all paintings he is so represented. Even so late as in Dryden's time, that poet describes Tonson as "like the man with left legs and Judas-colored hair."

There have always been a considerable number of red-haired Montgomerys, and we thought best to give this note in full, lest the red-haired ones might set up the claim of being the only true, genuine stock.

We have stated that most of the Montgomerys in the old country were royalists, yet you will observe from the preceding accounts that they had many conflicts with the powers that controlled the governments; and if the uprising in Scotland in 1639 be called a rebellion, the acknowledged chief of all the families of Montgomery—namely the sixth Earl of Eglinton—was among the leaders of this movement against the arbitrary cause of Charles the first.

And Their Descendants

CHAPTER III

"Hugh, second Earl and fourth Viscount Montgomery of the Great Ards, Was born 24th of February, 1650," and he was not thirteen years old when his father died. He or his sister Jane, or Jean, were entrusted to the care of William Montgomery, the author of the Montgomery Manuscript, who, with Elizabeth Montgomery, was a sister to the first Earl of Mt. Alexander.

This the second Earl's estate and finances became considerably entangled and involved in the courts to such an extent as to bring almost total financial ruin in 1675.

In connection with the settling of the second Earl's affairs, mention is made of Captain Hugh Montgomery. Note 27, page 267, Montgomery Manuscript says: "This gentleman was son of James Montgomery the clergyman. He was the first Earl's constant attendant and friend, and known as my Lords, Hugh. At this time there were living six other Hughs, not including the young earl-viz: Hugh, son of Hugh of Gransheogh; Hugh, son of the Seneschal; Hugh of Bollylesson; Hugh of Ballyheny: Hugh of Ballysheogh Hugh of Ballymaclady. Hugh mentioned in the text is styled of Dublin in 1663, but soon afterwards came to reside permanently at Ballymagowan, now Springvale.

Fortune again came to the second Earle in 1685 and he became governor of Charlemount, and it appears that he had become tired of the vexations connected with those unsettled and disturbing times, as note 47, page 271, Montgomery MS., says, *"Hugh the second Earl of Mt. Alexander, being in London in the year 1666 and seeing the design of the King against the Irish Protestants, returned to this country having sold a troop of horse which he had obtained from the Earl of Essex a few years before, and retired to his estate in Down resolving to live there in retirement so long as he could honorably do so. This retirement, however, was soon interrupted by the appearance of an anonymous letter claiming that a general uprising was to take place on Sunday, Dec. 9, 1688, in which man, wife and children of Protestants were to be overpowered and murdered. Episcopalians and Covenanters lost sight of their old quarrels and joined forces, and chose Hugh Montgomery as general to command the Protestant forces to defend themselves against this expected uprising, which, however, never materialized; but the fear, excitement and consternation were equal to those of 1641, during the Irish rebellion. This, however, served some good purpose. The Protestant churches, which had been so embittered against each other, now joined in one common cause against the Catholic foe, and did not now scruple to hear of the other way of worship and sermons."*

The Protestants made two unsuccessful attempts to capture Carrickfergus, the stronghold of the Catholic party, but finally compelled them to a very reasonable compromise, which was to remain in force as long as no Catholic force was raised nor sent into those provinces.

Note 51, page 274-5, Montgomery Manuscript says, *"Time and the discipline of events had taught both Episcopalians and Presbyterians. After a fierce struggle carried on with slight interruptions from the time of the Reformation until 1660, the Episcopalians remained masters of the situation. In 1661 the Government ordered the Covenant to be burned throughout Ulster by the hands of the common hangman, because it was then adjudged schismatical, seditious and treasonable;"* and Presbyterianism not only revived, but was in reality very much relieved by this conflagration. At all events the Presbyterians of 1688 as a body never thought of pledging the Prince of Orange to ends of the covenant, and aimed only at obtaining religious liberty for themselves, sweetened by a very moderate bounty from the state known as "Regnum Donum." And the Episcopalians, although the dominant party, obtaining at the restoration all and perhaps more than they ever expected in the way of power, soon came to understand that they had too hastily adopted their idol Charles II., and that, being so loyal in 1660 as to take no guarantees for constitutional government, they were compelled in 1688 to fight for those guarantees at a tremendous cost.

Both parties were therefore to some extent moderated in sentiments and aims, and had become more charitable toward each other; for such men as Milton and Jeremy Taylor had been reconciling the religious world, in the meantime, to the grand idea of religious toleration. The Episcopalians and Presbyterians not only became more lenient with each other, but more tolerant with the Irish Catholics.

The Protestant forces under Hugh Montgomery and others espoused the cause of William of Orange in 1688-9, and met with disastrous defeat with their unorganized and undisciplined troops against the well-trained soldiers of King James.

The Montgomerys

Some historians try to throw the entire blame of this defeat on the second Earl Montgomery, but in a lengthy report of this affair he clearly vindicates himself by showing that the council of war overruled his plan, and that while he had been appointed to the chief command really he only held the rank of a colonel, and that jealous partisan parties disputed his authority to the chief command and thus frustrated his plans.

However, this seems to have lost him his former popularity until 1691, when we find him a member of the Irish Parliament, in the House of Lords, and *"From the delivery of his writ in the House of Lords on the 5th of October, 1692, the Earl of Mt. Alexander was a leading and most indefatigable member. He was appointed on all important committees of the House and appears to have been most regular in his attendance at every sitting."* See Journals of the Irish House of Lords, volumes 1 and 2.

Hugh Montgomery the second Earl was in 1688 made master of Ordinances and made a brigadier-general, and finally—1701-2-3— was one of a council that ruled Ireland.

This second Earl Hugh Montgomery died in 1617 and his virtues are summed up as follows:

1. Paid all debts contracted by his father and grandfather.
2. Frugality.
3. Christian fortitude.
4. Liberality.
5. Always a true friend.
6. His splendid composition.
7. His abhorrence to public show in devotions.
8. His loyalty to his church.
9. Kind to citizens and soldiers.
10. Agreeable to servants.
11. His hospitality.
12. His poesy.
13. His strength in council.
14. His learning and fearless statement of his convictions in church and state.

It is stated that he obtained all honors and offices purely on his merits, unaided by powerful assistants to present his claims.

Henry Montgomery, brother of Hugh the second Earl, succeeded him to the earldom and became the third Earl of Mt. Alexander in Ireland, in 1716. He is represented as being of *"sweet temper and disposition, affable, courteous and complacent."* He had one daughter, Elizabeth, who never married. His oldest son was named Hugh, and the other son was named Thomas.

Henry was born at Mellifant, 1656, and died 1731. Nothing remarkable seems to have occurred during the 14 years that he enjoyed the title of an earl.

Henry was succeeded by his eldest son Hugh, who became the fourth Earl in 1631. In 1703 he married Elinor, daughter of Sir Patrick Barnwell, of Crickstown, by whom there were five children, who all died in childhood. The fourth Earl died in 1744 and was buried at Howth.—Note 10, page 293, M. MS. Thomas, second son of Henry the third Earl, became fifth and last Earl on the death of his elder brother Hugh in 1744. He was named after his uncle, Thomas St. Lawrence 25, Baron Howth, who died in 1727. The settlement of the Earl Montgomery is dated the 25th of May, 1725, and was made between Henry, Earl of Mt. Alexander, and the Honorable Thomas, his son, of the first part; Valentine Jones and Daniel De La Cherois of the second part, Luke St. Lawrence and Lewis Crummelin of the third part, and Daniel De La Cherois and Mary Angelica of the fourth part.

By his document the lands of Donaghadee, including the town. Ballybuttle, Templepatrick, Ballynora, Ballywilliam and other denominations were settled on certain trusts for the wife, with whom he received a large marriage dowry. This earl left his estate and other property to his countess, excepting an annuity of 20 pounds to Isabella, widow of Captain William Montgomery, the author's grandson, during her widowhood, and 50 pounds to each of their daughters, Elizabeth and Helena. He died in the eightieth year of his age, on the 7th of March, 1757. At his death the titles of Viscount Montgomery, of the Great Ards and Earl of Mt. Alexander, became extinct. By the following will of the Countess Mary Angelica De La Cherois, the reader will see how the remnant of the vast Mt. Alexander property descended to the families of De La Cherois and Crummelin.

This will is quite a lengthy document. She divides her landed estates equally between De La Cherois, the elder, a cousin, and Nicholas

Crummelin, and her personal property is divided up among about two dozen other parties.

And Their Descendants

CHAPTER IV

Sir James Montgomery, second son of the first Hugh Montgomery, the first Viscount of the Great Ards, was a very shrewd man and was elected a member of the Irish Parliament in 1641. He raised and equipped a regiment of soldiers in 1641, at the beginning of the Irish rebellion, and drove out the Maglinis's or Magnuses', from Locahill. This Maginnis province was one of the oldest in Ireland, running back to A. M. 3529. See Reeves Ecclesiastical Antiquities. "The old Castle Dundrun, the headquarters of the Maginises, was a military position from the remotest times, and was in good condition when Sir James Montgomery drove out the Maginises and McCartins in 1642. In 1652 the garrison placed in it was removed by order of Oliver Cromwell and the castle immediately afterward dismantled. See page 310-11, note 37, M. MS. Thus Sir James protected this section of country for months against the McCartins and Maginises.

The 20th of April. 1642, Sir James was recalled from Lacale to protect the country Comber and Dundonald, daily threatened by the Irish under Con Oge Oneil. He returned at the request of his brother Hugh, second Viscount Montgomery. This recall was just in time, and a man with any less judgment in military skill would have been utterly ruined. Sir James had about eleven hundred men. the Irish about 3000; yet he so maneuvered, planned and fought as to finally win the day and save the Protestants of that country from total ruin.

One reason assigned for those 1100 men repulsing a force of 3000 was the cruelties imposed upon the helpless friends of the Protestants by the Irish. On one occasion they tried to push them out on the ice, so that it might break and let them all drown; but they refused to go any further than their enemies would go with them. So they took the children from their mothers' breasts and threw them as far as they could on the weak part of the ice and as the mothers and nurses ran to rescue them the ice broke and they were all drowned. The soldiers of Sir James Montgomery having these things fresh in their minds, it was difficult to restrain them from being precipitate in their attack; but the confidence in their commander held them in check until the opportune moment, and the victory was complete.

The reader will bear in mind that the atrocities were not all on one side, as there are numerous instances where the Irish were murdered in cold blood—and that even sometimes by the direct order of officers whose rank was as high as captain.

This victory of Sir James Montgomery saved the entire country about Ulster from the ravages of the Irish and was of great benefit to the British. There were Captain Samuel Montgomery and two ensigns, William and Hugh Montgomery, with Sir James on this campaign.

After the disastrous defeat of the Royal forces at Lisnastrain, December 1649, Sir James suffered all the inconveniences connected with banishment similar to other royalist leaders, and especially that of Hugh, his brother and second Lord Viscount Montgomery of the Great Ards, which is fully detailed in a preceding chapter. And while he was attempting to make his way to London in a small boat, he was attacked by pirates, and in an engagement that followed was killed and buried in the sea. He was the father of William Montgomery, the author of the Montgomery Manuscript. This son erected a monument to the memory of Sir James, his father, which is as follows:

"The Honorable Sir James Montgomery, a person of knowledge, courage, piety and worth, well educated at schools and universities, as his manuscripts yet extant do show; traveled to France, Italy. Germany and Holland, learned those languages and made profitable observations relating to peace and war; returning home, studied at the inns of law, solicited his father's business at the .Royal court, at the council table, at the Parliament and prerogative in England and before the government and from counts in Ireland; was second son of Hugh, first Lord Viscount Montgomery of Ards, and gentleman in-ordinary of the privy chamber to King Charles; the Major-Colonel of foot and captain of horse, which he raised at his own expense and by his credit, and maintained by his prudence and industry fifteen months in the Barony of Lacale, which he preserved all that time from the Irish of this country and their assisting neighbors— and many other valuable services performed during all that war."

The Honorable George, named after his uncle George, the bishop, of whom we have spoken at length in another chapter, was quite different from other members of the family; not much inclined to a college education, as many of his kinsmen had been, but a lover of the chase, in hunting deer and other game. And yet he was a man of considerable note. He was born about 1606, and at the required age made the customary visit to his relatives. As he was not inclined to books it became necessary to send him abroad with an oral instructor to call his attention to important things and matters and impress them upon his mind.

"His person was portly, his discourse manly, and his heart stout."

His discourse was neither of philosophy, divinity nor physics, but good, round, home-spun, rational sense, and was very popular in society.

After returning home and meeting many friends, and also having been introduced to the King and kissing his hand he again took to travel and met the lady that was intended to be his bride; and he was so much fascinated and pleased with her that he prolonged his visit several days. These things were taking place about 1631-3. His wife died in 1646. He bore the commission of a captain and died in 1674.

On page 356, Montgomery MS., mention is made of the "Gransheagh" family and it tells of one John and his wife and servants being murdered by the Tories, and a son Hugh who was at the same time left for dead, but was found and recovered. Also in referring to that branch he brings up a genealogy and says: "This coat of armoreall on the Dexter side belongs to Wm. Montgomery, a son of Major Hugh, son of Hugh, son of Hugh, all Montgomerys, and freeholders of the lands of Gransheagh, in Donaghadee Parish, Barony of Ards and County of Down, Ireland; which last named Hugh was son of Robert Montgomery, second brother of Adam, the second of that name, The fifth Laird of Braidstane in Scotland. The first of which lairds was second brother to Alex, Earl of Eglintons, Lord of Ardrasson, a very ancient family of that rank in Scotland, all bearing the name of Montgomerie long before the battle at Atterburn, A. D. 1388, against the Lord Piercy, who was taken a prisoner by the hand of Lord John Montgomery of Ardrasson, who with the ransom money of Piercy, commonly called Hotspur, built the castle of Panune and caused carved a spur in the stone over the door thereof in memory of that action, and of the victory chiefly by his valor and conduct there obtained."

Note 29, page 316, M.MS., says: "The chief who so distinguished himself at the battle of Atterburn was Sir John de Montgomerie, who succeeded to the lordship of Andrasson in 1667, through his mother, a daughter of Sir Hugh Eglinton of Eglinton. Sir John's eldest son Hugh was slain at Atterburn, fighting by his father's side. The spear and Pennon of Piercy were carried along with the body of the gallant youth to Edinburg Castle, from thence no doubt conveyed to the family burying place at Eaglesham or Kilwinning, and the trophies still remain in the possession of the noble house of Eglinton. It is said that when the late Duke of Northumberland requested their restoration the late Earl of Eglinton replied, 'There is as good lea land here as any at Chevy Chase; let Piercy come and take them.'"

The author of the Montgomery Manuscript gives quite a lengthy account of Sir Hugh Montgomery of Ballymagoun, commonly called *"my Lords Hugh,"* because he was in the service of the third Lords Viscounts of the Ards. Hugh Montgomery was born in the north of Scotland. His brother was a minister.

This clergyman has already been mentioned by the author as attending the funeral of the first Viscount, to whom he was related. James Montgomery was of the Kessilhead branch and the first Viscount's mother was a daughter of the sixth Laird of Kessilhead.

His grandfather, Robert Montgomery, Sixth Laird of Kessilhead, who succeeded to that estate in 1602, obtained a grant from Bishop George Montgomery in Farmanagh in the year 1618. These lands he granted to his second son, James Montgomery, on the 13th of August, 1623.

From this Robert Montgomery sprang a large male family, but what became of them the author does not know. *"Whether removed by death or into a warmer, richer soil beyond our seas, I know not; but when they were alive and at home they were called the nine bold brothers of the Katonne."*

When the Presbyterians were in the ascendancy in 1643, this Rev. James Montgomery was not only deprived of his pulpit but vexed and harassed continually by one Mr. John Drysdale, causing him to be cited to appear before the Covenant. On those occasions he offered to meet any one or all of them in his own defense, but this was not allowed. Then he boldly refused to denounce the service book and swear by the Covenant, and told them that they were too many hounds to pursue so small a hare. But still Mr. Drysdale kept up his vexing. Finally the two men met one day on the public highway, when Montgomery said: *"You are determined to deprive me of my office and salary, and you harass me from place to place by your summons; but here I swear if you forbear not to trouble me more, or if you presume to give sentence of excommunication against me, I will take my amends on your bay and bones; for you shall wrong me too much to*

The Montgomerys

cause my salary to be given from me." These words mortified the said John, and he had care to stop further citations.

He was made chaplain to the regiment of Sir James Montgomery and proved to be a valuable one, too.

James Montgomery had an older brother, Samuel, who was senior captain in Sir James' regiment, and was a member of the courtmartial which met at Portaferry on the second of March, 1642, to try Sergeant Walter Kyle for the homicide of Lieut. William Baird. Samuel was at one time a Major in Scotland, and died unmarried.

Rev. James died in 1647 or 48. His son, called "our Hugh," was put under the care of William Montgomery, the author, who cared well for him and secured a lucrative position for him with the third Viscount Montgomery of the Ards, and with the exceptions of a few reverses he fared remarkably well, and died, in 1707 at the age of 72 years, having been born in 1635. His wife died in 1688. They had twelve children—six sons and six daughters viz: Hans, Hugh, Hamilton, James, Vere; Elizabeth, Catherine, Jane, Elinor, Alice and Christian. Hans was made a priest in 1691 and died in 1726, aged 58 years. He had four children—May, Lucy, Jane and Alice. His wife, Jane Hamilton, died in July, 1689, aged 37 years.

The large family of Hugh just mentioned, consisting of twelve children, are all again mentioned except Vere, Alice and Christian; but they are all referred to as a whole family as being *"well-conditioned and dutifully humble and observant towards their father,"* the mother having died 37 years before the father. She was a very estimable lady and transmitted many of her good qualities to her children, as is always true in such cases.

It is said of this large family, *"In a word, I do not see a more orderly, regular household anywhere, without cursing, swearing, obscenity and debauchery, every one being industrious, yet without noise."*

And Their Descendants

CHAPTER V

SOME OTHER MONTGOMERYS

In the preceding chapter we have briefly noticed the Montgomerys of Blackstane, Gransheogh, Creboy and Ballymagouns. We now turn to give some account of the man that was a chief instrument in assisting the sixth Laird to escape from prison in Holland, as referred to on page 22. His name was Robert Montgomery, and *"he brought his Dutch wife over with him."* The Sixth Laird settled him in upper Cunningham in the Great Ards in Ireland. The first three Lairds took good care of the title given to this Robert, but in the minority of their successors this title was fraudulently taken away from Robert's second wife.

William, the eldest son of Robert, moved to Scotland and died Unmarried.

Henry, the second son, was in troop of the Earl of Eglinton in 1689; was married and doing well. His daughter seems not to have married so well.

The Montgomery Manuscript, page 386, says that many Montgomerys of lesser note came over to Ireland about 1617. The following persons of that name received grants of denizenship at this date: John Montgomery of Ballimacrosse, Robert and William Montgomery of Donoghdie, Thomas Montgomery of Knochfergus, John Montgomery of Redene, Mathew Montgomery of Donoghdie, Robert Montgomery of Edenamany, Robert Montgomery of Moneyglosse and John Montgomery of Ballymagorrie. Mention is also made of other Montgomerys. John of Ballyhenry and John of Betta Rollie were both men of considerable estate in Ireland, but under a change of administration both were dispossessed of their lands, and John of Betta Rollie was forced to take lands in north-west Ireland.

It is claimed that the majority of all those Montgomerys were free from most of the vicious crimes and wickedness of their days, and yet they had their faults, one of which was an over-confidence in the goodness and honesty of other men and from this cause buffered many losses.

STILL OTHER MONTGOMERYS

Hugh Montgomery of Derrygonnelly was a justice of the peace and was a captain of horse and fought under Justin McCarty in 1689. He was the oldest son of Nicholas Montgomery, who was a lieutenant in Sir James' regiment in 1641. This Nicholas lived to be more than 84 j-ears old and was made Master of Arts in Glasco; and his father was Hugh Montgomery, who was made receiver of rents to Bishop George Montgomery at Clogher Dyoces. This Hugh died before 1641.

Robert, second son of Nicholas, was a lieutenant in the army. He had the honor of bearing the standard at the funeral of the first Viscount in 1636.

Andrew, the third son of Nicholas, was a good preacher and was possessed of the degree of A. M. He was married and had children.

Montgomery Manuscript, pages 390-1, mentions Captain Hugh and Captain James Montgomery as being quite prominent men in 1696. The author says that the families of these two men furnished him but very little to write about.

The same author says: *"There are other Montgomerys of greater name and fame for warlike feats than those two."*

They are grandchildren of Mr. Alexander Montgomery of Doe in the County of Donegal. Being debarred by the Presbyterians to use the word, he took the sword and fought against the Irish and secured a command. He served several years in the King's cause in the Irish rebellion before 1649. His epitaph is as follows:

> "Now he to Nature his last debt bequeaths,
> Who in life charged through a thousand deaths.
> One man ye have seldom seen on stage or to do
> The parts of Somwell and Samson too.
> Fit to convince or hew an Agog down;
> Fierce in his arms and priest-like in his gowns.
> These characters are due, as all may see,
> To our own Dwin and brave Montgomery.

The Montgomerys

> Now judge with what a courage will he arise
> When the last trumpet sounds ye great assize."

And for the grave-stone:

> "By what here underlies, you may conclude,
> Whate'er he be, how either great or good,
> Nor might nor meekness can from death secure us;
> Here lies a parson utrinsque Juris."

The following is the inscription on the tombstone of Alexander Montgomery's wife in Doe church:

> "Here lieth the body of Margaret Montgomery, Alias Cunningham, wife of Alexander Montgomery, who deceased the 18th of June, 1675."— Manuscript Notes by Brigadier General George Montgomery of the Bombay Army.

"This Alexander Montgomery had a son John, who was a major in the service of the third Viscount Montgomery, and he was taken prisoner probably at the battle of Lisnastrain, near Lisburn, and was sentenced to death; but two ladies, probably the third Viscount's wife and mother, Jean Alexander and Mary Moore, interceded in his behalf and saved his life. This Major John Montgomery lived at Craghan and his will was proven on the 28th of August, 1679. He directed that his body be buried in the Lifferd Church and left 100 pounds for funeral expenses. He mentions his brother William and his dear kinsman Dr. John Leslie. He bequeathed Gurron and Castle Oghry, still portions of the Convay estate, to his son with a charge on them to his dear wife. To his seven daughters —-Catharine, Nichola, Margaret, Mary, Eliza and Ann—he left legacies; the largest 150 pounds. To Nicholas, his personal estate amounted to 1400 pounds. This will he sealed with the Kessilhead arms. The seal has the initials "A. M." and probably belonged to his father. In Ulster Office there is a funeral entry of this John Montgomery which mentions his son John and his grandson also named John. I have followed this and made Colonel Alexander Montgomery a second son division of the Donegal, Cavan and Fermanagh estates. Croghan was sold by Robert Montgomery in the year 1800. Castle Oghry is near Invor, County Donegal." Manuscript Notes of Brigadier General George Montgomery of the Bornbay Army.

The author of the Montgomery Manuscript saw Alexander Montgomery in 1643. The author at that time was only ten years old.

The name of the first grandson, as has been stated, was John of Castle Oghry, and founder of the family of Beanlien, near Drogheda, County of Louth. William Montgomery, the author, also saw him in 1696. He married a very wealthy woman—Lady Moore. He died soon after, 1696, and left children, male and female, by his first wife.

Alexander, Jr., the second grandson of Alexander. Sr. was, in 1704, a major in the army. He married Elizabeth, daughter of Captain Coles, the heiress of the County of Managhan and now, 1704, lives in two miles of that town. He has one son and a good estate, and is a thriving man and a great tenant of the Duke of Ormond. He is the ancestor of the present family of Convay, near Raphoe, formerly of Ballyneck. His marriage with Elizabeth Cole occurred prior to 1696 and he died in 1726. His eldest son, Thomas Montgomery, is said to have been disinherited because he married without the consent or contrary to the wishes of his parents. He probably emigrated to America, for his third son, Richard, became afterward a general in the revolutionary service and was slain at the storming of Quebec on the 31st of December, 1775. These facts were communicated in 1864 by Lieutenant Colonel George Samuel Montgomery, Bornbay Army, to Thomas H. Montgomery of Philadelphia, author of the genealogical history of the several American families of that surname.—Manuscript Notes of Colonel F. O. Montgomery.

Robert, the youngest and third son of Alexander Montgomery, Sr., was ancestor of the Montgomerys of Bessmount. In Tyhalland Church, near Managhan, there is the following inscription on one of his descendants:

Alexander Nixon Montgomery, of Bessmount Park, died on the first of April, 1837, in the 76th year of his age. As a husband and father he was unequaled, and as a Christian will be held in veneration by all classes and denominations of society. Mark the prophet —*"Let me die the death of the righteous."*

Mrs. Eliza Montgomery, wife of Alexander Nixon Montgomery, died on the 8th of May, 1827, aged 40 years.

The Montgomerys

Mark Anthony Montgomery, late Ensign in the 76th regiment, died at Manchester on the 26th of April, 1844, aged 20 years.

The three Montgomery brothers—John, Alexander and Robert—mentioned in the text, were Sir Albert Cunninham's grand-nephews, being the grandsons of his eldest sister, married to Montgomery, Esq., of Bonnyglen, County of Donegal.—Lodges Peerage, edited Archdall, Vol. 7, Page 179.

The Montgomerys of Bonnyglen, or more correctly Bunnoglynn—foot of the glen, are descended from William Montgomery, fourth son of the first Earl of Eglinton. Hugh Montgomery of Andimhood and Bowhouse was grandson of this William. Robert, third son of Hugh of Bowhouse, came to Ireland, sojourning for a time at Rosemount, where he had a son born in 1660, and settling afterwards at Bun-no-glynn. His son, also named Robert, married the daughter of the Rev. Alexander Cunningham, Dean of Raphoe.
— Playfair Family Antiquity, Vol. 7, page 861, as quoted by T. Montgomery, page 120.

We here call attention to Alexander Montgomery, Sr., and Alexander junior, and the supposed distinguished son of Alexander junior, and the father of General Richard, his third son, and to their many descendants and legal heirs in Ireland, and then refer to the claims of parties in this country to the supposed fortune in New York, said to have been left by Alexander Montgomery, and you will find that the American biography says that General Richard had a brother John and a brother Alexander. Mr. Lair, one of the claimants, says that he had another brother, Ezekiel. Mrs. Brickins says that Alexander had issue and that she is one of his descendants, and E. H. Z. claims that said Alexander was a cousin to General Richard.

We don't know anything about the supposed fortune said to have been left in New York by Alexander Montgomery, but give these letters of newspaper accounts for what they are worth, and will here give the views of one who has had a large experience with litigations of different kinds. He says:

"I think the New York estate is a mere myth, gotten up by some scheming trickster to get money out of confiding people."

There was a Hugh Montgomery, seneschall to the third Viscount Montgomery. The seneschall is the person who has charge of the entertainment of the Lairds. One of his daughters married Mr. James

Montgomery, curate to Grey Abbey. His eldest son Hugh died unmarried. He was an officer in the army of the third Viscount, and was taken prisoner at the surrender at Lisnastiain and shot, contrary to the laws of surrender. This Hugh had another son, David, who went to Carolina.

Several other Montgomerys are mentioned by the Montgomery Manuscript, and he concludes by saying that *"Diverse other Montgomerys with their families and flocks are come out of Scotland since 1692 and have taken farms in Ireland."* And he says there are many rich yeomen whom he does not know.

CHAPTER VI

LEARNING

Bishop George Montgomery, already referred to, was the most learned of any of the Montgomerys of his day, as to being versed in Latin, Greek and other ancient Oriental languages. Others were better skilled in war and agriculture. Though many others were well-educated people, Sir James Montgomery took the degree of Master of Arts, and many of them learned the French, Dutch and Italian by coming in direct contact with those nationalities by visiting and residing in those countries for months and sometimes for years at a time. Continuing on this line we find reference made to some of the Montgomerys who were noted on account of their poetical works, and refer especially to Captain Alexander Montgomery. Note 63, page 400, Montgomery Manuscript says:

"Alexander Montgomery, one of the most justly renowned of early Scottish poets, was thus uncle of the sixth Laird of Braidstane, afterward first Viscount Montgomery of the Great Ards." This statement of the author is very interesting, as it confirms the testimony of Timothy Pant respecting the particular branch of the Montgomerys to which the celebrated poet belonged. In Pant's Topography of Cunningham, written about the year 1610, there is the following passage:

Hessilheid Castle, a strong old building environed with large ditches, seated on a leachveil planted and commodiously beautified: The heritage of Robert Montgomery, laird thereof. Faumes is the birth-place of that renowned poet, Alexander Montgomery. The poet was born in Germany, although he was of the family to which Hessilheid belonged. The old castle consisted principally of one capacious tower-shaped building, which formed the original manor place of the poet's family. The Hessilheid estate was a portion of the Barony of Giffen and passed into the hands of Frances Montgomery of Giffen in the year 1680. The latter on getting possession built certain additions to the old castle which, with the original structure, are now in ruins. It is curious that, although Montgomery's poetry must, have greatly contributed to the improvement of the generation in which he lived, no sketch of his personal history or career was written during his life or even at the time of his death. Being uncle to the first Viscount Montgomery, the poet must have been son to Hugh Montgomery— probably fifth Laird of Hessilheid, who is mentioned among the lesser barons of Ayrshire as one of those who signed the famous bond in 1562 for the maintenance of the reformed religion.

This Laird of Hazlehead, or Hessilheid, had one daughter married to the fifth Laird of Braidstano, father of our first Viscount, Hugh Montgomery, of the Great Ards in Ireland, and another married to Sir Mure of Rowallen. These ladies were sisters of the poet and their children partook largely of the poetical vein of their brother Alexander. Sir William Mure's son and successor, also named Sir William, was a poetical writer of no mean pretentions. In a poem addressed by him to the Prince of Wales, afterwards Charles the First, Sir William Mure thus refers to his uncle's celebrity:

> "Matchless Montgomery in his native tongue
> In former times to that great sire hath sung,
> And often ravished his harmonious ear
> With strains fit only for a prince to hear.
> My muse, which naught doth challenge worthy fame,
> Save from Montgomerys she her birth doth claim.
> Although his Phoenix ashes hath set forth
> Pan for Apollo, if compared in worth;
> Pretendeth little to supply his place,
> By right hereditor to serve thy grace."

The poet Montgomery is generally supposed to have been born about the year 1546; but whilst the year is not positively known, the poet himself has fixed the day on which he was born in the following lines:

> "Quhy was my mother blythe when I was borne:
> Quhy heght the weirds my weelfare to advance:
> Quhy was my birth on Easter day at morne;
> Quhy did Apollo then appear to dance;
> Quhy leugh he in his golden chair and lap.
> Since that the hevins are hinderers of my hap."

—Scottish Journal of Topography, vol. 1, page 563.

"Chery and the Slae."—This poem, which is better known than any other of Montgomery's poetical efforts, was first published in Edinburg by Robert Waldegrove in the year 1595; but manuscript copies of it had been in circulation several years prior to that date. James the 6th published in 1584 his *"Revalis and Cantetis of Scottis Poesie,"* which contained large extracts from the "Cherrie and the Slae". Several editions were printed in the interval between the close of the sixteenth and the middle of the eighteenth centuries.

It is interesting to know that the "Cherrie and the Slae" must have been one of the agencies which assisted in moulding the wondrous poetical genius of Robert Burns. The latter has some happy imitations of Montgomery's style, and even certain happy adoptions of his very expressions."—Note 64, page 400, Montgomery's Manuscript.

The celebrated "flyting" in verse between Alexander Montgomery and Sir Patrick Hume of Palwort must have been written prior to 1584, as it is quoted by King James in his Treatise on Scottish Poetry (see preceding note), published in that year. This "flyting," which does not possess much poetical merit, was undertaken by Montgomery and Hume in imitation of the earlier and more celebrated "flyting" between the poets Dunbar and Kenedy. Both flytings, however, are now only curious as illustrating the peculiar adaptations of the Scottish tongue to the expression of broad humor or satirical abuse. All the *"advocates of Edinburg"* were not admirers of Montgomery's "flytings", as might be inferred from our text, for Laird Hailes has said that the poem only *"tends to evince how poor, how very poor, genius appears when its compositions are debased by the meanest prejudices of the meanest vulgar."* This announcement, however, savors much of a critical spirit.—See Irvin's Lives of the Scottish Poets, vol. 2, pages 200-1.

Again and again in Scotland, besides the "Cherrie and the Slae", which appeared in 1595 and in 1597, there were editions of Montgomery's whole poetical works printed in the years 1605, 1615, 1629. 1663, 1645, 1668, 1675, 1711, 1722, 1754, 1779 and 1821. Besides "Cherrie and the Slae" and the "flyting" he has written a lengthy and beautiful poem entitled "The Mind's Melodie" together with a great number of sonnets, odes, psalms and epitaphs (and his "Dumb Salesquimn" and his "Confession of a Sinner".)

He is almost the only Scottish poet who has ventured to write sonnets in his native Scottish language. Of the seventy sonnets there are many truly beautiful both in thought and expression. Some of Montgomery's minor poems give us glimpses of his life which, like the lives of most poets, was seriously beset with evil in various shapes. Here is an illustration:

> "If lose of guids, if gritest grudge or grief,
> If poverty, imprisonment or pane,
> If for guid-will ingratitude agane,
> If languishing in laguor but relief,
> If det, if dolour and to become deif,
> If travel tint and labor lost in vane
> Do properlie to poets appertane,
> Of all that craft my chance is to be chief,
> With August, Virgil wanted his reward,
> And Ovid's late als lukles as the love
> Quhill Homer lived, his hap was very hard;
> Yet when he died seven cities for him strove.
> Though I am not like one of thame in arte,
> I pingle them per pyttie in that parte."

In another sonnet we meet the following in reference to his difficulties:

> "This is no lyfe that I leid up-a-land
> On raw red herring resisted in the reik,
> Syn' I am subject som tyme to be seik,
> And daily deing of my auld diseis.
> Ait bread ill aill and all things are ane eik
> This harme and blaidry buists up all my bees."

In the verses intended to celebrate the charms of Lady Margaret Montgomery, Countess of Wintonn and mother of Alexander Montgomery, sixth Earl of Eglinton, we meet these lines:

> "Quhose nobill birth and royal blind
> Her better nature does exceid
> Her native giftes and graces guid
> Sua bonteously declair indeid
> As waill and wit of womanheid
> That so with vertew dois ourfleit.
> Happy is he that sall posseid
> In marriage this Margareit."

These lines contrast favorably even with Tennyson's immortal chant—

> "Howe'er it be it seems to me
> 'Tis only noble to be good.
> Kind hearts are more than coronets,
> And simple faith than royal blood."

The Montgomery Manuscript, page 402, speaks in highly complementary terms of these poetical works, but they are probably lost.

And Their Descendants

CHAPTER VII

MONTGOMERYS IN FRANCE

Montgomery's Manuscript, pages 464-5, Note 66, speaking of the Acts of the Montgomerys in France, says:

"French historians mention two Montgomerys de Lorges—namely, Count James and Gabriel—whom they call the sons of James. The former James, it is said, in order to sustain the pretentions of his birth, in 1543 purchased the County of Montgomery in Normandy, which had belonged to his ancestors. In 1545 he succeeded John Stewart, Count of d'Aubigny, as captain of the Scotch guard. He died in 1560 at a very advanced age—between eighty and ninety—leaving several children, of whom Gabriel, the eldest son, was the most celebrated. In 1545 Gabriel commanded troops sent to Scotland by Frances I. to sustain the then Queen Mary of Lorraine, who had been appointed regent during the minority of their daughter, Mary Stewart, afterwards Queen of Scots. After the catastrophe mentioned in the preceding note he returned to Normandy and visited Italy and England." The preceding note, 65, says:

"This accident, which made way for Mary Stewart to the throne of France occurred at the jousts held in honor of the marriage of Philip II with Isabel or Elizabeth, daughter of Henry III., and of the marriage also of his sister Margaret to Emmanuel Philibert, Duke of Savoy: both happening on the 30th of June, 1559." Speed's account of the fatal accident to the King is as follows:

"The French King, thus over busy about Scotland's state, was over careless of his own, when at solemnifying the marriage of his daughter and sister he would needs be a challenger at tilt, seconded by the Duke of Guize and Ferrora, which triumphant joy was suddenly clouded by a sad catastrophe. For to run his best, and indeed his last course, in favor of his Queen, he sent a lance to the Earl of Montgomery with a command to have him enter the tilt; but he excused himself from running against His Majesty; alleged that fortune the day before afforded him not to break one staff; and now, as he feared, she would put him to a second shame. But the King, destiny so enforcing and his date fully run, sent him a second command, which Montgomery very unwillingly obeyed, and, breaking his lance upon the King's cuirasse, a splinter thereof, his beaver being somewhat open, struck him so deep in the eye that thereupon shortly he ended his life."

Note 66 continues:

"In 1562 the first of the religious wars broke out, desolating France for upwards of thirty years, during which Montgomery was greatly distinguished as a commander on the side of the Protestant party. He had several narrow escapes, the enemy being especially anxious to capture him. He and Coligny were formally condemned to death and executed in effigy. He was in Paris at the massacre of St. Bartholomew, but having had warning, Montgomery contrived to elude his pursuers."

He was eventually attacked by Mortignon, who commanded a very superior force, and who was anxious to capture him, knowing how cordially the cruel queen would hear of his destruction. Montgomery, who was forced to surrender at Domfraut, was immediately tried and condemned to death, his children being degraded from the rank of nobility. When he heard the latter part of the sentence he said: *"If they have not the virtue of nobles to raise themselves, I consent to the degradation."* He was executed on the 27th of May, 1547.

The following short notice of this family is written by Professor Le Herricher, of the College of Avrauches:

"Alexander de Montgomery, lord of Ardrasson and Eglinton, was cousin of James I., king of Scotland. From this nobleman descended Robert de Montgomery, father of Jacques (James), who was celebrated under the name of Captain de Lorges. In 1560 this Jacques died in the service of Frances I., king of France. His son, Gabriel I., who became the great Montgomery, and who was the person who mortally wounded King Henry II., succeeded to the estate of his five brothers and sisters. He married Isabean de Teral, lady of Lucy, and through her became seigneur of Lucy and of several parishes in Avranches, in Normandy. The family chateau, still known as the Chateau de Montgomery, but now unoccupied and going to ruin, is situated at Lucy, about three leagues from the town of Avranches. The present building is, however, comparatively modern, having been built about the year 1620 by Gabriel II, son of the great Montgomery. The ancient castle of the family stood at a short distance from it, on a cliff overhanging the river Lelune."— See Ulster Journal of Archeology, vol. 9, page 293.

This Gabriel, called the great Montgomery, was a leading Protestant general in France from 1562 to 1574, the date of his execution. This was a period of twelve years. He could out-general any man who met him with the same number of men, and at one time it appeared that he would succeed in maintaining the Protestant cause in France. Then it was determined to cause the destruction of his army at any cost, and Mortignon with that very superior and magnificent army was sent against him and compelled him to surrender; and it is said that his execution was in violation of the terms of surrender. Not so much on account of his Protestantism as on account of the very unfortunate affair with King Henry, the husband of Catharine, the Queen of France at that time.

Thomas H. Montgomery, pages 143-4, follows up the genealogy of Gabriel the great Montgomery, with Gabriel the second and third, Francis the fourth and Nicholas, the last of his line, which by its courage and great ability had identified itself with the history of its adopted country. Count Nicholas dying, it is said, in 1721, without children, the Count de Montgomerie reverted to his niece afterwards the Marchioness de Thibantot.

The author of the Montgomery Manuscript, page 470, speaks of meeting another Montgomery in France, 1664, and says:

"This Count de Montgomery was a little, black-haired man, very brave in his apparel and retinue. 1 visited him once, after I had first accosted him at Court. My French tongue was then a little out of use and he had no good Latin, as I believe, scarce more than to say his creed and prayers by. So far I could learn little of him concerning this family, but that his ancestors had been counts and great men in Normandy, and of large estates ever since and before Duke William conquered England. He was, as I fancied, ill-read in history and unskillful of his genealogy, as most men are careless of it. He said he had at home a tree of his predecessors. He was not then under any great command in France, and truly I find little of his family in the French Chronicles, although I searched De Serres de Girard and other authors of that kind; and so I leave him and them."

And Their Descendants

WILLIAM MONTGOMERY THE AUTHOR

As we have mainly followed the Montgomery Manuscript in the compilation of our foreign material, it will be proper to give a sketch of his life, written by himself.

It is supposed that he was born Oct. 27, 1633, at Aughaintain. He died in 1706, being 74 years old. His wife, Elizabeth, whom he married in 1660, was born in 1635 and died in 1677, aged 42 years.

William Montgomery remained a widower the remainder of his life.

Hugh, first Lord Viscount Montgomery of the Great Ards in Ireland, was, by his two sons, grandfather to both of them.

The author of the Montgomery Manuscript was a well-educated gentleman; could speak fluently in several languages besides his own. He suffered the perplexities in common with other royalists under the revolution of the Cromwell reign, and after much difficulty had his lands and rights restored to him. And he tells us that it is not necessary to write his life to perpetuate his name, as it will stand out in history as long as the records of his restoration are in existence.

In 1661 he was elected as one of the members of Parliament for the borough of Newtown.

At one time he was mistreated in business and says that it so happened because he had read books more than men and business.

He was High Sheriff in 1670. He takes great pleasure in narrating his social relations with and his visits to the nobility in Scotland, and was highly elated when they came into Ireland to repay the visit and enjoy his hospitality.

He was a very remarkable man in searching after and recording the history of the Montgomery family. Wherever he saw or heard the name he took time to investigate and record the history of the family.

The history that he has left us, giving an account of the family from 1603 to 1706, with the copious notes of Rev. George Hill in 1869, gives us one of the very best contributions to the history of the Montgomerys that have ever been published. The accuracy is surprising in a volume of its size.

Judge
Henry Partlow Montgomery
Georgetown, Kentucky

And Their Descendants

CHAPTER VIII

THE DESCENDANTS OF SAMUEL MONTGOMERY
By Judge H. P. Montgomery

Several years ago the writer became interested in the genealogy of the Montgomery family, and especially of the branch to which he belongs, being a descendant of Samuel Montgomery, who, with all his children but one, came to Kentucky from Wythe County, Virginia, in the year 1786, and settled in what was then Woodford County, but now Franklin County.

The object of the writer is not to write a history of the Montgomerys, but to present the names of the descendants of Samuel Montgomery, the Virginia emigrant to Kentucky in the year 1786, and present such scraps of history as the writer has been able to gather, that they may not be wholly lost—"*Which we have heard and known, and our fathers have told us . . . that the generations to come might know them, even the children which should be born; who should arise and declare them to their children.*"—Psalm lxxviii.

Thomas H. Montgomery in his History and Pedigree of Montgomery, published in 1863, claims that the first of the family of Montgomery who crossed the ocean was William Montgomerie of Brigend, who with his family, more than 160 years before his publication settled in the province of East New Jersey. This would place the date of the emigration of William Montgomery of Brigend about the year 1700. The writer claims that Thomas H. Montgomery is in error in his claim that William Montgomery of Brigend was the first of the name who crossed the ocean. The writer claims that his ancestors came to America and settled on the James River in Virginia in the year 1666, and sixty years after the first permanent settlement was made in Virginia.

The records of the Virginia Land Office, Colonial Series No. 6, page 678, shows grant to Robert Montgomery by Sir Henry Cheekdey of date April 30, 1679, of 850 acres of land, and the same Records. No. 7, page 615, of date Oct. 2nd, 1687, shows a grant from Francis Lord Howard to Hugh Montgomery for 250 acres of land. This Record shows that 21 years before the emigration of Wm, Montgomerie of Brigend there were Montgomerys in Virginia who were owners of large bodies of land.

The Montgomerys were early emigrants to America—as is shown by the records of the War Office of the United States, from which it appears that there were between three hundred and four hundred soldiers in the Revolutionary War by the name of Montgomery, and it is reasonable to suppose that there were as many more among the soldiers of this war whose mothers were named Montgomery. Among the soldiers of the Revolution named Montgomery were officers as follows: 2 Captains, 2 Lieutenants and 2 Ensigns from Pennsylvania; 1 Lieutenant-Colonel and 1 Lieutenant from Virginia; 1 Chaplain from Delaware; 1 Major-General and 1 Lieutenant from New York, and 1 Lieutenant from Massachusetts; which are convincing facts that they were early emigrants to America and bore a large part in the war for independence.

The family to which the writer belongs is Scotch-Irish. James Montgomery of Ireland was the father—besides other children, doubtless—of three sons, who emigrated to America in the year 1666 and settled on the James River in Virginia, and whose names were William, Robert and Hugh Montgomery, and for convenience in making up this genealogical statement we will call them the first generation in America, as follows:

No. 1. William Montgomery.
No. 2. Robert Montgomery.
No. 3. Hugh Montgomery.

Of these three brothers Hugh Montgomery returned to Ireland and died, never having married, and he and Robert Montgomery are the names of the two Montgomerys to whom the land grants were made by Sir Henry Checkdey and Francis Lord Howard.

SECOND GENERATION.
Children of William Montgomery (1):
4. Robert Montgomery.
5. Hugh Montgomery.
6. John Montgomery and four daughters.

THIRD GENERATION.
Children of Robert Montgomery (4):
7. William Montgomery.
8. Hugh Montgomery.
9. James Montgomery.

10. Samuel Montgomery married Margaret Nichols of Virginia —and three daughters, names not known.

The above Samuel Montgomery is the one who emigrated to Woodford County, Ky., from Virginia in 1786.

FOURTH GENERATION.

Children of Samuel Montgomery and Margaret Nichols, his wife:

11. William Montgomery, married —; 2nd, Mrs. Bryant.

12. Robert Montgomery, born April 23rd, 1762; died Feb. 8th, 1823; married, 1st, Mary Love; 2nd, Rachel Bohannon, April 22nd, 1798; 3rd, Patsy White Cotton, May 25, 1819.

13. James Montgomery died unmarried.

14. John Montgomery, born 1767, died 1848; married Mary Thomas.

15. Mary Montgomery married Frederick Edwards.

16. Elizabeth Montgomery married a Crockett.

17. Nancy Montgomery married Nathaniel Evans.

18. Samuel Montgomery died unmarried.

19. Joseph Montgomery, born Aug. 1, 1768, died Jan. 12, 1842; married Jane Sproule, 1796.

Robert Montgomery was a soldier of the Revolution and fought in the battle of Guilford's Courthouse, where he was severely wounded and left for dead on the battlefield.

James Montgomery was a lieutenant in the United States army and was in the Lewis and Clark expedition to the Pacific Ocean in the year 1805.

FIFTH GENERATION.

Children of Wm. Montgomery (11) and his wife.

20. Margaret (Peggy) Montgomery married Wm- Graham.

Children of Wm. Montgomery (11) and Mrs. Bryant (nee Graham) his wife:

21. Francis Graham Montgomery married Ann Stites.

22. James Hervey Montgomery married Malvina Trotter.

23. Samuel C. Montgomery, born April 15, 1802, died April 15, 1846; married Mrs. Lydia Easterday.

24. Jeptha Dudley Montgomery, born Oct. 29, 1807, died May 30, 1852; married Arabella Henry, Sept. 29, 1831.

25. Louisa Montgomery, born Jan. 25, 1811, died Feb. 7, 1880: married J. M. Bacon March 26, 1826.

26. Priscilla Montgomery married Archie Bryant.

And Their Descendants

Children of Robert Montgomery (12) and Mary Love, his wife:
27. Sallie Montgomery, born Jan. 6, 1789, died Jan. 30, 1863; married Robert Montgomery.
28. John Montgomery, born Nov. 6, 1791, died April 3, 1872; married Elizabeth Bohannon Dec. 26, 1813; married, second, Priscilla Montgomery, May 12, 1847.

Children of Robert Montgomery (12) and Rachel Bokannon, his wife:
29. Robert Montgomery, born Jan. 1, 1799, died May 15, 1800.
30. Hugh Montgomery, born Nov. 1, 1800, died in 1852; married Sallie Wilcoxon Dec. 10, 1820.
31. Mary (Polly) Montgomery, born Nov. 10, 1802, died Jan. 17, 1844; married Wm. Woods.
32. Margaret (Peggy) Montgomery, born Jan. 25, 1805, died Oct. 9, 1884; married Wm. Knox April 25, 1821.
33. Frances Montgomery, born Oct. 8, 1808; married Paschal Jackson.
34. Samuel Montgomery, born Nov. 1, 1810, died Dec. 30,
1885; married Susan H. Bacon; married, second, _____; married
third, Mrs. M. M. Walker, nee Owen, 1863.
35. Eleanor Montgomery, born Sept. 15, 1814; married Josiah Jackman.
Children of Robert Montgomery (12) and Patsy White Cotton, his wife:
63. Joseph L. Montgomery, born July 1, 1820.
37. Sarah Jane Montgomery, born Sept. 30, 1821, died Jan. 10, 1890; married John Meek, June 5, 1838.

John Montgomery (28) was a soldier in the war of 1812, and was with the expedition under Gov. Shelby to the Northwest Territory, but was not in any battle and after the close of the war, held for many years the office of Justice of the Peace, and held the office of Sheriff for one term in Gallatin County, Ky. For several years before his death he drew a pension for military service.

Hugh Montgomery (30) in 1852, during the excitement over the discovery of gold in California, "crossed the plains" to that state and died shortly after reaching the gold regions.

Samuel Montgomery (34) was a captain of Company 'I', of the first Illinois Infantry in the Mexican War, under Colonel Hardin, who was killed in the battle of Buena Vista. He was also major of the Second Battalion of the 6th Cavalry of Missouri Volunteers in the Union army. He fought in the battles of Wilson Creek, Prairie Grove and Pea Ridge. After the war he held civil positions, and among them mayor of Bloomfield, Mo., and president of the County court.

Children of John Montgomery (14) and Mary Thomas, his wife:
38. Samuel Montgomery, born 1796, died Feb. 1863. .
39. Robert Montgomery, married ——Christian.
40. Fountain Montgomery.
41. George Montgomery.
42. Malinda Montgomery died 1869; married Stephen Cook in 1819.
43. Matilda Montgomery married Robert Christian.
44. Margaret Montgomery never married.
45. James Montgomery.
46. William Montgomery.
47. Elizabeth Montgomery never married.

Children of Mary Montgomery (15) and Frederick Edwards, her husband:
48. Elizabeth Edwards married a Bartlett.
49. Edwards, a daughter.
50. John Edwards married Nancy Geiger.
51. Robert Edwards married Rebecca Sandusky.
52. James Edwards.

Robert Edwards (51) was a colonel of a regiment of Kentucky troops, and distinguished himself at the battle of the River Raisin, and his name is inscribed on a monument at Frankfort, Ky., erected in honor of Kentucky's distinguished soldier dead.

James Edwards (52) was also a soldier who fought in the battle of the River Raisin, and in that battle received a severe wound which ultimately caused his death in Webster County, Ky., about 25 years ago.

The writer has not been able to find the location of Elizabeth Montgomery (16), who married a Crockett, and has not been able to find her posterity; but it seems to be clear that she never moved to Kentucky, and is the only one of the children of Samuel Montgomery that remained in Virginia.

Children of Nancy Montgomery (17) and Nathaniel Evans, her husband:
52. Andrew Evans.
53. Jane Evans, born Nov. 6, 1786, died Jan. 9, 1867; married Peter Yaker.
54. Mary Evans, born March 31, 1792, died Oct. 18, 1872; never married.

55. Elizabeth C. Evans, born July 23, 1799, died Feb. 22, 1870; married Henry Sayers, Oct. 16, 87.

56. James Montgomery Evans, born Sept. 24, 80, died Jan. 2, 860; married Jane Phillips.

57. Martha Evans, born Nov. 23, 1806. Died Dec. 28, 1839; married Dean Megee about 1822.

Children of Joseph Montgomery (19) and Jane Sproule, his wife: 58. Jane Montgomery, born May 28, 1797, died Aug. 12, 1887 married Robt. Dean about 1815.

59. James Sproule Montgomery, born Nov. 7, 799, died Feb. 3, 1872; married Electa Oladine Wilson. Feb. 26.1828; married, second, Fannie Caroline Wert, Dec. 10, 1863.

60. Sarah Montgomery, born Nov. 17, 1801, died June 2, 1866; married Noah Davis, March 24, 1823.

61. Susan Montgomery, born Jan. 19, 1804, died in 1857; married George Hennegin, Aug. 28, 1828.

62. Samuel Montgomery, born May 27, 1806, died Jan. 29, 1889; married Mary Worley, Sept. 2, 1834.

63. Mary Montgomery died in infancy; age 3 months, born in 1807.

64. Catherine Montgomery, born Nov. 19, 1809, died April 2, 1894, 84 years old; a member of Baptist church; married Geo. W. Yocum, July 20, 1826.

65. Frances Montgomery, born 1812, died Jan. 1878; married Stephen Jenison, 1829.

66. Nancy B. Montgomery, born Sept. 18, 1814, died Dec. 15, 1877; never married.

67. Joseph Edward Montgomery, born May 6, 1817; married Clara Miriah Jenison, Sept. 24, 1840; married, second, Rebecca Phillips Graham, Sept. 24, 1845.

68. Elizabeth N., Montgomery born Sept. 30, 1820; married John Thomas Dashiell, Jan. 17, 1844.

69. John William Montgomery, born Aug. 30, 1824, died June 5, 1844, unmarried; drowned near Cincinnati, O.

James Sproule Montgomery (59) and Samuel Montgomery (62) lived many years in New Albany, Ind., and both died there; were both men of great energy and industry, fine ability and commanding presence. They both began life in the humble capacity *of* deck hands on steamboats plying the Ohio and Mississippi rivers, and arose to be captains of the largest boats on those rivers, amassed large means, and engaged in the banking business in their home city, and James S. Montgomery was honored with the position of president of the old mail line between Cincinnati and Louisville. They died in their home city full of years and honors, respected by all who knew them.

Commodore
Joesph Edward Montgomery

The following is taken from the Chicago Inter Ocean, issue of August 5. 1902, and it gives quite a life history of Commodore Joseph Edward Montgomery (67), whose death had just occurred:

"Joseph Edward Montgomery, one of the naval commanders of the Confederacy during the civil war, died early yesterday morning at the home of his son, Dr. James Montgomery, 183 Cass Street. He had been ill several weeks.

"Funeral services were held at the residence at 4 o'clock in the afternoon by the Rev. Dr. Brewer. Last night the body was taken to New Albany, Ind., for burial in the family lot. The immediate family and a few intimate friends accompanied it.

"Commodore Montgomery's health had not been good for several years. He was 85 years old, and his failing sight prevented him from leading the active life to which he was accustomed before he came to Chicago, twelve years ago. Gradually he lost interest in life, and when he caught cold the early part of last month his physicians predicted that he would not recover.

"During and preceding the civil war Commodore Montgomery was among the most noted of Mississippi steamboat commanders. It was his exact acquaintance with the river, coupled with his farsightedness and ability to command, that caused Jefferson Davis to place him in command of the fleet on the Mississippi river. He was an intimate friend of the President of the Confederacy.

"Montgomery's first engagement was at Fort Pillow in 1862, where he quit the fight with credit to his fleet. When he was attacked by the Union fleet at Memphis he was defeated and the entire Confederate fleet destroyed. After the loss of his fleet he superintended the construction of the gunboat Nashville, and when it was completed took it to Mobile. He attended to the mining of the Bay of Mobile. After the fight there in 1865 he attempted to cross overland to Texas and was captured by Union troops and held until the conclusion of the war, when he was pardoned by President Johnson.

"Commodore Montgomery would have been a widely-known man had there been no civil war. His name was known from end to end of the Mississippi river. It was he who taught Samuel L. Clemens how to pilot a river boat. He was a friend of Charles Dickens, having become acquainted with the English author while yet a river captain. At one time he was a Biblical student at Washington. D. C.

"Commodore Montgomery was a native of Kentucky, having been born at Carrollton May 6, 1817. His father was Joseph Montgomery, a soldier of the war of 1812 and of revolutionary descent.

"One of Commodore Montgomery's most daring feats was an attempt to capture General Grant at about the time of the battle of Belmont. He was head of a little band of scouts, and one of these, pretending to be a spy for the Federals, got General Grant to meet in a lonely spot. Grant was accompanied by only one aid, and Commodore Montgomery thought he surely had him; but all he got was the Northern leader's horse, the general riding away on his staff officer's steed.

"Mr. Montgomery came to Chicago in 1890, and since then Mrs. Clara White, his daughter, has been his constant companion. She is writing a history or his life, two volumes of which are finished. "There is pending before Congress a claim in favor of Commodore Montgomery amounting to §1,000.000 for twenty-five boats and cotton belonging to him which were confiscated by the Federal government at the time of the war."

The only other member of this generation still living is Mrs. Elizabeth N. Dashiell (68). She is the widow of J. T. Dashiell, who died in the year 1900, and who, during the exciting times of the civil war, was a member of the Indiana legislature, and altogether was one of the best men the writer ever knew.

SIXTH GENERATION.
Children of Francis Graham Montgomery (21) and Ann Stites, his wife:
70. Abraham Stites married Miss Moore.

Children of James Hervey Montgomery (22) and Malvina Trotter, his wife:
71. George Montgomery.

Children of Samuel C. Montgomery (23) and Lydia Easterday, his wife:
72. Priscilla Montgomery, born March 23, 1828; married John Montgomery, May 12, 1847.
73. William Montgomery, born Jan. 29, 1833; married Miriam Leechman, March 4. 1852.
74. Elizabeth Montgomery, born April 1, 1830; married Leander Harris in 1854.
75. Margaret Montgomery, born May 6, 1835, died Jan. 19, 1855.
76. Galveston Montgomery, born Feb. 24, 1838; married Mrs. Susan Easterday Dec. 12 1867.
77. Nancy B. Montgomery, born April 2, 1840; married James Satchwell, Dec. 6, 1860.

Children of Jeptha Dudley Montgomery (24) and Arabella Henry Barrett, his wife:
78. Sallie Graham Montgomery, born Nov. 13, 1832, died Feb. 6, 1889; married Rev. J. B. Tharp Nov. 2, 1858.
79. John Pope Montgomery, born June 2, 1834, died Jan. 14, 1881; married Irene Cook May 19, 1864.

80. J. Byron Montgomery, born April 18, 1837; married Eugenia Holt, June 13, 1867; married, second, Sallie Smith, May 22, 1888.

81. Elizabeth Montgomery, born Nov. 14, 1838, died August 8, 1839.

82. William Graham Montgomery, born May 29, 1840; died March 21, 1896; married Elizabeth Garner.

Mrs. Clara M. White

83. Anderson Gibson Montgomery, born Aug. 13, 1843, died Jan. 2, 1863.

84. Arabella Montgomery, born Nov. 27, 1845; married Rev. Samuel Preston Hogan, Aug. 25, 1870.

85. James Edward Montgomery, born April 19, 1847, died Oct. 25, 1861.

86. Prank Graham Montgomery, born Oct. 31, 1849; married Mollie Tompkins, May 10, 1882.

Galveston Montgomery (76) was a soldier in the Confederate army and a member of the regiment of Col. Giltner.

J. Byron Montgomery (80), William Graham Montgomery 8(2) and Anderson Gibson Montgomery (83) were in the Orphans' Brigade, C. S. A. The two first named were in the first Kentucky Cavalry. J. Byron was captain of Company "A," and William Graham was sergeant of same company. And the last named was in the Second Kentucky Infantry. The last named— Anderson Gibson Montgomery—was mortally wounded in the battle of Murfreesboro, Tenn.

Sallie Graham Montgomery (78) was the wife of Rev. J. B. Tharp, a prominent Baptist minister of Kentucky.

Arabella Montgomery, wife of Rev. Samuel Preston Hogan, a young Baptist minister of central Kentucky of great promise who died quite young—only a few years after entering upon his lifework.

Children of Louisa Montgomery (25) and J. M. Bacon, her husband:

87. Frank W. Bacon, born Aug. 11, 1827; married Rose A. Oliver, June 6, 1850; married, second. Sue -S. Spencer, April 14, 1862; married, third, Kate McLean, April 5, 1883.

88. Martha Priscilla Bacon, born Oct. 6, 1829, died April 29, 1888; married Frank S. Robinson, April 5, 1852.

89. George Robertson Bacon, born Nov. 15, 1831, died March 12, 1854; never married.

90. James Crawford Bacon, born Aug. 19, 1835, died Aug. 27, 1889; married Mary Hester Helton, Nov. 19, 1868.

91. Ann Mary Bacon, born Nov. 19, 1837; married Joseph W. Roberts, Feb. 25, 1863.

Children of Sallie Montgomery (27) and Robert Montgomery, her husband:

92. Nancy Montgomery, born Feb. 8, 1805; died July 29, 1839; married John Harper, March 29, 1827.

Children of John Montgomery (28) and Elizabeth Bohannon, his wife:

93. Sally Montgomery, born Dec. 14, 1814, died Sept. 8, 1887; married Ibsen Jackson, Feb. 9, 1832.

94. Belinda Montgomery, born Jan. 2, 1817, died Oct. 6, 1844; married May 14, 1836, to John Fothergill.

95. William Montgomery, born Oct. 13, 1818, married Elizabeth Hoggins, April 1, 1840.

96. Hugh Montgomery, born Jan. 12, 1820, married Mary Ann Rosell, Feb. 27, 1844; second, Nora Davis, Aug. 30, 1891.

97. Nancy Montgomery, born Sept. 30, 1821; died Sept. 3, 1897; married William McCreery, Nov. 13, 1389.

98. John Montgomery, born Dec. 22, 1823, died July 18, 1869; married Susan Easterday, Feb. 28, 1844.

99. Mary Montgomery, born Oct. 13, 1825, died March 19, 1891; married John Fothergill, Sept. 2, 1845.

100. Ezra Lee Montgomery, born June 1, 1827; died March 25, 1863; married Lizzie Lecompte, Feb. 20, 1857.

101. Thomas Jefferson Montgomery, born May 28, 1829, died April 6, 1866; married Phoebe Chrisman.

102. Emeline Montgomery, born June 27, 1901, married John S. Heady, Oct. 20, 1853.

103. George Washington Montgomery, born July 21, 1833, died Feb. 11, 1887: married Agues Clevinger May 6, 1858; second, Flora M. L. Childs, Nov. 12, 1872.

104. Elizabeth Ann Montgomery, born Jan. 19, 1837, died August 15, 1861; married Jacob Snyder, Sept. 14, 1854.

105. Henry Partlow Montgomery, born Feb. 8, 1839, married Nannie E. Kenney, Jan. 13, 1864; second, Alice P. Mundy, Jan. 1, 1889.

106. Andrew Jackson Montgomery, born Dec. 24, 1849, died August 27, 1891; married Elizabeth Porter Dec. 14, 1864; second, Vina Stevenson, Jan. 13, 1886.

Children of John Montgomery (28) and his wife, Priscilla Montgomery (72):

107. Samuel Montgomery, born March 18, 1848, married Mary Sidney Tompkins, June 15, 1885.

108. James Montgomery, born Nov. 29, 1849, married Victoria Montgomery, April 14, 1886.

109. Joseph Edward Montgomery, born April 1, 1852; married Gillie A. Smith. Dec. 26, 1876.

110. Margaret Frances Montgomery, born Jan. 27, 1854, died April 26, 1855

111. Jane Montgomery, born June 8, 1856, married James William Lancaster, Jan 22, 1877.

112. Lydia E. Montgomery, born April 16, 1861, died April 5, 1873.

113. Robert Love Montgomery, born Aug. 27, 1863; married Ella Runyan, Sept. 12, 1883.

Honorable
Hugh Montgomery
Warsaw, Kentucky

Hugh Montgomery (96) of Warsaw, Ky., a brother of H. P. Montgomery, mentioned in this work, is now closing the last days of his eighty-second year; has for many years been a Justice of the Peace of his County, and has by industry and business sagacity accumulated a large estate; but he is remarkable in this, that he seeks opportunities to befriend the poor and oppressed. His sympathies go out to save for the owners their property when creditors are about to take their homes from them. When a man has meritorious characteristics, and his property has been sold, Hugh Montgomery looks out for the time when right of redemption of the home expires, comes forward, furnishes the redemption money, gives the debtor time, and by his advice and influence enables him to pay off the oppressive debt. On one occasion the last day for redemption had come to a poor debtor, and the last hope of saving the home was gone when Hugh Montgomery came forward and paid the debt and divided the land with the debtor, gave one-half to him upon which to earn a living and took possession of the other half and managed it for a few years and made four crops, enough to pay all the debt, and then restored to the debtor all the land clear of encumbrance. Such men as these are rare but they understand and follow that rule the greatest of all—the Golden Rule. How much better would our race be if all men would copy his example!

George W. Montgomery (103) lived the greater part of his life in Ray County, Missouri, of which he was one of the associate judges of the County court. In the civil war he espoused the cause of the Confederacy and was a member of the regiment of Col. John T. Hughes of Missouri, and fought under General Price in his campaign in Missouri and Arkansas, and was wounded at the battle of Pea Ridge.

"Prominent Bankers of America," page 544: "Henry Partlow Montgomery (105), President of the First National Bank of Georgetown, Ky., was born in Gallatin County, Kentucky, February 8th, 1839. His grandfather, Robert Montgomery, was a revolutionary hero, and was wounded at the battle of Guilford Courthouse in North Carolina. Mr. Montgomery's lineage on both sides is eminently honorable. He was very carefully educated and, in 1860, graduated from Center College, Danville, Ky., with the second honor in a class of thirty-five. He then read law in the office of H. J. Abbett of Warsaw, and was admitted to the Bar of Gallatin County. Mr. Montgomery began practice in Shelby County, but after one year removed to Owenton, where he acquired and maintained a lucrative business until he transferred his office to Georgetown in 1882, where he now resides. While in Owenton he served seven years as County attorney, an office which involves the duty of public prosecutions. This position is considered recognition of superior abilities, especially when conferred on a young man. He has also held the position of Special Circuit Judge. It may be mentioned here that he was associate counsel for the defense in the celebrated case of the commonwealth of Kentucky against Thomas Buford, indicted for the murder of Judge John M. Elliott of the Court of Appeals. The organization of the First National Bank of Georgetown, in 1883, was partly facilitated by Judge Montgomery, and he has been its president since that date. He is also president of the Water Supply Company, which also furnishes electric light to the city, and he is active in all local matters tending to advance the education, morals and well-being of the citizens."

Note by D. B. M.:

I now have this to say further of Judge H. P. Montgomery, of Georgetown, Ky., in addition to the biography copied from "Prominent Bankers of America:" By invitation I visited him Nov. 28, 1900, and found him to be a prominent and wealthy man, probably worth one hundred thousand dollars. He owns thirteen hundred acres of land, nearly all in the very heart of the Blue Grass country, besides owning moneyed interests in nearly all the enterprises of his city. He is a lawyer of high standing and enjoys a lucrative practice. He is strictly honest in his dealings with plaintiff and .defendant; this I observed while in his busy office for one day. He is systematic in all his work; he opens business promptly at 8 o'clock A. M. and closes just as promptly at 4 in the afternoon; and all this time he is a busy man and thus it has been for forty years. He lives in the west part of Georgetown; his house, of stone and brick, is one of the finest in the city. The dwelling is near the center of a whole block and is elevated perhaps ten feet above the streets, the sides next the streets being supported by stone walls. Mr. Montgomery is a cripple, not having walked without crutches since five years old, and he weighs over three hundred pounds. He is happily surrounded with an interesting family. He has good social qualities, and, like other best of men, enjoys a little fun now and then. He is much interested in the history of the Scotch-Irish branch of the Montgomery family in America, and has rendered much valuable assistance in this direction.

Judge H. P. Montgomery has this to say about the part acted by the Montgomery family in the world: "In every war in Europe and America, since 900, the family has furnished its privates, captains, colonels and generals, and the muses have furnished poesy, and the halls of legislation have been benefited by their wisdom. The bar has been honored, and the pulpit adorned, and medical science advanced. You will say that I am vainglorious about my family, and I admit that I am proud of its record, whether on the tented field or the realms of literature, the pulpit or the forum, or in the humble sphere of the yeoman; and the more I learn of its history, the prouder I am of it."

And Their Descendants

Andrew Jackson Montgomery (106) was a soldier in the Confederate army, was a member of Graves Battery with Col. Roger Hanson's regiment, and fought at the battle of Fort Donaldson and at Chickamauga, and held several County offices in the state of Indiana.

Children of Hugh Montgomery (30) and Sallie Wilcoxon, his wife:

114. James Montgomery, born Jan. 19, 1822, died March 28, 1882; married Emma McConnell, Feb. 7, 1856.

115. Robert Montgomery, born March 14, 1825, died Aug. 5, 1852; married Lucy.

116. Samuel Montgomery, born June 28, 1827, died 1852; married Martha Miller.

117. Margaret J. Montgomery, born Feb. 15, 1830; married Thos. Lancaster Dec. 24, 1846; married, second, Wm. Oliver Bryan, Nov. 24, 1851; married, third, John T. Sheets, Feb. 4, 1858.

118. Frances Ann Montgomery, born March 9, 1833, died in 1833.

119. Lewis Montgomery, born 1834, died August 9, 1852. James Montgomery (114) was for many years a steamboat pilot in the Mississippi river.

"Children of Polly Montgomery (31) and William Wood, her husband:

120. Birch Wood, died in 1849.

121. Ella Wood married Silas Wood.

122. James L. Wood died March 3, 1869; married Margaret Stewart.

123. W. H. (Dink) Wood, died April 19, 1870; married Susan Kimbrough.

124. George S. Wood, born Sept. 16, 1839, died April 11, 1899; married Matilda Bowie, Feb. 17, 1874.

125. Sarah Wood, born____, died April 23, 1882; married Ben Martin.

126. Mary A. Wood, born Feb. 7, 1841; married J. J. Martin, Aug. 26, 1855.

127. Scott Wood, born April 8, 1842, married Susan Herron July 31, 1873.

Birch Wood (120) was a soldier in the Mexican war, and never returned home; is said to have been killed in the battle of Buena Vista. George S. Wood was a Confederate soldier; was a member of Graves Battery with Col. Roger Hanson's regiment, and fought at Fort Donaldson, and was afterward a lieutenant in Captain Barrett's company in Col. Gittnei's regiment, and fought at Mt. Sterling, Ky., in one of Gen. Morgan's raids, when he was severely wounded. He was a brave and faithful soldier.

The Montgomerys

Children of Margaret (Peggy) Montgomery (32) and William Knox, her husband:

128. John M. Knox, born Feb. 13, 1282, died April 22, 1892; never married.

129. Nancy Frances Knox, born Dec. 6, 1826, died March 1, 1888; married Randall L. Self, Jan. 19, 1848; married, second, Samuel L. Smith, Feb. 15, 1866.

130. Mary J. Knox, born Feb. 7, 1829, died Sept. 17, 1894; married Anderville Swails, Oct. 6, 1845; married, second, D. C. Williams, Feb. 24, 1856.

131. Josiah Knox, born June 20, 1832, died March 1, 1897; married Margaret Smith.

132. William H. Knox, born Nov. 27, 1837; married Emily Burns, July 1, 1858.

133. Eleanor Elizabeth Knox, born Oct. 30, 1835; married Hiram Rader, Jan. 1, 1854.

134. Jasper D. Knox, born Jan. 9, 1847; married Sarah E. McWilliams, Jan. 7, 1869.

135. Sally Ann Knox, born Sept. 20, 1824, died Sept. 20, 1833.

136. George R. Knox, born Dec. 8, 1840; married Ann Darnell, Jan. 6, 1875.

John M. Knox (128) and Josiah Knox (131) were private soldiers in the war of the rebellion, in Regiment 123, Indiana Volunteer Infantry.

Children of Frances Montgomery (33) and Paschal Jackson, her husband:

137. Jethro Jackson, M. D.

138. Samuel Jackson died unmarried about 19 years of age. Jethro Jackson is supposed to have died in Cuba in one of the filibustering expeditions to that island.

Children of Samuel Montgomery (34) and Susan H. Bacon, his wife:

139. Richard H. Montgomery, born Sept. 21, 1837, died Jan. 19, 1897; married Julia Couran, Dec. 1864.

140. Bacon Montgomery, born June 1, 1840, died 1888; married Mariah Homans.

141. Mary Eliza Montgomery, born Feb. 17, 1842, died Sept. 13, 1853.

142. William Wilson Montgomery, born Sept. 20, 1844, died July 8. 18—

143. Samuel Montgomery, born March 9, 1847, died Feb. 1, 1849,

144. John Jay Hardin Montgomery, born March 14, 1851.

145. Susan Alice Montgomery, born June 22, 1853; married Henry N. Phillips, Aug. 18, 1874.

Richard H. Montgomery (139) and Bacon Montgomery (140) and John J. Hardin Montgomery (144) were all Federal soldiers in the civil war, in the sixth Missouri Cavalry Volunteers. Richard H. was captain of Company E, and Bacon was the first major of his regiment, and after the close of the civil war was brigadier-general of the Missouri State Militia, and mayor of the city of Sedalia, Mo.

In the spring of 1862 he was commissioned lieutenant of Company E, and in the summer of the same year, after the death of Captain Hubbard, he was made captain. He was unusually kind to his men, giving particular attention to them in sickness. At the Wet Glade in Laclede County, Missouri, he and his brother Bacon distinguished themselves for their bravery, so testifies Alexander Zelmerger, a member of Captain Montgomery's company.

Susan Alice Montgomery (145) is the wife of Henry N. Phillips, an attorney of Poplar Bluff, Mo.

Children of Samuel Montgomery (34) and Mrs. M. M. Walker (nee Owens), his wife:

146. Addie Montgomery, born Nov. 2, 1864, died Oct. 26, 1879.

147. Mattie P. Montgomery, born Aug. 11, 1868; married G. W. Davis, Dec. 1, 1885.

148. Murtie P. Montgomery, born Aug. 11, 1868; married Dr. Elder Phillips, Dec. 31, 1885.

149. Laura Lollie Montgomery, born Nov. 20, 1872, died Nov. 24, 1877.

150. Reuben Pickett Montgomery, born Dec. 30, 1874; married Lizzie Jackson, Dec. 8, 1895; married, second, Hattie B. Haydock, Dec. 24, 1899.

Children of Sarah Jane Montgomery (37) and John Meek, her husband:

151. Robert S. Meek, born May 21, 1840, married Espa Patton, March 18, 1862.

152. William Meek, born June 25, 1842, died March 28, 1843.

153. Margaret E. Meek, born Dec. 25, 1844, married James B. Robinson May 19, 1863.

154. John Thomas Meek, born Feb. 13, 1846, married Florence Bonner, Feb. 18, 1871.

155. Louisa Martin Meek born Feb. 13, 1846; married John B. Meek, Feb. 16, 1870.

156. Adam Meek, born Aug. 30, 1850, married Adelaide Patton, June 27, 1878.

157. Jethro C. Meek, born Oct. 22, 1853, married Mila Meek, June 26, 1877.

158. Mary E. Meek, born June 25, 1855, married Andrew Brown, Aug. 31, 1875.

159. Tirzah Meek, born Jan. 2, 1858, died May 17, 1880; married M Lou Innis in 1878.

160. Anna E. Meek, born Oct. 13, 1861, married Strauther V. Pleak, Oct. 19, 1880.

161. Sarah Etta Meek, born July 10, 1863, died March 18, 1879; unmarried.

162. Lola Frances Meek, born Jan. 13, 1867, died Dec. 10, 1887; married Wm, Smith in 1887.

Children of Samuel Montgomery (38) and ____, his wife:
163. John Montgomery.
164. Thomas Montgomery died in 1900.
164. Frances Montgomery married J. B. Kevil.

Children of Robert Montgomery (39) and Christian, his wife:
165. John Montgomery.
166. William A. Montgomery.
167. Elizabeth A. Montgomery married Thomas Hammock.
168. Mathew Montgomery.
169. James Montgomery.
170. Matilda Montgomery married Holman.

Children of George Montgomery (41) and his wife:
171. J. Fountain Montgomery.
172. George Montgomery.

Children of Malinda Montgomery (42) and Stephen Cook, her husband:
173. Mary Jane Cook, born 1820, died 1888; married Isaac Hill.
174. George Washington Cook married Nancy Hammack.
175. John Doris Cook married Emily O. Jenkins.
176. Margaret Elizabeth Cook, married, first, John H. Davis; second, Basil Watson.

177. Permelia Cook died unmarried.
178. Matilda Cook died unmarried.
179. Robert Cook died unmarried.
180. Stephen Francis Cook married Perryman.

Children of Matilda Montgomery (43) and Robert Christian, her husband:
181. John G. Christian married Rebecca Givens.
182. Elizabeth Christian married Belmire.
183. Mathew C. Christian.
184. M. Campbell Christian.
185. W. Fountain Christian married Carter.
186. Samuel Christian.
187. Green Christian, M. D.

M. Campbell Christian (184) and Samuel Christian (186) were both Confederate soldiers, in the command of Gen. John H. Morgan.

Children of John Edwards (50) and Nancy Geiger, his wife:
188. Mary Ann Edwards married John Reinhardt.
189. John Edwards married Miss Knight, of Indiana.
190. Frederick Geiger Edwards, born in 1806; married Anna Pendleton Taylor in 1830.
191. Samuel Montgomery Edwards.
192. Franklin Edwards died unmarried.
193. Alfred Edwards died unmarried.
194. William Fitzpatrick Edwards died unmarried.

John Edwards (189) was a general in the Federal army and died in Washington City, D. C., a few years ago. Samuel Montgomery Edwards (191) was a soldier in the Texas war for independence, and was massacred with Col. Fanning's men at Goliad, Texas.

Anna Pendleton Taylor, the wife of Frederick Geiger Edwards (190), was a niece of General Zachary Taylor, the hero of Buena Vista and afterwards president of the United States.

Children of Robert Edwards and Miss Sandusky, his wife:
195. Robert Edwards married Miss Sandusky.

Children of Elizabeth C. Evans (55) and Henry Sayers, her husband:
196. William Sayers, born Nov. 13, 1818, died Dec. 13, 1884; married Jemima Jane Theobald, Nov. 15, 1838.

197. Nancy Jane Sayers, born April 3, 1820, died Feb. 9, 1838; married John Smith Dickerson, Feb. 17, 1839.

198. James Crockett Sayers, born July 2, 1832, died March 5, 1876; married Mary C. Sayers, Oct. 18, 1853.

Children of James Montgomery Evans and Jane Phillips, his wife:

199. William Wallace Evans, born June 2, 1832, died April 27, 1866.

200. Ann Eliza Evans married Henry Urmston, June 1869.

201. Martha Jane Evans, born Nov. 10, 1840, died July 16, 1864; unmarried.

202. Mary Hannah Evans, born Feb. 13, 1846, died March 16, 1864, unmarried.

203. John W. Evans, born Jan. 12, 1843, died May 27, 1868, unmarried.

204. James Henry Evans, born April 10, 1849, died June 1877; married Tomma Hughes, Sept. 13. 1871.

205. Edwin Franklin Evans, M. D., born July 8, 1854; married Mattie E. Scoville, Nov. 28 1889.

206. Harriett Montgomery Evans married George Harris.

Children of Martha Evans and Dean Megee, her husband:

207. James Megee, born July 30, 1825, died Sept. 8, 1832.

208. Mary Jessie Megee, born Dec .3, 1828, died July 7, 1829.

209. Presley Megee, born May 8, 1827, died July 15, 1848.

210. Dean Montgomery Megee, born April 19, 1830 died July 4, 1899; married Belie Switzer, Sept. 16, 1869; second, married Ella Moore.

211. Martha Jane Megee, born March 3, 1832, died July 23, 1863; married W. F. Cravens, July 19, 1805.

212. Anna E. Megee, born Aug. 22, 1834; married Joseph Clifton Cravens, Dec. 12, 1850.

213. Sarah Crockett Megee, born Aug. 15, 1846, married Wm. W. Adams, Jan. 26, 1588.

214. Marietta Megee, born Feb. 26, 1848; married James Gooch, May 15. 1860.

215. Margaret Ellison Megee. Born Dec. 12, 1839, died Dec. 3, 1865; married Louis C. Gooch, May 15, 1860.

Children of Andrew Evans and _____, his wife:

216. John Evans.

And Their Descendants

Children of Jane Montgomery (58) and Robert Dean, her husband:

217. Louisa J. Dean, born May 29, 1817, died March 2, 1893; married John Mastin, Aug. 6, 1844.

218. Josiah Dean married Chorena Scott.

219. John W. Dean, born Nov. 23, 1820, died Feb. 23, 1870; married Mary A. Tatman, Oct. 10, 1853.

220. James Dean, died unmarried.

221. Rebecca A. Dean, born Feb. 4, 1828; married Solomon Round, Oct. 14, 1847.

221. Sarah E. Dean, born June 16, 1830; married Stephen Bybault, Nov. 17, 1847.

222. William Dean, unmarried.

223. Samuel Dean, born Oct. 16, 1820, died July 14, 1847; married Margaret E. Crane, Oct. 23, 1856.

224. Mary Worley Dean, born Dec. 15, 1834, died Feb. 6, 1858; married Chas. B. Johnson, Sept. 26, 1849.

Children of James Sproule Montgomery (59) and Electa Ola, dine Wilson, his wife:

225. Washington Leonidas Montgomery, born Sept. 9, 1831, died at 18 months old.

226. Oladine Jane Montgomery, born July 17, 1833; married Benj. Frank De Vole, Feb. 23, 1853.

227. Mary Lowry Montgomery, born Dec. 21, 1828, died Nov. 22, 1852; married Marshall Mason Fitch, Feb. 26, 1850.

Children of James Sproule Montgomery (59) and Frances Caroline West, his wife:

228. Fannie Electa Montgomery, born June 18, 1865, married Alva W. Frazier, Sept. 20, 1893.

229. James Brooks Montgomery, born Sept. 19, 1867, married Emma J. Frazier, March 14, 1894.

Children of Sarah Montgomery (60) and Noah Davis, her husband:

230. Elizabeth Davis, born Dec. 19, 1824, died March 8, 1894; married Wm. S. Allen, Feb. 9, 1842.

231. Mary E. Davis, born March 27, 1830; married John C. Jenison, Oct. 2, 1856.

232. Emily A. Davis, born May 15, 1832; died Jan. 7, 1901; married Geo. Vernon Churchill, Nov. 25, 1852.

233. Joseph Montgomery Davis, born June 1, 1834; died Sept. 2, 1862, unmarried.

234. Henrietta Davis, born Oct. 31, 1836, married J. Wesley Johnson, Oct. 2, 1856.

235. James Brinkley Davis, born July 10, 1838, died June 1, 1864; married Sallie Boardman, Oct. 13, 1859.

236. Electa Davis, born July 19, 1840, married Alfred Henry Bainum, July 30, 1861.

237. Samuel Noah Davis, born June 16, 1842; died Dec. 9, 1861.

Joseph Montgomery Davis (233) was a pilot on gunboats and died after a few months' service in the Federal army during' the civil war.

James Brinkley Davis (235) was a Federal soldier and fought in the battle of Cold Harbor, and after he had fought through the battle, while talking to a friend, he was shot by a sharp-shooter and died instantly.

Samuel Noah Davis enlisted in the same army and after a few months' service sickened and died, never having been in any battle.

Children of Susan Montgomery (61) and George Hennegin, her husband:

238. Henry Hennegin, born June 13, 1829, died Jan. 31, 1887; married Myrtella O. Wilson, Aug. 4, 1859.

239. Josephine Hennegin, born Sept. 9, 1831, died Oct. 7, 1832.

240. Sarah J. Hennegin, born Sept. 28, 1833, died April 8, 1898: married William Gookins, Nov. 6, 1857.

241. James Hennegin, born Sept. 12, 1835, died Oct. 18, 1899; married Eliza J. Jones, Feb. 21, 1861.

242. Louisa Hennegin, born Jan. 18, 1838, married Cassander H. Spurlock, Oct. 20, 1867.

243. Mary Hennegin, born Nov. 4, 1839, died June 27, 1870; married Elias Jenison, Sept. 25, 1867.

244. Peter Hennegin, born Dec. 26, 1841, married Mary E. Ross, Sept. 18, 1866.

245. John Hennegin, born June 18, 1845, died Oct 27, 1847.

Children of Samuel Montgomery (62) and Mary Worley, his wife:

246. Harriet J. Montgomery, born July 16, 1835, unmarried.

247. Anna E. Montgomery, born April 14, 1846; married James P. Kintner, Dec. 8, 1870.

248. Lizzie D. Montgomery, born Sept. 28, 1851, unmarried.

And Their Descendants

Children of Catherine Montgomery (64) and George W. Yocum, her husband

249. William Yocum, born March 26, 1827, unmarried.

250. Joseph M. Yocum, born Feb 13, 1829, married Nancy Ann Hook about 1855.

251. Mathias Yocum, born April 14, 1831, married Martha Tunderback in 1866.

252. George W. Yocum, born June 27, 1833, died June 15. 1882, married Sarah J. Tunderback, March 14, 1861.

253. Sarah Jane Yocum born April 18, 1836; married A. B. Woolston, June 4, 1860.

254. John P. Yocum, born April 1, 1838; married Cynthia Hancock, Jan. 10, 1869.

255. Nancy B. Yocum, born March 18, 1840; married George Win. Iden, Oct. 21, 1680.

256. Edward Yocum, born May 6, 1842; died Feb. 8, 1891; married America Hancock; second, Dicy Ann Gordon; third, Mollie Bed.

257. Elizabeth Ann Yocum, born March 22, 1846, died Aug. 12, 1865.

258. Mary Ellen Yocum, born 1850, died Oct. 9 1851.

259. Catherine Emma Yocum, born Sept. 2, 1851; died Oct. 15, 1583.

Children of Frances Montgomery (65) and Stephen Jenison, her husband:

260. John Montgomery Jenison, born 1833, died 1836.

261. Diantha Ann Jenison, born Aug. 27, 1832, died 1861; married John Crowell 1857.

262. Josiah Jenison, born Feb. 27, 1834, died Sept. 23, 1873; married Ellen Love Watts, Dec. 4, 1853.

263. Lydia J. Jenison, born Aug. 27, 1835, died Oct. 10, 1877; married Simeon G. Bisinger, Oct. 3, 1850.

264. George Jenison, born 1837, died July 13, 1862.

265. Edwin Jenison, born June 10, 1840, married Sarah Jane Wilmot, Sept. 19, 1868.

266. Edward Jenison, born June 10, 1840, married Lucy Ann Hancock, Feb. 18. 1866.

267. Stephen Jenison, born in 1842, died Nov. 1842.

The Montgomerys

Children of Joseph Edward Montgomery (67) and Clara Mariah Jenison, his wife:

268. Leonidas Lycurgus Montgomery, born June 28, 1841, died Aug. 9, 1843.

269. Clara Mariah Montgomery, born March 3, 1844; married Capt. D. Forney Withers, May 18, 1864; second, Franklin C. White, Nov, 7, 1872.

Children of Joseph Edward Montgomery (67) and Rebecca Phillips, his wife:

270. James Montgomery, M. D., born May 6, 1849, married Emma Shoddy, Jan. 17, 1882.

271. Laura Graham Montgomery, born Jan. 12, 1847, died April 1850.

Children of Elizabeth N. Montgomery (68) and John Thomas Dashiell, her husband:

272. John W. Dashiell, born Oct. 8, 1844, married Fanny Myers, Nov. 19, 1872.

273. Mary Dashiell, born Feb. 1, 1848, married John H. Brown, March 17, 1866.

274. Noah D. Dashiell, born Dec. 16, 1850; married Adelia Reinstead, June 6, 1872; second, Edith Charling, Dec. 24, 1896.

275. Sarah Amelia Dashiell, born March 17, 1859; married George Risinger, April 2, 1882.

John W. Dashiell (272) is a prominent minister of the Methodist church; has been presiding elder, and now lives at Moore's Hill, Indiana.

SEVENTH GENERATION.

Children of Priscilla Montgomery (72) and John Montgomery, her husband:

These are the same as numbers 107, 108, 109, 110, 111, 112 and 113 of the sixth generation.

Children of Abraham Stites Montgomery (70) and ____ Moore, his wife:

276. James Moore Montgomery, born March 26, 1860, died March 10, 1891; married Lizzie W. Moore, Dec. 20, 1883.

Children of William Montgomery (73) and Miriam Leechman, his wife:

277. William Leonard Montgomery, born Nov. 10, 1853; married Corda Lowdenback, Oct. 31, 1878.

278. Emma Jane Montgomery, born March 1, 1855; married James Moberley Nov. 26, 1871.

279. Robert G. Montgomery, born May 29, 1857; married Lydia Giltner, Feb. 26, 1878.

280. Samuel P. Montgomery. Born Aug. 4, 1860, died Aug. 18, 1861.

281. Alvin Luther Montgomery, born July 5, 1862, died Oct. 15, 1982; married Flora Blackwell, May 5, 1888.

282. Mary A. Montgomery, born Nov. 10, 1864, died March 19, 1888; married Richard Searcy.

283. Cora P. Montgomery, born Oct. 4, 1869, died April 7, 1897 married Sandford Lowdenback, Nov. 29, 1887.

284. Harry P. Montgomery, born Aug. 9, 1874, died Oct. 21, 1874.

285. John L. Montgomery, born June 16, 1877; married Nora Anderson March 22, 1899.

Children of Elizabeth Montgomery (74) and Leander Harris, her husband:

286. Robert Samuel Harris.

Children of Galveston Montgomery (76) and Susan Easterday, his wife:

287. Betta Montgomery, married Addison Markland; second, John Doak.

Children of Nancy B. Montgomery (77) and James Satchwell, her husband:

288. Joseph S. Satchwell, born July 19, 1862, married Minnie Angie Moore, Aug. 21, 1889.

289. Lydia A. Satchwell, born Feb. 4, 1864; married John Y. Cleveland, Dec. 18, 1884.

290. Lewis E. Satchwell, born Oct. 17, 1865; married Mamie Craig, Feb. 22, 1894.

291. James Satchwell, born Nov. 15, 1867, died March 21, 1873.

292. Eva P. Satchwell, born July 17, 1870; married Thomas B. Craig, March 4, 1893.

293. Corda Satchwell, born June 18, 1873.

294. Nicholas B. Satchwell, born April 4, 1875.

295. Mamie Satchwell, born Oct. 21, 1877, died Oct. 5, 1882.

296. Virgie T. Satchwell, born May 27, 1881.

297. Mary Blanche Satchwell, born Nov. 21, 1885; died March 8, 1893.

The Montgomerys

Children of Sallie Graham Montgomery (78) and Rev. J. B. Tharp, her husband:

298. Jephtha Montgomery Tharp, born Jan. 8, 1860; married Maggie Ballard, Dec. 7, 1889.

299. Lizzie Belle Tharp, born Feb. 1, 1862; married Ben F. Million. Nov. 2, 1886.

300. Edward Gibson Tharp, born Dec. 7, 1863, died Nov. 11, 1865.

301. Joe Eddie Tharp, born Oct. 29, 1867; married Mary Buckner, May 1, 1892.

Children of Byron J. Montgomery (80) and Eugenia Holt, his wife:
302. Floried Holt Montgomery, born Jan. 1, 1872.

Children of J. Byron Montgomery (80) and Mrs. Sallie Smith, his wife:
303. Sarah Bella Montgomery, born March 18, 1889.

Children of Frank Graham Montgomery (86) and Mollie Tompkins, his wife:

304. Jeptha Edward Montgomery, born Sept. 17, 1884.

305. George Tompkins Montgomery, born Nov. 30, 1885; died Dec. 30, 1885.

306. John Holloway Montgomery, born Jan. 28, 1892.

307. Frank Graham Montgomery. Jr., born July 7, 1894, died Nov. 20, 1899.

308. Charles Kearns Montgomery, born March 21, 1896.

Children of Frank W. Bacon (87) and Rose Ann Oliver his wife:
309. Sallie Louise Bacon, born Oct. 6, 1851, died in 1856.

310. Emily Lilly Bacon, born Oct. 9, 1856; married Edwin Trafton Hatheway, June 11, 1874.

Children of Frank W. Bacon (87) and Sue S. Spencer, his wife:
311. Rosa Bacon, born 1859, died same year.

312. Flora Boyd Bacon, born 1865; married A. Messick, 1884.

313. Frank William Bacon, born 1867; married Alice McCane in 1883.

314. Daisy Bacon, born 1869; married Frederick P. Hibbard in 1887.

315. John Preston Bacon, born 1872; married Edith Swifee in 1895.

316. Sadie C. S. Bacon, born 1875; married A. E. Curtis 1899.

317. Fern Messick, born 1878; unmarried.

Children of Frank W. Bacon (87) and Kate McLean, his wife:
318. George Bacon, born 1885.
319. Louisa Bacon, born 1886.
320. Kate Bacon, born 1888.

Children of Martha Priscilla Bacon (88) and Frank S Robinson, her husband:
321. Lula Robinson, born Jan. 9, 1853; married H. H. Graves, April 19, 1871.

Children of James Crawford Bacon (90) and Mary Heston Patton, his wife:
322. William Ginn Bacon married Elizabeth Long.
323. Lizzie Bacon married John Vollman.
324. James Bacon.
325. Myra Bacon, died in infancy.
326. George Bacon, unmarried.
327. David Ginn Bacon married Myrtle Glenn.
328. Austin Bacon, unmarried.
329. Lydia Bacon, unmarried.

Children of Ann Mary Bacon (91) and Joseph W. Roberts, her husband:
330. Georgie Bacon Roberts, born Feb. 23, 1865; married Chas. C. Herrick, June 25, 1885.
331. John Stewart Roberts, born July 13, 1869; unmarried.
332. Joseph G. Roberts, born Feb. 29, 1872; married Edith Craig, Jan. 16.
333. Matt Abbett Roberts, born March 15, 1877, unmarried.
334. Richard Knott Roberts, born Nov. 14, 1878, unmarried.
335. William Todd Roberts, born Sept. 24, 1884, unmarried.

Children of Nancy Montgomery (92) and John Harper, her husband:
336. James C. Harper, born Mar. 25, 1828, died June 11, 1872.
337. Sarah J. Harper, born March 19, 1831, died Feb. 1, 1898.
338. John A. Harper, born Nov. 2, 1832.
339. Josiah Harper, born Nov. 30, 1834.
340. Louisa Harper, born Aug. 2, 1836, died Sept. 11, 1866.

Children of Sallie Montgomery (93) and Ibsen Jackson, her husband:
341. Martha J. Jackson, born Nov. 12, 1832, died Feb. 12, 1833.
342. Mary E. Jackson, born Nov. 18, 1833; married Abe Douglass Nov. 26, 1859; second, Jacob Snyder, Sept. 11, 1865.

343. Zerelda Jackson, born Sept. 16, 1834, died April 13, 1860; married James Helm, Sept. 18, 1856.

344. Francis A. Jackson, born April 27, 1837; married Sarah Lucille Newton, Sept. 13. 1866, second, Charlotta Eakins, Oct. 9, 1889.

345. Minerva Jackson, born July 9, 1839; unmarried.

346. Jasper N. Jackson, born Aug. 14, 1849; married Letta Todhunter, March 28, 1898.

Francie A. Jackson (344) was mustered into the Federal Army as a private, Aug. 22, 1861, Co. A, 3rd Indiana Cavalry (45th Regiment); was twice captured, the last time in Wilson's cavalry raid, in the rear of Petersburg, Va., and was held a prisoner one month in "Libby," Richmond, Va., and escaped on the road to Andersonville, and reported to Louisville, Ky., where he was honorably discharged. He fought at Fredericksburg, Chancellorsville, South Mountain, Antietam, Gettysburg, The Wilderness and was in the raids of Kilpatrick, Stoneman, Pleasanton, and Wilson.

Children of Belinda Montgomery (94) and John Fothergill, her husband:

347. Elizabeth Jane Fothergill, born Feb. 16, 1837; married James Helm, May 1, 1861.

348. Mary Susan Fothergill, born Sept. 24, 1836; died Feb. 4, 1839.

349. Angeline Fothergill, born Nov. 25, 1839; married J. Frank White, Oct, 25, 1865; second, Chas. Stevens, Feb. 16, 1873.

350. Sarah Fothergill, born June 26, 1841, married Herman Bradley, Nov. 11, 1870.

351. Martha E. Fothergill, born Feb. 24, 1843; married Ed. Craig, Nov. 5, 1874.

Children of Wm. Montgomery (95) and Elizabeth Hoggins, his wife:

352. Ellen Montgomery, born Feb. 2, 1841, married Bennett Sanders, March 6, 1862.

353. Mary Jane Montgomery, born March 7, 1842; married Wm. Henry Bohannon, Dec. 21, 1865.

354. Amanda E. Montgomery, born Aug. 12, 1844; married Hiram Bohannon, Sept. 11. 1867.

355. Letha Montgomery, born Jan. 27, 1847; died May 28, 1877; married Nicholas Forsee. Feb. 1870.

356. John James Montgomery, born Jan. 20, 1850; died April 29, 1872, unmarried.

357. Wm. Montgomery, born Jan. 20, 1856, died Aug. 6, 1897; married Mollie Hawkins, Dec. 24, 1883.

358. George Montgomery, born Feb. 25, 1858, married Mary Orr, May 5, 1881.

Children of Hugh Montgomery (96) and Mary Ann Roswell, his wife:
359. Sarah Elizabeth Montgomery, born Dec. 2, 1844; married John W. Griffin, Dec. 20, 1854.
360. Eliza Jane Montgomery, born Oct., 1847, died Nov. 28, 1867, unmarried.
361. Narcissus Emeline Montgomery, born June 18, 1849, died March 27, 18(58, unmarried.
332. Mary Ezra Jefferson Montgomery, born May 14, 1853, died June 9, 1862.
333. Ella Belinda Montgomery, born Aug. 22, 1857, died July 17, 1881; married Silas Montgomery. Dec. 27, 1875.
364. George Henry Montgomery, born July 3, 1860, married Sallie Orr, Sept. 6, 1881; married, second, Loadicia Carver, March 16, 1887.
365. Hughetta Eveline Montgomery, born Oct. 5, 1863, married John W. Brown, Dec. 27, 1881.

Children of Hugh Montgomery (96) and Nora Smith, his wife:
366. Jesse Lee Montgomery, born Aug. 10, 1892.

Children of Nancy Montgomery and (97) Wm. McCreery, her husband:
367. Sarah Elizabeth McCreery, born Feb. 19, 1841; married Joshua Dudley Wayland, Aug. 30, 1863.
368. David McCreery, born Dec. 28, 1842; died June 11, 1864.
369. Thomas McCreery, born July 29, 1848, married Mary L. Griffith, Dec. 22, 1880.
370. Belinda McCreery, born Nov. 21, 1844, unmarried.
371. John William McCreery, born Feb. 13, 1847, died Feb. 13 1847.
372. Alice McCreery, born Oct. 29, 1851, died May 4, 1871, unmarried.
373. Flora Belle McCreery, born Feb. 4, 1854; married Rev. Frank Asberry Savage, Dec. 20, 1876.
374. Henry Montgomery McCreery, born June 26, 1856; married Ella Snyder July 9, 1878.
375. Margaret Letitia McCreery, born Feb. 28, 1860, married Rev. Robert Henry Hiner Boswell, Dec. 27, 1882.
376. Robert McCreery, born May 4, 1865, married Lucy Stafford, Feb. 13, 1889.

The Montgomerys

David McCreery (368) was a soldier of the Confederate, army, and was with the forces of Gen. John H. Morgan at Cynthiana, and was killed in the capture of General Hobson by Gen. Morgan's forces in a fight at that place; and the Rev. Savage and the Rev. Boswell, the latter now deceased, were prominent ministers of the Methodist church in Kentucky, the latter at his death a professor in. the Methodist college at Wilmore, Ky.

Children of John Montgomery (98) and Susan Easterday, his wife:

377. Belinda Montgomery, born Sept. 15, 1845, died Dec. 31, 1874; married Elijah M. Lewis, June 28, 1833.

378. Lewis E. Montgomery, born Nov. 10, 1847, died March 10, 1887; married Hellen Ames, March 23. 1871.

379. John R. Montgomery, born Jan. 6, 1850; died Nov. 19, 1883; married Docia Jane Craig, Dec. 24, 1872; second, Bettie Montgomery, Feb. 20, 1879.

380. Frank E. Montgomery, born March 21, 1853; died June 23, 1886; married Lou A. Christian, May 14, 1878.

381. Silas Montgomery, born Aug. 10, 1855, died Oct .14, 1879; married Ella Belinda Montgomery, Dec. 27, 1875.

382. Marion Montgomery, born Sept. 23, 1858; married Kate Christian, Feb. 1881; second, Eva Tilton, Oct. 7, 1885; third, Emma Winters, March 13, 1890.

Children of Mary Montgomery (99) and John Fothergill, her husband:

383. John Taylor Fothergill, born June 22, 1846; married Nannie Easterday, March 18, 1875.

384. Win. W. Fothergill, born May 24, 1848; married Fannie B. Gardner, Jan. 14, 1873.

385. Mollie E. Fothergill, born June 27, 1851, died Sept. 2, 1875.

386. Margaret Susan Fothergill, born Oct. 22, 1855, died June 7, 1860.

387. Jefferson K. Fothergill, born April 7, 1860; unmarried.

388. Charles David Fothergill, born Aug. 15, 1866, died Oct. 10, 1867.

389. George Montgomery Fothergill, Born Aug. 15, 1853; died Oct. 17, 1855.

390. Jackson Lee Fothergill, born Nov. 25, 1868, died March 12, 1883.

Children of Ezra Lee Montgomery (100) and Elizabeth Lecompte, his wife:

391. Wm. Mitchell Montgomery, born Dec. 10, 1857, died March 19, 1859.

392. Elizabeth L. Montgomery, born Nov. 4, 1859; married John R. Montgomery, Feb. 20, 1879; second, Thos. M. Scott, Nov. 17, 1886.

393. South Carolina Montgomery, born Oct. 11, 1861; married 'Rev. Chas. M. Cooper, Jan. 30, 1884.

Rev. Chas. M. Cooper is a Methodist minister located in Colorado.

Children of Emeline Montgomery (102) and John S. Heady, her husband:

394. George Henry Heady, born Oct. 8, 1855, married Rebecca Frances Heady, Oct. 1, 1882.

395. Sarah Elizabeth Heady, born June 12, 1857, married David Rice, Oct. 3, 1876.

396. John Franklin Heady, born July 26, 1859, died March 4, 1890.

397. Jefferson Davis Heady, born June 3, 1861; married Sabina Kenney, Jan. 18, 1894.

398. Thomas Lee Heady, born Feb. 19, 1863, married Harriett Florence Bond, Oct. 21, 1896.

399. Owen Heady, born Dec. 13, 1864, unmarried.

400. Lena Heady, born Sept. 27, 1866; married Henry S. Peacock, Aug. 7, 1895.

401. De Witte Kemper Heady, born June 9, 1870, died Aug. 21, 1898.

Children of George W. Montgomery (103) and Agues Clevinger, his wife:

402. Ella Montgomery, born Feb. 19, 1859, died June 6, 1863.

403. Elizabeth Lee Montgomery, born Jan. 15, 1862; married George Edward Brock, Jan. 22, 1880.

404. Robert Emmett Montgomery, born Feb. 15, 1864; married Sallie Ada Page, March 1885.

405. Hugh A. Montgomery, born Dec. 7, 1866, died May 12, 1877.

Children of Elizabeth Ann Montgomery (104) and Jacob Snyder, her husband:

406. Erastus Snyder, born May 27, 1855, married Mattie Nave, Sept. 1882.

407. Sarah Ella Snyder, born Jan. 7, 1858; married Henry Montgomery McCreery, July 9, 1878.

408. John Henry Snyder, born Nov. 16, 1860.

Children of Henry P. Montgomery (105) and Nannie E. Kenney, his wife:

409. Elzora Lee Montgomery, born Oct. 28, 1864, died March 26, 1865.

The Montgomerys

410. Henry P. (Harry) Montgomery, Jr., born Feb. 19, 1866, married Kate Wooldridge, Aug. 14, 1897.

411. Elizabeth Montgomery, born April 2, 1839, married John H. Cooper, Dec. 7, 1887.

412. Nettie Montgomery, born Jan. 30, 1873, died May 20, 1874.

413. Staiar Montgomery, born Feb. 25, 1875, married Daisy Long, April 20, 1899.

Children of Andrew J. Montgomery (106) and Mamie E. Porter, his wife:

414. John S. Montgomery, born Sept. 21, 1865; married Emma G. Casteel, Oct. 7, 1886.

415. Delilah Belle Montgomery, born Oct. 15, 1867, died April 7, 1870.

416. Hugh T. Montgomery, born Aug. 17, 1870, married Nellie G. Perry, Nov. 11, 1891.

417. George E. Montgomery, born March 21, 1873, died Nov. 25, 1901; married Kate Smith, Sept. 12, 1894; second, Mattie E. Turner, July 6, 1901.

418. William P. Montgomery, born Feb. 13, 1876; married Ethel Bipus, Oct. 10, 1900.

Children of James Montgomery (108) and Sallie Victoria Montgomery, his wife:

419. Clyde Verner Montgomery, born April 26, 1887.

420. Emmett Lee Montgomery, born April 23, 1889.

Children of Joseph Edward Montgomery (109) and Gillie Smith, his wife:

421. Jennie Montgomery, Jan. 12, 1878, died Oct. 7, 1879.

422. Lucilla Montgomery, born Jan. 8, 1879, married John Mylor, Nov. 22, 1899.

423. Chester Dare Montgomery, born April 19, 1881.

424. Eva Alice Montgomery, born Jan. 24, 1887.

Children of Jane Montgomery (111) and James Win. Lancaster, her husband:

425. Eddie Lancaster, born Nov. 14, 1877, died Nov. 19, 1877. 426. Myrtle Lancaster, born Oct. 12, 1878; married Chas.

Stanley Crouch, Oct. 24, 1900.

427. James Walter Lancaster, born Dec. 3, 1883.

428. Harry Lancaster, born June 14, 1891.

429. Jennie May Lancaster, March 20, 1892.

Children of James Montgomery (114) and Emma McConnell, his wife:

430. Lillie Montgomery, born Dec. 26, 1856.

And Their Descendants

431. Adeline Montgomery, b. Feb. 28, 1863, d. Sept. 29, 18&5.

432. John Hugh Montgomery (a mute), born Sept. 13, 1866.

433. Sallie Victoria Montgomery, born Dec. 31, 1869; married James Montgomery, April 14, 1885.

434. Emma Montgomery, born Oct. 28, 1872, married George Bohannon, Sept. 12, 1894.

435. Myrtle Montgomery, born May 23, 1875, died Feb. 19, 1887.

436. Alice Montgomery, born June 11, 1878, married Everett Winn, June 20, 1898.

Children of Samuel Montgomery (116) and Martha Miller, his wife:

437. Lena Montgomery.

Children of Margaret J. Montgomery (117) and Thomas Lancaster, her husband:

438. Mary Anna Lancaster, born Feb. 6, 1848 died Aug. 3, 1853.

439. James William Lancaster, born March 4, 1850, married Jane Montgomery, Jan. 22, 1877.

Children of Margaret J. Montgomery (117) and Wm. Bryan, her husband:

440. Sarah Elizabeth Bryan, born Jan 28, 1853, died Aug. 4,

Children of Margaret J. Montgomery (117) and John Sheets, her husband:

441. Charles Edwin Sheets, born March, 1859, died Jan. 8, 1863. ,

422. Hugh Lucien Sheets, born June 1, 1861, died June 8, 1863.

443. Emma Ann Sheets, born Nov. 25, 1833, died Oct. 5, 1865.

444. Oscar L. Sheets, born Aug. 26, 1866, married Lucy E. Byers about 1887.

Children of W. H. (Dink) Wood (123) and Susan Kimbrough, his wife:

445. John Wood.

Children of George S. Wood (124) and Matilda Bowie, his wife:

446. Harry A. Wood, born Dec. 3, 1894: unmarried.

447. Robert Marion Wood, born May 23, 1876; unmarried.

448. Mary Alta Wood, born Sept. 18, 1877; married Calveston Robinson, Nov. 5, 1896.

449. Lafayette Wood, born Jan. 26, 1879; married Stella Sweeney, Dec. 19, 1900.

450. George F. Wood, born July 21, 1883, died Sept. 15, 1884.

Children of Sarah Wood (12) and Ben Martin, her husband:

451. Mary Elizabeth Martin married Green Derman.

452. Sarah Ellen Martin, born Sept. 5, 1851; married James .Herron, Oct. 24, 1865, second, Henry Herron.

453. Sylvanus Martin married Laura Maxwell.

454. Emily Martin married John Stevenson.

455. George Ann Martin married Alfred Day.

456. Frankie Belle Martin, born Dec. 9, 1869, married Ira Landsberry.

457. Mattie Martin, born Nov. 25, 1865.

458. James Martin died in infancy.

459. Harriett Martin died in infancy.

Children of Mary A. Wood (126) and J. J. Martin, her husband:

460. Isabella Martin, born Aug. 21, 1856, married Harvey Edward Johns, Nov. 26, 1875.

461. John James Martin, born March 21, 1858; married Millie J. Dunlap, Feb. 13, 1879.

462. Mary Ann (Polly) Martin, born June 10, 1860; married Wm. Day, Sept. 19, 1876.

463. Priscilla Martin, born May 2, 1862; married Samuel T. Kay, March 28, 1894.

Children of Scott Wood (127) and Susan Herron, his wife:

464. Cordelia Wood, born July 24, 1874, died June 23, 1875.

465. Sarah Jane Wood, born Sept. 16, 1875, died Oct. 5, 1875.

466. Viora Dell Wood, born May 26, 1877, died Aug. 21, 1877.

467. Maud Wood, born Oct. 31, 1879, died Dec. 2, 1891.

Children of Nancy Frances Knox (129) and Randall L. Self, her husband:

468. John F. Self, born Oct. 19, 1848, married Martha McWilliams, Dec. 22, 1869.

469. Ruth J. Self, born Oct. 15, 1851, died Feb. 27, 1874.

470. Presley F. Self, born Aug. 25, 1856.

Children of Nancy Frances Knox (129) and Samuel L. Smith, her husband:

471. Margaret A. Smith, born Sept. 23, 1868.

472. Wm. E. Smith born Jan. 11, 1871.

Children of Mary J. Knox (130) and Anderville Swails, her husband:
473. Elmira F. Swails, born Oct. 1, 1846; married David D. Seright, March 29, 1834.
474. Margaret A. Swails, born Feb. 22, 1852; married John W. Nation, March 17, 1870.

Children of Mary J. Knox (130) and D. C. Williams, her husband:
475. Wm. Addison Williams, born Jan. 1, 1858, married Julia F. Rogers, Sept. 19, 1881.
476. Ida J. Williams, born July 29, 1861, died Dec. 18, 1886.

Children of Josiah Knox (131) and Margaret Smith, his wife:
477. Sarah Knox married Robt. Scott.
478. Nancy Knox married Robt. White.
479. Martha Knox married Henry Martin.
480. William Knox.
481. Jasper D. Knox.
482. John Knox.

Children of William H. Knox (132) and Emily Burns, his wife:
483. Irro Knox, born April 13, 1858, married Thomas Fry. Feb. 10, 1881.
484. George Knox, born Sept. 11, 1861.
485. Thomas Knox, born Oct. 15, 1865.
486. Nora Knox, born Sept. 15, 1875; died July 4, 1894.

Children of Eleanor Elizabeth Knox (133) and Hiram Rader, her husband:
487. Mary Rader, born July 25, 1856, married David Solomon, Sept. 22, 1876.
488. Wm. Rader, born April 2, 1858, died May 29, 1884; married Lattie Woodard, Oct. 29, 1879.
489. Margaret Rader, born July 20, 1859, married Quincy Pounds, July 21, 1880.
490. John Rader, born Sept. 9, l806, married Emma Parish April 20, 1890.
491. Catherine Rader, born July 26, 1868, married Wm. Curtis, Feb. 25, 1891.
492. Walter Rader, born Aug. 21, 1870, married Lilly Rogers, July 30, 1891.

The Montgomerys

493. Lewis Rader, born March 16, 1873, died April 6, 1892.
494. Ida Rader, born May 17, 1875, married William Swindler, Dec. 24, 1900.
495. Porter Rader, born Dec. 15, 1880.

Children of Jasper D. Knox (134) and Sarah McWilliams, his wife:
496. Luna M. Knox, born' Oct. 27, 1870, married Halbert Lockhart, Oct. 26, 1890.
497. Mary Olive Knox, born July 26, 1873; married Lewis S. Bennington, Nov. 29, 1891.
498. Bertha Knox, born April 6, 1878; unmarried.
499. Lennie M. Knox, born Feb. 24, 1884; unmarried.

Children of George R. Knox (136) and Anna Darnell, his wife:
500. Daisy Knox, born Jan. 26, 1876; married Francis M. Smith, Oct. 17, 1898.
501. Benjamin H. Knox, born August 5, 1877.

Children of Richard H. Montgomery (139) and Julia Couran, his wife:
502. Julia Estelle Montgomery, born 1864, married Charles Wear in 1888.
503. Susan Alice Montgomery, born 1868; married C. E. Lewis in 1893.
504. Mary Montgomery, born 1866, died 1870.
505. Richard H. Montgomery, Jr. born 1871.

Children of Richard H. Montgomery (139) and Mrs. Sue Hardin, his wife:
506. Cecil Montgomery, born 1885.

Children of Bacon Montgomery (140) and Mariah Hemans, his wife:
507. Mont Montgomery, born 1865.
508. May Montgomery, born 1868; married Mr. King, 1894.

Children of Susan Alice Montgomery (145) and H. N. Phillips, her husband:
509. H. Ney Phillips, born June 7, 1875, died Nov. 13, 1877.
510. Samuel Montgomery Phillips, born June 20, 1878.
511. John B. Phillips, born Nov. 12, 1880, died July 31, 1882.
512. Pierre Soula Phillips, born Aug. 6, 1887.
513. Marcean Montgomery Phillips, born April 24, 1895.

And Their Descendants

Children of Mollie P. Montgomery (147) and G. W. McDavid, her husband r
514. Harriett McDavid, born March 6, 1887, died June 9, 1887.
515. Murtie McDavid, born Oct. 31, 1889, died July 3, 1892.
516. John McDavid, born Jan. 18, 1890.
517. Samuel McDavid, born April 11, 1893.
518. Bertha McDavid, born Oct. 12, 1895, died July 16, 1897.

Children of Murtie Montgomery (148) and Dr. Elder Phillips, her husband:
519. Maude Irene Phillips, born Nov. 1, 1886.
520. Henry Montgomery Phillips, born Nov. 17, 1887.
521. Mattie Marian Phillips, born August 5, J£89.
522. Eldon Paul Phillips, born May 9, 1892.
523. Edna Pearl Phillips, born May 9, 1892.
524. Hugh Douglass Phillips, born Feb. 11, 1898, died Sept. 27, 1899.

Children of R. P. Montgomery (150) and Lizzie Jackson, his wife:
525. Cecil Elmo Montgomery, born Oct. 29, 1896, died July 22. 1897.

Children of R. P. Montgomery (150) and Hattie B. Haycock, his wife:
526. Ruby Pauline Montgomery, born July 31, 1900.

Children of Robt. S. Meek (151) and Espa Patton, his wife:
527. Lydia F. Meek, born Feb. 11. 1871, died Nov. 28, 1883.
528. Delta Meek, died in infancy.
529. Mabel V. Meek, born Feb. 11, 1871, married Thomas Prim, Nov. 14, 1894.
530. Clyde L. Meek, born Aug. 17, 1874.

Children of Margaret E. Meek (153) and Jas. B. Robinson, her husband:
531. William E. Robinson, born July 31. 1864, married Clara Tainter, Dec. 31, 1889.
532. Stella Robinson, born Dec. 10, 1870; married Alva Reed, Jan. 27, 1891.
533. Clara J. Robinson, born Nov. 12, 1875.

Children of John Thomas Meek (154) and Florence Bonner, his wife:
534. Lura Meek, born Dec. 25, 1872, married Wm. McCoy, March 23, 1891.

535. Mildred Meek, born June 15, 1874.
536. Albert Meet, born Oct. 28, 1876.
537. Florine Meek, born Oct. 3, 1886.

Children of Louisa Martha Meek (155) and John A. Meek, her husband:
538. Sylvia Jane Meek, born June 30, 1874, married Rev. J. S. Swogger, Dec. 26, 1893.
539. Milo E. Meek, born Nov. 3, 1871; married Ellen H. Long, Sept. 28, 1898.
540. Ethel Meek, born Nov. 21, 1880.
541. Elmer Meek, born Oct. 7, 1882.

Children of Adam Meek (156) and Adelaide Patton, his wife:
542. Clifford Patton Meek, born May 1, 1882.

Children of Anna E. Meek and (160) Strauther V. Pleak, her husband:
543. Floy Della Pleak, born Sept. 18, 1881.

Children of John Montgomery (163) and ____, his wife:
544. Joseph G. Montgomery; unmarried.
545. Rosa L. Montgomery married N. B. Hays, att'y at law.

Children of Mary Jane Cook (173) and Isaac Hill, her husband:
546. John Hill, born ___, died 1898; married Ida Harkins.
547. Martha Hill, born___, died 1898; married Lindsay H. Martin.
548. George .Washington Hill, married Hepsy Dobbins.
549. Margaret Hill, unmarried.
550. Belle Hill, unmarried.
551. Malinda Hill, unmarried.
552. Green Hill, born 1850, married Miss Mallicks.
553. Hugh Davis Hill, born 1852, married Dobbins.
554. Rebecca Hill married James Davis.

Children of George Washington Cook (174) and Nancy Hammack, his wife:
555. Jeff Cook.
556. Annie Cook married W. A. Greene.
557. Morgan Cook.
558. Henry Cook.

Children of John Doris Cook (175) and Emily O. Jenkins, his wife:
559. John Davis Cook, unmarried.
560. William Ira Cook married Ida Smith.
561. Jimmina Tilden Cook died in infancy.
562. Cook, died in infancy.
363. Rosa May Cook, unmarried.

Children of Margaret Elizabeth Cook (176) and John H. Davis, her husband:
564. Ida Metcalf Davis, born 1848, died 1865.
565. Hiram Washington Davis married Frankie Parker in 1880. Mrs. Frankie Parker Davis was an authoress and published an interesting volume of poems.

Children of Margaret Elizabeth Cook (176) and Basil Watson, her husband:
566. Wilber Watson, born 1863, married Susie Burris in 1896.

Children of Stephen Francis Cook (180) and —Berryman his wife:
567. Mollie Cook married W. A. Donnelly.
568. Laura Cook married Allen.

Children of Mary Ann Edwards (188) and John Reinhard, her husband:
569. Edwin P. Reinhard, M. D., born Aug. 10, 1825.
570. Ann E. Reinhard married Francis Worley, June 27. 1877
571. Charles Reinhard died in infancy.
572. Sarah Reinhard died in infancy.

Children of John Edwards (189) and Knight, his wife:
537. Eugene Edwards.
574. John Edwards.
575. Marius Edwards.
576. Huldah Edwards married Dr. Maynard.

Children of Frederick Geiger Edwards and Ann Pendleton Taylor, his wife:
577. John Franklin Edwards married Virginia Louise McGill, Jan. 31, 1865.
578. Alfred Edwards married Caroline Doris.
579. Frederick Edwards.
580. Zack Taylor Edwards.

581. Elizabeth Gibson Edwards married Bernard A. Pratt.

582. Sallie Jovett Edwards married Dr. J. C. Olmstead, Nov. 24, 1880.

583. Mary Montgomery Edwards married Edward Pastell King, Nov. 20, 1880.

584. Virginia Randall Edwards, unmarried.

John Franklin Edwards (577) was a major in the Confederate Army; enlisted in 1861 at Bowling Green, Ky., in Captain Robert Biggs' company, 9th Kentucky Infantry, commanded by Col. Thomas H. Hunt. After serving as a private four months he was appointed to the staff of Major General McLaws, and held the position of chief commissary of his division, and served in this capacity until the repulse of Gen. Longstreet at Knoxville in East Tennessee, and was then transferred to the staff of Gen. Longstreet, and was then appointed chief commissary of the First Army Corps. He served in following important battles (besides many smaller ones): am No. 7, Warwich River, Williamsburg, Seven Pines, Second Manassas, Sharpsburg, Harper's Ferry, Fredericksburgh, Chickamauga, Knoxville, Wilderness, Gettysburg, Chancellorsville, and the seven days fight around Richmond; and in all these battles never received a wound.

Alfred Edwards (578) was a captain on General McLaw's staff. Frederick Edwards (579) and Zack Taylor Edwards (580) were both soldiers in the Confederate army, and lost their lives in that service.

Mrs. Elizabeth Gibson Pratt (581) is the widow of B. A. Pratt, who was also a soldier in the Confederate army.

Children of Robert Edwards, Jr., and Miss Sandusky, his wife:
585. Mary Ann Edwards.
586. Rebecca Jane Edwards.

Children of William Sayers (196) and Jemima Jane Theobald, his wife:
587. Elizabeth F. Sayers, born Aug. 29, 1840, died April 25, 18(53; married R. M. Carlisle. July 24, 1862.
588. John Durbin Sayres, born June 21, 1846, married Georgia Riggs, May 29, 1873.
589. Nancy Jane Sayres, born Aug. 20, 1844; unmarried.
590. James Watson Sayers, born Sept. 12, 1842, married Cornelia Johnson, April 18, 1873.
591. R. Henry Sayers, born Aug. 30, 1848, married Emma Sharp, Jan. 13, 1874.

592. Sanford T. Sayers, born Oct. 28, 1850, died June 20, 1873.

593. William Nunn Sayers, born Oct. 30, 1852, unmarried.

594. Edmond Hosier Sayers, born Jan. 15, 1855, died Sept. 21, 1865.

595. Thomas Ralston Sayers, born Oct. 3, 1856, died June 4, 1895; married Stella Hall, Nov. 1, 1883.

596. Mary Griffin Sayers, born June 8, 1861; married Horace Cambron, Nov. 9, 1880.

Children of Nancy Jane Sayers (197) and John Smith Dickerson, her husband:

597. William Henry Dickerson, born July 18, 1840; married Laura E. Thompson, Nov. 28, 1888.

598. John Newton Dickerson, born Oct. 6, 1842; married Mariah M. Thompson, March 13, 1884.

599. James Porter Dickerson, born Nov. 2, 1846; married Alice Wilkerson, Aug. 20, 1869.

600. Edwin F. Dickerson, born March 25, 1852, married Hattie Lee Stevens, Oct. 3, 1882.

601. Margaret E. Dickerson, born Oct. 6, 1855; married Eben Thompson, Feb. 3, 1886.

Children of James Crockett Sayers (198) and Mary C. Sayers, his wife:

602. John Finley Sayers, born Aug. 12, 1854, married Kate Ranton, Dec. 6, 1877.

603. Eugene Boyd Sayers, born Aug. 21, 1857; married Bessie J. Vickers, Nov. 7, 1882.

604. Charles Wallace Sayers, born March 6, 1860; married Anna Banister, Aug. 9, 1892.

605. William Henry Sayers, born Aug. 12, 1862; married Mrs. Mary J. Wilson. Oct. 10, 1889.

606. Elizabeth Lou Sayers, born Aug. 14, 1865; unmarried.

607. James Bruce Sayers, born Oct. 6, 1868; unmarried.

608. Sanford Dickerson Sayers, born March 2, 1872; unmarried. James Bruce Sayers (607) is a soldier in the army in the Philippines.

Children of Ann Eliza Evans (200) and Henry Urmston, her husband:

609. Thomas Harcourt Urmston, born Dec. 3, 1860, married Blanch Louise Edder, Oct. 12, 1895.

610. Henry Urmston.

611. Ann Eliza Urmston married Bud Crook.

The Montgomerys

Children of James Henry Evans (204) and Mary Tommie Hughes, his wife:

612. Jean Evans, born July 16, 1872, married William Merritt O'Neal, March 15, 1892.

Children of Edwin F. Evans (205), M. D. and medical lecturer, and Mattie E. Scoville, his wife:

We quote one of his strong sentences:

"We can and should rise above such petty trifles, and well panoplies in the dignity and noble charity of our humane profession, continue to serve God and humanity, as faithful ministers of the healing art, knowing no man, creed or policy, looking for no honors or glories outside our profession, trusting to it alone for the consummation of all earthly hopes we have rest, which is beyond our "ken,' to the God of the good Samaritan, who turneth not aside from the need, misery and want of his fellow-man. .Resisting evil and striving for the good, we leave the rest to that God who made us what we are. 'Tis He alone can decidedly try us; He knows each chord, its various tone; each spring, its various bias."

613. Cecil S. Evans, born Nov. 9, 1891.
614. Bartel W. Evans, born Nov. 9, 1891.
615. Ethel L. Evans, born Aug. 12, 1895.

Children of Harriet Montgomery Evans (206) and George Davis, her husband

616. Davis, born Sept. 28, 1870, died May 17, 1871.
617. William Adams Davis, born 1872, died 1874.

Children of Dean Montgomery Megee (210) and Belle Switzer, his wife:
618. Eugene Megee, born Dec. 14, 1872.
619. Jane Belle Megee, born Sept. 1874; married Edwin Megee, Feb. 20, 1900.
620. Walter Nathaniel Megee, born July 7, 1876.
621. William Presley Megee, born May 20, 1878.
622. Elizabeth Megee, born Feb. 1, 1880, died same year.

Walter Nathaniel Megee is a soldier in the Philippines.

Children of Martha Jane Megee (211) and William F. Cravens, her husband:

623. Margaret Ann Cravens, born June 19, 1852; married George H. Swinney, Feb. 15, 1872.

624. Presley Cravens, born July, 1854, died July, 1864.
625. George Washington Cravens, born Oct. 1859; unmarried.
626. Sarah Marietta Cravens, born April 9, 1859, died Sept. 22, 1859.
627. Thomas Dockens Cravens, born May 20, 1861.

Children of Ann E. Cravens (212) and Joseph Clifton Cravens, her husband:
628. James Montgomery Cravens, born Dec. 1, 1851, died April 23, 1873.
629. Sarah Elizabeth Cravens, born Sept. 4, 1853; married Rev. J. A. Boothe.
630. Joseph Dean Cravens, b. Dec. 19, 1865, d. Jan. 27, 1866. Rev. J. A. Booth is a prominent Baptist minister in Kentucky.

Children of Sarah Crockett Megee (213) and W. W. Adams, her husband:
631. Martha Jane Adams, born Sept. 7, 1860; married Owen J. Carpenter, Oct. 18, 1883.
632. Anna Lee Adams, born Sept. 26, 1861; married Thos. D. Coleman, M. D., June 18, 1890.

Children of Marietta Megee (214) and James Gooch her husband:
633. Mary Irene Gooch, born March 11, 1862; married William Singleton, Oct. 7, 1879.
634. Maggie M. Gooch, born Feb. 21, 1861, died in infancy.
635. Susan James Gooch, born June 20, 1863, died in infancy.
636. Sallie Adams Gooch, Sept. 11, 1867, died Sept. 18, 1889.
637. William Montgomery Gooch, born Feb. 11, 1870.
638. Bertha Gooch, born April 30, 1871.
639. Elizabeth M. Gooch, born Dec. 14, 1873, married Prof. John E. Smith, Oct. 9, 1895.
640. J. Warren Gooch, born April 10, 1876.
641. Logan Ellison Gooch, born Oct. 7, 1897.
642. Theodore E. Gooch, born Dec. 23, 1878.

Children of Margaret Ellison Megee (215) and Louis C. Gooch, her husband:
643. William Dean Gooch, born March 3, 1861; married Laura E. White, Nov. 8, 1893.

The Montgomerys

Children of Louisa J. Dean (217) and John Mastin, her husband:
644. Nancy J. Mastin, born June 28, 1846, died Sept. 25, 1846.
645. Johanna Mastin, born May 14, 1859, married Dyer Elder, Jan. 1, 1867.
646. James P. Mastin, born June 8, 1845, died June 8, 1845.
647. Zachariah T. Mastin, torn May 14, 1848, died May 16, same year.
648. John T. Mastin, born 1852, died 1860.
649. Mary B. Mastin, born April 18, 1861; married Harry L. Gaines, Dec. 24, 1895.

Children of Josiah Dean (218) and Chorena Scott, his wife:
650. Thomas Dean, died in infancy.
651. Scott Dean, died in infancy.
652. Alice Dean, born July 5, 1865; married R. D. Wadsworth, Dec. 24, 1885.
653. Amada Dean, born Nov. 4, 1868; married F. V. Wadsworth, Dec. 15, 1885.
654. Silas C. Dean, born July 27, 1873; married Helen S. Cahr, July 2, 1896.
655. Sarah J. Dean, born Aug. 2, 1875; married Dr. Arthur Wadsworth, Dec. 11, 1895.

Silas C. Dean (654) is a soldier in the Philippines, in First Colorado Regiment.

Children of John W. Dean (219) and Mary Tatman, his wife:
656. Jennie Montgomery Dean, born May 16, 1857; married Dr. Chas. Taylor, Oct. 5. 1887.
657. Julia Dean, born March 19, 1855.

Children of Rebecca A. Dean (221) and Solomon Rounds, her husband:
658. James Taylor Round, born Sept. 21, 1848; married Susan Thompson, July 12, 1876.
659. George W. Round, born Feb. 13, 1850, died Dec. 8, 1850.
660. John C. Round, born Jan. 22, 1853; unmarried.
661. Charles Warren Round, born Jan. 22, 1855; unmarried.
662. Parley Wilder Round, born Nov. 2, 1856; married Alice Matilda Landers, March 29, 1877.
663. Mary Ballard Round, born Feb. 24, 1859; married Robert Jethro Morris, May 2, 1878.
664. Laura Belle R Kind, born Feb. 24, 1859; died Sept. 2, same year.

And Their Descendants

665. Clara A. Round, born Sept. 12, 1861, died Sept. 12, 1862.

666. Florence Janie Round, born July 5, 1863; married Daniel Anderson, Dec. 6. 1883.

667. Delia Belle Round, born Feb. 5, 1865; married John A. Mallory Dec. 7, 1888.

668. George Scott Round, born Jan. 15, 1868; married Linda Jackson, Dec. 3, 1890.

669. Myrtle Luella Round, born April 2, 1870; married Marshall Atherson, Nov 10, 1890.

670. Alfred Burton Round, born April 30,1872; married Sarah E. J. Beckwell, Oct. 12, 1897.

Children of Sarah E. Dean (221) and Stephen Rybolt, her husband:

671. Mary Jane Rybolt, born June 13, 1849; married Byron C. Anderson. Jan. 1. 1868.

672. John Whelton Rybolt, born Nov. 6, 1851, married Mary M. Young, March 11, 1877.

673. Delilah Rybolt, born March 26, 1854, married David Spurgin, Aug. 14, 1881.

674. Josiah Rybolt, born July 25, 1857, married Mary Hudson.

675. Hezekiah Rybolt, born Jan. 15, 1859, married Anna Black.

676. Louise Belle Rybolt, born Sept. 10, 1861, married Wm. Clark, April 27, 1882.

677. Sherman Rybolt, born May 23, 1866, married Cressie Logan.

678. Grant Rybolt, born April 15, 1868.

679. Willis Rybolt, born Feb. 2, 1870.

680. Stephen Ballard Rybolt, born Dec. 2, 1873.

Children of Samuel Dean (223) and Margaret E. Crane, his wife:

681. Mary J. Dean, born July 20, 1849; married Samuel Gookins, June 14, 1877; second, Frank N. Dickerson, April 14, 1896.

682. John J. Dean, born Nov. 25, 1859; married Flora Campbell, Oct. 30, 1890.

683. William E. Dean, born June 30, 1861; married Lydia A. Rheinstedt, March 13, 1889.

684. Cornelius E. Dean, born July 27, 1863; died Jan. 23, 1864.

685. Winfield Scott Dean, born Dec. 20, 1866, died Oct. 30," 1897; married Caroline Sutherland, April 16, 1893.

Children of Mary Worley Dean and C. B. Johnson, her husband:

686. Mary Jane Johnson, born July 12, 1850, died April 4, 1875, married Isaac W. White, June 17, 1868.

687. Laura Belle Johnson, born July 31, 1853; married Samuel Anderson in 1875.

688. William Robert Johnson, born Jan. Jan. 5, 1855; died in infancy.

689. Louisa Luella Johnson, born Jan. 31, 1858; married Shaw.

Children of Oladine Jane Montgomery (226) and Benj. Franklin Do Vole, her husband:

690. James Montgomery DeVol, born Jan. 6, 1854; married Rose Badgley, March 15, 1876.

691. Willie DeVol, born March 20, 1856.

692. Clark DeVol, born Sept. 7, 1857, married Eunice J. Ed Oct. 19, 1881.

693. William Merwin DeVol, born March 26, 1860; died Sept. 27, 1866.

694. Charles Haines DeVol, born Aug. 4, 1871.

695. Mary Electa DeVol, born Feb. 12, 1864, d. Feb. 22, 1864.

Children of Mary Lowry Montgomery (227) and Marshall M. Fitch, her husband:

697. James Montgomery Fitch, born Dec. 23, 1850; died Dec. 15, 1853.

698. Mary Lowry Fitch, born Aug. 23, 1852; died Sept. 27, 1873; married John M. Bullock, June 6, 1872.

Children of Fannie Electa Montgomery (228) and Alva W. Frazier, her husband:

699. Fannie Edith Frazier, born June 29, 1894.

700. Clara Lenore Frazier, born Nov. 26, 1895.

701. Mary Frances Frazier, born March 2, 1900.

Children of James Brooks Montgomery, (229) and Emma J. Frazier, his wife:

702. Florence Minnie Montgomery, born July 24, 1895.

703. Shirley Frances Montgomery, born July 3, 1897.

704. Dorothy Alice Montgomery, born April 29, 1899.

Children of Elizabeth E. Davis (230) and William S. Allen, her husband:

705. John Claborn Montgomery Allen, born Feb. 3, 1844; died Aug. 31, 1845.

706. Mary Frances Allen, born March 26, 1846, married Lemuel Bledson, Sept. 21, 1869.

707. Davis B. Allen, born Feb. 3, 1848, died March 15, 1895; married Sallie Richards. June 5, 1873.

708. Joseph S. Allen, born March 14, 1851, died Sept. 13, 1853.

709. William S. Allen, Jr. born Jan. 15, 1854, died July 6, 1855.

710. Noah D. Allen, born Aug. 15, 1856; died Oct. 10, 1862.

711. Emma Allen, born April 5, 1858, died Dec. 16, 1858.

712. Louisa Bacon Allen, born Oct. 26, 1859; married Jo Odus Hanks, Oct. 17. 1894.

713. Sallie Allen, born Aug. 1, 1862; married James H. McDanell, Jr., March 15, 1887.

Children of Mary E. Davis (231) and John A. Jenison, her husband:
714. Luella Jenison, born Oct. 7, 1857, married Lewis G. Jameson, May 16, 1878.

Children of Emily A. Davis (232) and George Vernon Churchill, her husband:
715. Edgar Fremont Churchill, born Sept. 27, 1853.

716. Franklin Davis Churchill, born May 13, 1855; married Emma C. Edwards, Sept. 16, 1877.

Mr. Churchill has been superintendent of schools at Oakland City and Huntingburg, Indiana.

717. James Otis Churchill, born Jan. 23, 1857; married Minnie Russell, June 7, 1887.

718. Eva Churchill, born July 23, 1859, unmarried.

719. Fannie Churchill, born June, 6, 1863, died July 24, 1886; married Orlando E. Remy, Oct. 17, 1883.

720. Mary Churchill, born Oct. 4, 1864, married J. E. Schooley Dec. 24, 1887.

721. Noah Fred Churchill, born Sept. 14, 1869; married Sadie A. Slater, Nov. 4, 1891.

Children of James Brinkley Davis (235) and Sallie Boardman, his wife:
722. Ben F. Davis, born Aug. 22, 1860, married Emma Truitt, Aug. 2, 1882.

Children of Electa Davis (236) and Alfred Henry Bainum, her husband:
723. Bainum, born May 10, 1862, died May 23, 1862.

The Montgomerys

724. Hattie Belle Bainum, born July 24, 1863.

725. Noah Conaway Bainum, born Nov. 13, 1864.

726. Charles Alfred Bainum, born June 5, 1866; married Byrd Irwin, Nov. 13, 1890.

727. Sarah Electa Davis Bainum, born Nov. 12. 1867, died July 20, 1874. N

728. Infant son, Bainum, burn Aug. 12, 1871, died Nov. 8, 1871.

729. John Henry Bainum, born May 26, 1873, d. July 18, 1874.

Children of Henry Hennegin (238) and Myrtella O. Wilson, his wife:

730. George M. Hennegin, born Oct. 30, 1859, d. Jan. 3, 1883.

731. Jennie Electa Hennegin, born March 22, 1862: married Sterling Wood Tucker, May 10, 1882; married, second, Dan G, Jones, Dec. 28, 1899.

732. Annie Florence Hennegin, born June 26, 1864; died Oct. 11, 1866.

733. Harry W. Hennegin, born June 2, 1865.

734. Madge Wilber Hennegin, born Nov. 20, 1870.

735. Mary Bullock Hennegin, born June 27, 1874.

736. Percy Hennegin, born March 30, 1883, died Aug. 28. 1884.

737. Thaddeus Wilson Hennegin, born April 15, 1880, died Oct. 14, 1881.

Children of Sarah J. Hennegin (240) and William Gookins, her husband:

738. Henry H. Gookins, born Nov. 6, 1852; married Belle Moore, Dec. 8, 1874; second, Amanda Hyatt, March 2, 1883.

739. Meritt M. Gookins, born Nov. 8, 1853; married Jennie Holman, Nov. 8, 1883.

740. Tillie J. Gookins, born July 2, 1855; married Chas. F. Hazelrigg, July 11, 1886; second, Wm. G. Tremain, April 9, 1895.

741. Mary L. Gookins, born Aug. 12, 1857; married George Foster, Dec. 25, 1890.

742. Clara E. Gookins, born July 8, 1860; married R. N. Scherer, July 17, 1898.

743. William S. Gookins, born Nov. 2, 1864, married Emma Newman, Jan. 22, 1893.

744. George S. Gookins, born Feb. 10, 1866, married Anna Terhune April 25, 1893.

745. Peter. H. Gookins, born Nov. 9, 1868, married Clara Will, Feb. 11, 1894.

746. James N. Gookins, born Aug. 13, 1870; married Mary Hertenstein, June 1, 1891.

747. Oscar N. Gookins, born Oct. 7, 1872; married Nora Griffith, June 17, 1896.

748. Albert F. Gookins, born April 25, 1874.

Children of James Hennegin (241) and Eliza J. Jones, his wife:
749. Peter Segal Hennegin, b. Mar. 8, 1862, d. Aug. 26, 1863.
750. Myrtella Hennegin, born May 30, 1864, died Jan. 23, 1867.
751. Henry Montgomery Hennegin, born Sept. 29, 1866.
752. George L. Hennegin, b. April 1, 1869, d. Sept. 16, 1878.
753. Roscoe Sherman Hennegin, born April 2, 1872; married Adella Reed, Dec. 3. 1893.
754. William E. Hennegin, b. March 7. 1875. d. May 24, 1893.
755. Tacy D. Hennegin, born March 28, 1878.
756. Tillie E. Hennegin, born Dec. 13, 1881; married Charles Scott. June 17, 1900.
757. Moses Hennegin, born May 15, 1884.

Children of Louisa Hennegin, (242) and Cassander Spurlock, her husband:
758. Schuyler C. Spurlock, born July 6, 1868.
759. George Spurlock, born July 6, 1868.
760. Flora Spurlock, born Jan. 14, 1871, died Aug. 4, 1871,
761. Florence Spurlock, born Jan. 14, 1871, died Aug. 4, 1871.
762. Frederick Spurlock, b. July 24, 1872, died Sept. 22, 1879.
763. James Spurlock, born Aug. 31, 1874, died Oct. 30, 184.

Children of Mary M. Hennegin (243) and Elias Jennison, her husband:
764. William Clermont Jennison, born Aug. 15, 1868, died May 1, 1899; married Nora Duncan, Dec. 24, 1896.

Children of Peter Hennegin (244) and Mary E. Ross, his wife:
765. Laura E. Hennegin, born Sept. 18, 1867; married Jacob Wimer Jordan, Aug. 12, 1896.

Children of Annie E. Montgomery (27) and James P. Kintner, her husband:
766. Samuel Montgomery Kintner, born Dec. 11, 1871; married Elizabeth Edith Blanchard, Oct. 244, 1895.

767. Mary Elizabeth Kintner, born March 2, 1875.
768. Edwin Graham Kintner, born May 6, 1881.
769. William Charles Kintner, born May 26, 1884.
770. Julia Fay Kintner, born July 5, 1888.
771. James Shields Kintner, born Sept. 28, 1890.

Children of Joseph W. Yocum (250) and Nancy Ann Work, his wife:
772. James Yocum, born Feb. 28, 1855, died March 5, 1860.
773. George T. Yocum, born June 1, 1857.

Children of Mathias Yocum (251) and Martha Tunderback, his wife:
774. Rosetta Yocum, born June 3, 1869, married Chas. Gray, Oct. 13, 1886.
775. Minnie Yocum, born Jan. 2, 1869, married Nelson Lawrence, May 10, 1889.
776. John E. Yocum, born Dec. 9, 1871; married Nannie B. Foley, Dec. 18, 1892.

Children of George W. Yocum (252) and Sarah J. Tunderback, his wife:
777. Julia A .Yocum, born Dec. 31, 1861; married Daniel E. Bailey, Jan. 7, 1880.
778. Amanda Yocum, born Oct. 22, 1863, married Eugene B. McQueen, July 28, 1884.
779. Sarah E. Yocum, born July 17, 1865, died Nov. 17, 1893; married J. B. West. May 4, 1884.
780. Catherine J. Yocum, born Nov. 14, 1867; married N. B. Turpin, March 16, 1892.
781. Fernette Yocum, born Aug. 9, 1869, died Dec. 17, 1871.
782. Martha A. Yocum, born June 11, 1871; married George A. Vasse, Oct. 24, 1888.
783. Malinda locum, born Sept. 25, 1873, died July 20, 1887.
784. Isaac R. Yocum, born April 23, 1875, died Aug. 21, 1901; married Minnie Beagle, Oct. 23, 1895.
785. James N. Yocum, born April 23, 1877, died May 18, 1887.
786. Daniel W. Yocum, born April 25, 1878.
787. John A. Yocum, born Feb. 25, 1880, died March 13, 1880.
788. Maude M. Yocum, born April 20, 1881, married Gladdie Bailey, Oct. 31, 1895.

Children of Sarah Jane Yocum (253) and A. B. Woolston, her husband:

789. Annette Merrie Woolston, born July 30, 1861, married Elisha B. Barnes, Feb. 27, 188.

790. Noah Harris Woolston, born Jan. 8, 1863; married Carrie C. Butcher, Sept. 3, 1893.

791. John Edward Woolston, born Sept. 24, 1864; married Dola B. Coates, June 28, 1888.

792. George Alfred Woolston, born March 7, 1869; unmarried.

793. Catherine Woolston, born May 5, 1869, died Dec. 3. 1872.

794. Mary Woolston, born June 10, 1871, died Dec. 11, 1873.

795. Jervis Irie Woolston, born June 12, 1873, died June 24, 1873.

Children of John P. Yocum (254) and Cynthia Hancock, his wife:

796. Clara J. Yocum, born Jan. 6, 1870.

797. William Edward Yocum, born Oct. 28, 1871.

798. Cora May Yocum, born Oct. 27, 1873, died Aug. 14, 1878.

799. John Alfred Yocum, born Dec. 28, 1875, d. May 15, 1877.

800. Infant son, born dead, May 17, 1878.

801. George Franklin Yocum, born July 28, 1879.

802. Stella Merris Yocum, born Nov. 10, 1881, died Dec. 31, 1882.

803. Claude Everett Yocum, born May 25, 1884.

804. Golden Maude Yocum, born Feb. 1, 1887.

805. Myrtie Belle Yocum, born Dec. 23, 1889.

Children of Nancy B. Yocum (255) and George William Id en, her husband:

806. John F. Iden, born May 24, 1862, married Sarah R. Edwards, Nov. 13, 1895.

807. Ida J. Iden, born Feb. 20, 1864, died Feb. 13, 1890; married Winfield Jackson, Feb. 13, 1883.

808. Sarah C. Iden, born Nov. 13, 1866; married Oscar Adams, May 12, 1885.

809. Dorcas Ann Iden, born Aug. 21, 1867; married Joseph C. Black, March 10, 1889.

810. William D. Iden, born March 22. 1869, died April 3, 1869.

811. Mary Emma Iden, born April 4, 1870; married Chris. Farney, Sept. 4, 1889.

812. Lillie May Iden, born July 6, 1873; married Alfred D. Cunningham, Feb. 24, 1897.

813. George Juliette Iden, born April 1, 1876; married Chas. E. Harper, Feb. 24, 1897.

Children of Edward Yocum (256) and America Hancock, his wife:
814. Adda Yocum, born Jan. 7, 1870, died June 7, 1870.
815. Bertha Yocum, born July 4, 1871, died Dec. 20, 1871.

Children of Edward Yocum (256) and Dicy Ann Gordon, his wife:
816. Katie Yocum, born Dec. 22, 1876, married Elmer Hamilton, Dec. 25, 1890.
817. Mary Cynthia Yocum, born April 14, 1878, died April 30, 1888.

Children of Edward Yocum (256) and Mollie Red, his wife:
818. Nannie B. Yocum, born June 23, 1884.
819. Joseph E. Yocum, born Jan. 25, 1888.

Children of Diantha Ann Jenison (261) and John Crowell, her husband:
820. William Morgan Crowell, born July 5, 1852, died in 1855.
821. Margaret Ann Crowell, born Oct. 15, 1853, died May 24, 1885; married Dennis Chapin, 1877.
822. Emma Jettie Crowell, born Dec. 19, 1859, married Jacob Smith Coons, Oct. 7, 1886.
823. Isabella Crowell, born Sept. 13, 1861, died in infancy.
824. Benjamin Franklin Crowell, born Sept. 29, 1883, died in infancy.
825. Christiana Crowell, born Feb. 7, 1865, died in infancy.
826. Frances Jane Crowell, born 1855; married Phineas Ward, 1872.

Children of Josiah Jenison (262) and Ellen Love Watts, his wife:
827. Isabella W. Jenison, born June 30, 1854, married Eph. M. Croutz, Nov. 11, 1875.
828. Ann W. Jenison, born Feb. 27, 1857, died Dec. 1862.
829. Mary Frances Jenison, born July 29, 1599, married Geo. Ketchum, Sept. 11, 1S76; second, Joseph McKenzie, 1896.
830. William Ellsworth Jenison, born June 29, 1862, died Sept. 21. 1872.
831. Ida May Jenison, born March 27, 1865; married Joel Edward Brisco, Dec. 16, 1890.
832. Luella Jenison, born Nov. 7, 1867, married Edwin D. Septon, April 23, 1888.
833. Jeannette Jenison, born March 22, 1872, married Curtis Yuard, Oct. 10, 1893.

Children of Lydia J. Jenison (263) and Simeon G. Risinger, her husband:

834. Frances J. Risinger, born July 31, 1851 married David A. Duncanson, March 5, 1871.

835. Alice L. Risinger, born July 20, 1854; married Jerry Duncanson, Jan. 1, 1873.

836. Nancy A. Risinger, born Sept. 7, 1856; married John A. Rockwell, March 28, 1875.

837. Malinda E. Risinger, born May 26, 1858, died April 22, 1897; married Orange N. Risinger, July 4, 1878; second, W. E. Coles, Feb. 1892.

838. George E. Risinger, born June 1, 1860; married Otella J. Risinger, July 23, 1890.

839. Mary B. Risinger, born March 19, 1862; married Fred E. Blair, June 14, 1882.

840. Simeon S. Risinger, born May 2, 1865; married Mae L. Barrow Risinger, July 24, 1888; second, Aaron Henrietta Rolander, June 13, 1900.

Children of Edwin Jenison (265) and Sarah Wilmot, his wife:

841. Stephen Allen Jenison, born July 5, 1869; married Ada Molyneaux, Aug. 19, 1893; died Sept. 6, 1900.

842. Sarah Frances Jenison, born Oct. 6, 1870, died Jan. 7, 1895; married George E. Williams, July 23, 1887.

843. Cora Drusilla Jenison, born Feb. 8, 1872, married Edward Lefter, April 8, 1892.

844. Susan Elmira Jenison, born Oct. 21, 1874, died Oct. 22, 1888.

845. Bertha Isabella Jenison, born Sept. 30, 1876; married Elliott S. Sell. June 24, 1894.

846. Laura Elnora Jenison, May 5, 1880; married Walter Gill, Aug. 22. 1898.

847. Meritt Rollan Jenison, born Oct. 31, 1882.

848. Augustus Jenison, born Nov. 14, 1886.

849. Augusta Jenison, born Nov. 14, 1886.

850. Charia Jane Jenison, born Oct. 9, 1888, died Oct. 10, 1897.

Children of Edward Jenison (266) and Lucy Ann Hancock, his wife:

851. Ella Madora Jenison, born Nov. 19, 1866, died in 1867.

852. Edward Eugene Jenison, born June 19, 1869; married Ida Elton, 1897.

853. Lillie May Jenison, born August 22, 1872; married William S. Edwards, Sept. 28, 1897.

Children of Clara Mariah Montgomery (269) and Captain D. Forney Withers, her husband:
854. Sylla Edna Withers, born Dec. 26, 1868.

Children of Clara Mariah Montgomery (269) and Franklin C. White, her husband:
855. Charles Wallace White, born Nov. 20, 1875.
856. Clara Mariah White, born April 10, 1878.
857. Edward Montgomery White, born April 10, 1878.
858. Imogene Pearl White, born Sept. 23, 1884.
859. Frank Montgomery White, born Oct. 19, 1893.

Children of Dr. James Montgomery (270) and Emma Shoddy, his wife:
860. James Edward Montgomery, born Feb. 9, 1884.

Children of Rev. John W. Dashiell (272) and Fanny Myers, his wife:
861. Thomas Myers Dashiell, born Sept. 30, 1873; married Marie Boyle, June 21, 1899.
862. Emma Amelia Dashiell, born Dec. 7, 1874.
863. Newton Hayman Dashiell, born Sept. 6, 1876; married Rhoda Adams, June 12, 1900.
864. Edward Noah Dashiell, born May 1, 1878.
865. Lawrence Basil Dashiell, born Feb. 9, 1880.
866. Rachel Dashiell, born April 19, 1882.
867. Fanny Dashiell, born Sept. 25, 1883.
868. Edith Dashiell, born July 18, 1885.
869. John Frederick Dashiell, born April 30, 1888.
870. Stanley Dashiell, born Jan. 11, 1890; died Sept. 15, 1898.
871. Leland Elder Dashiell, born June 6, 1891.
872. Mary Dashiell, born Feb. 24, 1898.
Edward Noah Dashiell (864) is a student at Purdue University. Lawrence Basil Dashiell (865) in U. S. Navy, gunner on Battleship Kentucky.

Children of Mary Dashiell (273) and J. H. Brown, her husband:
873. Francis Brown, born Jan. 23, 1867, married Effie T. Draper, Feb. 22, 1887.
874. Charles Brown, born Sept. 9, 1870, married Emma Sefton, Oct. 21, 1891.
875. Nettie M. Brown, born May 22, 1873, married Charles N. Sefton, Sept. 24, 1895.

876. John T. Brown, born Dec. 5, 1875, married Zoo Myers, Jan. 3, 1899.
877. Sherman Brown, born April 2, 1880; married Elizabeth Roberts, Dec 21, 1900.

Children of Noah D. Dashiell (274) and Adeline Reinstead, his wife:
878. James Dashiell, born Dec. 26, 1873; married Elva Sefton, Feb. 6, 1895.
879. John Dashiell, born Aug. 20, 1881.
880. Robert Dashiell, born Dec. 12, 1894.
881. Thomas Dashiell, born June 27, 1896.

Children of Noah D. Dashiell (275) and Edith Charling, his wife:
882. Elizabeth S. Dashiell, born Oct. 19, 1900.

Children of Sarah Amelia Dashiell (275) and George Risinger, her husband:
883. Noah Risinger, born Dec. 29, 1882.
844. Flora Risinger, born Aug. 23, 1884.
885. Katie Risinger, born Jan. 21, 1892.
886. Mary Risinger, born April 17, 1894.

EIGHTH GENERATION.

Children of James Moore Montgomery (276) and Lizzie W. Moore, his wife:
887. J. Ashton Montgomery, born Aug. 13, 1889.
888. Mary F. Montgomery, born Aug. 31, 1891.

Children of William Leonard Montgomery (277) and Cordia Lowdenback, his wife:
889. Harry C. L. Montgomery, born July 31, 1879.

Children of Emma Jane Montgomery (278) and James Mobley her husband:
890. Perry L. Mobley, born Sept. 17, 1872.
891. Jesse M. Mobley born Aug. 8, 1873.

Children of Robert G. Montgomery (279) and Lydia Giltner his wife:

The Montgomerys

892. Frederick M. Montgomery, born Nov. 28, 1878, married Jerome Woodson Jan. 23, 1901.

893. Mamie J. Montgomery, born Aug. 30, 1880; married Edward Hardin, Feb. 15, 1898.

Children of Alvin Luther Montgomery (281) and Flora Blackwell, his wife:
894. William Luther Montgomery, born March 15, 1893.
895. Lucile Montgomery, born Mar. 6, 1891, died Mar. 6, 1896.

Children of Mary A. Montgomery (282) and Richard Searcy, her husband:
896. Pearl L. Searcy, born July 1, 1885.
897. Mary C. Parker Searcy, born March 22, 1888.

Children of Cora P. Montgomery (283) and Sanford Lowdenback, her husband:
898. Lloyd W. Lowdenback, b. July 6, 1891, d. Dec. 7, 1895.

Children of John L. Montgomery (285) and Nora Anderson, his wife:
899. Nellie Montgomery, born March 21, 1893.
900. Cordie T. Montgomery, born Jan. 13, 1900.

Children of Robert Samuel Harris (286) and _____, his wife:
901. Park Harris, born in 1889.
902. Ward Harris, born in 1891.
903. Harris, born in 1898.

Children of Betta Montgomery (287) and Addison Markland, her husband:
904. Allenvesten Markland.
905. Lena P. Markland married James Jacobs.
906. Chester Johnson Markland.
907. Ida Belle Markland.
908. Elvessa Markland.

Children of Bettie Montgomery (287) and John Doak, her husband:
909. Robert Lee Doak.
910. Robert Lee Doak.

Children of Lydia A. Satchwell (289) and John Y. Cleveland, her husband:
911. Perry C. Cleveland, born March 22, 1886.

912. Grover Cleveland, born Dec. 28, 1887.
913. Nannie B. Cleveland, Dec. 16, 1889.
914. Archie Cleveland, born Dec. 4, 1891.
915. Bryan Cleveland, Dec. 25, 1897.
916. Emma D. Cleveland, born March 6. 1901.

Children of Lewis E. Satchwell (290) and Mamie Craig, his wife:
917. Everett Satchwell, born Feb. 18, 1895.
918. Howard Satchwell, born July 4, 1897.

Children of Eva P. Satchwell (292) and Thos. B. Craig, her husband:
919. Pryor Craig, born July 29, 1894.
920. Estella Craig, born Aug. 23, 1896.
921. Floyd Craig, born Nov. 25, 1898.

Children of Jeptha Montgomery Tharp (298) and Maggie Ballard, his wife:
922. Ballard Montgomery Tharp, born Feb. 7, 1891.
923. William Ely Tharp, b. Sept. 26, 1892, d. Nov. 99, 1895.
924. Graham Tharp, born Sept. 1, 1894.
925. Rachel Mayo Tharp, born Nov. 3, 1898.

Children of Lizzie Belle Tharp (299) and Ben F. Million, her husband:
926. Sallie Belle Million, b. Aug. 16, 1888, d. March 4, 1889.
927. Belle Lee Million, born July 11. 1892, died Aug. 5, 1892.
928. Brent Million, born March 4, 1895.

Children of Joe Eddie Tharp (301) and Mary Buckner, his wife:
929. Coleman Buckner Tharp, born March 17, 1893.
930. Mary Joseph Tharp, born Nov. 27, 1896.
931. Sarah Elizabeth Tharp, born Nov. 28, 1900.

Children of Emily Lilly Bacon (310) and Edwin Trafton Hathaway, her husband:
932. Alvin Kaye Hathaway, b. May 19, 1876, d. Dec. 27, 1890.
933. Louise Hathaway, born May 2, 1880, died June 2, 1881.
934. Frank Bacon Hathaway, born Aug. 21, 1882.
935. Edward Trafton Hathaway, born Oct. 26, 1892.

Children of Flora Boyd Bacon (312) and Wm. A. Messink, her husband:
936. Frank Amita Messink, born in 1885.
937. William Messink, born in 1890.

Children of Frank W. Bacon (313) and Alice McCane, his wife:
938. Lucille Bacon, born in 1894.

Children of Daisy Bacon (314) and Frederick P. Hibbard, her husband:
939. Ina Hibbard, born Aug. 14, 1888, died Sept. 6, 1892.
940. Fred P. Hibbard, Jr., born July 25, 1894. ,

Children of John Preston Bacon (315) and Edith Swifee, his wife:
941. Fred P. Bacon, born in 1896.
942. Edith Bacon, born in 1898.

Children of Sarah C. S. Bacon (316) and A. E. Curtis, her husband:
943. Daisy S. Curtis, born Aug. 10. 1900.

Children of Lula Robinson (321) and H. H. Graves, her husband:
944. James Robinson Graves, born 1872.
945. Henry Hampton Graves, born Jan. 12, 1874, died Nov. 30, 1876.
946. Lula Belle Graves, born Aug. 18, 1876, died Oct. 14, 1883.
947. Archie Bryant Graves, born June 17, 1878.
948. Thurman B. Graves, born Dec. 3, 1880.
949. Nellie Graves, born March 22, 1883.
950. Eila Cleveland Graves, born March 20, 1885.

Children of Georgia Bacon Roberts (330) and Chas. C. Herrick, her husband:
951. Mary Louisa Herrick, born March 13, 1895.
Children of Joseph G. Roberts (332) and Edith Craig, his wife:
952. Edith L. Roberts, born Aug. 16, 1897.

Children of Mary E. Jackson (342) and Abe Douglass, her husband:
953. Abel F. Douglass, born Aug. 6, 1860, married Minnie Stewart, Nov. 25, 1885.

Children of Mary E. Jackson (342) and Jacob Snyder, her husband:
954. S. Harold Snyder, born Nov. 27, 1866; married Edith Sheldon, March 31, 1892.

955. Antoinette Snyder, born Feb. 22, 1868; married Prof. D. M. Nottier, Aug. 31, 1893.

Children of Zerelda N. Jackson (343) and James Helm, her husband:
956. Eugene A. Helm, born Aug. 18, 1858; married Rosa Lee Brown, March 6, 1890.
957. John Helm, born April 7, 1860, died July 4, 1860. Children of Francis A. Jackson (344) and Sarah Lucille Newton, his wife:
958. Alice F. Jackson, born Dec. 20, 1867; married Cornelius Hufford, Feb. 24, 1890.
959. Flora E. Jackson, born Sept. 26, 1869, died Dec. 28, 1869.
960. Earl F. Jackson, born March 16, 1873; unmarried.
961. Mary E Jackson, born May 28, 1876; married Henry W. Tangeman, Dec. 9, 1898.
962. Ella M. Jackson, born July 23, 1879; married Holland P. Long, May 30, 1900.

Children of Jasper N. Jackson (346) and Leila Todhunter, his wife:
963. Edith Jackson, born Feb. 20, 1899.
964. Jackson, daughter, born Dec 1, 1900.

Children of Elizabeth Jane Fothergill (347) and James Helm, her husband:
965. William T. Helm, born March 19, 1862, married Kate Anderson, April 19, 1888.
966. Belinda Helm, born Aug. 21, 1863, married James Ellis, Aug. 5, 1894.
967. Allen T. Helm, born April 20, 1868.
968. Ira F. Helm, born Dec. 4, 1869.
969. Irvin S. Helm, born Jan. 26, 1875, died Dec. 20, 1875.
970. George L. Helm, born Aug. 8, 1878, died March 18, 1880.
971. Harry B. Helm, born Sept. 1, 1881.

Children of Angeline Fothergill (349) and J. Frank White, her husband:
972. Luella White, born Dec. 3, 1866, died Dec. 1, 1867.
973. Irene White, born Nov. 1, 1867, married Rev. Grant Abbott, 1892.

Children of Angeline Fothergill (349) and Chas. Stevens, her husband:
974. Ida E. Stevens, born Aug. 8, 1875; married Jas. B. Powell, Jan. 1, 1899.

975. John R. Stevens, born Oct. 14, 1876; married Annie Petty, Nov. 9, 1899.

Children of Sarah Fothergill (350) and Herman Bradby, her husband:
976. Lemuel Bradby, born June 1871, married Kate Sheldon, Jan. 8. 1900.
977. Harry Bradby, born Nov. 6, 1877, unmarried.

Children of Martha Fothergill (351) and Ed Craig, her husband:
978. Mary E. Craig, born Dec. 29, 1875, died Sept. 11, 1896; married Elmer Forest Haydon, Oct. 7, 1894.
979. Arthur Craig, born June 23, 1877, died July 21, 1880.
980. Tabitha Craig, born Sept. 19, 1878.
981. John L. Craig, born Feb. 3, 1881.
982. Alice R. Craig, born July 25, 1882.
983. Edward Craig, born April 4, 1885.
984. William Carroll Craig, born Feb. 20, 1888.

Children of Fallen Montgomery (352) and Bennett Sanders, her husband:
985. Theodore Sanders, born May 18, 1863, died April 14, 1864.
986. Verney Sanders, born May 30, 1868.
987. Mary Ella Sanders, born Dec. 18, 1871.

Children of Mary Jane Montgomery (353) and Win. Henry Bohannon, her husband;
988. Candace Bohannon, born Nov. 8> 1866, died Jan. 20, 1869.
989. Win. Bohannon, born July 13, 1870, married Lydia Orr, Feb. 12, 1891, married second. Pearl Harrod, June 7, 1893.
990. George Bohannon, born Feb. 5, 1872, married Emma Montgomery Sept. 12, 1894.

Children of Amanda Montgomery (354) and Hiram Bohannon her husband;
991. Victor Montgomery Bohannon, born Sept. 28, 1868; married Pearl Middleton, Feb. 15, 1899.
992. Abram Bohannon, born March 15, 1870, married Girtrada Tharp, Feb. 25, 1896.
993. William Virgil Bohannon, born Sept. 10, 1871.

994. Mary Nicolas Bohannon, born March 3, 1873; married Byron Flood, Feb. 9. 1892.

995. Ella Bohannon, born May 23, 1878, married Elliott Estes, Feb. 2, 1898.

996. James Bohannon, born May 23, 1878, died Oct, 27, 1893.

Children of Letha Montgomery (355) and G. Nicholas Forsee, her husband:

997. Lilly Forsee, born Dec. 6, 1874, died March, 1880.

998. Letitia Forsee, born Sept. 3, 1876, died Aug. 4, 1877.

Children of George Montgomery (358) and Mamie Orr, his wife:

999. Richard Orr Montgomery, born Feb. 14, 1882.

1000. Bessie Montgomery, b. July 2, 1883, d. June 4, 1901.

Children of Sarah Elizabeth Montgomery (359) and John Griffin, her husband:

1001. Mary Jane Griffin, born Oct. 1, 1860; married John Richard Brown, Oct. 30, 1884.

1002. Hugh Griffin, born Dec. 7, 1866.

Children of Ella Belinda Montgomery (363) and Silas Montgomery, her husband:

1003. Jesse W. Montgomery, born May 1, 1877; married Minerva Potters Shoesmith, Oct. 25, 1899.

1004. John Silas Montgomery, born Nov. 15, 1878; died aged three mouths.

Children of Hughetta Eveline Montgomery (365) and John W. Brown, her husband:

1005. Claude Kirby Brown, born Dec. 6, 1884.

1006. Maude Allen Brown, born July 13, 1888.

Children of Sarah Elizabeth McCreery (367) and Joshua Dudley Wayland, her husband:

1007. Emmett Wayland, born July 24, 1864.

1008. Mary Frances Wayland, born May 30, 1866, died Nov. 12, 1869.

1009. Scott Tandy Wayland, born Dec. 10, 1867, married Lora E. Peak, Oct. 12, 1892; second, Kate G. Wayland, Feb. 9, 1898.

1010. Lenora Wayland, born Oct. 21, 1869, married Joshua F. Wallace. Aug. 17, 1892.

Children of Thomas McCreery (369) and Mary L. Griffith, his wife:
1011. Orliff McCreery, born Sept. 29, 1881.
1012. Mary Blanch McCreery, born June 22, 1884.
1013. Maude S. McCreery, born July 6, 1886.
1014. Azele McCreery, born March 6, 1888.
1015. Leslie Earl McCreery, born Jan. 19, 1890.
1016. Mary Alice McCreery, born Sept. 1, 1893.
1017. Ethel T. McCreery, born Sept. 14, 1900.

Children of Flora Belle McCreery (373) and Frank Asberry Savage, her husband:
1018. Daisy Meek Savage, born June 12, 1878.
1019. William Currans Savage, born Feb. 16, 1880.
1020. James Everett Savage, born Oct. 17, 1882.

Children of Henry Montgomery McCreery (374) and Ella Snyder, his wife:
1021. Walton H. McCreery, born June 1, 1879.
1022. Audley Malvern McCreery, born April 2, 1881.
1023. William Jacob McCreery, born May 20, 1883.
1024. Everett Harold McCreery, born March 13, 1885.
1025. Antoinette Belle McCreery, born Aug. 16, 1887.
1026. Claude Frank McCreery, born June 23, 1891.
1027. Robert Henry McCreery, born Sept. 1, 1896.
1028. Edith McCreery, born Oct. 19, 1899.

Children of Margaret Letitia McCreery (375) and Rev. Robert Henry Hiner Boswell, her husband:
1029. William Marvin Boswell, born Nov. 24, 1883.
1030. Robert Henry Hiner Boswell, born Feb. 4, 1886, died July 13, 1886.
1031. Charles Keen Boswell, born Feb. 28, 1892.
1032. Anna Clara McCreery Boswell, born Nov. 4, 1893.
1033. Edward Everett Boswell, born Aug. 23, 1896.

Children of Robert E. McCreery (376) and Lucy Stafford, his wife:
1034. Stella McCreery, born Dec. 31, 1890, died March 4, 1895.
1035. Josie Heath McCreery, born April 12. 1894.

Children of Belinda Montgomery (377) and Elijah W. Lewis, her husband:

1036. Otis Lewis, born March, 1864, died Aug. 21, 1886; married Lydia Funk, Oct. 1885.

1037. Beatrice Lewis, born April 7, 1885; married Dan B. Hanlon, July 6, 1885.

1038. Victoria Lewis, born Feb. 12, 1870; married Eliza J. McMillan. Feb. 12, 1893.

1039. Halle Lewis, born July 3, 1872, died Jan. 13, 1881.

1040. Franklin W. Lewis, born Dec. 10, 1874; married Sam J. Woody, Oct. 6, 1897.

Children of Lewis Montgomery (378) and Helen Ames, his wife:
1041. Nathan C. Montgomery, born Dec. 18, 1871; married Myretta Davis, July 25. 1895.

Children of John R. Montgomery (379) and Jennie Craig, his wife:
1042. Margaret Montgomery, b. Feb. 10, 1874, d. Feb. 13, 1874.
1043. Curtis Montgomery, born Feb. 10, 1875.

Children of Frank E. Montgomery (3S0) and Lou A. Christian, his wife:
1044. Milton Montgomery, born Aug. 28, 1881.
1045. Karl Montgomery, born July 25, 1883, died March 9, 1885.
1046. Frank L. Montgomery, born March 23, 1885.

Children of Silas Montgomery and Ella B. Montgomery his wife: Same as children of Ella Belinda Montgomery (363).

Children of Marion Montgomery (382) and Eva Tilton, his wife:
1047. Earle Montgomery, born July 31, 1886.

Children of Marion Montgomery (382) and Emma J. Winters, his wife:
1048. Pauline Montgomery, born May 25, 1893.
1049. Howard Montgomery, Sept. 28, 1897.

Children of John Taylor Fothergill (383) and Nannie Easterday, his wife:
1050. Lula H. Fothergill, b. Jan. 24, 1876, d. Dec. 14, 1879.
1051. Carrie B. Fothergill, b. April 1, 1879, d. Dec. 1, 1879.
1052. John Thomas Fothergill, born Sept. 14, 1877, died Nov. 28, 1879.
1053. Jesse Lee Fothergill, born Nov. 23, 1880.

1054. Lewis Fothergill, b. Sept. 20, 1882, d. Sept. 21, 1882.
1055. James Arthur Fothergill, born Jan. 9, 1884.
1056. Mary Susan Fothergill, born Dec. 25, 1885.
1057. William T. Fothergill, born Jan. 29, 1888.
1058. Hubert Brown Fothergill, born Sept. 21, 1890.
1059. Charles Davis Fothergill, born July 30, 1892.
1060. Martha Jane Fothergill, born Feb. 1, 1895.
1061. Luther Lee Fothergill, born June 24, 1898.
1062. Nannie May Fothergill, born March 3, 1901.

Children of William W. Fothergill (384) and Fannie B. Gardner, his wife:
1063. Lillie B. Fothergill, b. Aug. 15, 1876; d. Mar 18, 1880.
1064. Bessie L. Fothergill, b. Dec. 6, 1878, d. March 19, 1880.
1065. Carroll W. Fothergill, born March 31, 1881.
1066. Thomas S. Fothergill, born July 21, 1883.
1067. Lulie May Fothergill, born Aug. 2, 1888.
1068. Josie Brown Fothergill, born Feb. 11, 1895.
1069. Mattie S. Fothergill, born June 7, 1874, married G. G. Kelly, Jan. 1, 1879.

Children of Elizabeth L. Montgomery (392) and T. M. Scott, her husband:
1070. Charles Lecompte Scott, b. March 9, 1888, d. May 6, 1888.
1071. E. Bertha Scott, born July 6, 1889, died Feb. 13, 1893.
1072. Maurice Lee Scott, born Aug. 20, 1890.
1073. Walne Scott, born Aug. 30, 1893, died Aug. 30, 1893.
1074. Elizabeth Sophia Scott, born Oct. 20, 1894.
1075. Margaret Mitchell Scott, born Oct. 8, 1899.

Children of South C. Montgomery (393) and Rev. Chas. M_ Cooper, her husband:
1076. Robert Lee Cooper, born Aug. 6, 1885.
1077. Isaphine DeMoss Cooper, born Nov. 23, 1887.
1078. Carroll Cooper, born Feb. 1890, died Aug. 1895.
1079. Elizabeth Cooper, born Jan. 8, 1895.
1080. Joseph Lecompte Cooper, b. June 1896, d. Sept. 1, 1896.
1081. Margaret Cooper, born Nov. 27 1897.
1082. Charles Elswood Cooper, born Nov. 17, 1900.

Children of George Henry Heady (394) and Frances Heady, his wife:
1083. Emma Elizabeth Heady, born Sept. 9, 1885.

Children of Elizabeth Heady (395) and David Rice, her husband:
1084. Callie Rice, born Sept. 7. 1879.
1085. Grace Rice, born Nov. 14, 1881.
1086. Lola David Rice, born Dec. 29, 1885.

Children of Thomas Lee Heady (398) and Harriett Florence Bond, his wife:
1087. Helen Emeline Heady, born Aug. 10, 1897.

Children of Elizabeth Lee Montgomery (4403) and George Edward Brock, her husband:
1088. George Francis Brock, b. Nov. 18, 1880, d. Jan. 29, 1H90.
1089. Lean Brock, born Sept. 26, 1883.
1090. Anna Brock, born Jan. 27, 1887.
1091. Joe Hugh Brock, born Feb. 26, 1889.
1032. Nellie Agues Brock, born Sept. 30, 1893.
1093. William Robert Brock, born April 10, 1897.

Children of Robert Emmett Montgomery (401) and Sallie Ada Page, his wife:
1094. George W. Montgomery, Jr., born July 21, 1886.

Children of Erastus Snyder (406) and Mattie Nave, his wife:
1095. Omer Snyder, born Aug. 29, 1883.
1096. Florence Snyder, born Feb. 17, 1885.
1097. Everett Snyder, born March 10, 1887.
1098. Frank Snyder, born April 9, 1889.
1099. Daniel Snyder, born April 13, 1893, died Feb. 13, 1894.
1100. Orville Snyder, born March 14, 1891.
1101. William G. Snyder, born June 9, 1898.

Children of Sarah Ellen Snyder (407) are the same as children of Henry Montgomery McCreery (374).

Children of Elizabeth Montgomery (411) and John H. Cooper, her husband:
1102. Nannie M. Cooper, born March 16, 1889.
1103. Henry M. Cooper, born Aug. 3, 1891.
1104. John Lewis Cooper, born Sept. 23, 1894.

The Montgomerys

Children of Staiar Montgomery (413) and Daisy Long, his wife:
1105. Henry P. Montgomery, Jr., born Jan. 18, 1900.

Children of John S. Montgomery (414) and Emma G. Casteel, his wife:
1106. Montgomery, born Aug. 11, 1887, died in infancy.
1107. James Jackson Montgomery, born April 13, 1889.
1108. Marian Montgomery, b. June 26, 1891, d. Jan. 2, 1896. 1103. Maurice Montgomery, born Oct. 7, 1897.

Children of Hugh T. Montgomery (416) and Nellie G. Perry, his wife:
1110. Hazel H. Montgomery, born March 12, 1893, died May 12, 1896.
Children of Sallie Victoria Montgomery (433) are same as James Montgomery (108).

Children of Alice Montgomery (436) and Everett Winn, her husband:
1111. Montgomery Ellsworth Winn, born July 16, 1899.

Children of James William Lancaster (439), same as children of Jane Montgomery (111).

Children of Oscar L. Sheets (444) and Lucy E. Byers, his wife:
1112. George Sheets, born 1889.
1113. Nellie Sheets, born 1890.

Children of Mary Alta Wood (448) and J Calveston Robinson, her husband:
1114. Myra Robinson, born Dec. 22, 1898.

Children of Mary Elizabeth Martin (451) and Green Derman, her husband:
1115. George Derman married Ollie Southead.
1116. Ida Derman married George Hopperton.
1117. Laura Derman married Joe Southard.
1118. Angie Derman.
1119. Ellen Derman married Thomas Craig.
1120. Loula Derman. J

Children of Sarah Ellen Martin (452) and James Herron, her husband:

1121. Annie E. Herron, born March 10, 1870; married Jack McDonald, Nov. 22, 1885.
1122. Mollie Herron, born April 22nd 1867.
1123. Jennie Herron, born Feb. 3, 1873.
1124. John Herron, born Feb. 9, 1876.
1125. Nora B. Herron, born July 25. 1888.

Children of Sylvanus Martin (453) and Laura Maxwell, his wife:
1126. Benjamin Martin.
1127. Walter Martin.
1128. Lawrence Martin.

Children of Emily Martin (454) and John Stevenson, her husband:
1129. Lulie Stevenson married Bert Stewart.
1130. James Stevenson.
1131. William Stevenson.
1132. Carrie Stevenson.
1133. Frankie Stevenson.

Children of George Ann Martin (455) and Alfred Day, her husband:
1134. Lucy Day.
1135. Hattie Day.
1136. Ernest Day.
1137. Emmett Day.
1138. Archie Day.
1139. William Day.
1140. Claude Day.

Children of Franklin Bell Martin (456) and Ira Landsberry, her husband:
1141. Sallie Landsberry.
1142. Edith Landsberry.

Children of Isabella Martin (460) and Harvey Edward Johns, her husband:
1143. Lillie Johns, born Sept. 2, 1877, died Oct. 7, 1878.
1144. James Johns, born June 9, 1879, died Aug. 25, 1878.
1145. Jennie B. Johns, born Nov. 15, 1882; married Arthur Fon, March 6, 1901.
1146. Edna M. Johns, born Oct. 13, 1887.
1147. Homer Johns, born March 23, 18.14.

Children of John James Martin (461) and Mellie Dunlap his wife;
1148. Rellie Martin, born Aug. 13, 1880.
1149. Carrie Martin, born June 23 1883
1150. James Martin, born March 14, 1887.
1151. Jay C. Martin, born Sept. 26, 1888
1152. Fred Martin, born March 26, 1891.
1153. Priscilla Martin, born Feb. 4, 1894.
1154. Mary Martin, born Nov. 17, 1896.
1155. Ada Martin, born Aug. 12, 1900.

Children of Mary Ann (Polly) Martin (462) and William Day, her husband:
1156. Mary E. Day, born Oct. 10, 1880
1157. Walter Day, born Aug. 29, 1881.
1158. Effa Day, born Aug. 20, 1884.
1159. Nellie P. Day, born Dec. 20, 1886
1160. Nora Day, born Feb. 8, 1892.
1161. Fred Day, born Oct. 17, 1899, died Dec. 28. 1899.

Children of John F. Self (468) and Martha McWilliams, his wife:
1162. Laura Etta Self, born Oct. 18, 1870; unmarried.
1163. Prudence Self, born March 4, 1872; married Omer Sharp, July 29, 1897.
1164. Mary Maude Self, born July 20, 1874; married Anson B. Clark, No. 28, 1894.
1165. Nellie E. Self, born May 25, 1877; unmarried.
1166. Viola Ruth Self, born Feb. 4, 1884; unmarried.
1167. Earl Self, born Nov. 17, 1888.
1168. Carrie E. Self, born Aug. 31, 1890.
1169. John L. Self, born Aug. 3, 1879, died Sept. 17, 1880.

Children of Elmira F. Swails (473) and David D. Seright, her husband:
1170. Mary K. Seright, born Jan. 13, 1865, died Sept. 24, 1890; married James L. Harvey, Jan. 6, 1887.
1171. Margaret A. Seright, born March 31. 1867; married Noah C. Henagar, July 4, 1881.
1172. Andersville Morton Seright, born Dec. 8, 1869; married Mary Gilliland, July 16, 1899.
1173. Lou Seright, born March 8, 1873, died Feb. 17. 1895; married T. B. Goddard. Aug. 20, 1893.
1174. William A. Seright, born Feb. 25, 1877; unmarried.

1175. Robert Seright, born Sept. 30, 1879; unmarried.
1176. Harry Clay Seright, March 2, 1885; died April 5, 1889.
1177. Elsie Seright, born Sept. 12, 1887.

Children of Margaret A. Swails (474) and John W. Nation, her husband:
1178. Wilbur Ketchen Nation, born April 13, 1874.
1179. Kitty Clay pool Nation, born April 13, 1885.

Children of William Addison Williams (475) and Julia F. Rogers, his wife:
1180. Florence Gertrude Williams, born Dec. 18, 1883.

Children of Sarah Knox (477) and Robert Scott, her husband:
1181. Scott.
1182. Scott.
1183. Scott.

Children of Nancy Knox (478) and Robert White, her husband:
1184. Ernest White.
1185. William White.
1186. Allie White.

Children of Martha Knox (479) and Henry Martin, her husband:
1187. Lola Martin.
1188. Forest Martin.
1189. Ray Martin.

Children of Irro Knox (483) and Thomas Fry, her husband:
1190. Emma Fry, born Nov. 23, 1881.
1190. Earl Fry, born July 6, 1884.

Children of Mary Rader (487) and David Solomon, her husband:
1191. Charles Solomon, born Aug. 21, 1879.
1192. Bessie Solomon, born Aug. 30, 1881.
1193. Logan Solomon, born Oct. 18, 1885.
1194. Luzetta Solomon, born May 18, 1887.
1195. Katie Solomon, born July 4. 1890.
1196. Nolie Solomon, born April 8, 1893.
1197. Alice Solomon, born April 16, 1887.

Children of William Rader (488) and Lathe Woodard, her husband:
1198. Icie Rader, born Sept. 10, 1880.
1199. Onie Rader, born March 20, 1882.
1200. Pearlie Rader, born July 25, 1883.
1201. Carl Rader, born Sept. 23, 1884.

Children of Margaret Rader (489) and Quincy Pound, her husband:
1202. Mattie Pound, born Oct. 14, 1X83.
1203. John Pound, born March 29, 1886.
1204. Floy Pound, born May 21, 1888.
1205. Ovel Pound, born Jan. 20, 1892.
1206. Ethel Pound, born May 8, 1897.

Children of John Ruder (490) and Emma Parish, his wife:
1207. Wilber/ Rader, born April 8, 1891.
1208. Myrtle Rader, born May 2, 1893.
1209. Mary Rader, born Oct. 15, 1895.
1210. Fairy Rader, born July 23, 1898.

Children of Catherine Rader (491) and William Curtis, her husband:
1211. Madge Curtis, born July 27, 1893.

Children of Walter Rader (492) and Lilly Rogers, his wife:
1212. Corda Rader, born Sept. 9, 1892.
1213. Love Rader, born Oct. 18, 1894.
1214. Cora Rader, born Nov. 5, 1898.

Children of Luna M. Knox (496) and Halbert Lockhart, her husband:
1215. Bertie Earl Lockhart, born July 22, 1895.

Children of Mary Olive Knox (497) and Lewis Bennington, her husband:
1216. Lloyd R. Bennington, born Dec. 18, 1892.
1217. John Basil Bennington, born July 23, 1896.
1218. Orrin Bennington, born Nov. 6, 1900.

Children of Daisy Knox (500) and Francis M. Smith, her husband:
1219. Cecil R. Smith, born June 29, 1899.

Children of Susan Alice Montgomery (503) and C. E. Lewis, her husband:
Mercedes Lewis, born Feb. 25, 1894.

Daniel Lewis, born 1896.
Susan Alice Lewis, born 1899.

Children of William E. Robinson (531) and Clara Tainter, his wife:
1220. Mary Robinson, born June 12, 1890.
1121 Margaret Robinson, born Aug. 18, 1894.
1222. Mildred Robinson, born Dec. 20, 1899.

Children of Stella Robinson (532) and Alva Reed, her husband:
1123. Roland Reed, born Dec. 26, 1892.
Children of Lura Meek (534) and William McCoy, her husband:
1224. Mabel Glenn McCoy, born Nov. 29, 1892.
1225. Eugene McCoy, born Nov. 21, 1896.
1226. Herschel McCoy, born Oct. 18, 1898.

Children of Sylvia Jane Meek (538) and Rev. J. S. Swogger, her husband:
1227. George Glenn Swogger.

On this branch of the family the writer has only been able to learn that Rosa L. Montgomery (545) and her husband, N. B. Hays, have one child, a son; that John Hill (546) and Ida Haskins, his wife, have three children; that Martha Hill (547) and Lindsay H. Martin her husband, have six children; and that George Washington Hill (548) and Hepsy Dobbyn's, his wife, have five children.

Many others of this branch of the family, down to and including No. 568, have offspring; but the details could not be obtained.

Children of Alfred Edwards (518) and Caroline Doris, his wife:
1228. Frederick Geiger Edwards.
1229. Elizabeth Edwards, born ___, died in infancy.
1230. Ann Taylor Edwards.
1231. Alfred Edwards.

Children of Mary Montgomery Edwards (583) and Edward Postell King, her husband:
1232. Frederick Taylor King, born Oct. 17, 1879, died Nov. 16, 1889.
1233. John Gadsden King, born Dec. 4, 1882, died Dec. 8. 1882.
1234. Edward Postell King, Jr., born July 4, 1884.
1235. John Olmstead King, born April 25, 1887.
1236. Mary Edwards King, born Aug. 9, 1891.

Children of Dr. Edwin P. Reinhard (569) and ____, his wife:
1237. John Reinhard.
1238. Mary Reinhard.
1239. William Reinhard.
1240. Kate Reinhard.
1241. Helen Reinhard.
1242. Grace Reinhard.
1243. Charles Reinhard.

Children of Elizabeth F. Sayers (587) and R. M. Carlisle, her husband:
1244. John Griffin Carlisle, born April 20, 1863, died June 6,

Children of John Durbin Sayers (588) and Georgia Riggs, his wife:
1245. Hubert L. Sayers, born June 12, 1876.
1246. Stella Savers, born Aug. 16, 1880, died Sept. 28, 1896.

Children of R. Henry Sayers (591) and Emma Sharp, his wife:
1247. Charlie S. Sayers, born Nov. 9, 1874; married Max Wilson, May 8, 1895.
1248. Graham J. Sayers, born Jan. 12, 1878; married Elizabeth L. Pollock, July 5, 1900.
1249. Elizabeth Jane Sayers, born Oct. 13, 1888, died Aug. 3, 1889.

Children of Thomas Ralston Sayers (595) and Stella Hall, his wife:
1250. Harry Ralston Sayers, b. Nov. 14. 1885, d. Sept. 17, 1887.
1251. Roy Sayers, born Aug. 17, 1888, died Aug. 28, 1888.
1251. Watson Durbin Sayers, born Dec. 17, 1889.

Children of Mary Griffin Sayers (596) and Horace Cambron, her husband:
1252. Logan Carlisle Cambron, born April 23, 1883.
1253. Mary Horace Cambron, born March 19, 1885. ,

Children of William Henry Dickerson (597) and Laura E. Thompson, his wife:
1254. Maria Margaret Dickerson, born Jan. 18, 1890.
1255. Rose Eliza Dickerson, born April 16, 1891.

Children of John Newton Dickerson (598) and Mariah Thompson, his wife:
1256. Elbert Roy Dickerson, born July 16, 1885.
1257. Nellie Alice Dickerson, born Dec. 5, 1889.
1258. John Newton Dickerson, b. May 1892, d. Oct. 11, 1892.

Children of Edwin F. Dickerson (600) and Hattie Lee Stevens, his wife:
1259. Genia P. Dickerson, born May 25, 1884.
1260. Harry Wilber Dickerson, born Jan. 18, 1890.
1261. John Stanley Dickerson, born Sept. 21, 1888, died Jan. 14. 1889.

Children of Margaret E. Dickenson (601) and Eben Thompson, her husband:
1262. Laura Louise Thompson, born July 16, 1887.
1263. Jane Smith Thompson, born Dec. 11, 1889.
1264. Margaret Eba Thompson, born July 22. 1895.
1265. John L. Thompson, born Nov. 1, 1892, died July 15, 1893.
1266. James W. Thompson, b. Nov. 1, 1892, d. July 24, 1893.

Children of John Finley Sayers (602) and Kate Ranton, his wife:
1267. Bessie R. Sayers, born Sept. 28. 1878.
1268. Mabel Sayers, born June 21, 1883.
1269. Marie Sayers, born June 3. 1886.
1270. Sue Catherine Sayers, born June 3, 1893.
1271. James Bradley Sayers, born Feb. 10, 1896.

Children of Eugene Boyd Sayers (603) and Bessie J. Vickers, his wife:
1272. Paul Warner Sayers, born April 5, 1889.
1273. Geneva Prudence Sayers, born Jan. 10, 1891.
1273. Edna Sayers, born March 12, 1886, died Aug. 5, 1883.

Children of Jean Evans (612) and William Merritt O'Neal, her husband:
1274. Younger Evans O'Neal, born Dec. 21, 1892.
1275. Jennie Hardin O'Neal, born April 20, 1898.

Children of Jane Belle Megee (619) and Edwin Megee, her husband:
1276. William Montgomery Megee, born Jan. 7, 1901.

The Montgomerys

Children of Margaret Ann Cravens (623) and George H. Sweney, her husband:

1277. Charles S. Sweney, born Feb. 9, 1873, married Emma Ealy, Feb. 21, 1901.

1278. Marietta Gooch Sweney, born April 19, 1875; married Ernest J. Bell, June 11, 1896.

1279. G. T. Wallace Sweney, born April 21, 1887, died Aug. 2, 1890.

Children of Thomas Dochens Cravens (627) and his wife:

1280. John W. Cravens.

1281. Marietta Cravens.

Children of Sarah Elizabeth Cravens (629) and Rev. J. A. Boothe, her husband:

1282. Henry Manly Boothe, born June 19, 1876.

1283. Ann Cornelia Boothe, born Oct. 14, 1878.

1284. Ida Belle Boothe, born Feb. 2, 1880; married Leonard Andrew Branderick, May 2, 1900.

1285. Lennis Lee Boothe, born Aug. 11, 1884.

1286. Joe Cox Boothe, born Sept, 14, 1890.

1287. Eugene Montgomery Megee Boothe, born Aug. 13, 1893.

Children of Martha Jane Adams (631) and Owen J. Carpenter, her husband:

1288. William Adams Carpenter, born Sept. 9, 1884.

1289. Owen Coleman Carpenter, born Aug. 15, 1896.

Children of Annie Lee Adams (632) and Dr. Thomas D. Coleman, her husband:

1290. Sarah Starke Coleman, born March 2, 1891.

1291. Owen Adams Coleman, born Oct. 3, 1892.

1292. Martha McEwen Coleman, born Sept. 24, 1894.

1293. John Scott Coleman, born March 14, 1896.

Children of Mary Irene Gooch (633) and William E. Singleton, her husband:

1294. Janet Singleton, born Feb. 12, 1881.

1295. Frederick C. Singleton, born April 16, 1883.

1296. Marietta Megee Singleton, born June 29, 1885.

1297. Frank J. Singleton, born Oct. 7, 1887.'

1298. Corinne Singleton, born May 14, 1890.
1299. Edgar Singleton, born April 14, 1892.
1300. Percy G. Singleton, born March 4, 1894.
1301. Prewitt Ephraim Singleton, born Jan. 29, 1896.

Children of Johanan Masters (645) and Dyer Elder, her husband:
1302. Louella Elder, born Feb. 21, 1868, married Enos Porter, 1888.
1303. John Clay Elder, born Feb. 12, 1870; unmarried.
1304. Addie Belle Elder, b. April 24 1872, d. June 27, 1881,
1305. Margaret Pearl Elder, born Sept. 9, 1874: unmarried.
1306. Mary Kathleen Elder, born March 14, 1886.

Children of Alice Dean (652) and R. D. Wadsworth, her husband:
1307. Lowell D. Wadsworth, horn May 3, 1890.
1308. Aletha B. Wadsworth, born Jan. 17, 1893.

Children of Amada Dean (653) and F. V. Wadsworth, her husband:
1309. Eva J. Wadsworth, born March 3, 1889.
1310. Herbert C. Wadsworth, born Dec. 14, 1890.
1311. Herschel W. Wadsworth, born April 17. 1893.
1312. Robert J. Wadsworth, born Aug. 8. 1898.

Children of Sarah J. Dean (655) and Dr. Arthur Wadsworth, her husband:
1313. Charles D. Wadsworth, born Jan. 12, 1898.
1314. Wadsworth, babe unnamed.

Children of James Taylor Round (658) and Susan Thompson, his wife:
1315. Annie Round, born April 13, 1878
1316. Moses Round, born Jan. 20, 1881.
1317. Santa Round, born May 23, 1883, died Sept. 12, 1884.
1318. James Round, born Aug. 13, 1885.
1319. George Round, born June 5, 1888.

Children of Parley Wilder Round (662) and Alice Matilda Landers, his wife:
1320. Lura Round, born Feb. 3, 1879.
1321. Dow Round, born May 5, 1883.

Children of Mary Ballard Round (663) and Robert Jethro Morris, her husband:
1322. Lula Morris, born Feb. 5, 1880.
1323. Marshall Morris, born Jan. 26, 1882.
1324. Henry Morris, born Nov. 10, 1885.
1325. Carrie Morris, born March 11, 1890.
1326. Frank Morris, born Sept. 4, 1896, died Aug. 1897.

Children of Florence J. Round (666) and Daniel Anderson, her husband
1327. Jesse Irdell Anderson, b. Dec. 29, 1884, d. Feb. 28 1886.
1328. Daniel Isora Anderson, born March 17, 1886.
1329. Kirby Valeria Anderson, born Oct. 18 1887.
1330. Myrtle Alfred Anderson, born March 11, 1892.

Children of Della Belle Round (667) and John A. Mallory, her husband:
1331. Earle Dean Mallory, born Oct. 7, 1889.
1332. Grace Lazelle Mallory, b. Aug. 4, 1891, d. Aug. 16, 1895.
1333. Bruce Gordon Mallory, born April 26, 1893.
1334. Leone Lucile Mallory, born Jan. 7, 1895.

Children of George Scott Round (668) and Linda Jackson, his wife:
1335. Beulah Mariah Round, born May 3, 1895.
1336. Tamar Lura Round, born April 13, 1899.

Children of Mary Jane Rybolt (671) and Byron C. Anderson, her husband:
1337. Emma B. Anderson, born March 14, 1869; married Lafayette Brown. July 19, 1885.
1338. Minnie M. Anderson, born Oct. 28, 1871; married Ichabod Brown, July 15, 1888.
1339. Marietta Anderson, born Aug. 10, 1874; married John W. Joyce, June 13, 1893
1340. Nellie C. Anderson, born Aug. 6, 1876; married Fred B. Martin, July 15, 1897.
1341. Maude A. Anderson, born Feb. 22, 1880.
1342. Carrie L. Anderson, born Sept. 23, 1882.
1343. Edwin L. Anderson, born Jan. 14, 1885, d. Jan. 30, 1885.
1344. Dora E. Anderson, born July 18, 1891.
1345. Mabel Anderson, b. Feb. 1, 1886, d. Feb. 15, same year.
1346. Clark S. Anderson, born June 7, 1873; married Cora M. DeMotte, May 2, 1901.

1347. Byron L. Anderson, born June 10, 1887.

Children of John Whittier Rybolt (672) and Mary M Young, his wife:
1348. Willard Rybolt, born Nov. 18, 1880, died Aug. 12, 1881.
1349. Albert Rybolt, born April 27, 1878.
1350. Rena Ethel Rybolt, b. June 11, 1885, d. Oct. 16, 1898.
1351. Laura Gene Rybolt, born Oct. 19, 1888.
1352. Emma Jane Rybolt, born Feb. 20, 1891.
1353. Mabel Rybolt, born Dec 31, 1894.

Children of Delilah Rybolt (673) and David Spurgin, her husband:
1354. Nellie Spurgin, born July 15, 1882.
1355. George Spurgin, born March 21, 1884, died Sept. 11, 1885.
1356. Alpha Spurgin, born June 5, 1886.
1357. Cleveland Spurgin, born July 3, 1888
1358. Clarence Spurgin, born Dec 27, 1889.
1359. Dora Spurgin, born May 12, 1894.
1360. Maude Spurgin, born July 30, 1896.

Children of Hezekiah Rybolt (675) and Anna Black, his wife:
1361. ____Rybolt.
1362. ____Rybolt.

Children of Louisa Belle Rybolt (676) and William Clark, her husband:
1363. James Ralph Clark, born May 18, 1883
1364. — Clark, daughter, born May 8, 1885, died Aug. 19, 1885.

Children of Sherman Rybolt (677) and Crissie Logan, his wife:
1365. Myron Rybolt, born April 5, 1896.

Children of Mary J. Dean (681) and Samuel Gookins, her husband:
1366. Frank Gookins, born May 4, 1878.
1367. John Gookins, born Oct. 10, 1880.
1368. Frederick Gookins, born Sept. 29, 1885.

Children of William E. Dean (683) and Lydia A. Reinstead, his wife:
1368. Howard J. S. Dean, born Oct. 1, 1889.
1369. Ellsworth H. Dean, born Sept. 18, 1891.

Children of Winfield Scott Dean (685) and Caroline Soother, his wife:
1370. Robert William Dean, born Jan. 14, 1894.

Children of Mary Jane Johnson (686) and Isaac W. White, her husband:
1371. Lula White, born Oct. 22, 1869, died June 19, 1873.
1372. Laura B. White, born Feb. 7, 1871; married Albert Fearrangter, Not. 2, 1892.
1373. Charles W. White, born July 2, 1874; married Anna L. Smith, Nov. 13, 1895.

Children of James M. DeVol (690) and Rosa Badgley, his wife:
1374. Edna Louise DeVol, born Dec. 4.1876, died Aug. 3, 1877.
1375. Jennie Montgomery DeVol, born Oct. 20, 1878, died Sept. 14, 1900.
1376. Alice Belle DeVol, born Sept. 28, 1880.
Children of Clark DeVol (692) and Eunice J. Edson, his wife:
1377. Mary Ida DeVol, born July 18, 1883.
1378. Merwin Perase DeVol, born April 7, 1887

Children of Mary Lowry Fitch (698) and John M. Bullock, her husband:
1379. Mary Bradyon Bullock, born March 22, 1873, died July 22, 1873.

Children of Mary Frances Allen (706) and Lemuel Bledsoe, her husband:
1380. Bettie Allen Bledsoe, b. May 31, 1871, d. July 23, 1873
1381. William Allen Bledsoe, born Sept. 14, 1873; married Mattie Lee Gaines, Oct. 30, 1895.
1382. Lemuel Bledsoe, Jr., born Dec. 27, 1876; unmarried.
1383. Brymer Bledsoe, born May 7, 1881.

Children of Sallie Allen (713) and James H. McDanell, Jr., her husband:
1384. Elizabeth A. McDanell, b. May 16, 1897, d. April 5, 1898.

Children of Luella Jenison (714) and Lewis G. Jameson, her husband:
1385. Oliver P. Jameson, born April 14, 1897.

Children of James Otis Churchill 717) and Minnie Russell, his wife:
1386. Vernon R. Churchill, born Sept. §, 1888.
1387. Emily Churchill, born June 3, 1891.

And Their Descendants

Children of Mary Churchill (720) and J. E. Schooley, her husband:
1388. Lela Schooley, born Sept. 28, 1891.
Children of Noah Fred Churchill (721) and Sadie A. Slater, his wife:
1389. Fern Churchill, born Aug. 4, 1892.
1390. Vera Churchill, born Nov. 6, 1893.

Children of Ben. F. Davis (722) and Emma Truitt, his wife:
1391. Pearl Davis, born May 10, 1883.

Children of Jennie Electa Hennegin (731) and Sterling Wood Tucker, her husband:
1392. Sterling W. Tucker, born Dec 15, 1883
1393. Henry H. Tucker, born Jan. 14, 1888.

Children of Henry H. Gookins (738) and Belle Moore, his wife:
1394. Pearl A. Gookins, born Nov. 6, 1875; married Henry Ellinghouse, February 1896.
1395. Glenna A. Gookins, born May 8, 1879; married Otis Vines, April 28, 1897.

Children of Henry H. Gookins (738) and Amanda Hyatt, his wife:
1396. William Fielding Gookins, born Nov. 19, 1885.
1397. Laura Ethel Gookins, born Jan. 13, 1889.
1398. Jennie Varena Gookins, born July 1, 1891%
1399. Henry Orville Gookins, born Dec. 20. 1892.
1400. James Walson Gookins, born Oct. 21, 1894.

Children of Meret M. Gookins (739) and Jennie Holman, his wife:
1401. Flo Elsie Gookins, born Nov. 10, 1884.
1402. Earl Holman Gookins, born Sept. 24, 1888.
1403. Myrtle Madrid Gookins, born July 7, 1890.

Children of Mary L. Gookins (741) and George Foster, her husband
1404. Mabel Claire Foster, born May 18, 1892.
1405. William Hershel Foster, born April 23, 1895.
1406. Sallie Marie Foster, born May 27, 1896.
Foster, son, born Jan. 7, 1894, died Jan. 24, 1894.
Children of William S. Gookins (743) and Emma Newman, his wife:
1407. Florence Edna Gookins, born Dec. 24, 1893.
1408. Enos Earl Gookins, born April 3. 1900.

Children of George S. Gookins (744) and Anna Terhune, his wife:
1409. Bertha Gail Gookins, born April 24, 1894.
1410. William Harold Gookins, born Oct. 17, 1896.
1411. Mildred Ellen Gookins, born Sept. 30, 1898.
1412. Luke Terhune Gookins, born Nov. 1, 1900.

Children of Peter H. Gookins (745) and Clara Will, his wife:
1413. Robert Pierre Gookins, born Dec. 20, 1894.
1414. Helen Gookins, born April 19, 1896.
1415. Herbert H. Gookins, born March 15, 1899.

Children of Oscar N. Gookins (747) and Nora Griffith, his wife:
1416. Madge Gookins, born April 29, 1897.

Children of Roscoe Sherman Hennegin (753) and Adella Reed, his wife:
1417. Elsie May Hennegin, born Sept. 8, 1894.
1418. James Reed Hennegin, born Aug. 9, 1896.
1419. Lula Fern Hennegin, born Aug .26, 1898.'
1420. Anna Laura Hennegin, born Sept. 23, 1900.

Children of Tillie E. Hennegin (756) and Chas. Scott, her husband:
1421. Myrtle Grace Scott, born March 9, 1901.

Children of William Clement Jenison, (764) and Nora Duncan, his wife:
1422. Gerald Jenison, born April 8, 1898.

Children of Laura E. Hennegin (765) and Jacob Weiner Jordan, her husband:
1423. Jacob Weiner Jordan, Jr., born May 11, 1897.
1424. John Clay Jordan, born Oct. 31, 1899.

Children of Rosetta Yocum (774) and Chas. Gray, her husband:
1425. Stella Gray, born July 27, 1887.
1426. Gladys Gray, born Nov. 15, 1889, died March 16, 1891.
1427. Gracie Gray, born Nov. 15. 1889, died June 7, 1890.
1428. Olive Gray, born March 30, 1892.
1429. Frank Luthann Gray, born Jan. 7, 1894.
1430. Leta Gray, born July 26, 1897.
1431. Nellie Gray, born Feb. 19, 1899.

Children of Minnie Yocum (775) and Nelson Lawrence, her husband:
1432. Everett E. Lawrence, born Dec. 5, 1889.
1433. J. M. Lawrence, born Nov. 27, 1893, died April 5, 1895. '1434. Opal Lawrence, born Jan. 27, 1896.
1435. Oren Lawrence, born March 4, 1898, died July 5, 1899.

Children of John E Yocum (776) and Nannie B. Toley, his wife:
1436. Bertha B. Yocum, born Sept. 5, 1893, died Oct. 13, 1894.
1437. Gracy Yocum, born Jan. 26, 1895.
1438. Agnes Yocum, born Oct. 29, 1896.
1439. Vina Pearl Yocum, b. April 15, 1898, d. July 31, 1899.
1440. Leonard Yocum, born Feb. 1, 1900.

Children of Julia A. Yocum (777) and Daniel E Bailey, her husband:
1441. Amanda Inez Bailey, born May 18, 1894.

Children of Amanda Yocum (778) and Eugene B. McQueen, her husband:
1443. Fostal Lee McQueen, born Oct. 5, 1885, died Oct. 5, 1892.

Children of Sarah E. Yocum (779) and J. B. West, her husband:
1444. Ernest McGee West, born April 13, 1887.
1445. Everett West, born Dec. 26, 1890.
1446. Vernie West, born March 11, 1892.
1447. Everett Ruff West, born March 11. 1892.

Children of Catherine J. Yocum (780) and N. B. Turpin, her husband:
1448. Granville Eugene Turpin, born May 1, 1895.
1449. Sanford Leroy Turpin, born Jan. 13, 1898.

Children of Martha A. Yocum (782) and George A. Vosse, her husband:
1450. Grace Irene Vosse, born Sept. 8, 1890, died Jan. 13. 1896.
Children of Isaac R. Yocum (784) and Minnie Beagle, his wife:
1451. William Bryan Yocum, born March 5, 1899.

Children of Maudie M. Yocum (788) and Gladdie Bailey, her husband:
1452. Lillian Irene Baily, born Sept. 10, 1897.

Children of Annette Merris Woolston (789) and Elisha B. Barnes, her husband:
1453. Henry Alfred Barnes, born June 14, 1885.
1454. Walter Edward Barnes, b. July 28, 1887, d. July 7, 1889.

Children of Noah Harris Woolston (790) and Carrie B. Butcher his wife:
1455. Earl Woolston, born March 14, 1895.
1456. Nellie Pearl Woolston, born Feb. 13, 1897.

Children of John Edward Woolston (791) and Lola B. Coats, his wife:
1457. Birdie May Woolston, born March 4, 1889.
1458. Harry L. Woolston, born March 25, 1890.
1459. George William Woolston, born Feb. 28, 1892.
1460. Lillie Belle Woolston, born Oct. K 1894.
Children of John F. Iden (806) and Sarah R. Edwards, his wife;
1461. Zepha M. Iden, born Oct. 28, 1897.

Children of Ida J. Iden (807) and Winfield Jackson, her husband:
1462. Iva M. Jackson, born Jan. 8, 1884.
1463. Goldie Jackson, born Jan. 14, 1888.

Children of Sarah C. Iden (808) and Oscar Adams, her husband:
1464. Mary E. Adams, born Sept. 11, 1887, died July 8, 1889. 1465; Frank D. Adams, born March 4. 1890.
1466. Carl W. Adams, born June 27, 1892.
1467. Roy P. Adams, born Dec. 12, 1894.
1468. Pearl G. Adams, born Nov. 15, 1897.

Children of Dorcas Ann Iden (809) and Joseph C. Black, her husband:
1469. Ettie M. Black, born April 28. 1890.
1470. Willis C. Black, born Sept. 30, 1893.

Children of Mary Emma Iden (811) and Chris Farney, her husband:
1471. Pearl L. Farney, born Oct. 27. 1891, died Feb. 19, 1896.
1472. Roy Farney, born Feb. 23, 1894.
1473. Zella M. Farney, born Jan. 6, 1896.
1474. Christina Farney, born Feb. 8, 1898.

Children of Lillie May Iden (812) and Alfred D, Cunningham, her husband:
1475. Bonnie M Cunningham, born Dec. 4, 1897.

Children of George Juliette Iden (813) and Chas. E. Harper, her husband:
1476. Elsie M. Harper, born Dec. 27, 1897.

Children of Kate Yocum (816) and Elmer Hamilton, her husband:
1477 Nora Pearl Hamilton, born Oct. 3, 1891.
1478. Vera Pearl Hamilton, born Feb. 20, 1895.
1479. Orville Elmer Hamilton, born July 13, 1898.

Children of Margaret Ann Crowell (821) and Dennis Chapin, her husband:
1480. Charles Franklin Chapin, born April 23, 1878.
1481. Isaac John Chapin, born Aug. 30, 1880.
1482. Harris Arthur Chapin, born Oct. 12, 1881.
1483. Lucinda Dean Chapin, born April 2, 1885.

Children of Emma Jettie Crowell (822) and Jacob Smith Coons, her husband:
1483. Edith Pearl Coons, born Aug. 7, 1889.
1484. Walter Smith Coons, born Jan. 7, 1895.

Children of Frances J. Crowell (826) and Phineas Ward, her husband:
1485. William Belknap, Ward b. April 2, 1873, d. Aug. 3, 1873.
1486. Minnie Catherine Ward born June 30, 1876; married Asa Grant Ellis, March 18, 1897.
1487. Wallace Talbridge Ward, born Aug. 29, 1881.
1488. John Franklin Ward, born June 30, 1883.
1489. Phineas Cooper Ward, born June 20, 1886.
1490. Benjamin Franklin Ward, born July 9, 1889.
1491. Ruby May Ward, born April 4, 1893.

Children of Mary Frances Jenison (829) and George Ketchum, her husband:
1491. Harriett Ketchum, born Nov. 14. 1877.
1492. Isabella C. Ketchum, born Jan. 22, 1882; married Taylor Heaton, Sept, 4, 1896.
1493. Ellen Ketchum, born 1879.

The Montgomerys

Children of Ida May Jenison (831) and Joel Edward Briscoe, her husband:
1494. Juniata Briscoe, born Nov. 8. 1891.
1495. Cluquita Briscoe, born Aug. 1, 1893, died March 3, 1894. 1496^ Floyd W. G. Briscoe, born July 22, 1898.

Children of Jeanette Jenison (833) and Curtis Guard, her husband:
1497. Jenison Guard, born Nov. 5, 1894.

Children of Frances J. Resinger (834) and David A. Duncanson, her husband:
1498. Anna B. Duncanson, born March 5, 1872, married Lewis Deckrevel, Sept. 1892.
1499. Exelma A. Duncanson, b. Feb, 7, 1874, d. Feb. 19, 1874.
1500. Charles O. Duncanson, b. Feb. 5, 1875, d. Nov. 29, 1888.
1501. Simeon William Duncanson, born Feb. 14, 1877.
1502. Elsie Alice Duncanson, born Dec. 31, 1878, died June 18, 1887.
1503. George B. Duncanson, b. Oct. 15, 1881, d. June 28, 1887.
1504. Walter A. Duncanson, born May 4, 1883.
1505. Lester F. Duncanson, born Feb. 11, 1889.
1506. Stanley Montgomery Duncanson, born March 26, 1891.

Children of Alice L Risinger (835) and Jerry Duncanson, her husband:
1507. Delilah Jane Duncanson, born May 2, 1874.
1508. Frances L. Duncanson, born March 2, 1876; married John Boetcher. Oct. 3, 1894.
1509. Flora Duncanson, born Feb. 28, 1881, died May 23, 1887.

Children of Nancy A. Risinger (836) and John A. Rockwell, her husband:
1510. Isabella J. Rockwell, born Jan. 17, 1876.
1511. Albert S. Rockwell, born Aug. 14. 1877.
1512. Edith G. Rockwell, born May 13, 1880.

Children of Malinda E. Risinger (837) and Orange N. Risinger, her husband:
1513. Marion Risinger, born April 20, 1879,
1514. Alice Risinger, born Jan. 2, 1883.
1515. George Risinger, born June 1887.

Children of Malinda E. Risinger (837) and W. E. Coles, her husband:
1516. Mary Coles, born April 1893.

Children of George E. Risinger (838) and Otella J. Goodrich, his wife:
1517. Gerald O. Risinger, born Nov. 10, 1891.
1518. Jenison D. Risinger, born July 24, 1894.
1519. Myrtle S. Node Risinger, born Aug. 26, 1892; adopted March 11, 1899.

Children of Mary B. Risinger (839) and Fred E. Blair, her husband:
1520. Pearl Blair, born April 29, 1883, died June 27, 1887.
1521. Frank Blair, born Nov. 27, 1884, died June 21, 1887.
1522. Lydia B. Blair, born July 18, 1886.
1523. Ray Blair, born April 4, 1888.
1524. Vestra E. Blair, born July 5, 1889.
1525. Ina V. Blair, born Feb. 18, 1891.
1526. Helen S. Blair, horn Feb. 19, 1892.
1527. Irvena Blair, born Dec. 4, 1893.
1528. Bessie M. Blair, born May 4, 1899.

Children of Simeon S. Kisinger (840) and Mae L. Barrow, his wife:
1529. Buell B. Risinger, born Jan. 22, 1891.

Children of Simeon S. Kisinger (840) and second wife, Henrietta Bolander:
Zapher Inez Risinger, born Aug. 26, 1901.

Children of Stephen Allen Jenison (841) and Ada Molyneaux, his wife:
1530. Alfred Jenison, born June 8, 1896.
1531. Lillie May Jenison, born Dec. 22, 1897,
1532. Earl Dewey Jenison, born April 8, 1899.

Children of Sarah Frances Jenison (842) and George E. Williams, her husband:
1533. Marcus Elza Williams, born Dec 5, 1888.
1534. Asa George Williams, born April 28, 1891.

Children of Bertha Isabella Jenison (845) and Elliott S. Sell, her husband:
1535. Edith Clyesta Sell, born March 18, 1895.
1536 Ivey Leona Sell, born May 15, 1896.
1537. Cora Pearl Sell, born May 7, 1898.

Children of Laura Elnora Jenison (846) and Walter Gile, Her husband:
1538. Elza *Earl* Gile, born June 22, 1899.

Children of Edward Eugene Jenison (852) and Ida Elton, his wife:
1539. Cecil Edward Jenison, born Aug. 10, 1899.

Children of Francis Brown (873) and Effie T. Draper, his wife:
1540. Thomas Ernest Brown, born Nov. 28, 1887.
1541. Cecil M. Brown, born March 4, 1895.

Children of Charles Brown (874) and Emma Sefton, his wife:
1542. Mary Elizabeth Brown, born Aug. 27, 1898.

Children of John T. Brown (876) and Zoo Myers, his wife:
1543. Mary M. Brown, born Nov. 3, 1899.
1544. Milton Brown, born Sept. 25, 1900.
NINTH GENERATION.

Children of Mamie J. Montgomery (893) and Edward Hardin' her husband:
1545. William Robert Leonard Hardin, born Sept. 2, 1899.

Children of Abel F. Douglass (953) and Minnie Stewart, his wife:
1546. Goldie A. Douglass, born June 1, 1886:
1547. Howard N. Douglass, born Oct. 1, 1890.
1548. Steward D. Douglass, born May 6, 1894.

Children of S. Harold Snyder (954) arid Edith M. Sheldon his wife:
1548. Karl M. Snyder, born Feb. 26, 1899.
1549. Mildred J. Snyder, born March 5. 1896.

Children of Antoinette Snyder (955) and Prof. D. M. Mottier, her husband:
1550. Hartwig Mottier, born Nov. 11, 1895.
1551. Maude Mottier, born June 26, 1898.

Children of Eugene A. Helm (956) and Rosa Lee Brown, his wife:
1552. Earvin Thomas Helm, born May 29, 1891.
1553. Earl James Helm, born Nov. 12, 1893.

And Their Descendants

Children of William T. Helm (965) and Kate M. Anderson, his wife:
1554. Mary E. Helm, born Jan. 5, 1889.
1555. Maggie P. Helm, born March 21, 1891.
1556. James T. Helm, born Jan. 30, 1895.
1557. William W. Helm, born April 11, 1891

Children of Belinda Helm (966) and James Ellis, her husband:
1558. Jesse A. Ellis, born Sept. 22, 1898.

Children of Irene White'(973) and Rev. Grant Abbett, her" husband:
1559. Luella Abbett, born Nov. 25, 1893.
1560. Gladius Abbett, born May 17, 189S.
1561. Bernice Abbett, born Nov. 12, 1896.

Children of John R. Stevens (975) and Annie Petty, his wife:
1562. Esta Stevens, born Nov. 11, 1900.

Children of Mary E. Craig (978) and Elmer Forrest Hayden, her husband:
1563. Alline Jennings Hayden, b. July 4, 1896, d. Oct. 10, 1896.

Children of William Bohannon (989) and Pearl Harrod, his wife:
1564. Paul Alexander Bohannon, born July 11, 1894, died May 27, 1895.
1565. Guy Bohannon, born April 11, 1896.

Children of Victor Montgomery Bohannon (991) and Pearl Middleton, his wife:
1566. Victor Middleton Bohannon, born June 5, 1900.

Children of Mary Nicholas Bohannon (994) and Byron Flood, her husband:
1567. Harry Bohannon Flood, born Dee. 23, 1892.
1568. Effie Flood, born March 5, 1898.

Children of Mary Jane Griffin (1001) and John Richard Brown, her husband:
1569. Mary Elizabeth Brown, born Sept. 23, 1898.

Children of Jesse W. Montgomery (1003) and Minerva Peters Shoesmith, his wife:
1570. William Hugh Montgomery, born Nov. 5, 1900, died Nov. 8, 1900.

The Montgomerys

Children of Lenora Wayland (1010) and J. F. Wallace, her husband:
1571. Robert Homer Wallace, born July 17, 1893.
1572. Harry Raymond Wallace, born May 28, 1895.
1573. Lillian Elizabeth Wallace, born Jan. 16, 1897.
1574. Edwin Overton Wallace, born Dec. 8, 1898.
1575. William Golden Wallace, born Feb. 11, 1901.

Children of Otis Lewis (1036) and Lydia Funk, his wife:
1576. Otis L. Lewis, born Dec. 31, 1886.

Children of Beatrice Lewis (1037) and Dan B. Hanlon, her husband:
1577. Edna B. Hanlon, born March 5, 1887.
1578. Victor O. Hanlon, b. Feb. 22, 1889, .d. Aug. 12, 1892.

Children of Victor Lewis (1038) and Eliza J. McMellon, his wife:
1579. John W. Lewis, born March 17, 1895.
1580. Leland L. Lewis, born July 8, 1896.
1581. Vernon M. Lewis, born Sept. 26. 1897.
1582. Mary Frances Lewis, born Nov. 20, 1901.

Children of Frankie W. Lewis (1040) and Sam J. Woody, her husband:
1583. Lewis J. Woody, born July 24, 1898.
1584. Samuel G. Woody, born April 10, 1900.

Children of Nathaniel C. Montgomery (1041) and Myrtle Davis, his wife:
1585. Davis Montgomery, born Nov. 7, 1899.

Children of Mattie S. Fothergill (1069) and G. G. Kelly, her husband:
1586. William B. Kelly, born Dec. 26, 1889, died Oct. 27, 1890.
1587. Walter A. Kelly, born Dec. 26, 1889.
1588. Ray M. Kelly, born July 5, 1892.
1589. George Rowlett Kelly, born July 31, 1899.

Children of Lucille Montgomery (422) and John Mylor, her husband:
1590. Margaret Mylor, born Nov. 5,-1900.

Children of Prudence Self (1163) and Owen Sharp, her husband:
1591. Carl W. Sharp, born May 24, 1898.

Children of Mary Maude Self (1164) and Anson B. Clark, her husband:
1592. Rollin F. Clark, born Sept. 25. 1896, died Aug. 15, 1897.
1593. Glenn E. Clark, born June 10, 1899.

Children of Anderville Norton Seright (1172) and Mary Gilliland, his wife:
1594. Harry W. Seright.

Children of Lou Seright (1173) and T. B. Goddard, her husband:
1595. Hazel Goddard.

Children of Scharlie Sayres (1247) and Max Wilson, her husband:
1596. Huldah Frances Wilson, born June 18, 1898.
1597. Richard Porter Wilson, born Sept. 18. 1896, died July 15, 1897.
1598. James W. Wilson, born Aug. 12, 1901.

Children of Graham J. Savers (1248) and Elizabeth Pollock, his wife:
1599. Sarah Pollock Sayers, born March 26, 1901, died Sept. 9, 1901.

Children of Marietta Gooch Sweeney (1278) and Ernest J. Bell, her husband:
1600. Mary Louise Bell, born Aug. 19, 1897, died May 20, 1898.
1601. E. J. Bell, born April 26, 1900, died June 16, 1900.
1602. Galen Winn Bell, born April 1, 1901.

Children of Luella Elder (1302) and Enos Porter, her husband:
1603. William E. Porter, born July 2, 1889.
1604. Hester Myra Porter, born Feb. 5, 1894.

Children of Eunice B. Anderson (1337) and Lafayette Brown, her husband:
1605. David H. Brown, born Aug. 24, 1886, died Nov. 27, 1886.
1606. Ora M. Brown, born April 19, 1888.
1607. Clark S. Brown, born July 29, 1889.
1608. Clara B. Brown, born July 29, 1891.
1609. Mary C. Brown, born March 27, 1893.
1610. Bryan M. Brown, born Dec. 6, 1899.

Children of Minnie M. Anderson (1338) and Ichabod Brown, her husband:
1611. David L. Brown, born June 11, 1889.

1612. Freddie L. Brown, born Sept. 19, 1892.
1613. Charles B. Brown, born Feb. 23, 1894.
1614. Dewey H. Brown, born Dec. 14, 1898.

Children of Margaret M. Anderson (1339) and John W. Joyce, her husband:
1615. Helen A. Joyce, born Aug. 4, 1894.
1616. Mary K. Joyce, born Oct. 1, 1896.
1617. Elmer C. Joyce, born April 20, 1898.

Children of Charles W. White (1373) and Anna L. Smith, hi« wife:
1618. Edgar White, born Oct. 1, 1896, died Nov. 19, 1896.
1619. Robert S. White, born Nov. 5, 1897.
1620. Ruth White, born Dec. 2, 1899.
1621. Isaac W. White, born March 30, 1901.

Children of Pearl A. Gookins (1394) and Henry Ellinghouse, her husband:
1622. Lora Ellinghouse, born Nov. 21, 1896.
1623. Glenna Ellinghouse, born Feb. 20, 1898.

Children of Isabella C. Ketchum (1492) and Taylor Heaton, her husband:
1624. Carl Heaton, born March 12, 1897.

Children of Ann B. Duncanson (1498) and Lewis Deckrevel, her husband:
1625. Blanch Deckrevel, born April 9, 1893.
1626. Esther Deckrevel, born Aug. 22, 1894.
1627. John Deckrevel, born Oct. 6, 1895.

Children of Frances L. Duncanson (1508) and John Boettcher, her husband:
1628. Lois Boettcher, born Sept. 23. 1897.
1629. Lee Boettcher, born Sept. 23, 1897, died Sept. 24, 1897.

Children of Deltie May Jennison (1531) and W. S. Edwards, her husband:
1630. Merrill Jennison Edwards, born Jan. 15, 1902.

The writer regrets that he has been unable to obtain any information as to the descendants of Elizabeth Montgomery (16), who married a Crockett in Virginia and never came to Kentucky to live. It is also regretted that a more complete list of the descendants of John Montgomery (14) could not be procured.

William Montgomery (11) settled in Franklin County, Kentucky, and reared his family. Robert Montgomery (12) settled in Gallatin County, Kentucky, and reared his family, and finally moved to Rush County, Indiana, and there died. John Montgomery (14) moved to Webster County, Kentucky, where he raised a family. Mary Montgomery (15) moved to Jefferson County, Kentucky, where she reared her family. Nancy Montgomery (17) settled in Woodford County, Kentucky, between Versailles and Lexington, and reared her family. Joseph Montgomery (19) first settled in Henry County, Kentucky, and moved from there to Ripley County, Indiana, and reared his family.

It is a remarkable fact that since 1786, when Samuel Montgomery (10) came to Kentucky, his descendants now live in the following states: Kentucky, Tennessee, Georgia, Indiana, Ohio, Illinois, Missouri, Kansas, Arkansas, Texas, Michigan, Iowa, Nebraska, South Dakota, and California— one-third of the states of the Union —an evidence of the enterprise of the family.

AN ANCIENT DEED

This Indenture, made this fourth day of October, in the year of our Lord one thousand Seven hundred and ninety-one. Between Samuel Montgomery of the one part and Robert Montgomery of the other part, witnessed that the said Samuel Montgomery, for and in Consideration of the sum of one hundred and thirteen pounds, Virginia Currency, to him in hand paid by the said Robert Montgomery, Before the sealing and delivering hereof, the receipt whereof is hereby acknowledged and the said Robert Montgomery, acquitted and Discharged, hath Bargained and Sold by these presents, doth bargain. Sell and Convey Unto the Said Robert Montgomery his heirs and assigns, a Certain tract or parcel of land Containing two hundred and twenty-six acres, lying on the Waters of the lower dry Run. The Waters of south Elkhorn, in the County of Woodford, and Bounded as followeth: part of Andrew Lewis's military Claim for 3000 Acres, Beginning at a White oake horn been two Iron Woods and hicory on Benjemine Craigs line, thence the Same South fifteen and two thirds degrees, West one hundred and seventy Six and one half pole, to two large White oakes, Corner between Craig and Montgomery on the Southward line of the old

Survey, thence the same North Seventy four Degrees West two hundred and six poles to three hicory Saplins, South West Corner, to the Said Survey. Thence a line of the Same North Sixtn Degrees, East one hundred and seventy six and one half poles to two White oakes and White ash one the same, thence south Seventy Four, East two hundred and five and one fourth poles to the Beginning; to have and to Hold the above granted premises. With all the appurtenances thereto Belonging, with all and singular Benefits and emoluments thereunto Belonging and Therefrom to arise unto the said Robert Montgomery his heirs or assigns, to them only. We for Ever, and the said Samuel Montgomery for himself and his heirs and Assigns, Exs, Adms. doth hereby Covenant and agree to him and with the said Robert Montgomery his heirs and assigns that unto him then he and they the land and primcies aforesaid hereby Intended to be Conveyed Will Warent and for Ever hereafter Defend against the Claims and Demands of all persons lawfully Claiming, in Witness Whereof the said Samuel Montgomery hath hereunto set his hand and affixed his seal the day and year above Written.

Sind and Delivered
In the presence of   Saml Montgomery (seal)
Bennet Pemberton
John Price, Jun.
Woodford County, to wit October Court, 1791
This Indenture was produced in Court,
Acknowledged by Samuel Montgomery as party thereto,
and ordered to be recorded.
                                   Teste
                                   Cave Johnson, C. W. C.

This is a true copy, even to the misspelling of words and the wrong use of capital letters. It will show for all time that Samuel and Robert Montgomery lived in Kentucky at the time this deed was made, and that the above genealogy represents the descendants of these two men. Samuel was the father of Robert. This deed was recorded 111 years ago.

And Their Descendants

CHAPTER IX.

As an introduction to the history of the Montgomery family in America, especially some of the branches that settled in Virginia, near Jamestown, and their descendants who subsequently lived in Green briar, Wythe, Roanoke, Montgomery and other nearby counties during the years of the French and Indian and Revolutionary wars, and then in great numbers emigrated to Kentucky, and finally many of them settled in the various western states, we here insert a most interesting letter written by Judge Henry P. Montgomery, of Georgetown Ky. It goes farther back and throws more light on the ancestors of the Montgomerys of Kentucky and south-western Indiana than any other information that we have obtained. It not only does this, but it connects the Montgomerys of south-western Indiana with that numerous family to which Judge Montgomery belongs. Mr. Montgomery says:

"The oldest one living of my branch of the family is Commodore J. Ed Montgomery, now (in 1902) living in Chicago, Ill. 85 years old. He is the man who commanded the Confederate fleet and fought before Memphis, June 6, 1862; and his niece. Mrs. Jennie M. DeVol, of New Albany, Ind., gives me the following statements as made by Commodore J. Ed Montgomery. (These notes were taken down by his daughter. Mrs. Clara White, now of Chicago, Ill., referred to elsewhere).

"'My grandfather was Samuel Montgomery. He married Miss Margaret Nichols of Virginia. My father's name was Joseph Montgomery, born Aug. 1, 1768. He was the youngest son, and at the time of his death his parents lived near Petersburg, Va., on the Appomattox River. When my father was twelve years old—1870— they moved to London County, on New river. They lived in the valley called the Cove. My parents were married in Wytheville, Wythe County, Va., in 1796. My mother was Miss Jane Sproule, daughter of James and Frances Sproule, nee McCutchen. My mother was raised in Rockbridge County, Va. A few weeks after their marriage they moved to Kentucky. Five families formed a colony. It was called the Montgomery colony. Their names were ' Graham, Scott, Major, Sproule and Montgomery. The colony settled in Franklin County, Ky., at the forks of the Elkhorn River.

"'In 1801 my father settled in Henry County, on the Kentucky river. There he discovered some valuable springs, known as Drennon. In 1808 my father sold this farm to Thomas Smith, then moved to the mouth of Kentucky River just above Carrolton; lived there twelve years, or until 1820, when he sold to General W. O. Butler and brothers, and moved to Ripley County, Ind. The state had only been admitted to the Union of States four years. Father died Jan. 12, 1842. Mother died July 16, 1842. Uncle Robert Montgomery settled in Gallatin County, Ky., on the Ohio River. He married in Virginia, but was a widower with four children when they moved to Kentucky. His second wife was Miss Catherine Bohannon. She was a very large lady, being over six feet tall. Uncle Robert's eldest son, John, married his second wife's youngest sister, Elizabeth Bohannon. Uncle Robert had eight children. Cousin John had twenty-one children—fourteen by his first wife and seven by his second wife. The Montgomerys originated in the north of France. Here they spelled their name Montgomerie, but in Scotland the name subsequently changed to Montgomery.

"'We have always called ourselves Scotch-Irish. Three brothers, sons of James Montgomery, viz, William, Robert and Hugh, came to America in 1666. This was more than one hundred years before we had a United States. They landed at Jamestown on the James River, in Virginia. Some years after they landed, Hugh returned to Ireland and died without issue. William and Robert remained in Virginia and married there. William had three sons and four daughters. The sons were Robert, Hugh and John.

"'Robert, Sr., also had seven children—four sons and three daughters. The sons were William, Hugh, James and Samuel. Samuel was my grandfather and had five sons and four daughters. The sons were William, Robert, John, James and Joseph.'"

Judge H. P. Montgomery says: "The foregoing quotations 1 find quoted in a letter to me from my cousin, Mrs. DeVol, of New Albany, Ind.. and is copied from a published statement made by Commodore J. Ed Montgomery, from notes taken down by his daughter, Mrs. Clara White, now of Chicago; and from a careful examination of the names and other facts in my knowledge, I believe the same to be correct. I call your attention to the statement claiming the emigration to America in 1666; and if you will count generations as we count them, it is altogether probable that your Hugh Montgomery, Sr., was a brother to Samuel Montgomery, my great-grandfather, and a son of Robert, who was a son of James in Ireland. Does this not seem a reasonable deduction from the preceding facts?

"I had this letter when you were at my house in November, 1900, but it did not strike me so forcibly as it did on reading it since you were here.

"I had been led to believe that I was descended from John Montgomery, named in the Houston-Montgomery branch. But the foregoing is the best evidence I have of my genealogy, and I shall adopt it as correct. It takes me back to old Ireland.

"By a close comparison you will discover that Hugh Montgomery, Sr., and Samuel Montgomery were contemporary, living in the same state, and each had one or more sons in the Revolutionary War. But Hugh was the oldest—probably the oldest of the entire family. Samuel must have been born as early as 1740, and probably several years earlier, to have had a son born in 1762, the birth of my grandfather, Robert Montgomery. Hugh must have been born as early as 1705, as he had ten children, the youngest born probably about 1745.

"You will notice that Hugh, Sr., and Samuel Montgomery had a brother William. You will see in Green's Historic Families of Kentucky that one William Montgomery, the father-in-law of General Ben. Logan was killed by the Indians in Lincoln County, Ky., in 1779 at or near Ft. St. Asaph; and this was about the time that Col. John Montgomery came with a body of men and relieved the fort. This William Montgomery was the ancestor of "Mark Twain" (Mr. Clements) and other distinguished Kentuckians. I think it important in your history to trace this branch of the family back as far as possible. They came to Kentucky from the Holston River country, the same as my family. May it not be a fact that this William Montgomery was a brother to Hugh, Sr., and Samuel? You might obtain this information from "Mark Twain," or from Mr. Green, author of "Historic Families." or from some of the Montgomerys living in Lincoln County, Ky. Stanford is their County Seat."

Later, Judge H. P. Montgomery consulted Mr. Green, referred to above, and D. B. Montgomery consulted "Mark Twain" (Mr. Samuel L. Clemens) without obtaining any more information than has already been published in the histories of Kentucky, which will be given here.

And Their Descendants

This William Montgomery must have been born as early as 1730, and perhaps several years earlier, as Anna Montgomery, his daughter, who married Gen. Ben. Logan was born in 1752, and the probability is that John, William and Mrs. Russel were all older than Gen. Logan's wife.

This is the history of William Montgomery as gleaned from the Kentucky histories—Green, Collins and others:

Collins, volume 2, pages 471-2.—In the fall of 1779, William Montgomery the elder, the father-in-law of General Logan, who married Anna Montgomery in Virginia, with his family and son-in-law, Joseph Russel moved from the Holston settlement in Virginia to Kentucky and took refuge in Logan's Fort, near the headwaters of Green river. Here they remained but a few months, when, apprehending no danger from Indians, the old man with his sons, William, John. Thomas and Robert, and his son-in-law, Russel, left the fort and built four log cabins on the head waters of Green river, about twelve miles in a south-east direction from Logan's Fort, to which they removed in the latter part of the winter or early in the spring of 1780. They had, however, been there but a short time when the savages discovered and attacked the colonies. In one of the cabins lived William Montgomery the elder and wife, and his sons Thomas, and Robert, and daughters Jane and Betsy, with two younger children, James and Flora. Mrs. Montgomery, with her youngest child, Flora, were then at Logan's Fort, and Thomas and Robert were absent, spying.

William Montgomery, Jr., his wife and one child, the late Judge Thomas Montgomery, son of a former wife, and a bound boy, occupied another.

John Montgomery, then but lately married, occupied a third, and Joseph Russell, wife and three children, the fourth. These were all the white persons, but there were besides several slaves.

In the month of March, 1780, at night a small body of Indiana surrounded the cabins, which were built close to each other and rather in a square. On the succeeding morning, between daylight and sunrise, William Montgomery the elder, followed by a Negro boy, started out at the door of his cabin. They were immediately fired at and both killed by the Indians, the boy's head falling back on the door-sill. Jane, the daughter, then a young woman—afterward the wife of Col. Wm. Casey, late of Adair County—sprang to the door, pushed out the Negro's head, shut the door and called

The Montgomerys

for her brother Thomas's gun. Betsy, her sister, about twelve years of age, clambered out of the chimney, which was not higher than a man's head, and took the path to Pettit's station, a distance of about two and one-half miles. An Indian pursued for some distance, but, being quite active, she was too fleet for him and reached the station in safety. From Pettit's a messenger was immediately dispatched to Logan's Fort.

For some cause or other—probably the call of Jane for her brother's rifle, which was doubtless overheard by the Indians—they did not attempt to break into the cabin. William Montgomery, Jr., on hearing the first crack of a gun, sprang to his feet, seized a large trough which had been placed in his cabin to hold sugar-water, placed it against the door and directing the apprentice boy to hold it, grasped his rifle, and through a crevice over the door fired twice at the Indians in rapid succession before they left the ground, killing one and severely wounding another. John Montgomery was in bed, and in attempting to rise was fired upon through a crack and mortally wounded, his door forced open and his wife made prisoner. Joseph Russell made his escape from his cabin, leaving his wife and three children to the mercy of the savages. They, with a mulatto girl, were also made prisoners.

The Indians commenced an early retreat, bearing off their wounded companion and taking with them their captives. A few minutes after their departure, and when they were hardly out of sight, the Indian who had pursued Betsy Montgomery returned and, being ignorant of what had occurred in his absence, mounted a large beech log in front of the younger William Montgomery's door and commenced hallooing. Montgomery, who had not yet ventured to open the door, again fired through the crevice and shot him dead.

As soon as the messenger reached Logan's Fort, General Logan with his horn sounded the well-known note of alarm; and in a few minutes, as if by magic, a company of some twelve or fifteen men, armed and equipped for battle, were at his side. They instantly commenced their march; passed the cabins where the attack had been made, and took the trail of the Indians. By the aid of some signs which Mrs. Russell had the presence of mind to make by occasionally breaking a twig and scattering along the route pieces of white handkerchief which she had torn into fragments, Logan's party found no difficulty in the pursuit of the Indians. After traveling some distance they came upon the yellow girl, who had been tomahawked, scalped and left for dead, but who, on hearing the well-known voice of General Logan, sprang to her feet and afterward recovered.

The Indians, as was known to be their habit when expecting to be pursued, had a spy in the rear who was discovered by Logan's party at the same instant that he got his eyes upon them, and a rapid march ensued. In a few minutes they came in sight of the savages, when Logan ordered a charge, which was made with a shout, and the Indians fled with great precipitance)-, leaving their wounded companion, who was quickly dispatched. A daughter of Mrs. Russell, about twelve years of age, upon hearing Logan's voice, exclaimed in ecstasy, "There's Uncle Ben'!' Then the savage who had her in charge struck her dead with his tomahawk. The remainder of the prisoners were recaptured without injury. As the force of the Indians was about equal to that of the whites, General Logan now encumbered with the recaptured women and children, wisely determined to return immediately, and reached the cabins in safety before dark on the same day.

The particulars of the foregoing narrative have been received from the Montgomery family, but principally from Mi's. Casey, who was an actor in the drama.—History Kentucky, Collins, volume 2, pages 471-2-3.

Silver Creek, Madison County, Ky., Feb. 5, 1901.

H. P. Montgomery, Esq., Dear Sir: I very much regret my inability to give you any information concerning the antecedents of William Montgomery, Sr. I know that he lived in Augusta County before he removed to the Holston County. It is almost certain that he was not born in Augusta County, in which there were no settlers prior to 1732. He either removed to Augusta from Pennsylvania or came direct from Ireland. I think the latter is the more likely to have been the fact. At one time his wife's people lived in Amherst County.

The Montgomerys of Ireland were descendants of Scotch people of the name who had settled in Ireland and, as their name indicates, were descendants of Anglo-Normans who settled in Scotland. But I have no means of identifying William Montgomery with any other family of the name than his own in this County, much less with any in Ireland or Scotland. Some of his descendants claim that he was a descendant of General Richard

Montgomery of the Revolution, but so far as I know this is wholly without proof, and my judgment is that the identity of the name is its only basis.

Yours very truly,

"T. M. GREEN.

"Traditions ascribing to Anne Montgomery, wife of General Ben Logan, a relationship to the hero of Quebec are of no value and are entitled to no respect. It was not near, nor can the most remote connection be traced. The identity of the names suggest to the imagination the probability that both may have sprung from families—possibly his kinsmen and clansmen—planted by Hugh Montgomery in Ireland upon the lands obtained from O'Neill as the price of his liberty, or from the subsequent emigrations of Protestant Scotch.

"All that is certainly known of Anne Montgomery's ancestors is that they were of the Scotch-Irish Presbyterians who peopled the valley; that they were in every way respectable, that their names are found among the valiant soldiers, among the civil officers deemed worthy of trust, and among the preachers of God's Word. With the Logan's, Gambles, McClures and Campbells they struck out to the Holston, then the frontier. They did not acquire wealth, but became independent; and, the stuff of which they were made being good, maintained in excellent credit the names they had inherited. "The fate that befell her father and others of her kindred has already been stated, and is found in detail in the pages of Collins.

"Thomas Montgomery, one of the sons of her brother William, won distinction as the able judge of his circuit district. He was the father of the late Dr. Montgomery of Lincoln, and of the first wife of Dr. Lewis W. Green, the learned president of Hampden Sidney and of Center College, and one of the most eloquent and scholarly of pulpit orators.

"Anne Montgomery's sister Jane was the wife of Col. William Casey of Adair, after whom a Kentucky County was named, and was, as has been stated, the grandmother of "Mark Twain," the author and humorist.

"A niece of Anne Montgomery married a brother of Col. Joseph Hamilton Daviess, and after his death became the wife of the late Thomas Helm of Lincoln. The wife of the eloquent Joshua F. Bell was her daughter.

"A niece of Anne Montgomery was the wife of Judge Ben Monroe of Frankfort, an upright judge, a valued reporter of the court of appeals, and a humble Christian. This niece was the mother of Col. George W. Monroe, a soldier of the Federal army, and of the first wife of Judge Wheat of the Kentucky court of appeals. Mrs. Wheat was the mother of Mrs. Cornelia Bush, the first woman elected public librarian of the state.

"Did prescribed limits permit, few pleasures would be more gratifying than that of following these Montgomerys through all of their ramification—Caseys, Russells, Clemens, Wheats, Adamses, Helms, Bells, Monroes, and others. The numerous descendants scattered far and wide over the South and West, both men and women, generally staunch Presbyterians, everywhere by their intrepidity, self-reliance and strong good sense, vindicate the laws of heredity.

"After the death of General Logan, his widow Anne Montgomery married General James Knox, by whom she had no issue. General Knox was a native of Ireland, of Scotch descent, a man of great force of character, and as a leader of the "long hunters" was one of the earliest as well as one of the most intelligent of the explorers of the Kentucky wilderness—his expedition setting out in 1769. He raised corn in what is now Jefferson County in 1775; was a soldier in the Revolution, and represented Lincoln County in the legislature from 1795 to 1800. He died in Shelby County, Dec. 14, 1822. The widow, Anne Montgomery, of both these gallant men, died in Shelby Oct. 18, 1825, aged 73 years."—Green's Historic Families of Kentucky pages 41-2-3.

John Montgomery, one of the seven sons of Hugh Montgomery, Sr., of Virginia, as stated in his genealogy, was one of the "long hunters" with General Knox in Kentucky for three years.

Green, following Foot's account of the early settlers, has this to say concerning the courtship of General Ben Logan and Anne Montgomery. Referring to the preaching of Mr. Cummings, a Presbyterian minister among the early settlers of the Holston country, he says, "Mr. Cummings' universal habit before entering the house was to take a short walk alone while the congregation were seating themselves. He would then return, at the door hold a few words of conversation with some one of the elders of the church, then walk gravely through this crowd, mount the steps of the pulpit, deposit his rifle in a corner near him, lay off his shot-pouch and commence the

The Montgomerys

solemn worship of the day. He would preach two sermons, having a short interval between them, and go home. Such were the lessons by which Logan and his kindred were imbued—where the religious and military spirit went hand in-hand; such the scenes amidst which their characters were formed, broadened and heightened. There he (Logan) met with Anne Montgomery, the daughter of one of his neighbors, of the Scotch-Irish race, escorted her home from these martial-religious exercises, whispered into her willing ears the tender words of love even while his hands grasped the rifle, and, as the years rolled by, won and married her."

She was about 22 years old, having been born in 1755, and married about 1774. Logan soon after came to Kentucky, and she followed in 1776. The accounts of Logan's life and services will be found ii all the histories of Kentucky and the Northwest, as he operated extensively in Ohio.

As already slated, the descendants of William Montgomery, Sr. are very numerous and are among the best families in the state of Kentucky and other states. But all efforts to learn who his ancestors were have so far failed. We wrote "Mark Twain" several letters, and he thought the desired information could be obtained; hut as yet it has not been found.

The Logan's of Kentucky are related to the Emmersons of Indiana. One of the Emmersons who early settled in Indiana married a Logan: hence the name Logan in the family here.

"'Wildcat McKinney' was the sobriquet won and worn by the faithful schoolmaster, John McKinney by the singular incident detailed below:

"Early in the spring of 1785 a traveler arrived at Lexington, Ky., having a newspaper containing articles of peace agreed upon with Great Britain but not yet ratified by our Congress. The stranger would take the paper with him when he should renew his journey next morning. This was nearly three years and a half before the establishment of the Kentucky Gazette, the first newspaper in the district. The sight of one was a rare treat, but one with such important and joyous news could not be given up. Mr. Me Kinney was appealed to for a copy of the articles of peace, and fur this purpose arose before daylight and went into the schoolhouse which stood outside the fort a few rods, and was engaged at this work when the strange visitor appeared.

"Some years after this he (Mr. McKinney) removed to Bourbon County and was one of the five members from that County in the convention of 1792 at Danville, which formed the first constitution of Kentucky, and on June 4th took his seat as a representative in the first legislature at Lexington. In 1820 he removed to Missouri and lived to a good old age. Here is the story:

"In ITS5 Lexington was only a cluster of cabins, one of which, near the spot where the court-house now stands, was used as a schoolhouse. One morning in May, McKinney, the teacher, was sitting alone, busily engaged in writing (copying the terms of peace as noted above) when, hearing a slight noise at the door, he turned his head and beheld—what do you think, readers?—a tall Indian in his war paint, brandishing his tomahawk and handling his knife? No! An enormous wildcat with her fore-feet upon the step of the door her tail curled over her back, her bristles erect and her eyes glancing rapidly through the room as if in search of a mouse.

McKinney's position at first completely concealed him, but a slight and involuntary motion of his chair, at the sight of this shaggy inhabitant of the forest, attracted Puss's attention and their eyes met. McKinney, having heard much of the prowess of 'the human face divine' in quailing the audacity of wild animals, attempted to disconcert the intruder by a frown. But Puss was not to be bullied. Her eyes Hashed fire, her tail waved angrily, and she began to gnash her teeth, evidently bent upon serious hostility. Seeing his danger, McKinney hastily arose and attempted to snatch a cylindrical rule from a table which stood in reach, but the cat was too quick for him. Darting upon him with the proverbial activity of her tribe, she fastened upon his side with her teeth and began to rend and tear with her claws like fury. McKinney's clothes were in an instant torn from his side and his flesh dreadfully mangled by the enraged animal, whose strength and ferocity filled him with astonishment. He, in vain attempted to disengage her from his side. Her long, sharp teeth were fastened between his ribs and his efforts but served to enrage her all the more. Seeing his blood flow very copiously from the wounds in his side, he became seriously alarmed; and not knowing what to do he threw himself upon the edge of the table and pressed her against the sharp corner with the whole weight of his body. The cat now began to utter the most wild and discordant cries, and, McKinney at the same time lifting up his voice in concert, the two together sent forth notes so doleful as to alarm the whole town. Women, who are always the first in hearing or spreading news, were now the first to come to McKinney's

The Montgomerys

assistance. But so strange and unearthly was the harmony within the schoolhouse that they hesitated long before they ventured to enter. At length the boldest of them rushed in; and seeing McKinney bending over the corner of the able and writhing, his body in great pain, she at first supposed that he was laboring under a severe fit of the colic. But quickly perceiving the cat, which was now in the agonies of death, she screamed out: 'Why, Mr. McKinney, what is the matter?' 'I have caught a cat, madam,' replied he, gravely, turning round while the sweat streamed from his face under the mingled operation of fright and fatigue and agony.

"Most of the neighbors had now arrived and attempted to disengage the dead animal from her antagonist; but so firmly were her teeth locked between his ribs that this was a work of no small difficulty. Scarcely had it been effected when Mr. McKinney became very sick and was compelled to go to bed. In a few days, however, he had entirely recovered, and as late as 1820 was alive and a resident of Bourbon County, Ky. where he has often been heard to affirm that he at any time would rather fight two Indians than one wildcat.

"This John McKinney was the grandfather of Wm. H. Montgomery, of Orleans, Ind., on his mother's side, and he told me that McKinney could not press the life out of the cat; that every time McKinney relaxed his efforts the cat would renew the fight. Finally with one hand (as previous to this he had lost the use of the other hand) he managed to get out a pen-knife that he used to make quill pens for the school-children and entered it between two ribs of the cat and pierced its heart, when it died. Mr. McKinney had been a man of Herculean strength and great daring and wonderful endurance."

Incidentally we made the acquaintance of R. E. Carter, of Abilene, Texas, an extensive real-estate agent, who is a descendant of the elder William Montgomery, who was killed near Fort Asp, in Kentucky, 1779. His mother was Mary Wright Ellis Montgomery, daughter of Wm. Montgomery, Jr., who killed the two Indians and wounded another at the time his father was killed. He was a prominent lawyer, an able judge, and a member of Congress. It was while he was in Congress that he took his wife back to Amherst County, Va., to visit her people, and she gave birth to Mr. Carter's mother and died there. Mrs. Carter was raised in Virginia by her uncle, Richard Ellis and others at Amherst court-house, Va., and married Col. Champ Carter and remained in Virginia until seven children were born. Then they moved to Stanford, Ky. Col. Carter was a lawyer, and County clerk of

Lincoln County, Ky., from 1850 to 1858. His wife died in 1858, and in 1859 he and his family moved to Milford, Ellis County, Texas, and Col. Carter died while on a visit to his son, R. E. Carter, Chapel Hill. Washington County, Texas.

Col. Carter's wife had a half-brother, Dr. Thomas B. Montgomery, who was born at Stanford. Ky., and lived and died there. His widow, a Miss Chenault, and several children, now live at Columbia, Miss. I believe that William Montgomery has a monument at Frankfort, Ky.

Mary Wright Ellis Montgomery, who married Col. Champ Carter, had ten children to survive her—eight sons and two daughters: 1—Thomas Montgomery Carter graduated at the University of Virginia in 1855; was a Presbyterian minister awl chaplain of Parson's Brigade, of Texas, C. S. A.; and during military period after the war he went with a Texas colony as chaplain to Brazil in 1866, and died at San Paul. Brazil. 2—Edward Hill Carter died in Waco, Texas, in 1901, after a residence there of 30 years, and left five children. 3—Champ Carter Jr., a lawyer in Franklin, Robertson County. Texas died in 1885, leaving five daughters. 4—Jennie Ellis Carter, unmarried, lives in Texas. 5—Powhester Ellis Carter died of yellow fever in Waco, Texas, in 1887, unmarried. 6— Charles Lee Carter, with large family, moved from Ellis County, Texas, to Portals, New Mexico. 7—J. M. Carter lives in Plainview. Texas. 8—Patrick Henry Carter lives in Hill County, Texas. 9— Eva M. Carter Halbert lives in Wichita, Falls County, Texas.

Col. Champ Carter was the sixth generation from John Carter of England and Cozotoman, Va., as shown by a tree made by R. R. Carter of Shirly, Va., in 1880, and his mother, a Miss Wood, was niece of Patrick Henry; and President Win. H. Harrison and grandson as well as Gen. R. E. Lee are in this tree. E. H. Champ, P. E. and R. E. Carter, were all in Co. E, 15th Texas Vol. Int., Polynic Brigade, Morton's Division Ex. C. S. A. Three of them were wounded in Louisiana. Thomas M. and C. L. were in Parson's Cavalry, all from Texas.

10—R. E. Carter is now adjutant-general and secretary of Morton's Division of Dallas Reunion since April. 1902. He married Ella Montgomery, of a Mississippi family. Four children: 1— Ernest S. Carter; 2—Rich. E. Carter, a lawyer; 3—Kate V. Carter is teaching in public schools; 4—Oliver M. All single in 1903.

Mr. R. E. Carter was born in 1842 and was 17 years old when the family left Kentucky for Texas. He says: "We lived at the old Montgomery home at Stanford, Ky., until we came to Texas, which was sold to Winford Baily. Logan's Creek is within a mile of Stanford, on which was our old home and Logan's Fort. I have crossed it many times."

CHAPTER X.
DESCENDANTS OF HUGH MONTGOMERY, SR.

In the preceding chapter we have made an effort to approximately find the date of birth of Hugh Montgomery, Sr., which is probably 1705. We do not know where he was born, but we do know that Jamestown and Williamsburg on the James River, Virginia, were two important points from which emigrants pushed out into the unsettled interior of Virginia. One route was up through the center of the state, through a mountain pass, into Augusta County. Other emigrants penetrated the interior by following up to the headwaters of the Roanoke and its tributaries, and other rivers; and it is quite probable that Hugh, senior, came up into Roanoke County, Virginia, by way of the Roanoke River route, or by the James River route, as his descendants were known to have lived in Roanoke, Montgomery, Greenbrier and other surrounding counties. Tradition in our family represents that he was wealthy, educated and refined, and these facts give rise to the supposition that he must have emigrated to America from Ireland; but I have looked in vain for proof to sustain the supposition that he came from Ireland, and the accounts given by Commodore J. Ed. Montgomery, late of Chicago, and H. P. Montgomery, of Georgetown, Ky., are the most reasonable that I can obtain Besides, Samuel N. Montgomery, now of Cynthiana, Ind., a Federal soldier in Company F, 80th regiment Ind. Vol., met and became well acquainted with Samuel Montgomery during the Civil War who was an older brother of Commodore J. Ed. Montgomery. This Samuel Montgomery was well versed in the relationship existing between his family and those in south-western Indiana, which proves conclusively that the account given by J. Ed. Montgomery related in the preceding chapter is true.

It is not known who Hugh Montgomery married, but he had ten children—seven sons and three daughters. All the sons took part in the Revolutionary War, and all lived to return home. After the war, it is reported, Hugh found himself destitute of property, and the family scattered—some going to Montgomery, Alabama, some to Tennessee, some to Kentucky, and probably some remained in Virginia. It is claimed by some that Hugh, senior, came to Kentucky and died near Lexington in 1785 at a very advanced age.

As already stated, he had ten children. Of the oldest, Hugh, born 1727, we have no information. There is a bare possibility that the grandfather of Mrs. Bankerston of Ringold, Ga., and of Anthony Montgomery of Boy, Tenn., was this Hugh; but this is rather improbable, as it is claimed that Hugh came from Ireland and Hugh above was probably born in America.

2.—Robert, born 1729. We know absolutely nothing of him.

3.—Of Joseph, born 1731, we have no information unless he was the Captain Joseph Montgomery who accompanied George Rogers Clark on his expedition from the falls of Louisville, Ky., to Vincennes in 1778 and 1779.

4.—Of William, born 1733, we know nothing concerning his family except Squire Samuel, one of his sons, who was probably born about 1770 in Virginia and came to Kentucky, and then to Gibson County in 1814. He was wounded in Harmer's defeat in 1793 or '94. He married Hannah Copeland in Kentucky. They had eight children: 1—Sarah, born 1793; married Samuel Montgomery, Jr., Nov. 15, 1814. This was the second year after the Gibson County was organized, and the thirty-eighth wedding in the County. (See index. Samuel Montgomery, Jr.) 2—Jesse Montgomery was born in Kentucky in 1795, near Danville. He remained in Kentucky to complete the trade of blacksmith, and came to Gibson County, Indiana, in 1816 and settled on the south-east quarter of section 25, town 3, range 12 west, and carried on his trade. Along toward the close of his life he moved to Owensville and died there of cancer in 1861. He married Manece Mounts. They had five children:

1—Louis Montgomery, born Aug., 1820; died Feb. 3, 1890; married Mary A. Wilson, nee Daugherty. Dec. 23, 1841. He settled on part of section 3, town 3, range 11 west, and lived there till 1859, when he built a fine, large residence a short distance east of the Bethlehem General Baptist Church to which he and his wife belonged and they were remarkable in hospitality in entertaining company from that church. His wife was born in Adair County, Ky., 1822. They had eight children: 1—Manece J., born March 30, 1844; died March 4, 1882. 2—Stephen, born Oct. 11, 1846; died small.

The Montgomerys

3—Jesse, born April 19, 1848; died small. 4—Henry C., born May 27, 1849; married, first, Susan Lowe; no children; second, married Cordelia Knox. Oct. 12, 1871 and had six children: 1 -Minnie, born July 12. 1872; died May 19, 1900; married Louis Allen Montgomery, March 19, 1896; one child: 1—William Clancy, born May 3, 1900.

2—Jesse, son of Henry C. Montgomery, born 1874; single 1902.
3—Lillian, died single at the age of 21 years.
4—Tina, died single, Feb. 18, 1891.
5—Daisy, died single.
6—Ross, single 1902.

5—Mary C, daughter of Louis Montgomery, born Nov. 9, 1852; died—.
6— Wm. L., born April 17, 1854; died—.
7—Sarah Ella, born Feb. 17, 1858; married Thomas Emerson Jan. 1, 1880; children three: 1—Vivian H., born 1881; single 1902. 2—Virgie, died at 8 years old. 3—Virlie E., born 1894.
8—Flora N., daughter of Louis Montgomery, born June 29, 1861; married C. W. Redman, Oct. 28. 1882. Children three: 1— Vaughn, died 12 years old. 2—Infant. 3-Oval, born 1890.

2—Susan, born 1822, daughter of Jesse Montgomery, married Hiram Westfall, who died July 23, 1890. He was at one time trustee of Montgomery Township. Mrs. Westfall now (1902) lives in Owensville, Ind. Children four: 1—Mat., died single; 2, 3, 4, died small.

3—Mary, born 1824, daughter of Jesse, married Absalom Pritchett. He was a corporal in Co. E, 42nd Regt. Ind. Vol.; died at Mattoon, Ill. His wife lives there now (1902). Children three: 1—Nora, married a Mr. Teague. 2—Alice, married Oscar Wilson, who is quite a good artist. 3—Edward, married____.

4—John, born 1826, son of Jesse, married Susan McClure. Moved to Midland, Ill., then to Missouri, where he died. Children four: Eugene, Coreen, Jesse and _____.

5—Nancy, born 1828, daughter of Jesse, first married a Mr. Kirkpatrick of Mattoon, Ill.; second, married Rev. Thomas Walker, Oct. 2, 1878, a C. P. minister of Owensville, Ind., who was a very useful pastor in that church for more than 30 years. He died Oct. 9, 1887. Third, she married Joseph Fleming Sharp. Oct. 25, 1888. She left no children.

3—Nancy Montgomery, born 1797, sister to Jesse and daughter of Squire Samuel, married Jesse Nash.

4. Her sister, Maria, born 1794, married Andy Nash.

5—Polly, another sister, married Preston Tolbert; no children.

6—Eliza, another sister, first married John Spilman, Sr.; two children; second, married Lee Cleveland; one child: 1—John Spilman, Jr., was raised by his uncle, Jesse Montgomery, and married Almarinda Finch and moved to Chauncey. Ill.; children five: 1—Sarah; 2, Alice; 3, George; 4, John; 5, James. ,

7—Jennie Montgomery, born 1805, another sister of Jesse, married Montgomery Alcorn. (See index.)

8—Samuel Montgomery, brother of Jesse, born 1807, known as "Blind Sam the Gunsmith," on account of having weak eyes. He had a shop on north-east quarter section 25, Township 3, range 11 west. He married_____, and had three children: 1—Benjamin, born Dec. 1838: married first Hannah Sharp; children eight. She died March 3, 1874. Second, married Harriet Skelton, who died June 25, 1890, children one: 1—Molly, born 1859; married Will Welman, a carpenter, Nov. 20, 1887; children one: 1—Lena, born 1890. 2—Martha, born 1861, died small. 3—Corene, born 1863; married Frank Mauck, Jan. 31, 1886 who has a government position at Washington, D. C, 1902; children five: 1—Robbie, born 1887; 2—Glenn, born 1890; 3—Russell, born 1892; 4—Elmer, born 1897: 5—Clifford, born 1899. 4—Samuel Montgomery, born Jan. 23, 1865: married Lena Rathrock, Dec. 25, 1899; one child—infant, dead. 7—Wilmina, born 1872; married George W. Smith, who has been County commissioner and is now on a four-year term as trustee of Montgomery; children five: 1—Lyle W., born 1892; 2—Chauncey M., born 1895; 3-Willis F., born 1896; 4—Helen W., born 1898; 5—Margaret, born 1900. 8—Augustus W. Montgomery, born Feb. 28, 1874; was raised from an infant by Hiram W. Smith and wife; is a teacher in the common schools; married Bertha Martin, March 11, 1896; children 2: 1. Ralph; 2. Hazle. 9—Lawrence O. Montgomery, born Sept. 23, 1890; married Sarah E. Fisher, March 8, 1899; children one: 1. Franklin W., born 1900.

2— Samuel N. Montgomery, born 1845, son of Blind Sam; married twice; children seven, of whom five are dead. His son, B. F., died in 1901. His daughter, Mary, born 1876, married a shoemaker. Edith, born 1888. This family lives in Missouri.

The Montgomerys

Of the three daughters of Hugh Montgomery, Sr., 5—Mary, born 1735; 6—Martha, born 1737: 7—Jane, born 1739, we only know that Mary married a Mr. Blair of Maryland, Martha married a Mr. Robinson of Virginia, and Jane probably never married.

DESCENDANTS OF JOHN MONTGOMERY
(One of the Seven Sons of Hugh, Sr.)

8—John Montgomery, born 1741. This John Montgomery was rather a remarkable character. It is pretty certain that he was the John Montgomery of whom Collins speaks when he says:

"This same John Montgomery had been on a hunting expedition in 1771, on Dick's River, near where a Baptist church, Mt. Gilead now stands—now Green County, on Cany Fork, Greensburg, Ky., the County Seat. They were known as 'the long hunters' under General Knox. Most of them afterward settled in Kentucky. This same John Montgomery was at the garrison of Harrodsburg, which is now the County Seat of Mercer County, Ky., from Dec. 16, 1777, to Oct, 16, 1778."—Collins, Ky., volume 2, page 624.

He must have married about 1777 as Wm. Montgomery now (1901), of Orleans. Ind., a grandson, says that he came down the Ohio River and landed at Louisville, or the Falls, in 1779, when his oldest child was one year old. Collins, page 127, volume 2, says that the first settlement in Christian County, Hopkinsville, the County Seat, was made by John Montgomery and James Davis, who came from Virginia in 1785 and settled on the west fork of Red River, where they built a block house. At or near the block house was a large cave which served as a hiding place for themselves and families against the attacks of Indians. From this statement it seems that while he was a Virginian he had been in Kentucky since 1779, and then in 1785 pushed on further west where he would be more at home, as most of his life had been on the wilds of the frontier. He was one of the seven sons of Hugh Montgomery, Sr., and was in the war of the Revolution. All these statements are corroborated by Wm. H. Montgomery, of Orleans, Ind. He had three sons, viz:

1—John Montgomery, born 1778; married Clarissa Harlow McKinney, daughter of John, or "Wild Cat" McKinney.

This John Montgomery left Kentucky in 1828 and moved to Madison County, Ind.—Anderson, the County Seat, and then in 1850 moved to Orange County, Ind.—Paoli, County Seat—and settled near Orleans, where he died. He had ten children, all of whom lived to be grown. He must have left Christian County, Ky., where he was raised, and moved up to Fayette County, as one of his children, Elizabeth, was born near Lexington, Ky., in 1827. 1—Wm. H., born Feb. 1815: died Aug. 1902, aged 87 years. He died on the old homestead of John Montgomery, his father, near Orleans, Ind. He was in comfortable circumstances, owning a large farm about two and one-half miles from Orleans. I visited him Nov. 23, 1900. He related to me the circumstances of his grandfather, John Montgomery, born 1741, building the block house near the cave, in Christian County, Ky., in 1785; and also the "Wild Cat" McKinney encounter. These were related to me before I found them recorded in Collins' "History of Kentucky". For this reason I made a record of both of them.

Wm. H. Montgomery first married Margaret Finley; born Aug. 9, 1825; died Jan. 24, 1870: children five: 1—Theopolis Montgomery, born Feb. 29, 1844; died Feb. 1865. He was a soldier in Co. B, 66th regiment Ind. Vol., and died in the hospital at New Albany, Ind. 2—Wm. M. Montgomery, born Aug. 14. 1846; died Jan. 30, 1873; married Miriam Fisher, April 20, 1869; children one: 1—Clara Y. Montgomery, born probably 1870; married James A. Tegarden, Dec. 18, 1894. They now (1901) live in Nashville, Tenn.; children three: 1. Lera; 2. Myrtle; 3. Infant daughter. 3—Clarissa H., daughter of W. H. Montgomery, born April 2, 1850; married Loveall M. Nicholson, April 1835. He died Aug. 4, 1895, aged 57 years He was an elder in the Christian church at Vincennes, Ind. Mrs. Nicholson has rendered me valuable assistance in this work. She now (1901) resides with her father near Orleans, Ind. 4—Preston Montgomery, born April 28, 1857; first married Cora R. Hallowell. April 5, 1879. She died Jan. 2, 1881. She was a grand, good woman with a cheery disposition; she was called "Sunshine" by her many friends. Children one: 1—Claudia H., born Jan. 12, 1881. Preston Montgomery married, second, Mettie McIntyre Sept. 13, 1884; children one; 1—Vanclair, born 1890. 5—Eugene N. Montgomery, son of W. H, born Dec. 14, 1865; married Clara Hardeman, Oct. 19, 1893: children 3: 1—Margaret L.; 2. Mary E., 3. Hugh.

Wm. H. Montgomery, born 1815; second married Mrs. Elizabeth C. Finley, March 23, 1871; children three: 1—Mary, born July 28, 1872. 2—

John E., born Aug. 4, 1874: died Aug. 9, 1876. 3—Laura Ethel, born Oct. 31, 1876; single 1900.

We here insert a letter from Mrs. Jessie Margaret Welch Gibson, of Jonesville, Va. which gives a condensed account of the ten children of John Montgomery, born 1778:

"Mr. D. B. Montgomery, Owensville, Ind.

"Dear Sir:

A copy of the Adair County News, published at Columbia. Ky., April 11, 1900, containing your letter of April 1, to the editor of that paper—concerning certain members of the Montgomery family—accidentally fell into my hands this morning, and as I am a descendant also from the same family and have never been able to find out a great deal about them. I determined to write you as a means of learning more of my ancestors.

"My mother was Mary Ellen Welch, nee Cunningham. Her mother was Elizabeth Cunningham, nee Montgomery. She was the daughter of John Montgomery (born 1778) and Clarissa Harlow McKinney, and was born May 30, 1827, near where the city of Lexington, Ky., now stands. She accompanied her father, John Montgomery, to Madison County in 1828, and then to Orange County in 1850. She is still living, in Illinois. I remember to have heard her speak of Uncle Hugh Montgomery, whom I presume was one of the seven sons of Hugh Montgomery Sr.

"My great-grandfather, John Montgomery (born 1778) fought in the war of 1812, and was more or less disabled all the rest of his life from the exposure of the campaign in Canada, where he had both feet frozen. He lived to be more than 80 years old. His wife died in Missouri, at the home of my grandmother, in her 89th year.

"John Montgomery (born 1778) raised ten children, all they ever had, to be married and have families. Wm. H. is living near Orleans, Ind., and is now (1900) 85 years old, but is still active and hearty. Mary married Pascal Jackson, and died many years go. Martha is living near Kewanna, Ind. Emma married James Finley, and died many years since. James was a Federal soldier, and died soon after returning home. John Alexander was a soldier in Co. B, 66th regiment Ind. Vol., and died about eighteen months after being discharged. Sarah married a Mr. Boulby and now resides with her daughter in Indianapolis. Clarissa Harlow married Adam Alexander, who died many years ago, and she is now (1900) practicing law in Los Angeles, Cal. Andrew lives on a farm near McPherson, Kansas.

"I would be very much pleased to learn more of the first Hugh Montgomery, who settled in Roanoke County, Va., early in 1700; also if you are positive that all seven of these sons fought in the Revolutionary War.

"Most sincerely yours,

"MRS. JESSIE MARGARET WELCH GIBSON,
"Jonesville, Virginia."

You will observe that this letter gives in a very short space some account of all this large family of Montgomerys. I regret very much that I could never obtain any further correspondence with this lady. But through her relatives at Orleans, Ind., I learned that she was born about 1872, and that she is an intelligent and cultured lady, as her letter plainly indicates.

2—William Montgomery, born 1780, and a son of John (born 1741), settled in Scott County, Ky. — George town County Seat—and raised a family there, and finally moved to Shelby County, Ind.— Shelbyville County Seat—and became wealthy. I understand that many of his descendants are in that County at this time.

3—Katie Montgomery, his sister, born 1782, married a Mr. Ireland and moved to Ohio, and died there.

CHAPTER XI.
DESCENDANTS OF SAMUEL MONTGOMERY. SR.

He was born in Virginia, probably about 1743, and was one of the seven sons of Hugh Montgomery Sr., all of whom, our family tradition says, were in the Revolutionary War. He was a quiet, peaceable, industrious and religious man, and highly esteemed by all his neighbors.

He married Polly McFarland in Virginia and moved and settled within about eight miles of Perryville. Ky. In 1811 he came with most of his family to Indiana and settled on the north-east quarter of section 24, town 3, range 12 west, in Knox (now Gibson) County, which was organized in 1813. This farm had been taken up by his nephew, Walter C. Montgomery who had settled here in 1806. The farm is now known as the Wm. Benson farm. Samuel Montgomery died in 1815 and was buried on his own farm. His children were: Polly, born 1775; Rachel, born Nov. 26, 1777; Katie, born Nov. 19, 1779; Robert, born 1781; James, born 1783; Benjamin, born 1785; Dorcas, born 1887; John, born 1790; and Samuel, the youngest, born 1794.

Just at what time Samuel Montgomery, Sr., came to Kentucky, we are not prepared to say; but he was there as early as 1794, as his youngest son, Samuel, Jr., was born there in that year. We have already shown that his brother John had been all over that section of Kentucky as early as 1774, as he was a member of the "longhunters" under General Knox and afterward settled in Kentucky in 1779.

1—Polly Montgomery, daughter of Samuel Sr., born probably in 1775, married David Swope, of Kentucky, about 1795. Mr. Swope died in 1845. His wife had died some time before this, as Mr. Swope was living with his second wife when he died. Polly Swope had six children: 1—Montgomery Swope, born 1796: never married. 2--Morgan, born 1798. 3—Martin, born 1810. 4—Dorothy, born 1804. 5—David, born 1807. 6—Mary Elizabeth, born 1810.

Morgan Swope, No, 2, first married Sonia Robinson, of Girard County, Ky., and had two children: 1. Emily E., died 27 years old; 2. Elizabeth, who married Benedict Swope, a cousin, and had seven children. Morgan Swope married, second, Martha Ruby in 1835. He died in 1876, aged 78 years. By his second wife he had four children: 1. Montgomery; 2. I. M.; 3. Morgan; 4. Wm. Henry.

Montgomery Swope, born Dec. 22. 1836, married Eliza Martin of Owensville, Ind. Mr. Swope was a Captain in the Confederate Army three years under Forest and Johnson. He had three children: 1—Leroy is married and lives at Cottonwood Falls, Kansas. 2 —Hargrove, is married and lives in Houston, Texas. 3—Rena, is married and lives in Stafford, Kansas.

1. M. Swope, born March 2, 1838, married Cordelia Scantland Jan. 22, 1862: children four: Annie, Walter, William, Early, and Martha C.

Morgan Swope, born Feb. 28, 1841, married Louisa Flanders; children four: 1—Samuel, who is chief physician in the sanitarium at Deming, New Mexico. 2—Martha married Robert Hicks and lives in Ballard, Ky.; children 9. 3—Breton, died 1900 aged 23 years. 4—Morgan, killed 1895, aged 12 years.

William Henry Swope, born Oct. 1, 1845; first married Ella Swope, a distant relative; one child: Eugene Swope; married and lives in Cincinnati, Ohio. William Henry Swope married second a Miss Dawson; children two: 1—Lemuel, married and lives at Paducah, Ky.; 12, Logan, single 1901.

Martin Swope, son of Polly Montgomery-Swope, born 1801; married a Miss Owen; two children: 1—James D., a painter by trade; 2—Taylor, a farmer.

Dorcas Swope, daughter of Polly Montgomery-Swope born 1804; married Benedict Swope, her cousin; children five: Hardin, a farmer; Benedict, a physician: Mary, married a Dawson; Dorcas, also married a Dawson; Eliza was deaf and dumb.

Mary Eliza Swope, daughter of Polly M. Swope, born 1810, married A. Spidell; children ten: 1—John D. 2—Christopher, was in Confederate army. 3—Thomas, was in Confederate army. 4—Richard, was in Confederate army. All three of these lived to return home without wounds. 5—Benedict. 6—Mary. 7—Jacob. 8, 9, and 10—three daughters born in Tennessee after 1850.

The Montgomerys

RACHEL MONTGOMERY—THE MOUNTS FAMILY.

Rachel Montgomery, second child of Samuel Montgomery, Sr., married Smith Mounts; and we here give some account of this family. The Gibson County History says, page 57:

"The Mounts families in this county are descended from John and Providence Mounts, natives of Switzerland. They were among the early settlers of Philadelphia, Penn. and subsequently moved to Virginia, and then to Kentucky, where they became noted Indian fighters."

Mathias and Smith Mounts, sons of John Mounts, were with General Wayne during the Indian wars of 1794 and took part in several engagements in north-western Ohio. They became residents of south-western Indiana in 1807. Mathias Mounts married Mollie Montgomery, eldest daughter of "Purty Old Tom," an account of whom will be given in another place.

Smith Mounts was born in 1770, probably in Virginia. When he came to Indiana he settled on section 24. Town 3, range 12 west, where he lived until his death, Sept. 13, 1834. He was also in the war of 1812 and fought in the Battle of Tippecanoe. It is regretted that so little is known of the ancestors of these people. There is a tradition handed down by John D. Mounts, a grandson of Smith Mounts, Sr., that the name "Smith" came into the family from one of the Mounts family having married a Smith in Virginia. Smith Mounts Sr. married Rachel Montgomery, about 1796. She was born Nov. 26, 1777; died May 5, 1851.

There is strong evidence that the names Mountz, Mounce, Mounts, Mount, are all derived from the same original name. There are old papers in Gibson County showing that the family here has spelled the name three different ways since 1807. It was first Mounce or Mountz; now all of them spell it Mounts. The early generations of the family here were wonderful developments of physical strength. Garrad Mounts had not an equal in this particular in all south-western Indiana. Children 8: Garrad, Moria, Manece, Montgomery, Polly, Dorcas, Smith, and Thomas A.

1—Garrad Mounts, born 1797; died July 12, 1878; married Patsy Montgomery, daughter of Joseph Montgomery. Sr., born April 22, 1803; died July 17, 1892. She was a remarkably shrewd woman. They were married Dec. 14, 1819, at Owensville, Ind., by Samuel Montgomery, a justice of the peace, who was an own cousin to her father and came to Indiana in 1814.

Garrad Mounts, whose mother was Rachel Montgomery, was at one time County Commissioner and held other offices of trust. He was one of the best physically developed men in Gibson County. Notwithstanding his Herculean strength, he was a remarkably peaceable man for that day, when it was a very common thing for men to contest each other's strength simply for the victory. His brother, Montgomery Mounts, was not as large as Garrad, nor so peaceably inclined. At one time he proposed to whip Garrad, who reasoned with and tried to convince him how disgraceful it would be for brothers to fight; but without avail. So the two men prepared for battle. Garrad stood sparring while Montgomery madly rushed at his antagonist. Garrad, instead of striking him, caught and lifted him up and dropped him on the opposite side of a high fence, then mounted his horse and rode away.

A story used to be told to the effect that Garrad Mounts, while Constable, lifted up a house-log and burst in a door where a dangerous criminal was barricaded. The truth of the matter is that he allowed other men to place the log on his shoulder then he moved forward and hurled it against the otherwise impenetrable door and crushed it to pieces. To the surprise of every one present, the man surrendered without resistance, saying: *"What is the use to contend with a man that can carry a house-log?"* Mr. Mounts was a man of very great force of character, and a highly respectable citizen. They had twelve children:

1—Nancy Mounts, born Feb. 17, 1821; died Feb. 11, 1880. She married James L. Emerson, Nov. 7, 1839. He was born 1817, died about July 5, 1890. They raised their family on a farm about five miles south of Owensville, in Johnson Township, Gibson County, Ind. Mr. and Mrs. Emerson were recognized as being among the best citizens in the County. Mrs. Emerson was generous and always had a word of cheer and comfort for the distressed and afflicted. Mr. Emerson was one of the best farmers in the County. The assessors' reports show that his farm made the best average of crops of any large farm in Johnson Township. He was plain and unassuming. He favored the public school system and gave his family the full benefits of its advantages. Several of his children taught in the public schools, and three of his sons graduated from first-class colleges—namely, Garrad M., Z. T. and Logan. Mr. Emerson's grandmother was a sister to General Ben. Logan of

The Montgomerys

Revolutionary fame, who operated in Virginia, Kentucky, and Ohio; hence the name Logan in the family. Mr. Emerson had peculiar financial views. He was opposed to sureties on notes and preferred to lend his money to young men of industry and good habits, just starting in life, without sureties, rather than loan to older ones with sureties; and probably he never lost much money on this plan.

The manner of assisting his children is to be commended. At the age of 21 years he gave each $1000 and took a receipt for the same, which at his death were all found carefully filed among his papers. He held the greater portion of his estate until his death. No man and wife ever held the respect and esteem of a large family in a more satisfactory, manner than did James and Nancy Emerson. Children 14—namely:

1—John W. Emerson, born Aug. 11, 1840, was a Second Lieutenant in Co. F, 58th regiment Ind. Vol. He taught several years in the common schools after the Civil War. The old soldiers of his regiment enjoy a good camp-fire story at his expense. At one time during his service in the army he had a terrible struggle with typhoid fever, and the report reached home that he was dead. His father procured a good metallic coffin and sent for John's body, but when the coffin reached camp he was still alive and finally recovered and remained in the army until the close of the war. The boys now tell it that John was too contrary to use the coffin after it had been sent to him. John was delirious for several days and wandered about the camp at will. Dr. James C. Patton, a relief surgeon, saw John at this time and was much interested in him, but did out get his name. Afterward the doctor enlisted in the 58th regiment and became intimate with Mr. Emerson, but never dreamed of his being the sick man that he had attended mouths before. Sometime after the war the doctor and Mr. Emerson met and were discussing that terrible scourge of fever among the soldiers, when the doctor related the above circumstance and remarked that he had always regretted that he did not learn the man's name. To his great surprise and joy Mr. Emerson said, "I am the man."

John W. Emerson first married Nancy J. Knowles, Dec. 10, 1865. She died March 29, 1875. Children six:
    1—Cora M. Emerson, born Dec. 9, 1867, married Perry Pritchett, June 21, 1890; children 3: 1. Lake Pritchett, born Jan. 17, 1891, 2. Leslie Pritchett, born Feb. 1899, 3. Infant, born ____.

2—Dr. Ralph VV. Emerson, born Oct. 23, 1869; is a graduate from Merom College in Indiana. June 13, 1895, and of the Eclectic Medical College at Cincinnati, Ohio, March 10, 1898; located in Owensville, Ind., March 20, 1898; married Ella Johnson, Aug. 28, 1898. She was born Sept. 9, 1877. Children one: Wash. Johnson Emerson, born Sept. 1. 1901.

3— Alice C. Emerson, born March 31, 1871; died July 1, 1871.

4—Martha R. Emerson, born Aug. 23, 1872; died Oct. 25, 1872.

5—Erastus D. Emerson, born Oct. 2,1873; was a soldier in Co. K, 159th regiment Indiana Vol., in the Spanish-American War; married Ada Steel, Dec. 23, 1900; no children.

6—Sally Emerson, born Feb. 1, 1875; married James Swader of Texas City, Ill., no children.

John W. Emerson married Sarah Ellen Yeager, Nov. 26, 1878; children six: 7—Grace Emerson, born Nov. 1, 1879; married William E. Bixler, Aug. 16, 1898; no children. 8—Floral Emerson, born Aug. 24, 1882; married Elmer Murphy, Dec. 29, 1901; live near Poseyville, Ind.; children one: Murphy, horn Oct. 26, 1902; 9 ---Frank P. Emerson, born Dec. 17, 1885; died Jan. 19, 1888. 10—Chauncey R. Emerson, born July 9, 1887; died March 24, 1888. 11—Nicholas H., born June 30, 1890. 12--- James R. Emerson, born Jan. 3. 1893.

Patsy Emerson, born June 20, 1842, second child of Nancy Mounts-Emerson; married John W. Carter, Oct. 3, 1861. He was a soldier in Co. F. 80th regiment Ind. Vol. He was severely wounded at the battle of Resaca, Ga., May 15, 1864, from which he never fully recovered. He was trustee of Patoka Township, Gibson County Ind., from 1894 to 1895. He died in Princeton, Ind., Nov. 15, 1895; children three: 1—Dr. Virgil R. Carter, born Jan. 7, 1863; located at McGary station, Ind. He graduated from an Eclectic medical college in Cincinnati: first married Turie Buff, June 4, 1890. She died March 3, 1891; children one—Jesse B. Carter, born Jan. 26, 1891; died June 11, 1892, second, married Clara M. Logan of Toledo, Ill., Nov. 28, 1895. She died March 15, 1897, children one: Emerson C. Carter, born Jan. 15, 1897; died Sept. 11, 1899, third, married Mattie R. Eaton of Princeton, Ind., Feb. 2, 1901. Children one: Lowell Carter, born Nov. 15, 1901. 2—Albert L. Carter, barn July 18, 1866; died Jan. 18, 1890; single. 3—Laura Carter, born April 7,

1868, third child of Patsy Emerson Carter; married G. E. Daugherty, April 9, 1890. She died Feb. 20, 1898; children 1: John B. Daugherty, born Oct. 26, 1892; died April 16, 1895. Mr. Daugherty is married again to Miss Eliza Kirkpatrick, and is in the hardware business in Owensville.

Eliza M. Emerson, born Oct. 6, 1843; died Sept. 22, 1844; third child of Nancy Mounts-Emerson. G. M. Emerson, fourth child, born June 15, 1845, was a soldier in 137th regiment Ind. Vol. He is a graduate of Medina College, in Ohio, and has been surveyor of Gibson County, Ind., for seven or eight terms; married Julia Wheatley, who is a graduate of Medina College. They live in Princeton, Ind. (1902): children three: 1—Infant, 2—Infant, 3—Rex, Emerson, born ____.

Z. T. Emerson, born April 1, 1847, fifth child; is a graduate of Medina College, Ohio. He taught in the high schools of Indiana several years; was a real estate agent; was at one time Deputy Sheriff; is now (1902) in the banking business at Cynthiana, Ind.; never married.

Permelia E. Emerson, born Feb. 7, 1849; died Feb. 19, 1850; sixth child.

Thomas H. Emerson, born Jan. 18, 1851; died Feb. 1898; seventh child of Nancy Mounts-Emerson; taught in the common schools; was County commissioner for several terms; died in office in the very zenith of his usefulness and the whole County mourned on account of his death. He married Sarah Ella Montgomery, daughter of Louis L. Montgomery Jan. 1, 1880; children three: I—Vivian Emerson, born Oct. 20, 1881; 2—Virgie, died small; 3— Verlia, born March 8, 1894.

Mary J. Emerson born Aug. 29, 1853, eighth child; married Wm. Johnson Oct. 8, 1872. He was a soldier in Co. F 80th regiment Ind. Vol. Children one: Hebert Johnson, born ____.

Lydia Emerson, born Aug. 29, 1850, a twin to Mary J., and ninth child. Lenora Emerson, born Sept. 6, 1855, died ____; tenth child; was the second wife of John L. Short, a furniture dealer in Owensville, Ind. She also attended school at Medina College and was well educated and a most excellent woman. She died Sept 20, 1898; no children. Mr. Short died March 14, 1901.

And Their Descendants

Almira Emerson, born June 5, 1858; 11th child; married Henry Brush, of near Texas City, Ill.; children four: 1—Anna Brush; 2— Bernice; 3—Roy; 4—Jesse.

Jesse P. Emerson, born Jan. 18, 1861; 12th child married Virginia Randolph, Aug. 25, 1897. She is a graduate of three colleges: 1. Merom, Ind.; 2. Indiana State Normal; 3. State University of Indiana. They now (1903) live on the old home place of his father. James L. Emerson. Children one: Virgil Emerson.

Anna L. Emerson, born May 27, 1863; thirteenth child; married T. A. Mangrum, March 23, 1884, a farmer and stock-raiser who was born Dec. 11, 1859; and they live east of Bethlehem church of General Baptists, in Gibson County, Ind., on the Bailey Williams farm; children three: 1—Cloyd E. Mangrum, born July 22, 1880: 2 and 3—Ola and Ida Mangrum, twins, born Dec. 17, 1891.

Logan L. Emerson, born Aug. 19, 1866; died Feb. 21, 1902. He graduated from Stanford University, California, in the classical course, and was considered one of the best-educated men in Gibson County. He was the youngest of the family, being the fourteenth child. He died in Evansville, Ind., where he had gone to have an operation performed for appendicitis.

Almira Mounts, born June 3, 1823: died Feb. 15, 1884: second child of Garrad Mounts: married Wesley Redman, Sept. 14, 1847. He died Dec. 23, 1886. They lived east of Ft. Branch, Ind.; children two: 1—Cordelia Redman, married Elias Barker, and died without issue; 2—Wm. Crit. Redman, married Fanny Rogers; children 8: 1. John W. Redman, married Ellen Nordhorn, children two—Isel and Gertie; 2. Dora Redman, single, 3. Cordelia Redman married Wm. Steefel, 4. Jesse Redman, single, 5. Katie Redman, married Russel Showers, children three—Hazle, Noble, Lester, 6. George Redman, single, 7. Stella Redman, single, 8. Norman Redman, single.

Wesley Mounts, born March 28, 1825, died Aug. 16, 1861; third child; married Mary Boren, April 4, 1850; children three: 1, John Mounts, born 1851; married Josie Numan; no children. 2. Bertha A. Mounts, born 1853 married Joseph Nass; no children. 3. Martha A. Mounts, born 1855, second wife of Joseph Nass; no children.

The Montgomerys

Garrad Smith Mounts, born April 23, 1827, fourth child of Garrad Mounts, Sr., married Lydia Sword, May 14, 1870; children three: 1. Henry Mounts, born — was marshal of Cynthiana at one time. 2. Leonard Mounts. 3. Martha Mounts.

Eliza Mounts, born April 3, 1829, fifth child of Garrad Mounts died single, Dec. 8, 1887.

Permelia Mounts, the sixth child, born Nov. 13, 1831; died Mar. 13, 1857. She was handsome, intelligent and a splendid conversationalist and a teacher in the common schools.

Margaret E. Mounts, born May 25, 1834, seventh child of Garrad Mounts Sr. married George Trible, Jan. 6, 1857. They live a short distance west of Haubstadt, Ind. children twelve: 1. Samuel N. Trible, born 1858 has taught in the public schools for many years, lives in Ft. Branch, Ind.; first married Molly Draper, Dec. 27, 1888, children one: infant. Married second, Ida B. Gray; children one: Eula. 2. John B. Trible, born 1800; taught in the common schools several terms, and served one term as sheriff of Gibson County, Ind.; has been on the police force at Princeton, Ind.; married Lizzie Drysdale, Sept. 15, 1886; children two: 1. Deirdre Trible 2. Fay Trible. 3. I. L. Trible, born 1862, lives in Bridgeport, Ill.; married Jennie Finney; children one: Bernie Trible. 4. Nancy Trible, born 1864, died small. 5. W. R. Trible, born 1866, married Mary Singer; children three: 1. Joseph G. Trible 2. Leofla Trible 3. George N. Trible. 6. Emeline Trible, born 1866, twin to W. R. Trible, died small. 7. Ida W. Trible, born 1868, married E. K. Dutton; children two: 1. George R. Dutton; 2. Roy Dutton. 8. George S. Trible, born 1870; married Ida Cleveland; children one: Nina M. Trible. 9. Martha Trible born 1871; single, 10. Charles C. Trible, born 1872, died small. 11. Mary J. Trible, born 1875, died Sept. 22, 1901. 12. O. P. Trible, born 1881; single.

John D. Mounts, born Aug. 16, 1836; eighth child of Garrad Mounts; taught in the common schools in Indiana; lived several years near Chancy, Ill.; then lived in Kansas, then in Terre Haute, Ind.: died in Princeton, Ind., 1900. He left a small genealogical manuscript, from which I have gathered many things that would otherwise have been lost. He first married Anna McCrary of Owensville, Ind., Aug. 16, 1863. She died Sept. 14, 1875; children 4: 1. Isaac Mounts, born 1864 somewhere in the West. 2. Mattie, born 1866, single in 1902. 3. Mary, born 1868; married a Mr. Evans. 4. John Mounts, born 1870: lives near Pond Creek, Oklahoma Territory, and is in good circumstances; single 1902. Second, John D. Mounts married Mrs. Hannah Baldwin, nee DePriest, Aug. 20, 1880; children one: Freda Garrad Mounts.

I. L. Mounts, born Aug. 14, 1839, ninth child of Garrad Mounts, was a soldier in Co. F, 58th Ind. Vol. The writer heard Mr. Mounts relate an incident in his war experience which was solemn and distressing. It was at the battle of Chickamauga. It was a little after dark on Saturday night, Sept. 19, 1863, at the close of the second day's fight. The 58th Indiana regiment was lying down in line of battle when a Confederate command in line, which appeared in the darkness to be three deep, approached in front of them. The Federals were commanded to hold their fire until the Confederates came dangerously near, when they suddenly arose and sent a volley with terrible effect into the Confederate ranks. This closed the contest for that day but the wounded and dying remained there all night moaning and crying for help and praying for mercy. At what time those who escaped death or being wounded left the field is not known, but no truce was sent and no favors asked by the repulsed Confederates. Therefore the Federals could not venture to render any assistance. Mr. Mounts says this was the most miserable night he ever spent in all his life. Lieutenant John W. Emerson, of the same company, says the same; and Rev. J. J. Height, chaplain of the 58th regiment, refers to this matter on page 183 of his history of the regiment and says:

"And a terrible night it was; cool and no fire could be permitted; all around were the dead and dying. The cries and moans of the wounded are most distressing. The most horrible features of a battle are the experiences of the living soldier on the field the night after the battle."

Mr. Mounts married Sally E. Pritchett. Jan. 1. 1871; children one: John Mounts, born Oct. 1, 1871. He is an engineer and thresher.

Martitia Mounts, born July 25, 1841; tenth child of Garrad Mounts; married Win. Redman, Oct. 20, 1855, who was a soldier in Co. F, 58th regiment Ind. Vol. He has been dead several years. Mrs. Redman lives in Owensville, Ind.; children 5: 1. Perry Redman, born 1866: is a mail-carrier on a rural route from Owensville. Ind.; married Mary McReynolds, April 1901: no children. 2. Patsy Redman. 3. Janie Redman. 4. Annie Redman. 5. Flora Redman. All single 1903.

The Montgomerys

Crittenden Mounts, born Sept. 27, 1843, died April 16, 1844; eleventh child of Garrad Mounts.

Indiana Mounts, born July 1, 1848; twelfth child of Garrad Mounts; married Charley Raines, May 3, 1887; no children.

Moria Mounts, born 1799; second child of Rachel Montgomery Mounts, married John Armstrong, probably about 1824; children eleven: 1. Wm. Armstrong, born 1825; married Pop. McGary; no children. 2. Manece Armstrong born 1827; married, _____ 3. Malinda, born 1829. 4. Elizabeth Armstrong, born 1831; married Merida Greer. 5. Montgomery Armstrong, born 1833; never married. 6. Thomas Armstrong, born 1835, married Pap. McGary Armstrong. He has been seriously crippled for a long time. He now (1902) lives in the west part of Owensville, Ind., and is 67 years old; children, seven: 1. Mira Armstrong married George Mellinger of Patoka, Ind.; children two: 1. John Mellinger; 2. Floyd Mellinger. 2., Daniel Armstrong, first married Errena Witherow; no children; second, married Emma Ewing; no children. 3. Amelia Armstrong, married Harrison Doane, Feb. 14, 1889; children two: 1. Benjamin Doane; 2. Richard Doane. 4. John Armstrong married Anna Tichenor, Dec. 1901. 5. Eliza Armstrong died 12 years old. 6. Millard Armstrong died small. 7. Millard (Kise) Armstrong, single. Menece Mounts, born in Kentucky, third child of Rachel Montgomery-Mounts, married Jesse Montgomery, Sr., who was born 1795.

Montgomery Mounts, born 1803, fourth child of Rachel Montgomery-Mounts, married Jane Rosborough about 1826; children eight; 1. Polly Mounts, born 1827, married Wesley Montgomery. (See index—"Col. William Montgomery of Indiana.")

Rachel Mounts, born 1829; second child of Montgomery Mounts; married Jordan Clark, 1847; children four: 1, Jane Clark, born 1848, died March 18, 1894, married John L. Brown, June 17, 1869. He was a soldier in the 120th regiment Ind. Vol. He has large possessions in land; is a stockholder in the First National Bank of Owensville, Ind.; is an extensive fruit-grower, and has mining stock in the Dakotas. Children seven: 1. infant, a daughter, born Nov. 8, 1869, died Nov. 8, 1869; 2. Eliza E. Brown, born Nov. 24. 1870; married George W. Woods in Princeton, Ind., Sep. 4, 1889; children two: 1. Carl L. Woods, born Oct. 20, 1890; 2. Hazel D. Woods, born Oct. 8, 1893. 3. Amanda E. Brown, born Oct. 20, 1872; married Madison M. Knowles, of near King's Station, Ind.; children one: 1. Ovela Knowles. 4,

Arthur Brown, born Aug. 21, 1874, lives near King's Station, Ind.; married Belle Tichenor, Aug. 5, 1896; children one: 1. Eunice J. Brown, born April 20, 1899. 5. James E. Brown, born Aug. 16, 1876, died Aug. 20, 1896. 6. Forney B. Brown, born Oct. 8, 1877; married Othneal Hollis, a farmer, Aug. 6, 1896; children two: 1. John P. Hollis, born May 13, 1897; 2. Bartlet P. Hollis, a twin to John P., born May 13, 1897. 7. Eva E. Brown, born Dec. 17, 1885; single 1902. 8. Harvey O. Brown, born April 29, 1889.

John L. Brown married, second, (Feb. 20, 1895) Melissa Clark, daughter of Rev. Wm. Clark, and cousin to his first wife; children three: 1. Zella V. Brown, born Sept. 26, 1896; died Jan. 10, 1897. 2. Arvel C. Brown, born Nov. 7. 1899. 3. Darwin D. Brown, born Dec. 22, 1901.

Joseph Clark, born 1850; second child of Rachel Mounts-Clark; lives in Carmi, Ill., and is a large land-owner. At one time in early life he was completely broken up, financially, but by industry, economy and perseverance he accumulated property and satisfied all his creditors and is now in the enjoyment of his hard-earned wealth; married Kate Allen, from Tennessee; children three: 1. Ida Clark; 2. Effie Clark; 3. Flora Clark.

William Clark, third child of Rachel Mounts-Clark, born Jan. 25, 1852, near Owensville. Ind. married Amelia Campbell at Oakland City, Ind. Nov. 7, 1872 by the Rev. Jacob Speer. His wife was born Nov. 5, 1855. Moved to Burnt Prairie, Ill., then to Kansas, then to near Spencer, Iowa, and died there Aug. 26. 1902. He was a member of the Free Baptist Church in Iowa. Children nine: 1. Jennie S., born Dec. 2, 1874. 2. Franklin J., born Nov. 30, 1878. 3. Elmina P., born April 30, 1884. 4. George E., born June 9, 1886. 5. Lillie M., born March 24, 1888, died July 24, 1891. 6. Bessie O., born Oct. 8, 1890. 7. Eva, born July 15, 1892. 8. Pearlie A., born Jan. 20, 1894. 9, Vinetta F. born July 1. 1895.

Columbus Clark, fourth child of Rachel Mounts-Clark died small.

Margaret Mounts, born 1831; third child of Montgomery Mounts; married Dow Simpson; children one: 1. Jane Simpson; married Henry Gambrel, who was born March 1, 1858; children one: 1. Lawrence Gambrel; single 1902.

William Mounts, born 1833; fourth child of Montgomery Mounts: died single.

Garrad Mounts, Jr., born 1835; married Malinda Harmon, sister to John Wesley Harmon of Owensville, Ind.; children four: 1. Mat Mounts, married Henson Pegram, Aug. 15, 1875; no children. 2. Alice Mounts married John McCrary, Nov. 27, 1S79. He was born in 1855 and lives near Oakland City, Ind. Children nine: 1. Bernie, born 1881. 2. Delphy, born 1883. 3. Barney, born 1885. 4 and 5, John and Grace, twins, born 1887. 6. Minie, born 1889. 7. Evaline, born 1892. 8. Iva, born 1894. 9. Ruth, born 1899.

Lizzie Mounts, third child of Garrad Mounts, Jr., deceased; married James Wilhite; one child.

Jule Mounts, fourth child of Garrad Mounts, Jr., single 1902.

Nancy Mounts, born 1837; sixth child of Montgomery Mounts, died single.

Sarah Mounts, born 1840; seventh child of Montgomery Mounts.

Jasper Mounts, born 1844; eighth child of Montgomery Mounts; was a soldier in the 65th regiment Ind. Vol. When last heard from he was in the South-west, probably in Arizona; married Kate Powell of Owensville, Ind.; children three: 1. Ina Mounts; 2. Delia; 3. John.

Folly Mounts, born 1805; fifth child of Rachel Montgomery Mounts; married Roan Ike Montgomery. (See index.)

Dorcas Mounts, born 1807, died about 1850; sixth child of Rachel Montgomery-Mounts; married Harrison Newsom in Illinois, probably in 1831. He came from Massachusetts and was probably of German descent. He was at different times connected with gristmills, saw-milk, shingle machines and merchandise, and was a Justice of the Peace for many years. He died on a farm near Friendsville, Ill., Nov. 5, 1882; children seven: 1. Smith Newsom, born Sept. 9, 1832. He was a soldier in the 42nd regiment Ind. Vol., was captured at the battle of Chickamauga and died in Andersonville prison, Georgia, in 1864; never married. 2. Rachel Newsom, born Feb. 22, 1835; married Charles Jones of Owensville, Ind. He was born May 10, 1832. She now lives in Newkirk, Okla.; children five: 1. Senorita Jones, born 1855; married Charles McNair of Friendsville, Ill.; children two: 1. Maggie McNair; 2. infant. 2. Viola Jones, born July 24, 1857; married Albert B. Thurman; children six: 1. George A. Thurman, born March 19,

1877. 2. Charles E. Thurman, born Oct. 24, 1878. 3. Nora E. Thurman, born Nov. 12, 1880. 4. Wm. M. Thurman, born June 9, 1883. 5. Mary M. Thurman, born Sept. 12, 1885; died July 28, 1890. 6. Thomas L. Thurman, born June 13, 1889. 3. Edson Jones, born 1860; married in Mt. Carmel, Ill.; children one. 4. Bertha Jones, born May 5, 1863; married Belle Willis of Newkirk, Okla., who was born Dec. 29, 1870; children six: 1. Blanch Jones, born April 6, 1889; 2. Bessie Jones, born Dec. 10, 1890: 3. Virgil Jones, born Nov. 21, 1892; 4. Jyla Jones, born Dec. 2, 1894; 5. Ruth Jones, born April 8, 1897; 6. Earl Jones, born May 18, 1899.

Wilmot G. Jones, born July 19, 1870; fifth child of Rachel Newsom-Jones; married Ida Fay, July 15, 1895.

Martha J. Newsom, third child of Dorcas Mounts-Newsom, born 1838; married Samuel Simpson, Dec. 11, 1864. He died Dec. 7, 1886, in Indianapolis, Ind. after undergoing a surgical operation. Mrs. Simpson has valuable lands in the bottoms west of Owensville, Ind.; children two: 1. Maggie Simpson, born Sept. 16, 1865. 2. Infant. Maggie Simpson married Samuel Scott. Jr., Sept. 16, 1886. They own good lands in the bottoms; children four: 1. Hazel C., born Sept. 3, 1888. 2. Ronald Scott, born Dec. 18, 1889. 3. Darby C. Scott, born July 17, 1893. 4. Laura, M. Scott, born March 17, 1897.

Thomas Newsom, born Feb. 21, 1840: taught in the public schools in Indiana; lives in Belmont, Ill., and is in good circumstances; married Pauline W. Await, Jan. 8, 1876. She was born Aug. 18, 1854; children five: 1. Lola Newsom, born Dec. 14, 1876: married Peter Joachin, June 27, 1900; children one: Roy Joachin, born June 14. 1901. 2. Wm. O. Newsom, born Oct. 22. 1878. 3. Thomas J. Newsom, born Nov. 28, 1881. 4. John E. Newsom, born Dec. 14, 1883. 5. Lloyd Newsom, born Feb. 12, 1889.

William Newsom, born Dec. 7, 1843; fifth child of Dorcas Mounts-Newsom; was a soldier in the 58th regiment Ind. Vol. He lives north of Mt. Carmel, Ill., near Friendsville; married Sarah J. Chaffee; children three: 1. Jasper Newsom, born Nov. 5, 1884. 2. Harrison Newsom, born April 8, 1888. 3. Pierson Newsom, born Sept. 14, 1890.

Andrew Newsom, sixth child of Dorcas Mounts-Newsom, born Nov. 24, 1844; died Feb. 15, 1874; single. 7, Romelia Newsom, born April 15, 1847; lives with his brother William near Friendsville, Ill., single.

The Montgomerys

Smith Mounts, born 1809, died____; seventh child of Rachel Montgomery-Mounts. He lived northwest of Owensville, Ind. where he owned a fine body of land. He first married Lucy Montgomery, daughter of Judge Thomas Montgomery, Jr. Children one: Isaac Mounts, born probably 1840; owns good farm near Brown's Crossing, Ill.; married Anna Malone; children five: 1, Lucy. 2. John. 3. Thomas. 4.____ 5. Nelly. Smith Mounts, born 1809, married second Permelia Davis; children 12: 1, 2, 3, infants. 4. Abijah Mounts, born 1854, married Oassa Spriggs, July 3. 1880: moved near Varner, Mo., 1901; children eight: 1. Wm. L. 2. Flora J. 3. Howard. 4. Ella. 5. Dale. 6. Harvey. 7. Hazel. 8. Clarence.

5. Joseph L. Mounts, born 1856, died 1858. 6. Silas Lender, born 1858, died Jan. 18, 1885. 7. Elijah, born 1860, died 1873. 8. Lucy, born 1862, married Jacob W. Mauck: children sis. See index J. W. Mauck. 9. Mary A. Mounts, born 1874; single 1902. 10. Ida Mounts, born 1806; married Jeff. Wellborn, farmer. They live north-west of Owensville and own a fine farm near Mt. Vernon, Ind.; no children. 11. Martha J. Mounts, born 1868. 12. Flora Mounts, dead. 13. Oscar Mounts, born 1872: married Clara Armstrong, April 15, 1894: children four: 1. Harold Mounts, born Feb. 13, 1895; 2. Everett Mounts, born Dec. 22, 1895; 3. Laverne Mounts, born July 7, 1897; 4. Evangidale Mounts, born June 6, 1900.

Thomas A. Mounts, born in 1818, eighth child of Rachel Montgomery-Mounts, was born and raised on the farm that "Purty Old Tom" Montgomery intended to settle on, as noted elsewhere, which is section 24, town 3, range 12 west. He lived here all his life and, being a good farmer and having fine black river land to cultivate, he became quite a wealthy man. He died Dec. 31, 1888; first married Manece Boren, about 1840; one child: Smith Mounts, born Sept. 11. 1841. He married Mary Ann Brumfield, Feb. 2, 1865. She was born Jan. 2, 1841. They settled two and one-half miles south-east of Owensville, and are in favorable circumstances; children two: 1. infant, born Nov. 11, 1865. 2. Manece Mounts, born March 21, 1869. She married Marion Witherspoon, Nov. 17, 1887. He was born Aug. 29, 1866. They own the old M. E. Shiloh camp ground, established probably in 1830, south of Owensville. Children one: Harvey Witherspoon, born Dec. 9, 1888.

Thomas A. Mounts married, second, Minerva Redman probably about 1854. Children 12. 2. Manece J. Mounts, born 1855; married James M, Wright. 3. George W. Mounts, born 1856; died small. 4. James B. Mounts, born Sept. 23, 1857; married Maranda J. Harris, Nov. 4, 1880. Children four: 1. Melva Mounts, born Feb. 8, 1881, died Feb. 25, 1900. 2. Hertus O.

Mounts, born Oct. 13, 1884. 3. Nannie W. Mounts, born July 15, 1889. 4. Ralph W. Mounts, born Nov. 13, 1891.

5. Julia W. Mounts, born 1858, died _____; daughter of Thomas A. Mounts married James Montgomery of Beason, Ill.; children five: 1. Lafayette. 2. Samuel. 3. A daughter, dead. 4. Rolla. 5. Welzie. 6. Robert Mounts, born Feb. 10, 1859. First married Lillie Green of Owensville, Ind., March 8, 1883 and now, in 1902, lives in Poplar Bluff, Mo.; children five: 1. Maud; 2. Wilber; 3. Burt; 4. Roy; 5. Eva F. Second, married _____.

7. Elzathan Mounts, born Jan. 9, 1861; owns the old C. P. campground south of Owensville, Ind., established probably 1835; married Flora Marvel, Nov. 25, 1886; children four: 1. Claude Mounts, born Aug. 21, 1887. 2. Lawrence Mounts, born Feb. 1, 1889. 3. Zella Mounts, born April 14, 1891. 4. Percy Mounts, born Feb. 16, 1897, died Aug. 14, H97.

8. Nora Mounts, born 1863, married Wm. Westfall in Indiana: they now (1902) live in Grayville, Ill., and have charge of the telephone exchange at that place. Children four: 1, Gertie; 2, Ila; 3. Retha; 4.

9. William Mounts, born Feb. 1865; first married Ollie Stone, May 3, 1885. She was born Feb. 6, 1866, died Oct. 3, 1890, second, married Bettie Reed, April 5, 1891. She was born Sept. 13, 1869; children three: 1. Rufus O.; 2. Mina E.; 3. Floyd.

10. Alcephas Mounts, born Sept. 14, 1867: married Anna Stone. Sept. 5, 1889; children two: 1. Lester A. Mounts, born Aug. 1, 1890. 2., Goldie L. Mounts, born Aug. 4, 1896.

11. and 12. Rachel and Thomas J. Mounts died small. 13. Alta Mounts married Jack Massey. She died in Princeton, Intl., 1901.

Katie Montgomery, third child of Samuel Montgomery, Sr., born Nov. 19, 1779, married Thomas Alcorn, Sr., who was born Feb. 6, 1777. They had eleven children: 1. Montgomery Alcorn, born Nov. 23, 1800- died Aug. 7, 1821: married Jane Montgomery, daughter of Squire Samuel Montgomery, and had two children: 1. Samuel, born probably 1820, and was a physician, 2. Montgomery Alcorn, Jr., born 1821: married Jane Stone, daughter of Silas Stone. Their children were Mary, Andrew, Maranda, Mag, Minnie, John, and others. Among these were a pair of twins.

The Montgomerys

2. Jane, born March 9, 1801, died Aug. 7. 1838; daughter of Katie Montgomery-Alcorn; married John Smith about 1819. Their children were: 1. Thomas, born April 16, 1820: died Feb. 12, 1902: married Jane Harris 1847; she was born Nov. 16, 1827, died Oct. 1, 1898. They had eleven children: 1. Isaac H., born July 6, 1848, married Eunice Boren, no children: 2. Matilda C., born Jan. 11, 1850, died March 2, 1872; 3. Kate, born ____, married Ellison Williams, had live children: 1. Stephen, a carpenter, married—, no children; 2. Myrtle, married Louis Goad, a carpenter; 3. Pearl, married John Shafer, a farmer. (Mr. Shafer was killed Dec. 10, 1901, west of Owensville. Ind., near the farm of John Waters, by a wagon running over him.) Had one child—Kenneth Shafer. 4. Jesse, married Amy Hopkins; 5. William, single 1902. 4. Stephen L. Smith, born Aug. 28, 1853; died Oct. 5, 1882, single. 5. Eliza M. Smith, born June 3, 1856; married George Cater, a farmer; one child—Frank Cater. 6., Mary E. Smith, born Oct. 22. 1858; first married Frank Dyer: one child— Dovie Dyer. Mr. Dyer died Feb. 5, 1888. Mary married, second, Louis Whitenbaugh, a carpenter; no children. 7. James W. Smith, born Dec. 24. 1810; married Josie Cater; children two—Stephen and Ethel Smith. 8. Louella Smith, born Aug. 20, 1833; married McGrada Daugherty, a farmer and fruit-grower and an elder in the C. P. church. He is now (1903) living in Yoncalla, Oregon; children two—Elmer and Gertrude Daugherty. 9. Josie Smith, born Sept. 16, 1865; single. 10. Malinda J. Smith, born March 10, 1869; dead. 11. Dora Smith, born June 4, 1872; married Thomas Westfall, a farmer. They moved to Yoncalla, Oregon, in 1902; one child—Ruby Westfall.

2. Malinda Smith, daughter of John Smith, born 1822, was the second wife of Archie Knowles, born 1810 and died 1849; children: 1. Nancy J., first wife of John W. Emerson of Owensville, Ind. (See index). 2. Kate, first wife of Sanford Howe, who was a soldier in the 24th Ind. Vol. They had one child, William Howe, who is a graduate of Lincoln University. Lincoln, Ill. and is a C. P. minister.

3. Lydia Smith, daughter of John Smith, born 1824; married Benjamin Earl Robinson, of Bowling Green, Ky., about 1843. He died April 27, 1881, at Oakland City, Ind. They had seven children: 1. John, born Feb. 2, 1845; was a soldier in Co. F, 80th regiment of Indiana Vol. and was killed in the battle at Resaca, Ga., May 11, 1864. 2. Sallie Robinson, born 1847; married James S. Blythe, a soldier in Co. A, 58th regiment of Ind. Vol. They had three children: 1. Ella, 2. Mattie 3. Luther, born Nov. 24, 1873; married Nelly M. Kesterson,

Aug. 9, 1900. She died in 1902. 3. James Robinson, born 1848, married twice but I do not know the name of either of them. 4. Malinda Robinson, born 1850, first married Samuel Parker, a Federal soldier: second, married a Mr. Esque. 5. Emma Robinson, born 1852, married Lon Steel, a Federal soldier. 6. Pearl Robinson, married_____. 7. George Robinson, married____; dead.

4., Isaac Smith, born 1826, son of John Smith, married Matilda Harris and had seven children: 1. Wm. Frank Smith, a teacher for several years; is now a physician at Vincennes, Ind.; first married Rosa Williams; one child, Ray Smith, who was second lieutenant in a company in the 159th Ind. Vol. in the Spanish-American War, and is now (1902) a minister in the Disciple or Christian church. 2. Thomas Smith, son of Isaac Smith, died when about grown. 3. Benjamin died when about grown. 4, George, married Elvira Gudgel. They have two children: Thomas and Dale. 5. Otis Smith has served as constable of Montgomery Township; married Eliza Simpson and has two children: Walter and Flora. 6. Ralph. 7. Permelia, died when about grown; 8, Marion, married Etta Julian; children 3: 1. Emit. 2. —. 3. —.

5, Kittie, daughter of John Smith, born 1828, died March 1902; married Wm. Wright, who was a very prominent elder in the C. P. church and a very useful man in Christian work. They had ten children: 1. James M. Wright, married Manece Mounts, June 14, 1876; children 4: Idessa Wright, married Clarence Clark; children 2: Carlton H. Clark and ——. 2, Providence Wright. 3. Aggie Wright. 4. Willie Wright.

2. John Wright, a barber in Ft. Branch, Ind.; married Georgia Wood. They have five children: Wm. T., Elva, Robert, Eva and Roosevelt. 3. Lizzie Wright, married W. L. Smith, a farmer, Dec. 24, 1881; one child—Versa. 4. Wm. Wright, died 1899; married Myrtle Martin, 1899; one child—dead. 5. Thomas Wright, married Martha Montgomery; one child— Loran. 6. Isaac Wright, married Mary Wallace and have two children—Ida and Ray. 7. Samuel Wright died small. 8. Amos Wright, single 1903. 9. Benjamin Wright, married Retha Massey and they have two children—Tela and Vela. 10. Marv Wright, married Schuyler Muck, a jeweler, and they have two children—Victor and Cecil.

Benjamin Alcorn, born Dec. 8, 1803, son of Katie Montgomery Alcorn, married Orpha Marvel; children three: 1. Elisha, born 1829, died 1901; at one time was deacon in the Bethlehem G. B. church, afterward an elder in the Mt. Mariah C. P. church; was an excellent, good man; married Mary Martin April 17. 1851. She was born Feb. 27, 1831 children six: 1. Orpha, born June 29. 1854. 2. Francis. E. born Jan. 8, 1857; married Thomas Sides, Sept. 18, 1878; children three: 1. Etta Sides married Thomas Wiseman, 1900, no children; 2. Jesse Sides, born July 13, 1881; 3. Ralph W. Sides, July 4, 1885. 3, Sarah Alcorn, born March 2, 1859, died July 18. 1877. 1. Thomas Alcorn, born March 20, 1861; taught in public schools; was at one time candidate for the legislature on Democrat ticket; married Ella Jones, March 8, 1883; children five: 1. Curtis M., born June 6, 1884; he weighed 262 pounds at 16 years of age. 2. Alva F. 3. Willie. 4. Leila A. 5. Harvey S.

5. Simeon Alcorn, son of Elisha Alcorn, born Nov. 23, 1863; married Anna Pritchett, Nov. 15, 1887; one child—Zella, born June 26, 1888.

6. Lucinda Alcorn, daughter of Elisha, born Nov. 23, 1866; married Sylvester Sides, Feb. 11. 1866; children four: 1. Albert R., born Feb. 19, 1888. 2. Mabel M., born May 23, 1890. 3. Ethel, born Sept. 26, 1891. 4. Charles, born Nov. 20, 1893. 7, Matilda Alcorn, daughter of Elisha, born Jan. 1, 1869; married Matthew Peacock, Oct. 4, 1891; no children.

8, Mary A. Alcorn, daughter of Elisha, born Jan. 1, 1874; married Grant Gibson, July 30, 1899; one child—Orville, born Feb. 5, 1901.

2, Benjamin Alcorn, Jr., born 1831; son of Benjamin, Sr., and brother of Elisha; married Rebecca Palmer and had several children. One of them, named Thomas, married a daughter of Elisha Mead: both are dead. One of their daughters, Delia, lives in Owensville, Ind.

3, Thomas, another brother of Elisha Alcorn, born 1833. Died single.

4, Nehemiah Alcorn, born 1805, son of Katie Montgomery-Alcorn; died June 24. 1856. I only know of one child—Johnson, born probably about 1827. He lived many years south-east of Princeton. Ind., and has many descendants in the neighborhood of Columbia church; first married a Cawhorn; seven children: 1. Ellen, who is blind. 2. William, married Carrie McCrary; children seven: 1. George; 2. Jesse; 3. Maggie; 4., Oscar; 5. Arthur; 6. Homer; 7. Pleasie; 3. May Alcorn, married John Lucas; no children. 4. Fanny Alcorn married and lives in Texas. 5. Gusta Alcorn., married Hallie Strawn; three children. 6. George Alcorn married a Philips. 7. Ida Alcorn, single 1901.

And Their Descendants

Johnson Alcorn married, second, a Mrs. Whitaker; children six:

1. Philip Alcorn; first married Maggie Anderson; one child, Hazle. Second, married Florence Covington; one child.

5, Thomas Alcorn, son of Katie Montgomery-Alcorn, born Jan. 25, 1808; died July 2, 1858; married Jane Haynes. I only know of one child—James T. Alcorn, born probably about 1839. He was a soldier in the 1st regiment Ind. Cavalry; married Anna Boren, Jan. 1866; children three: 1. James Grant Alcorn, born Nov. 17, 1866. At the age of 16 he knew absolutely nothing of the common-school branches save arithmetic and reading, yet at the age of 19 he made a six-month teacher's license. He taught his first school at the Willey school-house, Montgomery Township, Gibson County, in 1889. He taught four terms at the Buttermilk school-house, Smith Township, Posey County commencing in 1890. He sold his interest in the old home, Blackriver farm, to his brother David and moved in the fall of 1884 to the David E Craig farm, where he now lives— 1902. He united with the Christian Church at Union, Montgomery Township, Gibson County, in 1892. He is an enthusiastic third party Prohibitionist, claiming that, as sure as there is a God, right will prevail. He married Florence Lee Craig, Sept. 23, 1891; children six: 1. Maurice Lee, born Aug. 25, 1892. 2. James Oral, born Oct. 25. 1893. 3._____. 4. Jesse M., born Nov. 24, 1895. 5. _____. 6. Manford Craig, born Dec. 21, 1899.

2. David Colfax Alcorn born Oct. 3, 1868, and a brother to James Grant Alcorn; is a graduate from the Terre Haute Commercial College. He is a wealthy and enterprising farmer in Smith Township, Posey County, Ind.; is a member of Old Union church. He is also a bitter enemy to the rum power— because he desires to save his fellow-men from this curse. He married Ella Saulmon, Oct. 27, 1894; children two: 1. Cora, born June 26, 1897. 2, Alma, born Dec. 18, 1899.

3, Ada Alcorn, sister to Grant and David Alcorn, born Oct. 21, 1870; is also a member of Old Union church; first married Joseph R. Davis, Dec. 11, 1889. He died in the early part of 1886. Second, she married John Wilsey, Dec. 1, 1897.

6. Dorcas Alcorn, born Dec. 23, 1809, daughter of Katie Montgomery-Alcorn. 7. Rachel Alcorn, born April 12, 1812. 8. Pauline Alcorn, born March 9, 1813; died Feb. 25, 1828. 9. Katie Alcorn, born Feb. 26, 1816; married a

Mr. Travis and moved to Illinois. 10. Robert Alcorn, born Feb. 21, 1819; married Elizabeth Dyhouse.

11. Agnes Alcorn, born Dec. 20, 1820; died June 20, 1840.

Robert Montgomery, born 1782, fourth child of Samuel Montgomery, Sr., was in the battle of Tippecanoe, Nov. 7, 1811. On this expedition he caught a severe cold, from which he never recovered. He died in 1815 and was the first person buried in what is now known as the Wm. Benson cemetery, two miles south of Owensville, Ind., on the south half, north-east quarter section 24, range 12 west. His father, Samuel Montgomery, Sr., had selected this place to be buried, as he did not expect to live long; but his son died first and was interred in this cemetery. The father also died in 1815 and is buried here. Robert Montgomery married a Miss Cook in Kentucky: children seven:

1. and 2. Hugh and Houston, twins. Hugh had four children: 1. Larkin; 2. Dudley; 3. Henry; 4. Fielding. Houston married Sally Sterrett; children five: 1. Rachel, born June 17, 1840; first married Thomas Montgomery, son of Roan Ike Montgomery, Dec. 22, 1861; children four: 1. Permelia, born June 3, 1863, died Aug. 20, 1863; Burgess, born March 19, 1868. He was a soldier in Co. K. 129th regiment Ind. Vol., in the Spanish-American War; enlisted June 18, 1898; discharged Nov. 25, 1898; single 1903. 3. Oscar, born Feb. 2, 1870; died Aug. 16, 1871. 4. Thomas, born June 7, 1871; died small. Rachel Montgomery married, second, Victor Woods; children two: Dora and Cora Woods—twins, born Dec. 81. 1878. Cora married Frank Danfort, of Friendsville, Ill. March 1901.

2. Polly Montgomery, daughter of Houston Montgomery, married William Bradum. 3. Hugh died small. 4. Roxy married Henry Kemper. John Franklin, born ____ lives near Owensville, Ind.; single.

Russell Montgomery, third son of Robert, Sr., had four children: 1. Robert. 2. Henry. 3. Rumania. It is said she was a very handsome woman; married John Mandy: one child.

4. Sally Montgomery, fourth child of Robert Montgomery, Sr., married John Summers; one child William Summers, who lived near Pane, Ill. when last heard from. Second, she married a Mr. Carmine; one child—Lafayette Carmine.

5. Tandy B. Montgomery, fifth child of Robert Montgomery Sr., married a Johnson. He was a cripple and educated for a teacher; taught probably thirty or more years in the schools of Indiana. He was a splendid scribe; was the sixth recorder of Gibson County. Ind., and died in office. Children five:

1. Mary, married Brown Campbell, In Nov. 1902, of Oakland City, Ind.; children three: 1. Mat married Ed. Richardson: no children. 2. Jennie, dead. 3. Montgomery married Clara, daughter of Col. Wm. Cockrum of Oakland City, Ind. They have a handsome residence not far south of the Oakland City College; child one. Mary Lou Campbell. 2. Frank, second child of Tandy B. Montgomery, a soldier in Co. E, 80th regiment Ind. Vol., and killed in the battle of Perryville, Ky., Oct. 8, 1862; single. 3. Charles Montgomery, son of Tandy B., was a First Lieutenant in Co. D, 58th regiment Ind. Vol. He died at Olney, Ill., several years after the war, single. 4. Alexander Montgomery, son of Tandy B., was a First Lieutenant in Co. E, 80th regiment Ind. Vol. He was at one time auditor of Gibson County, Ind.; practiced medicine several years in Olney, Ill.; was well educated and did much work for Gibson County in the way of making up public records. He died in Princeton, Ind., about 1890, single. 5. Julia Montgomery, fifth child of Tandy B., lived most of her life in Owensville and Princeton, Ind. and died in the latter place about 1900 single.

James Montgomery, Sr., born 1784, fifth child of Samuel Montgomery Sr., died probably 1827; was quite a wealthy man of his day. He owned, and raised his family on the north-west quarter of section 24, town 3, range 12 west. He owned a Negro, called Pete, who had almost full control of his affairs and contributed largely to his success in life. He retained more Irish characteristics than any other member of his family, as he talked in a very brusque Irish brogue. He built a horse grist-mill in 1811. He was overseer of the poor in 1814, and was one of the commissioners to adjust the accounts of the overseers of the poor in 1818. He married Nancy Cook, in Kentucky, probably about 1805; came to Indiana probably 1811; children eleven:

Greenberry Montgomery, first child of James Montgomery, Sr., born 1806; died Dec. 27, 1875; married Eliza Gerald about 1834. She died July 4, 1894. He settled south-west of Princeton, Ind.; children twelve: 1. James, Jr., born 1835; married Nancy Griffin; children nine: 1. Ollie Montgomery, who married John Bisker of Princeton, Ind.; children three: 1. Arvis Bisker; 2. Liana Bisker; 3. Elwood Bisker. 2. Willis, son of Jas. Montgomery Jr., born 1864; died Aug. 4, 1872. 3. Forna, daughter of James, Jr., born 1867; died Sept. 10, 1872. 4. Grant, son of James, Jr., married Maggie Woods; children three: 1. Ruby Montgomery; 2. Mary Montgomery; 3.____. 5. Oscar

The Montgomerys

Montgomery, son of James, Jr., born 1873; died Sept. 15, 1875. 6. Rose, daughter of James, Jr. 7. Fanny, daughter of James, Jr., married Ech. Woods; one child—Lowell. 8. Harvey, son of James, Jr., married Lizzie Bada; one child: Hilda Montgomery. 9. Horace, son of James, Jr., deaf and dumb; single.

John W. Montgomery, second child of Greenberry, born 1837; first married Sarah Perkins; no children, second, married Becky Pritchett; no children, third, married Maggie Barnett; child one: Dora E. Montgomery; married Harvey Kendle, July 23, 1902.

Wm. M. Montgomery, born 1840; died 1897; was a soldier in the 65th Ind., Vol., Co. B.; married Anna J. Woods; children ten: 1. Delia Montgomery married Charles Knight. Princeton, Ind.: one child, Virgil Knight born 1895. 2. Charles Montgomery, son of William, married Anna Cherry; children two: 1. Florence Montgomery; 2. Lilly Montgomery. 3. James Montgomery, son of William, born Dec. 1881; died Aug. 28, 1882. 4. Clarence Montgomery, son of William, born Sept. 1897; died Dec. 18, 1897. 5. Elmer Montgomery, 6. Jennie Montgomery. 7. Arthur Montgomery. 8. Maggie Montgomery married Walter J. Arburn, Feb. 27, 1902. 9. Ross Montgomery. 10. Freda Montgomery.

Thomas Montgomery, born 1842, fourth child of Greenberry, was a soldier in the 120th regiment Ind. Vol.; married Cordelia McDowell; children eight: 1. infant. 2. Infant. 3. Katie. 4. Albert. 5. Infant. 6. Infant. 7. Hattie. 8. Alfred.

Garrad Montgomery, fifth son of Greenberry, born 1844; died 1848.

Richard Montgomery, sixth son of Greenberry, born 1846; was a soldier in the 80th regiment Ind. Vol.; children eight: 1. Martha Montgomery; married Thomas Wristlet; one child—Loran Wright.

Emilia Montgomery, second child of Richard, married Major Wright: children two: 1. Versie Wright; 2. Otto Wright.

Lorenzo Montgomery, third child of Richard, married Minnie Newberry; one child—Ray.

Pearl Montgomery, fourth child of Richard, married Samuel Sisson, a teacher in public schools; children three: 1, Eldon; 2 and 3, _____.

John, fifth child of Richard.

Jesse Montgomery, sixth child of Richard, married Florence Embry; one child—Gertrude Montgomery.

Elmer Montgomery, twin to Jesse and seventh child of Richard, married Nancy Powers; one child, Montgomery.

Grace Montgomery, eighth child of Richard, married Arba Luhring.

Permelia Montgomery, born 1848, seventh child of Greenberry Montgomery, married Sanford Emberton: children two: 1. Victoria Emberton; married John Alsop, a brick mason of Ft. Branch, Ind. Feb. 13, 1884; died March 1885; no children. 2. Echlass Emberton died single, Nov. 14, 1899. Permelia Montgomery Emberton married, second, James Woods; no children.

Martha Montgomery, born 1851, eighth child of Greenberry, married Samuel L. Olmstead: children eight:
1., Lillie Olmstead, married Lewis Wirth; one child—infant.
Second, Eva Olmstead married Samuel Embree; children five: 1. James; 2. Earl; 3. Eunice: 4. Fornia; 5. ____
.3, Nora Olmstead married Robert Boyle; children two: Florence and Ralph Boyle.
4. and 5. Willie and Maggie Olmstead single.
6. Ella Olmstead married Edgar Townsend: one child, Claude Townsend.
7. and 8. Florence H. and Alma Olmstead, single.
Willis Montgomery, born 1854, ninth child of Greenberry, married Elizabeth H. Fauquier: children four: 1. Abbie 2. William 3. Otto 4. Ina May.

Victory Montgomery, tenth child of Greenberry, born 1855; married Robert Cam; children five: 1. Harvey 2. Essa: 3. Edgar. 4. Mabel 5. Divie.

Artimeca Montgomery, born 1857, eleventh child of Greenberry, died 1857.

Nora Montgomery, born 1850, twelfth child of Greenberry, married Charles Florica; children three; 1. Infant; 2. Ada Florica: married Anda Maxim; no children. 3. Sophia Florica.

Matilda Montgomery, born Oct. 8, 1808; died March 10, 1874; second child of James Montgomery, Sr., married Peter Smith, 1825; he was born Oct. 17, 1803; died Dec. 15, 1870; children thirteen:
1. Infant.
2. Nancy Smith died at two years old.
3. Infant.
4. America Smith, married Charles Cleveland; children eleven: 1. Cornelia A. Cleveland, married Theodore Smock; children two: Roy and _____; 2. Laura E. Cleveland, married Franklin Stallins; children —. 3. John F. Cleveland, married; children six: —. 4. Pheba Cleveland married Win. Vaughn; children —5. Saphronia Cleveland married_____ 7. Louis Cleveland, married_____. 8. Sanford Cleveland, married _____. 9. Rana Cleveland, married_____. 10. George Cleveland died young. 11. Infant._____.

Sarah Ann Smith, fifth child of Peter Smith, married Robert Eaton; children eight: 1. Peter Eaton, married_____. 2. Harriet Eaton married John Eaton. 3. Matilda Eaton, married_____. 4. Elizabeth Eaton. 5. Louisiana Eaton married a Mr. Jones. 6. Indiana Eaton, twin to Louisiana, married a Mr. Jones. 7. Lovina Eaton. 8. Nerva Eaton.

Mary Smith, sixth child of Peter Smith, married Robert Eaton; children three: 1, Louisa Eaton, 2. ___ 3. _____.

Gilbert L. Smith died 1832, seventh child of Peter Smith; married Jane Jordan; children five: 1. Thomas J. Smith, 2. Matilda Smith, 3.___, 4.___, 5.___.

Patsy Smith, born Oct. 29, 1834, eighth child of Peter Smith, married George Finch, March 13, 1851. He was born July 18, 1829. They settled in the neighborhood of the Providence church of Regular Baptists, in Gibson County, Ind. Mr. Finch was County commissioner three years. They celebrated their golden wedding in 1901 and she carries, as the testimony of love and respect of her children, a nice gold watch presented on that occasion! Children 13:
1. William P. Finch, married Lucinda Spencer; children four: George W. Finch, Belle Finch, infant and Amy Finch.

And Their Descendants

2 and 3, Lemira J. and Matilda A. Finch, dead.

4, Isabella Finch, married James Holcomb; children five: Jefferson, Arel, Lester, Jesse, _____.

Malinda A. Finch, fifth child of Patsy Finch, married Charles Holcomb, a lawyer and ex-judge of Broken Bow, Neb., and a brother to ex-Governor Holcomb of Nebraska: children five: 1. Wilber, married____. 2. Versa. 3. Mabel. 4. Edna. 5. Roy.

James F. Finch, sixth child of Patsy Finch, married Ellen DePriest; children eight: 1. Myrtle. 2. Claudia. 3. Zelmie. 4. Roy. 5. Lester. 6. Carl. 7. Effie. 8. Edna.

Ida May Finch, seventh child of Patsy Smith, married Calvin Glaspie; children five: 1. Claudia. 2. Ethel. 3. Bertha. 4. Lora. 5. Flora.

Nancy Ellen Finch, eighth child of Patsy Smith, married Harry Morrison; children, six: 1. Leila. 2. Arthur. 3. Verdi. 4. Bessie. 5. Herral. 6. Lula.

Oscar Finch, ninth child of Patsy Finch, married Emma Hutchinson: children three: 1. Onie. 2. Arvel. 3. _____.

John S. Finch, tenth child of Patsy Finch, married Nannie Rana; children five: 1. Oscar, 2. Zetteda, 3. Mabel, 4. Rosa, 5. Willis.

Bertha D. Finch, eleventh child of Patsy Smith, married George Gladish; children two: 1. Infant, 2. Ray.

Ella E. Finch, twelfth child of Patsy Smith, married Louis Seaman; children two: 1. Virgil, 2. Eunice.

John W. Finch, thirteenth child of Patsy Smith, taught in the public schools; married Stella Strawn; children two: 1, Jesse; 2, Patsy.

Thomas J. Smith, ninth child of Peter Smith, died at 21 years old.

George F. Smith, tenth child of Peter Smith, died at 18 years old.

Lucinda Smith, eleventh child of Peter Smith, married Wm. McGee. She died in Arkansas; children two: 1. Wm. M. McGee, a druggist in northern Indiana; married Emma McFredrica; children two—boys. 1. James W. McGee married Adaline Reavis: children three.

James M. Smith, twin to Lucinda Smith, twelfth child of Peter Smith, married Jane Stella; children five: 1. Peter; 2. Matilda. 3. Nancy. 4___, 5___.

John Mac Smith, thirteenth child of Peter Smith, first married Julia Wilson; children two: 1. George F. Smith; married Anna Heironimous; children one—Roy Heironimous. 2. Thomas J. Smith, son of John Mac Smith. Second. John Mac Smith, thirteenth child of Peter Smith, married Anna McReynolds; no children.

America Montgomery, born 1810, third child of Jas. Montgomery Sr., married John Baker, of Mt. Vernon, Ind. He was a wealthy man of that place; was a merchant and miller and did considerable speculative business on the Mississippi River. Children six:
 1. Jesse Baker, who married America Montgomery, daughter of Robert McFarland Montgomery, Sr. They had two children: 1. Eddie died small; 2. Willie Baker married Essie Albright.
 2, Isaac Baker, son of America Montgomery, married Lizzie Hovey; children three: 1, Nelly Baker, married_____; children ____; 2. Frank Baker; 3. Jesse.
 3. Aaron Baker, son of America Montgomery, was one of the best surveyors in southern Indiana; was a soldier in the 80th regiment Ind. Vol.
 4. Mary Baker, daughter of America Montgomery, married Wm. Simondson; children two: 1. Jesse Simondson, lives in Little Rock, Ark.; 2. Charley Simondson.
 5. Charley Baker, son of America Montgomery, died single.
 6. Kittie Baker, daughter of America Montgomery, married a Mr. Thomas; one child—Baker Thomas.

Jesse Montgomery, born 1812, son of James Montgomery, Sr., died single.

Robert McFarland Montgomery, Sr., born Sept. 7, 1814; died in Owensville, Ind., of cancer, Dec. 7, 1881, aged 74 years and seven mouths. He was the fourth child of James Montgomery, Sr.; settled on south-west quarter section 13, town 3, range 12 west, in Montgomery Township,

Gibson County, Ind., married Julia Ann Richards in 1836. She was born 1817, died Aug. 20, 1901 aged 84 years; children ten:

1. Jesse, born July 30. 1836, died single.

2. America, born Oct 11, 1838, died Feb. 24, 1888; first married Jesse Baker as above; second, married George Rowe, near Mt. Vernon, Ind.; children five: 1. Lincoln Rowe, married Clara Huntsinger, March 12, 1891; children five: 1. Mabel born Jan. 5, 1892; 2. Ethel, born Sept. 11, 1893; 3. Claude, born April 23, 1896: 4. Herbert, born July 27, 1898; 5. Joseph born Sept. 15, 1900. 2. Mattie Rowe, daughter of George Rowe, married Walter Curtis, Sept. 7, 1886; children six: 1, George, born Sept. 29, 1888; 2, America, born Jan. 1, 1890; 3. Belle, born March 21, 1894; 4. Harry O., born Oct. 2, 1895; 5. Macky, born July 17, 1896; died Oct. 17, 1896; 6. Willie, born June 18, 1900. 7. Harry, son of George Rowe, married Mattie Bradford, Sept. 12, 1898; children one—Homer Rowe, born March 21, 1899. 4. Thomas, son of George Rowe, single 1902. 5. Infant. June 25, 1902, an engine boiler exploded and killed George Rowe, his son Thomas, and Harry's son Homer.

3. Martha Crockett-Montgomery, born Feb. 13, 1840. Third child of Robert McFarland Montgomery, Sr.; married Hiram Willis Smith; children five: 1. Allison Smith, born 1857; married Victoria Williams; children three: 1. John Clark Smith; 2. Menzie: 3. infant. 2. Leroy Smith, son of Hiram Willis Smith, born 1859, died ___. 3. America Smith, daughter of Hiram Willis Smith, born 1861; married James Cantrell; children eleven: 1. Myrtle Cantrell, married Andrew Heine; children one—Zola Heine. 2. Thompson Cantrell; 3. Mackie, died six years old. 4. Bertha; 5. Dalpha; 6. Saphronia; 7. Lera; 8. Jalia; 9. James: 10. Myrle; 11. Tirie. Anna, fourth child of Hiram Willis Smith, born 1864; single. Saphronia, fifth child of Hiram Willis Smith, born 1866; married George Alexander; children five: 1. George died in infancy. 2. Constance 3. Nettie. 4. Forest. 5. Greetheth.

4. Sarah Montgomery, fourth child of Robert McFarland Montgomery, born Aug. 20, 1841; married Silas Pollard, Jr.: children thirteen:

1. Elzathan Pollard, married Martha Jane Anderson: children eleven: 1. Nora Pollard, married Thomas Frelan, no children: 2. McFarland Pollard, died in infancy; 3. Virgil B.; 4. Sarah E.; 5. George Ed.; 6. Benjamin; 7. Mamie; 8. Mida; 9. Mattie; 10. Edith May; 11. Carson.

McFarland Pollard, second son of Sarah Montgomery Pollard, died at one year old.

Amanda V. Pollard, third child of Sarah Montgomery Pollard, married Charley Smith: children three: 1. Sarah Ann. 2. Florence Ida. 3. Elsie.

George E. Pollard, fourth child of Sarah Montgomery-Pollard, married Elizabeth Whetstone: children one—Wm. Silas Pollard.

Sarah Ann Pollard, fifth child of Sarah Montgomery-Pollard, married Wm. Vopel; children one—Otto Vopel.

William Pollard, sixth child of Sarah Montgomery-Pollard, married Mary Belle Frelan; no children.

Thomas Pollard, 7th child of Sarah Montgomery-Pollard married Ida Whetstone; children two: 1. Jesse P. Pollard; 2. Charley Pollard.

Florence Pollard, eighth child of Sarah Montgomery Pollard, married Martin D. Huntsinger; children three: 1. Loren E. 2. Owen S.; 3. Sarah E.

Jesse Pollard. 9th child of Sarah Montgomery Pollard married Win. Vaught: no children.

Jalia, the tenth child, died in infancy.
11. Ida.
12. Mattie.
13. Gertrude, single 1901.

5. Nancy J. Montgomery, born Sept. 28, 1844, died 22 months old. 6. Louisa Ann Montgomery, born July 8, 1846 died eight months old. 7. Mary Matilda Montgomery, born Nov. 13, 1847, died small. 8. Infant. These four last mentioned are children of Robert McFarland Montgomery, Sr.

Robert McFarland Montgomery, Jr., ninth child of Robert McFarland Montgomery, Sr., born Aug. 2, 1851, lives on the old home place of his father and is a farmer and stock-raiser and deals especially in fine hogs and Hereford cattle, and also grows fruit extensively. His fine residence occupies one of the finest sites in Montgomery Township, on the right of the public road leading from Owensville to Cynthiana, about two miles from the former town. He married Spicie Johnson, Jan. 2, 1873; children eight: 1. infant, born Sept. 24, 1873, died Sept. 24, 1873. 2., Elsie, born April 3, 1875: is a graduate of the Owensville high school, has taught in the public schools of Gibson County for several years; single 1902.

Benjamin Montgomery, third child of R. M. Montgomery, Jr., born Nov. 14, 1878; married Nellie P. Crawford, Nov. 22. 1899; children two: Dwight C. and Darby Montgomery.

Sarah Montgomery, born March 6, 1880, fourth child of R. M. Montgomery. Jr., was for several months a clerk in James Montgomery's store in Owensville, Ind.; married Clarence Mauck, Dec. 25, 1901; one child, Mary Etta.

Ella Montgomery, born Feb. 1, 1882, fifth child of R. M. Montgomery, is secretary and book keeper for her father in his stock business; single 1903.

Jesse Montgomery, born Nov. 17, 1884, sixth child of R. M. Montgomery, is also engaged in the fine-stock business; single 1903.

Infant Montgomery, seventh child of R. M. Montgomery, Jr., born May 6, 1886, died May 6, 1886.

Vada Montgomery, eighth child of R. M. Montgomery, Jr. born July 30, 1891.

Victoria Ann Montgomery, born Jan. 28, 1853, tenth child of Robert McFarland Montgomery, Sr., married William Redman, a farmer and thresher; children three: 1. Jessie Redman, a teacher in the public schools, married Prof. A. V. Mauck of Owensville, Ind., March 26. 1903. He is well educated and a thrifty farmer. 2. Robert M. Redman, married Nellie Tichenor; children two: 1. Eva Linn Redman, born Feb. 17, 1901; 2. Arthur Howe Redman, born Aug. 18, 1902. 3. Jalia Redman married Jacob Shafer, Sept. 12, 1901; one child—Velma Shafer.

Garrad Montgomery, born 1816, sixth child of James Montgomery, Sr., married Sarah Phillips, sister to Maj. John Phillips, now (1901) of Evansville, Ind.; children eight: 1. James; 2. Mary; 3. David: 4. Lee. Mary was living in 1902, but I do not know whether any other member of the family is living or not.

Polly Montgomery, born Aug. 24, 1819, married John W. Robb, a merchant of Stewartsville, Ind., July 23, 1844. He was born Oct. 23. 1816; was a large land-owner in Posey County, Ind., at one time being in possession of nearly 4,000 acres. His start in life was from small beginnings.

He was strictly honest in his dealings with his fellow men. He died April 11, 1894. He often told his children that the happiest days of his life were when all his children were small and he could place them on straw in a two-horse wagon and come in one day and visit the mother of his wife, near Owensville, and return next day. This was when he was a man of small means. He had eleven children: 1. Lenora Robb, born Sept. 16, 1845, married F. M. Wellborn, of Owensville, Ind., Feb. 7, 1867. She has good landed possessions. Mr. Wellborn was at one time engaged in the general mercantile business, also engaged in buying wheat and corn; probably has handled as much of these products as any man in the County. One child—George R. Wellborn, born March 7, 1868, married Lillie Heston, Oct. 11, 1893, daughter of Joseph Heston, one of the largest land-owners in Gibson County. George R. Wellborn is a graduate of DePauw University, at Greencastle, Ind.; is now (1902) proprietor of the large department store in Owensville, Ind., and is also a stockholder in the state bank of Owensville: one child—Harold Heston Wellborn, born Sept. 23, 1894, died Feb. 23, 1895.

America Robb, born Nov. 17, 1846, married Edwin W. Carr. May 9, 1875. They have a fine property not far from New Harmony. Ind.; children seven: 1. Edwin W. Carr. Jr., born March 2, 1876, married Grace E. Thomas, Aug. 9, 1894; children five: 1. Grace M.; 2. Muriel, dead; 3. Muriel; 4. Cyril C.; 5. Edwin. 2. Everett, son of Edwin W. Carr, Sr., born Aug. 19, 1877, died in infancy; 3. Nora Carr, born Oct. 7, 1878, died in infancy: 4. Ida, born March 11, 1880; 5. John W., born Oct. 23, 1881; 6. Clarence F. born June 14, 1884, died June 4, 1887; 7. Alice, born April 3. 1889.

Eliza J. Robb, third child of John W. Robb, born March 17, 1849, died Sept. 10, 1850.

Lona E. Robb, fourth child of John W. Robb, born Nov. 10, 1850, died Aug. 3, 1852.

Mary Alice Robb, born March 22, 1853, fifth child of John W. Robb, has good bodies of land in Wabash bottoms; married Dr. F. A. Kelly. Aug. 3, 1873; children eight: 1. Frank, dead, 2. Infant, 3. Robbie, dead, 4. Mary, is a graduate of Bloomington University, in Indiana, class of 1900, 5. Elnora, dead, 6. Infant, 7. Alice C. dead, 8. Greta.

John E. Robb, born Nov. 4, 1854, died Feb. 1, 1869; sixth child of John W. Robb.

And Their Descendants

Minerva A. Robb, born March 14, 1856, died Oct. 6, 1857; seventh child of John W. Robb.

8. Leroy Thomas Robb, born Sep. 27, 1857, married Flora Lucas, Sept. 7, 1879. He owns a good farm west of Owensville; children four: 1. Mary Robb married Asa Mauck in 1902. 2. Lou Nora Robb married Benjamin Mauck, April 1901; died Aug. 1901. 3. John Robb. 4. Minerva.

Ida Robb, ninth child of John W. Robb, born March 9, 1859, married Benjamin Hyne; one child—Carl Hyne. Mr. and Mrs. Hyne have a fine residence in New Harmony. Ind.; have large possessions in the Wabash bottoms and deal extensively in stock, especially in cattle. Mrs. Hyne is now (1902) in poor health.

James F. A. Robb, born Aug. 4, 1860, has a large farm in the bottoms and lives at Stewartsville, Ind.; married Lucretia Defur, who died 1896; children five: 1. Infant. 2. Mary. 3. Roy. 4. Erline. 5. Paul.

Preston, Robb, born July 15, 18512, has considerable land: married Emma Rutledge, Sept. 13, 1883; children two: 1. Ralph Robb, born Feb. 8, 1885. 2. Mary E. Robb, born Feb. 21, 1887.

Patsy Montgomery, born 1820, eighth child of James Montgomery, Sr., married (Black) Logan McCrary, and died soon after; no children. Her twin sister Sally, born 1820, the ninth child, died single.

Jane Montgomery, born 1824; died Nov. 21, 1888; married Franklin Daugherty who from a poor boy accumulated property until he was reckoned among the wealthy men of Montgomery Township; children nine: 1. Garrad Daugherty, born Nov. 1844. He was a soldier in the 120th regiment Ind. Vol. He moved to Winstead Lake, McLead County, Minn., and died there 1902; first married Fanny McCrary, in Indiana; children four: 1. Almeda J. Daugherty, born March 12, 1869, in Gibson County, Ind.; married Luther Tichenor, Dec. 25, 1888. He was born Dec. 7, 1863. Children four: 1. Mary E. Tichenor, born Nov. 6, 1889; 2, Anna B. Tichenor, born March 25, 1891; 3. Willie M. Tichenor, born Nov. 12, 1892; 4. Hazel G. Tichenor, born July 10, 1895. 2. Minnie Daugherty married Charley Strom, near Winstead Lake, Minn.; one child—Nellie Strom. 3. Anna Daugherty. 4. Edgar Daugherty.

The Montgomerys

Emily Daugherty, born Dec. 1846, second child of Jane Montgomery-Daugherty, married James P. Stone, Aug. 10, 1874. He is a retired farmer and a stockholder in the Owensville Milling Co. Children three: 1. Frank Stone. 2. Jane Stone. 3. Lona Stone.

Rosalia Daugherty, born 1848, third child of Jane Montgomery Daugherty, married Newton F. Westfall, a soldier in Co. F, 80th regiment Ind. Vol. They live at Francisco, Ind.; children six: 1. Win. S. Westfall, married Melissa Combs; children two: Carl and Arthur. 2. Thomas Westfall married Dora Smith, 3.___, 4. Mamie Westfall dead, 5. Janie Westfall married Wm. Combs, children two: Clarence and____, 6. Anna Westfall, single 1902, Marion Westfall was a soldier in the 159th regiment Ind. Vol., in Spanish-American War.

Mary Ann Daugherty, born Sept. 1851, fourth child of Jane Montgomery-Daugherty, first married Joseph DePriest, March 4, 1874. He died March 27, 1878; children one, Arthur DePriest. Second, she married C. C. Emerson, Oct. 9, 1879. He was a soldier in the 65th regiment Ind. Vol.

James F. Daugherty, born Jan. 18, 1854. He is an elder in the C. P. Church; married Mat. J. Skelton, Oct. 9, 1873; moved to Yoncalla, Douglass County, Oregon Aug. 8, 1894. They visited Owensville, Ind. 1902. He is in the fruit business. Children five: 1. Frank, born July 1, 1874; died March 16, 1876. 2. Leonard Daugherty, born March 11, 1876; married Clara Helliwill, Feb. 5, 1899; children one—Frankie Daugherty, born Nov. 4, 1899, at Yoncalla, Oregon. 3. Charles Daugherty, born Nov. 14, 1879, married Gertrude Helen Lamb Dec. 17, 1902. 4. Blanch Daugherty, born Aug. 24, 1882; married Ross King, May 7, 1902. 5. Luther Daugherty, born Sept. 4, 1888.

Louisa Daugherty, born Feb. 1856, sixth child of Jane Montgomery-Daugherty; married George Allen, of Kentucky, Aug. 11, 1873. They live near Oakland City, Ind.; children nine: 1. Garrad Allen, born 1875; married; one child. 2. Samuel Allen. 3. George. 4. Frank. 5. Lula. 6. Thomas. 7., Claude. 8. Cora. 9. Roy.

John Daugherty, born 1859; seventh child of Jane Montgomery Daugherty; married Florence Tichenor, Dec. 25, 1888: children two: 1. Oscar Daugherty, born 1889. 2. Frank Daugherty.

America Daugherty, born June 1861; eighth child of Jane Montgomery-Daugherty; married Wm. Marvel, in Gibson County, Ind., and they now live not far from Mt. Carmel, Ill.; no children.

McGrada W. Daugherty, born Feb. 3, 1864; ninth child of Jane Montgomery-Daugherty; was a farmer and fruit-grower near Owensville, Ind. and an elder in the C. P. Church. He moved to Yoncalla, Oregon, 1902; married Louella Smith, March 29, 1895; children two: 1. Elmer Daugherty, born Nov. 17, 1888; 2. Gertrude Daugherty, born Aug. 15, 1899.

James Montgomery, Jr., born 1828, eleventh child of James Montgomery, Sr., was a merchant in Owensville, Ind., and became quite a wealthy man. He was a man of perseverance and good judgment in the merchandise business, He died March 7, 1891; married Louisa Lucas, who was an excellent good woman: children five: 1. Julius died small. 2. Parnasha, died small.

3. James Montgomery, born June 18, 1862; son of James, Jr.: succeeded his father in the merchandise and grain business in Owensville, Ind., and is now, 1902, a stockholder in the Owensville Milling Co., also in the Owensville state bank. He married Hattie E. Beardsley, who was born in New York but married in Bourbon, Ill., Sept. 26, 1883; children two: 1. Ruth Trauch Montgomery, born June 1, 1891. 2. Martha Louisa Montgomery, born Nov. 23, 1899.

Maggie Montgomery, born July 8, 1855: fourth child of James Montgomery, Jr.; married Dr. John M. Williams, who graduated from the Eclectic Medical Institute, Cincinnati, Ohio, in the class of 1881. He first practiced at Fort Branch; located at Owensville, Ind., 1882; owns lands in Vanderburg and Gibson counties. He is a stockholder in the First National Bank of Owensville; children one—Gertrude Williams, born April 10, 1889.

Harvey Montgomery, born Nov. 6, 1877; now (1902) lives in Owensville. Ind., and is a clerk in the clothing department of his brother; single.

Benjamin Montgomery, sixth child of Samuel Montgomery, Sr. married Polly Smith, in Kentucky—sister to Dr. Willis Smith; children eight: 1, Sally, born 1807; married Nick Lawson and moved to Texas. 2, Martin Montgomery, born 1809, married and had one son. Louis.

The Montgomerys

Smith Montgomery, born Mar. 10, 1811; died Oct. 15, 1865; third child of Benjamin. Sr. married Minerva Hawkins, who was born *Feb.* 10, 1818; died Oct, 7, 1862; children 12:

1. John S., born Aug. 9, 1834; died Sept. 29, 18:34.

2. Willis, born Sept. 16, 1855; married Rebecca Taylor: children seven: 1. Lydia, married -James Scott, no children; 2. Frank; 3. Jane: 4. Lou; 5. Oscar; 6. Clarence; 7. Oliver. The circumstances connected with the family of Willis Montgomery are rather peculiar. He was born Sep. 16, 1835, married and had a family of seven children; one of them married, and the entire family are now dead, leaving no issue whatever.

3. Louisa, born Nov. 29, 1837.

4. Lucinda, born May 18, 1840.

5. Lewis, born June 7, 1842; died Aug. 29, 1844.

6. Manece A., born Nov. 10, 1844. These four are also children of Smith Montgomery.

7, William W., son of Smith Montgomery, born Nov. 2, 1845; was a soldier in Co. F, 80th regiment Ind. Vol., and now lives in Cynthiana, Ind.; married Gemima Cater; children three: 1. Mary, 2. Nancy married Jesse Garrett; children two, Everett and Walter, 3. Martha;

8. Aaron Montgomery, born Oct. 23, 1848, son of Smith, was a soldier in Co. D. 31st regiment U. S. Regulars, 1866 to '69; is a barber in Owensville, Ind.; first married Nancy Mitchell; children three: 1. Nelly K., married a Mr. Turner and lives in Eureka, Kansas. 2. Manece. 3. Belle. Second, Aaron Montgomery married Olivia Day, nee Blythe; children three: 1. Almie. 2. Rosa. 3. Alte.

9. Jesse Montgomery, born 1851, ninth child of Smith first married Susan Thompson, no children. Second, married Martha McConnell; children ten: 1. Alice. 2. William. 3. Aaron. 4. Emma. 5. Ida. 6. Infant. 7. Infant. 8. Lizzie. 9. Maggie. 10. James.

10. Amos Montgomery, born 1854, tenth child of Smith, married Sarah Cater: children six: 1. Myrtle. 2. Adelaide. 3. Ella. 4. Charley. 5. Jimmie. 6. Martha.

11. Lucinda Montgomery, born 1859, eleventh child of Smith, married Win. T. Hill; children eight: 1. Smith. 2. John. 3. Mary. 4., Jane. 5. Rosa. 6. Frank. 7. Willis. 8. Florence.

12. Betty Montgomery, born 1861, twelfth child of Smith, married James Gibson; children six: 1. Bertha. 2. Ada, married Frank Stewart; one child—Carry F. Stewart. 3. Burton, son of Betty Montgomery. 4. John. 5. Guy. 6. Fred.

Betty Montgomery, born about 1814, fourth child of Benjamin Montgomery, Sr., married James B Downey: children six: 1. Rachel, born 1834. 2. and 3. Robert and John, twins, born 1836, 4. Martin, born 1840. 5. and 6. Nancy and Benjamin, twins, born 1843,

Willis Montgomery, born about 1848, fifth child of Benjamin., Sr., was drowned in the Wabash River at Mt. Carmel, Ill.

Dorcas Montgomery, born Oct. 27, 1820, sixth child of Benjamin Montgomery Sr. is now (1903) 83 years old. She lives about three miles east of Cynthiana. Ind.: married Samuel Boren, Oct. 13. 1839, Mr. Boren was an excellent singer and was nearly all his life a leader in the old Southern Harmony. Children eleven:

1. Mary Boren, born Aug. 21, 1840; married Patrick Epperson, Feb. 27, 18151; children two: 1. Hiram N. Epperson, married Sophia A. Grotius, Jan. 24, 1894; one child—Lewra F. Epperson, born Jan. 8, 1896. 2. Ellis R. Epperson, son of Patrick, married Sally Martin. Feb. 10, 1887; children three: Julia M., born Aug. 14, 1889: Henry X., born March 28, 1893; Mary F., born Nov. 18, 1899.

2. Martha Boren. second child of Samuel Boren, born Oct. 16, 1842; married R. B. Bixler, March 29, 1856. who was a soldier in Co. F, 80th regiment Ind. Vol., and was wounded in the arm at Perryville, Ky., Oct. 8, 1862; children five: 1, Essie M. Bixler, born Jan. 15, 1867; married D. P. Bird of Owensville, Ind., June 17, 1891; she died Oct. 7, 1899; no children. 2. Dr. Otto Bixler, born Dec. 29, 1868: graduated at the Ohio Dental College, 1899; is located in Owensville, Ind.: married Ella Montgomery, April 19, 1893, daughter of Hon. Jesse Montgomery of Cynthiana. Ind.; one child, Wilhelmene May Bixler born Jan. 24, 1901.

3, Agnes Bixler, born July 29, 1872; married Dr. I. L. Turman of Cynthiana, Ind., Aug. 22, 1894; children one—Kenneth Turman, born Dec. 14, 1895.

4. John Bixler, born June 29, 1875; married Effie Montgomery, April 24, 1895, daughter of James H. Montgomery: children one— Essie Chlotile Bixler born 1896.

5. William Bixler, born March 22, 1878; graduated at Lafayette, Ind. and is a teacher in the college at that place; married Grace Emerson, Aug. 16, 1898; no children.

3. Abner Harrison Boren, born March 12, 1845; died April 13, 1S99; son of Samuel; a dealer in farm implements, Eldorado, Ill.; married Cordelia C.

The Montgomerys

Shelton, Dec. 14, 1865: children five: 1. M. C. Boren, born June 13, 1867; married Oscar Martin, April 19. 1885 children three: 1. Flora, born June 24, 1886; 2. Roy L. born Oct. 18, 1895; 3. Pauline M., born May 12, 1900.
    2. Edgar E. Boren, born Oct. 8, 1870; died April 15, 1871.
    3. Elva E. Boren, born Aug. 8, 1875; died June 22, 1895.
    4. George R. Boren, born Dec. 18, 1879.
    5. Walter A. Boren, born May 1, 1886.

Caroline Boren, fourth child of Samuel Boren, born June 17, 1847; married Rana Carter, March 28, 1868. He was a soldier in the 137th regiment Ind. Vol. Children two:
    1. Abner Alvah Carter, born June 19, 1870, married Ella B. Sides, April 2, 1895; children two: 1. Mildred Carter, born Aug. 7, 1896, died Feb. 20, 1897; 2. Ina Carter, born Sept. 22, 1901.
    2. Hampson Curtis Carter, born May 2, 1875, son of Rana Carter, married Effie Brumfield, Oct. 30, 1901; no children.

Eunice Boren, born Sept. 18, 1849, fifth child of Samuel Boren, married Isaac H. Smith, Jan. 27, 1878; no children.

John Boren, born Jan. 26, 1852, sixth child of Samuel Boren, married Amelia Shelton, Feb. 22, 1874; children five:
    1. Loran E. Boren, born April 2, 1877; married Nora Shultz, Nov. 6, 1898; one child—Clifford E. Boren, born Jan. 13, 1900; died Feb. 17, 1900.
    2. Cora E. Boren born Nov. 27, 1878, died May 13, 1900; married John W. Newman, Dec. 25. 1898; one child—Norman B. Newman.
    3. Hattie G. Boren, born Oct. 20, 1881.
    4., Wilber C. Boren, born Dec. 13, 1888.
    5. Edith E. Boren, born Jan. 3, 1892.

William R. Boren, born Sept. 14, 1859, seventh child of Samuel Boren, married Emma L. Pruitt, Oct. 12, 1880; children two:
    1. Eva E. Boren, born May 29, 1881, married Charles G. Carter, Dec. 29, 1898; one child—Harold B. Carter, born April 3, 1900; died May 17, 1900.
    2. Gilbert P. Boren, born Feb. 16, 1888, second child of Wm. Boren.

Miranda Boren, born May 30, 1857, eighth child of Samuel Boren; single 1902.

Asberry Boren, born March 8, 1860, ninth child of Samuel Boren, married Amanda McNeely, Sept. 5, 1888; one child—Arley Boren, Nov. 2, 1889.

Ida W. Boren, born March 21, 1863, tenth child of Samuel Boren; married G. F. Martin. June 14, 1885; children seven: 1. Arthur, born Oct. 11, 1887; died Oct. 30, 1887. 2. Edna A., born Oct. 28, 1889. 3. Ross, born March 10, 1891, died Sept. 25, 1891. 4. Abner, born Oct. 7, 1892, died Nov. 26, 1893. 5. Grace, born Oct. 4, 1894. 6. Ida, born May 9, 1897. 7. George W., born Jan. 7, 1900.

Dr. Samuel Wesley Boren, born March 8, 1867, eleventh child of Samuel Boren: is located (1902) at Poseyville, Ind.; married Gertie Lockwood, Sept. 3. 1896; she died at Wadesville, Ind., probably in 1897; no children, second, married Miss Rosa Kight, of Poseyville, Ind., Jan. 14, 1893.

Lucinda Montgomery, born probably about 1823, seventh child of Benjamin Montgomery, Sr., married Aaron Wilkinson, who was one among the earliest correspondents to local newspapers in southern Indiana. He was quite an interesting writer. He died near Cynthiana probably about 1890; children eight:
1. Susan Wilkinson married Jack Reed, a Federal soldier. They moved to Arkansas and she died there; children two—Wall and Clay Reed.
2. Rana Clay Wilkinson was a soldier in Co. F, 80th Ind. Vol.; was wounded in the Battle of Perryville, Ky., Oct. 8, 1862. He is an attorney at Evansville. Ind.; married a lady in Ohio; No children.
3. Masten Wilkinson, was a soldier in the 137th regiment Ind. Vol.; died 1901; married Clara Huff; children two: Nellie and Hattie Wilkinson.
4. Elisha Wilkinson first married Maggie Stern; children two: Infants, twins. Second, married Ada Stem; children four: Maggie, dead; John, infant, Maggie.
5. John Wilkinson lives in Princeton, Ind.; is a marble workman: married Lena Weir; one child—Lucy Wilkinson.
6. Scott Wilkinson died single.
7. Add. Wilkinson, married_____; no children.
8. Lizzie Wilkinson, married James H. Montgomery; children three: Sheridan, John and Effie.

The Montgomerys

8. Lydia Montgomery, born probably about 1825, married Joseph Massey, Sr., of Owensville. Ind. Mr. Massey died several years ago. Mrs. Massey now (1902) lives in Owensville; children four:

1. Amanda Massey, married Millard Dyre, Sept. 22, 1881; children three: 1. Romelia; 2. John; 3. Rudolph.

2. Belle Massey, second child of Joseph Massey, married Tony Wetter; both dead; no children.

3. Fannie Massey, third child of Joseph Massey, married Perry Stone; both dead; children four: 1. Elsie; 2. James; 3. Naomi; 4. Floyd.

4. Henry Massey, fourth child of Joseph Massey, married Winnie Thompson; one child—dead.

Dorcas Montgomery, born 1787, seventh child of Samuel Montgomery, Sr., married Thomas Stone in Kentucky, and they came to Indiana probably 1811. Mr. Stone was quite a prominent man of that day. He was at one time Sheriff of Gibson County, Ind. He died in 1822, and is buried in what is known as the Wm. Benson cemetery, two miles south of Owensville, Ind.; children nine:

1. Catherine Stone, born 1808. first married Robert T. Leach; children seven: 1. Celestial Leach, born July 10, 1825; 2. Wm. Leach, born 1827, died when about grown; 3. Rebecca Leach, born 1829, died when 12 years old; 4. Thomas Leach, born 1831, died single; 5. Eli Leach, born 1833, married___; 6. John Leach, born 1835, was a Major in the first regiment Ind. Cavalry and was killed in the battle of ____: never married; 7. Mary Leach, born 1837, married a Mr. Burrett. Catherine Stone-Leach second married Robert McReynolds; one child —Joseph McReynolds.

2. Samuel Stone, Sr., born May 3, 1810: died Feb. 11, 1883; was a large, well-proportioned man, fine-looking, and above the average in natural abilities, and at the time of his death was considered quite a wealthy farmer. He was noted for keeping fine horses. He married Lucy Maddox, Feb. 28, 1830. She was born June 2. 1814, and is now. Dec. 3, 1902, still living but in very poor health. She is a very shrewd woman, and Mr. Stone always attributed his success in life largely to her good judgment in financial affairs. She was a daughter of Jane Montgomery-Warrick, later Jane Maddox. Children eighteen: six died in infancy; twelve lived to be grown and have families of their own; eleven are now (1902) living.

1. Willis Stone, born March 9, 1831, married Margaret Baker, July 20, 1854. She was born Sept. 30, 1834, and died Sept. 10, 1899. He moved to

Manard County, Ill., in 1852, and to Tolono, Ill. in 1865, where he now lives (1902); children seven: 1. John B. Stone, born Feb. 4, 1856; is an abstractor: married Stella G. Gunn, Dec. 30, 1885. She was born May 4, 1865: children two: 1. Delia D. Stone, born Dec. 26, 1886; 2. Mabel G. Stone, born Aug. 10, 1889. 2. Eva Stone, daughter of Willis Stone, born Nov. 19, 1857: married Charles D. Merry. Dec. 24, 1884. He was born June 6, 1860; is working for Armour & Co. Children three: 1. Carl E. Merry, born Feb. 19, 1886; 2. Elda M. Merry, born May 14, 1887; 3. Dean S. Merry, born July 6, 1891. 3. Lucy W. Stone, daughter of Willis Stone, born Aug. 12, 1861; married John H. Pettit, Sept. 3, 1884. He was born Sept. 24, 1860: is a carpenter. Children five: 1. Nelly Pettit, born July 2, 1885, 2. Jaunetta, born Jan. 22, 1888, 3. Myrtle L., born Jan. 1, 1890, 4. Harry R., born March 2, 1892, 5. Frederick E., born Dec. 26, 1893, 4. Anna Stone, daughter of Willis Stone, born Aug. 6, 1860, single, 5. Martha Stone, born Jan. 4, 1868, died Sept. 23, 1874, 6. Mary Ellen Stone, born Jan. 12, 1872; died Oct. 3, 1874, 7. Edith Emma Stone, born Nov. 10, 1878- single.

Mary Jane Stone, born Jan. 12, 1833; second child of Samuel and Lucy Stone; first married Elihu Gambrel, Sept. 8, 1851; children six: 1., John Gambrel, born Aug. 1852; married Laura Cunningham, Jan. 13, 1876; children five: 1. Bertie Gambrel, born 1879; 2. Clarence Gambrel, born 1881; 3. Oma Gambrel, born 1885; 4. Gracie Gambrel, born 1885, died 1891; 5. Henry Gambrel, born 1887, died 1893.

Mary Gambrel, born April 26, 1855; second child of Elihu and Jane Gambrel; married Jesse M. Sloan, Jan. 23, 1870; children seven: 1. Henry W. Sloan, born Dec. 12, 1870; married Emma Harris, Oct. 23, 1895; children one—Vernon Sloan, born Nov. 4, 1898. 2. Julia A. Sloan, born Dec. 24, 1872; died Aug. 19, 1896; married George White May 29, 1895; one child—Laura B. White, born April 18, 1896, died April 18, 1896. 3. Lucy J. Sloan, born Sept. 26, 1874; died Dec. 4, 1877. 4. Ella May Sloan, born Feb. 16, 1877; married Gilbert Wiggle, April 6, 1898; children two: 1. Cecil Roy Wiggle, born March 25, 1899; 2. Jesse Evan Wiggle, born May 9, 1901. 5. Ida F. Sloan, born Nov. 12, 1879. 6. Emma L. Sloan, born June 21, 1882; married Guy Johnson, Feb. 22, 1901; one child—Donald Johnson, born July 7, 1901. 7. Lola M. Sloan born Sept. 29, 1889.

Henry T. Gambrel, third child of Elihu and Jane Gambrel, born March 1, 1858; married Margaret J. Simpson, April 2, 1881. She died Nov. 11, 1887;

children one -Lawrence Gambrel, born ___. Second, married Eliza E. Seaman, Nov. 5. 1888; children _____.

4. Samuel Gambrel, born July 3, 1860; married Emma Mauck, June 1, 1880; children five: 1. Willie Gambrel, born 1881. 2. Mary Gambel, born 1883. 3. Charley Gambrel, born 1885. 4. Julius Gambrel, born 1888. 5. Frank Gambrel, born 1891.

5. Philecta W. Gambrel, born Jan. 1863; died___.

6, Julius Gambrel, Sr., born July 1865; married Emma Kendle, Feb. 2, 1885; one child—James H. Gambrel, born, died Nov. 10, 1891.

Jane Stone Gambrel, born Jan. 12, 1833, second married James Kroh, July 27, 1868; one child—Ina Kroh, born 1869; first married Albert Douglass; children Grace Kroh and Florence Douglas. Second, married Nicholas Yeager; children three—Gladys Fay and Roy. Third, married ____Seymour.

Margaret Stone, born Oct. 27, 1836; third child of Samuel and Lucy Stone; married Rev. Wm. Clark, Sept. 27, 1853, a General Baptist minister. He was an able, sincere, upright, honorable man and truly a great help to his denomination and Christianity in general; born Aug. 11, 1835. He died Nov. 8, 1899. Children seven:

1. Samuel Clark, born Dec. 4, 1854; first married Annie Owens; children one—Molly Clark, born Jan. 26, 1875; married Gilbert Pearson; children one—Annie Pearson. Samuel Clark married, second, Carrie Massey, Feb. 18, 1877; children one: William Clark, born Aug. 17. 1890.

2. Isaac Clark, born Nov. 6. 1858: married Alice Massey, Nov. 12, 1879. She was born July 14, 1858; children two: 1. Clarence M. Clark, born May 16, 1882; married Idessa Wright. Jan. 18, 1901; children two: 1. Carrolton M. Clark, born Aug. 27, 1901; 2._____.

2. Fannie Clark, born Feb. 26. 1884; single 1903.

Third child of Wm. and Margaret Clark died at eight days old.

4. Melissa Clark, born May 30. 1861; married John L. Brown.

5. Emma Clark, born Nov. 11, 1863; died Aug. 20. 1888: one child—Harvey Clark, born April 12, 1884; married Ida Kelley, Nov. 24, 1901; one child - infant.

6. Mary Clark, born Sept. 23, 1865; married Marion Knowles, Sept. 16. 1885; children four: 1. Stella Knowles. 2. Nola Knowles. 3. Erse! Knowles. 4. Adrian Knowles.

7. Lucy Clark, born Nov. 21, 1870; married James Weedman 1892. They lived for a while in Little Rock, Ark., but now (1902) live three miles south of Owensville, Ind.; children five: 1. Rolla Weedman, born Oct. 1894. 2. .W. R. Weedman, born Dec. 1896. 3. Hope Weedman, born Nov. 1899. 4. George Weedman, born Sept. 1900. 5. Hassel Weedman, born Feb. 1902.

7. George Clark, born Aug. 1, 1875; married Flora Smith, Aug. 5, 1896. They live one mile north of King Station, Ind.; one child —Jerald Clark, born Sept. 15, 1897.

Henry Stone, born Oct. 1, 1838; fourth child of Samuel and Lucy Stone; married Sarah E. Stillwell, Sept. 10, 1863. They live on a farm near New Harmony, Ind.; children five:

1. Dalton Stone, born March 27, 1865; married Nora Miller, Nov. 1892. They live in Evansville, Ind.; children four: 1. Bertha Stone, born June 1893, died Dec. 11, 1895; 2. Ida Stone, born May 7, 1895; 3. Willie Stone, born Sept. 1897; 4. Louis Stone, born Sept. 1899.

2. Nora Stone, born Dec. 7, 1867; married. Allison Clark, Oct. 5, 1884; children four: 1. Everett Clark, born Sept. 29, 1885; 2., Edith Clark, born Oct. 24, 1887; 3. Laverne Clark, born Oct. 2, 1889; 4. Versa Clark, born Sept. 3, 1892.

3. George Stone, born March 17, 1869; married Laura Grubb, Dec. 31, 1899; no children.

4. John Stone, born Oct. 20, 1871; single 1902.

5. Mell Stone, born Dec. 3, 1876; single 1902.

Nancy Stone, born July 18, 1840, fifth child of Samuel and Lucy Stone, married James Spore Dec. 24, 1861. He died Dec. 27, 1880; children seven:

1. Louella Spore, born Sept. 18, 1862; married Oscar Stone, Feb. 18, 1886; children four: 1. Ethel P. Stone, born Jan. 26, 1887; 2. Clarence E. Stone, born July 29, 1889; 3. Letha O. Stone, born March 29, 1896, died Oct. 29, 1899; 4., Jesse Burl Stone, born May 8, 1900.

The Montgomerys

2. Perry Spore, born July 14. 1864; married Clara Garrett, Dec. 1, 1892; children two: 1. Hazel E. Spore, born Nov. 23, 1893; 2. Denzel Spore, born Dec. 5, 1900.

3. Lucy Spore, born May 4, 1866; married George McCrary, 1897; children one—Ova D. McCrary, born April 30, 1898, died Aug. 4, 1898.

4. Samuel Spore, born Jan. 16. 1868; single 1902.

5. Anna Spore, born Feb. 10, 1869; single 1902.

6. Willis Wesley Spore, born Dec. 25, 1874; married Anna Finch.

7. Henrietta Spore, born March 6, 1881, died July 9, 1881.

Nancy Spore second married Thomas Thompson, June 9, 1898; no children. They live at Oakland City, Ind.

Thomas Stone, Jr., born Dec. 26, 1841; sixth child of Samuel and Lucy Stone; moved to Manard County, Ill., then moved to near Tolono, Ill.; married Pearl Knowles in Ind., Nov. 10, 1867, who was born June 13, 1848; children twelve:

1. John S. Stone, born Oct. 31, 1868; married Odessa Hoover, March 5, 1890. She died April 16, 1899.

2. Lucy E. Stone, born Oct. 31, 1868; is a twin to John S. Stone; married Charles R. Baker, Nov. 10, 1892, a farmer and road commissioner of Leroy, Ill.

3. Willis Stone, a farmer, born June 10, 1871; married Lydia E. Barnhart, Jan. 30, 1895; children four: 1. Leila G. Stone, born Dec. 8, 1895. 2. Thomas T. Stone, born Jan. 27, 1897. 3. Chauncey L. Stone, born Nov. 19, 1899. 4. Grace M. Stone, born Oct. 1901.

4. Infant son, born Dec. 20, 1871; died Dec. 22, 1871.

5. May Stone, born March 4, 1876; died Feb. 28, 1880.

6. Alice Stone, born March 7, 1878; married Alonzo Wolf, Aug. 19, 1896, a farmer of Wayne County, Ill.; children two: 1. Hattie P. Wolf, born May 20, 1898; 2. Ida H. Wolf, born Jan. 5, 1901; died small.

7. Martha C. Stone, born Oct. 25, 1880; married Robert M. Gooden of Louisville. Ky., Oct. 10, 1901. He is farming near Homer, Ill.

8. Lewis B. Stone, born Oct. 25, 1880, a twin to Martha C, above; married Minnie Harmer, July 25, 1901.

9. and 10. Twins, Harry F. and Clara E. Stone, born May 2, 1883, single 1901.

11. Grover C. Stone, born Aug. 11, 1886; died Sept. 23, 1889.

12. Scott Stone, born July 20, 1889. The reader will observe that there are three pairs of twins in this family.

Ellen Stone, born Sept. 1, 1846; seventh child of Samuel and Lucy Stone; married Samuel Burk. They live north-west of Oakland City, Ind.; one child—Luther Burk.

Elizabeth Stone, born Oct. 26, 1848; is the second wife of James C. Pruitt, married Nov. 19, 1874. Mr. Pruitt has been a merchant in Owensville, Ind., for about thirty years, and is a stockholder in the Farmers department store. He taught many years in the public schools, and is an elder in the C. P. church and a radical prohibitionist. Children two: Clarence Pruitt, born June 18, 1876; died April 13, 1877. 2. Minnie Pruitt, born June 18, 1878; is a teacher in the public schools.

Newton Stone, born Aug. 4, 1850; is the ninth child of Samuel and Lucy Stone. He is a farmer near Burnt Prairie, Ill.; married Zerelda Cleveland, Dec. 31. 1872. She was born July 3, 1852; children ten:
1. Infant son, died Sept. 1873.
2. Samuel M. Stone, Jr., born Jan. 19, 1875; married Minnie Funkhouser, Oct. 21. 1894; one child—Clyde Stone, born Oct. 22. 1895.
3. and 4. Infant sons, twins, died Jan. 10 and Feb. 4, 1877.
5. Amanda A. Stone, born June 3. 1878; married John Vaught, Feb. 26, 1897; one child—Orville Vaught, born June 26, 1900.
6. Winfield S. Stone, born Aug. 7, 1880; died July 20. 1881.
7. Ethel Pearl Stone, born June 12, 1882; married John Renfro, Aug. 30, 1900; one child—Irene Renfrew, born June 8, 1901.
8. Cayce Stone, born March 4, 1887.
9. Henry Stone, born Feb. 26, 1890.
10. Lucy Stone, born Dec. 4, Martha Stone, born May 14, 1852; tenth child of Samuel and Lucy Stone, married William Gordon, Aug. 14, 1871). They now live in Owensville, Ind.; children three: 1. Zada M. Gordon, born Sept. 2. 1880; married Charley Maus, of Mt. Vernon, Ind., March 10, 1901; now live in Princeton, Ind.: one child, Iona Blanch Maus, born May 22, 1902. 2. James Hervey Gordon, born Sept. 27, 1881; single. 3. Dovie Gordon, born April 13, 1884; married Harry Switzer, of Princeton, Ind., Aug. 27, 1902.

The Montgomerys

Dorcas Stone, born Sept. 11, 1853; eleventh child of Samuel and Lucy Stone; married Thomas J. Spore, Sept. 15, 1875. They moved north of Oakland City, Ind., where she died March 16, 1896; children three: 1. Mattie Spore, born Aug. 16, 1876; married Frank Eskew, Aug. 25, 1895; children one—Paul Eskew, born Aug. 31, 1897. 2. Lenora Spore, born Aug. 7, 1879; died Oct. 14, 1880. 3., Arthur Spore, born Aug. 25, 1883; single 1903.

George C. Stone, a farmer, born Feb. 23, 1857, twelfth child of Samuel and Lucy Stone, married America Montgomery, Oct. 31, 1878: one child—Florence Stone, died Dec. 23, 1899, when about 23 years old; an excellent young lady; single.

Peggy Stone, born 1812; third child of Dorcas Montgomery Stone; married Col. Wm. Montgomery. (See index—"Col. Wm. Montgomery, of Gibson Co., Ind.")

Nancy Stone, born 1813, fourth child of Dorcas Montgomery Stone; married Jesse Knowles. They moved to Manard County, Ill., in the forties, and later moved to Greenwood County, Kansas, and Mr. Knowles was drowned in the Verdigris River. We have failed to find out any more about this family.

Dorcas Stone, born 1814; fifth child of Dorcas Montgomery Stone; married "Big" Asa Knowles and moved to Manard County, Ill. Their children were Samuel, John, Jacob, Martin, Thomas, Eli, Prettiman, and others.

Samuel Knowles, born 1841, is a lawyer; made speeches in southern Indiana in 1860 in behalf of Stephen A. Douglas. He was then 19 years old. He was several times a member of the legislature of Illinois.

Manece Stone, born 1816, ninth child of Dorcas Montgomery Stone; married Martin Knowles, 1834; moved to Manard County, Ill.; children eight: 1. Wiley Knowles, born Aug. 17, 1835, furnished the data for this family. He was a soldier in Co. A, 58th regiment Ind. Vol.: was licensed to preach by the C. P. church in 1859; graduated from Lincoln College, Ill., 1872; is still active in the ministry—1902—and lives at Madera, California; married Ann Ripson. Dec. 1, 1864; no children.

And Their Descendants

2. Mary Knowles, born probably 1837; died March 13, 1866; married James Eldredge; children two: 1. Manece E. Eldredge, 2. Vernetta E. Eldredge.

3. Thomas A. Knowles, born Jan. 16, 1840; was a soldier in the Federal army; married Henrietta Lockhart, Nov. 14, 1861; children fourteen: 1. Lou A. Knowles, born Aug. 26, 1862. 2. Captolia, born Aug. 2, 1866. 3. Flora K., born Oct. 12, 1867. 4. Arena, born April 28, 1869. 5. Sylvester B., born July 22, 1871. 6. Halsey, born April 6, 1873. 7. Jerome, born Feb. 20, 1875. 8. Nora, born April 6, 1877. 9. Delco, born May 18, 1878. 10. Estella M., born Feb. 25, 1880. 11. Virella, born Sept. 30, 1882. 12. Claudius, born April 25, 1885. 13. Henrietta, born Aug. 21, 1887. 14, Thomas, born Aug. 21, 1887; a twin to No. 13.

William Knowles, born Oct. 9, 1813; died Dec. 29, 1897; fourth child of Martin Knowles; was a soldier in the Federal army: married Abigail Rice March 10, 1870; children four: 1. Harry W. Knowles, born 1871, died 1871. 2. Minerva O. Knowles, born Jan. 3, 1873. 3. Wrinta G. Knowles, born March 27, 1883. 4. Rachel R. Knowles, born July 30, 1885.

Levira Knowles, born 1844 or 5; fifth child of Martin Knowles, married Abner Blaine March 16, 1859. They live in Greenview, Ill.; children eleven: 1. Joint W. Blaine, born Feb. 29, 1860. 2. Mary E. Blaine, born Oct. 8, 1862. 3. Martha A., born March 22, 1864. 4. Edward W., born Feb. 8, 1866. 5. Eliza M., born Feb. 28, 1868. 6. Melinda J., born June 1, 1870. 7. Huldah G. born Sept. 21, 1872. 8. Verda A., born Sept. 20, 1874. 9. Frederick W. born Sept. 13, 1876. 10. Abner P., born May 19, 1879. 11. Elva E. born March 14, 1887.

Dorcas Knowles, born 1846 or 7: sixth child of Martin Knowles; first married James Cummings, 1863; children two: 1. Melissa K. Cummings; 2. Mary E. Cummings. Second, married E. D. Powers and had several children whose names are not known.

Jasper N. Knowles, born 1848; seventh child of Martin Knowles; was in the Federal army; first married Harriet C. Knowles, Sept. 18, 1867, granddaughter of Benj. Montgomery, who located in Manard County, Ill., in the fifties: children five: 1. John W. Knowles, born Sept. 4, 1868. 2. Lizzie M. Knowles, born Dec. 8, 1869. 3. Arthur L. Knowles, born June 25, 1871. 4. Lenora L. Knowles, born June 17, 1872. 5. Clara B. Knowles, born March 13, 1874. Second, married Margaret Smith, Jan. 15, 1880; children four: 1.

Manece J. Knowles, born Nov. 16, 1880. 2. Ethel D., born Feb. 4, 1886. 3. Cora L., born March 9, 1891. 4. George M., born Oct. 31, 1892.

George W. Knowles, born Oct. 8, 1852; eighth child of Martin Knowles; married Mary Allison, Oct. 3, 1875; children ___: 1. Perry T. Knowles, born Nov. 21, 1876. 2. Roy L. Knowles, born July 13, 1878.

Silas Stone, born 1816, sixth child of Dorcas Montgomery-Stone; died Aug. 14, 1888; married Polly Woods, who died July 21, 1891; children six:

1. Rilis Stone, married Litha Spore; children five: 1. Joseph J. Stone, married Ella Woods;-children ___; 2. May Stone, dead; 3. Charley Stone, single; 4. Ella Stone, married John Brokaw, children ___; 5. Win. Stone, married_____.

2. Wm. Stone, second child of Silas Stone, married Margaret Perkins; children four: 1. James Stone; 2. Thomas Stone; 3. Trecie Stone; 4. Infant.

3. Jane Stone, third child of Silas Stone, married Montgomery Alcorn; children eight.

4. Margaret Stone, fourth child of Silas Stone, married James Mauck, who died in Owensville in 1902; she died several years earlier; children four: 1. Peter Mauck, first married Eliza Massey, Sept. 15, 1883: one child, dead. Married, second, Fanny Musick, Sept. 13, 1887; children three: 1. Hazle Mauck; 2. Eunice Mauck; 3. Maggie Mauck, dead.

5. Thomas Stone, fifth child of Silas Stone, first married Malia Alberta; children two: 1. Willie Stone, died at one year old; 2. Manus Stone; 3. Letha Stone. Thomas Stone, son of Silas Stone, second married Mary Ted; children four.

Thomas Stone, Jr., born probably about 1818; seventh child of Dorcas Montgomery-Stone; married Jane Daugherty of Owensville, Ind. They moved to Iowa probably in the fifties. Mrs. Stone has been dead several years and I understand that Mr. Stone now (1903) lives at Winterset, Iowa: eighty or more years old; children eleven:

1. Sarah Stone, married Stewart Propit in Iowa; children five: 1. Charles Propit. 2. Edward Propit. 3. Willie Propit, dead. 4. Delbert Propit. 5. Clyde Propit.

2. Lucy Stone, second child of Thomas Stone, Jr., died small.

3. Louisa Stone, third child of Thomas Stone, Jr. died small.

4. Martha J. Stone, fourth child of Thomas Stone, Jr., married Berry Knowles in Iowa; children four: 1. Albert Knowles, dead. 2. Isaac Knowles. 3. Lizzie Knowles. 4. Elsie Knowles.

5. Logan Stone, fifth child of Thomas Stone, Jr.; single. He is a poet of considerable note.

6. Stephen Stone, sixth child of Thomas Stone, Jr., died small.

7. Samuel Stone, seventh child, died single at 24 years old.

8. John Stone, eighth child, died at 8 years.

9. Thomas H. Stone, ninth child, has been superintendent of public schools in his County; married Kate Roon in Iowa: children three: 1. Lloyd Stone; 2. Roscoe Stone, dead: 3. Harry Stone.

10. Ella Stone, tenth child of Thomas Stone Jr. married W. J. Clark in Iowa; children three: 1. Harvey Clark; 2. and 3. Ruby and Pearl Clark, twins.

11. Robert B., eleventh child of Thomas Stone, Jr., has been superintendant of public schools in Des Moines, Iowa; single.

Sarah Stone, born 1820: eighth child of Dorcas Montgomery Stone: married Thomas Jefferson Montgomery. See index—Montgomery. Thos. Jefferson.

John Montgomery, Squire John, born about 1790; eighth child of Samuel Montgomery. Sr. He took part in some of the Indian wars. Some claim that he was in the Battle of Tippecanoe, but we are not positive about this. He was a fine looking, well-built man with considerable of the Irish characteristics; married Juno Cook in Kentucky and came to Indiana about 1811; children ten: 1. Nathan Montgomery, born about 1812; first child of Squire John Montgomery; married Melissa Sullivan of Evansville, Ind.; children ten: 1. America Montgomery, married Robert Hunter: children five: 1. Mat; 2. Archie; 3. 4. and 5. Names not known; 2. Martha Montgomery married a Voorhees, near Terre Haute, Ind. 3. Abel Montgomery, married a Pritchett; children four. 4. John Montgomery, was a soldier in the Federal army; first married a Smith; children five: 1. James Montgomery; 2. John Montgomery; 3. a daughter; 4. Kirk Montgomery, married Orie Thompson, near Owensville, Ind., and moved to a place nine miles east of Oklahoma City, Okla.—no children; 5. Lawrence Montgomery, married:____ children___. Paulina Montgomery, fifth child of Nathan Montgomery, Sr., married____. Mary Montgomery, sixth child of Nathan Montgomery, married a Mr. Drummond; children one, ___. Nathan Montgomery had other children: 7. Vicie; 8. Ruth; 9. Lawrence; 10. Florence. 11. Infant.

The Montgomerys

Artimeca Montgomery, second child of Squire John, married John Witherspoon, an elder in the C. P. church of Owensville, Ind.; children five: 1. Jane Witherspoon married Robert Summers. (See index —Summers, Robert.) 2. Thomas Witherspoon, was a soldier in the 58th regiment Ind. Vol.; married Cordelia Woods; children five: 1. Hattie, born 1863, dead; 2. Etta, born 1865, dead; 3. Edward Witherspoon, born 1868, a carpenter at Princeton, Ind., married Nannie E. Erwin, children one—Donald Erwin Witherspoon; 4. Charles Witherspoon, born 1871, dead; 5. Alice Witherspoon, born 1874, married Orien Knowles, proprietor of a restaurant in Owensville, Ind.—one child, Julia F. Knowles, dead. Sally Witherspoon, third child of John Witherspoon, married Samuel Stubbles in Missouri. Melissa Witherspoon, fourth child, married Dr. Chandler of Owensville, Ind.; they moved to Arkansas, where the doctor died; children one—Richard Chandler. Indiana Witherspoon, fifth child, married Joshua Haley of Missouri.

Sally Montgomery, third child of Squire John Montgomery, married John Woods; children ten: 1. Esther Woods, married Thomas Spore; children five: 1. David Spore, married Dora Rains, children two—Bessie and Edith Spore; 2. Will Spore, married Mary Pierce, children two—Jesse and Nellie Spore; 3. Daniel G. Spore, married Rosa Braselton, children three: Roy, Herschel and Opal; 4. John F. Spore, son of Esther Woods-Spore, single; 5. Alice Spore. 2. Margaret Woods, daughter of Sally Montgomery Woods, died small. 3. Isaac Woods, married Mary Stroud; children nine: six died in infancy; 7. Henry; 8. Maud Woods, married James Hall; children one—Frankie Hall; 9. Bertha Woods. 4. David Woods, son of Sally Montgomery-Woods, died in Federal army. 5. Bettie Woods married David Hart, who represented Gibson County in the state legislature a part of the term in 1899, on the Democrat-Populist ticket. A Republican legislature gave his seat to his opponent, James M. Cockrum. Mr. Hart had six children: 1. Frankie Hart died at 4 months old. 2. Elsie J. Hart, dead; 3. Arthur Hart; 4. Pearl Hart; 5. Ornie Hart; 6. Gracie Hart, dead. 6. Manece Woods, married William Binkley: children four: 1. Elmer Binkley, dead: 2. Nelly Binkley married Eck. Mason—one child, Viola Mason; 3. Rod. Binkley, married Ella Watkins—children one, Victor Binkley; 4. and 5. Infants.

Samuel Woods, seventh child of Sally Montgomery Woods, married Lizzie Q. Brazleton; children nine: 1. Ivy Woods, married Marion White; children one—Lottie White. 2. Effie Woods, married Eula Rothbrock;

children two: 1. Hazle Rothbrock; 2. infant. 3. Ellis Woods. 4. Sarah. 5. Ethel. 6. Orpha. 7. Verna, 8. and 9. Infants.

John Woods, eighth child of Sally Montgomery-Woods, married Mary Baten; children three: 1. infant. 2. Anna Woods, married Joe Brown; children two: Claude and Harvey Brown. 3. Louie Woods.

Sarah Woods, ninth child of Sally Montgomery Woods, dead.

Thomas Woods, tenth child of Sally Montgomery-Woods, married Eliza Baton; no children.

"Big" David Montgomery, fourth child of Squire John Montgomery, married a Hopkins; children five:

1. Elvina Montgomery, born about 1840; married Nathan Wilson of Owensville. He was a soldier in the 120th regiment Ind. Vol. Children five: 1. Pinkney Wilson, married____; three children. 2. Perry Wilson, married Kate ____; children two. 3. Ollie Wilson; married a Mr. Breeses; children two, Freddie and Ervina Breeses. 4. Tula Wilson, married twice. 5. Willie Wilson, single.

2. Amanda Montgomery, born Jan. 18, 1842, daughter of "Big" David Montgomery, married Reuben Emerson, a carpenter of Ft. Branch, Ind. March 29, 1860; he was born Dec. 25, 1837; children eight: 1. Ida Emerson, born Feb. 15, 1861, first married Joseph Jones, Sept. 15, 1886; children five: 1. Roscoe Jones, born May 7, 1887; 2. Elda Jones, born June 22, 1888; 3. James C. Jones, born Feb. 11, 1890; 4. Edna Jones, born March 4, 1893; 5. Edith Jones, born March 17, 1895, died Nov. 7. 1897. Ida Emerson second married Jacob Green; children one—Zona Green, born Aug. 10, 1899. 2. Charles Emerson, born May 24, 1863, married Allie Rule, May 4, 1893; children four: 1. Carl Emerson, born March 11. 1894; 2. Lythe Emerson, born Jan. 8, 1896; 3. Verl Emerson, born Feb. 4, 1898. 4, Glenn Emerson, born Dec. 31, 1899. 3. Lemuel Emerson, born Sept. 11, 1864; was a soldier 18 months 1902-3 in Co. H, 20th regiment U. S. Regulars. He was also a soldier in a Georgian regiment in the Spanish-American War. 4. Lucy Emerson, born Dec. 14, 1866; supposed to have drowned in 1883. 5. Lilly Emerson, born March 4, 1868; died Oct. 3, 1883. 6. Elzora Emerson, born Nov. 22, 1872; married Wm. Rogers in 1893; children one—Onie D. Rogers, born April 21, 1894; now (1902) living with his grandparents, Emersons, in Ft. Branch, Ind.

The Montgomerys

7. Clara Emerson, born Sept. 29, 1881, died Oct. 9, 1881. 8. James Emerson, born Aug. 16, 1885, died Aug. 24, 1885.

3. Samuel Montgomery, third child of "Big" David Montgomery, was a soldier in the 120th regiment Ind. Vol.; married Ophelia Brokaw and now lives in Evansville, Ind.; children ten: 1. Etta Montgomery. 2. Cora. 3. Arle. 4. Arie. 5. Lloyd. 6. Lela. 7. 8. 9. and 10. Infants. You will observe a peculiarity in the names of this family, which is that the six names given are all spelled with four letters. This is the only instance of this kind that I have observed.

4. Margaret E. Montgomery, fourth child of "Big" David Montgomery, married Isaac Ayers; children five: 1. James Ayers, born Nov. 23, 1871, lives in Chicago, Ill.; married Herresa Cardwell; children three: 1. James Joseph Ayers; 2. Dorothy Ayers; 3. Elsie M. Ayers. 2. Ida Ayers, born May 3, 1874; lives in Princeton. Ind.; married Clarence Binkley; one child—Frank Binkley. 3. Elsie M. Ayers, born April 18, 1876; is a teacher in the public schools and a stockholder in the Owensville Milling Company; single 1903. 4. Ora Ayres, dead. 5. Infant.

5. Sylvester Montgomery, fifth child of "Big" David Montgomery, married Otilda Alberta; children nine: 1. Austin Montgomery. 2. Louis. 3. Flora, dead. 4. Wilber. 5. Oral. 6. Sylvester. 7. 8. 9. 10., Infants.

William Montgomery, fifth child of Squire John Montgomery, married Margaret Hawkins; children eight: 1. Nelson. 2. Martha. 3. John. 4. Clara. 5., Henry. 6. Columbus.

Big Tom Montgomery, sixth child of Squire John Montgomery, engaged in a personal combat with Henry Pullen in Owensville about 1850. They were the best of friends, but under undue political influences engaged in this contest, which is referred to by the old citizens of this day. He married Clara Hawkins, and they moved to the neighborhood of Flora, Ill., in the fifties. Children seven: 1. Martha J. Montgomery. 2. Micah Arm. 3. James. 4. Henry. 5. Maggie. 6. Allie Belle. 7. Infant.

Hiram Montgomery, seventh child of Squire John Montgomery, died single.

Margaret Montgomery, eighth child of Squire John Montgomery, married Samuel Hawkins; children four: 1. Jane Hawkins; 2. Martha: 3. John 4. Samuel.

John Montgomery, ninth child of Squire John Montgomery, died at 12 years old.

Samuel Montgomery, tenth child of Squire John, died small.

I have been informed that Squire John Montgomery was in the Battle of Tippecanoe.

Samuel Montgomery Jr.
Cynthiana, Indiana

Samuel Montgomery, Jr., born 1794, in Kentucky, ninth and youngest child of Samuel Montgomery, Sr. He belonged to the state militia, and at the time of the call by Gen. Harrison for assistance to fight the Battle of Tippecanoe he was absent on a visit. On returning home and being informed that the company to which he belonged had joined General Harrison he procured a horse and hastily followed them; but he met his company at Vincennes, returning home. He was about 17 years of age at this time. He first married Sarah Montgomery, Nov. 15. 1814, was born 1793, died Aug. 1829. This was the 38th license issued in Gibson County, Ind. He was on the first jury drawn in Gibson County. It was in a justice's court, held in a small log cabin south-west of Princeton, on the McCurdy farm, on the flat to the left as you go to Princeton, just after crossing the branch, on the old road. The first regular court was held in a stone house built by Judge Isaac Montgomery, now known as the John Hudelson and Joseph McCarty farms. The children of his first wife were five:

The Montgomerys

1. Robert Montgomery, born Aug. 17, 1815; he enlisted in the 58th regiment Ind. Vol., Oct. 1861; discharged for disability April 22, 1862; enlisted in Co. I, 120th regiment Ind. Vol., in March, 1864, discharged Sept. 7, 1865, as a corporal. First married Patsy Boren: children four: 1. Sarah Montgomery, born 1833; married James Dougan; children seven: 1. Louisa Dougan, first married Henry Clark, 1882; he died Jan. 1, 1888; children two—Verna Clark, born 1884 and Netta Clark, born 1888. Louisa Dougan second married John McIntyre, 1889, a soldier in Co. F. 33rd regiment Ind. Vol.; lives near Ft. Branch, Ind.; no children. 2. Rose Dougan, born March 16, 1861, married George M. Clark of Gibson County, Ind., Dec. 24, 1883. He was born Dec. 9, 1862, and is a licensed preacher in the General Baptist church. He now lives at Maunie, Ill.; children one—Ethel Clark, born Nov. 20, 1884. 3, Andrew Dougan, single. 4, Samuel R. Dougan, born 1866, died 1882, 14 years old. 5. Charles Dougan, married Vina Powers about 1891; children four. 6. Clara Dougan, married John Linn, about 1891; children three. 7. Pleasant Dougan married and has two children.

William Montgomery, born 1835, second child of Robert Montgomery: married Polly Douglass, 1863, and lives at Cynthiana, Ind.; children five: 1, Albert Montgomery, is in a grocery store in Cynthiana; married Ida Jones: no children. 2. John Montgomery. 3. Anna Montgomery married Glenn Kimble. 4. Ernest Montgomery, single. 5. Leslie Montgomery, single.

3. Rosa Montgomery, born 1837, married Berry Carter; children two: 1. Marion C. Carter, married ____. 2. Magdalene Carter married a Mr. Oldham.

4. Mary Montgomery, born 1839, married Wm. Dougan: children four: 1, Wesley Dougan. 2. Etta Dougan. 3. Anna Dougan.
4. Rosa Dougan.

Robert Montgomery married, second, a Mrs. Perkins; children three:

1. Martha Montgomery, born 1841, married Harvey Burton; children two: 1, Maggie Burton; 2. a son.
2. Nancy Montgomery, born 1845, married James Hitch of Princeton, Ind.; children five.
3. John Montgomery lives in Princeton, Ind.; married Anna Brown; children____.

Ira Montgomery, a farmer, born Jan. 4, 1818, died 1883; second child of Samuel Montgomery, Jr.; married Zerelda Knowles, who now (1902) lives in Poseyville. Ind., about 81 years old and remarkably active for one of her age; children six:

1. Temperance Montgomery, born about 1840, married Casey Calvert of Posey Co., Ind. He has been postmaster at Poseyville, and is now (1901) in charge of the Posey County infirmary; children three: 1. Grace Calvert, single 1901. 2. Andrew Calvert has been a railroad postal clerk; is a serious cripple from rheumatism; married Belle Hudson of Mt. Vernon, Ind.; children two: 1. Harry Calvert, 2. Allen Calvert.

2. Andrew Montgomery, born 1842, married Anna Johnson, born 1814. Mr. Montgomery has been Marshal of Poseyville for about four years and holds that office now (1902). Children four:
1. Frank M. Montgomery, Jr., born 1871, is now, 1903, Marshal of Owensville, Ind.; was unanimously elected in May, 1901. Previously he had conducted a grocery store; married Myrtle Marvel, 1893; children three: 1. Harold Montgomery, born 1894. 2. Russell Montgomery, born 1896. 3. Margaret Montgomery, born 1901.

2. Enos P. Montgomery, second child of Andrew Montgomery, born 1873, married Anna Eaton, 1899; children one—Dorothy Montgomery, born 1901. Mae Montgomery, third child of Andrew Montgomery, born 1875, single. Roscoe Montgomery, born 1877, fourth child of Andrew Montgomery; is a clerk in a grocery store in Poseyville, Ind. married Estella Reaves, 1898; children one—Athel Montgomery, born 1899.

3. John Montgomery, born , third child of Ira Montgomery, is a farmer near Poseyville, Ind.; taught in the public schools; married Polina Cox; children four: 1. Lillian Montgomery, born 1875. 2. Wilber Montgomery, born 1884. 3. Estella Montgomery, born 1880. 4. Chester Montgomery, born 1888.

4. Frank Montgomery. Sr. born ____, a farmer near Poseyville, Ind.; married Elizabeth Fitzgerald, 1873; children four: 1. Ada Montgomery, born 1874, taught in the public schools, single 1901. 2. Cleo Montgomery, born 1876, taught in the public schools; married Thomas Brown, 1901, a commercial traveler of Terre Haute, Ind. 3. Louis Montgomery, born 1878, single. 4. Ernest Montgomery born 1880, single.

5. Dr. Nathan Montgomery, born____ , died 1903; fifth child of Ira Montgomery, graduated at an Eclectic medical school of Cincinnati, Ohio, 1896, and is now (1903) practicing in Norman, Oklahoma; first married Florence Fitzgerald; children three: 1. John Montgomery, dead. 2, Evans Montgomery, single; taught in the public schools. 3. Daniel Montgomery, a farmer in Oklahoma, married; one child. Second, married Molly Montgomery; no children. Third, married a Williams; no children.

6. S. B. Montgomery, born 1860, sixth child of Ira Montgomery, is an attorney in Poseyville, Ind.; married Alice Tharling; children three: 1, Charley Montgomery. 2. Iona Montgomery.

Louisa Montgomery, born Oct. 8, 1819, third child of Samuel Montgomery, Jr., married Hiram Green, a farmer. 1838; she died 1854; children six: 1. John Green, a farmer, born 1839; was a soldier in the 17th regiment Ind. Vol.; lives in Richland County, Ill.; single. 2. Dr. Samuel Montgomery Green, born 1842 was a soldier in the 17th regiment Ind. Vol. After the war he graduated at the Rush Medical College, Chicago, Ill. He practiced in Bureau County, Ill. 24 years. He then located in Dixon, Ill., and is a specialist in the eye and ear. He first married Lydia Johnson of Princeton, Ind., 1865, one child—John Green. Second, married Maria Mishner of Bureau County, Ill.; children one, _____ Mishner.

Sarah Ann Green, born 1845, third child of Hiram Green, Sr., married Alexander McClure, 1865, a miller at Patoka, Ind. He was a soldier in the 17th regiment Ind. Vol.; children two: 1. Katie Louisa McClure, single; she is a nurse by profession. 2. Mary Ellen McClure born 1870 married Christ. Opperman of Evansville, Ind.: children one—Sophia Opperman, born 1892.

Nancy Green, born 1817, fourth child of Hiram Green, Sr., died in infancy.

Dr. William Green, born 1850, died 1879; fifth child of Hiram Green, Sr.; enlisted in Co. H, 17th regiment Ind. Vol., 1864, not quite 15 years old, and served till the close of the war after which he graduated from the Rush Medical College, Chicago, Ill. He practiced in Whiteside County, Ill.; married Elizabeth Kane, 1871; children two: 1, Kate Green, married and lives in Iowa. 2. Hiram Green. Jr., single.

And Their Descendants

Louisa Green, born 1852, sixth child of Hiram Green, Sr., married Wm. H. McMurtry, in 1872, of Richland County. Ill.; children two: 1. Mary Ruby McMurtry taught in the public schools of Illinois for three years; married John S. C. Nichols, a grain merchant of Noble. Ill.; children five: 1. Fred Green Nichols; 2. Lee Curtis Nichols, a twin to Fred G.; 3. Horace L. Nichols; 4. Elizabeth C. Nichols; 5. Esther L. Nichols. 2. Elizabeth McMurtry, single; graduated in the scientific course in the Northern Illinois Normal at Dixon, Ill., in the class of 1901. She is a post-graduate in the oratorical department of that school and at present, 1902, is teaching in the public schools of Texas.

Romelia Montgomery, born June 12, 1823, fourth child of Samuel Montgomery, Jr. He was a Federal soldier in an Illinois regiment; married Eliza Cleveland, 1848; children six: 1. Samuel L. Montgomery, born Jan. 23, 1848, died 1871. 2. Nancy L. Montgomery, born April 22. 1849. 3. Sarah E. Montgomery born Jan. 7, 1854, married John Fairchilds, a farmer, Nov. 2, 1878 moved to Oklahoma, 1902; children three: 1. Ira W. Fairchilds, born Sept. 12, 1880, died Aug. 11, 1898; 2. John E. Fairchilds, born April 23, 1887, died July 15, 1887; 3. Loral E. Fairchilds, born Aug. 1889.

4. John Montgomery, a farmer, born 1856, married Susan A. Eaton in 1880; lives south of Cynthiana, Ind.; children four: 1. Effie D. Montgomery, born____, died 1882. 2. Alma Montgomery married Willis Smith, 1901, a farmer near Mounts Station, Ind. 3. Wilber B. Montgomery died 1891. 4. Eva F. Montgomery.

5. George W. Montgomery, born 1858, married Emma Young; children six: 1. Ira P. Montgomery. 2. Alice M. Montgomery. 3. Ada E. Montgomery. 4. Walter Montgomery. 5. Adrian Montgomery. 6. Opal Montgomery. 6. Alice Montgomery, born May 7, 1868, married W. C. Williams, May 4, 1889; one child—Halbert Williams, born Dec. 28, 1892; died Jan. 7, 1893.

Rana C. Montgomery, born 1825, fifth child of Samuel Montgomery, Jr., died small.

Samuel Montgomery, Jr., second married Nancy Robb, nee Davis, probably 1833; children five:

Dr. David B. Montgomery, born March 26, 1834, died Sept. 1, 1885; sixth child of Samuel Montgomery, Jr.; graduated from the Rush Medical

College, Chicago, Ill., 1858, and immediately began practice at Cynthiana, Ind., and became quite a wealthy man. He was one of the best scribes in the Hush Medical College of the class of 1858, and received the compliments of the professors for the same. He was a man of fine personal appearance and a splendid conversationalist; married Margaret Whiting, about 1858; children one, Ada Montgomery, born July 2, 1867; she married Samuel Adams, Princeton, Ind., June 26, 1885. Mr. Adams is now (1903) on his second term as Auditor of Gibson County, Ind., and has an interest in the Princeton Clarion-News; children one—Fay Adams, born April 14, 1887.

Sarah E. Montgomery, born Dec. 8, 1836, seventh child of Samuel Montgomery, died single, Sept. 1854.

Dr. T. J. Montgomery, born Sept. 15, 1839, eighth child of Samuel Montgomery, Jr.; graduated from Rush Medical College, Chicago, Ill., 1833; practiced in Cynthiana, Ind., five years, then took a review course at the same school in 1869; then located in Owensville, Ind.. Oct. 17, 1869, where he is now (1903) comfortably settled in one of the best offices in town, on Main Street. He has been one of the leading physicians of this place all these years and has accumulated sufficient means to enable him to build a fine residence. Besides, he has considerable land possessions a few miles south of town, also is a stockholder in the First National Bank of Owensville, Ind. He married Lydia A. Whiting. Dec. 2, 1863; children two: 1. Jessie M. Montgomery, born Oct. 9, 1864; married Woodfin D. Robinson, Sept. 4. 1884, who is now, 1903, on a third term as Judge of the appellate Court of Indiana. He is considered one of the safest judges in the state; is a graduate of the State University at Bloomington, Ind., and a trustee of that institution. He attended law school in Virginia, and graduated in the law department at Ann Arbor, Mich. Represented Gibson County in the Legislature in 1895-6. He lives at Princeton, Ind.; children one—Virginia, born Dec. 20, 1902.

Elsie Montgomery, born Dec. 2, 1866, daughter of Dr. T. J. Montgomery, married C. B. Smith, Sept. 14, 1887. They own a fine body of Blackriver land south of Owensville, Ind. Mr. Smith is president of the First National Bank of Owensville and a stockholder in the Farmers department store at that place; also a breeder of Angus cattle. Children, two infants.

Samuel N. Montgomery, born Feb. 4, 1842, in Montgomery Township, Gibson County, Ind.; ninth child of Samuel Montgomery Jr. He was a

Corporal in Co. F, 80th regiment Ind. Vol., and served until close of the war. He was seriously wounded at the Battle of Perryville, Ky., with a musket ball, Oct. 8. 1862. Perryville is about eight miles from where his father was born in 1794.

While in the hospital at New Albany, Ind., a Mr. Samuel Montgomery, a cousin of Judge H. P. Montgomery and a brother to Commodore J. Ed. Montgomery, who commanded the Confederate fleet at Memphis, 1861, opened a letter to the soldier through a mistake. He immediately sought out the soldier and made due apology, and they traced back their relationship, which was clear at that time but is not remembered at this date. However, he would have the soldier visit him in his elegant mansion and insisted that he should make his house his home as long as he remained at New Albany. There were some young ladies in the family at that time and the soldier spent many pleasant hours with them. I understand that two of these ladies still live in that town and the soldier now (1903) lives about one and one half miles north of Cynthiana, Ind., on part of the farm on which he was raised. He married Melissa Redman of Cynthiana, Ind., Nov. 2, 1865. Children eight: 1. Essie Montgomery, born Oct. 8, 1860, died Oct. 26, 1895. She finished her education at the Danville, Ind., normal; taught several years in the public schools; married C. E. Wilkinson of Cynthiana, Ind., Sept. 27, 1889; children one— Lela Wilkinson, born July 18, 1890. 2. Otis Montgomery, a farmer, born Nov. 10, 1868, single 1903. 3. 4. and 5. Children--died small. 6. James R. Montgomery, born Sept. 16, 1879; graduated at the Independent Normal at Valparaiso, Ind.; taught in the public schools; is a student in the P. S Medical College at Chicago, Ill.; single 1903. 7. Ruby Montgomery, born Sept. 23, 1881; single 1903; is taking the scientific course in the Independent Normal at Valparaiso, Ind. 8. David W. Montgomery, born Aug. 21, 1886; is taking the high-school course at Cynthiana, Ind.

Jesse M. Montgomery, a farmer, tenth child of Samuel Montgomery, Jr. born May 15. 1845, in Gibson County, Ind.; is a staunch Republican and represented Gibson County in the legislature in the 55th regular session, which began Jan. 10. 1887; now, March 17, 1902, lives about one mile north of Cynthiana, Ind.; married Lemira Benson. Nov. 22, 1866. Children three: 1. Oscar Paul Montgomery, born Aug. 21, 1808, died May 20, 1895, graduated in the scientific course at the National Normal University of Lebanon, Ohio, in the class of 1891; taught in the public schools. He was a member of the McReynolds & Montgomery hardware and furniture firm, Cynthiana, Ind. He married Olive L. Smith, June 29, 1892: children one—Jessie Corrine Montgomery, born May 27, 1893. 2. Ella L. Montgomery, born Dec. 21, 1870: received her education in the Gibson and Posey County schools and taught successfully in the Cynthiana schools of Posey County; married Dr. U. O. Bixler, April 19, 1893; children one, Wilhelmina Mae Bixler born Jan. 24, 1901. 3. Dr. Samuel Benson Montgomery, born July 6, 1874; graduated in the Owensville, Ind., high-school, class of 1892: finished his education at Wabash College. Ind.; graduated from the University Medical College, Louisville, Ky., 1898; commenced practice immediately in Posey County and is now (1903) enjoying a nice practice at Cynthiana. Ind.; children one, Mary Leona Montgomery, born March 5, 1901.

And Their Descendants

CHAPTER XII.

THOMAS MONTGOMERY, SR, OR "PURTY OLD TOM MONTGOMERY THE DEER KILLER," BORN 1745.

In the preceding chapters we have given some account of nine children of Hugh Montgomery, Sr. We now take up the tenth and youngest, Thomas Montgomery, known all over Gibson County in his day as "Purty Old Tom the Deer Killer." The prefix "Purty" was attached to his name on account of his upright, lithe carriage and portly appearance. It is said that he was straight as an arrow. The "Deer Killer" came from the fact that he killed 160 deer around the springs on the Colonel Jones farm, now owned by Lieutenant Wm. Jones, his great-grandson. This was on the south-west quarter of section 12, town 3, range 12 west.

He came to Indiana in 1805 and marked an oak tree by the spring on what has for a long time been known as the Smith Mounts farm; then the Thomas A. Mounts, and now (1902) as the C. B. Smith farm—south-east quarter of section 24, town 3, range 12 west.

He then returned to Mount Sterling, in Montgomery County, Ky., in order to bring his family to Indiana; but for some reason he did not return to Indiana until 1806. When he arrived at the quarter-section on which he had marked the oak tree he found the land occupied by a man, in a rail pen for a house, by the name of Hamer —now known as Heubner. George Heubner of near Poseyville, Ind., is a descendant of that man.

So "Purty Old Tom" drove on north to those springs a little south-west of Owensville and made a temporary stop on the Jones land above referred to. It appears that he did not desire this land, as shortly afterward he moved a little south-east to the south-east quarter of section 13, town 3, range 12 west and entered that land in 1807. This was 95 years ago. This land descended to his youngest son, Walter Crockett Montgomery, and is now in possession of Smith Miller Montgomery, the youngest son and the 19th child of Walter Crockett Montgomery.

"Purty Old Tom" was born in Roanoke County, Virginia, 1745; was married to Martha Crockett in Virginia, 1767. She was a sister to Col. Joseph Crockett, of the Revolutionary War, and an own cousin to the famous Davie Crockett of Tennessee, "who so gallantly gave up his life at the old Alamo, bravely fighting for Texas independence."

"Purty Old Tom," when a boy 12 years old, with his gun defended from a block-house his mother and several other women and children, killing one Indian and wounding several others. On some one complimenting his courage and bravery he remarked that it was a case of necessity—"foight or doi" (in the Irish brogue). This circumstance was often related by "Roane" Ike Montgomery, *a,* nephew of his, who was born 1799 and died May 14, 1900, aged 91 years.

"Purty Old Tom" was one of the seven sons of Hugh Montgomery. Sr., and took part in the Revolutionary War; after which he lived in Montgomery County, Va., near the head waters of the Roanoke Springs, not far from Shawsville, Va., until 1796, when be moved to Mount Sterling, in Montgomery County, Ky., and remained here until they emigrated to Indiana in 1806. He was the first of the family to settle in Knox, now Gibson County; children eight: 1. Hugh, 2. Molly, 3. Joseph, 4. Jane. 5. and 6. Thomas and Isaac—twins. 7. Patsy, 8. Walter Crockett.

1. Hugh Montgomery, Jr., born 1768, died in Virginia, 1780, at the age of 12 years.

2. Molly Montgomery, born 1770, married Mathias Mounts, in Kentucky and came to Indiana in 1806. He was a soldier in the war of 1811-12 and fought in the battle of Tippecanoe. Nov. 7, 1811. They settled on the northeast quarter of section 27, town 3, range 11 west, on a farm now owned by John Embree. Children twelve.

It seems that at one time we had almost lost trace of this family, but further research brought considerable information concerning them. There are quite a number of the descendants of Patsy Mounts, No. 9. of this family, who married Henry Ayers, Sr., in Gibson County, Ind., whose genealogy will follow in this connection. We here insert a very interesting letter concerning other members of this family; and also the genealogy of Nancy Mounts, No. 11. Will follow in its proper place.

The Montgomerys

Albion, Ill, April 6, 1901.

Dear Mr. Montgomery:

Yours of the 4th instant received. In regard to the descendants of Molly Montgomery, N2G5, who married Mathias Mounts, personally I know very little. But I referred the matter to my father, Alhanan Emmerson, who is a grandson of hers, and found that he knew all of them and something of the history of most of them. All in the family are now dead. Stephen is buried in Edwards County. Ill.; Smith. Jr., in Iowa; Milton, somewhere in the South; Hugh, about Davenport, Iowa; Joseph and Silas, in Bluegrass, Iowa; Polly Stennett, at or near Red Oak, Iowa; Selia Hunt and Jane Morse, in San Bernardino, Cal.; Nancy married Allen Emmerson, Sept. 17, 1810, and died Dec. 5, 1876, and lies in the Little Prairie cemetery, three miles west of Albion, Ill. We have no record of any of the family except Nancy, the mother of my father, and consequently I cannot give exact dates. Father knows considerable about several of the before-mentioned family, and if you desire I can write you more in detail about some of them. Jane and Selia have especially interesting histories, both being Mormons and emigrating westward with that sect. Wayne Stennett, of Iowa, a son of Polly Mounts-Stennett, could no doubt give you information regarding several of the family.

Yours truly,

JOHN W. EMMERSON.

With the above information we will now give the genealogy of Patsy Mounts, the ninth child in this family. She married Henry Ayers, Sr., about 1817; children 10:

1. James Ayers, born Oct. 26, 1818, died Feb. 20, 1877; first married Margaret Woods, who was born Aug. 1, 1821, died June 3, 1851; children three: 1. David Ayers, born April 19, 1842, died Feb. 22, 1851,

2. Martha J. Ayers, born Aug. 18. 1845; married William Brokaw, Nov. 1868, a farmer and grain dealer of Ft. Branch, Ind.; children nine: 1, Eva Brokaw, married Ellis Woods—children two Oscar and Fay Woods; 2, Lucy Brokaw, married Albert Miller—children two, Raymond and Dale Miller; 3. John Brokaw, married Anna French, no children; 4. Arthur Brokaw married

Nannie Long, one child; 5. Albert Brokaw, married Clyde Glasby, one child; 6. Weslie Brokaw, single; 7. Rosa Brokaw, died at 16 years; 8. Florence Brokaw, single 1901; 9. Jesse Brokaw, single 1901.

3, Isaac Ayers, born Sept. 11, 1850; married Margaret E. Montgomery, Feb. 1, 1871; children five.

James Ayers, Sr., second married Sarah Ann Davis, Sept. 1, 1851; she was born July 3, 1828; children three:

1. Infant.

2. Azariah Ayers, born Dec. 14, 1855; married Alice Cooper, Dec. 8, 1877, and now (1903) lives near Dyersburg, Tenn.; children seven: 1. Galion Ayers.
2. Claude Ayers, 3. Maud Ayers, 4. Eva Ayers, 5. Grover Ayers, dead, 6. Mary Ayers, 7. Infant.

3. Margaret Ayers, born Nov. 22, 1857, married Jonah Lagrange, Dec. 23, 1880, who was born July 27, 1858; he is a large farmer and a business man of Princeton, Ind.; children three: 1. George Lagrange, born Oct. 28, 1881, died Sept. 21, 1894. 2. Freddie Lagrange, born March 11, 1890, died April 18. 1890. 3. Clarence Lagrange, born Feb. 21, 1894.

Nancy Ayers, born about 1820, second child of Henry, Sr.
David Ayers, born about 1822, third child of Henry, Sr., died single.
Azariah Ayers, fourth child of Henry, Sr., born about 1824; married Abagail Alexander; one child—Albert Ayers, a lawyer in Indianapolis, Ind.; married Emma Lewis; children three: 1. Raymond Ayers. 2. Maria Ayers. 3. Infant.
Azariah Ayers, born 1824, second married Elizabeth Gambrel; children seven: 1. Henry, married Ida Thornburg; children four: 1. Elsie; 2. ___; 3. Fred; 4.___. 2. Hiram, dead. 3. George, dead. 4. James, dead. 5. Joseph. 6. Abbie; married Ben Symonds: children three: 1, Grover; 2.___; 3.___. 7. Edward, married___.

Azariah Ayers, born 1824, third married Mary Westfall; one child, ___.
Eliza J. Ayers, fifth child of Henry Ayers, Sr., born about 1826, married William Alexander, who lives near Emden, Ill.; children live: 1. Henry. 2. Fannie. 3. David. 4. William. 5. Infant.

The Montgomerys

Henry Ayers, Jr., born about 1828, sixth child of Henry Ayers, Sr., was at one time chief of police at Evansville, Ind.; married Ellen Mauck; children nine: 1. Infant. 2. Joseph Ayers, married; children two: 1. Henry Ayers; 2. ___.

William Ayers, third child of Henry Ayers, Jr., married Mary Kingsbury; one child—Edith Ayers.

Ben Ayers, fourth child of Henry, Jr., dead.
5. Alice Ayers, married Henry Kriphy; children three.
6. Hattie Ayers, married Wm. Gray; children three.
7, Julius Avers, married___; children one—Ray Ayers.
8. Pearl Ayers.
9. James Ayers, dead.

Louise Ayers, born about 1830, seventh child of Henry Ayers, Sr., first married Louis Marvel; one child—Amelia Marvel, married Wm. Swanson, a lumber dealer in Evansville, Ind.; children one— Albert Swanson.

Louise Ayers, second married Hiram Farquhar; one child—Lilly Farquhar, married Robert Davis; no children.

Louise Ayers third married Wm. Crawford of Owensville, Ind.; no children; she now lives in Garden City, Kansas.

8. Francis Ayers, born about 1832, son of Henry Ayers, Sr., married Lucy E. Orastead. They have a good farm north-east of Fort Branch, Ind., and now (1903) live in Ft. Branch; children four: 1. Abbie Ayers, died one year old. 2. Elizabeth Ayers, married Henry Davis; children three: 1. Frank Davis; 2. Mollie Davis; 3. Harry Davis. 3. Harvey Ayers, died 25 years old. 4. Hamilton Ayers, died 25 years old.
9. Polly Ann Ayers, born about 1834, daughter of Henry Ayers, Sr. married Perry Hargrove; children two: 1. Willis Hargrove, married Louella Mauck; children two: 1. Charles Hargrove: 2. Mabel Hargrove. 2. Nannie Hargrove, married Douglass Barker; children two: 1. Perry Barker; 2. Martha Barker.
10. Julia Ayers, born about 1836, daughter of Henry Ayers, Sr., died small.

Nancy Mounts, eleventh child of Molly Montgomery-Mounts, married Allen Emmerson, 1810, and moved to Albion, Ill.; children thirteen: 1. Martha Emmerson, married Isaac Greathouse; children four:

1. Francis Greathouse, first married Eunice Wright, children five; second married Jane Shilling, children three: 1. Timothy Greathouse, a farmer near West Salem, Ill, married, children four; 2. Nancy; 3. Jane; 4. Ellen Greathouse—no information. 2. Jersey Greathouse married Henry Vandeveer, a farmer near West Salem, Ill; children three: ___. 3. Alta Greathouse married Wm. Vandeveer: children three, ___. 4. Mary Greathouse, married Richard Roby; children four, ___. 5. and 6. Walter and Ella Greathouse. 7. Chester Greathouse, married; children one, ___. 8. Cleveland Greathouse.

Indiana Emmerson, second child of Nancy Mounts-Emmerson; no information.

Jesse Emmerson, third child of Nancy Mounts-Emmerson, was a prominent man in Edwards County, Ill. He was County clerk for several terms; was also sheriff of the County and filled other responsible positions in the County; married Samantha Sperry: children four: 1. Morris Emmerson is editor and publisher of the Register at Mt. Vernon, Ill.: children four: 1. Annie; 2. Ray; 3. George; 4. Ethel. 2. Charles Emmerson is a banker at Albion, Ill.; married Mary Bomhill. 3. Louis Emmerson is a merchant and banker at Mt. Vernon, Ill; married Onnie Matthews; children two: 1. Aline; 2. Dorothy. 4. Louise Emmerson married Otto King, a merchant at Sullivan, Ind.: children five: 1. Arthur; 2. Emmerson; 3. Elsie; 4. Marie; 5.___.

Sanford Emmerson, fourth child of Nancy Mounts-Emmerson, married Sarah Willis; children six: 1. Allen Emmerson is a minister in the Christian church and an ex-County judge of Eureka, Kansas; married___, children two: 1. ___Emmerson; 2. Oriel Emmerson, now Mrs. French. David Emmerson, second child of Sanford Emmerson, is a farmer in Oklahoma; married, children two, ___. Martha Emmerson, third child of Sanford Emmerson, married Jason Bunting, a retired farmer of Albion, Ill.; children four: 1. Fanny Bunting married John May, a farmer near Albion, Ill.; one child, ___. 2. Hattie Bunting married Orange Edwards, a farmer near Albion, Ill.; children two: 1. Mattie Edwards: 2, ___, 3. Sarah Bunting, married John Shepard, a farmer living near Albion, Ill.; children two, ___. 4. Kate Bunting married Henry Longborn, a farmer near Albion, Ill.; children two, ___. Nelly Emmerson, fourth child of Sanford Emmerson, married Frank Coles, a furniture dealer in Albion, Ill.; children four: 1. Eva. 2. Frederick, dead. 3. Kate. 4. Constance. Eva Coles married George Smith, a dentist in Virginia, Ill.: one child—Rova Venetta Smith.

Hugh Emmerson, fifth child of Sanford Emmerson. married Selina Bunting; children five: 1. Mary Emmerson, married Osel Willis, a farmer in Edwards County, Ill.; children five: 1. America Willis, married Morris Johnson, a farmer near Taylorville, Ill.; children five: 1. Lottie; 2. Alice; 3. Albert; 4. Kate; 5. Chester. 2. Lucy Willis, married Thomas W. Gibson, a farmer near Grayville, Ill.; no children. 3. Frank Willis; no information. 4. Mary Willis married Edson Brickett, dead. 5. Jennie Willis, married David Lewis; no children. 2. Rosa.

3. Bradford. 4. Delbert. 5. Olive Emmerson—children of Hugh Emmerson; no information.

Charles Emmerson, sixth child of Sanford Emmerson, married and has several children: no further information.

Mary Emmerson, fifth child of Nancy Mounts-Emmerson — no information.

Jane Emmerson, sixth child of Nancy Mounts-Emmerson, married B. F. Willis, a farmer; children four: 1. Sarah. 2.___. 3. Jesse. 4. James Willis, a farmer near West Salem, Ill., married Ma/Tilton; children four: 1. Mabel; 2. Hollis; 3___ and 4.___.

Elizabeth Emmerson, seventh child of Nancy Mounts-Emmerson, married James C. F. Hall, a minister in the Christian church; both dead; no children.

Harriet Emmerson, eighth child of Nancy Mounts-Emmerson, married George Green, a retired farmer near Albion. Ill.; children three: 1. Charles Green, dead. 2. Henry Green, dead. 3. Ida Green married Wm. Cindlend, a harness dealer in Albion, Ill.; children two: 1. Edith Cindlend; 2. Marion Cindlend.

Nancy Emmerson, ninth child of Nancy Mounts-Emmerson, married Wright W. Willis, a blacksmith in Ellenery, Ill.; children four: 1. Olive Willis, dead. 2. Sanford Willis, a restaurant keeper in Eureka, Kansas; married, one child. 3. Louis Willis Liveryman, Golden Gate, Ill., married Jane Gilliard; children two: 1. Lottie; 2. Alva Gilliard. 4. Edward Willis—no information.

Alhanon Emmerson, born April 13, 1830, tenth child of Nancy Mounts-Emmerson, retired farmer of Albion, Ill., married Emily Woods; children five:

1. Harry Emmerson, who once made application for a cadet at West Point Military Academy and was rejected on account of physical disability; is well educated and talks fluently in several languages; has traveled extensively and is a civil engineer and railroad builder, and is now (1901) in New Chwang, North China. He visited Col. Denby, the United States minister to China, and was cordially received and invited into his house and introduced to the colonel's family.

2. Wm. W. Emmerson is local editor on the Mt. Vernon (Ill.) daily Register.

3, Frank Emmerson is a passenger brakeman on the Big Four railroad, Indianapolis, Ind.; married Katie Howard; children three: 1, Beulah. 2, Jesse. 3, June.

4. John W. Emmerson, fourth child of Alhanon, is well educated; is superintendent of the Albion, Ill., schools, and has done considerable work in County normals, and has been untiring in assisting me in collecting material of this branch of the family. On account of the poor health of his wife he contemplates moving to Colorado in the near future. Wherever Mr. Emmerson locates he will prove a welcome and useful citizen. He married Margaret Hitchcock; children one—Theodora Emmerson.

5. George Emmerson is a farmer in Wayne County, Ill.; married Lucy Giel; children two: 1. Emily. 2., Elhanan.

Allen Emmerson, eleventh child of Nancy Mounts-Emmerson. Married___; one child—Isalena Emmerson; first married David McCullum; children four: 1. Charles McCullum, a farmer in Wayne County, Ill.; married Kate Limes; children four: 1. Alma; 2. Alta; 3. David; 4. Lyman.

2. Frances McCullum married Wm. Kessler, a mechanic in Vincennes, Ind.; children four: 1. Clara; 2. George; 3. Grace; 4. Frank.

3. Daniel McCullum, a farmer in Wayne County, Ill., married Alma Parks; children two: 1. Ruth; 2. Louis.

4, Martha McCullum, married Charles Rose; children four: 1. Harry: 2. Mabel; 3. Ethel; 4, Blanch.

Isalena Emmerson second married Marion Williams; children four: 1. Henry W. Williams, married Mary Snelling; children three: 1. Laura; 2. Nelly; 3. Virgil. 2. Wm. Williams, married Mary Wade; children one—Mamie. 3.___. 4. Mary Williams married Jesse Gray.

Lucy Emmerson, twelfth child of Nancy Mounts-Emmerson, married Edwin Dickson of Paskin, Wisconsin; children four: 1. William, 2. Elmer, dead. 3. Charles. 4. Francis Dickson, traveling salesman, Minneapolis, Minn.

Eliza Emmerson, thirteenth child of Nancy Mounts-Emmerson, married James T. Craig; children four: 1. Horace J. Craig, a merchant at Ordmore, I. T.; married Anna Tribe; children one—Burnett Craig. 2. Allen Craig. 3. Alice Craig, married Harry Brown, deputy postmaster, Albion, Ill.; no children. 4. Harry Brown.

JUDGE JOSEPH MONTGOMERY.

Joseph Montgomery, third child of "Purty Old Tom" Montgomery, was born in Virginia, March 3, 1773: died in 1824. He married Nancy Davis in Kentucky and came with his father to Indiana, 1806, and settled on the north-east quarter of section 33, town 3, range 11 west. This place is now known as the Emily Armstrong farm. By some means he lost this valuable tract of land and then moved to the neighborhood of Poseyville, Ind., and settled on what is known as the Wesley Jacques farm. He probably owned two farms in that locality, as at one time he lived on another farm in that neighborhood. He was in the war of 1812, in the company of Captain Warrick, and took part in the battle of Tippecanoe. He was one of the associate judges of Gibson County in 1814, and held other offices of trust. His wife, Nancy Davis, was born Jan. 1, 1874; died Nov. 20, 1849. They were buried on the farm of their son, Roane Ike Montgomery, on the south-east quarter of section 2, town 3, range 12 west, now owned by America Keneipp. Children seven: Isaac, William, Patsy, Thomas Jefferson, Polly, Betsy, and Nancy.

And Their Descendants

1. Isaac Montgomery, born 1799, died May 14, 1890, aged 91 years; was known as "Roan Ike," on account of his hair having become a mixed roan by the time he was 18 years of age. He was a large, well-built man, six feet tall, and weighed over 200 pounds. He was the most active man in Gibson County in his day. He could run and jump 22 feet and then turn around and jump 22 feet back over the same ground. Other men could jump 22 feet one way, but could not do the same back over the same ground. He was constable of Montgomery Township for seven years. He first married Polly Mounts, sister to Garrad Mounts. Children, three.

Second, married Caroline Sharp, who died April 18, 1885; children five:
1. Permelia Montgomery, born April 18, 1825, died small.
2. Thomas Montgomery, born Sept. 20, 1827, married Rachel Montgomery, Dec. 22, 1861, daughter of Houston Montgomery, children four: 1. Permelia A. Montgomery, born June 3, 1863, died Aug. 20, 1863. 2. Burgess Montgomery, born March 19, 1868: was a soldier in Co. K, 159th regiment Ind. Vol., in the Spanish-American War; enlisted June 18, 1898; discharged Nov. 25, 1898; single in 1903. 3. Oscar Montgomery, born Feb. 2, 1870, died Aug. 16, 1870. 4. Thomas Montgomery, born June 7, 1871, died small.
3. Elizabeth Montgomery, born Nov. 8. 1829, died small.
4. Benjamin Montgomery, first child by his second wife, born July 5, 1840; first married Emily Kesterson, 1863, who died March 1885; children 3: 1. Wm. S. Montgomery, born July 29, 1864. 2. Florence L. Montgomery, born June 8, 1866. 3. Clara Montgomery, born July 16, 1869. Benjamin Montgomery second married___, children two: 1. Isaac Montgomery. 2. Juanita Montgomery.
5. Wm. Montgomery, born Jan. 1842, was a soldier in the 65th regiment Ind. Vol.; died at Henderson, Ky., June 29, 1863, single.
6. Joseph C. Montgomery, born April 7, 1846, died at the home of his brother-in-law. J. M. F. Montgomery, Dec. 6, 1885, single.
7., James D. Montgomery, born Sept. 10, 1848, died May 16, 1849.
8. George W. Montgomery, born July 4, 1850; died in Missouri, March 16, ___; married Amanda Osborn; children five: 1. Addie. 2, Charley. 3. Maggie. 4. Tommie. 5. Nettie.
9. Isaac Montgomery, born 1852, died small.
10. Mary E. Montgomery, born June 20, 1854, married J. M. F. Montgomery, a farmer, May 6, 1875; he taught several years in public schools; has stock in the Owensville Milling Co.; lives southeast of

Owensville, Ind.; no children, but they raised Burgess Montgomery (see above) and Elsie Ayers, relatives.

Roane Ike Montgomery, above mentioned, was a grandson of "Purty Old Tom" Montgomery, and not a nephew, as stated on page ___, and he died in 1890 instead of 1900.

Colonel William Montgomery, born 1801, second child of Joseph Montgomery, Sr., was a colonel in the Indiana State Militia, and was a remarkably shrewd and fine-looking man. He was a County commissioner 1837 to 1842; was a member of the state legislature of Indiana 1843-4. He lived on the south-east quarter section 17, town 3, range 11 west, and died there in 1847, and was the second person buried in what is known as the Joseph Clark cemetery, on the above quarter-section of land. A child of his was the first one buried there. He had sold his farm in 1847, preparatory to moving to Manard County, Ill., to which County his family moved after his death. He married Peggy Stone about 1826; children 12: Wesley, Patsy, Joseph, Dorcas, Sarah Jane, Nancy, Lucy, Thomas, Levi, Elizabeth, Kate, and William.

Wesley Montgomery, born 1827, married Polly Mounts, in Gibson County, Ind. They moved to Manard County, Ill., probably about 1847 or '48, and he now (1902) lives in Mason City, Ill.; children seven: 1. Larkin Montgomery, a farmer, married Jane Davidson; children two: 1. Charley Montgomery; 2. Nancy Montgomery. John Montgomery, second child of Wesley Montgomery, single. Thomas Montgomery, third child, a farmer, married Laura Barnell; children seven: 1. Jesse; 2. Edward; 3. Roy; 4. Alice; 5. Nola; 6. Mary; 7. Lucilla. Asa Montgomery, fourth child of Wesley Montgomery, married Dora Smith; one child—Millard Montgomery. Charley Montgomery, fifth child of Wesley, married Elizabeth Sutton; children two: 1. Earl Montgomery; 2. Gladys Montgomery. Mary Montgomery, sixth child of Wesley, married G. S. Bollinger, a merchant; children two: 1. Bennie Bollinger; 2. Alice Bollinger. Louella Montgomery, seventh child of Wesley, born Feb, 10, 1868 married F. B. McKinnan, a lawyer in Bloomington. Ill.; children four: 1. Thomas Wesley, 2. Ruth; 3. Rachel; 3. Esther. Ruth and Rachel were twins.

2. Patsy Montgomery, born May 4, 1828, married John Lowery Knowles about 1846 who was born March 1, 1823; lives on southeast quarter of section 23, town 3, range 12 west, known as the Nicholson farm, and later

as the Green Raspberry farm, near Antioch church, in Montgomery township, Gibson County. They have attended strictly to farming and have accumulated quite a good fortune, being considered among the wealthiest people in Montgomery Township. They had fifteen children: 1. Lucinda; 2. Zerelda; 3. Isaac N.; 4. Calvin; 5. Charity; 6. Cordelia; 7. George A.; 8. William Henry; 9. Samuel Nathan; 10. Ellis; 11. Francis Marion; 12. Martha Wilmina; 13. James; 14. Cynthia; 15. Sarah Ellen.

1. Lucinda Knowles, born Oct. 4, 1847, married George Garten, Feb. 27, 1867. He was born Jan. 13, 1845. They moved to Solomon City, Kansas, where she died Dec. 23, 1887; children seven: 1. Nancy E. Garten, born Dec. 15, 1868, married Wm. Shultz, May 25, 1887, a farmer of Gypson, Kan.; children six: 1. Alvin Shultz, born Jan. 18. 1888; 2. A. Elizabeth Shultz born April 1, 1889; 3. Henrietta E. Shultz, born Sept. 16, 1890: 4. J. Elmer Shultz, born March 24, 1892; 5. W. Roy Shultz, born June 18, 1897, died Feb. 4, 1899; 6. Ethan Shultz, born Oct. 5, 1900. 7. Martha Garten, born Sept. 25, 1870, married Lawrence O. Simpson, a farmer, Feb. 14, 1900. They live four miles west of Owensville. Ind. She was a teacher in the public schools for several years; one child—Laurie A. Simpson, born July 18, 1901.

3. Mary F. Garten, born March 16, 1872, married Robert Gump, a farmer, Feb. 12, 1896. They live at Holland, Kansas; children three: 1. Benny F. Gump, born May 27, 1897; 2. Pearl L. Gump, born June 1, 1898; 3. Deborah Gump, born May 23, 1900.

4. Rebecca J, Garten, born Sept. 3, 1873, married Oliver Darling, a poultry dealer in Gypson, Kansas, Sept. 27, 1893. He was born Sept. 15, 1872; children two: 1. Hattie O. Darling, born Oct. 8, 1894; 2. Vercie Darling, born March 10, 1898.

5. Rosa Garten, born Dec. 16, 1875, married Samuel W. Montgomery, a mechanic of Kansas City, Mo., May 22. 1901.

6. John L. Garten, a farmer, born Aug. 16, 1878, of Abilene, Kansas, married Jessie Leslie, Oct. 13, 1897; children one—Luther Garten, born Aug. 29, 1899.

7. Marshall Garten, born April 3. 1881—single.

2. Serelda Knowles, born____; married Samuel Hunter about 1876; children four: 1. Leslie Hunter, born 1877, is a teacher in the public schools; single, 1903. 2. Versa Hunter, born 1879, married Harry Pollard, 1897, a farmer; children two: 1. Ruth Pollard, born 1898; 2. Blanch Pollard, born 1900. 3. Cleopatra Hunter, born 1881. 4. Infant

3. Isaac N. Knowles, a farmer, born Jan. 23, 1853; is a deacon in the Owensville General Baptist church; married Martha E. Cantrell, Dec. 5, 1875, Rev. D. M. Shoemaker officiating. She was born July 2, 1854. Children seven: 1. Ada Knowles, born Sept. 22, 1876, married John Gardner, a miller, Dec. 3, 1902. 2. Lere Knowles, born July 5, 1878. 3. Cora Knowles, born Nov. 11, 1882. 4. Luther Knowles, born April 30, 1885. 5. and 6. Loy and Soy, twins, born June 25, 1887. 8. Ensel Knowles, born April 29, 1895.

4. Calvin Knowles died small.

5. Charity Knowles, born March 23, 1856, married Joseph Wellborn, a farmer, Jan. 4, 1877; children three: 1. Ellis Wellborn, a farmer, born Nov. 15, 1877, single 1903. 2. Ethel Wellborn, born Sept. 20, 1880, died April 26, 1901. 3. Arvey Wellborn, born June 13, 1883, is a clerk in the Farmers department store at Owensville, Ind.

6. Cordelia Knowles, born Sept. 19, 1858: married Harvey Lucas, a farmer, Aug. 16, 1881. He was born Nov. 12, 1856: is a deacon in the Owensville General Baptist church. Children three: 1. Infant, born Oct. 16, 1882, died Oct. 16, 1882. 2. Lora D. Lucas, born Oct. 12, 1883. 3. Edgar W. Lucas, born Feb. 13, 1885.

7. George A. Knowles, a farmer, born ___, married Eliza Smith, Aug. 6, 1882: children three: 1. Grace Knowles, born 1883. 2. Infant, born 1885. 3. Letha Knowles, born 1888.

8. William Henry Knowles, a farmer, born___, married Flora Daugherty, Feb. 22, 1883; children four: 1. Elsie Knowles, born Feb. 1884. 2. Orie Knowles, born 1885. 3. Elva Knowles, born 1887. 4. Infant, born 1891. 5. Fay Knowles, born 1893.

9. Samuel Nathan Knowles, a farmer, born June 3, 1864; was a candidate on the Democrat ticket for County treasurer in 1902; married Zerelda Martin, July 1, 1886; no children.

10. Ellis Knowles died small.

11. Francis Marion Knowles, a farmer, born July 3, 1867, married Mary Clark, Sept. 15, 1885. She was born Sept. 23, 1866; children four: 1. Stella Knowles, born Aug. 22, 1887, died Jan. 9, 1892. 2. Nola Knowles, born July

19, 1891. 3. William Ersel Knowles, born May 8, 1895. 4. Vesper Adrian Knowles, born July 22, 1897.

12. James Knowles.

13. Cynthia Knowles.

14. Mina Knowles, born March 1871, married Jesse Lucas, a farmer, Jan. 10, 1897; children four: 1. Elmer Lucas, 1898. 2. Hazel Lucas, born 1899. 3. Ethel Lucas, born 1900. 4. Ralph Lucas, born 1901.

15. Sarah Ellen Knowles.

Joseph Montgomery, third child of Colonel William Montgomery, born 1831, was a soldier in the Federal army in the Civil War: married Mahala Montgomery, daughter of Martin Montgomery; children one—Ella Montgomery.

Dorcas Montgomery, born 1833, fourth child of Col. Wm. Montgomery, married Isaiah Wilkinson in Missouri; children___.

Sarah Jane Montgomery, born 1835, fifth child of Col. Wm., married John Roberts, a farmer north of Owensville, about 1858. He died April 21, 188-1; children three: 1. W. T. Roberts, a farmer, born June 26, 1859; taught in the public schools; married Mary Stone, Aug. 31, 1882, and she died Aug. 28, 1902; children three: 1. Arthur F. Roberts, born Aug. 26, 1883, died April 9, 1893; 2. Mabel J. Roberts, born May 8. 1896; 3. Myrtle L. Roberts, born June 30, 1899. Louisa Roberts, born Aug. 22, 1862, second child of Sarah Jane Montgomery-Roberts, married D. C. Tichenor, a farmer and thresher, June 17, 1883; one child—Elsie L. Tichenor, born Jan. 28, 1887. Martha Roberts, born Oct. 2, 1864, third child of Sarah Jane Montgomery-Roberts, married Pinkney Armstrong, a large farmer and fruit-grower living near Bethel church, north of Owensville, Ind.; no children.

Nancy Montgomery, born 1837, sixth child of Colonel Wm. M., was the second wife of "Big" Asa Knowles; children four. Second, married James Eldredge; one child: 1. Ella Knowles. 2. Maggie Knowles. 3. and 4. Cinda and Minda Knowles, twins. 5. William Eldredge.

The Montgomerys

Lucy Montgomery, born 1819, seventh child of Col. Wm., married Ben Ellis; children three: two sons and one daughter. Thomas Montgomery, born 1841, eighth child of Col. Wm., married Mahala Montgomery, daughter of Martin Montgomery and the wife of his brother Joseph.

Levi Montgomery, born 1843, ninth child of Colonel William, was a soldier in the Federal army in the Civil War; married____.

Elizabeth Montgomery, born 1844, tenth child of Col. Wm., married a Watkins; children___.

Kate Montgomery, born 1845, eleventh child of Col. Wm., married Henry Stone in Manard County. Ill., who was a Federal soldier in the Civil War; children three: 1. Dr. Charley Stone. 2. Newton Stone. 3. Luther Stone.

William Montgomery, born 1847, twelfth child of Col. Wm., was only a few weeks old when the family moved from Gibson County, Ind., to Manard County. Ill. He is a mechanic in Mason City, Ill.; children eight: 1. Frank Montgomery. 2. James Montgomery married Grace Chesley. 3. Etta Montgomery, married Lemuel Anderson; children four: 1. John; 2. Bessie; 3. William; 4. Charles. 4. Lucy Montgomery. 5. and 6. Bertha A. and Myrtle A. Montgomery, twins. 7. Addie Montgomery. 8. Florence Montgomery.

Patsy Montgomery, born April 22, 1803, in Kentucky; died July 17, 1892; third child of Joseph Montgomery, Sr.; married Garrad Mounts, Dec. 14, 1819. She raised a large family.

Thomas Jefferson Montgomery, born Jan. 1805, in Kentucky; fourth child of Joseph Montgomery, Sr. He was quite a good business man. At one time he was justice of the peace, when those officers acted as County commissioners. He was exceptionally strong in drafting instruments of writing, such as wills, contracts, etc. He was a member of the Owensville General Baptist church, and was moderator of Liberty association of General Baptists in 1846. He was collector of taxes in Gibson County, Ind., in 1841. He was defeated for representative on the Whig ticket in 1843 by Col. Wm. Montgomery, his brother, who was on the Democrat ticket. I have understood that he was defeated by only one vote. He moved to Manard County. Ill., Nov, 1849 and located at Bee Grove. His wife died April 1865. He died Dec. 1868. He married Sally Stone, who was born 1813; Children eighteen:

And Their Descendants

1. Richard Montgomery, born probably 1830, was a soldier in the 73rd regiment Ill, Vol. Inf.; was wounded at Stone River and died in a hospital 1863; married Lucilla Knowles.

2. Wm. Montgomery, born; married Sarah Dunning; died probably 1879.

3. Catherine Montgomery, married Ira Sikes; died one year afterward; no children.

4. Elizabeth Montgomery, married J. D. Hughes and lives in Grandview, Ill.

5. James Montgomery, born in Gibson County, Indiana, Sept. 27, 1838, was a soldier in Co. G, 38th regiment Ill. Vol.; enlisted 1861, and discharged at Huntsville, Ala., 1865; married Sarah E. Steel, Sept. 20, 1866. She died March 8, 1876. Mr. Montgomery is now (1902) living in Atlanta, Ill.: children four: 1. Calvin C. Montgomery, born Jan. 3, 1868, is a physician in St. Louis, Mo.; married Lucia Ray burn; children two: Alma and Eva Montgomery. 2. Arthur Montgomery, born Aug. 8, 1869, a farmer at Middletown, Ill. married Maud Pond; one child—Herbert E. Montgomery. 3. E. W. Montgomery, born March 15, 1871, is a lawyer at Atlanta, Ill.; married Carrie Stone, Sept. 1, 1897; one child—Dean C. Montgomery, born April 8, 1899. A. D. Montgomery, born March 5, 1873, a farmer at Middletown, Ill.; married Lavina Montgomery, Jan. 3, 1901; one child—Eugene H. Montgomery, born Jan. 3, 1902. Samuel Montgomery, born 1839, was a soldier in the 10th regiment Ill. Cavalry, for three years; was hurt in a raid and died in Texas. 1864.

7. Permelia Montgomery, born____, married William Y. McLemore; died soon after; no children.

8. Charles Montgomery died 1858, 15 years old.

I understand there were ten other children in this family. They must have died small.

Polly Montgomery, born 1807 in Indiana, fifth child of Joseph Montgomery. Sr., married Richey Sumner, Sr. He was a captain in the state militia. He settled as administrator many estates in Gibson County, and was clerk of the Owensville church of General Baptists for many years; died Jan.

The Montgomerys

7. 1873; children five: 1. Louisa Sumner, born 1831, married B. F. Skelton, a farmer; children twelve: 1. Mary Skelton died small. 2. Mat Skelton married James Daugherty (see index, Daugherty, James). 3. Manerra Skelton died small. 4, Amanda Skelton, married Albert Lagrange, and they moved to Missouri, where she died; children eight: 1. Allie L.; 2. Maud; 3. Louisa L.; 4. Infant son; 5. Henry; 6. Frank; 7. Grace; 8. Ollie. 5. Infant son. 6. Ollie Skelton, married David Cleveland, Oct. 9, 1879; children four: 1. Henry; 2. Florence; 3. Horace; 4. John. 7. Ida Skelton, married Marshall Stone, a sawmill man, Aug. 4, 1881; children three: 1. Jesse Stone, born 1882; 2. Pearl Stone, born 1884, married Samuel L. Harmon, Dec. 1902; 3. John Stone, born 1886. 8. Joseph Skelton died small. 9. Richard Skelton died small. 10. Henry Skelton, single 1903. 11. Ophelia Skelton, married Edgar Lowe, a miller of Ft. Branch, Ind., June 11, 1891; children three: 1. Gertrude; 2. Lester; 3. Walter. 12. Nannie Skelton married James Williams, a liveryman in Haubstadt, Ind.; children three: 1. Arlene; 2. Leonard; 3. Van Ray.

Joseph Sumner, born 1833, second child of Richey Sumner, Sr., was an excellent good citizen; married Minerva Montgomery, daughter of Judge Thomas Montgomery, about 1852; children five:

1. Mary Sumner, born 1853, married George Pritchett of Fort Branch, Ind., Sept. 16, 1874, and they moved to Oakland City, Ind. where she died; no children. Mr. Pritchett was at one time marshal of Oakland City.

2, Louisa Sumner, born 1855, died Jan. 5, 1881; married Frank Yeager, a farmer, who died Dec. 8, 1885; children one—Harvey Yeager, a soldier in the 161st regiment Ind. Vol. in the Spanish-American War; married Mary Thompson.

3. Thomas Sumner, born 1857, lives in Evansville, Ind.; married Maud Matthews of Owensville, Ind., March 23, 1877; children six: 1, Weslie Sumner, married. 2, John Sumner, was a soldier in the 161st regiment Ind. Vol. in the Spanish-American War and afterward in the 17. S. Regular Army and served in the Philippines. 3, Aggie Sumner. 4. George. 5, Maggie. 6, Earl.

4. Oscar Sumner, born Aug. 22, 1859, retired farmer; married Elizabeth Emmerson, March 11, 1880; no children.

5. Emma Sumner, born 1831, died Nov. 18, 1884.

Robert Sumner, born Oct. 5, 1835 died Dec. 9, 1878; first married Jane Witherspoon; children two. Married second Mary E. Goodnight March 14, 1864; she died June 10, 1882; children seven:

1. Charles Sumner, born Feb. 13, 1858, single 1902.

2. Thelma Sumner, born July 3, 1863, died Nov. 5, 1886; married John Stone, July 9, 1882, who was accidentally killed by his gun slipping in his buggy.

3. Frank Sumner, born Jan. 27, 1835, died single in Alabama, June 26, 1888, while working with Sumner Bros, saw-mill.

4. Mattie Sumner, born Oct. 14, 1867, married Oscar Cantrell, Sept. 18, 1885, a barber, now in Grayville, Ill.; children three: 1. Floyd O, Cantrell, born Sept. 7, 1883, died Aug. 17, 1888; 2. Frank Cantrell, born Aug. 8, 1888; 3, Edna A. Cantrell, born July 28, 1892.

5, Effie Sumner, born Oct. 19. 1870, married Nial R. Nye, March 12, 1890, a marble dealer in Mt. Vernon, Ind.; no children.

6. Agnes Sumner, born Feb. 26, 1872, married Ross Strain of Princeton, now of Indianapolis, Ind., Oct. 19, 1892; died Sept. 22, 1893.,

7. Richard Sumner, born 1874; was killed June 3, 1889, by horses running away with a wagon.

8. Otto Sumner, born Aug. 27, 1876, died July 25, 1893.

9. Roberta M. Sumner born Nov. 26, 1878, married Frank Burgos, Nov. 12, 1899.

Isaac Sumner, born 1837, married Mary E. Richards; children two: 1. Effie C. Sumner, born ___, married W. G. Brady, April 27, 1892, who is one of the leading attorneys of Gibson County, Ind., and came within 53 votes of being elected circuit judge, thus reducing the usual majority of about 700. He graduated in the law department of the University of Virginia, June 1888, and has been a partner of the Hon. C. A. Buskirk of Princeton, Ind., since July 1, 18S8; children two: 1. John Sumner Brady, born Feb. 6, 1893. 2. Thomas Richards Brady, born March 3, 1899.

2, Florence Sumner, born ___, married John Shull, Nov. 12, 1889, a liveryman in Princeton, Ind.; children two: 1. Gladys Shull, born Sept. 30, 1890. 2. George Wyatt, born Dec. 24, 1893.

Kate Sumner, born probably 1840, died Aug. 22, 1874, married Alfred Pritchett, a farmer, who was a soldier in the 42nd regiment Ind. Vol.; children two): 1. Annie Pritchett, married Simeon Alcorn, Nov. 6, 1897; one child—Zella Alcorn. 2. Aubrey Pritchett died Dec. 12, 1884.

The Montgomerys

Betsy Montgomery, born 1809, sixth child of Joseph Montgomery, Sr., married John McFadin, 1830, in Owensville, Ind. John McFadin, with his father, Wm. McFadin, settled on what is known as McFadin's Bluff, at Mt. Vernon, Ind., in 1798. John McFadin moved to Owensville about 1825, being a widower at that time. He was a prominent man in the business affairs of Owensville. He moved to Missouri and settled near Lexington, sometime in the fifties. He was a slaveholder and a very strong partisan. During the Civil War he strongly sympathized with the Confederacy. One night he was called out of his house by a guerilla band and shot to death. Children four:

1. Nancy McFadin, born July 31, 1831. During the troubles incident to the Civil War she came to her brother-in-law, the Hon. J. W. Montgomery, of Gibson County. Ind., who was the husband of Jane McFadin, a half-sister of hers, and died here July 7, 1872.

2. Martha McFadin, born May 15, 1836, died Jan. 10, 1900. She married Mr. Morehouse, of Missouri, who was a colonel in the Federal army, and lieutenant-governor with Gov. Marmaduke of Missouri, who was a general in the Confederate army. Mr. Marmaduke died in office and Mr. Morehouse succeeded to the governorship of Missouri. Children three: 1. Nannie Morehouse. 2. Ned Morehouse. 3. Topsy Morehouse.

3. Fortunatus McFadin, born Oct. 15, 1839, was a soldier in the Confederate army from the beginning to the close of the war; married Mary M. McDowell, April 5. 1881. She was born March 15, 1841; died Jan. 3, 1902; children four: 1. and 2. Infants. 3. John Daniel, is now (1902) in the U. S. Regular Army in the Philippines. 4. Mary, at home, single. Mrs. McFadin was a graduate of the Baptist Female College, of Lexington, Mo., class of 1860, and taught many years.

Joseph McFadin, born Nov. 15, 1841; was a soldier in the Confederate army.

Nancy Montgomery, born 1811, seventh child of Joseph Montgomery, Sr., married Henry Gambrel, who was a commissioner in Gibson County, Ind., 1836-7, 1861; Children four: 1. Maria Gambrel, married David Wilhite, of Princeton, Ind.; children three—Charley, Harvey and May. 2. Mat Gambrel married Isaac Combs, of Illinois. 3. Mary Gambrel married Judge Poe of Kansas. 4. Maranda Gambrel married a Mr. Riggs of Illinois.

And Their Descendants

Jane Montgomery, born in Virginia, 1774, fourth child of "Purty Old Tom" Montgomery, married Captain Jacob Warrick in Kentucky, 1795. Captain Warrick was one of the distinguished citizens of Gibson County, Ind. He was the son of John Warrick, Sr., who was a Revolutionary soldier. Jacob Warrick was born in Greenbrier County, Va., 1773. At the age of eleven years, or in 1784, he moved to Fayette County, Ky., and settled about seven miles from Lexington. At the age of 21, or in 1794, he enlisted under the command of General Anthony Wayne. Soon they marched by Fort Defiance, in Ohio. On the 20th of August, 1794, Jacob Warrick took part in the battle at the Rapids of the Maumee River.

An incident occurred at this battle relating to Jacob Warrick which I will here relate in the language of a daughter of one of the soldiers:

"As soon as General Wayne came up with the Indians, who were in line of battle on the left bank of the river, the firing commenced. The Indians, who had more than double the number of the Americans, soon made a desperate effort to turn the left flank. General Wayne ordered a charge to be made, which was executed with great promptness. The Indians gave way. They were pursued in full speed. The company to which Warrick belonged was on the flank of the enemy next to the river. Warrick's horse was in full speed on the river bank a few paces ahead of the company, when an Indian who had concealed himself in the thicket, finding that he would be run over, darted under the neck of Warrick's horse to reach the river. Warrick, quick as thought, grabbed him by the hair of the head. (It must be understood here that a horse is as much afraid of an Indian as he would be of a bear; therefore when Warrick caught the Indian his horse reared and plunged into the air.) The shock caused Warrick to careen in the saddle, which carried him, the Indian and the horse over the precipice, headlong down the bank, to the water's edge. Warrick, being a giant in strength as well as size, clung to the Indian, who was his equal, and just at the moment when each was preparing for the combat one of Warrick's compeers leaped from the saddle down the bank of the river, and with one deadly blow of the tomahawk sent the Indian to his long home."—From an old copy of Evansville Journal, now (1903) in the possession of J. W. Jones, Midland, Ill.

Mr. Warrick's people here stoutly deny this statement of assistance by a comrade and claim that Mr. Warrick dispatched his antagonist alone and single-handed. Someone did fire a shot, and General Harrison ordered him to desist, saying that Warrick was capable of taking care of himself; at the same time saying, "You may shoot Warrick."

In 1806 Jacob Warrick came with his father-in-law, "Purty Old Tom" Montgomery, to Indiana and settled in Knox County (now Gibson), west of Owensville, on what is now (1903) known as the J. D. Thompson farm, in section 11, town 3, range 12 west , He brought with him to Indiana fine cattle, fine horses, several slaves and money. He was a close, intimate friend of Henry Clay, and often consulted with him in regard to Indiana finally becoming a slave state. Mr. Clay, who at one time later on bad eighty thousand dollars invested in slaves, always told Mr. Warrick that Indiana would not be a slave state.

Jacob Warrick, at the outbreak of the Indian war of 1811, *"raised a company of eighty men known as rangers, and at the request of General Harrison joined the main army at Vincennes, and with it marched against the Indians, and while gallantly leading a charge at Tippecanoe was mortally wounded,"* Nov. 7, 1811, and *"Major Smith, the old surveyor and schoolteacher of Gibson County, wrote Captain Warrick's will on the battle field after the battle was over. He lived two days and was buried on the battlefield where he had so bravely fought for the preservation of the lives of those he held dear, and for the safety of the homes and firesides which were so sacred to the settlers. General Harrison in his official report of the battle took occasion to commend in the highest terms the bravery and intrepid conduct displayed by Captain Warrick."*

We know but little of Captain Warrick's ancestors. We find in a history of the Montgomerys and Summervilles of Virginia and Ohio, written by Prof. Frank Montgomery, now in the signal service at Davenport, Iowa, a reference to a Jacob Warrick taken from the Pocahontas Journal, in Greenbrier County, West Virginia, who was probably an uncle of Captain Jacob Warrick.

"Warrick County, Indiana, was named in honor of Captain Warrick." It is claimed by Mr. Warrick's close friends that Gibson County, Ind., by all right and fairness should have been named in honor of Captain Warrick.

There is no monument marking the graves of those who fell at the battle of Tippecanoe. There is a plot of ground arranged something like this, the squares with names and dates being slightly raised and set in sod, with the names and dates set in gravel:

	Heroes of 1811	
Nov. 7, 1811		**Nov. 7, 1811**
	Tippecanoe	

It seems that the state should erect some kind of monument in memory of these heroes. Jacob W. Jones, of Midland, Ill., a grand-son of Captain Jacob Warrick, has said that he was willing to assist in this matter.

Jane Montgomery, his wife, was also a very remarkable woman. She was large and rather coarse-featured, but was a woman of rare good sense and fine judgment. Her carriage and every-day appearance indicated intelligence. She was a woman of wonderful endurance and courage; born in Virginia, 1774, married Jacob Warrick here in 1795; removed to Kentucky in 1796, and came to Indiana in 1806; had seven children by Captain Warrick. After his death she married Dr. John Maddox, of Kentucky, about 1813, and moved with him to the Red River country in Texas, and finally settled in Alexandria, Louisiana, 1824. Not liking that country, they returned to Indiana in 1825.

She remained in Indiana while Dr. Maddox made a prospecting visit to Illinois, near where Lincoln is now located. He died while on that visit, in 1826, and was buried in Illinois. She had three children by Dr. Maddox.

Dr. Maddox while in Indiana filled the office of assessor, in 1813 justice of peace, and represented Gibson County in the legislature probably about 1814 and '15—at least it was before Indiana became a state. After the death of Dr. Maddox his wife made herself familiar with his medical works and practiced midwifery successfully for many years. The weather never became too cold, dark or rainy for her to answer a call. Although she was large, she could ride like an Indian. Many times she rode through the thick, dark woods, guided only by the knowledge of the horse returning to its home. She was bold and courageous, and no one ever attempted to interfere with her nocturnal rides. She died in Gibson County, Indiana, Sept. 3, 1846. Her children by Captain Warrick were: 1. Montgomery; 2. Nelly; 3. Nancy; 4. John; 5. Harry; 6. Jacob G.; 7. Patsy. Children by Dr. Maddox: 1. Lucy; 2. Polly: 3. Thomas.

1. Montgomery Warrick, born 1797, near Lexington, Ky., moved to Indiana in 1806; married Patsy Jones, a sister to Col. Charles Jones, and settled on the Capt. William A. Waters farm, section 3, town 3, range 12 west, now (1903) owned by John Waters; moved to near Lincoln. Ill., 1830; children six:

1. Polly Warrick, married Herod Music; children seven. Second, married a Mr. Jackson; children five:

1. Harriet Music, married Philip Baker; children four: 1. Henry Baker died 19 years old. 2. Eliza Baker married a Delicia. 3. Samuel Baker. 4. Margaret Baker married a Mr. Morrison.

2. Charles Music married Margaret Thompson, whose father was very wealthy. Mr. Music died in about six weeks after his marriage; no children.

3. Margaret Music married George Barney. They live at Marshall. Minn. Children five: 1. Anna Barney. 2. Mary Barney. 3. Lillie Barney. 4. Samuel Barney. 5., Lizzie Barney.

4. Samuel Music, lives at Liberal, Mo.; married Nelly McFarland; children three: 1. Mabel Music; 2. William Music; 3. John Music.

5. Janie Music married Joseph Kinan of Logan County. Ill. They now (1903) live near Shelby, Neb. Mr. Kinan was a Federal soldier in the Civil War, in an Ohio regiment. This family deals largely in stock and has become very wealthy. Mrs. Kinan is a sister to Mrs. John W. Harmon of Owensville, Ind. Children seven: 1. Mattie Kinan was endowed with a fine poetical talent; married a Mr. Cotalett and died a few months after. 2. Jessie Kinan. 3. Alberta Kinan. 4. Spencer Kinan. 5. Joseph Kinan. 6. Alice Kinan married an Ellsworth. 7. Dolly Kinan.

6. Annie Music, married Henry Whitsel; children two: 1. Mary Whitsel married Albert Waterly. 2. Gertrude Whitsel.

7. Bettie Music, second wife of John W. Harmon of Owensville, Ind.; married Dec. 12, 1878. Mr. Harmon is half-owner in the Harmon & Wallace flouring mill at Owensville, Ind.; also a stockholder in the First National Bank and the Farmers department store at that place, besides having large possessions in land. Mrs. Bettie Music-Harmon, his wife, has large possessions inherited from Mr. and Mrs. Robert Skelton, her uncle and aunt, near Lincoln, Ill. Children one--Grace Harmon, born Oct. 22, 1880; married Rufus Barnett, May 29, 1901, who was in the jewelry business in Owensville; children one —Robert Harmon Barnett, born July 4, 1902.

Following are the children of Polly Warrick-Music by Mr. Jackson: 1. and 2. John and Phoebe Jackson, twins. John married Opha Fletcher; children two: Imogene and Ola Jackson. Phoebe married Henry Babbitt; children eight. 3. Willard Jackson; married____. 4. Permelia Jackson married a Jackson. 5. Susan Jackson, married a Foley; children one—Grace Foley.

Henry Clay Warrick, second child of Montgomery Warrick, died four years old. 3. Child, died small. 4. Jacob Warrick died single. 5. Martha J. Warrick married Robert Skelton, a wealthy farmer living east of Lincoln, Ill. The fine residence is at Skelton. These large possessions he and his wife, having no children, gave to Mrs. Skelton's niece, Bettie Music, whom they raised, and she married John Wesley Harmon of Owensville, Ind., just referred to.

6. Julia Warrick, the youngest child of Montgomery Warrick, married Curb Turley; children one—George Ann Turley, married James Townsend.

The Montgomerys

WILLIAM HUBBARD
A SLAVE OF MONTGOMERY WARRICK.

In connection with the history of the Montgomerys and Warricks we have made mention of the fact that they brought slaves with them to Indiana. Just here we will give a more detailed account of one of those slaves, known all over Gibson County as William Hubbard.

"Purty Old Tom" Montgomery gave "Hub," as he was commonly called, to his grandson, Montgomery Warrick, in Kentucky. Montgomery Warrick and "Hub" were about the same age, having been born in 1797. While "Hub" wore clothes the same as other people, in addition to these he always wore what was known as a hunting shirt, which was a coat, or rather a gown, which came nearly to his feet, with a leather belt buckled around the waist . The writer remembers seeing him many times, but never saw him without the "hunting shirt."

In the days of "kidnapping" in southwestern Indiana, some parties suggested to Montgomery Warrick that he had better sell "Hub," as someone would steal him, anyway. To this Mr. Warrick replied: *"I had just as leave sell a brother as Hub, therefore I will not sell him; and if any one steals him they will have to suffer the consequences."* It is not likely that it would have been very healthful to have stolen any kind of property from the Warricks of that day, and much less so to have stolen "Hub," as he could have been identified anywhere in the world, and the Warricks had the means and grit to have found him and punished the kidnappers.

"Hub" was a man of remarkable constitution, of heavy build, rather round-shouldered, with a very full breast and a very heavy, thick, short neck—so much so that there was no way that he could lie down that his head would touch the floor; therefore his large, heavy head always hung clear of the floor. He would never sleep in a bed, but always on a pallet on the floor in front of the large fireplaces of that day with his head next the fire. After he became a free man (he was always about the same as free) he at first, for a part of his time, made his home with the widow of Captain Warrick, the mother of Montgomery Warrick; and when in 1813 Dr. Maddox began to pay some attention to Mrs. Warrick "Hub" made vigorous protests and proposed doing all the work on her farm for just his board and clothes if she would not marry; at the same time giving fair warning that if she married, Hub was relieved of all further obligations. Mrs. Warrick, disregarding his protests, married Dr. Maddox—probably in September, 1813. From this date on, in a great measure, Hub became a local tramp, stopping for a few days at a time with some of the Montgomery connection, as he claimed relationship with all of them. As the Montgomerys were very numerous it generally took him about six months to make the rounds, in the meantime doing a vast amount of hard labor—principally breaking and hackling hemp and flax. It took a giant to handle these old heavy breaks, but Hub was equal to the emergency.

He was wholly without education; never was able to count twenty. He could reach nineteen, and then, like a child, would go back to 18 — 6—11, etc. He kept the time he worked by cutting notches on a stick, then he would carry that stick and the money received to the next man to see if he had been fully paid. I am not aware, however, that anyone ever tried to cheat "Hub."

He had an unquenchable appetite for whiskey, and once while he was under the influence of liquor some boys placed a wagon-bed over him and awaited the results. When he awoke he looked about and muttered to himself: "Dead—dead, and buried under a wagon bed!" After this occurred someone met him and said: "Hub, I heard you were dead." "Yes," he answered, "I did too, but I knew it was a lie as soon as I heard it."

His feet turned out very seriously, and it was told on him that one time he crossed a wheat-field, nearly ready to be harvested, and on his way back when he reached this field he discovered that someone had gone through the wheat with a sled. This caused him to Income very indignant, and he was cursing and swearing and heaping vengeance on any one that would treat a neighbor in that way, when someone passing called his attention to the fact that the damage had been caused by himself with his turned-out feet. This is an old story and may not have happened in this way.

A few years after this the Hon. Thomas Jefferson Montgomery, while a candidate on the Whig ticket for representative—against Col. William Montgomery, his brother, nominated by the Democrats —made a speech in the old public building on the public square in Owensville, in which he related the circumstances above, and said that if the Democrats would do likewise and look backward over their own record and note the devastation behind them, they would have no just cause to complain of their neighbors.

The Montgomerys

A few days after this came the election, and "Hub" as usual was on hand. The Democrats called his attention to the exposures that Jeff had made and prompted him with all manner of counter exposures at Jeff's expense. Jeff at this time was just around the corner of a house and heard it all; so the Democrats good-humouredly told Jeff that they were now willing to square off with him. When the count was made, after the election, he only wanted one vote to elect him.

"Hub" died south west of Owensville, at the Henry Hobbs residence and is buried in the potter's field in the Owensville cemetery.

NELLY WARRICK.

2. Nelly Warrick, born near Lexington, Ky., 1799; married Col. Chas. Jones of Kentucky, about 1819, who was born 1791, died Feb. 1864. He came to Indiana 1812 and settled on Barren Creek, on the old Jess Wells farm, section 17, town 3, range 12 west, which is now known as the Jim Jordan farm. Then he moved to the Frank Jones farm, section 10, town 3, range 12 west. Then he moved to the farm on which "Purty Old Tom" Montgomery first settled, now owned by Lieut. William Jones, his son. He was a tall, straight erect, fine-looking man, and wielded a strong influence in the County. He was a soldier in the war of 1811 and '12, under the command of General Hopkins. He was also in the Wat Anderson volunteer company that followed the Indians from the massacre of Rochester, Ill., and assisted in the burial of the bodies of Canon and Buroway. He was colonel of the state militia, and was County commissioner in 1822-3-4, and in 1831. Children twelve:

1. Eliza Jones, born Jan. 2, 1820; died Feb. 3, 1901; married Captain W. A. Waters, March 22, 1838. He was born March 31, 1813, and was a wealthy farmer, living west of Owensville on the farm now owned by John Waters, his son. He was a first lieutenant in Co. E 42nd regiment Ind. Vol., for eighteen months. He was well read on the current events of the day as well as in general literature and history. He died Aug. 5, 1866, and is buried in Owensville cemetery. Children eleven:

1. Charles C. Waters, born Aug. 25, 18}9, single 1903.

2. Nancy J. Waters, born Nov. 8, 1841; died April 9,1879; married Thomas J. Johnson, Feb. 25, 1864, a soldier in the Federal army, in Civil War; he died May 1, 1890; children six: 1. George W. Johnson, born 1866; died 1891. 2. James A. Johnson, born 1868. 3. Elmer Johnson, born 1871 was serving on his third term in the U. S. Regular Army at the time of his death,

And Their Descendants

July 4, 1901. 4. Mary Johnson, born 1873, single. 5. Ella Johnson, born 1876, died Nov. 3, 1884. 6. Infant son, born 1879, died April 9, 1879.

3. James B. Waters, born Sept. 26, 1844, single 1903; was a soldier in Co. E, 42nd regiment Ind. Vol.

4. Eleanor Waters, born Feb. 28, 1847, single 1903.

5. Eliza A. Waters, born March 20, 1849; died Sept. 3, 1850.

6. Infant daughter, born Dec. 4, 1850; died Dec. 4. 1850.

7. Elizabeth L. Waters, born April 16, 1852; married Frank P. Yeager, Oct. 12, 1882. He died Dec. 8, 1885; no children.

8. Jacob J. Waters, born Dec. 4. 1854; died Aug. 20, 1881; single.

9. Mary Waters, born May 14, 1857; died Sept. 25, 1858.

10. John F. Waters, born Aug. 8, 1860; single 1903.

11. Martha Waters, born June 12, 1862; single 1903.

The above family received a comfortable inheritance from their parents, and through industry and economy have very materially enlarged it. They, like their parents, are ready readers and keep well abreast of the times in literature.

2. Jacob W. Jones, born in Gibson County, Ind. Jan. 25, 1821: never married. He moved to DeWitt comity, Ill., 1856, and invested in the fine lands of that County near Midland, and has accumulated quite a good fortune. He is a good talker, and a sly joker, and enjoys company to the fullest extent He enjoys the cherished blessing of a good memory and is familiar with the history of America through all its military and civil struggles and advancements, which makes him a very agreeable and instructive conversationalist. He and his brother, John Jones, have rendered me valuable assistance in this work. On Jan. 25, 1903, he was 82 years old.

3. Franklin Jones, born Dec. 4, 1823, married Comfort Sharp, Dec. 16, 1847. She was born April 28, 1828. He lives about two miles west of Owensville, on a farm that his father, Col. Jones, once lived on. He has retired from the active duties of farming and is in the enjoyment of a handsome living. Children eight: 1. Ellen W. Jones, born Dec. 19, 1848, single 1903. 2. Maria Jones, born Feb. 28, 1850, single 1903. 3. John Jones, born March 14, 1852, farmer and stock-raiser; married Dovie Kell, Aug. 30, 1899; children one— Infant, born Sept. 1900. 4. Mat. T. Jones, born Feb. 6, 1854, single 1903. 5. Eliza J. Jones, born July 14, 1856, single 1903. 6. Mary E. Jones, born May 22, 1861; married Theodore W. Crawford, a farmer, Oct. 16, 1884; children six: 1. Eva M. Crawford, born Oct. 19, 1885; 2. Franklin L.

Crawford, born March 29, 1887; 3. Opha T. Crawford, born July 31, 1889; 4. Minnie J. Crawford, born Feb. 5, 1892; 5. Delia A. Crawford, born Sept. 5, 1894; 6. Mary Mabel Crawford, born Dec. 19, 1900, died July 14, 1901. 7. Sarah Alice Jones, born Jan. 2, 1865, married W. Oscar Jones, a farmer, Sept. 3, 1885; children six: 1. Elsie C. Jones, born June 5, 1886; 2. Eme E. Jones, born Nov. 15, 1887; 3. Fannie F. Jones, born Dec. 9, 1889; 4. Alfred T. Jones, born Jan. 24, 1893; 5. Roxia A. Jones, born April 13, 1894; 6. Ruth M. Jones, twin to Roxia A. Jones, born April 13, 189 died Aug. 15, 1894. 8. William F. Jones, a farmer and stock-raiser, born Aug. 23, 1874, son of Franklin Jones; married Bertie G. Stephens, Aug. 19, 1900; children___, infants.

John Jones, son of Col. Chas. Jones, born March 13, 1825; died Sept. 22, 1902; married Permelia Montgomery, daughter of Hon. J. W. Montgomery, of Indiana, and moved with his brother, J. W. Jones to Midland, Ill, 1856—one of the most beautiful sections in the state, and shares in the wealth they accumulated there; children six: 1. Ella J. Jones, born March 23, 1860; married Thos. Marvel, April 28, 1882; lives between Waynesville and Midland, Ill.; is a farmer and has one of the best and most convenient gas plants on his farm for house use—such as lights, fuel and power— that I have seen anywhere; children four: 1., John E. Marvel, born June 2, 1883; 2. Eva M. Marvel, born Dec. 3, 1885, died Jan. 8, 1902; 3. Ethel Marvel, born Feb. 27, 1892; 4. Opal Marvel, born June 15. 1897. 2. Warrick Jones, a farmer and stock raiser, born Oct. 22, 1853, single 1903. 3. Charles Jones, a farmer and stock raiser, born Feb. 13, 1866, married Minnie B. Cross. Sept. 14, 1892; children three: 1. Carl D. Jones, born March 3, 1894; 2. Clella Jones, born Oct. 13, 1897; 3. Floyd Leland Jones, born 1902. 4. Frank Jones, a farmer, son of John Jones, born March 5, 1869. 5. Mat Jones, born Nov. 24, 1871, single 1903. 6. Mary Jones, a twin to Mat, born Nov, 24, 1871, married Guy A. Randolph, Nov. 19, 1896. He is a banker in Warrensburg, Ill.; is also engaged in writing a genealogical history of the Randolph family; children one— Virginia Pauline Randolph, born March 6, 1899. 5. Robert Jones, born 1827, son of Col. Charles Jones, died 1830.

6. Nancy Jones, born 1829, married Abraham Mauck, about 1848, who was at one time engaged extensively in the milling business at Mt. Carmel, Ill. He died in Princeton, Ind.; children five: 1. William Mauck died small. 2. Eliza Mauck married Henry Tichenor of Princeton, Ind. He died a few years since. 3. Elizabeth Mauck, dead. 4. Charley Mauck lives in Iowa. 5. Jacob Mauck killed by a railroad train about 1898 or '99.

7. William Jones, a retired farmer, born Sept. 22, 1832, was a first lieutenant in Co. E, 42nd regiment Ind. Vol.; served with the regiment from the time it was mustered in until it was mustered out of the service. He lives on the farm where his great-grandfather, "Purty Old Tom" Montgomery settled in 1806—section 12, town 3, range 11 west. Around the springs on this farm "Purty Old Tom" killed 160 deer. No wonder he took the name of "The Deer Killer"! Mr. Jones says that previous to the rebellion he had read a great deal about wars, but when it came to taking an active part in the civil struggle he found a vast difference between reading war and fighting in war. Mr. Jones was seriously wounded in the battles of Chickamauga and Resaca. He owns a large body of land southwest of Owensville, Ind., and is a stockholder in the First National Hank of Owensville, and also in the Farmers department store in that place. He married Martha Massey, March 8, 1874; children two: 1. Fannie Jones, born Feb. 13, 1875, died Feb. 17, 1875. 2. Florence Jones, born March 29, 1878; single 1903.

8. Charles Jones, born 1835; died 1865, single.

9. Martha Jones, born 1837; died Jan. 28, 1890, single.

10. Thomas Jones, a farmer, born 1839, married Mary Kesterson; children four: 1. Ella Jones, born___; married___. 2. Elmer Jones, born ___. 3. George Jones, born ___. 4. William Jones, born___.

11. Marshall Jones, born 1841, was a soldier in Co. E, 42nd regiment Ind. Vol.; married Edgington and moved to Nebraska, children___.

12. James Jones, born 1843, died single.

NANCY WARRICK.

3, Nancy Warrick, born Nov. 1, 1800, near Lexington Ky., came with her parents to Gibson County, Ind., 1800; married Col. Robert McClure, son of Thomas McClure, Dec. 25, 1825. Col. McClure was born near Hopkinsville. Ky., June 24, 1792, and came when a young man with his parents to Posey County, Ind., and settled on what was known as the Overton farm, on the New Harmony road. He was in the war of 1812, and was a colonel in the Blackhawk war. He lived in Indiana until 1821, when he moved to what is now known as Lincoln, Ill., where they remained for five years. Then they moved to what was then known as Stout's Grove, now Dover, Ill. He died

Aug. 8. 1835, at Stout's Grove, and is buried in that cemetery. Children six: 1. Permelia. 2. Jacob W. 3. Charles Jones. 4. Thomas Bassel. 5. Susan Jane. 6. John Willis.

Permelia McClure, born April 18, 1820, N1G7; married Henry C. McClure, Feb. 6, 1842, at Stout's Grove, Ill. At that time he was a teacher. In July, 1843, they moved to Mrs. McClure's father's farm, near Princeton, Ind., where they resided for three years. During this time Mr. McClure completed a course at Hanover College in Indiana. Then they returned to Stout's Grove, Ill., and resided on a 240-acre tract of land belonging to Mrs. McClure's father, which afterward fell to Mrs. McClure as her part of her father's estate. They lived at Stout's Grove from this time until 1885, when they moved to Gibson City, Ford County, Ill., where Mr. McClure owned 900 acres of land. There he engaged in the banking business under the firm name of H. C. McClure & Sons, which continued until March 16, 1899, the date of his death. Mr. McClure was a man of broad intellectual culture, an industrious and persevering student, and traveled extensively, having visited many interesting points in the United States, Alaska, Old Mexico, and twice abroad— once in 1880 and again in 1898. The latter trip was to the Orient and the Holy Land. Mrs. McClure always accompanied her husband in his travels, and continues to travel extensively for one of 83 years. She is a remarkably interesting conversationalist, seemingly with a memory as strong as in the days of her youth; and her letters to me are among the best I have received in connection with this genealogy. She is said to very much resemble her grandmother, Jane Montgomery, wife of Captain Jacob Warrick. Children six:

1. Robert Augustus McClure, born Jan. 3, 1843, was a soldier in the 93rd regiment Ill. Vol., and served during the entire war. He is a banker in Gibson City, Ill.; married Ann McLaughlin; children five: 1. Elizabeth McClure, married J. P. Lamey, who is one of the editors of the Gibson City Courier; children two: 1. ___ Lamey; 2. Mildred Lamey. 2. Mary McClure married William Stathers, a hardware dealer in Melvin, Ill.: children two: 1. Hazel Stathers; 2. Helen Stathers. 3. Katherine McClure, single 1902 4. John Clay McClure, cashier in bank at Gibson City, Ill.; married Bertha Beardsley, Oct. 17, 1900; one child—Frederic Robert McClure. 5. Ethel Lyle McClure, single 1902.

2. Susan Augusta McClure, born June 5, 1850, daughter of Permelia McClure; died Sept. 15, 1851.

3. Horace Adrian McClure, born Sept. 26. 1852, is a real estate agent in Gibson City, Ill.; married Ella Martin of Indiana; children two: 1. Ethel A. McClure, born Nov. 23, 1881, single 1902. 2. Lewis M. McClure, born Feb. 11, 1885 is with his uncle in a bank at Mahomet, Ill.

4. Herman Warrick McClure, born Aug. 16, 1865, lives at 1712 N. Nevada Ave., Colorado Springs, Colo. He is a banker at that place; first married Ella May Vance, March 16. 1881; she died July 30, 1894; children five. Second, married Harriet Montgomery, daughter of Henry Montgomery of Atlanta, Ill., Oct. 22, 1895; she assisted in gathering material concerning the McClure family; no children. 1. Mabel L. McClure, born March 16, 1882. 2. Vance E. McClure, born Jan. 5, 1884. 3. Julia McClure, born Dec. 31, 1885. 4. Cora McClure, born March 6, 1889. 5. Adell McClure, born April 15, 1891. All these are by the first marriage, and are now (1902) in school in Colorado.

5. Frances Olivia McClure, born Dec. 6, 1858, died March 15, 1897; married Jonn Jones, a farmer; children two: 1. Marshall Jones, born 1885. 2. Ruth Jones, born 1892.

6. George L. McClure, born Sep. 27, 1863; is a banker at Mahomet, Ill.; married Alice Kirkpatrick; one child—Infant.

2. Jacob Warrick McClure, born near Lincoln, Ill., Dec. 18, 1822, son of Col. Robert McClure; married Alice Hall; children two: 1. Israel McClure, dead. 2. Mary McClure married a Mr. Harris of Memphis, Tenn. She is dead. Mr. McClure when last heard from—1899—was in Huntsville, Ala.; supposed now (1901) to be dead.

3. Charles McClure, son of Col. Robert McClure, born Feb. 9, 1824, moved to Ft. Riley, Kansas years ago; married Serepta Van Sickle of Danvers, Ill. He died in 1898 and is buried at Ft. Riley. Children four: 1. Winfield McClure. 2. Clara McClure. 3. Harry McClure. 4. John McClure, dead.

4. Thomas B. McClure, born Sept. 15, 1827, son of Col. Robert McClure, married Emma Clark, who is living (1902) with her two daughters, Mrs. C. E. and Mrs. John Vance, at Danvers, Ill. Mr. McClure died at Memphis, Tenn. 1898 and is buried there.

5. Susan J. McClure, born June 13, 1831, daughter of Col. Robert McClure, married Robert McClure, a brother to Henry C. McClure; children

six: Two died in infancy. 3. Robert is a druggist in Wheaten, California. 4. Laura is in Kansas City, Mo. 5. Nancy married Irvin Wilson, of Sutton. Mo. Ii, Cora, is living with her father in Lawrence, Kansas, where Mrs. McClure died in 1896.

6. John Willis McClure, born May 14, 1833 died at 14 years of age: son of Col. Robert McClure.

Nancy Warrick, wife of Col. Robert McClure married second Benjamin Conger. She died at Stout's Grove. Ill., Jan. 7, 1861 and is buried beside her husband and child at that place. The Conger children were: 1. Isaac Conger was a Federal soldier and was never heard of after the Battle of Shiloh, at Pittsburg Landing. Tenn. 2. Elizabeth Conger, married Jesse Benson and now (1901) lives at Colfax, Ill., and has an interesting family of three boys. 3. Robert Conger lives at Burlington, Kansas.

4. John Warrick, born 1803, near Lexington, Ky.; son of Jane Montgomery-Warrick: married a Miss Prince, and at one time was engaged in the tannery business in Princeton. Ind. He was given a good start in the world by his father, and made good use of his opportunities. He engaged in business in Owensville, Ind., about 1835, where he carried an extensive business besides being a large land owner. He also did a large business in shipping by flat-boats, to New Orleans market, large quantities of pork, corn, and other products. His store stands on the corner south east of the public square. It was a frame building, one story high, part of which now forms a portion of Thomas Emmerson's residence, now (1903) occupied by Aunt Betsy Emmerson. Mr. Warrick was an energetic, careful business man, and acquired a large fortune. He erected a large warehouse on the Wabash River, where his pork and grain were stored during the winter, and when navigation was opened in the spring they were loaded on great flat-boats which had been constructed for that purpose, and floated down the rivers to New Orleans. He was the first postmaster of Owensville and owned and controlled the village for several years.

About 1836 or 1838 he built a steam saw and flouring mill. It had three runs of burs and was considered a large mill in that day. He also built several frame dwellings and invited and encouraged other business men to locate in the town. He built a large two-story house on the lot now occupied by Dr. Martin A. Montgomery, but died before it was completed. At his death, January 9, 1847, he was carrying on probably the heaviest mercantile business and had the largest estate of any man in the County. He had no children: an adopted son inherited his estate. He also died, and his mother, a Mrs. Blair, inherited the estate.--Gibson County History, pages 51-199.

5, Henry Clay or "Harry" Warrick, born 1805, near Lexington, Ky. was born cripple-having crooked feet. His father, Captain Warrick, had arranged for him to have a good education, intending to make a business man of him. Elsewhere I have referred to the organization of kidnapers, who were stealing free and indentured Negroes and running them south and selling them into slavery. This began about the year that Indiana was admitted to the Union as a free state. This had been carried on to such an extent that all Negroes were in continual dread of being kidnapped; and Pete Irons, at the suggestion of some white friends, prepared for such an emergency.

Mr. Irons, to whom Pete once belonged, lived on the Silas Pollard land, south-west quarter of section 11, town 3 range 12, now owned by J. D. Thompson: and Harry Warrick was raised on the farm where J. D. Thompson now lives—north-west quarter of section 11, town 3, range 12; the houses being about a half mile apart. Pete always had a strong liking for Harry and spent much of his leisure time in carrying him around on account of his crooked feet. There are several traditions concerning this matter; the most probable is this:

Someone had told Pete Irons that the kidnapers intended to run him off south and sell him. With this fear in his mind he armed himself with a gun, and while traveling on the public highway, which then ran across a farm known as the Thomas Sumner farm, now owned by Mrs. Anderson Thompson, northwest quarter of section 6, town 3, range 11 west—at a point probably two hundred yards south-east of the house he met Harry Warrick coming home from school, taught by Major Smith, in company with Dr. Maddox, his step-father, and other parties. He rode up to Pete Irons and, in order to have a little fun, said: "Pete, you are my prisoner!" Pete quickly drew his gun on Harry and fired. Harry swung over and caught the limb of a tree with a death-grip which peeled the bark from the limb, and died. Some of Harry's friends wrenched the gun from Pete's hands, knocked him down and left him for dead, but he recovered and was some time afterward killed, either in Posey or Vanderburg County near what was called The Drifts, on Big Creek.

The Montgomerys

Another account says that it was evident that Pete intended to kill someone else who was in the company and Harry knocked the gun aside and the ball hit him in the neck, under the chin, and that a negro boy who was with them grabbed Pete's gun and knocked him down.

Harry Warrick was probably about 19 years old at the time of his death, about the year 1824.

6. Jacob J. Warrick. Jr. born Mar. 2, 1807, died Mar. 16, 1858; son of Jane Montgomery-Warrick; was a soldier in the Blackhawk War; remained on the old homestead of his father. Captain Jacob Warrick married Palsy Skelton in Indiana, May, 15, 1827. She was born in Kentucky, Sept. 23, 1809; died in Logan County, Ill. March 23, 1875. They moved near Lincoln, Ill., 1831; children twelve:

1. Montgomery Warrick, Jr., born Jan. 21, 1828, in Indiana; died Dec. 18, 1818; married Cynthia Marvel, May 15, 1848, no children.

2. Sarah Warrick, born June 14, 1829, in Indiana; died April 1, 1851, in Illinois; first married James Music, Oct. 28. 1850; he died Jan. 9, 1858; children two: 1. Sarah E. Music, born Nov. 30. 1851; married Thomas P. Cochran. Aug. 28, 1873; children one—Edith O. Cochran, born Sept. 20, 1880, single. 2. James C. Music, born Sept. 3, 1853; married Josephine Cochran, July 28, 1875; children five: 1. Clarence A. Music, born Sept. 5, 1876, died Jan. 19, 1890: 2. Grace M. Music, born Sept. 5, 1885, died Feb. 14, 1886; 3. Thomas H. Music, born March 22, 1895; 4, Nora L. Music, born Nov. 3, 1898; 5, Dora L. Music, twin to Nora L., born Nov. 3, 1898. Sarah Warrick-Music second married John Thomas, Jan. 29, 1856; children one—Jacob Warrick Thomas, born Sept. 30, 1857; died Aug. 1864. 3. Robert M. Warrick born Jan. 24, 1831 died May 21, 1S56, single. 4. Emily Warrick born March 14, 1833, died Sept. 12, 1833. 5. John C. Warrick, born Nov. 20, 1835 married Maggie Laper Aug. 28, 1870; no children. 6. William Warrick, born Dec. 26, 1837 was a soldier in Co. C, 105th regiment Ill. Vol.; died Feb. 28. 1863.

7. Benjamin C. Warrick, born Jan. 30, 1840, married Bettie Rankin, Aug. 8, 1861. They have a large estate near Lincoln, Ill.: children five: 1. Edward K. Warrick, born July 9, 1862; married Ella C. McCellecher Feb. 1, 1891; children three: 1. Jacob E. Warrick, born Aug. 5, 1892; 2. Lydia E. Warrick, born June 1, 1898; 3. Ethel C. Warrick, born Sept. 1, 1900. 2. William P.

Warrick, son of Ben Warrick; born April 1, 1863, married Sarah E. Morris, March 6, 1888; children five: 1. Infant son, born Aug. 19, 1888, died Aug. 19, 1888; 2. Benjamin C. Warrick, Jr., born Sept. 24, 1889; 3. Infant son, born Jan. 11, 1891, died Jan. 15, 1891; 4. Sarah E. Warrick, born Aug. 18, 1896; 5. Wilmarie Warrick, born July 30. 1898. 3. John A. Warrick, son of Ben Warrick, born June 1, 1867, married Mary A. Apple, Oct. 6. 1896; children two: 1. Margaret E. Warrick, born July 1, 1872; 2. Mary A. Warrick, born Dec. 1, 1898. 4. Sinnett K. Warrick, daughter of Ben Warrick, born July 9, 1870, died March 20, 1893, single. 5. Seth A. Warrick, born Sept. 30, 1872; single.

8. Nancy E. Warrick, born July 6, 1842, died Dec. 22, 1879; married Moses H. Fletcher, Aug. 1, 1861; children four: 1. Ophelia W. Fletcher, born July 9, 1862; married John W. Jackson, June 1, 1881: children___ . 2. Jacob Eli Fletcher died small. 3. Ella Fletcher, born March 20, 1868, married J. Lawrence, March 14, 1897; children___.

9. Martha C. Warrick, born June 17, 1845; first married William A. McCord. Sept. 15, 1870. He was a soldier in Co. D, second California cavalry regiment: one child—Madie A. McCord, born July 9, 1871, died June 7, 1889; single. Mr. McCord died Aug. 24, 1872, and Martha C. Warrick second married James Cochran, Dec. 14, 1881; children three: 1. Lutina Cochran, born Aug. 15, 1883.

2. Roy B. Cochran, born May 7, 1885. 3. Lela Cochran, born Dec. 21, 1887, died Oct. 6, 1895

10. and 11. Infants, twins, born 1847.

12. Louisa Warrick, born Aug. 13, 1849, first married Joseph Mauck, of Owensville, Ind.; children two: 1. Charley W. Mauck, born Dec. 5, 1875. 2. Richard Mauck, born Sept. 29, 1877. Second, married W. H. Turner, Oct. 25, 1881; children two: 1. Matilda E. Turner, born Dec. 21, 1883; single. 2. William E. Turner, born March 21, 1890.

PATSY C. WARRICK.

7. Patsy C. Warrick, born June 3, 1809 died Sept. 22, 1868; No. 7, Gen. 6. She married Dr. Willis Jackman Smith, born in Danville. Ky., about 1800, who died near Owensville, Ind., Aug. 17, 1835. He was a very remarkable man of that day. The Hon. Jacob W. Montgomery, late of Owensville, Ind., said Dr.

Smith was at least two generations in advance of his day in south-western Indiana. But Jacob W. Jones, of Midland, Ill., who was a nephew of Dr. Smith's wife, reverses this statement and says that Dr. Smith was not two generations in advance of the times, but that south-western Indiana was two generations behind the times. Dr. Smith was educated in Danville. Ky. He was not only well versed in medical jurisprudence, but also in the literature of his day. He appeared when alone to be of rather a meditative frame of mind; but engage him in conversation and he would rally, straighten himself up and assume a dignity characteristic of the southern people; his countenance would brighten, and ho would appear a different man. He is said to have been one of the most interesting conversationalists of that day. He enjoyed a large practice and was rapidly becoming a wealthy man; but his strength was not sufficient for the work. He died at an early age, respected by all south-western Indiana. I have heard it said that the whole township was in tears at his death.

Patsy Warrick-Smith settled on what is now known as the Jacob Paden farm, about two miles west of Owensville, Intl. Mrs. Smith also at one time owned the Wm. Armstrong farm, north-east quarter of section 3, town 2, range 11 west; her father, Captain Warrick, having willed this to her while mortally wounded on the battlefield of Tippecanoe. By Dr. Smith she had four children. By a second marriage, to Jacob Paden, three children:

Emily Smith, born Nov. 24, 1827, died Jan. 1, 1902; first child of Patsy Warrick-Smith married William Armstrong, Feb. 25, 1846, a farmer. He was a deacon in the Regular Baptist church of Owensville, Ind.; was a highly respected citizen. His ancestors came to Indiana in an early day, and we find honorable mention of the name running back to the days of the Revolutionary times; children six: 1. Willis Armstrong, born May 25, 1847, a farmer and sawmill man, married Naomi (Mark, Aug. 16, 1868; children eight: 1. Elmer Armstrong, a farmer, born May 28, 1869, married Dora Hopkins. Feb. 26, 1896; children four: 1. Essie V. Armstrong, born Dec. 8. 1896, died Feb. 22. 1898; 2. Herschel P., born Nov. 1, 1899, died Oct. 15, 1900; 3. and 4. Darwin E. and Dorothy M., twins, born March 23, 1901. 2. W. C. Armstrong, born March 14, 1871, single 1903. 3. George Armstrong, born April 5. 1873, died July 14, 1873. 4. Emily F. Armstrong, born Jan. 7, 1875, married John G. Benson, a farmer, Sept. 27, 1896; children three: 1. Gladys Benson, born July 21, 1897; 2. Virgie Benson, born Aug. 12. 1898: 3. Florence Benson, born ___ 21, 1902. 5. Elza G. Armstrong, born May 25, 1878, single 1903. 6. Stella B. Armstrong, born Sept. 7, 1880, married W. F.

Rainey, Aug. 10, 1902. 7. Arthur P. Armstrong, born Feb. 8, 1883, single 1903. 8. Ora K. Armstrong, born Nov. 15. 1888.

Warrick Armstrong, born Feb. 6, 1849, second child of Emily, was a teacher in the schools for several years; now a large farmer north of Owensville, Ind., on Indian Camp creek, on what is known as the Jacob Mauck farm: married Nancy Mauck: children twelve: 1. Clara Armstrong, born Nov. 29, 1872, married Oscar Mounts. 2. Arthur, born June 11, 1874, died Oct. 1, 1877. 3. Clarence, born Sept. 13. 1876; single 1903. 4. Henry, born March 22, 1878. 5. Mary, born Feb. 25, 1880. 6. Florence, born Feb. 20, 1882, married Oscar Bruce, Oct. 1902. 7. Ada. born Nov. 4, 1883. 8. Luther, born Jan. 8, 1886. 9. Clemma, born Nov. 9, 1887, died April 9, 1889. 10. Willard, born Sept. 11, 1889. died May 3, 1890. 11. Chester, born Aug. 24, 1891. 12. Ensel, born Feb. 26, 1897, died July 9, 1897.

3. Infant, born April 17, 1851; died April 24, 1851.

John F. Armstrong, born Oct. 11, 1852, fourth child of Emily, was a teacher for several years; married Lucinda Mauck in Indiana, Sept. 6, 1874; moved to Kansas in 18—; deals largely in cattle and horses; children four: 1. Frank Armstrong, born 1876, married Alice Jones Feb. 5, 1899, a teacher in the public schools of Kansas. 2. Dell, born 1878. 3. Dora, born 1882. 4. Dickie, born 1885.

Morgan Armstrong, born May 28, 1855, died March 4, 1859; fifth child of Emily.

James H. Armstrong, born March 31, 1858, sixth child of Emily, lives on part of the old Armstrong farm, on which he was raised, north-east of Owensville; married Leila Grace Bingham, July 6, 1879; she was born April 8, 1860; children ten: 1. Charley Armstrong, born Aug. 13, 1880, died Sept. 26, 1881. 2. Mary L. born July 22, 1882. 3. Harvey, born May 7, 1885. 4. Lemuel Garner, born Feb. 18, 1887. 5. William Edgar, born Feb. 18, 1887, twin to Lemuel G. 6. Elva F., born July 7, 1889. 7. John B., born Dec. 13, 1891. 8. Flora L., born April 27, 1895. 9. Ruth, born Aug. 10, 1897. 10. Hershel, born Feb. 19, 1899, died Aug. 11, 1899.

Mary L. Armstrong, born April 22, 1860, died June 6, 1888; seventh child of Emily; married Joseph Knowles, Oct. 6. 1880; children three.

Pinkney S. Armstrong, born Nov. 24, 1866, is a large farmer and fruit-grower: lives north of Owensville on the Princeton road; married Martha Roberts, Dec. 1, 1887; no children.

Louisa Smith, born June 12, 1829, second child of Patsy Warrick-Smith, married Levi Johnson, Oct. 21, 1848, who was born Dec. 25, 1824. He is a deacon in the Maumee Union General Baptist church. He has served as trustee of Montgomery Township, elected on the Republican ticket. He owns considerable land west of Owensville, and some in the Wabash bottoms. Altogether he is considered a well-to-do man. He has always been interested in the public schools and has assisted his children in obtaining a liberal education. He is one of the prime movers in sustaining and perpetuating the annual reunion of the Johnson family, the descendants of Arthur Johnson, in south-western Indiana and south-eastern Illinois. Children six:

1. John W. Johnson, born Dec. 19, 1849 (No. 1, Gen. 8); died Oct. 1901; married Lucinda J. Thompson, Nov. 23, 1876. He taught in the public high schools. He was a very popular man in Gibson County; was elected and served two terms as County auditor; was chairman of the Republican central committee for a number of years: was president of the Gibson County Fair Association; was internal revenue collector for the 1st congressional district of Indiana in 1900. He owned a substantial residence in Princeton and possessed considerable land in Montgomery Township. He died in Princeton when not quite 52 years old. Children three: 1. Luella Johnson, born Sept. 28, 1878. 2. Elsie Johnson, born Feb. 1, 1887. 3. John W. Johnson, born March 11, 1890.

2. G. W. Johnson, a farmer, born June 2, 1852, married Marovia Johnson, Jan. 21, 1877. He lived until recently just west of Owensville on the farm which was owned in an early day by Judge Roland B. Richards; later known as the John Simpson farm. Besides this he owns lands in the Maumee and Wabash bottoms. He was a teacher in the high schools. He now lives in Owensville and is a stockholder in the Owensville state bank. One child—S. Ella Johnson, born Sept. 9, 1877; married Dr. Ralph W. Emerson, Aug. 28, 1898. One child-Wash Johnson Emerson, born Sept. 8, 1901.

Martha Johnson, third child of Levi Johnson, born April 27. 1854; single 1903.

4. Emma A. Johnson, born Oct. 14, 1858, married J. D. Thompson, Sept. 5, 1878. He was born Nov. 20, 1858. Mr. Thompson owns considerable land, and deals in Jacks and Jennets and line horses; is a stockholder in the state bank of Owensville, Ind. They live on the old home farm of Captain Jacob Warrick, who was great grandfather of Mrs. Thompson. The old family cemetery of the Warricks is located on this farm, which is about two miles west of Owensville. Children three: 1. Archie Thompson, born Sept. 6, 1880. 2. Will S. Thompson, born Dec. 16, 1881. 3. Albert Thompson, born March ___. 1883 is a teacher.

5. Warrick D. Johnson, a farmer, born Feb. 1, 1865, married Phena A. Boren, May 12, 1887. He taught in the high schools of the County, and is an elder in the C. P. church. Mrs. Johnson was also a teacher in the public schools. Mr. Johnson is the author of an excellent paper on the genealogy of the descendants of Arthur Johnson, his grandfather. I do not know whether this paper was ever published or not. It should be. Children five: 1. Mattie F. Johnson, born Nov. 21, 1887. 2. Warren B. Johnson, born Feb. 13, 1890. 3. Warner L. Johnson, born Jan. 25, 1895. 4. Geo. W. Johnson, born Dec. 18, 1897. 5. Ella Marie Johnson, born Nov. 25, 1899.

6. Laura E. Johnson, daughter of Levi Johnson, born Aug. 19, 1871, died Nov. 16, 1876.

Warrick Smith, born Sept. 23, 1831, near Owensville, Ind. third child of Patsy Warrick-Smith: first married Margaret M. Simpson, Feb. 1856, who was born Dec. 4, 1838, died Jan. 14, 1895. Children five. Married second Serelda Smith; no children. He moved to Atlanta. Ill., 1856, where he was a successful farmer. He returned to near Owensville, Ind., in 1868 and purchased the John Simpson farm north of town and carried on farming and stock raising there until a few years since, when he moved into Owensville. Mr. Smith laid out a nice new addition to the town of Owensville, on Main Street. While living at Atlanta, Ill., three children were born: 1. John Willis Smith, born Jan. 10, 1857; is a well-to-do farmer and owns a fine farm west of Owensville, Ind., in the Wabash bottoms; also owns land north of Owensville, and is a stockholder in the state bank of that town; unmarried 1903. 2. George W. Smith, born June 22, 1859 owns a farm north of Owensville, Ind. He has served a term as commissioner of Gibson County; is now, 1903, trustee of Montgomery Township, and lives in Owensville, where he owns a nice residence. He married Mina Montgomery; children five. 3. Infant son of Warrick Smith, born Sept. 1, 1866. 4. Cora Smith, born

Dec. 31, 1871, died Aug. 4, 1874. 5. Lilly Smith, born July 26, 1875, married _____Murnahan, 1902.

Elizabeth Smith, born Feb. 12, 1834, fourth child of Patsy Warrick-Smith; professed religion at Antioch church in 1852; first married Morgan Williams, in Indiana, 1853, and moved to Atlanta, Ill. Mr. Williams died March 2, 1871. Second she married Alfred Martin of Owensville, Ind., April 30, 1872, and died there June 12, 1887, of cancer. She was an accomplished and handsome woman. She and Mr. Martin raised an orphan boy whom they named Richard Clemens. She brought him from Atlanta, Ill. They educated him at Valparaiso, Ind. He is somewhere in Oklahoma connected with the educational enterprises of that state. Mr. Alfred Martin has been township assessor, also township trustee, and has held other positions of trust.

PATSY WARRICKSMITH'S PADEN CHILDREN.

1. Nancy Paden, born March 1, 1837. 2. Jane Paden, born Dec. 26. 1839. These two own and control and manage for themselves a good and valuable body of land west of Owensville, Ind. They have always lived on the farm and have raised and cared for several orphans; never married. 3. Frank Paden, born June 1, 1841, was a soldier in an Illinois regiment; returned home and died Aug. 14, 1872, married_____ ; one child_____, dead.

Children of Jane Montgomery-Warrick by Dr. John Maddox:

1. Lucy Maddox, born June 2, 1814, is now (1903) in a very low state of health; she married Samuel Stone

2. Polly, or Mary Maddox, born Aug. 9, 1816, married Newton A. Wasson, son of Rev. Joseph Wasson, Sept. 11, 1832. Newton A. Wasson was a very excellent man. He was born Dec. 3, 1810, and came to Indiana about 1812; children eleven:

1. John W. Wasson, born Aug. 14, 1834, near Owensville, Ind.; died in Lincoln, Ill., Oct. 22, 1896. His wife lives in that town now —1903. He married Caroline Sharp, Sept. 11, 1854 and moved to Logan County, Ill., 1856, where he lived until 1863, when he moved to DeWitt County. Ill., near Midland; moved in 1891 to Lincoln, Ill. He was a deacon in the C. P. church and an elder in the same for 25 years. Children ten: 1. Byron F. Wasson, born June 17, 1885, taught in the public schools; is an electrician and is in

the telephone business; married Lilly Clay, of Atlanta, Ill., Aug. 24, 1886; children two: Earl, born Dec. 23, 1889; Dean, born Aug. 10, 1891.

2. Bray V. Wasson, born Nov. 7, 1856; died March 25, 1864.

3. Van R. Wasson, born Sept. 11, 1858, was educated at Merom. Ind., and at the University of Illinois; is now superintendent of schools at St. Peters, Minn.; married Nelly Ingersoll, June 27, 1888; children four: 1. Iva, born Jan. 22, 1890; 2. Lewis, born Oct. 2, 1891; 3. Van, born Nov. 5, 1896; 4. Selma, born March 23, 1898.

4. Elmer Wasson, born Aug. 26, 1861, died Sept. 8, 1862.

5, William L. Wasson, born Nov. 30, 1862, Was educated at Merion College in Indiana; taught in the public schools and is now engaged in the implement trade in Lincoln, Ill. He visited Europe in 1901; single 1902.

6. Charles L. Watson, born Sept. 14, 1866. was educated at Merom, Ind. and Lincoln, Ill.; is engaged in business with stereopticon views, with headquarters at Decatur, Ill. He visited Europe in 1894 and traveled extensively in that country. Children two: 1. Eugene, born March 11, 1894; 2. Hellen, born Feb. 3, 1897.

7. Mary L. Wasson, born Feb. 27, 1868; taught in the public schools of Illinois; married John T. Marvel, March 11, 1888, a farmer near Waynesville, Ill.; children four: 1. Edith May, born March 6, 1889. 2. Infant, born 1883. 3. Carl, born Sept. 11, 1893. 4. Sadie Marie, born Nov. 7, 1899.

8. Sarah E. Wasson, born Nov. 7, 1869, graduated in Lincoln, Ill., college, June 15, 1896; taught in the public schools for many years; married Charles W. Marvel, Nov. 29, 1900, who is a farmer near Waynesville. Ill.

9. Calvin Wasson, born May 3, 1872 was educated at Lincoln College and is now, 1901, associated with his brother. William L. in the implement business in Lincoln, Ill., and is considered an excellent business man.

10. Katie A. Wasson, born 1874, graduated at Lincoln College in 1896; has taught in the public schools and is now, 1901, engaged in a book and notion establishment in Lincoln. Ill.

Jane Wasson, born Sept. 4, 1836; died Aug. 30, 1845; second child of Polly Maddox-Wasson.

Permelia Wasson, born Feb. 7, 1838, third child of Polly Wasson, married John Summers, Sept. 1856, in Owensville, Ind., and moved to Atlanta. Ill., and lived there about 31 years; then moved to Clarion, Iowa, in 1887. Mr. Stunners died in Iowa Sept. 9, 1894. Children two: 1. Fidela Summers, born Oct. 12, 1858, married John Summers; one child—Harvey Summers, born May 15, 1877; married Jessie A. King, born June 23, 1879; no children. 2. Charles L. Summers, born April 9, 1868; married Cora B. Chapman, born April 7, 1874; children three: 1. Cecil P. Summers, born June 17, 1896; 2. Bessie M. Summers, born May 29, 1899; 3. Gladys I. Summers, born Oct. 26, 1900.

4. Joseph T. Wasson, born April 26, 1840, was a soldier in Co. K, 24th regiment Ind. Vol., and was killed in the battle of Champion Hill, Miss., May 16, 1863.

5. Louisa Wasson, born Oct. 22, 1842, married Rev. Austin Hudson, 1800, of the Christian church. Mr. Hudson was a very prominent minister, popular with his own church and other denominations as well. He was of a commanding personal appearance, and was a remarkably fluent speaker, strong in the pulpit, and did much to build up and sustain his church in south-western Indiana and elsewhere. He represented Gibson County in the state legislature in 1869-70: children two: 1. Clara Hudson, born Aug. 9, 1867, married Prof. Otho Fairfield in 1886. He is a professor in Alfred College, of the Seventh Day Baptists, New York. Children three: 1. Irving, born Nov. 9, 1887; 2. May, born 1891; 3. Marie, born 1898. 2. Ellis Hudson, son of Louisa, died at two years.

6. James Larkin Wasson, born June 15, 1845: enlisted in Co. F, 80th regiment Ind. Vol., in 1862, and was mustered out with the regiment in 1865, as a sergeant. He died at his home in Cynthiana, Ind., July 1, 1899; married Manecia J Boren, Nov. 8, 1866; children seven: 1. Arthur C. Wasson, born June 6, 1868; married Minnie E. Williams, Dec. 13. 1891. He taught in the public schools of the state of Indiana; residence, Poseyville; a farmer; children one—Herald Wasson, born April 1, 1897. 2. Oscar Wasson, born Oct. 7, 1870; died May 9, 1872. 3. Lulu A. Wasson, born Oct. 27, 1873; taught in the public schools of the state; married Dr. U. G. Whiting, Aug. 3, 1892. Mr. Whiting graduated from the University Medical College, of

And Their Descendants

Louisville. Ky., in the class of 1897, and is now located at Wadesville, Ind., and has a line practice: children two: Edna Fay, born Aug. 20, 1893; Van, born May 12, 1895. 4. Ora A. Wasson, born Feb. 23, 1878, taught in the public schools; married Arthur J. Endicott, Nov. 27, 1900; one child—Edith F., born Oct. 13, 1901. 5. Joseph F. Wasson, born Sept. 8, 1880; died May 8, 1900. 6. John B. Wasson, born Feb. 26, 1883. 7. Bertha Wasson, born Nov. 5, 1889.

7. Lucy W. Wasson, born July 11, 1848, died Feb. 28, 1868.

You will observe that her mother, Polly Maddox-Wasson, died the next day—Feb. 29. 1868. Lucy W. Wasson had just graduated from the Merom College, in Indiana, and had commenced teaching. She was a beautiful and accomplished young lady.

8. Sarah E. Wasson, born Jan. 22, 1851, was the second wife of Julius Mauck who was raised near Owensville, Ind., but has lived for many years on a farm near Apple ton City, Mo. They were married in 1870; children four: 1. Corwin Mauck was a graduate of Appleton City Academy: had taught school. He was drowned in the Arkansas River, in 1900, while working on a dredge-boat; was seen only once after he fell into the water. 2. Mary Mauck, was a graduate of Appleton City Academy, and had taught school, died of measles in 1895 unmarried. 3. Mattie Mauck, born ___. 4. Clay Mauck, born ___, will soon graduate from the Appleton City Academy, Mo.

9. Chas. S. Wasson, son of Polly Wasson, born in Gibson County, Ind., Nov. 15, 1853; taught in the schools; married Fanny Parker, near Midland, Ill. July 12, 1882; lived near Owensville, Ind. a number of years, then moved to Illinois and lived just north of Midland. He sold his farm there in 1901, for $100 per acre, and has purchased 525 acres about 25 miles south of Des Moines, Iowa, and will move there in the spring of 1902. He is in the stock business. Children one—William P. Wasson, born June 4, 1884; graduated at the Waynesville Academy in 1901, at the age of 17 years.

10. Mary E. Wasson, twin to Martha, born Nov. 12, 1856, was educated at Merom College, in Indiana; taught in art, literature and music; married Rev. William M. Hollett of the Christian church, June 16. 1891. They are now, 1902, located at Perry, Oklahoma. Children five: 1. Lucy Marie Hollett, born Aug. 1, 1892. 2. Barton Otho Hollett, born Feb. 12, 1894. Carle Ellen

Hollett, born April 14, 1896. 4. Charles Marion Hollett, born Nov. 6, 1897. 5. Anna Louise Hollett, born Oct. 13, 1900.

11. Martha Wasson, twin to Mary E., born Nov. 12, 1856: was educated at Merom College, Ind.; taught art and literature; married Matthew Berry, a merchant in Merom; he is now a farmer near that place. Children three: Earl Berry, born June 8, 1884, graduated in the high school at 16 years; Carl, born 1887; Jessie F., born 1893.

10. Thomas Maddox born Sept. 1, 1819, is the youngest child of Jane Maddox. whose first name was Montgomery and who first married Captain Jacob Warrick. Mr. Maddox was raised near Owensville. Ind., and married Betsy Teel in Indiana, Oct. 2, 1842, who was born April 2, 1822 and died June 3, 1880. Mr. Maddox moved to DeWitt County, Ill., in 1846, and settled about three miles south-west of Waynesville, and has always been considered one of the best citizens of that section of country. He is now, 1902, past 83 years old and is in comfortable circumstances. He married Ann Summas, July 14, 1881, and they are now living on the old home place near Tabor church, on the Waynesville and Midland road. By his first wife he had seven children: by the second, none.

1. John Maddux, born Sept. 20, 1843; was a well-informed man on the current events of the day. He first married Minerva Kenton in Illinois, April 9, 1866. She died in the fall of 1870. He moved to Kansas, 1870, and married Dora Pamers; who now lives near Beulah, Colorado.

2. W. H. Maddox, born Sept. 18, 1845; died July 22, 1847.

3. Joseph Maddox, born Jan. 15, 1848, is a well-to-do farmer and is a great admirer of fine horses, and has bred and raised a great many horses as well as good cattle. He is considered one of the substantial men of his County. He lives now, 1902, near a station called Tabor, on the railroad, between Waynesville and Midland, Ill; was elected treasurer of DeWitt County, Ill., in 1902, with a large majority, on the Democrat ticket; married Mary C. Curry, Oct. 16, 1878. Children four: 1. Elmer T. Maddox, born Sept. 1, 1879, just 60 years after Thomas Maddox, his grandfather, was born. He continues to live on the home farm and carries on the business of raising fine horses and pure-bred cattle. He married Helen F. North, of DeWitt County, Ill., Jan. 15, 1903. She was born June 30, 1881. 2. Maud Maddox,

born Jan. 26, 1882. 3. Dora Elizabeth Maddox, born July 25, 1886. 4. Wilmer C. Maddox, born Sept. 13, 1890; died Feb. 3, 1891.

4. Nancy Jane Maddox, born April 15, 1850, married James Hall, a farmer living near Hallsville, Ill., Dec. 16, 1869; children one—Lula Hall, born Jan. 31, 1871, at Hallsville; married E. Wallace Dunham, an attorney at Clinton, Ill., July 1. 1896; children three: 1. Kent W. Dunham, born Nov. 8, 1897. 2. Helen Dunham, born May 7, 1899. 3. Lulu C. Dunham, born July 21, 1900.

5. and 6. Infant and Morgan W. Maddox, twins, born April 22, 1856; Morgan died May 16, 1857.

7. Jacob W. Maddox, born Sept. 6, 1858, died Feb. 7, 1879.

JUDGE ISAAC MONTGOMERY
FIFTH CHILD OF "PURTY OLD TOM."

Isaac Montgomery, a twin to Thomas Montgomery, Jr. born 1776, in Virginia, in what is now Montgomery County. At the age of 19, or in 1795, he and his father came to Kentucky on a hunting and prospecting tour. In 1796 his father moved to Kentucky. Some of the family settled near Lexington, and some in Montgomery County near Mt. Sterling.

Isaac Montgomery married Martha McClure, a daughter of James McClure, and came with that family and settled in Giteou County, Ind., in 1800, on what is now known as the Finney farm, south-west of Princeton. At this place it is said that he built the first horse grist-mill in the County. He was a soldier in the war of 1811-12, and was in the battle of Tippecanoe. He was one of the judges of the Court of Common Pleas, in 1813, that laid off the County into five townships—viz, Madison, Blackriver, Patoka, Montgomery and White river. The first two named have lost their identity; the three last have been somewhat modified. He was in the state senate from 1818 to 1821, and again from 1825 to 1829; and in the House of Representatives in 1840. The Gibson County History says that he served twelve years in the legislature. He was a probate judge from 1830 to 1832, and held many other offices of trust in the County. In fact, he was almost continuously in office of some kind from 1813 until 1851. He probably attained the most prominence in the County of any of the family. He was a large, athletic man, and in physical appearance was one of the best-looking

The Montgomerys

men in the County. He was fond of hunting and was regarded as the best shot in the County. He had a large gun made at Princeton on purpose to kill bears.

About 1851 Mr. Montgomery and his youngest son, McGrada, moved to Texas; and soon after he reached that country he with others went on a hunting expedition. They struck camp, and "Uncle Isaac," as he was called, was left to keep camp while the younger members of the party went out in search of game. Isaac was on the alert and kept a close outlook for anything that might chance to come that way, and he was soon rewarded by the appearance of a large black bear. He took aim, and his unerring shot brought down the much-prized bear. The writer, then a lad of six years, remembers well the congratulations of his friends here in Indiana. Uncle Isaac was at that time at least 75 years old. Children nine:

1. Jane Montgomery, born 1800, married General John I. Neely in 1829. He was born Jan. 20, 1790; died Nov. 9, 1867. He was a very prominent man here in early days. He was an aid-de-camp to General Harrison in the war of 1811-12; was one of the first trustees of the board of incorporation of Princeton, Ind. in 1818. In 1880 he was one of the justices of the County, who acted as County commissioner. He was the second recorder of Gibson County and served 21 years in that office. He was also the second County clerk. Along in the fifties he lived in Owensville. Ind., in a house that occupied the lot on which now stands the department store of Geo. R. Wellborn. John Robert Thomas, a grandson, lived with him in Owensville, of whom mention will be made hereafter. Mr. Neely and wife are buried in the Montgomery cemetery, near Oakland City, Ind. Children eight:

Martha Ann Neely, born 1830, married Berry L. Briar, of Fountain County, Ind. She and her three children are all dead.

2. Caroline Neely, born 1832, first married William A. Thomas of New Harmony, Ind. They moved to Mt. Vernon, Ill., and had six children—three dying in infancy. 4. Rosalie Thomas married James H. Draper, of St. Louis, Mo.; now living in Pennsylvania; had but one child—Carrie Draper, who is married and now lives in Washington, D. C. 5. John Robert Thomas, son of Caroline Neely Thomas, referred to as once living in Owensville, subsequently lived in Oakland City, Ind. and finally in Mt. Vernon, Ill. While living with his grandparents in Owensville, he was a good-natured, quiet, peaceful boy, and the last boy in town that would have been expected to become a politician. Yet he represented the Cairo district of southern Illinois

in Congress for ten years, and is now (1901) a United States judge in Oklahoma. He was a captain in the Federal army, in an Illinois regiment. John R. Thomas was married the second time, and one of his sons, _____, is a lieutenant in the regular army in the Philippines.

Ellen Thomas, daughter of Caroline Neely-Thomas, married a Mr. Haine, a lawyer, now of Chicago, Ill.; no children.

Caroline Neely was married a second time, to a Mr. Berryhill, and had five children—one in Washington, D. C.; one a surgeon in the U. S. navy, now stationed in New York; one living in Australia, a physician; two are dead.

Moria Neely, No. 5, married Hugh B. Montgomery, son of John R. Montgomery. She had three children. Mother, father and children all dead.

6. Isaac Montgomery Neely married May C. Elstine, in Benton, Ill. He was a surgeon in the civil war, and has been since 1886 registrar of vital statistics in Cook, Ill. Children five: 1. and 2. died in infancy. 3. Charles G. Neely is married: children seven; one dead. Mr. Neely lives in Chicago, and is one of the circuit judges of Cook County, Ill. 4. John R. Neely is a physician in Chicago, Ill.; children five: four boys and one girl. 5. Kate Neely, single.

7. Joseph W. Neely, was a minister in the Church of God, and lived in central Illinois; subsequently came back to Gibson County, Ind., and united with the General Baptist church; married Elizabeth Clark; children four. He has been dead several years.

8. Elizabeth Neely married David Bryant, who died in Nashville, Tenn., during the civil war, children two. The daughter is dead, and Mrs. Bryant now (1901) lives with her son in Washington state.

9. Mollie Neely, married Ezra Woods of Illinois; three children — all girls and married.

10. Margaret Neely, who was born in Owensville, Ind., 1839, married Rev. William Crawford of Princeton, Ind. 1860. He was born in Owensville, Ind., 1839. He was a minister in the Cumberland Presbyterian church; was a soldier in the 58th regiment Ind. Vol., and was a prisoner seven months and

ten days in Libby Prison at Richmond, Va. He died in Princeton, Ind., Sept. 15, 1902.

Returning home from the war he entered the ministry; was ordained in 1870. He held most acceptable charges at Union, Pike County, Ind. eight years: Patoka eight years; Oakland City seven and a half years. He had the happy satisfaction of seeing twenty of the young men who made professions of religion under his preaching become ministers of the gospel and zealous workers in the vineyard of the Lord.

Dr. W. J. Darby, a life-long friend of Rev. Crawford, conducted the funeral services. He was buried in the Montgomery cemetery near Oakland City, Ind. The remains will rest exactly beneath the spot where once the Montgomery church pulpit stood, at which he professed religion, and from which he was ordained a minister of the gospel. He had three children: 1. Edith Crawford married Orien Peed; has one child. 2. Hattie Crawford, single. 3. Stanley Crawford married Emma Erwin: Mr. Crawford while at work in a saw-mill at Oakland City, Ind., 1900, had the misfortune to lose an arm. He is now engaged as traveling salesman for the Princeton clock company. Children two: Gertrude and Edith Crawford.

2. Joseph Montgomery (Big Joe), son of Judge Isaac, lived in Princeton, where the Dr. Lewis residence now stands, near the E. & T. H. railroad. He died in 1845. He had a son, William Montgomery, who moved to Texas between 1845 and 1850. Joseph Montgomery had two daughters, but I know nothing of them.

3. John R. Montgomery, born 1804, son of Isaac, was a well-known and popular citizen of his day. He was clerk of Gibson County, Ind. eight years; married Kittie Brownlee, of Princeton, Ind., probably about 1824; children seven:
   1. Hugh B. Montgomery, born 1825, was a lawyer and fine speaker; moved to Illinois in 1842; was a presidential elector in 1844 and died soon after; married Moria Neely, his cousin; all his family are dead.
   2. Dr. George B. Montgomery, born Aug. 12, 1827, died at Huntingburg, Ind. Jan. 4, 1901. He served in the Mexican war, in Co. D, 16th regiment Ky. Vol., Capt. Richard Owen's company. He served as a surgeon in an Indiana regiment in the civil war. His widow now lives at Huntingburg, Ind. Two daughters also live there—Viola and Helen; the latter married Mr. Leo H. Fisher, prosecuting attorney of the 57th judicial district of Indiana.

John R. Montgomery's other children were: Adaline, who married a Dr. DeTar and died soon after; Martha, who married a Mr. Longbottom of Evansville, Ind.; no children; John, who died at the *age* of 15 years; Isaac, who died in infancy, and Warren, who served in a Michigan regiment in the Federal army and died in Andersonville prison just before the war closed.

Thomas Montgomery, born 1806, fifth child of Judge Isaac Montgomery, married Elizabeth Edmonson, in Indiana, April 16, 1833. She was born Oct. 20, 1809. He located near where Oakland City now stands, about 1833 or '34; came to Petersburg, Pike County, Ind., and engaged in the merchandise business, and also shipped produce on flat-boats to Southern markets. He was well and favorably known throughout the County as a successful business man and a worthy Christian. He was a member of the C. P. church and a Whig and Republican in politics. He died July 24, 1871. His wife died Dec. 21. 1894, in Lincoln, Neb., and was buried at Petersburg, Ind. Children nine:

1. James Montgomery, born May 16, 1834, died Sept. 18, 1837.
2. Isaac Newton Montgomery, born Sep. 11, 1835, died Aug. 18, 1837.
3. Eliza Ann Montgomery, born Oct. 20, 1837, at Petersburg, Ind.; married Burr Polk, March 22, 1858; officiating minister, Rev. H. D. Onvett. Mr. Polk was a captain in the Federal army; was born in Taylorsville Ky., Jan. 15, 1835, died in Lincoln, Neb., May 1, 1886; children five: 1. Carrie S. Polk, born in Princeton, Ind., Dec. 17, 1858, died Dec. 17, 1877; married James M. Irwin, in Lincoln. Neb. Oct. 10, 1883. He was born Mar. 2, 1855; children three: 1. Anna Montgomery Irwin, born in Tecumseh, Neb., Sept. 1884, died Aug. 18, 1885; 2. Burr Polk Irwin, born Dec. 25, 1885: 3. James Matthews Irwin, born in Quincy, Ill., March 7, 1889. 2. Ida Polk, born March 6, 1861, died May 8, 1863. 3. Frank M. Polk, horn in Petersburg, Ind., Feb. 28, 1864, was in the U, S. army; died in San Francisco, Cal., April 29, 1901. 4. Charles Edna Polk, born in Vicksburg, Miss., Dec. 31, 1874. 5. William Polk, born, died Dec. 17, 1877.
4. Thomas F. Montgomery, son of Thomas Montgomery, Sr., born Aug. 31, 1839, died March 20, 1855.
5. Mary E. Montgomery, born Oct. 25. 1841, married John H. Miller at Petersburg, Ind., March 31, 1868, by Rev. James Richey. Mr. Miller was born at Rockport, Ind., Dec. 9, 1840; was a first lieutenant in the 10th Indiana Cavalry; practiced law at Petersburg, Ind., after the war; moved to Princeton, Ind., 1884, and is practicing law there now (1903). Children five:

The Montgomerys

1. Montgomery Leslie Miller, born July 28, 1869, attended commercial school in Cincinnati, Ohio, and the law school in Virginia; was a partner in law with his father in Princeton, Ind., and was an honorable and highly respected citizen. He died in Princeton, Ind. Feb. 11, 1902, unmarried. 2. Henry Scott Miller, born April 17, 1871, died July 4, 1871. 3. Bessie Atwood Miller, born Aug. 28, 1872. She furnished the data for the genealogy of Thomas L. Montgomery, her grandfather. She is single (1903). 4. Frank Miller, born Nov. 11, 1874, died Aug. 3, 1877. 5. Fred Miller, born Oct. 31, 1876 died Nov. 20, 1878.

6. Martha Hellen Montgomery, born Feb. 25, 1843 married R. M. Howell Oct. 12, 1875 by Rev. A. F. Hutchinson at Petersburg, Ind. Mr. Howell was born Feb. 13, 1840, died Aug. 11, 1893. Mrs. Howell now lives in Lincoln, Neb.; children two: 1. David Howell, born Dec. 5, 1876, died Dec. 18, 1876. 2. Thomas Howell, born April 23, 1882 is with a publishing company in Chicago, Ill., in 1902.

7. John L. Montgomery, born Jan. 20, 1845, died Aug. 17, 1847.

8. Charles E. Montgomery, born in Petersburg. Ind., Aug. 5. 1848, married Alice M. Logan, Oct. 25, 1871 by the Rev. Abel Sterrett, Washington, Ind. She died Sept. 19, 1872, at 4 P. M. Mr. Montgomery moved to Lincoln, Neb., and became quite wealthy, and died there May 26, 1892. Rev. J. E. Jenkins preached the funeral sermon and deceased was buried at Petersburg, Ind.

9. Emma Montgomery, born Oct. 28, 1851, married Charles W. Chambers, Oct. 12, 1875 by Rev. A. F. Hutchinson, Petersburg. Ind. Children two Mary G., and Lyle.

6. Archelaus Montgomery, born 1808, sixth child of Judge Isaac Montgomery; died June 21, 1835 and is buried in Montgomery cemetery, near Oakland City, Ind. He married Rachel___. She was born March 25, 1815: died Sept. 9, 1883. Children five: 1. Mary J. Montgomery, born Nov. 13, 1837 died March 15, 1867; married a Mr. Jennings. 2. Eliza Montgomery Wheeler, born Feb. 15, 1839, died Nov. 1, 1866. 3. Joseph P. Montgomery, born Sept. 29. 1841, was a Federal soldier; died at Chattanooga, Tenn., 1864. 4. John R. Montgomery, born___, died Dec. 12, 1866. 5. Martha A. Montgomery, born___, died April 7, 1859.

Harvey Montgomery, born April 10, 1810; seventh child of Judge Isaac Montgomery; married Betty Whitman. He is buried in the Montgomery cemetery, near Oakland City, Ind. Col. William Cockrum of Oakland City speaks of him in highly commendable terms, as being an upright, honest man, particularly interested in giving wholesome advice to young people. Children seven: 1. Ann Eliza Montgomery, born 1830, died Nov. 18. 1854, aged 18 years; married David Bryant, who was a soldier in Co. M, 58th regiment Ind. Vol. 2. George W. Montgomery, born 1837, died Sept. 6, 1890: was a soldier in Co. D. 58th Indiana regiment. 3. Theodore Montgomery was a soldier in Federal army; married Elizabeth McGinnis. 4. I. M. Montgomery was a soldier in Co. D, 58th regiment Ind. Vol. 5. Radcliff Montgomery. 6. Katie Montgomery married a Mr. Crow and now (1902) lives in Oakland City, Ind., a widow. 7. John Montgomery, born July 19, 1848, died Sept. 23, 1853.

Maria Montgomery, eighth child of Judge Isaac Montgomery, married Philander Woodard.

McGrada Montgomery, tenth child of Judge Isaac Montgomery, married a Miss Lucas of near Owensville, Ind., and moved with his father to Texas in 1851. He has at least two children living in or near Semfronius, Austin County, Texas—Fielding L. and Miss Maggie Montgomery.

JUDGE THOMAS MONTGOMERY.

Judge Thomas Montgomery, born in Virginia in 1876, sixth child of "Purty Old Tom" and twin to Judge Isaac Montgomery. He was a Democrat, and his twin brother a Whig. The two parties in Gibson County, Ind. nominated them for the legislature. Thomas was defeated in this race. However, he was a very prominent and popular man. He was elected County commissioner in 1817. In 1820 he was elected one of the associate judges of Gibson County, and continuously elected to that office for 26 years. He first married Betsy Warrick, in Kentucky, a sister to Captain Jacob Warrick. He settled on what is known as the old James Stewart farm in Montgomery Township, Gibson County, Ind. They had six children:

1. Polly Montgomery, born 1806, died 1869: married Major James Skelton who died in 1866. He was major of the State Militia. He lived about four miles south-west of Princeton near Marsh Creek, on the Owensville and Princeton road. Children ten:

The Montgomerys

1. Betsy Skelton, born 1825, married Samuel Mauck, Sr. He at one time owned a fine, large farm north of Owensville, part of which is now owned by Marion Thompson. He sold his farm and moved to Owensville, then to Princeton; met with reverses, and finally lost most of his property. Children four: 1. Julius Mauck first married Cordelia McNeely of Princeton, Ind. second, married Sarah Ella Wasson, daughter of Polly Maddox-Wasson. 2. James Mauck married Sarah Malone; children ___; he died in 1903. 3. Joseph Mauck married Louisa Warrick of Lincoln, Ill. 4. Mary Mauck, first married Luther Abner; children one—Hattie Abner, dead. Second, married Louis H. Wheeler, a merchant in Princeton; children one—Joseph W. Wheeler.

2. Amanda Skelton, born 1827, married Henry Mauck, Sr.; children seven:

1. Sarah Mauck, born Feb. 18, 1848, died Nov. 27, 1899; married William Forbis, Oct. 19, 1865; children ten: 1. Henry E. Forbis, Irwin Aug. 5, 1866, died March 9, 1869. 2. Maria Forbis, born March 23, 1869; married J. A. Mahan, Sept. 3, 1885; children four: 1. Albert L. Mahan, born July 4, 1887, died Aug. 10, 1887; 2. Ora M., born Aug. 20, 1888; 3. James C., born Oct. 4, 1893; 4. Sarah M. born Aug. 10, 1900. 3. Henry E. Forbis. Jr., son of Sarah Mauck Forbis, burn Feb. 27, 1871. 4. Amanda J. Forbis, born June 14, 1873, died Sept. 22, 1874. 5. Larkin C. Forbis, born April 1, 1875. 6. America Forbis, born Sept. 3, 1877 married William F. Meyer, Dec. 23, 1894; children four: 1. Robert F. Meyer, born Sept. 21, 1895. died Oct. 10, 1895; 2. Benjamin F. Meyer, born Dec. 16, 1897; 3. Jefferson D. Meyer, born Feb. 21, 1899, died Aug. 10, 1899; 4. Margie Meyer, born May 13, 1900. 7. Lucinda Forbis, born Aug. 15, 1879, died Sept. 2, 1881. 8. John B. Forbis, born Oct. 9, 1881. 9. Howard J. Forbis, born April 25, 1891. 10. Ella P. Forbis, born Nov. 1, 1892, died Nov. 15, 1892.

2. James F. Mauck, born Dec. 19, 1851, single 1903; second child of Henry Mauck, Sr.

3. Samuel Q. Mauck, born Sept. 14, 1854; married Julia E. Stewart, Feb. 5, 1885. She was born March 1, 1865; children six: 1. Amanda E. Mauck, born July 28, 1886. 2. C. Henry Mauck, born March 13, 1888. 3. J. Frank Mauck, born July 5, 1890. 4. Nora M. Mauck, born Feb. 17, 1892, died April 19, 1897. 5, S. Noble Mauck, born Sept. 3, 1897. 6. Mary M. Mauck, born March 30, 1901.

4. Mary Mauck, born Jan. 7, 1857, daughter of Henry Mauck, Sr., married J. I. Moore, a farmer, July 23, 1873. He was born in Jefferson County, Ill., March 17, 1852; children nine: 1. Ida F. Moore, born Sept. 2,

1874, died Oct. 2, 1875. 2. William H. Moore, born July 24, 1876, died April 11, 1880. 3. Henry A. Moore, born Jan. 8, 1879. 4. Nora M. Moore, born Feb. 11, 1883. 5. John F. Moore, born June 16, 1885. 6. Grace O. Moore, born Nov. 27, 1886. 7. Sarah E. Moore, born June 20, 1889. 8. Clarence L. Moore, born Nov. 13, 1892. 9. Eliza M. Moore, born May 20, 1895.

Charles Mauck, born 1859, fifth child of Henry Mauck, Sr., is somewhere in the West; has been married, but I have no report from him.

6. Frank S. Mauck, born May 15, 1862, is a government clerk at Washington, D. C.; married Rena Montgomery, Jan. 31, 1886. She was born July 8, 1864. Children five -see page ___, Corene Montgomery.

7. Howard W. Mauck, born March 4, 1865, died Sept. 5, 1902. He was at one time trustee of Montgomery Township; married Lavina J. Clark, April 15, 1885. She was born Nov. 15, 1860; children seven: 1. Ada A. Mauck, born Dec. 8, 1885. 2. Rudolph B. Mauck, born Aug. 23, 1887, died Aug. 25, 1888. 3. Osborn G. Mauck, born May 18, 1889. 4. Lydia D. Mauck, born May 12, 1891. 5. Hettie E. Mauck, born Aug. 8, 1893. 6. Howard R. Mauck, born Sept. 4, 1895. 7. Henry Lee Mauck, born Feb. 7, 1898.

Barnes Skelton, born 1829, third child of Maj. James Skelton, married Lucinda Mauck; children two: 1. Nancy J. 2. Elizabeth, first married Joseph Thompson, 1875; children one—Maria Thompson. Elizabeth Skelton-Thompson second married A. N. Bennett, a farmer, Dec. 28, 1878; children six: 1. Albert Bennett, born 1879; 2. Cuba Bennett, born 1881; 3. Fred Bennett, born 1883; 4. Barney Bennett, born 1885, died 1901; 5. Vaughn Bennett, born 1887; 6. George Bennett, born 1889.

Thomas Skelton, fourth child of Maj. James Skelton, born 1831, died 1852.

Benjamin F. Skelton, fifth child of Maj. James Skelton, born 1833, did quite an extensive business in the way of settling up estates of deceased persons; married Louisa Summers.

Sarah Skelton, born 1835, sixth child of Maj. James Skelton, married John Hollis of Princeton, Ind. He was a soldier in Co. B, 58th regiment Ind. Vol., and was wounded three times in the battle of Chickamauga, Tenn. They have good property in Princeton and a farm south-east of that place. Children two: 1. Mary E. Hollis. 2. Newton Hollis. Both are dead.

Newton O. Skelton, born 1837, died June 28, 1880; seventh child of Maj. James Skelton; taught in the public schools; was clerk of Liberty association of General Baptists for many years; moved to Princeton and engaged in the farm implement business. He left his family well provided for; married Catharine Richards of Owensville, Ind.; children five: 1. William R. Skelton, single 1901. 2. Mattie Skelton died at 12 years. 3. Mary Skelton, married Jerald Wellborn, a merchant in Princeton, Ind.; children one—Mary C. Wellborn. 4. Jesse Skelton; 5. Nelly Skelton died small.

Infant Skelton, born 1839, eighth child of Maj. James Skelton.

Maria Skelton, born 1840, died 1900, ninth child of Maj. James Skelton; married John Ervin, who taught in the public schools for many years; children three: 1. Lilly Ervin, married Joseph French of Patoka, Ind., a commercial traveler; children four: 1. Henry French; 2. Anna; 3. Lucina; 4. Sylvester J. 2. Emma Ervin, married Stanley Crawford; children three: 1. Gertrude; 2. Edith; 3. Infant.

Emily Skelton, born 1842, tenth child of Maj. James Skelton; married Samuel Reavis. He was a soldier in the 17th regiment Ind. Vol.; lives in Princeton and is a contractor; children ten: 1. Allie, dead. 2. Harry, dead. 3. Frank. 4. Mattie, dead. 5. Arthur, dead. 6. 7. and 8. Infants. 9. John H. Reavis, married Grace Milburn; children one—Margaret Reavis. 10. Fred Reavis was a soldier in the 101st regiment Ind. Vol., in the Spanish-American War.

Nelly Montgomery, born 1808, second child of Judge Thomas Montgomery; married James Roberts; children___: 1. Joseph Roberts, married Eliza Waters; no children. 2. Thomas Roberts died single. 3. Dr. William Roberts, was a soldier in the Confederate army; is now (1903) a practicing physician in Terre Haute, Ind. and is an influential citizen and owns considerable property. He married Octavia Brown; children three: 1. Ella; 2. and 3. ___.

Moses Montgomery, born 1810, third child of Judge Thomas Montgomery---no information.

Nancy Montgomery, born 1812, died March 8, 1884, fourth child of Judge Thomas Montgomery, married Joseph Skelton; children twelve:
1. Mary R. Skelton, born Jan. 27, 1831, died Sept. 18, 1850.

And Their Descendants

2. Ellen Skelton, born May 3, 1833.

3. Martha Skelton, born July 9, 1835.

4. Louisa Skelton, born March 22, 1839, died Sept. 22, 1850.

5. Elizabeth Skelton, born Sept. 30, 1840, died Aug. 31, 1873: married N. Wood Martin, near Owensville, Ind. They moved to Iowa; children two: 1. Lee Martin. 2. Edward Martin.

6. Levi Skelton, a farmer, born Aug. 31, 1842; lives north-west of Owensville; married Elizabeth J. Humphrey; children four: 1. Etta Skelton, born Jan. 1867, married Millard Lucas, Nov. 1, 1885, a farmer north-west of Owensville; children one—Arthur Lucas. 2. Mary Skelton, married John P. Moore, a farmer, Sept. 7, 1887; children three: 1. Willis Moore, born June 1889; 2. Prentice Moore, born July 1895; 3. John L. Moore, born Oct. 1897. 3. Nannie Skelton born___, married Greenberry McCarty; children one ___.

Adolph McCarty, born 1894. 4. Arthur Skelton married Pearl Sharp in 1902.

7. Sarah Skelton, born June 25, 1845 married Columbus Emmerson, a retired farmer. He was a soldier in the 65th regiment Ind. Vol.; lives in Owensville, Ind. Children five: 1. Florence Emmerson, born Dec. 21, 1867, married Morton Woods, a farmer; children one—Edith Woods, born May 5, 1894. 2. Joseph L. Emmerson, a farmer, born Sept. 29, 1870; married Agnes Pegram, May 12, 1897; children two: 1. Herman L. Emmerson born April 26, 1898; 2. Hildreth Emmerson, born May 4, 1901. 3. Dr. Jesse D. Emmerson, son of Columbus C. Emmerson, born Sept. 22, 1872: graduated at the Indiana Dental College, Indianapolis, Ind., March 27, 1895; commenced practice in Owensville, Ind.; then in Evansville, then in Princeton; then in Junction City, Kansas; and now, 1903, in Owensville, Ind.; married Ada Bixler, April 26, 1899. She died April 17, 1902; no children. 4. Otis Emmerson, son of Columbus, a farmer, born Aug. 19, 1875; married Anna Cushman, Sept. 12, 1900; children one Emmerson, born 1902. 5. Gussie Emmerson, born April 15, 1878; married Oscar Daugherty, a restaurant man in Owensville, Ind.; children one—Doris E. Daugherty, born May 5, 1901.

John E. Skelton, eighth child of Maj. James Skelton, born April 10, 1847, died Sept. 26. 1850.

9. Elisha E. Skelton, born Nov. 4, 1849, died Sept. 19, 1850.

The Montgomerys

10. Thomas M. Skelton, a farmer, born Aug, 14, 1851; married Sarah E. Smiley, Aug. 20, 1878; children two: 1. John Skelton, born May 25, 1879; 2. Infant, born 1881.

11. Harriet Skelton, born June 5, 1853 married Benjamin F. Montgomery, Aug. 1875; children one—Lawrence O. Montgomery, born Sept. 1880.

12. James Skelton, born Nov. 20, 1855; died June 27, 1856.

Jacob Montgomery, born 1814, fifth child of Judge Thomas Montgomery—no information.

Thomas Montgomery, born 1816, sixth child of Judge Thomas Montgomery, was known as "Little Tom." He speculated considerably on the Mississippi river and finally lost all he possessed, and died west of Owensville probably about 1870; first married Millie Harris and had one daughter, Mary Ellen Montgomery. She has been dead many years. Second he married Nancy Malone, nee Skelton, a sister to Maj. James Skelton; no children. Third he married Hannah Forbis; no children. Fourth he married Christina McCleveland, a mere girl, whom he married in his old age, which proved to be rather an unfortunate marriage.

Judge Thomas Montgomery second married Katie Teel, about 1818: children six:

1. Julia Montgomery, born 1819, died May 30, 1860; seventh child of Judge Thomas Montgomery; married Thomas Sumner about 1837, who was born Aug. 30, 1811 and died July 25, 1863. He was in the Blackhawk war. He superintended the repairing of the levee road through the Wabash bottoms the first time it was repaired. At one time he was a wealthy man. Children eleven:

1. Molly Sumner, born 1838, died Dec. 12, 1882, in Illinois. She was a bright woman, of rare intelligence, and possessed exceptional conversational powers; married John Jolly, a large farmer on Kickapoo creek, about four miles south of Atlanta, Ill. Mr. Jolly was raised near Stewartsville, in Posey County. Ind., and was a brother to Mrs. James Cale of near Poseyville. Mr. Jolly moved to Kansas and died there; children two: Richard Jolly, born 1867, is a real estate agent in Kansas City, Mo., 1901. Wilber Jolly, born 1833, is a telegraph operator.

2. Maria Sumner, born 1840, died Aug. 28, 1879, taught in the public schools for many years; was the second wife of the Hon. Jacob F. Bird of Owensville, Ind., married Oct. 11. 1874. He is a native of the state of Tennessee, and represented Gibson County in the legislature in 1866-1867, and was the first superintendent of the public schools in Gibson County. He was also a principal in the high schools of the County for several years. He is a graduate of Tusculum College, Tenn.; has practiced law and conducted a profitable mercantile business in Owensville. He is now (1903) growing old and feeble.

3. Richard Sumner, born 1843, was a soldier in the 17th regiment Ind. Vol. By good judgment, good management and honesty he has accumulated quite a nice fortune. Now (1903) he is the owner of thirteen hundred acres of profitable land in the Wabash bottoms; is a stockholder in the new mill at Owensville, also has stock in the state bank of that place. He had the misfortune to lose a leg, a few years after the Civil war, by being thrown by an unruly horse. He married Roxie Jacques in 1875; children three:

1. Ida Sumner, born 1882, married Burl Stunkel, Dec. 20, 1902. 2. Infant, born 1888. 3. Richie Sumner, born 1894.

Willis, fourth child of Thomas Sumner, born 1845, died March 1859, single. McGrada, fifth child of Thomas Sumner, born 1817, died small. Louisa, sixth child, born 1819, died small.

7. James Sumner, born Dec. 20, 1850, is a saw-mill man and lumber dealer; also owns several hundred acres of bottom land, and now (1903) lives in Owensville, Ind. He married Ida C. Wilson, March 14, 1878. She was born Aug. 20, 1860. Children eleven:

1. Infant, born Dec. 13, 1879. 2. Mary Belle Sumner, born Aug. 6, 1882, a clerk in Montgomery's store 1903. 3. Lula Fern, born Dec. 20, 1884. 4. Maurice Summer, born Oct. 31, 1885, died Oct. 1, 1886. 5. Harry Encil Sumner, born Nov. 28, 1887; a clerk in Wellborn's department store 1903. 6. Ruth Sumner, born June 1889, dead. 7. Richey Sumner, born 1891, dead. 8. Gilbert Wilson Sumner, born April 20. 1894. 9. James Wallace Sumner, born March 7, 1886, died July 6, 1886. 10. Catherine Sumner, born March 11, 1899.

11. James Charles Sumner, born Oct. 20, 1901.

Infant, eighth child of Thomas Sumner, born 1854.

Henry Sumner, born 1857, ninth child, was once a merchant in Owensville. Ind., then moved to Kansas and engaged in the stock business, and then in the milling business, where he met with financial reverses and returned to Owensville in 1898, and died Aug. 20, 1900. He first married Ida Herring, March 1, 1877. She died Sept. 28, 1879; one child—infant. Second, married Mat. Forester Oct. 15, 1881; children two—infant, and Dale.

Belle Sumner, born 1859, tenth child of Thomas Sumner, was educated at Lincoln, Ill., and married Rev. Walter Baugh, a C. P. minister who was a graduate of Lincoln University. They now (1901) live in San Jose. Cal.; children two: 1. Arlene Baugh. 2. Lucien Baugh.

Infant, born 1860, eleventh child of Thomas Sumner.

2. Lucy Montgomery, born 1821, eighth child of Judge Thomas Montgomery, married Smith Mounts.

3. Minerva Montgomery, born 1823, ninth child of Judge Thomas Montgomery, married Joseph Sumner.

4. Henry Montgomery, born Oct. 13, 1825, tenth child of Judge Thomas Montgomery, moved to Atlanta, Ill., when a young man, and became wealthy—owning many hundred acres of fine land. He is now (1903) a retired farmer, living in Atlanta, Ill.; first married Celinda Andrews, Jan. 7, 1854. She died July 7, 1857, children two: 1. Harvey T. Montgomery, born Dec. 27, 1855, is a commercial traveler and lives at Bloomington, Ill.; married Florence A. Staler, Feb. 12. 1879; children two: 1. Catharine Montgomery, born Jan. 29, 1880, single 1901; 2. Henry M. Montgomery, born Oct. 1, 1881. 2. W. H. Montgomery, son of Henry, born July 7, 1857, died in infancy.

Henry Montgomery second married Luna Ann Beardsley, Oct. 23, 1858; children five: 1. Thomas E. Montgomery, third child of Henry, born Aug. 8, 1859; married Abigail Hoblet, Feb. 7, 1880; children three: 1. Mabel I. Montgomery, born Jan. 19, 1882, died Feb. 2, 1901; 2. Herbert L. Montgomery, born March 17, 1887; 3. Bernice Marie Montgomery, born March 23, 1891. Judson Montgomery, fourth child of Henry, born Sept. 17, 1861, died Aug. 11, 1862. Harriet M. Montgomery, born May 4, 1864, fifth child of Henry, married Herman Warrick McClure, Oct. 22, 1895. She furnished the data for Henry Montgomery's family, and also aided in furnishing that of the McClure family; no children.

Minnie Belle Montgomery, born Nov. 5, 1867, sixth child of Henry, married Arthur Thurston Kenyon, a farmer, Oct. 6, 1887; children two: 1. Infant son, born June 29, 1888. 2. Rowena Belle Kenyon, born March 28, 1896.

Judson Willis Montgomery, a farmer, born March 25, 1876, seventh child of Henry. This man's grandfather, Judge Thomas Montgomery, was born in Virginia in 1776, one hundred years prior to this birth. Judson W. Montgomery married Frances Kindred, Nov. 20, 1898; children two: 1. Arthur Kindred Montgomery, born Aug. 25, 1900. 2. Anna Frances, twin to Arthur K., born Aug. 25, 1900.

Isaac Montgomery, born 1827, eleventh child of Judge Thomas Montgomery, moved to Benton, Ill., many years since; was a soldier in an Illinois regiment in the Civil War; died probably 1895, married___ ;children five: 1. Pinkney. 2. Joseph. 3. Henry, 4. Mary. 5, ___, a daughter.

Catherine Montgomery, born 1829, daughter of Judge Thomas Montgomery, lived for many years with her sister Minerva Sumner near Owensville Ind.; also lived for several years with her brother Henry Montgomery near Atlanta. Ill., and died there several years since.

PATSY MONTGOMERY.

Patsy Montgomery, seventh child of "Purty Old Tom," was born in Virginia in 1780; married Col. Robert McGary in Kentucky and cams to Indiana in 1806 and settled about two miles east of Owensville. She was the second wife of Col. McGary. His first wife was a Miss Davis, a sister to the wife of her brother, Joseph Montgomery, Sr. It is believed that these two Davis women were in some way connected with Jefferson C. Davis, late president of the Confederacy—probably his aunts. It is reported that Mr. Davis at the outbreak of the Civil War made inquiries of parties living at Evansville. Ind. if any of the descendants of Robert McGary or Joseph Montgomery, Sr. were living in or near Evansville. Patsy Montgomery-McGary probably had three children: 1. Thomas. 2. Eliza, who married

Wright Pritchett of near Owensville. They have one son James Pritchett, an able lawyer, living (1903) at Vincennes. Ind.

3. Robert McGary, Jr., married Amanda Poe: children five:

1. Thomas McGary, married Lydia Heinman; children six: 1. John died small. 2. Ella McGary, married John Miller; one child—Toby Miller. 3. Harrison McGary, single. 4. William McGary, married___. 5. Amanda McGary, married George Williams; no children. 6. Emma McGary married George Ekerson, no children.

Martha McGary, second child of Robert McGary, Jr., married Thomas Johnson; children three—Thomas, Amanda and Mary. Pop McGary, third child of Robert McGary, Jr., first married William Armstrong, and second married Thomas Armstrong.

Emily McGary, fourth child of Robert McGary. Jr., married Samuel Rumble; children eight: 1. Frankie Rumble married John Dragoo of Owensville, Ind. He died several years ago. Children four: 1. Elsie Dragoo, once a clerk in Pruitt's store in Owensville. 2. Willie, 3. Arthur, 4. Theodore, 2. Amanda Rumble, married Ed. Byrd; children four: Elsie, Bertha. Emma and Charley. 3. Mary Rumble, married Charley Hall; children two—Lillie and Charley. 4. Lyda Rumble, married George Selby; one child—Walter. 5. William Rumble, married Bertha Hoover; no children. 6. Daisy Rumble, dead. 7. David Rumble, single. 8. Burl Rumble, single.

Henry McGary, fifth child of Robert McGary, Jr.—no information.

WALTER CROCKETT MONTGOMERY

Walter Crockett Montgomery was born at the head of Roanoke Springs, Virginia, in 1784. He came with his father, "Purty Old Tom," to Mt. Sterling, Ky., 1796, and then to Gibson County, Ind., in 1806. He designated himself as "Old Virginia Walter." He was known all over Gibson County as being the owner of the stallion "Old McKinney Roan," the noted race-horse of those early days in Indiana, which was never outdistanced on the race track. This noted horse was admired by all parties when he was on dress parade on public occasions, such as election days and muster days. He had been trained from a colt to leap over a pole held up for that purpose, and on those public occasions he took as much pride and interest in his exploits as did his admirers and owner. The pole at first would be held at three feet. "Old McKinney Roan" always leading in the leap, nearly all the other horses on the ground would follow suit up to five feet, then they would fail, or try to run under the pole. Then the pole would be raised by inches, and "Old McKinney" would clear it at a height of six feet. Then he would curl his tail over his back and prance so elastically that "Old Virginia Walter" would declare "the horse could walk on eggs and not break them."

Mr. Montgomery and Gen. William Henry Harrison were well acquainted in Virginia and renewed their acquaintance in Indiana, and the general often stopped over night with Mr. Montgomery while he was looking after the interest of Indiana Territory between Vincennes and Mt. Vernon. Mr. Harrison appointed Mr. Montgomery sheriff of Knox County, out of which several comities were afterward formed. He was a soldier in the war of 1811-12, in the company of Capt. Jacob Warrick, who was his brother-in-law. Mr. Montgomery died Jan. 14, 1856, and was buried in the old family cemetery in which his father, "Purty Old Tom," was buried in 1818, on the farm he settled on in 1807. He first married Nancy Roberts, born June 1790, died Jan. 1815, of the disease then known as "black-tongue," which proved so fatal in that day. Children-thirteen. Second he married Margaret Powell, Nov. 23, 1845, who was born Feb. 4, 1812, died Dec. 11, 1894; children six:

1. and 2. Thomas and Matilda, twins. 3. Jacob W. 4. Joseph. 5. Isaac. 6. John. 7. Martha Crockett. 8. Nelly. 9. Walter Crockett. Jr. 10. Robert. 11. William W. 12. Infant, twin to Wm. W. 13. Andrew J. 14. Infant. 15. Elizabeth J. 16. Mary A. 17. James P. 18. Infant. 19. Smith M.

1. Matilda Montgomery, born June 23, 1809, died June 13, 1857; married Asa Knowles, born March 5, 1802, died July 6, 1898, therefore he was 93 years old. He was born in Georgia; lived on a farm west of Owensville, Ind., until most of his family was grown. Then he sold out his farm, probably about 18(50, and went into the hotel business at Princeton, which was a very bad move. He moved from Princeton, Ind., to Greenwood County, Kansas, when probably 70 years old. He was a Democrat, and a staunch Cumberland Presbyterian, and a few years before his death he wrote a little pamphlet setting forth his views on baptism and other matters and sent many of them back to Indiana to his relatives and friends. The Knowles people in Indiana wished to hold a reunion in the grove of John

Lowery Knowles, a half brother of Asa. "Uncle Asa" was a disbeliever in such things and opposed it vigorously; but finally, through the pressure of old friends, he consented to be present, and he afterward made a full confession of his error in this matter, saying: "I believe I have met one thousand of my relatives and friends, since coming to this two-days reunion, that possibly I never would have met again in this life if I had not attended this meeting." He was a Knowles and married a Montgomery, which connected him to nearly all the people in Montgomery Township. He was a disbeliever in the medical profession. He was quite sick at the reunion, and the writer suggested that he call a physician. He said: "No, sir; I never had a doctor to see me but once in my life, and he came pretty near getting me that time, so I take no more medicine."

Matilda Montgomery, his wife, was a grand, good woman, horn 1809; was a twin to Thomas Montgomery. This is a characteristic which belongs to the Montgomery family in Gibson County, and it has more or less followed the family ever since 1776, when Judge Isaac and Judge Tom, sons of "Purty Old Tom," were born in Virginia: and I have noted 55 pairs of twins, the majority of them being descendants of "Purty Old Tom." Children seven:'

1. America Knowles, born Oct. 16, 1830, married Thompson G. Mauck, Sr., Nov. 13, 1851. He was born Sept. 6, 1830. He belongs to an old and well-respected German family; lives west of Owensville, Ind., and has been engaged in farming all his life. He is a member of the Regular Baptist church of Owensville. America Knowles, his wife, was an exceptionally good woman. She was a member of the C. P. church. She died Oct. 20, 1892; children five: 1. Jacob W. Mauck, a farmer, born Aug. 25, 1852; married Lucy Mounts Nov. 30, 1876. She was born Aug. 21, 1857. Children six: 1. Nora V. Mauck, born Oct. 16, 1877, died Sept. 9. 1879. 2. Asa L. Mauck, born July 14, 1879; married Mary Robb, Dec. 3, 1902. 3. Eliza E. Mauck, born May 15, 1882, died Aug. 5, 1897. 4. George T. Mauck, born Sept. 8, 1883. 5. and 6. Infant twins. Abraham Mauck, born Sept. 18, 1854, second child of T. G. Mauck, married Maggie Johnson, May 12, 1876. She was born Aug. 31, 1855. Mr. Mauck and his entire family now (1902) live in Denver, Colorado; children seven; 1. Harvey A. Mauck, born Aug. 22, 1877, single. 2. Mary M. Mauck, born Nov. 24, 1878, single. 3. John A. Mauck, Jr., born Aug. 24, 1880; married Grace Reid of Denver, Colorado, Sept. 7, 1900. 4., Myrtle A. Mauck, born March 29, 1882, single. 5. Joseph C. Mauck, born July 1, 1883, single, 6. Maggie C. Mauck, born Oct. 15, 1884, single. 7. Thompson Mauck, born Oct. 24, 1887, single.

Asa K. Mauck, born May 21, 1857, died Aug. 20, 1870; third child of T. G. Mauck.

Matilda J. Mauck, born Jan. 1860, fourth child of T. G. Mauck; married Henry W. Smith, a farmer, Oct. 27, 1881. He was born Jan. 18, 1859; is a deacon in the C. P. church and a stockholder in the Owensville Milling Company. Children three: 1. Nora Pearl Smith, born April 28, 1884. 2. America Bertha Smith, born July 31, 1890, died April 28, 1892. 3. Earl Ross Smith born June 18, 1893.

John A. Mauck, born Oct. 12, 1862, fifth child of T. G. Mauck. Mr. Mauck was head clerk in the Farmers department store in Owensville, and is now (1903) in the department store of G. R. Wellborn; married Ada Robinson, Aug. 10, 1887; children two: 1., Bernice Mauck born Mar. 11, 1893; 2. Hilda Louisa Mauck born May 17, 1902.

Sarelda and Nancy Knowles, 2 and 3, children of Asa Knowles, died in infancy.

Sarah Knowles, born Dec. 3, 1833, fourth child of Asa Knowles, married Thomas Fisher, Feb. 4. 1865. He was a soldier in the 24th regiment Ind. Vol.; was severely wounded, from which he finally died, probably about 1895. Mrs. Fisher now lives in Virgil, Kansas; children two: 1. Albert S. Fisher, born June 19, 1867, died April 10, 1883. 2. Joseph W. Fisher, born Jan. 9, 1875.

Elizabeth Knowles, born about 1835, fifth child of Asa Knowles; married William Tolbert. He was a soldier in the first regiment Ind. Cav.; died in Virgil. Kansas, where his wife now lives; children seven: 1. Minnie R. Tolbert, dead. 2. Luella C. Tolbert married Horace G. Marshall: children four: Elsie, ____, Ben and Beulah. 3. Asa M. Tolbert. 4. Eugene Tolbert, dead. 5. Myrtle Tolbert, married Grant Hollins; children two—sons 6. Matilda J. Tolbert, married Earl Russell; one child. 7. Gilbert Tolbert.

Patience Knowles, sixth child of Asa Knowles, married Clinton Simpson. He died in Owensville, Ind. and she lives in Virgil, Kansas; children three: 1. Sarah. 2. Laura died Sept. 16, 1877. 3. Georgia.

Martha Knowles, born Sept. 19, 1846, seventh child of Asa Knowles, married Alfred Mauck, Oct. 1868, in Indiana; moved to Toronto, Kansas, and Mr. Mauck died there Dec. 31. 1888. Mrs. Mauck and nearly all her family moved to Salubria, Idaho, in 1902; children four: 1. Mary T. Mauck born July 8, 1869, in Indiana; married Andrew Case, Oct. 31, 1895 at Toronto, Kansas; no children. 2. Nannie A. Mauck, born April 20, 1871 in Indiana, married Thomas Harris. July 2, 1894; children three: 1. Janie O. Harris, born April 27, 1895: 2. Alice L. Harris, born Feb. 14, 1898; 3. Jesse W. Harris, born Aug. 7, 1900. 3. Cornelia A. Mauck, child of Martha Knowles-Mauck, born Feb. 6, 1874, in Indiana; married Oliver J. Grider, Nov. 25, 1894, at Toronto, Kansas; one child, Velva M. Grider, born Nov. 29, 1895, died Dec. 6, 1896. 4. Matilda J. Mauck, born Jan. 4, 1880, in Indiana, married James A. King, Aug. 1, 1899 at Virgil, Kansas; one child—Louis D. King, born June 26, 1900.

Thomas Montgomery, born June 24, 1809; a twin to Matilda above, and second child of Walter Crockett Montgomery, Sr.; married Betsy Gambrel, sister to Henry and Thompson Gambrel. They moved to Atlanta. Ill., Oct. 1848, and he died there in 1853.

Hon. J. W. Montgomery, born Feb. 6, 1811, third child of Walter C. Montgomery, Sr. married Jane McFadin Oct. 4, 1835. She was born Oct. 15, 1814; was the daughter of John McFadin, Sr. She lived in Owensville when only four families lived in the town; she lives there now (1903), though most of her life has been spent in the country on a farm. She is one among the best women I ever knew.

J. W. Montgomery was a great reader, kept up with news of the day. He had a remarkable memory and was one of the best-posted men in the country. He knew something of the history of every representative in the National Congress, from Jackson's administration down to the closing years of his life. He represented Gibson County in the Indiana legislature in 1875-6. He was generous to a fault; never turned a neighbor away empty-handed when it was in his power to help him. He never refused lodging to a traveler in his life.

To illustrate, probably about 1850, Earl Robinson, who was full of pranks and jokes had been to Owensville one day and late in the afternoon, on his return toward home, he fell in with a stranger on horseback who was traveling his way. When they reached a byroad leading off to Robinson's house, the stranger asked to be entertained over night. This was Robinson's opportunity for a little fun. He replied: "I would keep you, sir, but it would not be treating the U. S. government right, as it has a station just over the ridge there and employs a man by the year to entertain all strangers free of charge"—at the same time describing the man, house and surroundings so there could be no possibility of a mistake.

Hon. J.W. Montgomery
Owensville, Indiana

The stranger found Mr. Montgomery just starting out to do up the night feeding, and asked for a night's lodging. "Certainly," replied Mr. Montgomery, at the same time blowing open a large gate that led into a wood-lot adjoining the yard, allowing the stranger to ride in, then saying: "Hitch up your horse, go into the house, make yourself comfortable. The boys will soon be in and take care of your horse."

As soon as Mr. Montgomery came in from work the sharper said: "This is certainly a very fine arrangement the government has for entertaining the traveling public," and then related what Mr. Robinson had told him. Mr. Montgomery carried out the joke, asking no questions as to what kind of man it was, saying afterward that he knew very well who the informer was.

The next morning when the boys caught, bridled, saddled and brought out the horse, the stranger said: "Mr. Montgomery, this is a remarkable arrangement; but, notwithstanding the government pays all expenses, it seems to me that I should at least pay you something, as you have treated me with so much consideration."

The Montgomerys

"No, sir, the government has made ample provision for me, sir."

The stranger reluctantly put his money back in his pocket, and with many thanks proceeded on his journey—probably never finding another government station equal in hospitality.

Mr. Montgomery was very entertaining in conversation. He had an almost inexhaustible fund of ready material to attract and interest his hearers. He had eight children:

1. Permelia Montgomery, born Aug. 27, 1836, married John Jones, Sr., in Gibson County, Ind., Oct. 30, 1856, and moved to near Midland, Ill., which is one of the most beautiful sections of the state; children six.

2. Lucinda Montgomery, born April 21, 1838, died March 17, 1872; married James C. Pruitt, Nov. 27, 1862. Mr. Pruitt is a merchant in Owensville, Ind.; children two: 1. Leonardo Pruitt, born March 24, 1864, died Nov. 8, 1865. 2. Joseph Pruitt, born March 10, 1872, died July 24, 1872.

3. Walter Crockett Montgomery, born Dec. 6, 1839; lives in Owensville, Ind., and deals in nursery stock; first married Theodosia McCrary, Nov. 18, 1862. She was born Dec. 19, 1845, died Sept. 25, 1870. Children five: 1. Emma E. Montgomery, born Nov. 20, 1863; died Sept. 18, 1870. 2. Clarence E. Montgomery, born Sept. 16, 1865; died Oct. 1, 1870. 3. Permelia J. Montgomery, born Aug. 1, 1867; died Sept. 1, 1868. 4. Julius A. Montgomery, born Jan. 19, 1839; died Sept. 29. 1870. 5. Infant, died Sept. 18, 1870. There was a terrible epidemic of flux in the fall of 1870, and you will observe that Mr. Montgomery lost his wife and four children—his entire family except one, which died in 1868.

Mr. Montgomery married, second, Mary E. Jacques, Jan. 16, 1873. She was born Dec. 15, 1840; children five: 1. Martha Montgomery, born April 25, 1874, died May 4, 1888. 2. Roxie S. Montgomery, born Jan. 9, 1876; taught in the public schools; married John Newman, June 18, 1902. They live in Evansville, Ind. 3. Delia J. Montgomery, born Sept. 3, 1878; married Henry Merritt, Feb. 1901. He is a mechanic in Indianapolis, Ind. 4. Mary L. (Molly) Montgomery, born Sept. 4, 1879, married Everett H. Cook, a hardware dealer, Dec. 25, 1902. They live in Indianapolis, Ind. 5. Warrick M. Montgomery, born Feb. 18, 1882, died Aug. 14, 1882.

And Their Descendants

Martha J. Montgomery, born July 29, 1841, fourth child of J. W. Montgomery; married Henry Clark, a farmer, July 25, 1861. He died Feb. 22, 1880. He was a brother to Rev. Win. Clark and a very useful man in Christian work. Mrs. Clark lives in Owensville, Ind.; children nine:

1. Allison Clark, born June 2, 1862, died Dec. 29. 1896; married Lenora Stone, Oct. 5, 1884: children four.
2. Oscar Clark, born May 3, 1864, died 1864.
3. Edgar Clark, twin to Oscar, born May 3, 1864, died 1865.
4. Ida Clark, born Feb. 13, 1867, died Oct. 23, 1870.
5. Joseph W. Clark, born Aug. 14, 1869, died Oct. 10, 1870.
6. Perlia J. Clark, born Sept. 22, 1871; married Gaias Hoar, of Ft. Branch, Ind., Aug. 1890. They have charge of the telephone exchange there. Children five: 1. Hazle, born April 1892. 2. Dale, born 1894. 3. Roscoe, born 1896, died 1898. 4. Percy, born 1899. 5. Infant, born Jan. 1903, died Feb. 1903.
7. George W. Clark, born Oct. 22, 1873; is in a restaurant in Owensville. Ind.; has taught in the public schools: single 1903.
8. W. D. Clark, born Dec. 12, 1876, married Ada Sprague. They moved to near Poplar Bluff, Mo., then in 1901 moved to Kingfisher, Oklahoma; then to Oregon; children two--Freda and Rollin.
9. Nerva Clark, born Sept. 20, 1878: has taught in the public schools; lives in Owensville, Ind. and single 1903.

Nancy J. Montgomery, born Sept. 28, 1896, died Sept. 21, 1847; fifth child of J. W. Montgomery.

J. M. F. Montgomery, a farmer, born May 6, 1848, sixth child of J. W. Montgomery; taught in the public schools; married Mary Montgomery, daughter of "Roan Ike" Montgomery, May 6, 1875. They are stockholders in the Owensville Milling Company; no children, but they raised Burgess Montgomery and Elsie Avers.

William W. Montgomery, born March 7, 1852, died Aug. 19, 1856; seventh child of J. W. Montgomery.

Joseph Montgomery, a carpenter, born July 17, 1854, eighth child of J. W. Montgomery; taught in the public schools; lives near Midland, Ill.; married Mary A. Yeager, Oct. 6, 1879; no children.

The Montgomerys

Joseph Montgomery—"Long Armed Joe"—born Oct. 27, 1813; fourth child of Walter C. Montgomery, Sr. married Nancy Hughs, about 1837. He cut trees, and rolled in logs on the first levee to Mt. Carmel, on the Indiana side, and ditched both sides. Most of his work was accomplished by his own strength and labor. He was 6 feet 4 inches tall and weighed 204 pounds; raw-boned, with arms about four inches longer than those of most men of that day, which made him a disagreeable opponent in the common contest of that time. He was always smiling, even in the contests in which he frequently engaged—always with success. He never was the aggressor. There was only one way that he could be made to fight, and that was for a man to strike him first which frequently happened; but no man ever desired to bring on a second contest. In assisting to let a loaded wagon down a hill, on the farm now owned by Marion Thompson, a wheel struck a root and switched the wagon-tongue, throwing him down, and one wheel ran over his neck. He spoke and said, "My neck is broken," and died. This occurred Oct. 23, 1848. He had four children:

1. Thomas Montgomery, a farmer, born Aug. 5, 1839; married Louisiana Rutledge, Nov. 5, 1863 in Indiana; moved to Neodesha, Kansas, in 1886; died there Oct. 20, 1899; children six, all born in Indiana: 1. Willard, born Dec. 28, 1864, died in Kansas, Jan. 20, 1894. 2. Edward N., born Nov. 11, 1866; was in the California Heavy Artillery in the Spanish-American War. 3. William Joseph, born Oct. 24, 1868, enlisted in the Spanish-American War but was rejected. 4. Arthur, born Feb. 16, 1874, enlisted in the Spanish-American War but was rejected. 5. Leona, born Dec. 13, 1875, taught in the public schools of Kansas; died Dec. 23, 1901, in Pueblo, Cal., from having stepped in a vat of scalding water, at the machine shop, where someone had neglected to shut down the door. He was a graduate of a high school; at the time of his death was in the employ of a railroad. 6. Lawrence, a twin to Leonard, born Dec. 13, 1875; lives with his mother near Neodesha, Kansas.

2. Isaac Montgomery, a twin to Thomas, born Aug. 5, 1839, died small.

3. Frank Montgomery, born June 2, 1841 and 4. Mary E. Montgomery, his sister, born Feb. 22, 1846; both single 1903 and living in Neodesha, Kansas, in comfortable circumstances.

Isaac Montgomery, born May 5, 1815, fifth child of Walter Crockett Montgomery, Sr.; first married Polly Teel, in Indiana, probably about 1837. He was rather a small man, never weighing over 135 pounds. She was over six feet tall and an ideal, good woman. They moved to Atlanta, Ill., in 1854, and she died there; children six. He married a second time, but I do not know whom; one child, ___. Isaac came back to Indiana in 1856 and died the same year. Children seven:

1. Walter C. Montgomery, born probably 1838, was a soldier in the 24th regiment Ind. Vol.; never married; died in Owensville a few years after the war.

2. Dr. W. T. Montgomery, born probably 1840, was a soldier in the 33rd regiment Ind. Vol.; lived with Asa Knowles, who married his father's sister, Matilda, already mentioned, after 1856 until he enlisted in the army. He entered and remained in the army until the close of the war, when he prepared himself for teaching. In 1838 he entered Lincoln College, in Illinois. In 1869 or '70 he entered Rush Medical College, in Chicago, Ill., from which he graduated in a regular course; practiced medicine in Chicago for several years, then became a specialist in eye and ear.

Later he visited Europe in the interest of his profession. In 1900 he again visited Europe, and remained abroad several months. He is now located in the new Marshall Field building, Washington Street, Chicago, and is enjoying' a very lucrative practice. He has been married twice, but no living children; had one infant by his first wife.

3. and 4. Infant twins, born about 1843, children of Isaac Montgomery.

Thomas Montgomery, born probably 1846, fifth child of Isaac: engaged in the stock business in Kansas, and died there unmarried.

Nancy Montgomery, born probably 1850, sixth child of Isaac, married Nicholas Boren, of Princeton, Ind.: no children.

7. Louis Montgomery, born 1856, in Illinois, son of Isaac by a second wife; visited Indiana after he was grown. The last I heard of him he was in Missouri, unmarried.

So far as I know there is not a living grandchild of Isaac Montgomery.

John Roberts Montgomery, born May 4, 1817, married Rachel B. Brumheld about 1840. He died 1856. His wife died 1879. He was of rather heavy build, sandy curly hair, and blue eyes. She was slender with straight, black hair and black eyes. Children six:

1. Richard Montgomery, born June 16, 1841, was a soldier in Co. F, 80th regiment Ind. Vol. He was captured at London, Tenn., in 1863 while repairing the telegraph line. He was several months at Belle Island, opposite Richmond, Va., then taken to Andersonville, Ga., where he died Aug. 15, 1864. His remains are supposed to have been removed to Chattanooga, Tenn. His name is recorded on the family monument of D. B. Montgomery, his brother, in the Joseph Clark cemetery in Montgomery Township, Gibson County, Ind. He was never married.

2. Walter C. Montgomery, born May 26, 1843, second son of John Roberts Montgomery, was a soldier in Co. F, 80th regiment Ind. Vol.; was in the Perryville fight with the regiment, Oct. 8, I 802, which had left Camp Gibson, at which it was organized, just one month to a day. He was severely wounded at Kenesaw Mountain, from which he is a great sufferer at the present time. He lives in Owensville and is in comfortable circumstances. He married Louisa Clark, a sister to Rev. William Clark, Sept. 8, 1870. She was born Oct. 13, 1847; children five:

1. Lillie B. Montgomery, born July 5, 1871, married George N. Yeager, March 13, 1890, a farmer and breeder of poultry and stock. One child—Lulu Yeager, born July 20, 1891.

2. John Montgomery, born July 6, 1873, is a liveryman in Owensville, Ind. and treasurer of the Town Board of Owensville, 1902; married Minnie Marvel, Dec. 13, 1893; one child—Ureta F. Montgomery, born Sept. 22, 1894.

3. Maggie Montgomery, born Oct. 27, 1875; married Luther Boren, a farmer and stock-raiser, Aug. 15, 1895; children two: 1. Doyle Boren, born Oct. 24, 1896. 2., Jesse Boren, born Aug. 2, 1901.

4. Myrtle Montgomery, born April 13, 1880; dead.

5. Ada Montgomery, born Oct. 18, 1884; a clerk in James Montgomery's store; single 1903.

D. B. Montgomery
Owensville, Indiana

David B. Montgomery, born Oct. 20, 1845, third child of John Roberts Montgomery. He taught several years in the common schools; united with the General Baptist church at Owensville, Ind., 1865; licensed to preach in 1867; ordained in 1874. He was one of editors of the General Baptist Herald from January 1874 to January 1875. He published a history of the General Baptists in 1882. He has in manuscript a Life of Rev. Dr. A. D. Williams, late president of Oakland City College, Oakland City, Ind. He is also the compiler of this Genealogy. He married Nancy Jane Smith, daughter of John Martin Smith, Oct. 1, 1874. She was born Jan. 25, 1852, and died March 21, 1899. Children two:

1. Dr. Martin A. Montgomery, born June 20, 1875, graduated from the Owensville high school in 1893; graduated from the University Medical College at Louisville, Ky., 1898, and began practice at Owensville, Ind., in April, 1898. His residence and office are on the old John Warrick residence lot; married Josie Strehl. Oct. 1, 1899. She was a teacher in the public schools of Owensville and was born Sept. 26, 1878. One child—Herald Martin Montgomery, born July 2, 1900.

2. Lewra A. Montgomery, born April 2, 1878, married George R. Simpson. Feb. 15, 1894, a farmer and stock-raiser. He was born June 20.

The Montgomerys

1871. Children two: 1. Martin Doyle Simpson, born Sept. 21, 1894, died Jan. 24. 1895. 2. Darwin Montgomery Simpson, born Sept. 25, 1896; has been in school during the fall and winter since 1900.

John R. Montgomery, Jr., born May 13, 1848, died 1864—17 years old; fourth child of John Roberts Montgomery.

Mary June Montgomery, born April 25, 1851, fifth child of John Roberts Montgomery, married John B, Thompson, Dec. 2, 1877. He died about nine miles east of Oklahoma City, O. T., Oct. 14, 1S89, They were married in Indiana and moved to Udall, Kansas, in 1886; took a claim in the Territory in 1888, and he died in 1889, She was left with four small children, therefore she was allowed to return to Indiana and remain until the final proving up of her claim. She remained in Indiana until the fall of 1899 when she and all her family except Jessie returned to their farm in Oklahoma. She married George W. Brown, of Oklahoma, a contractor in good circumstances, Sept. 29, 1902. Thompson children six: 1. Infant, born Sept. 5, 1878, died Sept. 9, 1878, 2. Ora Lee Thompson, born Dec. 31, 1879, married Kirk Montgomery, Sept. 23, 1896, in Indiana, and moved to Oklahoma City, 1899; no children. 3. Jessie E. Thompson, born March 4, 1882, was a clerk in Welborn's department store in Owensville, Ind., 1902. 4. Wilber A. Thompson, born Aug. 13, 1884. 5. Noma Thompson, born June 18, 1887, died Mar. 25, 1890. 6. Walter Thompson, born Feb. 22, 1890.

Andrew J. Montgomery, born March 10, 1854, sixth child of John Roberts Montgomery, moved to Udall, Kansas, in 1878, came back to Indiana on a visit in 1879 and has been in the West ever since. He has traveled all over the Southwest. He is now in the Indian Territory and is said to be in favorable circumstances. He married Polly McCrary, in Kansas; children four: 1. John Montgomery, born____.

Martha or Patsy Montgomery, born March 13, 1819, seventh child of Walter C. Montgomery, Sr.; died Feb. 27, 1888; married Louis Barr, in Indiana, Sept. 18, 1844. Mr. Barr was born April 18, 1818, died June 21, 1895. Mr. Barr had moved from Gibson County, Ind., to Atlanta, Ill., many years before this marriage—probably as early as 1830. Immediately after their marriage, in 1844, they returned to the home of Mr. Barr which was about four miles south of Atlanta, Ill., just south of Kickapoo Creek, about three-fourths of a mile distant. They raised their family there, and died on their old home place. Mr. Barr was a whole-souled, generous-hearted

Irishman, always full of life and ready to encourage the deserving. Children seven:

1. Jane Barr, born Sept. 16, 1845; married A. T. Hays of Logan County, Ill., Jan. 3, 1867. He was a soldier in the 7th regiment Ill. Vol. of first 75,000, called in the Civil War, and then a first sergeant in the 4th Ill. Cavalry and served until the close of the war.

Mr. Hays, by good management and industry, has gained quite a good fortune. He served three terms as trustee of his township, and four years as deputy sheriff and four years as sheriff of Logan County, Ill. He owns a fine body of land five miles south of Atlanta, and has a fine residence in Lincoln. Mr. and Mrs. Hays enjoy company and are admirable entertainers. Children three: 1. and 2. Infant sons, twins, born Feb. 22, 1868. 3. Infant, born Aug. 5. 1871, died Aug. 5, 1871.

2. John W. Barr, born May 15, 1847, by trade a carpenter; was postmaster under Cleveland; later a merchant in Atlanta, Ill. He has a very handsome income. He is in poor health and is encumbered with 275 pounds in weight.

3. James T. Barr, born Aug. 13, 1850, died July 17, 1852.

4. Matilda E. Barr, born May 15, 1853; married Alexander Rhodes, June 26, 1873. He has a nice residence in Lincoln, Ill. and a good farm south of Kickapoo Creek. He is a carpenter by trade; has retired from the farm. Children three: 1. Louis Rhodes, born Feb. 16, 1876, graduated from Lincoln College in 1899; graduated from a Chicago medical college in 1902, and is now located in Lincoln, Ill. 2. David Rhodes, born Dec. 4, 1878, is a fireman on the Chicago and Alton railroad (1902). 3. Mattie Rhodes, born May 2, 1888, is a bright student in the Lincoln schools.

5. Rebecca Barr, born May 20, 1856, married Charley McKean of Indianapolis, Ind., Sept. 16, 1886. He died Jan. 12, 1893. She sold her interest in the old home farm and now (1902) lives in Lincoln, Ill., in comfortable circumstances.

6. Andrew J. Barr, born April 27, 1858. He was educated at Lincoln College, and at the Wesleyan College, Bloomington, Ill. He is a brilliant young attorney and has a remarkably fine practice. He was defeated for

Congress in the landslide in politics in the 13th Illinois district in 1894. He is fine-looking and is a silver-tongued orator. It will be a long time before his oratory and strength as a campaign speaker in 1894 will be forgotten. Those speeches attracted the attention of the St. Louis Globe-Democrat and the Chicago Record. He married Miss Bessie Scroggs, of Champaign, and now (1902) lives in a handsome residence in the most beautiful part of Bloomington, Ill., and ranks among the best lawyers in the state.

Nelly Montgomery, born April 13, 1821 died April 7, 1877; eighth child of Walter C. Montgomery Sr. married John Knowles of Gibson County, Ind. He was born Sept. 14, 1815. He was an elder in the C. P. church. Besides a large family of their own, they raised several orphan children, viz: John and Louisa Wells, Bill Knowles, W. C. Montgomery, Dan Henly, and perhaps others. He died Aug. 20, 1869, in Owensville. Ind. He was, at the time of his death, one among the wealthiest men in Montgomery Township. Nelly Montgomery-Knowles was the mother of one pair of twins: her oldest daughter, Nancy, had two pairs; her third daughter, Per*melia had three pairs,* her ninth child and third son, James L., one pair; her tenth child and fourth daughter, Callie, one pair—making seven pairs of twins among her grandchildren. She had one granddaughter to have one pair, and one to have two pairs. Counting Nelly's own twins, this makes eleven pairs in her family descent. In all she has about 120 descendants. Children thirteen:

1. Martha Knowles, born Jan. 6, 1838, died small.

2. William B. Knowles, farmer, born April 27, 1839 was teacher in the common schools; was an elder in the C. P. church 33 years. He was a graduate of a commercial college. He died at Bird's Point, Mo., on his way home from Texas, where he had been for his health. He first married Maria Mauck; children three: 1. John F., dead. 2. Elmer E. Knowles, born Jan. 16, 1864 married Minnie Bradley, Jan. 8, 1892. 3. Infant.

William B. Knowles married, second, Janie Smith; children four:

4. Madison M. Knowles a, farmer, born Oct. 11, 1873, married Lizzie Brown, Aug. 23, 1892; one child—Ovela Knowles, born June 2, 1893.
5. David W. Knowles, born Jan. 31, 1876, single.
6. Fannie Lake, born May 9, 1882; single.
7. Nelly, born Feb. 11, 1887, died March 5, 1887.

3. Nancy Knowles, born June 4, 1847, daughter of Nelly, married James R. R. Hill, Jan. 14, 1864. He was born in Barren County, Ky., 1838; taught in the public schools and came to Indiana when quite young. He was a soldier in the 80th regiment Ind. Vol.; moved to Greenwood County, Kansas in 1877, and Mrs. Hill died there Aug. 19, 1897. She was a member of the C. P. church from 16 years old. Children twelve:

1. John W. Hill, born___; married Ella Pinkerton, in Kansas, May 8, 1887. Children two: 1. Maggie Hill, born___. 2. James R. R. Hill, born ___. They live at Bush, Oklahoma.

2. Annetta Hill, born____, married Samuel A. Richey in Kansas, Jan. 4, 1882. They live at Ukiah, California; children eleven: 1. Isaac. 2. Henry. 3. Etta. 4. Archie. 5. Guy. 6. Anna. 7. Bertie. 8. Lemmie. 9. Glenn, twin to Lemmie. 10. Matilda. 11. Victor H.

3. Mollie A. Hill, married A. R. Lindermond, at Yeats Center, Kansas, Dec. 5, 1900; no children.

4. Maggie Hill.

5. Matilda F. Hill married Ferdinand C. Jones, March 8, 1899; one child, ___. They have a claim at Cache, Oklahoma.

6. Frank J. Hill, twin to Matilda F. 7. Arthur H. Hill. 8. Charles D. Hill, dead. 9. Bertha E. Hill. 10. Edgar Hill. 11. and 12. Ollie and Dollie Hill, twins.

4. Thomas Knowles, born April 19, 1843, son of Nelly Montgomery-Knowles; married Lizzie Mauck, in Indiana; moved near Moran, Schofield County, Texas; children seven: 1. Nettie Knowles, married C. W. Carter; children five: Elizabeth, Myrtle, Jacob W., Birdie, and Marietta. 2. Jacob W. Knowles, single. 3. Carrie Knowles, married David R. Carter; children three: Mary B., W. J. Bryan, and Earl. 4. Effie Knowles, married Luther Alstone; children three: Pearl, Lonnie, and Bertha. 5. May Belle Knowles, born___, married Mark L. McDonald; one child—Erie Pearl. 6. Thomas E. Knowles, single. 7. Pearl Knowles, single.

5. Matilda Knowles, born Feb. 4, 1845, daughter of Nelly Montgomery-Knowles; was a teacher in the public schools; married Richard Brumfield, who lives about two and one-half miles west of Haubstadt, Ind., and is a

farmer. He taught in the public schools; was trustee of Johnson township four years; children twelve:

1. James H. Brumfield, born Aug. 26, 1866, died June 2, 1888, single; taught in the public schools.
2. Laura Brumfield, born July 1, 1868; single 1903.
3. Sarah E. Brumfield, born March 2, 1871; taught in the public schools; single 1903.
4. Rosina Brumfield, born Feb. 11, 1873, taught in the public schools; married Charles B. Patrick, April 18, 1894. He is a railroad engineer. He has operated in the north-west and south-west, from Oregon to Old Mexico. Children five: Pansy P. and Myrtle M., twins; John M. and Richard, twins (dead); and Clara F.
5. John A. Brumfield, born Feb. 16, 1875; taught in the public schools; graduated from a dental college in Cincinnati. Ohio, in 1900; is now (1902) practicing in Princeton, Ind.; married Myrtle Smith, of Owensville, June 28, 1900; one child.
6. William Victor Brumfield, born July 27, 1877; taught in the public schools; is now (1902) in the farm-implement business in Owensville; married Malinda Kight, Oct. 10, 1901; no children.
7., Infant, born June 12, 1879.
8. Mary P. Brumfield, born Jan. 19, 1881; single.
9. Richard M. Brumfield, born Nov. 9, 1882, taught in the public schools; single.
10. Ernest W. Brumfield, born May 24, 1884.
11. Matilda F. Brumfield, born June 5. 1886.
12. Clara J. Brumfield, born Aug. 31, 1888.

6. Permelia Knowles, born June 13, 1848, daughter of Nelly Montgomery Knowles; married Thomas Stone, a farmer, Nov. 10, 1857. They were raised near Owensville, Ind.: moved to Manard County, Ill., then to Tolono. Ill. Children twelve.

7. and 8. Infant Knowles twins, born Sept. 1, 1850; children of Nelly Montgomery-Knowles.

9. James L. Knowles born Aug. 28, 1851, in the farm-implement business in Owensville, Ind.; married Julia Givens; she died Feb. 26, 1877; children two: 1. Nellie Knowles, died two and one-half years old. 2. Orien Knowles, is in restaurant business in Owensville, Ind.; married Alice Witherspoon; one

child, Julia F. Knowles, dead. Second, J. L. Knowles married Susan Herring, nee Massey. Oct. 18, 1878; children two: 1. Gertie, died 6 years old. 2. Grace died 7 months old; twin to Gertie.

10. Caroline Knowles, born Jan. 10, 1854, died 1894, daughter of Nelly Montgomery-Knowles; married John Rutherford; children three: 1. and 2. Twins. 3. Infant.

11, John W. Knowles, born July 4, 1856, son of Nelly Montgomery-Knowles; was killed by a wagon running over him when small.

12. Joseph M. Knowles, born May 15, 1858, son of Nelly Montgomery-Knowles; lives at Tolono, Ill.; first married Mary Armstrong; in Indiana, Oct. 6, 1880. She was born April 22, 1860, died June 6, 1888; children three: 1. Minnie Knowles, born July 10, 1882; married Wesley Douglass; one child— Earl Douglass. 2. Emma Knowles, born Dec. 28, 1883, married Wesley Witherspoon. He died 1902; no children. 3. Mary L. Knowles, born May 23, 1888.

Joseph M. Knowles second married Edith Baker, of Tolono, Ill. She was born April 10, 1872; children four: 1. Zerlena J., born June 20, 1894. 2. Charlie A., born July 7, 1898. 3. Floyd M., born April 29. 1900. 4. Melvin C., born Aug. 31, 1902.

13. Ida Bolle Knowles, born May 23, 1860, daughter of Nelly Montgomery-Knowles; married William Rutherford: children two— Ella and William.

9. Walter Crockett Montgomery, born April 11, 1823, son of Walter C. Montgomery, Sr.: was a soldier in the seventh regiment Ill. Vol., from Aug. 1861 to Feb. 1862. He was in the battle of Shiloh. He has been a man of wonderful endurance. He was born one and one-half miles south of Owensville, Ind., moved to Atlanta, Ill., about 1850. In 1866 he moved to Ft. Scott, Kansas; then to Webster City, Iowa; then back to Indiana; and now, 1902, lives near Sebree, Ky. He first married Lucinda Ash, of Indiana, Feb. 6, 1844. She was born Feb. 26, 1826; children twelve. Second he married Mahala Gardner of Atlanta. Ill. about 1869; children three. Third he married Ruth Ashley, nee Madden, of Sebree, Ky.; no children.

The Montgomerys

1. Louisa J. Montgomery, born May 5, 1846, married John Barr, of near Waynesville, Ill., and moved to Webster City, Iowa, and became quite wealthy. She died a few years after they were married. One child—James Barr, married ___; children four.

2. Warrick Montgomery, born Aug. 27, 1847; enlisted Feb. 12, 1864, in the 106th regiment Ill. Vol.; discharged July 12, 1865. He lives about two miles west of Atlanta, Ill.; is a well-to-do farmer. He has made two trips to Europe for the purpose of buying and importing fine-bred draft horses. He married Mrs. Emma Johnson, nee Dunn, an estimable lady, who also has considerable property in her own name.

3. James Montgomery, born Oct. 29, 1849, married___, and was in Kansas when last heard from.

4. Joseph Montgomery, born May 16, 1851; first married Rose Sullivan, in Logan County, Ill.; children one, ___. Second; married Mary King, in DeWitt County, Ill.; moved to Denver, Colorado and was killed in a mine disaster. 1. Thomas Montgomery, son of Joseph, now lives near Beason, Ill.: married a Miss Kester.

5. Lorenza Montgomery, born 1853.

6. Levi Montgomery, born 1855, married Miss Brassfield; lives north of Lincoln, Ill.; children four: ——.

7. Alfred Montgomery, born 1856, married Bessie — — and lives in Bloomington, Ill. He is an artist of considerable note. He has traveled considerably in the interest of his profession. Children four: ___.

9. Ollie Montgomery, born 1859, married a Mr. Patterson near Lincoln, Ill. They have eleven children, but I have failed to obtain their names.

10. Emma Montgomery, born 1861, married___; have no information. Children, four.

11. Charley Montgomery, born 1863, lives in Peoria, Ill., and is connected with the livery business; married___; children___.

12. William Sherman Montgomery, born 1865 was a United States soldier in the Philippines, in Co. H, 28th regiment. When last heard from he was in Colorado, 1902; single.

13. David Lewis Montgomery, married a Miss Hatch; children___.

14. Marion Montgomery, single.

15. Infant.

10. Robert Montgomery, born Jan. 9, 1826, son of Walter Crockett Montgomery, Sr.; died Jan. 28, 1845, of "black-tongue."

11. William W. Montgomery, born Jan. 18, 1829 was a twin to a brother who died small; first married Elizabeth Jonson, Sept. 13, 1853; children five. She died Feb. 13, 1862. Second he married Sarah Carnahan, Aug. 7, 1864; children twelve. She died Dec. 17, 1881, near Millshoals, Ill. She was a daughter of Hon. M. T. Carnahan, who was a noble-looking man and represented Posey County, Ind., for 21 years in the state legislature. Mr. Montgomery was also of portly appearance—six feet tall, erect, black eyes and black hair, and the finest set of white teeth I ever saw; never had a decayed tooth. He moved from Owensville Ind., about 1872 to Burnt Prairie, White County. Ill. Later he moved north of Millshoals, Ill., and died there Jan. 21, 1892, on the same day his brother, Hon. J. W. Montgomery, died, near Owensville, Ind.; children seventeen:

1. Permelia Montgomery, born Sept. 11, 1854 married Joseph Welborn, Nov. 6, 1890. She is his second wife; no children of her own, but she has truly been a mother to Mr. Welborn's three children and tenderly cared for Ethel through a long and serious affliction which ended in death.

2. Wilmina Montgomery, born July 22, 1856, in Indiana, and moved to Burnt Prairie, Ill.; later to Atlanta, Ill.; then to Lincoln. Ill. and now (1903) lives in Gibson County, Ind.; in a very low state of health; never married.

3. America Montgomery, born, Jan. 11, 1858, married George C. Stone, Oct. 31, 1878. Mr. Stone is a farmer and stock-breeder; one child—Florence Stone, died Dec. 24, 1899. She was a beautiful and good-hearted girl.

4. Elnora Montgomery, born July 18, 1860, married Pinkney A. Clark, a farmer, Aug. 5, 1880. They moved to Spencer, Iowa, March 1899, and are living there now—1902. They have no children of their own but raised Eugene Montgomery, a half-brother, from infancy, and he is with them at this time.

5. Lizzie Montgomery, born Jan. 12, 1862, died June 1862.

6. Louisa M. Montgomery, born June 3, 1865, married Win. Files of Millshoals, Ill., June 4, 1883 who was born Feb. 27, 1855. He has been telegraph operator at that place; is postmaster there now. Children five: 1. Pearl E. Files, born Oct. 15, 1884. 2. Grace M. Files, born Aug. 14, 1886. 3. Roy B. Files, born July 7, 1891. 4. Dorsey Dee Files, born July 25, 1900. 5. Delmar Lee Files, born July 25, 1900 died July 25, 1900; twin to Dorsey Dee.

7. Martha B. Montgomery, born Aug. 7. 1866, married John M. Scudder of Millshoals, Ill., March 12, 1885. He is a railroad carpenter. They now live at Yeates Center, Kansas; children live: 1. Verna E. Scudder, born Oct. 17, 1886. 2. Roscoe P. Scudder, born July 1, 1888. 3. John M. Scudder, Jr., born Dec. 12, 1893, at Springfield, Ill. 4. Ethel Scudder, born Feb. 6, 1896,

The Montgomerys

Eldorado, Kansas. 5. Ray H. Scudder, born May 26, 1898, Ft. Smith, Ark.; died Feb. 6, 1899.

8. Louis Allen Montgomery, a farmer, born Oct. 29, 1867, lives north of McGary Station; married Minnie Montgomery, March 17, 1896. She died May 19, 1900. One child — William Clancy Montgomery, born May 3, 1900.

9. M. T. Montgomery, born July 8, 1839, is a liveryman in Owensville, Ind.; married Ethel Marvel, Dec. 14, 1898: no children.

10. Walter A. Montgomery, born March 8, 1871, died Dec. 14, 1881.

11. Charles Ed. Montgomery, born March 2, 1873, is working with the Missouri Pacific railway, with headquarters at Ft. Smith, Ark.

12. and 13. Infant twins, born Jan. 25, 1875; died Jan. 25, 1875.

14. Carrie A. Montgomery, born Dec. 6, 1875, married William Phelps, a farmer, near Millshoals, Ill., May 16, 1894, who was born March 2, 1870. Children two: 1. Ernest N. Phelps, born Jan. 16, 1896. 2. Nolen Phelps, born Dec. 7, 1897.

15. Clara A. Montgomery, a twin to Carrie, born Dec. 6, 1875; died June 1876.

We note here that four children were born in this family in less than one year.

16. John W. Montgomery, born Feb. 27, 1878; never has walked or talked.

17. Eugene Montgomery, born Oct. 4, 1881, lives with his sister, Elnora Clark, in Spencer. Iowa.

13. Andrew J. Montgomery, born March 17, 1831, son of Walter C. Montgomery Sr., was born and raised on a farm south of Owensville and lived there until a few years before his death. He died in Owensville, Ind., Dec. 14, 1895. He first married Mary McCrary, Nov. 1858. She died Nov. 30, 1884. Children five. Second, married Mary E. Chandler, June 19, 1889. She died April 7, 1899; no children.

1. Willis E. Montgomery, born Nov. 4, 1859; taught in the public schools; was a graduate of the Danville, Ind., Commercial School; was a soldier in Co. K, 159th regiment Ind. Vol., in the Spanish-American War. He was freight agent at Princeton, Ind.; never married.

2. Virgil V. Montgomery, a farmer, born March 1, 1861, lives in Owensville, Ind.; married Anna B. McCrary, May 1, 1887; children two: 1. Bertha Montgomery, born May 15, 1888. 2. Gilbert Montgomery, born March 10, 1890.

3. Infant, twin to Henry, born June 3, 1863, died June 17, 1863; third child of A. J. Montgomery, Sr.

4. Henry Montgomery, born June 3, 1863, died April 30, 1864.

5. Walter Logan Montgomery, a farmer, born July 14, 1866, died near Cynthiana, Ind., July 9. 1890; married Carrie Williams Oct. 3, 1886. She died___; children one—Ethel Montgomery, born July 5, 1887. She lives at Cynthiana, Ind.

14. Infant of Walter C. Montgomery, Sr., born Feb. 16, 1848, died Feb. 16, 1848.

15. Elizabeth J. Montgomery, daughter of Walter C. Montgomery, Sr. born March 2, 1849: lives in Owensville, Ind. She is quite an enthusiastic worker in the Methodist church; never married.

16. Mary A. Montgomery, born July 23, 1850, died Aug. 9, 1850.

17. James P. Montgomery, a farmer, born Dec. 30, 1851, son of Walter C. Montgomery, Sr.; lives in Vanderburg County, Ind., on the old John Powell farm, on the Owensville and Evansville road, about two and one-half miles west of St. James: first married Fanny McFadin, June 3, 1876, granddaughter of John McFadin— page ___. She died Nov. 12, 1884; children two. Second married Carrie Muth Feb. 9, 1886. She died May 25, 1898; children seven: 1. Eddie Montgomery, born Aug. 19, 1877, died in infancy. 2. Harvey Montgomery, born Aug. 29. 1880; was in California in 1901. 3. James A. Montgomery, born 1887. 4. Walter L. Montgomery, born July 29, 1888. 5. Comad E. Montgomery, born April 16, 1890. 6, Margaret E. Montgomery, born Sept. 18, 1891, died. 7. Lena Y. Montgomery, born Feb. 8, 1893. 8. Gilford M. Montgomery, born Sept. 1, 1894. 9. Eleanor M. Montgomery, born Feb. 9, 1895,

18. Infant, born July 9, 1853, died July 9, 1853; child of Walter C. Montgomery, Sr. 19, Smith Miller Montgomery, born Feb. 22, 1855; the nineteenth and last of the children of W. C. Montgomery, Sr.—"Old Virginia Walter." He was named for Smith Miller, who was representative in Congress at that time from the "pocket" of Indiana. Mr. Miller was a radical Democrat. Mr. Montgomery is a staunch Prohibitionist. He owns most of the quarter-section which was taken up by his grandfather, "Purty Old Tom," in 1807—96 years ago. This farm has continuously remained in the possession of the family for all these years. He married Martha Ella Lane, Nov. 14, 1878. She was born in North Carolina, June 9, 1859; children three:

1. Oscar C. Montgomery, born Aug. 17, 1879; died Sept. 17, 1888.

2. Alvah O. Montgomery, born Nov. 21, 1880; married Angeline M. Chism, of Princeton, Ind., Dec. 1, 1901; one child—Carroll Edgar Montgomery, born Sept. 18, 1902. 3. Ellis Roscoe Montgomery, born Jan. 26, 1884; single.

And Their Descendants

CHAPTER XIII

CROCKET FAMILY NO. 1.

On Sept. 20, 1895, the "Crockett Clan." composed of members of this illustrious family who live in Tennessee, Kentucky, Texas, Arkansas and Illinois, met at the Alamo, in Crockett County, Tenn. Several addresses were made by members of the Clan—notably Col. K. H. Crockett, of Stuttgart, Ark., Chief of the Clan.

"The Fall of the Alamo" was read by Ingram Crockett, of Henderson, Ky. and a historical sketch of the Crockett family was read by Mrs. Anna Belle Tuck, of Plymouth, Ill. This paper is full of interest to the descendants of the family, and I take the liberty of reproducing it in connection with the few historical facts I have collected concerning this family:

The first record we have of the Crockett family dates back and prior to 1643. Gabriel Crocketagni lived at that time in the south of France. His son, Antoine Peronnett De Crocketagni, was born at Montanbon, France, July 10, 1643. In 1664 Gabriel Crocketagni obtained for his son a position in the house of Louis XIV. This son of Gabriel Crocketagni was, according to tradition, one of the handsomest young men in the south of France, an excellent horseman, and devoted to his calling. By his fine appearance and love of duty he drew the personal attention of the king, who was anxious to retain him in his service and make him second in command of the household guards.

In 1669 Antoine Crocketagni was married to Louise De Soix. There is a tradition among us that the Crockett family was related to Lafayette. It must have been through this union, for history says that the Lafayette and De Soix families were related. The family originally was Catholic, but was converted to Protestantism.

Antoine, under the direct instrumentality of John De Le Fontaine and the distinguished French Protestant, Matthew Maury, whose descendants are very numerous in the South today and whose great-grandson, Matthew F. Maury, was founder of the National Observatory at Washington. D. C.

Soon after his marriage, Antoine resigned his commission and removed to Bordeaux, where he entered the merchants' service of the Fountaines and Maurys, who had the monopoly of the wine and salt trade in the south of France at that time. Antoine's first child, Gabriel Gustave, was born at Bordeaux, Oct. 12, 1672. In that year the Bishop of Lyons, through the king, ordered all heretics (Huguenots) to leave the south of France within twenty days. Prior to this, other members of the Crockett family had been forced into exile and had taken up their abode in England, and afterward in Ireland.

Antoine Crocketagni and wife, Louise De Soix, having become members of the Church of England, were among the exiled members still in the employ of the Fountaines and the Maurys. They took up their abode in Ireland, near Bartry Bay, where the following children were born to them. In Ireland the name was changed to Crockett. As above stated, they had one son born in France—Gabriel Gustav, born Oct. 12, 1672. The following were born in Ireland:

James Crockett, born Nov. 20, 1674.
Joseph Louise Crockett, born Jan. 9, 1676.
Robert Watkins Crockett, born July 18, 1678.
Louise DeSoix Crockett, born March 15, 1680.
Mary Frances Crockett, born Feb. 20. 1682.
Elizabeth Crockett, born April 13, 1685.

We have no record as to whom Gabriel Crockett married. "James Crockett married an Irish girl by the name of Martha Montgomery, daughter of Thomas Montgomery, who was a sailor in the naval service of England."

This is the first instance we have noticed of a marriage between the Crockett and Montgomery families, and probably occurred about 1700.

Joseph Louise Crockett, the third son of Antoine Crockett, born 1676, married Sarah Stewart of Donegal, Ireland, and was the father of ten children:
1. Joseph Crockett, Jr., born in Donegal, Ireland, May 6, 1702.
2. Thomas Stewart Crockett, born in Donegal, Ireland. March 9, 1704.
3. John Crockett, born in Bantry Bay, Ireland, June 10, 1707.
4. William Crockett, born in New Rochelle, N. Y., Aug. 10, 1709.
5. James Edwin Crockett, born in Virginia, Nov. 1811.
6. Jason Spotswood Crockett, born in Virginia, Nov. 1713.
7. Elizabeth Crockett, born in Virginia, Jan. 30, 1715.
8. Martha Ellen Crockett, born in Virginia, Sept. 10, 1719.

Please notice in the above that some of the children were born in the north of Ireland, some in the south, one in New York, and four in Virginia.

Joseph Louise Crockett, born 1676, revisited France, but the hatred was still so strong against the Huguenots that he came to this country and settled at the Huguenot colony of New Rochelle, and finally in Virginia. I have not time to trace all the record, but wish to refer to John Crockett of the fourth generation, born (at Bantry Bay, Ireland), 1707, who was my great-great-grandfather. He married Eliza Bemly, a French lady who came to Virginia with the Maurys. He taught school for thirty years in Virginia. Three of his sons fought for American independence during the Revolution. One of them, Col. Joseph Crockett, served with distinction through the entire war.

It is through his patriotic devotion to his country that I am entitled to wear this badge of the Daughters of the American Revolution—an honor I esteem very highly.

A brother of John Crockett, Jason Spotswood Crocket, born in Virginia, 1713, is thought by almost all who have given this matter any attention to have been the grandfather of the immortal "Davy," and consequently the great-great-grandfather of our Chief. Now I am aware that this idea does not coincide with "Davy's" own statement, for in his Autobiography he says: "My grandfather came from Ireland." Might it not have been his great-grandfather instead? This is a question I have tried hard to solve, and as yet have not fully succeeded. My own opinion is sustained by considerable proof, that Jason Spotswood Crockett was the grandfather of David Crockett. He married Margaret Lacy of Lancaster County, Pa., in 1770. He lived in Pennsylvania for seven months, and then removed to North Carolina. He had a large family of children. The descendants of James, Joseph, Louis and James Edwin are very numerous throughout the South. We have no record of Gabriel or Robert Watkins Crockett ever having come to this country.

It is my opinion that they are the ancestors of the Irish, English and Scottish branches of the family.

There are a large number of Crockets in the New England States, but unfortunately we know but little of their early history and in some cases can only name back to grandfather. I received a letter recently from S. R.

Crockett, the now famous novelist of Penacrick, Scotland, which read as follows:

"I know but little of my early ancestry. I only know they came from Ireland to Scotland, and tradition says they were French refugees. That establishes the relationship to us beyond a doubt. It is very unfortunate that our forefathers cared so little for family history. Old letters and records were often ruthlessly destroyed that would be priceless now. It is hard to find the "missing link," but I have faith that it will be found, and then all Crockets, whether coming from England, Scotland or Ireland, will be found to have come from one common French parentage.

"We have reason to be proud of our Huguenot ancestry. It is an honor to have come from people of whom it is said no other class of immigrant, save the Puritans of England, cast such healthful leaven amid the elements that proved the new world."

In our family the mixture of Gallic with the French has produced a hardy, robust race. Much of the wit and humor among us comes from the Irish strain, and patriotic devotion comes from our French ancestry.

As a family or clan the Crockets rank high. In it are found some of our eminent lawyers, doctors, preachers, poets, journalists and professors. The halls of Congress have often resounded to the voices of members of our Clan. Members in our Clan, among whom stands our honored Chief, rank below none as orators and word-painters. As a family the Crockets are warm-hearted and impulsive; quick to resent an injury, and quick to forgive. Given to hospitality, their latch-strings are always on the outside and all friends are welcome. There are doubtless some black sheep in the flock. What flock has them not? But they only serve to make the whiteness of the rest the more apparent. The Crockets have proved their devotion to what they believed was right, in every war in which this country has been engaged. We find no less than eight fighting for American independence during the Revolution; a number for American rights in 1812; again in the Mexican War they are not found wanting.

How many of their brave young lives went out during our civil war I know not, but the number was great. Some wore the blue, some the gray. Would that I had the pen of a ready writer, that I might add one leaf to the laurel wreath encircling the brow of our hero, the "Immortal Davy." But what words of mine could add to his renown? You all know the story of his life and death. It was learned at your mother's knee. Many a young life has been made better by the recital of his deeds. His love of liberty, which led him to a martyr's death, has been an inspiration to thousands and will so prove to thousands yet unborn. His unswerving honesty and devotion to what he believed to be right has become proverbial. "Be sure you are right and then go ahead" echoes around the world upon the members of the Clan.

I would urge the necessity of gathering up all the information regarding the family history possible. I have had excellent success during the past year in my labor of love, but each one must assist if ever the history is completed. I have had letters from all over the United States, one from Germany, one from Scotland, and several from Canada.

For much of the above history I am indebted to Mr. S. M. Duncan, of Nicholasville, Ky., who obtained it from Mr. David Maury, of Essex County, Va., in 1858. It is taken from an old record of the Crockett family which was brought to this County by some member of the family early in 1700. A copy of the letter by Mr. Maury is in my possession. There may be some slight errors in it in regard to dates and births, etc., but in the main it is doubtless correct.

Hoping to meet you one and all, from our dear and honored Chief to the last little child among you, at our next reunion, I will say good-bye. "God be with you till we meet again."

ANNA BELLE TUCK,
Secretary Crockett Clan.

And Their Descendants

CHAPTER XIV.

CROCKETT FAMILY NO. 2.

John Crockett and Esther, his wife, came to America about 1715, and in 1728 they came to Philadelphia and soon afterward settled at Lancaster, Pa., from which place they moved to Monocracy, Maryland. In 1749 most of the family moved to Wythe County, Virginia— then Augusta County. It must be borne in mind that at that time Augusta County embraced the entire south-west part of Virginia. They lived at Fort Chiswell, where they remained until after Braddock's defeat in 1755. On account of Indian depredations they returned East as far as Winchester, Va., and after collecting fresh supplies of stock and provisions returned to Wythe County. Yet some of them, including Hugh Crockett and his father, Joseph, Sr., settled on the south fork of the Roanoke River, in what is now Montgomery County.

Joseph Crockett, Sr., was born in Londonderry, Ireland, and married Jane DeVigne, the daughter of a French exile. He died in the year 1767, at his home in Montgomery County, near the present village of Shawsville.

Their sons were Walter, Hugh, Joseph, Robert and Samuel; daughters Mattie, Mary, Elizabeth and Nancy.

Walter Crockett was the first clerk of Wythe County, Va. He married Miss Margaret Steel-Caldwell and lived on New River in Wythe County. He had a son, Samuel, Jr., who married a Miss Carter who lived on the James River near Richmond; they moved to Scott County, Ky., and raised a large family.

Samuel Crockett, Sr., was born in March, 1740: married Jane Armstrong, daughter of William Armstrong and Susan Johnson. They lived on Reed Creek, near Kent's Mill, in Wythe County, Va. Their sons were Joseph and Robert; daughters Susan and Jane. Samuel, Sr., served in the Revolutionary War, on the staff of General Green, in the rank of major. He died at his home on Reed Creek in 1782, and his widow, Jane Armstrong-Crockett, married John Draper, grandfather of John S. Draper, of Draper's Valley, Va.

Joseph Crockett also served in the Revolutionary War as colonel of a regiment. He was afterward appointed marshal of the Territory of Kentucky and settled in Jessamine County of that state. A grandson of his, J. B. Crockett, was elected to the supreme bench of California. He died at his home near Fruitdale, in that state, a few years since.

Hugh Crockett married Rebecca Tarlton, or Charlton, of Jersey City, N. J. She was one of the few who escaped massacre with the settlers of Long Cane, on the Savannah River, South Carolina, by the Cherokee Indians. They lived on the old Crockett farm near Shawsville, Montgomery County, Va.

Hugh Crockett was appointed colonel of a regiment of colonial troops by Lord Dun more, the governor of Virginia. He was also appointed colonel of a regiment by Thos, Jefferson, when governor of Virginia, and served on the staff of General Green. He died in 1816 and was buried in the old family burying ground on the farm. His descendants are still living in or near Shawsville in Montgomery County, Va., and up to a few years ago were the owners of the celebrated Crockett springs.

Robert Crockett remained single and was killed by Indians while on an exploring expedition in Tennessee.

Mattie or Martha Crockett married Thomas Montgomery and moved to Kentucky, 1796, where she died. Then Mr. Montgomery came to Gibson County, Indiana, in 1806, and is known in this book as "Purty Old Tom the Deer Killer."

Mary Crockett married Jacob Kent, of Montgomery County, Va., and was the mother of Col. Joseph Kent, who lived near Max Meadows, in Wythe County, Va., and also of Jennie Quick Beauford.

Elizabeth Crockett married William Robertson and moved to Kentucky. Nancy Crockett married Henry Davis.

Hugh Crockett, Sr., had one brother and two cousins who came to America with him. Some of their descendants settled in Wythe County, Va., others moved to Tennessee and Kentucky. He also had two sisters who were born in Londonderry, Ireland, and came over with him. One of them married a Mr. Long. The other married Ezekiel Calhoun. A son of theirs married a Miss Montgomery, of Wythe County, Va.; and their son, Patrick Calhoun, married Martha Caldwell, and they were the parents of Hon. John C. Calhoun, who was born in South Carolina Mar. 18, 1782, just three months after leaving their home at Bowling Green, near Wytheville, Va., where the Hon. R. C. Kent now resides.

The descendants of Joseph Crockett were always known as the Roanoke Crockets, to distinguish them from the descendants of his brother, who were known as the Wythe Crockets and also those of the Kentucky and Tennessee branches of the family.

The main part of the history of the Crockett family was copied from articles that appeared in The Enterprise, of Wytheville, Va., beginning Sept. 12, 1895, written by Dr. John T. Graham, of Wytheville, Va. We have given it a place here because it corresponds with a well-known tradition of the families of Montgomerys in south-western Indiana—to the effect that the Montgomerys and Crockets had intermarried in Ireland and continued to do so in America.

In this same series of articles we find that James Crockett , born in Ireland, Nov. 20, 1674, married an Irish girl by the name of Martha Montgomery, daughter of Thomas Montgomery, who was a sailor in the naval service of England," as stated in the paper of Anna Belle Tuck, page 276.

Samuel Crockett, of the second generation in the United States, married Elizabeth Montgomery.

Then Thomas Montgomery, born probably in 1740, married Martha Crockett, in Virginia, probably about 1764. And then, one Joseph Crockett married, in Wythe County, Va., Catharine Montgomery, in 1800.

Now, as to the location of the Crockets and Montgomerys in Virginia, they are found in many parts of the state; but of these just mentioned the same article says:

"In 1770 Virginia formed from Augusta County a new County covering all this western region, and called it "Botetourt," after Governor Botetourt and two years later, 1772, another County was formed, extending from the head-waters of the Roanoke river northwest to the Ohio river and west to the Mississippi. This County was named "Fincastle," from the seat of Lord Botetourt in England. The County Seat of this County was at Fort Chiswell, now in Wythe County, and the home of the McGavoch family. The fort was built by the state in 1858, under direction of William Byrd, and named by him after his friend, Col. John Chiswell. Fincastle County did not long continue. In 1776 the territory covered by it was divided up into three new counties—Montgomery, Washington and Kentucky—and Fincastle County abolished.

In 1791 Kentucky was made a state and admitted to the Union. This was the first child of Virginia, the mother of states, and the first admitted to the original thirteen.—Hale.

Mr. Graham gives the following accounts of some of the early Montgomerys in Virginia:

Though we cannot trace their ancestry and descendants perfectly, they are certainly related to the Montgomerys of south-western Indiana.

John Montgomery, born about 1700, came to America from Scotland. He crossed the Atlantic when a mere boy, not over 15 years of age, and fell in love with a Scotch-Irish infant daughter of John and Esther Crockett, who came to America on the same vessel, about 1715. On that voyage he played with this baby on deck of the ship, and what at first seemed to be a childish interest and friendship soon ripened into love, and before leaving the vessel at New York, John Montgomery asked John and Esther Crockett for their daughter to be his wife. They were much amused at his request, but promised him their child, little thinking that the first love of his warm young heart would last very long among the hardships of the new world; but as soon as Nancy Agnes Crockett was old enough John Montgomery claimed her as his bride. They were married before 1750 and lived in Wythe County, Va., where they raised a large family, who were instrumental in defending and developing the country. John Montgomery was in the Revolutionary War, and there are good reasons to believe that he was Colonel John Montgomery, mentioned in Heitman's Historical Register as colonel of a Virginia regiment from 1778 to 1781. If that was the John Montgomery in question, he was in Gen. Geo. Rogers Clark's campaign in the Western Territory. At any rate his granddaughter, Mrs. Amanda Cox, who was living in Wytheville, Va., remembers having heard her mother say that John Montgomery was in the Revolutionary War; and in the records of the War Department at Washington, D. C, it is found that one John Montgomery enlisted as a private in Captain Arthur Smith's company, 4th Virginia regiment, to serve two years. August, 1777, he is reported sick at Cross Roads. To January, 1778, with General Scott; February, 1778, discharged.

John Montgomery was one of the first magistrates of Wythe County, Va., and rendered many interesting and original decisions. On one occasion two of his neighbors got into a dispute about a hog and came to him to decide the case. Each man made oath to having raised the hog, consequently each claimed it. As there were no other witnesses in the case it was rather difficult to decide the rightful ownership. After walking the floor for some time, trying to arrive at a decision, Montgomery suddenly turned to the claimants and said: "Well, the man who can repeat the Lord's Prayer best gets the hog." Both men made the attempt to repeat the Lord's Prayer for a hog, and one of them knew it almost perfectly, so he got the hog. Montgomery's idea for giving such a decision was that a man who knew the Lord's Prayer would have more regard for the obligation of an oath than a man who did not know it. Reader, you may draw your own conclusion about the correctness of the decision.

This John Montgomery, Sr., born 1700, who married Nancy Agnes Crockett, as already narrated, had fourteen or fifteen children: 1. John Montgomery, born 1759, 2. Robert, 3. Samuel, 4. William, 5. Silas, born 1775, 6. Stephen, 7. Joseph, 8. Aim, born 1782, 9. Rachel, born 1779, 10. Esther, 11. Nancy, 12. Catharine, 13. Elizabeth.

Of this large family the first six died without issue. Mr. Graham in his papers associates John Montgomery, Jr., with Dr. Graham as a teacher in Liberty Hall Academy. This is an error. That John Montgomery belongs to the Montgomery-Houston family and was born in 1752, and had seven children; while this John Montgomery had none.

Mrs. Amanda Cox, granddaughter of John Montgomery, Sr., has his old family Bible, which was printed in Edinburg, 1737. From it I have gotten the family record, which is peculiar and quaint in expression. In recording the births of their fourteen or fifteen children everything is put down with an exactness that would seem superfluous to one of this fast age. For example I give one or two records:

"John Montgomery, Jr., born Jan. 29, 1759, at 4 o'clock in the morning.
"Ann Montgomery, born Jan. 10th day, being Thursday, 1782, at 2 o'clock in the morning, the thirteenth day of the moon's age.

"Rachel Montgomery, born 2nd day of Oct. in the year 1779, the 23rd day of the moon's age, on Saturday.

"Silas Montgomery, born 20th day of Jan., 1775, at 5 o'clock and 4 minutes in the morning of the 20th day of the moon's age. Poor Silas died young; probably he was born under an unlucky moon."

Joseph Montgomery married Betsy Draper and moved to Arkansas, but nothing was ever heard from them.

John Montgomery, Jr., married a Miss Finley. They died without issue and were buried in the lot now owned by Mrs. C. L. Fox, in whose garden their gravestones may be seen to this« day, 1895.

Esther Montgomery married a Crockett or a Montgomery, but nothing is known of their history.

Ann Montgomery married James Craig.

Rachel Montgomery was born near Fort Chiswell, in Wythe County, Va., Oct. 2, 1779, and died Oct. 10, 1843, near Chatham Hill, in Wythe County. She married Major Samuel Graham and bad thirteen children—eight daughters and five sons: 1. Nancy Montgomery Graham. 2. Polly Craig Graham. 3. Amanda (Cox of Wytheville, Va.) 4. Eliza Friel Graham. 5. Margaret Ann Graham. 6. Helen Maria Graham. 7. and 8. Robert Craig and Catherine Graham, twins. 9. John Montgomery Graham. 10. Samuel Livingston Graham. 11. James Monroe Graham. 12. William Leander Graham. 13. Rachel Graham.

Robert Craig Graham, son of Maj. Samuel Graham and Rachel Montgomery, was born at Black Lick, Wythe County, Va., about the year 1813, and moved to Tazewell County, Va., about 1837, where he lived an uneventful life as merchant and farmer. In those days the goods were hauled in wagons from Lynchburg, Va. It is said that in 1838 Robert Graham bought the first sack of coffee that was ever in Tazewell County, and after keeping it eighteen months was compelled to return it as unsalable. Robert Graham was fond of manly sports, a great hunter, and possessed an inexhaustible supply of humor and had few superiors in telling a good story. He persistently refused office of any kind. He was frank, open and honest, not only in his dealings, but boldly so in his opinions. His first wife was

Elizabeth Witten. Their two children were Samuel C. and Rebecca. After the death of Elizabeth he married Cynthiana McDonald.

Judge Samuel C. Graham, grandson of Rachel Montgomery Graham, was born in Tazewell County, Va., Jan. 1, 1846. He volunteered in Co. I (Capt. W. E. Peery), 16th regiment Virginia Cavalry, in the fall of 1863. He was in service in north-west Virginia the valley and Piedmont. He was wounded in the ankle in the skirmish with Hunter's men on their retreat from Lynchburg, in the summer of 1864, known as the battle of Hanging Rock, near Salem, Va. He was again wounded, in the knee, at Monocracy Junction, in Maryland, on Early's march to___. He was severely wounded at Moorefield, in Hardy County, W. Va., in August, 1864. A rifle ball passed clear through his body, penetrating the upper lobe of his left lung. He was captured by the enemy, but left on the field as dead, and was carried off the field by friends when sufficiently recovered. He was very young when he entered the army, and never rose above a private.

On returning home after the war he studied law, and began practicing in 1871, in Tazewell County, where he has lived ever since. He says of himself:

"I have worked hard at my profession, and while it is said that a prophet is not without honor save in his own country, my people have been the best friends I have found on earth."

William Leander, son of Major Samuel Graham and Rachel Montgomery, married Vickie Thompson, daughter of Col. Archie Thompson, of Tazewell County, and lived a similar life to that of his brother until the Civil War, in which he served as colonel in the Confederate forces. He was in command at Crockett's Cave and repelled Gen. Averill in his march toward Wytheville just a few days before the battle at Cloyd's farm, near Dublin, Va. During the latter part of the war he was captured, and kept a prisoner at Columbus, Ohio, for several months. By his innate humor he made himself a favorite both with friends and foes, and fared better than many of his fellow-prisoners. At the age of 78 he is still hale and hearty and as fond of sports as men of forty.

Nancy Montgomery married James Graham, who was born March 28, 1776. He lived on Locust farm, near Graham's Forge, in Wythe County. He died Jan. 31, 1846, of apoplexy, or was killed by a fall from his horse at Reed Creek, near his home. Nancy Montgomery-Graham died when her three children, Elizabeth, Catherine and Robert, were quite young. Elizabeth was taken by her aunt, who herself died soon after so that Elizabeth Graham was left in care of the aunt's young daughter, Sophia Friel. Sophia Friel never married, and at her death left her estate in Wythe County to her young cousin, Elizabeth Graham, and she continued to live there after her marriage to Charles Tate. The widow of John Friel Tate, the eldest son of Elizabeth Graham-Tate, now resides at the old Friel farm, now called Maplewood.

Catherine Graham married William Hanson, of Wytheville.

Robert Graham was a minister of the gospel, and married late in life a Miss Fannie Frazier, of Memphis, Tenn. He died without children.

Elizabeth Montgomery married Samuel Crockett. One of their sons, John Crockett, married Nancy Graham . . . From this union came that family known as the Case-Crocketts, with the exception of Allen Crockett's family, who are descendants of Samuel, brother of John Crockett.

Catherine Montgomery was the second wife of Joseph Crockett: married Jan. 16, 1800, father of the late Dr. Robert Crockett, of Wytheville, Va. Their children were the late Dr. Robert Crockett, Lucy, Eliza, Susan, and Julia Ann.

Dr. Robert Crockett, son of Catherine Montgomery-Crockett, was born Feb. 16, 1804; married Elmira Craig, the 19th of May, 1829. He studied medicine under Dr. Jacob Haller and attended the medical department of Transylvania University, at Lexington, Ky., and also at the University of Pennsylvania. His practice extended over the present counties of Wythe, Pulaski, Grayson, Wythe, Bland and Tazewell. He was a man with decided views on every subject he discussed, and was said to have been one of the best and most polished conversationalists in the state. In politics he was a Democrat. He was in the legislature of Virginia one or two sessions during the war, but was strongly opposed to secession. Early in his professional career he was offered a professor's chair in a medical college in St. Louis. Mo., but family ties kept him in Virginia. He was well informed on every branch of his profession, and especially so on surgery, and was for a number of years the only surgeon in south-west Virginia. He was thoroughly systematic in his work and with him everything was done according to a preconceived method. He was scrupulously clean as to the care of his instruments and his practice in general, and that long before the days of Lister and his doctrine of antiseptics.

He had the sad misfortune to lose his wife in 1838, and three or four children in the next four years. He died at his home in Wytheville on the 10th of February, 1877, leaving three children surviving him—namely: Mrs. Colonel Robert Sayers and Capt. Robert Crockett, both of Wytheville, and the late Dr. Charles Crockett of Bluefield, W. Va. Joseph Crockett, a younger son, was killed at Cold Harbor, on the 27th of June, 1862. He was assistant surgeon to the 4th Virginia regiment (infantry) of the Stonewall Brigade, and was a man of marked talent and great promise in his profession.

Lucy Crockett, daughter of Catherine Montgomery-Crockett, born March 6, 1806, became the second wife of John B. Propit, Feb. 2, 1847. She never had any children of her own, but raised her husband's first wife's children with such care and kindness that they always looked upon her as their real mother.

Julia Ann Crockett daughter of Catherine Montgomery-Crockett, married Thomas Morrison, Nov. 3, 1835, and lived in Newburn, Pulaski County, for many years, but finally came back to Wytheville.

Susan Crockett, daughter of Catherine Montgomery-Crockett, married William H. Spiller, Dec. 22, 1831. Their children are well known to the readers, and four of them live in Wytheville to this day.

And Their Descendants

CHAPTER XV.

MONTGOMERYS OF DECATUR COUNTY, INDIANA.

1. Hugh Montgomery, born in Ireland, probably about 1760, came to America at an early age and settled in Pennsylvania. He had one full-brother, William Montgomery, and a half-brother, George Montgomery.

1. and 2. Hugh and William both served in the war of the Revolution. William was lost in the war, and nothing more is known of his history.

Hugh was severely wounded several times, but finally returned and enjoyed the blessings of a comfortable home until the war of 1812, when he again enlisted and again returned to his home. He died in 1830. He married Eva Hartman, 1784, who was born in Germany. She died in 1823. Children thirteen:

1. Mary Montgomery, born June 14, 1785; married a Mr. Alexander Grant.

2. Elizabeth Montgomery, born Feb. 20, 1787: married a Mr. Thompson.

3. Thomas Montgomery, born April 24, 1788, married Elizabeth Bingham, at Beaver, Pennsylvania, 1809. They then joined a colony moving out for the far west, and came down the Ohio River on flat-boats and settled in Butler County, Ohio. He was in the war of 1812. He died Sept. 22, 1845; his wife died Nov. 26. 1860. Children ten: 1. Rebecca. 2. Henry. 3. Sarah. 4. Eva. 5. John. 6. Hugh. 7. George. 8. Martha. 9. Thomas. 10. Robert S.

1. Rebecca Montgomery, born Feb. 10, 1810, died July 8. 1844. 2. Henry Montgomery, born Dec. 12, 1812, died June 9, 1835. 3. Sarah Montgomery, born March 6, 1814, died Dec. 1. 1886. 4. Eva Montgomery, born 1817, died Nov. 1879; married A. J. Draper.

5. John B. Montgomery, son of Thomas. Sr., born Jan. 10, 1820, died Dec. 15, 1890; married Elizabeth Gageby, Jan. 16, 1844: children seven: 1. John G. 2. Thomas H. 3. James I. 4. Elizabeth B. 5. Sarah G. 6. Susan M. 7. Rebecca A.

And Their Descendants

1. John G. Montgomery, son of John B., born 1845, died April 18, 1891; married Elizabeth J. Elder, Sept. 30, 1874; children two: 1. Rena Glendara, born 1875; 2. Maggie May, born 1877.

2. Thomas H. Montgomery, son of John B., born 1847, died April 8, 1883.

3. James I. Montgomery, son of John B., born 1849.

4. Elizabeth B. Montgomery, daughter of John B., born 1851; married James Watson Craig, Sept. 11, 1872; children six: 1. Robert B. Craig, born 1873. 2. Oliver G. Craig, born 1875, married Louisa Wetzler, Dec. 16, 1896; children two: Mary E. and Francis C. 3. Thomas Craig, born 1877. 4. John W. Craig, born 1879. 5. Charles H. Craig, born 1881. 6. Elizabeth Craig, born 1883.

5. Sarah G. Montgomery, daughter of John B., born 1853. 6. Susan M. Montgomery, born 1855. 7. Rebecca A. Montgomery, born 1857.

6. Hugh Montgomery, son of Thomas Montgomery, Sr.—no information; born March 25, 1822, died Oct. 8, 1851. 7. George Montgomery, born June 18, 1824, died Oct. 10, 1851. 8. Martha Montgomery, born Aug. 25, 1826, died June 26, 1901. 9. Thomas Montgomery, Jr., born April 1829, died Nov. 24, 1874. 10. Robert S. Montgomery, born May 18, 1831, died March 10, 1901.

4. Henry Montgomery, son of Hugh of 1760, born April 29, 1790.

5. Margaret Montgomery, born June 17, 1792, died small.

6. William Montgomery, born Aug. 26, 1793, married Anna Damine. He was killed in a battle in 1812.

7. Sallie Montgomery, born Sept. 3, 1795, married a Mr. Watson.

8. Hugh Montgomery, son of Hugh of 1760, born Aug. 29, 1797. He came with his parents from Pennsylvania to Ohio when he was a small boy and remained until 1817; then he made a visit to Kentucky on horseback. There he first met Elizabeth Montgomery, the second daughter of George

Montgomery, his father's half-brother, who is No. 3 in the beginning of this chapter and whose genealogy will be given later on.

At this pleasant Kentucky home Hugh Montgomery, Jr., met and greatly admired this lady, Elizabeth, to whom, it is said, he was very courteous during his visit. He soon returned to his home in Ohio, but he could not forget, nor cared he to forget, this somewhat shy, black-eyed damsel of the Bluegrass country, though she was his half-cousin: so about one year after this, when he was about 20 years old, he returned to the sunny south land to wed this beautiful young lady, whom he preferred as the most suitable for him among all the kindred, tribes and tongues. Therefore the wedding occurred, on October 14, 1818, and they began housekeeping in Shelby County, Ky.; but they afterward came to Indiana, in 1830, settling two miles north of Greensburg, on a farm rented. Later he moved one mile southeast of Greensburg and purchased a small tract of land and made a nice, pleasant home, where they lived until separated by death. She died Dec. 4. 1858.

During the Civil War Hugh enlisted in the 134th regiment Ind. Vol., at the age of 66 years, but he was rejected on account of age. So with good cheer and God-speed he bade the boys good-bye and returned home and continued in the peaceful pursuits of life until his death, April 22, 1872, at the age of 75 years. Children seven: Five boys—three dying in infancy—and two girls, who are still living in Decatur County. Ind. The old homestead has now passed into the possession of his oldest daughter, Sarah Ann.

1. John G. H. Montgomery, born Aug. 14, 1819, in Kentucky: a farmer, but a natural genius; married Sarah Shadrick, Jan. 30, 1840. She was of southern birth and came to Indiana with her father's family when she was a gentle maiden of 16 years, leaving behind her many sweet, sweet memories of the glad days of her youth in the sunny south-land, and of the happy moments spent at the little Bethel Baptist church, where at a tender age she had been received to membership after embracing the religion of Christ. She was gifted in song, and though sometimes pining for her happy home in the South, her mellow voice was often heard upon the gentle zephyrs over Indiana, where she had settled with her people in Decatur County. Here she met and married John G. H. Montgomery. In 1849 they purchased almost three acres of land one and one-half miles southeast of Greensburg, Ind. They gradually added to this until it grew into a large, fine, productive farm, and here they raised a family of eight children till they all had homes of their

And Their Descendants

own; but even after this the children delighted to refer to the old homestead as "Home, sweet Home." Children eight: 1. Nancy Jane. 2. Sarah E. 3. Mary F. 4. Henry H. 5. Robert W. 6. Anna Eliza. 7. John Q. 8. George.

1. Nancy J. Montgomery, born Nov. 1, 1840, married N. S. Poiler, Jan. 5, 1860. She died April 8, 1870; children four: 1. Celestia J. Poiler, born 1861, married Charles Gray, a German, April 22, 1879; children four, ___. 2. Sarah L. A. Poiler, born 1863, married John Carnut, Jan. 1, 1884; children three, ___. 3. Infant son, born 1867. 4. Minnie May Poiler, born 1870, married Joseph Tilton, of Cincinnati, Ohio.

2. Sarah E. Montgomery, born Jan. 25, 1842, married Leonard F. McCune, June 1861. She died March 5, 1874; children two: 1. Edward F. McCune, born___. , died at 14 years. 2. Clifford McCune, born___, died at 18 months. All these lay sleeping side-by-side in the old Sand Creek cemetery.

3. Mary F. Montgomery, born 1844, married J. E. St. John, July 30, 1861; children one—Frank H. St. John, born May 6, 1863; died Dec. 6, 1893.

4. Henry H. Montgomery, born 1846, was a soldier in the 134th regiment Ind. Vol.; is a blacksmith near Greensburg, Ind.; married Amanda Beocraft, Dec. 1876. She died May 5, 1880; one child. Second, married Jane Hudson, 1882; children five: 1. Dedrick Montgomery, born ___, died Aug. 18, 1880. 2. Albert. 3. Ida. 4. Ona. 5. Epha.

5. Robert W. Montgomery, born 1848, married Minnie Williams, of Greensburg, Ind., Aug. 19, 1880. He lives in Greensburg and is connected with the printing and book-binding business. Children four: 1. Ernest Montgomery, born June 7, 1881; died Feb. 7, 1884. 2. Mary Louisa Montgomery. 3. Charles Robin Montgomery. 4. Sarah Dorothy Montgomery.

Anna Eliza Montgomery Cobb
Greensburg, Indiana

6. Anna Eliza Montgomery, born 1850 lives at Greensburg, Ind. She furnished the larger part of the genealogy of this Decatur County family; also the poem that follows, entitled "The Old Homestead." She married Jasper Cobb, a farmer, March 13, 1873; one child—Robbie Cobb, born Feb. 16, 1876; died Sept. 5, 1880.

7. John Q. Montgomery, born Sept. 26, 1853, near Greensburg, Ind.; located in Vinton, Benton County, Iowa, 1874, and was an overseer and contractor of buildings till 1884, then he opened a carriage and wagon shop; married Sallie E. Parker of Shellsburg, Iowa, Dec. 5, 1878, by Rev. Amos Weaver of Vinton, Iowa. She was born June 9, 1851; children seven: 1. Gratie C. Montgomery, born April 27, 1882; died Aug. 2, 1883. 2. Effie E. Montgomery, born Aug. 29, 1883. 3. John Q. Montgomery, born Sept. 24, 1885. 4. Ivea M. Montgomery, born Jan. 30, 1888. 5. Vena W. Montgomery, born Feb. 15, 1890. 6. Wayne O. Montgomery, born April 15, 1892.

8. George Montgomery, born 1854, first married Lizzie Layton, of Greensburg, Ind., in 1878 who died July 28, 1880; no children. Second he married Julia Gray, of German descent, both her parents having been born in Germany. He is located near Greensburg, Ind., and is proprietor of machine shops which manufacture and repair wagons, buggies, etc. Children two: Sarah L. E. Montgomery and Roy Montgomery.

John G. H. Montgomery, born Aug. 14, 1819, the father of the above family and companion of Sarah, his wife, for 56 years, broke the earthly union in death Sept. 24, 1894, aged 75 years. Sarah, the loving wife and patient mother, followed March 17, 1898, leaving six children surviving her.

5. Sarah Ann Montgomery, born Dec. 30, 1826, daughter of Hugh, Sr., married Daniel McCormick, Jan. 27, 1848, in Decatur County. Ind.; children two: 1. McCormick, born Jan. 15, 1849, married Clark Hamilton, Feb. 19, 1867. She died June 17, 1880: no children. 2. Mary Olive McCormick, married John Harland, of Greensburg, Ind., May 23, 1876; children two: 1. Lena Harland, married Orla Barnard; children two—Ethel and Edith.

6. William A. Montgomery, a farmer, born in Indiana, April 30. 1833, was a soldier in Co. E, 7th Ind. Vol., for three years and returned home without a single wound. He died May 13, 1902, at Shellsburg, Benton County, Iowa; married Nancy J. Potter, Oct. 20. 1858. She died April 9, 1902; children four—three born in Indiana, one in Iowa: 1. John W. P. Montgomery. 2. Charlotte A. Montgomery. 3. Mary E. Montgomery. 4. Frank H. Montgomery.

7. Mary E. Montgomery, born July 19, 1836, in Indiana, married J. W. McCune, March 1855; children four—two of them dying in infancy. Corintha Jane, the second child, born May 8, 1857, died March 1, 1887; leaving only one living child—Vanbuskirk McCune, who is married and has one son, named Grover McCune.

9. Nancy Montgomery, daughter of Hugh of 1760 born June 29, 1799, married a Mr. Hindman.

10. George Montgomery, born April 2, 1801, in Pennsylvania, came to Indiana with his father, then moved to Iowa in an early day; married ___; children three: 1. John Montgomery, near Vinton, Iowa, who has sons George and Fred, Vinton, Iowa. 2. Mike Montgomery, who has sons Marion, Vinton, Iowa; Edson and Frank, of Braden, Iowa. 3. Henry Montgomery, justice of the peace at Spikardsville, Mo.

There is a James Montgomery, a hardware dealer at Rock Island, Ill., and S. B. Montgomery, an attorney at law, Vinton, Iowa; but I know nothing of their genealogy. John Q. Montgomery of Winton, Iowa, furnished the sketch of George and Robert Montgomery. Generation 1, Nos. 10-13. Miss Belle

Montgomery of Greensburg furnished that of Thomas Montgomery, Generation 1. No. 3.

11. Peggy Montgomery, born Oct. 3, 1803, married a Kercheval.

12. Michael Montgomery, born March 28, 1806, died May 12, 1845; married Ann F. Robertson, July 23, 1826. She died April 29, 1890. Children ten:
   1. Eva Montgomery, born May 8, 1827, died May 19, 1902; married Joseph R. Peery, April 17, 1861; no children, but she became the stepmother of two little girls, Mary and Lou Peery, and tenderly nurtured them to womanhood.
   2. Amy Montgomery, born March 21, 1829, married Joseph A. McKee. Feb. 15, 1849, and died Sep. 12, 1865; no children.
   3. Rebecca J. Montgomery, born April 1, 1831, died Dec. 25, 1888, single. She left an invalid mother to whom she had devoted her life.
   4. Malinda Montgomery, born 1833, married Hugh Heinman, Aug. 17, 1854; one child—Michael M. Heinman.
   5. Sarah Ann Montgomery, born July 30, 1835, died Jan. 9, 1892; married John O. Wood, Dec. 17, 1855; children four—three daughters and one son.
   6. Riley S. Montgomery, born April 15, 1837, died April 17, 1895; married Laura Hamilton, Jan. 22, 1869; children two: 1. Clayton Montgomery. 2. Orville Montgomery.
   7. Hugh Montgomery, was a soldier in Capt. Granger's company, 9th regiment Iowa Vol., and died from wounds received in the battle at Tullahoma, Alabama, Jan. 2, 1864; never married.
   8. William H. Montgomery, born 1841, married Lucy E. Bunker, of Greensburg, Ind., Feb. 8, 1870. He was a soldier three years in the 7th regiment Ind. Vol., Co. G.; is now located with his family at Chattanooga, Tenn. Children five: 1. Grace Montgomery, born, married Harry C. Burriss, Oct. 2, 1895; children three: 1. Paul Burriss; 2. Victoria Burriss; 3. Isabel Burriss. 2. Bessie Montgomery married F. A. Provence, Oct. 16, 1895; children two—Thomas and Amy. 3. Ada Montgomery, died July 13, 1898. 4. Amy Montgomery. 5., Waldo L. Montgomery, died at Little Rock, Ark., Dec. 17, 1901.

10. Louisa M. Montgomery, born 1843 married Wm. S. Peery, Dec. 12, 1865; children five—four boys and one girl. Only the two youngest boys are now living.

13. Robert Montgomery, burn May 1807 in Pennsylvania; came to Ohio with his father in 1809; moved to Decatur County, Ind., 1822. The heavy work of clearing up the new farm was done under Robert's care. Shortly after this his mother and father died, and were the first to be laid to rest in what is known as the Watts cemetery. Robert served in the war of 1812; married Miss Louisa Robinson, Oct. 2, 1834. She was born in Massachusetts in 1817 and united with the Greensburg Baptist church. They lived happily together for 46 years, when Robert died May 1, 1881. He moved to Lynn County, Iowa, 1849; afterward to Benton County, Iowa, 1851. He was fortunate in good health, never having taken any medicine until within the last eighteen months of his life. Children two: 1. Mrs. David Geiger, who died 1899. 2. Michael Montgomery, who has sons Frank and Hugh, of Sioux City, Iowa.

Having finished the genealogical history of Hugh Montgomery, No. 1. Generation 1. Of this branch of Montgomerys, who married Eva Hartman, in Pennsylvania, 1784, we take up the history of his half-brother:

3. George Montgomery, born probably 1770, married Polly Aiken, whose mother was born and raised in Ireland; and although she emigrated to America, where all her children were born and raised, she was never able to speak one word of English. Her daughter, Polly Aiken, was raised in Pennsylvania, near the Alleghany Mountains, where from the breezy summit, mid the wild scenery of the mountains so beautifully bedecked by the hand of the Creator, Cupid had shot his arrow down, and the two hearts of George Montgomery and Polly Aiken were transformed into one, for good or ill, for weal or woe, and pledged to walk together henceforth through the shadows and the sunshine of life's transient journey; and after a few years happily spent together in Pennsylvania, they with their little family moved to "Old Kentucky," settling in the forest of Shelby County, which lies between Louisville and Frankfort. At what date he settled here we do not know, but it was in the days of Daniel Boone, when the beautiful blue grass region was but a dense, dark forest with Indian wigwams scattered here and there amid the wild thickets of underbrush. And it was here, in the homely log-cabin with its one window and one door, which were often-times barred—not by the polished steel lock and bolt of today, but with huge logs and rough poles which were dragged from the forest for the purpose of securing the lives of our early ancestors, who were likely to be attacked in the silent hours of the night while they were resting in the quietude of sleep, which was no doubt as sweet to these early pioneers

amid all the hardships and dangers of their lives and toils as are the slumbers of the child of luxury and ease in the cushioned parlors, with their costly drapery, of this our modem day. And Elizabeth Montgomery, the second daughter of this family, who married Hugh Montgomery, her half-cousin, in 1818, testifies to the happiness and contentment and exceedingly warm and generous hospitality so characteristic of the people of those southern climes, in that day.

They had eight children: 1. Alexander Montgomery. 2. Elizabeth. 3. Sarah. 4. Abagail. 5. Mary. 6. William. 7. John. 8. James. The dates of birth of these are not known, neither do we know that they were born in the order named; but they were all married in Shelby County, Ky., and Alexander, William and John died there; but James and his family moved to Crawfordsville, Ind., in 1832, and he died there.

The William Montgomery of this family is said to have accumulated a great deal of wealth in Kentucky. He owned a large plantation and many slaves. The civil strife between the states proved disastrous to the financial prosperity of this family, which consisted of several children; but nothing is known of them or their descendants at this time.

Of Elizabeth Montgomery, the second daughter of George Montgomery, No. 3. Generation 1—a full account has been given of her and her husband, Hugh Montgomery.

We will proceed to give some account of Alexander Montgomery, the oldest child of George. He was a soldier in the war of 1812, and had an arm broken in battle and was captured by the Indians. He was placed with other prisoners in a pen built of poles, to await their doom, which they supposed would be death in its most cruel form. But instead of this they were given tasks to perform, and if their endurance were sufficient their lives would be spared; if not, they would immediately be scalped by the chief and his barbarous crew.

Alexander had to run the gauntlet, which was to run between two rows of Indians with clubs to knock him down if they could. The distance is not known, but at the end of the race was a gulf or creek with steep banks, to be cleared by him, or they would pounce upon him and kill him. This would seem like desperation and despair for a man with a broken arm, but he made the effort, and, summing up all his courage and strength, made a dash which seemed like leaping into the very jaws of death—but lo, his fate was such that he cleared the trench and landed on the score-mark beyond. He was then turned over to an old Indian squaw, who gave him the kindest treatment, pretending to charm his pains by witchcraft, at the same time applying liquids of wild herbs until his arm was entirely healed. Seemingly he was satisfied and content, but he watched every opportunity for escape, and after about one year succeeded; but they made a diligent search for him, and he could often hear them in their pursuit as he was hidden in a hollow log or lying low among the thick brush. He could hear them galloping by, chattering and singing their war songs, which meant death to some poor victim like himself. Finally, through shrewdness, perseverance, privation and almost starvation, he reached the river and swam across, and finally reached his own door, where his family had mourned him as dead. The shock was too much for the good wife and mother, who fainted. When she recovered, Alexander related his suffering for the first time.

Alexander became the father of three children—Maranda, Eliza and Samuel.

"THE OLD HOMESTEAD"

For they say the old home of our childhood is sold,
And strangers will soon enter there to abide,
Where back into memories of the past, long ago,
I see a bright vision of sweet faces glide;
Where with father and mother, and brothers four,
In the gable-roofed cottage we had named retreat.
We are greeting, as time turns backward once more,
Four sisters in a home of affection complete.

There the busy old clock, on the mantel-piece,
With its merry chimes the time doth keep
Of our childish songs and joyous laugh,
While our parents sow, that children may reap.
'Twas 'neath time's enchantment and love we abode,
Under the sheltering wings of their tender care,
As from innocent childhood and thoughtless youth
Up to manhood and womanhood we were nurtured there.

The Montgomerys

Ne'er thought we how with the years that were to come
Their steps should totter and their eyes grow dim
Through service wrought to build this home
To rear and shield their children in.
'Tis through memory magic that my father I see,
When his long summer day's work was done,
Sitting on the back porch in his old low chair,
Resting in the shades of the slow-sinking sun.

As he bids, we children go, hasten along,
And bring home the cows through the bars of the lane.
In the sell-same path we his footsteps trace,
When from the field with pony and plow he came.
As quick from the door of the porchway we bound,
With Major, the old watch-dog close by our side,
Pausing not till we reach the woods-pasture field,
Where awaited our come, Rose, Lill and old Pide.

Then, trusting dog Major to drive home the cows
Through the bars, from the woods to the meadow lane,
We children would gather the pretty wild flowers,
Dreaming not of their cost, in our childish game,
As we carried them home, where around mother's feet,
We built great castles through the bright hopes of youth.
She called us her jewels, and shared in our joys
As she patiently taught us some lesson of truth.

In the dreamy distance, my fancy seems to see the form
Of mother just now, in her quiet, old-fashioned way
Preparing the meal for her children so dear,
Who will all be at home for dinner today.
There is Janie, and Lizzie and Mary, grown up;
Next comes Henry, then Robert and Lide;
Then Johnnie (our father's own namesake he was),
And George was the baby—all by love's toil supplied.

Now the sound of the bugle-horn rings through the air.
And in melody we hear "A charge to keep I have—a God to glorify."

And Their Descendants

Then in ray dreams I see again her smooth, dark, shining hair.
I list, and lo, she's singing now of that "sweet bye-and-bye."
'Tis mother's tender voice again that soothes away our care.
Oh, memory dear, 'tis sweet to know that thou art with us still!
And as the angels' song makes glad the courts of heaven above,
The thought of mother ever shall the living heart-cords thrill.

   Clinging to the eaves of the porch and the bell-flower tree
   Are the morning-glories mother has planted; but the door
     Is ajar, and with her pan and tray in hand, it seems I see
     Her trudging from the smoke-house again, as of yore.
   With the sweet-savored hain or some sausage to brown.
     In the bright, rosy morn we children of her birth
   Are gathered 'round the table and— no one can tell how,
   But to us it seemed to be the very best breakfast on earth.

And there's the old milk-house, with its moss-covered roof
And entrance-way cool, from the waters of the deep curbed well,
   With its door carved, by youthful hand, a memorial proof
   That, mingling there, we had our joys and sorrows to tell.
And there, too, is the old shop with its shavings and coal,
   Where our father's hammer, in the days now gone by,
   Carved the wood and the steel into many shapes, of old,
   For the tiller of the fields of the wheat, corn and rye.

   In the barn-yard corner stands the broad, low wood-shed,
   And just beyond is the orchard, that my fancy now sees,
     Where hang the ruddy apples, so mellow, ripe and red;
     And we children are now climbing up the old fruit-trees
That father's own hands planted. There too's the cedar grove,
     Where softly the zephyrs fan out on the breeze
   And send the sweet-sounding notes of red-bird afloat
     Through the waving branches of the evergreen trees.

   And there's the truck-patch planted just back of the barn,
   Where the corn and the beans and the muskmelons grew;
     And a scene of us children picking cucumbers there.
     Through the years that have flown, is still on my view.
   Near by was the old mill that crushed the sugar-cane,
With its long sweep revolving and its rollers going 'round,

The Montgomerys

Till the tubs were filled full of the juicy liquid, sweet,
That away to the evaporator furnace did bound,

Where over the fire it would sputter, steam and skip:
And now with cup of measure in his sunburned hands
I see my father standing by the polished pan to dip
The dainty, odorous syrup, to supply the great demand.
His was an honest measure, filled full to the brim,
And this was the lesson that he taught us day by day.
While in field, shop or shed he toiled on with care—
"Honesty is always the best policy," he would say.

But I see another picture that is now shining out:
From the chimney fire-place, one cold winter night.
As my father at the hearthstone corner sits and reads
His paper, by the tallow caudle's pale, dim light,
And my quiet mother with her gentle grace—
f see her nimble fingers around the stockings go,
And I hear the quick sound of her needles' click
That clad our young feet from the ice and the snow.

But youth's path is through many a vale;
And slowly old Time's wing, on his craggy cliff,
Fans in the changed light, till in years to come
He varies life's scenes alike into clouds that drift.
And another picture is now brought to my view;
For the pencil of time has marked with care
My mother's face; her form is bent, her step is slow;
Silver threads have found a place in her black, silken hair.

But her children, though scattered near and far.
She still hold dear within her gentle, loving heart
While their wayward steps, if such there should be,
Through her bosom throb like an arrow's dart.
Now when we gather in the old homestead,
The Book she loved best in her lap we find;
In softest accents we hear her while she reads—
"On earth peace, and good will to all mankind."

These words, her Christian faith, like good seed sown.

And Their Descendants

Daily into life's woven web the Christ impressed:
"Seek for God's kingdom and His righteousness to know.
Till His own time shall crown the saved and blessed."
My father, less ambitious and more submissive grown,
I see; and lo, his feeble form, and on his brow ringlets of frosted
hair! We hear him say: "Children, my work is done; 'tis but a little
while; But I can trust in Him who doeth all things well; I'll soon be
over there."

And now no more from the wayside mounds
Shall we carry tributes of daisies and violets and ferns
To father and mother, from the soil where they sacrificed
For their children's sake, for their pleasure earned;
For here is a vision where they passed over the tide;
In the church-yard yonder, near the old home's door,
Their bodies lie peacefully slumbering, and they
Will welcome their children to the Homestead no more!

But when the autumn comes, or the gentle spring-time brings
The flowers that speak with silent, inspiring speech,
I shall think of the Homestead, with its unbroken ties;
Of our father and mother in their humble life, each,
And of the dear sisters who first left us here;
Then of the old home circle, with its sad broken ties.
As we saw them pass with their spirits enrobed—
Pass from earth in a plumage for paradise.

But we know, like the roses and violets that fade,
The old homesteads of childhood are all passing away,
As one by one we are passing over Jordan's dark wave.
But shall these sweet memories, too, soon all decay?
No, never! for a hope from the dead past is springing,
As I dream, oft there comes from the far crystal strand
A bright band of loved ones, hovering 'round
To guide us to the "house not made with hands."

They would pilot us when we are sad and weary,
Saying, "Come unto Jesus and rest and wait."
They would cheer our pathway when lone and dreary,
Till the angels beckon through the golden gate,

And then to our Father's house we would go—
To that home where forever shall dwell the dear ones all;
And the heart's sacred memories recorded here
Will be painted in garlands on heaven's high wall.

And though this is but a phantom dream
And these scenes are not what they seem.
Time's pulse beats on with respiring breath,
And such is life, and such is death!
And as through fleeting dreams we see
The what has been, the what shall be,
Shall to faith's vision some time unfold,
Beyond, the beautiful pearly gates of gold!

"And God shall wipe away all tears from their eyes, and there shall be no more death, neither sorrow, nor crying; neither shall there be any more pain; for the former things are passed away."— Rev. 21:4. (Composed and written by Lida Montgomery-Cobb, March 7, 1900.)

MONTGOMERYS OF DAVIESS COUNTY, INDIANA

There is a family of Montgomery's at Montgomery, Daviess County, which town was named in honor of Valentine B. and James Montgomery, 1858.

The great grandfather, whose given name we have not learned, came from Ireland and settled in Maryland in 1810 then moved near Springfield, in Washington County, Ky. The family came to Daviess County, Ind., in 1835, and organized the town of Montgomery, 1858 as stated above.

The grandfather's name was James Montgomery; children six:

1. Valentine B. Montgomery, born 1815, married a Miss Wasson. They had six children: Henry, James, Frank, John, Lizzie and Sallie.

2. Eliza Montgomery born 1817, daughter of James, Sr., married James O'Brien; children two-dead.

3. John Montgomery, born 1820, died 1846; married Liza Hawker; no children.

4. James C. Montgomery, born 1822, now (1901) lives at Montgomery and is in good circumstances. He owns a large farm near Montgomery and does quite an extensive business in furnishing mining supplies, as a very large mining business is carried on at Montgomery and in the surrounding country. He first married Jane Buby; one child—dead; Second wife, Susan Brown; no children. He also carries on merchandise and deals in grain.

5. William Montgomery born 1825, son of James, Sr., married Mary Ellen Berliew; children ten:

1. George F. Montgomery is quite a business man and is now (1901) general manager of the Tombigbee and Northern railway company. His address is now Mobile, Ala. From what I can glean, there is much more of interest connected with this man's history, but he seems too modest and reticent to give full particulars. He has not lived at Montgomery, Ind. for several years. He married Idora Railing; children two—William H. and George W. Montgomery.

2. Martha A. Montgomery married John Murphy; children three; John. May and George Murphy.

3. James A. Montgomery, married at Brunswick, Ga., and now (1901) lives there; children four, but have not learned their names.
4. John H. Montgomery, single.
5. Charles A. Montgomery, married and now (1901) lives at No. 22 Dearborn street, Chicago; no children.
6. Estella Montgomery, single.
7. William O.
8. Ella.
9. Maggie.
10. Cora.

6. Rose Ann Montgomery, daughter of James, Sr., married John Fagan; children two—Jane and Elizabeth.

THE MONTGOMERYS OF EDWARDSPORT, INDIANA

The Montgomerys

A Montgomery, given name not known, came from Ireland (date not given) and settled in Maryland. He had several children, but we know the names of only two: 1st, Clark, who is supposed to have had no family; 2nd, Thomas, who probably left Maryland when a small boy and settled near Mackville, in Washington County, Ky. He married a Miss Stevens, claimed to have been related to Hon. Alexander H. Stephens of Confederate fame. He was a shoemaker by trade. He moved to Bruceville, Knox County, Ind., sometime between 1852 and 1858. He was noted for his uncommon neatness in his every-day appearance. So far as we know he only had two children—Courtney Louis, and Thompson. Courtney Louis, it seems, first settled at Carlisle, Ind., and there married Christian Weller. He moved to Bruceville, Ind., and spent most of his life there. The last few years of his life were spent in Edwardsport, Ind. He died there Dec. 30, 1870. He was engaged in the harness trade. His wife died Sept. 1, 1902. Children seven:

1. Thomas Montgomery died at 2 years.

2. Oliver Thompson, born 1860, is a farmer and grain dealer of Edwardsport, Ind. He married Martha Killion of that place, June 1883; children six: Dale, David, Roy, Ruth, Clinton and Ivy.

3. James died in infancy.

4. Frank S., born Aug. 1863, is a freight agent at Vincennes, Ind.; married May Lynch of Edinburg, Ind.; children two—Courtney L. and Ralph P.

5. Jessie B., was educated at Bardstown, Ky., Ind. State Normal and University of Chicago, and has been teaching 15 years. She has been principal of the City Normal at Fort Wayne, Ind., for the training of teachers, five years. Previously she taught in the State Normal at Ypsilanti, Mich. She is well posted in educational work, not only in her native state, but in other states as well.

6. Fannie Edith died small.

7. Mattie W., born June 1869, married James L. Toops, of Edwardsport, Ind., Nov. 1888. Mr. Toops immediately moved to Fort Branch, Ind., and engaged in the poultry business, and has a very extensive trade in that line; children two: 1. Roger Leslie Toops, born Aug. 7, 1891, who is named for the 4th Roger Montgomery, who successfully led the cavalry charge under King

William at the battle of Hastings, Oct. 14, 1068. 2. Mary Frances Toops born Dec. 30, 1893.

MONTGOMERYS OF SEYMOUR, INDIANA

Richard Montgomery married Annabel Clarkson at Glasgow, Scotland. They emigrated to this country about 1812, stopping at Philadelphia. Later they came over the mountains and down the Ohio River to Louisville, and finally settled in Jackson County, in 1820. The children who lived to maturity were Richard, John C, William, Theophilus W., Thomas K., Henry, Mary J., James R., and Robert H. The children are all now dead, except three. My father's name was Theophilus W. The descendants of the entire family are now quite numerous, but I can furnish the list almost complete in a short while, if it will be of any use to yon. Very truly yours,

O. H. MONTGOMERY.

MONTGOMERYS OF NEW ALBANY, INDIANA

Robert Montgomery came from Ireland and settled in Indiana in an early day. He had a son, James Helms Montgomery, who was born in Indiana but raised in New York City by an aunt. From there he came to Kentucky and married Letitia Nation, daughter of Edward Nation. He was a Baptist minister. Just how many children he had we do not know, but he had a son, Captain John Robert Montgomery, who was a steamboat captain from Jeffersonville, Ind., for many years, and died there in 1873. And he also had a daughter, Mrs. Mary Partlow, living in Jeffersonville in 1901. Captain John Robert Montgomery had at least two children: Dr. Harry C. Montgomery, of Jeffersonville, Ind. (1901), and Miss Sarah L. Montgomery, principal of the training school for teachers (1901) at Springfield, Ill.

SOME OTHER MONTGOMERYS OF GIBSON AND POSEY COUNTIES, INDIANA

Robin Montgomery came to Indiana from Georgia in an early day and stopped with a Mr. Moore, near Patoka, now in Gibson County, Ind. Later, when the Knowles and Marvel families, with whom he was acquainted in Georgia, came to Indiana and settled on Black River, Robin Montgomery came down to this locality in 1812 and married Patience Marvel, daughter of Prettiman Marvel, Sr. This was the first marriage in that neighborhood. Mr. Montgomery was a soldier in the war of 1812 and fought in the battle of Tippecanoe. He raised a large family. His sons were William, Prettiman, Samuel, John, Robert, James, George, Thomas, and perhaps others. One of his daughters married John Benine. The descendants of this family are numerous in Gibson and Posey counties. I made two efforts to obtain a genealogy of this family, but did not succeed.

COLONEL WILLIAM COCKRUM.

In reply to inquiries made by William Cockrum, of Oakland City, Ind., colonel of the 42nd regiment Ind. Vol., in regard to the Cockrum family being identified with the Montgomerys in Scotland and Ireland—believing that Coghran, Cochran and Cockrum originated from the same name.

We find a Col. Hugh Cochran serving in the war of 1641-1652, with Sir James Montgomery, and that his grandmother was a daughter of Sir Robert Montgomery of Skelmorlie.

At the funeral (1663) of the Third Viscount Montgomery, afterwards the First Earl of Mt. Alexander in Ireland, Lieutenant Colonel Cochran is mentioned among the kinsmen of the deceased. You will observe that the great-grandmother of Colonel Hugh Cochran, wife of Sir Robert Montgomery, was the daughter of Sir William Douglass; which adds no little prestige to the genealogical line of his ancestors. The beauty of this lady, Margaret Douglass, is the subject of two sonnets by Captain Alexander Montgomery, author of "The Cherie and the Slae."

If these names all belong in common to the same family which it is believed they do, they constitute a very large, influential family both in the United States and across the waters, who are leaders in advanced thought and work, in almost every department of life's work.

SOME EARLY MONTGOMERYS IN THE UNITED STATES

Oak Park, Ill., April 14, 1902

Mr. D. B. Montgomery, Owensville, Ind.

Dear Sir:

Am in receipt of your favor of 10th inst., and in reply would say the Montgomery family with which the writer is identified removed from Scotland to the north of Ireland in the seventeenth century. A descendant, a widow whose maiden name was Mary Montgomery, came to this country in 1731 or 1732 to marry Mr. James Patterson, of Scottish descent, who was born in County Antrim, Ireland, in 1708, and came to this country from the north of Ireland in 1728. Settlement was made in Little Britain Township, Lancaster County, Pennsylvania, on a large tract of land purchased by Mr. Patterson, the greater portion of which is held at the present day in the Patterson name.

Mary Montgomery had two brothers, Thomas and James Montgomery, and a sister Jane, who came to this country and settled in South Carolina. Jane married James Ramsay. They were parents of David Ramsay, M. D., the historian, and president (pro tempore) of the Continental Congress during the illness of Hancock in 1785. Of the brothers, Thomas and James, the writer has no record. Mary Montgomery was niece of Hon. John C. Calhoun's mother's father, or rather first cousin of that statesman.

James and Mary Montgomery-Patterson had ten children. Hannah, their third child and oldest daughter born in 1736 or 1737, married William Montgomery, a relative who came from the north of Ireland. His family removed from Mongomo, Scotland, and settled in the north of Ireland in 1680.

The children of James and Mary Montgomery-Patterson were: William, born 1733; married, first, Rosanna Scott; had five children. Second, married Elizabeth Brown; ten children. John married Eleanor Milligen; eight children. Hannah, born 1736 or 1737, married William Montgomery; nine children. Mary, married John McKnight; trace lost. Samuel married Mary Wylie; two children. Jane, married Hugh Brown; trace lost. Isabella married James Brown; one child. James, born 1745, married Letitia Gardner; nine children. Elizabeth died in 13th year. Thomas, born 1754, married Mary Tanyhill; nine children.

The children of William and Hannah Patterson-Montgomery were: Elizabeth, who married William Baily. Hannah married James McKnight. William married Nancy Brawley. John first married Martha Brawley, sister to Nancy Brawley. Second married Nancy Busick. Frances married William

Buchanan. Rebecca married Thomas Aydlott. James Patterson, died aged 21, not married. Mary married Moses Hanks. David married Araminta Breden.

When William, the third child and oldest son, was ten or eleven years old, this family removed from Lancaster County, Pennsylvania, with the intention of going to Abbeville district, South Carolina, where resided the Calhoun family, who were relatives. In Guilford County, N. C., old friends from Ireland were met, who persuaded Mr. Montgomery to locate in their vicinity. Settlement was made near Bethel church, east of Greensboro. This was about the year 1768 or 1770. William and Nancy Brawley-Montgomery's children were: Hugh, Hannah, who married James Benefield. William, born Dec. 29, 1789, married Sarah Albright. Nov. 13, 1817. Martha, no record. James Patterson married Sarah Brower. Margaret married James Prier.

Of Hugh, little is known by the writer except that he was a volunteer in the war of 1812 after the close of which he was postmaster at Ashville, N. C., and from there went to Rome, Georgia, where trace of him was lost.

James Benefield was of Guilford County N. C.; removed to Tennessee, and later to Martin County, Indiana; was in the war of 1812, and under General Jackson at New Orleans.

William Montgomery was a mechanic, physician and politician.

His first public service was in the state senate. He was in the convention to amend the Constitution of North Carolina, 1835, and was elected and served six years in Congress; served his state in legislature a number of terms. His wife, Sarah Albright, was of Orange County, N. C. They were parents of ten children—three sons and seven daughters. At the present date all are dead but two sons. Their children were: Elizabeth; Eliza; Daniel A., physician of Burlington, N. C., living 1902, aged 83 years; Delila; James R.; Mary; Harriet; Cornelia; Maria B., and William.

Daniel A. Montgomery, M. D., was born May 16, 1819; married Josephine, daughter of Captain John Berry, of Hillsboro, Orange County, N. C.; had issue of five sons and two daughters. (Their names I have not got at present date, but am in the way of getting them). Dr. Montgomery was surgeon in the 3rd North Carolina regiment in the Civil War, under appointment by the governor. "Stockard's History of Alamanee" says of him:

"Dr. Daniel A. Montgomery is one of the oldest residents of Burlington; was for many years a physician with a very large practice; represented his people many times in the General Assembly. He is an old-time, high-toned gentleman, courtly in his bearing, kindly in his speech, rather tall, straight, with gold-gray hair and blue eyes."

James Patterson Montgomery, born in Guilford County, N. C., March 12, 1793, was a fine cabinet-workman and made musical instruments. His wife was daughter of Hon. Abram Brawer of Randolph County, N. C. Their children were: Nancy C., born Sept. 10, 1818. William E., born Feb. 3, 1823. Caroline R., born Nov. 13, 1824. Daniel V., born April 29, 1830. Nathaniel P., born July 2, 1836. This family removed from Guilford County, N. C., in 1838, and settled in Ipava, Fulton County, Ill.

I have nearly a full list of the descendants of James P. and Sarah B. Montgomery.

John, son of William and Hannah Patterson-Montgomery, married first, Martha Brawley. Their children were Martha, Isabella, Samuel, Thankful, John, Anne, Jesse and David Caldwell. The children by his second wife, Nancy Busick, were William, James, Nancy, Enoch H., Eliza W., Betsy W. and Frances D.

Of this family Anne married John Boone, of Guilford, N. C. He was a relative of Daniel Boone, of Kentucky notoriety, and had issue of Julia Boone.

David C. returned to Arkansas. His first wife was Ann Theamster, of Batesville, Ark.; no issue. Second wife was Mary A. Rutherford, of North Carolina; no issue. David C. was a mechanic and was a member of the state legislature of Arkansas several terms.

I am in correspondence at the present time with Montgomerys of Arkansas, Illinois, Minnesota and North Carolina, and in almost daily receipt of letters of information from many different branches of the family of James and Mary Montgomery-Patterson. If there is anything in this communication which you would care to put into print, cut out and use what you care for; and if I can serve you in any way in the future please advise me.

The Montgomerys

Respectfully yours,
GEORGE M. BLACK.

The seventh child of James and Mary Montgomery-Patterson was James Patterson, Jr.; married Letitia Gardner, born 1803. They had nine children, one of whom was Rachel, who married John Black, of Scotch-Irish descent, in 1826. She is the mother of George M. Black, of Oak Park. Ill., who furnished the above sketch of the Pattersons and Montgomerys. He is preparing a special register on this line and may publish it in the near future.

(Cincinnati, Ohio, Library, Pennsylvania Genealogy by William Henry Egle, 1866.)

"Rev. Joseph Montgomery, son of John and Martha Montgomery, emigrants from Ireland, was born Sept. 23, 1733 (O.S.) in Paxton Township, then Lancaster, now Douphin County, Pennsylvania. He was educated at the College of New Jersey, from which he graduated in 1755, and was afterward appointed master of the grammar school connected with the college. In 1760 the College of Philadelphia and Yale College conferred upon him the Master's degree. About this time he was licensed to preach by the presbytery of Philadelphia and soon after, by request, entered the bounds of the presbytery of Lewis, from which he was transferred to that of Newcastle, accepting a call from the congregation at Georgetown, over which he was settled from 1767 to 1769. He was installed as pastor of the congregations at Christiana Bridge and Newcastle, Delaware, on the 16th of August, 1769, remaining there until the autumn of 1777, when he resigned, having been commissioned chaplain of Col. Smallwood's (Maryland) regiment of the Continental Line. During the war his home was with his relatives in Paxtoug. On the 23rd of November, 1780, he was chosen by the General Assembly of Pennsylvania as one of its delegates in Congress, and was re-elected the following year. He was elected a member of the Assembly of the State in 1782, serving during that session. He was chosen by that body Feb. 25, 1783, one of the commissioners to settle the difficulty between the state and the Connecticut settlers at Wyoming. When the new County of Douphin was erected, the Supreme Executive Council appointed him recorder of deeds and register of wills for the County, which office he filled from March 11, 1785, to Oct. 14, 1794, the date of his death.

"Mr. Montgomery filled conspicuous and honorable positions in church and state in the most trying period of the history of the country. In the church he was the friend and associate of men like Witherspoon, Rogers and Spencer, and his bold utterances in the cause of independence stamp him as a man of no ordinary courage and decision. . . . He enjoyed to an unusual extent the respect and confidence of the men of his generation."

The Rev. Mr. Montgomery was twice married; first in 1765, to Elizabeth Reed, who died March 1769; daughter of Andrew and Sarah Reed of Trenton, N. J., and they had issue: 1, Sarah Pettit, born July 1766, married Col. Thos. Foster. 2, Elizabeth, born July 17, 1768, died Oct. 12. 1814, in Harrisburg, Pa.; married Samuel Land.

Mr. Montgomery married second, July 11, 1770, Rachel (Rush) Boyce, born 1741, in Byberry, died July 28, 1798, in Harrisburg, Pa. She was the widow of Angus Boyce and daughter of Thomas and Rachel Rush, who were the parents of the celebrated Dr. Benjamin Rush. They had issue: 3, John, born Dec. 23, 1771; probably dead.

PENNSYLVANIA MONTGOMERYS

Charles Montgomery, who lives in Harrisburg, Pa., makes inquiry of a very old man by the name of Barnes Montgomery, who formerly lived in Hightstown, N. J., but now of Asbury Park, N. J.

MONTGOMERYS OF PENNSYLVANIA AND SOUTH CAROLINA

(By Dr. J. B. Landrum, of Campobello, S. C.) The original ancestor of the Montgomery family that made settlement in the present County of Spartanburg was John Montgomery. Scotch-Irish, who emigrated from North of Ireland to Pennsylvania before the Revolution, and subsequently to Spartanburg in 1785, and settled north of Tyger River near Swoddy's Bridge. He married in Pennsylvania. Rosa Roddy, and had seven children: 1. Alexander. 2. John. 3. James. 4. Robert. 5. Hugh. 6. Margaret. 7. Mary.

1. Alexander Montgomery, who married Miss Samons and had thirteen children, among whom we have the names Alfred, Arnoldus, Robert, Mathias, Edward, Elias, John, and Minerva, who married Curtis Bradley.

2. John Montgomery, Jr., son of John from Pennsylvania, first married Margaret Miller. He was a man of considerable prominence and influence in his day, being above the average in intelligence and general information. He

was a progressive farmer and carried on the business of blacksmithing and wood-work. He was a manufacturer of wagons at a time in the history of Spartanburg District when imported wagons were unknown. By honest industry he accumulated a handsome property. He was a good provider, hospitable in his home, and a progressive citizen. He was for many years a magistrate, appointed by enactment of the General Assembly of South Carolina, and was an efficient officer in this capacity. He was a soldier in the war of 1812, being Orderly Sergeant of the company of Captain James Brannon, which for a half-century or more paraded at Timmons' old field prior to the outbreak of the Civil War. His death occurred in 1847 or '48.

As already stated, he married Margaret Miller, daughter of Michael Miller, who was a very remarkable woman for her day and generation. She was born near the close of the Revolutionary War, Sept. 16, 1786, and died in 1882, in the 96th year of her age. For eighty years or more she had been a consistent and faithful member of the Presbyterian church of Nazareth. Her life was marked by her love of the Bible and her intelligent comprehension of its contents. As her physical constitution was of the iron type, so her mental faculties were strong and vigorous. She studied the Bible attentively, carefully and prayerfully all through life and committed to memory large portions of it; and also many of Newton's hymns. The treasures which she gathered in early youth proved to be of great comfort to her in old age. All through her long life, duty was to her a word full of meaning. Living remote from her church (Nazareth), she and John Smith—a neighbor and a useful and acceptable elder in the same—organized and conducted a Sunday school near her dwelling, which was sustained for thirty years. Old and weary of the world, she passed away as gently as the wave dies along the shore when the storm is over.

John Montgomery, Jr. and Margaret Miller had thirteen children:

1. Nancy Montgomery first married Dr. Andrew B. Moore; second, married Col. Samuel N. Evans. One of her sons, Andrew Charles Moore, was in the 18th South Carolina Volunteer regiment, and was killed at the second Manassas fight.

2. Rosa Roddy Montgomery married John Chapman, Jr. One of her sons, Warren Davis Chapman, was in the battalion, was wounded below Richmond and died a few days afterward.

3. Mary Montgomery married William Cunningham, Esq. Captain Michael M. Cunningham, one of her sons of the 6th regiment S. C. Vol., was killed in Virginia.

4. Benjamin Franklin Montgomery first married Harriet, daughter of James Moss; second, married Juliet Moss, her sister. By his first wife he had twelve children: 1. John Henry. 2. James M. 3. Nancy Elizabeth. 4. Robert Scott. 5. Benjamin Landrum. 6. Emily Margaret. 7. Francis B. 8. Mary Crawford. 9. William C. 10. Anna Caroline. 11. Sarah Cornelius. 12. Joseph Oscar.

Robert Scott Montgomery, No. 4, son of Benjamin, was in a Texas regiment and killed in the battle of Franklin, Tenn. At this writing, 1899, only four of this family are living—John Henry, Benjamin Landrum of Hillsdale, near Enoree, S. C, and Elizabeth, wife of Dr. E. R. W McCrary, and Anna Rogers reside in Texas.

CAPTAIN JOHN HENRY MONTGOMERY

Captain John H. Montgomery, eldest of the twelve children referred to, of Benjamin F. and Harriet (Moss) Montgomery, was born fourteen miles west of the city of Spartanburg, December 8, 1833. He was brought up on his father's farm, receiving the best education that could be afforded in the common schools of his neighborhood. One of his instructors was Richard Golightly, whom we have mentioned at another place in this volume. Not possessing what might be called a strong constitution, he was at the age of 19 years placed in the country store of James Nesbitt in the southern portion of the present County of Spartanburg. He held this position for a year, for which he was paid $5 per month and board. During this year, without questioning the propriety, he performed all the requirements of his employer. He worked around the house and barn, and though hired as a clerk his first work was to drive a four horse team loaded with flour to the iron works at the present site of Clifton, S. C, a distance of thirty miles, loading back with iron and nails.

From Mr. Nesbitt's store he went to Columbia and worked as a clerk for four months in the store of Robert Brice, which was during the winter of 1853-54. The next spring he entered into a partnership with his brother-in-law. Dr. E. R. W. McCrary, in the mercantile business at Hobbyville, S. C, which was but a few miles from the store of his old employer.

The Montgomerys

In the fall of 1855 the parents of Mr. Montgomery, his four brothers and six sisters, together with his brother-in law and partner, removed to Texas, leaving him the sole member of the family remaining in South Carolina. With a limited capital he continued in the mercantile business at Hobbyville for three years or more, meeting all the obligations which had been contracted by the firm in good faith, but under trying difficulties.

In 1857 he married Miss Susan A. Holcomb, daughter of David Holcomb, a native of Union County, S. C, who settled in Spartanburg in 1845. In 1858 he moved his stock of merchandise to a store owned by his father-in-law two miles distant, where he continued in the business of a merchant in connection with a small tannery until the outbreak of the Civil War. In December, 1861, he volunteered his services to his country and was enrolled as a private in Co. E. 18th regiment S. C. Vol. Upon the organization of said regiment, however, he was appointed regimental commissary with the rank of captain. This office, under new army regulations, was abolished in 1863, and Captain Montgomery was made an assistant commissary of the brigade, which office was also abolished in 1864, and he was then made an assistant division commissary, continuing as such until the close of the war, surrendering with General Lee at Appomattox. April, 1865.

Returning home after the war, he began life anew, as it were. Besides owning a small farm, upon which he had depended for the support of his family during the war, he had a small stock of leather, the accumulation of his small tannery, which was the only property he possessed.

In 1866 he began the use of commercial fertilizers upon his farm, and soon demonstrated to his neighbors the importance of stimulating plant growth. He at once engaged in the sale of fertilizers to his neighbors and surrounding country, which was the dawning of a new era of prosperity in his business career. He had all the while successfully conducted the business of his tannery, and in 1870 resumed his merchandising at the same place.

His sale of commercial fertilizers had assumed such proportions as to make it necessary to give up farming, and later, all other brandies of business. In 1874 he removed to Spartanburg and turned his attention exclusively to fertilizers, associating himself with Colonel Joseph Walker and Dr. C. E. Fleming, under the name of Walker. Fleming & Co.

In 1881 this firm purchased a water power on Pacolet River, known as Hough Shoals, and in 1882 commenced the erection of the Pacolet Manufacturing Company, which was completed the following year. The company was incorporated in 1881 with Captain Montgomery as its president and treasurer, which position he still holds. In 1887, the capacity of the mill was 26,224 spindles and 840 looms; but it was again enlarged in 1894, making it the third mill of the company, containing in the aggregate 57,000 spindles and 26,000 looms. Its annual consumption of cotton is about 300,000 bales, and its capital about $500,000.

In 1889, Captain Montgomery was made president and treasurer of the Spartan Mills. For information as to the capacity of these mills, the reader is referred to our review on the progress of manufacturing in Spartanburg, at another place in this volume.

Captain Montgomery is a stockholder and director in the Whitney Mills, the Lockhart Mills, Morgan Iron Works, and the Clifton Mills.

Aside from his business relations to the companies referred to, he is in every sense of the word a model gentleman, fully alive to every enterprise and business industry looking to the development and up building of his country. Notwithstanding he has been successful in his business investments and has accumulated a handsome fortune, he has been liberal with his means and a generous contributor to every worthy object of charity with which he has been confronted.

He has been for nearly a half century a consistent member of the Baptist church, which he has most always represented in the annual meetings of the association. In his church he is among the foremost in the support of his pastor and of all the claims of missions and charity coming before it.

In another place in this volume we have endeavored to state the circumstances under which the Hon. Peter Cooper of New York donated the valuable property comprising the Institute building and surrounding grounds at Limestone Springs to the Spartanburg Baptist Association, the history of the progress of which we have recorded.

In 1888 Captain Montgomery succeeded to the presidency of the board of trustees of the Cooper Limestone Institute, now known as Limestone

College, and its marked success from year to year has been mainly due to his indomitable energy, excellent judgment and contributions from his private means which have already amounted to some $15,000 or more. He still presides at the head of an able board of trustees of this college, which, by reason of the work of remodeling and its modern equipment, will for all time to come add additional honors to his name and character. In all these generous gifts, however (at one time the sum of $500 for the library of the college, he has had no reference whatever to the perpetuation of his name or memory. He has simply done what he felt to be a duty in the distribution of the means with which he has been so abundantly blessed by his own perseverance and the assistance of a kind Providence.

In the ordinary walks of life he is the same humble and unassuming citizen that he was when a country boy on his father's farm at the age of 18 years. The humblest operative in his employ can approach him with as much freedom as the wealthy capitalist with whom, in a business way, he is much associated.

Captain Montgomery, by his marriage with Miss Holcomb, had eight children, only three of whom are now living—viz: Victor M., Walter S., and Benjamin W. Those who have died were: David F., Mary, John, Katy Lois, and an infant unnamed.

A true patriot, a philanthropist, Captain Montgomery stands before the people of Spartanburg as one of the best, most influential and progressive citizens.

5. Elizabeth Montgomery, daughter of John Montgomery and Margaret Miller, married the Rev. John G. Landrum. Dr. J. B. Landrum is their son and is an author of note, and wrote this sketch.

6. John Crawford Montgomery died small.

7. Michael Miller Montgomery married Martha Cora, of Neuse District, S. C. Their son, John Oscar Montgomery, was in the 18th regiment S. C. Vol. and killed at second Manassas.

8. Chevis C. Montgomery married Mary McCarrell of Greenville District, S. C.

9. Hannah Amanda Montgomery, married Col. S. N. Evans— second wife.

10. Catherine Montgomery married Edward Ballenger.

11. Heron Earl Montgomery married Sarah Ballenger.

12. Robert Scott Montgomery, Sr., married Catherine Gaudelock, of Neuse District, S. C.

13. Margaret Montgomery married William Moore of Morgantown, N. C.

3. James Montgomery, son of John Montgomery from Pennsylvania, married a Miss Walker and had two sons—John W. and Robert Montgomery.

4. Robert Montgomery, son of Pennsylvania John, never married.

5. Hugh Montgomery, son of Pennsylvania John, had eight children: John, James, Thomas, Walker, David, Elias, Mary and Elizabeth. Of these, Mary married a Gross and Elizabeth married Shadrach Barton.

6. and 7. Mary and Elizabeth Montgomery, daughters of Pennsylvania John—no information.

"BOYNE WATER" MONTGOMERY FAMILY, OF DELAWARE, PENNSYLVANIA AND OTHER STATES

1. Major William Montgomery, great-grandson of Lord Nicholas Montgomery, who married the daughter and only heir of Lord Lyle about 1500. This great-grandson, Major William Montgomery, was killed in the battle of Boyne Water, which was fought near the town of Drogheda, Ireland, July 1, 1690. Captain William Montgomery, son of Maj. William Montgomery, was wounded in this same battle and had two brothers killed in the same. He was afterward promoted to major in his father's regiment, and in all the records of this family he is known as the "Boyne Water Major." He married the daughter of William Dunbar.

"Boyne Water Major" William Montgomery came to America about 1720 and settled in Delaware. He had several brothers, but all died without issue. He had sons as follows: John, the eldest, who went to sea and was never heard of afterward; however, there are several things that tend to show that he went to Virginia and was the father of the John Montgomery who was a lieutenant colonel of George Roger Clark's regiment, which on July 4, 1778, captured Kaskaskia, in Illinois, and later captured Vincennes, Ind., from the English. See index—Col. John Montgomery.

Robert, the second son of "Boyne Water Major" Montgomery, had children—Margaret, Sarah, William, Hugh, Matthew, Jane and Robert. Of this family little is known—all living at this time (1844) in Delaware—from old papers in this family.

Alexander, the third son of "Boyne Water Major" Montgomery, came to America in 1740; died 1747. He married a lady named Mary ___, in Ireland, and had four sons and two daughters: 1. John; 2. Moses; 3. William, born in 1736; 4. Daniel, born probably 1738; 5. Margaret, born probably 1740.

John Montgomery, son of Alexander Montgomery, born probably 1732, married and moved to North Carolina, on Deep River, above Fayetteville about 30 miles. He had six or eight daughters, but no son. One of his grandsons took his name and at this time (1836) is said to be a respectable member of the legislature.

Moses Montgomery, born about 1734, son of Alexander Montgomery, had at least one son who settled in Williamson County, Tenn., about 1838.

William Montgomery, born Aug. 3, 1736, in Chester County, Pennsylvania, afterward of Danville, Pa., makes the following interesting statement concerning himself and family, which is found recorded in the old family Bible, later in the possession of Mrs. Hannah Lawhead:

"By the goodness of Divine Providence, Aug. 3, 1809.

"I have this day numbered seventy-three years (not noticing the change of style), and it is but right that I should have a record of something of God's goodness to me in so long a life. I was the third son of Alexander and Mary Montgomery, who both died, leaving me an orphan ten or eleven years old, but by the restraining grace and goodness of God I was led up through the slippery paths of youth up to manhood. I early married Margaret Nivins; she was all that could be expected in a woman; she was pious, sensible and affectionate. She lived with me about 13 years and had issue— Mary, who died at the age of 23 years; Alexander, who died in infancy; Margaret, who died in the same year with her sister; William, who is still alive and has a large family—is now about 47 years old, born 1762; John, who is about two years younger, and also has a large family; Daniel, who is two years younger, born 1766, and has a family; Alexander, who died about one year old. About 22 months after her decease I married Isabella Evans, a most distinguished and delightful woman, by whom I had issue—Robert, born in April, 1773: Hannah, born 22nd of January, 1775; Alexander, born October 2, 1777; and Margaret, born January, 1784. The three former are still living, but she died soon after her marriage with Thomas Woodaide: but their mother was called away from me in August, 1791 and in April, 1793, I again married a worthy and eminent woman. Her maiden name was Boyd and she was the widow of Col. Matthew Boyd, by whom she had issue—John, who died with the dysentery, aged about 23 years; also Rebecca, who is married to the Rev. John Patterson; lives happy and is raising a fine family. But I have had no issue by my present wife nor has any uneasiness arisen in consequence of it, nor can it be said that any of my children have had a step-mother, being always treated with as much tenderness and respect as they could have expected from their own mother. Another instance of my happiness, and for which I ought to be very thankful, is the untarnished morality of my children and the peace and harmony that has always subsisted among; them. Through all this long life I have been abundantly provided for; have enjoyed honors enough unsought by any other means than honestly endeavoring to do my duty to my God and my country; great health and much comfort, retaining my natural powers with little diminution till about five or six years past, since when I feel sensibly the advance of old age; but 1 hope that the goodness and mercy which have followed me all through life will not forsake me when gray hairs appear, but continue to conduct me safely down to death; after which, through the merits of our Lord Jesus Christ alone, and the mercy of God our Savior, I hope to obtain eternal rest and happiness.

"WILLIAM MONTGOMERY.

"Note.—This year the woolen factory at Danville was established under my care."

(The above is a true copy of what appears to be an original draft made by James Montgomery, who is the son of Jeff. T. Montgomery of Sumner

Co., Tenn., who was the son of Wm. Montgomery of the same place, who was the son of Wm. Montgomery of Danville, Pa.)

This William Montgomery was a gentleman or strong mind. He was censor of Pennsylvania in 1776. A peculiar office under the constitution of Pennsylvania at that date. (Charter and Constitution of United States. Part II., pages 1540-42-43.) He was prominent in settling the disputes concerning the boundary lines of northern Pennsylvania; was County judge, mayor, general of militia, and owned many thousand acres of the best land in Pennsylvania. In 1776-7 he commanded a regiment of state militia for six months in service. His son William, born 1762, was 15 years old at that time, and served with him in the Revolutionary service. The elder William Montgomery served in the legislature of Pennsylvania, and in Congress. He died in 1816, aged 80 years.

The younger William Montgomery, named above, born 176?, married Jane McMillan about 1788, and soon after settled on Drake's Creek, Sumner County, Tenn., where he died in 1838. They had sons Daniel, John, Robert, William. Jefferson T.; and daughters Margaret, Jane, Hannah, Polly—who died in infancy and Elizabeth.

John Montgomery, son of William, Jr., had sons William, Fielding T., John, Robert and Daniel.

John Montgomery, born in Pennsylvania in 1764, and died in that state in 1834 or '35, son of William Montgomery, Sr. married Elizabeth Bell in 1788, who died in 1836; children, William, James. Daniel, Jane, Margaret, John, Rebecca, Mary, Elizabeth, and four others who died in infancy.

About 1822 or 1823 William (son of John) married Jane Robison; they went to Arkansas as missionaries. His wife died shortly after the birth of her first child; the child died soon after. He married for his second wife Mary Weller, who died shortly after giving birth to her first child. Mary Weller His third wife was Harriet Woolley: she had one child—James Lawhead. William) Montgomery died of cholera in 1834; he and his three wives and oldest child are all buried on mission ground in Arkansas. Mary Weller in 1847 married Rev. T. P. M. Walker and is living in Hancock County, Ill. Their children are William M. Alexander F., James M., Maggie M., Thomas M. and Charles G. William M. died of consumption when about 22 years old. Alexander married, 1874, Nettie Mull, and is living in Rack Island, Ill. James Lawhead, son of William Montgomery, died in New York City, unmarried.

James, son of John Montgomery, married Margaret Reed, March. 1821. Their children were Jane Elizabeth, born Feb. 23, 1822; John, born March, 1823; Caroline, born Aug. 13, 1824; Louis R. born April 14, 1826. John died in infancy. James Montgomery died in Pennsylvania, Aug. 1826, aged 35 years. In 1836 his widow and three daughters moved to Monmouth, Ill. Jane E. died in Mercer County, Ill. Aug. 1843.

Caroline Montgomery born Aug. 13, 1824, daughter of Capt. James Montgomery, married George Poage Rice Feb. 4, 1841. He was born Oct. 27, 1812, in Greenup (now Boyd) County, Ky. He died July 7, 1890, in Omaha, Neb., and was buried in Monmouth, Ill. He studied for the Presbyterian ministry in Clarksville, Tenn.; moved with mother and brothers from Christian county, Ky., *to* Monmouth, Ill., in 1835. With his brother he kept store in Monmouth a few years; farmed in Henderson County. Ill. till 1857, then moved to Oquawka and entered the mercantile firm of Phelps &, Rice, which continued four years, when he retired. He was 40 years a ruling elder in the Presbyterian Church. His children were: James Montgomery, born March 8, 1842; John Hopkins, born Feb. 14. 1844: William Gyrus, born April 30, 1846, died May 8, l850; Jane Elizabeth, born July 30, 1848, died May 18, 1849; Mary Louise, born June 15, 1850; Carrie M. born April 15, 1853; Ann, born Oct. 1856, died in infancy; Charles Edward, born Nov. 3, 1858.

James Montgomery Rice, born March 8, 1842, at Monmouth. Ill., son of Caroline Montgomery-Rice, lived in Henderson County, Ill., on a farm until 1847; home in Oquawka; freshman Monmouth College, class 1850 to 1851. Aug. 20, 1861, he enlisted as a private in Co. E, 10th regiment Ill. Inf., for three years; was corporal and sergeant, and detailed clerk at brigade headquarters; was in many battles— Corinth, Pittsburg Landing, Missionary Ridge, Ringold, Buzzard Roost, Resaca, Peach Tree Creek, Ezra Church, Jonesboro. Capture of Atlanta, and others; a member of National Guard of Illinois from May 30, 1875; General Inspector R. P. of Illinois National Guard for many years—resigned Jan. 1896; member of state legislature 1871-1872, which revised statutes after adoption of the new constitution; member of General Assembly, Presbyterian church in the United States 1898, 1899 and 1900. He was the author of the new method of electing standing committees—see Appleton's American and English Encyclopedia 1900. He was also author of the declaration of war with Spain. He graduated at law school, Michigan University, LL. B. 1866: was admitted to Supreme Court of Illinois. April 14, 1866; in 1877 city attorney of Peoria, Ill.; member of State Bar Association;

principal organizer of Peoria Law Library Association; admitted to practice in Supreme Court of United States, March 26, 1890. He married Eliza F., daughter of Col. Charles Ballance, a lawyer of Peoria, Ill., who was first colonel 77th Ill. Vol. Inf., and Julian Margaret, nee Schnebly. Eliza was born at Peoria, Ill., Jan. 26, 1844; graduated at Monticello Seminary, Godfrey, Ill., near St. Louis; died Feb. 17, 1895, and was buried at Peoria; a faithful member of Presbyterian church and several patriotic ladies' societies. Their children were: Lillian Ballance, born March 26, 1873; Julia Margaret, born Oct. 28. 1874; died March 4, 1875; Caroline Montgomery Rice, born March 18, 1876, student of Smith College, Northampton, Mass. taught in public schools of Peoria, Ill., and Denver, Col., member of second Presbyterian church; Mary Virginia, born Oct. 18, 1880, graduated A. B. of Michigan University, June 1902; Montgomery Gordon, born Aug. 24, 1882, student Sophomore Bradley Polytechnic Institute, Peoria. Ill.; Willis Ballance, born Dec. 6, 1884, graduate of June, 1901, Peoria high school.

John Hopkins Rice, born Feb. 14, 1844, married Dec. 29, 1869, to Margaret J., daughter of Judge Preston Martin and Ann Elizabeth, nee Taylor; enlisted Aug. 10, 1862, in Co. C. 91st Ill. Vol. Inf.; promoted corporal sergeant, 1st sergeant, and 1st lieutenant; mustered out July 12, 1865. On Dec. 26, while guarding the bridge over Salt river, Ky., was captured by Gen. John Morgan, the raider, and paroled; remained in parole camp at St. Louis, Mo., until exchanged June 5, 1863; moved to Vicksburg, Port Hudson, New Orleans, Morganzia, La., Brownsville, Tex., Brazos de Santiago, Texas, Palo Alto, Mobile. He was a farmer, justice of the peace, school director, treasurer school board, member of Presbyterian Church: moved to a farm near Wichita, Kansas, Feb. 14, 1900. His children are: Frank Montgomery, born Sept. 1, 1871; lives near Wichita, Kansas; is a farmer. Ann Louise, born Sept. 2, 1873; died Dec. 17, 1873. Sallie Plumer, born July 31, 1876; member of Presbyterian Church; is teaching school near Wichita. William Cyrus, born March 9, 1880; member of Presbyterian Church; is a farmer near Wichita. Mary, born Oct. 2, 1884, died Sept. 24, 1885. Eva M. born Aug. 3, 1886.

Mary Louise Marriott, nee Rice, born June 15, 1850, married John Thomas Merriott, May 29, 1879; taught school at Mineir, Ill., Brimneld, Ill.; was assistant principal of Elmwood high school; member of Presbyterian church; studied at Peoria County normal school, and at Valparaiso, Ind.

And Their Descendants

John T. Merriott is a merchant and broker at Wakefield, Neb.; was born March 6, 1855, in Brimfield, Ill.; son of William and Sarah (nee Percy) Merriott, who were born and married in Lincolnshire, England.

John T. Merriott and family moved to Wakefield, Neb., in 1881, and still live there. Their children are: Caroline Montgomery, born March 24, 1886; graduated at Wakefield high school, class of 1902, and lives with her father and mother. William Henry, born Sept. 16, 1888; student at Wakefield high school.

Carrie M. Rice, born April 15, 1853, Henderson County, Ill., married in Monmouth, Ill., Lyman Weeks Case who was born Dec. 1, 1853, at Swanton, Vermont—son of Samuel Montague Case, born June 6, 1821, Fairfax, Vt., and Ann Maria Babcock.

Lyman W. Case is a loan broker and loan agent. He moved from Peoria, Ill., in Sept. 1889 to Omaha, Neb., where he still resides. The children are: Bertha Case, born Aug. 19, 1873, graduate of Neb. State Normal, Peru, Neb.; united with Westminster Presbyterian church. Omaha, 1889; teacher in Omaha public schools since 1899. Frederick Albert Case, born April 13, 1880; died June, 1881. Montgomery Babcock Case, born Feb. 11, 1882; student of University of Nebraska.

Charles Edward Rice, born Nov. 3, 1858, married Emma Lyon; graduate of Monmouth College 1877; graduate Omaha, Neb., Theological Seminary, 1875; ordained a Presbyterian minister March, 1894; pastor of Carey and other small churches in Nebraska since 1895; was engaged in work for the American S. S. Union from 1887 to 1892; now resides at Hotchkiss, Colorado.

Lillian Rice Brigham, nee Rice, born March 26, 1873, married Sept. 4, 1896, Daniel Rufus Brigham, son of Daniel Morgan Brigham mid Lillian Brigham, nee Card, of Milwaukee, Wis. Lillian graduated from Smith College. Northampton Mass., June, 1894; was professor of history and English literature in Normal School of Arizona, 1896-7. Her husband, Daniel Rufus Brigham, born April 10, 1865, died at Denver. Colorado, Feb. 19, 1902: was son of Daniel Morgan Brigham and Lydia Brigham, nee Card, of Milwaukee. Their children are: Daniel Morgan, born May 8, 1899. Caroline Rice, born March 1, 1901.

The Montgomerys

Nov. 22, 1872, Louisa R., daughter of James Montgomery, married William B. Jamison, a widower with three children—Alphens, Alma and Janie, aged respectively 22, 20 and 10 years.

Alphens married Carrie Monteith, Oct. 5, 1875, and is living on a farm in Henderson County. Ill.

Alma married Joseph Carter, Sept. 1871. They have one child —Ernest O., aged 4 years. They are living on a farm in Henderson County. Ill. Janie is living with her parents in Biggsville, Ill.

Daniel, son of John Montgomery, married Christiana Giffin, 1826, who died of consumption when her first child, William G., was about nine months old. In 1835 he married Margaret Simington. Their children were Robert S., John, Daniel and James. William G. married Jennie Titterington. John married Miss___. Daniel married Aurilla Parks. James is a merchant, unmarried, living in the city of Rock Island, Ill. The four married brothers are farming in Rock Island County, Ill. Their father, Daniel Montgomery, died of spinal disease in 1848. His widow is living with her maiden sister in Milan, Rock Island County, Ill.

Jane, daughter of John Montgomery, married Rev. William Requaro, missionary to the Indians, in 1834. She died childless shortly after reaching the mission ground.

Margaret, daughter of John Montgomery, married Thomas Candor, 1824. Their children were John M., Robert, Josiah, Elizabeth, Mary and Daniel Montgomery. John died just as he had finished his theological course at Princeton, N. J., aged about 23.

Robert married Rebecca Lynn; their children are John, Thomas, Ward, Loomis, Maggie, Sadie and Mary. Josiah married Nellie ___; their children are Carrie, May and Robert. Elizabeth died in infancy. Mary married Graham Lee; their children are Elisha, Maggie, Milo, Fannie, and an infant who died shortly after its mother in 1874. Maggie died a few months afterward. Mr. Lee is married again.

D. Montgomery Candor married Miss___. The Candor brothers are all living near each other in Rock Island and Mercer counties, Ill. Mrs. Margaret Candor died in 1841, not quite two years after Mr. T. M. Candor married his second wife, Mary L. Broadman. He died in 1870 or 1871, in Aledo, Ill., and his widow died about a year after at the residence of her step-son, D. Montgomery Candor.

John, son of John Montgomery, was a Presbyterian minister. He married Sarah, daughter of Rev. Wm. Vail, missionary to the Indians. Their children were Joseph V., William F., Christiana S., Asenath, Elizabeth, Daniel and Sarah. Joseph V. married Anna___ and is living in Kewanee. Ill. Christiana S. married Washington I. Moore, a retired sea captain, and is living in Lynn, Conn. Their oldest child is named Kathleen. William F. is in Cincinnati. Asenath is married and living in Iowa.

Mr. John Montgomery, his wife and twin children—Daniel and Sarah—all died in 1843. Elizabeth died about a year before.

Rebecca, daughter of John Montgomery, Sr., married Rev. Matthew Patterson, a widower with two children—John and Sarah; they are both married and living in Freeport, Ill. Rebecca died childless. Mr. M. Patterson is at present in Freeport, Ill. Mary married Hopkins Boone; their children were H. Montgomery, Jane Elizabeth, Hannah B., and nine others who died in infancy. Montgomery died in battle in New Mexico during the late war. Elizabeth married Benjamin Burroughs. She died in 1870 leaving four children—Anna, Eva, Mary and Libby. Mr. Burroughs has since married again and is living in Quincy, Ill. Hannah married John Geddes; their children are Thomas Boone, Mary M., Alexander Walker, and Frank. They are living at Farlow's Grove, Mercer County Ill.

Elizabeth, daughter of John Montgomery, Sr., married William Sheriff and died childless.

Mary Montgomery, wife of Hopkins Boone, died in 1858.

About two years after, Mr. Boone married his second wife, Mrs. Hinds, a widow with two children—Fannie and Jennie. Mr. Boone is living in Aledo, Ill. Fannie and Jennie are married and living in Mercer County, Ill.

Each member of the family of John Montgomery, Sr., that had any descendants living was represented in the late war.

Rev. T. P. M. Walker, son-in-law of Wm. Montgomery was chaplain, and his son William was also in the army. Jas. M. Rice, who furnished part of the data for the above history, and his brother, John H. Rice, grandsons of Captain James Montgomery, each served three years—the former as sergeant and the latter as first lieutenant. Robert S. Montgomery, son of Daniel, was captain of a cavalry company and was wounded at Lexington, Mo.—supposed to be mortally, but he recovered and served out his time. Wm. F., son of John Montgomery had his horse killed under him at the battle of Wilson Creek, Mo., but he escaped unhurt. Montgomery Candor, son of Margaret Montgomery, was a captain in the army. Montgomery Boone, son of Mary Montgomery, was a member of a Colorado regiment and was killed in New Mexico. Elizabeth and Rebecca Montgomery had no children. General William Montgomery's son John, born 1764, was a colonel of the state militia of Pennsylvania. There is an interesting circumstance about this Gen. William Montgomery, the Revolutionary colonel. Later in life he was made a major-general of the militia. His son Daniel was a brigadier-general and commanded one of the brigades in his father's division. His other son, John, was a lieutenant colonel of one of the regiments in Daniel's brigade, and James Montgomery, a son of John, was a captain in his father's regiment; so that a paper forwarded from him to the governor would go first to his father, John, then to his uncle, Daniel, and then to his grandfather, William Montgomery.

Daniel, born 1766, son of William Montgomery, Sr., was a member of Congress for several years. He married Christiana Strawbridge of Scottish descent; their children were Hannah, Margaret, William, Mary, Strawbridge, and several others who died in infancy. Hannah married John Boyd, Margaret and William died unmarried, Mary married Dr. McGill, Strawbridge married Sarah Breadenburg, a daughter of a German reformed minister; they had one daughter who married a Presbyterian minister.

Robert, born April, 1773, son of William Montgomery, Sr., married for his first wife Miss Boyd; their children were Mary Nivan and one son. His second wife was Mrs. Louisa Edwards, by marriage niece of Rev. Jonathan Edwards; she had two children when she married Mr. Montgomery, and two afterward. Hannah, daughter of Gen. Wm. Montgomery, born Jan. 1775; married James Lawhead; they died childless.

Alexander, born Oct. 2, 1777, son of William Montgomery, Sr., married Jane Boyd: their children were Mary Eliza, Isabella, Hannah, Margaret, and a son who died in infancy. Isabella married Michael Grier, son of Isaac Grier, D. D., a brother of Judge Robert Grier. She died leaving five or six children. Shortly afterward Mary Eliza married her brother-in-law, Michael Grier. They are living in Danville, Pa. Hannah married Andrew Russel; they have a large family and are living in Danville, Pa. Margaret is unmarried.

Alexander Montgomery died a number of years ago. His wife, Jane Montgomery, is still living (1876). I think she must be nearly 100 years old.

William Boyd, step-son of William Montgomery, Sr., died unmarried.

Rebecca, step-daughter of William Montgomery, Sr., married John B. Patterson, a Presbyterian minister; their children were Margaret, Matthew, William, John, Jane, Rebecca, Hannah, Robert and Elizabeth. William and John died unmarried. Matthew is a Presbyterian minister. He married for his second wife Rebecca Montgomery. The daughters are all unmarried living at the old homestead, Montour County, Pa. Robert married Josepha McCoy and is living in Centralia, Ill., in the railroad business.

Captain Daniel Montgomery, born probably 1738, fourth son of Alexander Montgomery, was with Washington at the battles of Trenton and Princeton, in the Revolutionary War. He married Margaret Willard, a descendant of Rev. Samuel Willard, First Presbyterian minister of Boston. Captain Daniel Montgomery moved from Philadelphia to Northumberland County, Pa., and founded the town of Danville. He died 1823 or '24.

Hon. William Montgomery, born in Philadelphia, 1774, only child of Captain Daniel and Margaret Montgomery, was for many years judge in Northumberland County, Pa. He married Jane Hayes, niece of the Hon. Andrew Hayes, member of the Continental congress. Judge Montgomery died in 1847.

Rev. Samuel Montgomery, third child of Judge William and Jane Montgomery, was born April 15, 1814, in Danville, Pa.; married Mary E., daughter of Dr. Samuel McKeehan, of West Alexander, Pa. Samuel Montgomery preached in Pennsylvania and Ohio, and died in Oberlin, Ohio, March 19, 1887; children—Elizabeth M., who died in infancy. 2. Elizabeth B., single; lives in Cadillac, Mich. 3, Narcissa Y. Montgomery, married H. H. Couchman, of Ft. Calhoun, Neb.; children two: 1, Mary E. Couchman, married Rev. Charles A. Arnold, Ord, Neb. 2, Anna C. Couchman, married Henry Roberts, Arlington, Neb. 4. Samuel Whitefield Montgomery died Aug.

19, 1863. 5, Anna W. Montgomery married Joseph Chase, of Seattle, Wash. 6, Aristae J. Montgomery, married Dr. J. M. Wardell, of Cadillac, Mich.; one child-Montgomery Wardell, born July 15, 1893.

Margaret Montgomery, born probably 1740, one of the daughters of Alexander Montgcmeiy, married a Mr. Strawbridge, near Danville, Pa., and died about 1839 at the age of 98 or 99 years.

MONTGOMERY-HOUSTON FAMILY
OF PENNSYLVANIA, VIRGINIA AND OTHER STATES

William G. Montgomery, of Birmingham, Ala., has kindly sent me the book containing the Montgomery-Houston genealogy, with whom the Montgomerys are connected. This book was published about 23 years ago. He says:

"Our records are not entirely complete. Our family is also Scotch-Irish—descended, we think, from the Skelmorlie branch. Our ancestor, John Montgomery Sr. (Generation 3), came to America about 1730 or before; came to Pennsylvania or Delaware; married Esther Houston, daughter of John Houston, probably 1751, and moved from Pennsylvania to Augusta County, Va., settling between Stanton and Lexington, Va., near New Providence church.

Esther Houston came with her father, John Houston, from Ireland about 1735. She was born about 1724. They settled in Pennsylvania and remained there until the three oldest children were married, when they emigrated to Virginia, as above stated. Children twelve: 1. John. Jr. 2. Mollie; 3. Ann: 4. James; 5. Dorcas; 6. Jane; 7. Robert; 8. Esther; 9. Alex; 10. Isabella 11. and 12. Two daughters.

1. John Montgomery, Jr., born 1752 (No. 1, Gen. 4), was a Presbyterian minister, highly respected for his talents, piety and usefulness. He was a popular preacher, a good scholar, an esteemed relative and an admirable man. He began his education in one of those famous Scotch-Irish log colleges; this one being located on Timber Ridge, Augusta County, Va., and being conducted successfully by the Rev. John Brown and William Graham. Rev. John Montgomery completed his education at Princeton College, New Jersey, graduating 1775; and returning to Virginia was ordained by Hanover Presbytery at Tinkling Springs Church, Augusta County. Va., April 26, 1780.

He settled first in Fredric County, Va., and preached in Winchester, Opequon and Cedar Creek churches for a time, and then moved to Rocky Springs church, in the "Pasture'" of Rockbridge County, Va., in 1789, where he died in 1818 at the *age* of 66 years. This church is situated not far from where "Windy Grove" and Lebanon churches now (1879) stand. He married Agnes Hugait, 1772, daughter and only child of Col. Thomas Hugart and Rebecca Estill, near Rocky Springs, Va. Mr. Waddell. in his history of Augusta County, Va., says Colonel Hugart was colonel of a Revolutionary regiment under Lafayette, and was also high sheriff of Augusta County, Va., and a wealthy planter, owning large grants of land and the greater part of Deerfield valley in that County. Rev. John Montgomery had seven children: 1. Esther; 2. John; 3. Thomas; 4. William; 5. Isabella: 6. Hugart; 7. Esttelline.

1. Esther Montgomery, born 1785 (No. 1, Gen. 5), died Feb. 1850. She lived single for many years and then married Rev. James C. Wilson, pastor of the Presbyterian church of Waynesborough, Augusta County, Va., an excellent, able minister who died not long afterward, very suddenly, while receiving his mail at the post office. She was a truly pious, intelligent and estimable lady, extensively known and much beloved. A large circle of relatives and acquaintances called her familiarly "Cousin Hettie." Her social qualities were of a high order. She died at 67 years of age without children.

2. John Montgomery (No. 2, Gen. 5), born 1788, died 1829; married Elizabeth Nelson, of Augusta County, Va., Nov. 11, 1813. Elizabeth Nelson's father came from Ireland when he was 17 years of age; had been well educated and taught school for some time. A merchant friend of his, Robert Manis of Philadelphia, the celebrated financier, told him to purchase largely of molasses on which to speculate, and he would advance the money. Young Nelson accepted the kind and liberal offer, obtaining on his sales a very handsome profit. He served as clerk for his friend for some time, but afterward established an independent business and, prospering greatly in trade, finally became sole proprietor of three ships, importing largely from abroad. But, war ensuing, his ships were captured by the French and he was reduced almost to penury; but by industry and tact for business he recovered so far from his prostration that he lived in comfort the rest of his days.

John Montgomery (No. 2, Gen. 5) was an elder in the Presbyterian Church and his home is near where Goshen depot is situated, in Rockbridge County. Va. His wife, Betsy Nelson, had a brother James with whom the distinguished Conrad Speed, D. D., made his home for many years, in Augusta County, Va., and he often entertained his friends by telling them of the sayings and doings of that very learned but somewhat eccentric divine.

Elizabeth (Betsy) Montgomery was a rather small woman and somewhat delicate, remarkably lively and cheerful in disposition, much loved by her children and friends. She told the writer on one occasion, when we were trying to trace out an exact kinship but could not succeed as well as we desired, "Well, I always claim kin pretty far off, if it is good."

We are only able to present brief accounts of the children. We regret that it is so, since they have always been regarded as occupying high ground among the best of our citizens in Virginia and elsewhere. They lived at Goshen, Rockbridge County, Va. Their graves near Goshen are close to the railroad, west of town, and have a large flat stone in a good state of preservation (1902). Children seven:

Their eldest son, Alexander N. Montgomery (No. 1, Gen. 6), born 1814, never married; was a member of the Episcopal Church and died in 1859 aged about 45 years.

John J. Montgomery (No. 2, Gen. 6), born Dec. 19, 1816, died June 13, 1892: was an elder in 1881 in McElhaney church, Greenbrier County, Va.; was a good Christian man, faithful as an officer of the church, took much interest in Sabbath schools; unassuming and retiring, with much good, practical common sense and quiet humor. He lived for many years in the town of Lewisburg, W. Va. His wife was Margaret, the daughter of T. Craigh, who was a well known and wealthy merchant and land-owner of Greenbrier County, Va. John J. Montgomery and Margaret Craigh had eight children: Lilly E., Bettie A., John T., Louis W., Nannie C, James A., Maggie C. and Samuel A.

Lilly E. Montgomery (No. 1 Gen. 7), born Aug. 23, 1857, married Robert W. Harrah, April 4, 1878; no children. They now (1901) live in Greenbrier County, W. Va.

Bettie A. Montgomery (No. 2, Gen. 7), born May 8, 1860, no information.

John T. Montgomery, born June 29, 1862, married Fannie E. Plubman, Dec. 28, 1897; one child—Margaret L. Montgomery, born Nov. 4, 1898; lives in Greenbrier County, W. Va.

Louis W. Montgomery, born Feb. 14, 1864, no information.

Nannie C. Montgomery, born Nov. 25, 1866, married J. N. Lowry, Sept. 1894; children four: 1. Oliver E. Lowry, born July 6, 1895, died Sept. 13, 1895. 2. Samuel C. Lowry, born June 28, 1896. 3. John B. Lowry, born Nov. 13, 1897. 4. James F. Lowry, born Feb. 8, 1900; residing (1901) in Greenbrier County. W. Va.

James A. Montgomery, born Oct. 26, 1869, married Julia Smith. Feb. 1896: children two: 1. Ruth Montgomery, born Oct. 1897. 2. Charles Joseph Montgomery, born Dec. 1900. Residence (1901) in Birmingham, Ala.

Maggie C. Montgomery, born Nov. 25, 1872, married W. P. Wyles, Oct. 9, 1895; children three: 1. Julia E. Wyles, born July 21, 1896. 2. John A. Wyles, born Feb. 13, 1898. 3. Joseph P. Wyles, born Feb. 13, 1900. Residence, Greenbrier County, W. Va.

Samuel A. Montgomery, born March 16, 1875, died Dec. 25 1875.

James N. Montgomery (No. 3, Gen. 6), born Nov. 15, 1818, died June 1, 1886; married Ann S. Jacob of Wheeling, Va., Nov. 16, 1847: children five: 1. Nannie; 2. John Alex; 3. Sallie E.; 4. Mary E. N.: 5. William G.

W. G. Montgomery
Birmingham, Alabama

The children are all sprightly, interesting, and a great comfort to their parents. John Alex. Montgomery has served as a civil engineer successfully and William G. stood high in his class in college and received some of the honors of the institution. Their mother is an intelligent, amiable, pious, active member of the Presbyterian church of Lewisburg, W. Va.; stands among the first in sustaining and promoting the benevolent operations of the church and of the community. Mr. Montgomery is an elder in the Presbyterian Church, faithful and judicial in council, exemplary and active. He has for many years superintended the Sabbath-school, and frequently represents his church in the courts of presbytery and synod. He has served for many years also as an officer in the Lank, to tie acceptance of all concerned. He has had delicate health; resides in town, but superintends his valuable farm in the vicinity. Children five:

1. Nannie Montgomery (No. 1, Gen. 7), born July 24, 1849, died Sep. 2. 1861.

2. John Alexander Montgomery (No. 2, Gen. 7), born Aug. 31, 1851, first married Fanny R. Bright Nov. 16. 1880; children three: 1. Guy Bright Montgomery, born Sept. 5, 1881. 2. James Nelson Montgomery, born March 20, 1884. 3. Cochran Montgomery born July 3, 1885. John Alex Montgomery second married Carrie G. Lewis, of Tuscaloosa, Ala., Dec. 27, 1888: children four: 1. Carol Lewis Montgomery, born Dec. 14, 1889. 2. Ann

Jacob Montgomery, born July 22, 1893. 3. Lewis Garland Montgomery, born Sept. 31, 1895. 4. Hugh Nelson Montgomery, born April 10, 1899.

3. Sallie Estella Montgomery (No. 3, Gen. 7), born March 24, 1854, married William Abner Frantz, of Virginia, Aug. 23, 1882; children three: 1. Sousana Montgomery Frantz, born July 7, 1883. 2. Estella V. Frantz, born Aug. 6, 1887. 3. Mary Belle Frantz, born April 5, 1894. They live in Lewisburg, W. Va.

4. Mary E. N. Montgomery (No. 4, Gen. 7), born Feb. 2, 1857, married Oct. 17, 1877, Frank Chilton Brown of Virginia; children five: 1. James Montgomery Brown, born Sep. 3, 1878. 2., Emma Granville Brown, born Sept. 16, 1880. 3. Ann Mitchell Brown, born Dec. 1. 1882. 4. Edna Marshall Brown, born March 7, 1886. 5. Frank Chilton Brown, born July 4, 1890, Residence (1901) Lewisburg, W. Va.

5. William G. Montgomery (No. 5, Gen. 7), born June 3, 1861, married Oct. 5, 1886, Sophia Perkins of Birmingham, Ala. Children three: 1. James Nelson Montgomery, born July 19, 1887. 2. Hattie Earl Montgomery, born June 28, 1889. 3. William G. Montgomery, born Aug. 13, 1899.
W. G. Montgomery, Sr. residence (1901) Birmingham, Ala., and is in the book and stationery business, and has rendered me much assistance in this work.

William H. Montgomery (No. 4, Gen. 6), born May 5, 1821, has been a successful merchant for many years at Lewisburg, W. Va. He and his family are members of the Presbyterian Church and mining the most worthy and respectable citizens of the town. They have a very pleasant and agreeable family. He married Ruth E. Jacobs, of Wheeling, Va.; children six: Elizabeth M., James F., Zachariah J., Martha M., Anna P., Jane C.

Elizabeth M. Montgomery (No. 1. Gen. 7), born Sept. 30, 1851, married Silas B. Mason, of Virginia, June 25, 1873; children nine: 1. Ruth Mason, born April 30, 1874. 2. Claborn Rice Mason, born June 22, 1875, dead. 3. William Horatio Mason, born Feb. 19, 1877. 4. James Montgomery Mason, born Aug. 12, 1879. 5. Dora Tate Mason, born Dec. 26, 1881. 6. Annie Clifford Mason, born April 5, 1884; dead. 7. Elizabeth Montgomery Mason, born March 2, 1887. 8. Winifred Boxley Mason, born Jan. 2, 1891. 9. Charlotte Eugene Mason, born Jan. 4, 1895. Residence (1901) Lewisburg, W. Va.

The Montgomerys

1. Ruth Mason (No. 1, Gen. 8), born April 3, 1874, married Oct. 11, 1899, Samuel C. Beard of near Lewisburg, W. Va.; one child— Esta Montgomery Beard, born July 25, 1900.

2. James F. Montgomery (No. 2, Gen. 7), born March 29, 1854 married June 24, 1884, Annie Matthews Witherow of Lewisburg, W. Va.; residence (1901) Frankfort, Ky.; children three: 1. William Mason Montgomery, born May 15, 1885. 2. James Witherow Montgomery, born Oct. 26, 1887. 3. Zach. Dangerfield Montgomery, born Oct. 26, 1887.

3. Zach. Jacob Montgomery (No. 3, Gen. 7), born July 19, 1859, married Oct. 10, 1883, Claudia A. Maer of Columbia, Miss. Children three: 1. Elizabeth Mason Montgomery, born Jan. 19, 1885. 2. Annie Montgomery, born Oct. 3, 1886. 3. Elsie Shattuck Montgomery, born May 26, 1888; residence (1901) Frankfort, Ky.

4. Martha W. Montgomery (No. 4, Gen. 7), died young.

5. Annie P. Montgomery (No. 5 Gen. 7) born May 30 1861 died June 12, 1886.

6. Jane Clifford Montgomery (No. 6, Gen. 7), born April 26, 1867, married June 25, 1890, Mason Matthews of Lewisburg, W. Va. (1901); children two: 1. Alex. F. Matthews, born Aug. 23. 1895. 2. Elizabeth Montgomery Matthews, born Feb. 19, 1900.

Franklin T. Montgomery (No. 5. Gen. 6), born March 13, 1824; married Elizabeth, Kerns. He was a deacon in the Lewisburg church: a pious, worthy man. For many years his health was delicate, rendering him to a considerable extent unfit for active business. He died in 1872. His wife had died some years before. Children three: 1. Martha K. Montgomery (No. 1, Gen. 7), married June 24, 1884, James M. Roder, of Greenbrier County, Va.; residence 1901, Lewisburg, W. Va.; children three: 1. Franklin K. Roder: 2. James W. Roder; 3. Martha Montgomery Roder. 2. Bettie K. Montgomery (No. 2, Gen. 7), dead. 3. Nannie Waddell Montgomery (N. 3, Gen. 7), married Nov. 20, 1890, William D. Slaver of Monroe County, Va.; residence, 1901, Lewisburg, W. Va.; children two: 1. Sant Roder Slaver; 2. Alex. Nelson, died Oct. 13, 1894.

Nannie E. L. Montgomery (No. 7, Gen. 6), born June 2, 1829, married Lyttleton Waddell, an editor of Virginia; children eight: Montgomery,

Elizabeth, St. Clair, Alex. L., Lucy D., James N., Charles E., Franklin S., and William W.

Of the above children and grandchildren of John Montgomery No. 2, Gen. 5, we are informed that 21 are members of the church— and probably more than that number.

1. Montgomery Waddell (No. 1, Gen. 7), born May 4, 1853, died Feb. 1858.
2. Elizabeth S. Waddell (No. 2, Gen. 7), born July 7, 1855, married W. H. McGee, Sept. 3, 1884; children four: 1. Alice Montgomery McGee, born July 24, 1885. 2. Nannie L. McGee, born May 30, 1887. 3. Lucy E. McGee, born June 3, 1891. 4. Elizabeth D. McGee, born Jan. 30, 1895.
3. Alex. Waddell (No. 3, Gen. 7), born March 25, 1857, died Oct. 25, 1857.
4. Lucy D. Waddell (No. 4, Gen. 7), born March 14, 1860, married James B. Wood, Sept. 3, 1884; children two: 1. Lyttleton W. Wood, born March 17, 1889. 2. Laura P. Wood, born Sept. 24, 1894.
5. James N. Waddell (No. 5, Gen. 7), married Margaret R. Daniel, Aug. 25, 1897; children two: 1. Cornelia Waddell, born Oct. 30, 1898. 2. Margaret Montgomery Waddell, born Jan. 27, 1901.
Charles E. Waddell (No. 6, Gen. 7), born July 25, 1861, died June 2, 1886.
Franklin S. Waddell (No. 7, Gen. 7), born Jan. 10, 1867.
William Wirt Waddell (No. 8, Gen. 7), born July 9, 1869, married Martha Payne, Dec. 10, 1890: children three: 1. James N. Waddell, born Nov. 29, 1891. 2. William Wirt Waddell, Jr., born Aug. 10, 1894. 3. Mary Walker Waddell, born Aug. 26, 1898. Residence, 1901, in Charlottesville, Va.

Nannie Estaline Lockhart Montgomery, the mother and grandmother of the parties above, was the seventh child of John Montgomery and Elizabeth Nelson. She was married Oct. 4, 1850 to Lyttleton Waddell. He was a grandson of the Rev. James Waddell, whom the Hon. Wm. Wirt, in his sketch-book entitled "British Spy" immortalized under the name of "The Blind Preacher." During the first year of their married life they lived in Stanton, their birth-place, where Mr. Waddell was editor of the "Stanton Spectator."

In 1861 he volunteered as a private soldier in the "Stanton Artillery," then commanded by Captain Imboden. He remained with this battery until

1862. He afterward served in the signal corps of the army until the close of the war.

In 1874 he moved his family to Charlottesville, Va., where he remained until his death in 1886. For many years he was editor of the Chronicle of Charlottesville.

He was for many years a ruling elder in the Presbyterian Church. Failing health led him to give up journalist work and engage in the boot and shoe business.

His widow is living at Charlottesville, Va., surrounded by her four remaining children and nine grandchildren. She was born in 1829. She was for many years very active in Christian work, Sunday-schools and ladies' benevolent societies. For fifteen years she has been distressingly afflicted with rheumatism, and for ten years not able to walk. This seems to be an inheritance in the Montgomery family. Still, amid all this suffering she maintains the sparkle in her bright, dark eyes, and her remarkably fair complexion still shows that she has been very handsome; and she still retains rare intelligence and industry, preferring to labor for the little ones of her grandchildren.

Her husband, her son Charles E., her brother James Montgomery, and a niece named Annie P. Montgomery, all died within two days of each other.

Frank S., her seventh child, a bright and loveable boy, received an injury to one of his eyes from a ball thrown by a playmate, and the sight gradually failing, he became depressed and restless, giving up his position in the "People's National Bank" of Charlottesville and accepting another with a firm in New York, February, 1889. One month after reaching New York he left his boarding-house, telling his landlady he would not be back to tea; that he would take tea with a friend. That was the last ever seen or heard of him. It is supposed that he was either drowned or killed.

Elizabeth St. Clair Waddell married, Sept. 3, 1884. Rev. W. H. McGee, of Mississippi, of the Episcopal faith, and her family is the only non-Presbyterian. Her husband is at present a "missionary to Cuba" and is doing a good work there.

And Their Descendants

Lucy Douglass Waddell married James B. Wood, on Sept. 3, 1884, of Charlottesville, Va., an energetic young business man; deacon and treasurer of the Presbyterian Church. His wife says he is always busy but never too busy to make his home a happy one with his cheerful disposition.

James Nelson Waddell married Margaret Daniel of Memphis, Tenn., Aug. 25, 1897. He succeeded his father in business and carries it on successfully. He is a worthy Christian man, taking an active part in the Sunday-school work of the Presbyterian Church.

William Wirt Waddell married Martha Payne of Charlottesville, Va. He is teller at the "People's National Bank" of that place. He is the third son of the family who has filled satisfactory positions in that bank, Charles E. and Frank S. having been employed before him.

Thomas Montgomery (No. 3, Gen. 5), born 1790, died 1848, married Juliet Dalhouse, of Augusta County, Va. They had five children: John L., William, Wallace, Thomas Edwin, Mary Jane and Dr. James H.

1. John L. Montgomery, (No. 1, Gen. 6), died early.
2. William Wallace Montgomery (No. 2, Gen. 6), married Elizabeth Irvine, his cousin; children two: 1. Agnes H. Montgomery (No. 1, Gen. 7), married D. B. Taylor, a merchant in Baltimore, Md., they have one child—Maysie G. Taylor. 2. Eugene I. Montgomery (No. 2, Gen. 7), married Virginia McV. Jordan; children four: 1. Agnes E. Montgomery. 2. William McV. Montgomery. 3. Cornelius F. Montgomery. 4. Elizabeth C. Montgomery. Residence Clare, Augusta County, Va.

Thomas Edwin Montgomery (No. 3, Gen. 6), married Caroline E. Crawford. They lived in Augusta County. Va. His end was tragical. Driving his wagon, his team took affright and ran furiously away, and he was killed (1870), leaving three sons and two daughters: Mary V., Hettie J, James T., John W., Charles R.

1. Mary V. (No. 1, Gen. 7), married John W. Glenby; no children.

2. Hettie J. Montgomery (No. 2, Gen. 7), married Wm. S. McClintic of Bath County, Va.; children nine: 1. Ernest H. McClintic. 2. Thomas. 3. Emmett W. 4. Robert. 5. Charles. 6. Stanley. 7. Edmonia. 8. Caroline. 9. Mary Agnes. Residence, 1901, Bath County, Va.

3. James T. Montgomery (No. 3, Gen. 7), married Maggie McCorkle of Rockbridge County, Va.; children five: 1. Thomas E. Montgomery. 2. William J. 3. Lina. 4. Samuel. 5. Alfred.

4. John W. Montgomery (No. 4, Gen 7.), married Alice Rhodes of Albemarle County, Va.; residence there in 1901; children nine: 1. Juliette M. Montgomery. 2. R. M. C. Montgomery. 3. Nathan H. 4. Mattie Taylor. 5. William M. 6. Robert E. H. 7. Ethel V. 8. John C. 9. Thomas McC.

4. Mary Jane Montgomery (No. 4, Gen. 6), married Robert J. Glendy; children eight: Juliet, Isabella, Thomas Hugart, John William, Maysie Estelline, Charles, Edmonia.

1. Juliet Glendy (No. 1, Gen. 7), married Summerfield Moon of Albemarle County, Va.; children two: Maria Daisy Moon and Mary Belle Moon.

1. Maria Daisy Moon (No. 1, Gen. 8), married July 1, 1888, T. M. Taylor, civil engineer, of the University of Austin, Texas, 1901; children two: 1. Summerfield Mood Taylor (No. 1, Gen. 9), born May 8, 1889. 2. Julia Louisa Taylor, born Sept. 26, 1898-No. 2, Gen. 9.

2. Mary B. Moon (No. 2. Gen. 8) married a Mr. Ball, being a student in Baum University, Germany, 1901.

Isabella Glendy (No. 2, Gen. 7), married John Guy of Augusta County. Va.; children two: 1. Maysie M. Guy (No. 1. Gen. 8) married F. M. Sumtnerville of Clark County, Va. 2. Estella Guy (No. 2, Gen. 8) married Sanford Carson of Monterey, Va.

3. Thomas H. Glendy (No. 3, Gen. 7), lives in Bath County, Va.; unmarried.

4. John William Glendy (No. 4. Gen. 7) married his cousin, Mary W. Montgomery, who died without issue.

5. Charles Glendy (No. 5, Gen. 7) married Belle Heylef, of Mexico, Mo.; one child—name not known; live in Missouri.

6. Maysie Glendy (No. 6. Gen. 7) married Harvey Francisco. She died in 1872; one child —Maysie G. Francisco.

7. Estella L. Glendy (No. 7. Gen. 7) married Samuel Irvine, Bath County, Va. Children nine: 1. Robert Ervine. 2. Margaret. 3. Jane. 4. William. 5. Douglass. 6. Lina. 7. John Guy. 8. Thomas. 9. Lyle.

Dr. James Hugart Montgomery, the last child of Thomas Montgomery (No. 3, Gen. 5), single in 1879; lived for some time in Texas, but now makes his home with his brother William W. Montgomery, in Augusta County, Va.

4. William Montgomery, Jr. (No. 4, Gen. 5) the fourth child of Rev. John Montgomery (No. 2, Gen. 4) and grandson of Esther Houston (Generation 111). He studied medicine and became a very skillful physician; was very popular as a man, being intelligent, cheerful and of a most amiable temper. He never married, and died at 35. He practiced his profession extensively in Lexington, Va., and the surrounding country.

5, Isabella Montgomery (No. 5, Gen. 5), married Maj. Eugenio Ervine, of Rockingham County, Va.; children five: Elizabeth C., Esther, John M., Francis E. and James Estelle.

1. Elizabeth C. Irvine (No. 1, Gen. 6), married her cousin, William W. Montgomery (No. 2, Gen. 6).

2. Esther J. Irvine died young.

3. John M. Irvine (No. 3, Gen. 6), married Mary Coulter. Children two: 1. Lucy Belle Irvine. 2. Charles E. Irvine.

4. Francis E. Irvine (No. 4, Gen. 6), married Neoria Coulter; children two: 1. William Montgomery Irvine. 2. Clement M. Irvine.

5. James Estil Ervine (No. 5, Gen. 6), married Hannah M. King, of Waynesboro, Va.; children eight: 1. Wm. K. Ervine. 2. Eugene C. Ervine. 3. John Montgomery Irvine, unmarried; deputy surveyor, Augusta County. Va. 4. George F. 5. Wayle A. Irvine. 6. James E. Irvine, Jr. 7. Hugart Irvine. 8. Agnes M. Irvine.

The Montgomerys

1. William K. Irvine (No. 1, Gen. 7), married Anna Brown: children five: 1. Stewart Irvine. 2. Anna K. Irvine. 3. 4. and 5._____.

2. Eugene C. Irvine (No. 2, Gen. 7), married Sophia Hunter; children six: 1. Mary Irvine. 2. Houston. 3. Nealis. 4. Virgie. 5. Leta. 6. Eugene.

3, John Montgomery Ervine (No. 3, Gen. 7), of Augusta County, Va., is deputy surveyor; unmarried.

4. George F. Irvine (No. 4, Gen. 7) married Mamie Winfree; children one—name not known.

6. James E. Irvine, Jr. (No. 6, Gen. 7), married Mary Stewart, of Augusta County, Va. The mother of these five children died in 1880, being 82 years of age.

6. Hugart Montgomery (No. 6, Gen. 5), born 1801, died 1844. He never married; was a physician of much skill, like his brother William; practiced in the "pastures" of Rockbridge County, and died in 1844, aged 43.

7. Estaline Montgomery (No. 7, Gen. 5), born 1807, died 1829. She was an exemplary, amiable young lady; was affianced to a worthy young man, a student of Union Theological Seminary, Va., but before the consummation of their cherished hopes she died of a fever and he, having contracted the same malady by attending her during her sickness, died also in a short time. His name was James Robinson.

Those of the above children of Rev. John Montgomery who were married—namely John Thomas and Isabella—now (1878) have 50 grandchildren and 15 great-grandchildren, and none of his descendants have ever brought disgrace on the Montgomery name.

Mollie Montgomery (No. 2, Gen. 4), daughter of John Montgomery, Sr., and Esther Houston, married a Mr. Edmonson and had children:

Ann Montgomery (No. 3, Gen. 4), daughter of John Montgomery, Sr. and Esther Houston, married a Mr. Crasky and had children.

James Montgomery (No. 4, Gen. 4), son of John Montgomery, Sr., and Esther Houston, married a Miss Weir and moved south to the Holston settlement, near Abington, in south-west Virginia, as did several other brothers, with some of the Houstons. All were staunch Presbyterians. We lost connection with those who moved south except a few records mentioned in the Houston genealogy. Of the sons and daughters that remained in Augusta County, Va., we have complete records.

James Montgomery, mentioned in the paragraph above, had eight children—namely: John, James, Hugh, Jane, Peggy, Polly, Samuel, Esther. Of these children we have been informed by Mr. C. W. McCord, of Mississippi, who married into the family that Hugh (Generation 5), the third child of James, was married twice and raised a large family in Franklin County. Tenn.; and that Jane (Gen. 5), the fourth child of James Montgomery, married William Moore; they also lived in Franklin County.

Polly Montgomery (No. 6, Gen. 5), married James Cowan, a United States officer in the war of 1812; children six: Samuel M., Betsy, Ann, Julia Doak, Martha, John.

Samuel M. Cowan (No. 1, Gen. 6) married Nancy Clemens: one child—James C. Cowan (Gen. 7), living in Tullahoma, Tenn.

Betsy Cowan (No. 2, Gen. 6), married William Montgomery, her own cousin, a son of Hugh (No. 3) above mentioned; children three: 1, James Chester. 2., Mary Ann. 3. Eva.

Mary Ann Montgomery (No. 2, Gen. 7) married Gen. Nathan B. Forest, of Confederate fame, of Tennessee; children one—Captain William Forest.

Eva Montgomery (No. 3, Gen. 7) married Rev. Lewis C. Taylor; no children.

Ann Cowan (No. 3, Gen. 6) married Alfred M. Cowan; no children.

Julia Doak (No. 4 Gen. 6) married John Davis; children six: 1. James C. Davis. 2. Elizabeth Davis. 3. Mary Polk Davis. 4. Nannie Davis. 5. Thomas Davis, 6. Samuel Davis.

Martha M. Cowan (No. 5, Gen. 6) married first John C. Griffith; second, C. W. McCord; one child—Donna McCord, No. 1. Gen. 7.

John Cowan (No. 6. Gen. 6) married Anna Brown; one child— William Cowan, No 1, Gen 7.

The Montgomerys

Dorcas Montgomery (No. 5, Gen. 4) daughter of John Montgomery Sr. and Esther Houston married a Mr. Lowery and had five sons: 1. John M. 2. David. 3., Robert E. 4. James. 5. William.

John M. Lowery (No. 1, Gen 5) married_____; children___.

David Lowery (No. 2, Gen. 5) married_____; children___.

Robert Lowery (No. 3, Gen. 5) married Elizabeth Moore, daughter of Wm. Moore and Elizabeth Steel, of Augusta County, Va.; children William Moore (No. 1. Gen. 6) John Moore (No. 2, Gen. 6) and some others.

Jane Montgomery (No. 6, Gen. 4), daughter of John Montgomery and Esther Houston, married Samuel Newel; had a large family: Samuel B. Newel (No. 1, Gen. 5), married ——: only know of one son, Samuel A. Newel (No. 1, Gen. 6). A daughter of Jane Montgomery and Samuel Newel, Sr., married a Mr. Owen and had three sons.

Robert Montgomery (No. 7. Gen. 8), son of John Montgomery, Sr., and Esther Houston, married a Coleville; children six (Gen.7): Juliet Montgomery, A. C. Montgomery, John C. Montgomery, Polly Montgomery, Jane Montgomery and Sallie Montgomery.

Esther Montgomery (No. 8, Gen. 4), daughter of John Montgomery, Sr., and Esther Houston, married Rev. Samuel Doak, D. D.; children two: Samuel and John W.

Samuel Doak, D. D., Jr. (No. 1, Gen. 5) married Sarah McEwen, his step-sister; no children.

Rev. John W. Doak (No. 2, Gen. 5) married Miss Alexander, a sister to Dr. A. Alexander of Princeton Theological Seminary; one son.

Rev. Archibald Alex. Doak (No. 1, Gen. 6), married Miss Cowan, daughter of Sallie Paxton-Cowan, sister of John D. Paxton. D. D., of Kentucky; children seven (Gen. 7): 1. H. M. Doak, clerk of the U. S. court at Nashville, Tenn. 2. James Hall Doak, died in the Confederate army, 1862. 3. Rev. Al. Sidney Doak, lately pastor of Alabama Street church in Salem; now at Wood lawn, Ala. 4. Samuel Tyler Coleridge Doak lives in Nashville, Tenn. 5. William Edmonson Henry Doak lives in Nashville, Tenn. 6. Mabel Doak died young. 7.

Sarah Jane Doak died young. 8. Sallie Doak, married Benjamin Shaw and lives at Clarksville, Tenn.

Dr. Samuel Doak, Sr., married second Margaret McEwen, the widow of Alex. McEwen and sister to Rev. Samuel Houston of Rockbridge County, Va., by her first husband she had four sons and one daughter. By her second marriage she had no children. Her only daughter married Samuel Doak, D. D., Jr., her stepbrother, as stated above.

Alexander Montgomery (No. 9, Gen. 4), son of John Montgomery, Sr., and Esther Houston—of him we have no positive knowledge. We hear that he lived in Aione County, Tenn., at Scoverville, and was a justice of the peace for the County in 1796. He was a Ranger in 1794 and 1796.—See Ramsey's Annals of Tennessee.

Isabella Montgomery (No. 10, Gen. 4), daughter of John Montgomery Sr., and Esther Houston, married Mr. Brinkman.

There were two other daughters in the family of John Montgomery, Sr., but we have no knowledge of their descent.

MONTGOMERYS OF PENNSYLVANIA, TENNESSEE, MISSOURI, ILLINOIS, AND OTHER STATES.

Sometime after the Irish Rebellion, in 1649, when peace was brought about by the methods and management of Cromwell, the Montgomerys of the branch of the family herein mentioned moved from Scotland into Ireland, where they settled in the northern part of the province of Ulster. There they lived, and after the manner of the country grew and prospered, except that in their religion and philosophy they were Scotch, and that part of Ireland in which they lived became—and so remains to this day—rather a part of Scotland than of Ireland. For with these people came and continued to come their neighbors, kinsmen and friends from Scotland, and though they married and inter-married among the Irish people to such an extent that they became known as Scotch-Irish, still, except for a new energy and impulsiveness picked up from the Irish blood, they stamped Ulster with Scottish ideas and religion and customs almost as much as if they had transferred to their new homes their native land. But the government of Great Britain, as dispensed in Ireland, has never been satisfactory to the

Irish people. and it was impossible to oppress the Irish in Ireland without oppressing also their Scotch-Irish neighbors and friends, so that the feeling among the Irish and the Scotch-Irish became one of general complaint as it was one of general suffering; and the Scotch-Irish, and the Montgomerys among them, were not backward in making their complaints and grievances known and when an opportunity was presented to secure greater liberty under both law and conscience by moving to America they eagerly seized it and made the best of it.

Under the impulse just mentioned, about the year 1768 or 1769, Thomas Montgomery, then a young man about 20 years of age, with four brothers, emigrated from Ireland to America. He did not have to be Americanized, for that had taken place in him before he came, so that in the contest then on between the colonies and the mother country he was in full sympathy with the colonies: and when the War of the Revolution came on he fought with the Americans for freedom in America, enlisting and serving in the state of Pennsylvania; his first act of war being a personal encounter with a British recruiting officer who was offering special inducements to one of his companions to enlist with the Tories; in which encounter, because of his great strength and activity, he did not come off second best. He served as a private, and after the close of the war went with his family through Kentucky into that part of North Carolina which afterwards became a part of Tennessee, now known as Blount County, Tennessee, where he settled near the city of Knoxville.

Although a young man, he was married when he came to America, his wife being a woman of rare intellect and character, speaking the Scotch dialect with perfect accent, who became a great Indian interpreter, readily acquiring and conversing in the language of all the Indian tribes living or trading in the section of country in which she lived. She learned their languages with great ease and spoke them fluently.

Thomas Montgomery was a man over six feet in height, of great strength and courage, of ruddy complexion, with blue eyes and a well-marked Roman nose; a lover of horses and dogs, and rather too much inclined to the race-course to match with the revival spirit that rolled like a wave over the country at the opening of the eighteenth century; and though he fell in with it and gave it his influence finally, he transmitted to all his children a fondness amounting to almost a passion for fine horses, fine cattle and fine dogs. He and his wife lived and died in Blount County,

Tennessee, and were buried in the cemetery of a Presbyterian church on Baker's Creek, he having died in 1830 and she two years later.

To him were born eight children: David, William, John Patton, George, Samuel, Margaret, Elizabeth and Susan.

Samuel Montgomery was born in the year 1786 in that part of North Carolina which afterwards became the eastern part of Tennessee. He grew with his brothers to a vigorous and manly manhood —tall, active, strong, and for his own good rather too full of physical courage; for his physical recklessness resulted in the breaking of both his arms and one of his legs—a very serious matter in a new country where surgery was practically an unknown art. At the age of twenty-one, on the 20th day of August, 1807, he was united in marriage with Nancy Jones, a daughter of Col. Richard Jones, who had been a playmate of George III, King of England, when he was Prince of Wales, and who had emigrated to America, through Canada, and settled in Washington County, Tennessee, then a part of North Carolina. This marriage was performed by the Rev. Samuel Doake, a minister of the Presbyterian Church, and the founder of Doake College, in East Tennessee.

Nancy Jones Montgomery, whose brother was a lawyer of the firm of Nixon, Burnett, & Jones, of Knoxville, Tenn., and at the time of his death a young man of great promise, was no ordinary woman. Her intelligence, piety and perseverance made her a marked and marvelous woman, one who impressed her personality not only upon the members of her family, but upon every community in which she lived. She spent her long and useful life in a new, wild country, but she tamed it wherever she went; and no sower ever cast seed into the ground with greater confidence or better results. Her fields were the lives and consciences of her husband, her children and her neighbors, and she lived to rejoice in a perpetual harvest, and died in the 79th year of her age, having lived to see the accomplishment of her heart's highest hope—the establishment of a well-grounded and well-fruited hope and faith in her Savior and His mission among men. With her many family cares and the pioneer country in which she spent the whole of her life, she knew not many books, but one Book she constantly studied and earnestly strove to know; and her life became like unto, if short of, her highest conception of that Book.

Samuel Montgomery enlisted as a private with Captain James Gillespie, at Knoxville, Tenn. in the Second War with Great Britain, and after completing the term of his service was honorably discharged at the same place. In the year 1831 or 1832 he moved to Carroll County, Tenn., where he lived till the year 1851, at which time he moved to Dade County, Missouri, where he continued to live till the day of his death, July 26, 1856, when he was buried in Greenfield, in that County. His wife survived him 14 years, having died at the home of her son, the Rev. George W. Montgomery, in Coles County, Illinois, in the year 1870, where she was buried in the cemetery of the West Union Cumberland Presbyterian church, loved and honored of all who knew her.

To Samuel and Nancy Montgomery were born eleven children: Archibald, Lavina, Francis, Jones, Jane Ann, Mary, Elizabeth, Richard, George Washington, Sophia, Samuel Nelson, and Nancy Isabella Davis.

The children all lived to be grown, and all reared families except Mary, who was engaged to be married to a man since that time grown to be widely known as the Rev. J. L. Cooper, D. D., but who died in her 20th year.

George Washington Montgomery, the eighth child of Samuel and Nancy Montgomery, was born July 7, 1824, in Blount County, Tennessee. He moved with his parents to Carroll County, Tennessee, in the eighth year of his age, where he grew to manhood with his many brothers and sisters amid the stirring scenes and robust conditions of a new country, where men were planting homes in the virgin forest and contending with conditions almost as new and untried as those that confronted our first parents when they were informed that "In the sweat of thy face shalt thou eat bread." They had the forests to fell and the beasts of the fields to conquer. And the open hand of Samuel Montgomery—open, so open to the needs and requests of his friends that two fortunes, for that time, his own and that received from his wife's father, went in the payment of security debts that brought to him and his family no returns—made his home in the wilderness one rather of robust and vigorous toil than of effeminate luxury; and to this George W. Montgomery, together with his five brothers, owed much of their princely good health and manly character, and habits of industry. And about the only luxury he enjoyed, aside from the companionship of a community of young stalwarts of the forest like himself, came to him through the use of the fine horses to which his father, amidst all his reverses, had still clung. The old out-door camp-meeting was then in it« glory, and old Bethel Camp Ground was the annual place of gathering for worship for from twenty-five to fifty miles around. And there it was, when but fourteen years of age that he made a public profession of faith and connected himself with the

Cumberland Presbyterian church, a profession and an action upon it filled with wide-reaching consequence to himself, to his family, and to the people in whatever section of the country he lived. Connected with the old Camp Ground was established Old Bethel College. To this he went as soon as he was prepared, and there he received both his literary and his theological training; and from that place he moved, in 1850, to Dade County, Missouri, where he began his pioneer life as a young preacher, and at intervals a teacher of day schools and of writing schools as the circumstances demanded. He was strong as a lion and gentle as a lamb; a man of sound judgment, and gifted in oratory. He had perfect command of himself and of his audience; and when occasion made it necessary he would carry his point by argument, in which he had no superior; by persuasion, of which he was a master; or by eloquence—through all of which his sincerity and his deep earnestness ran like the gentle and almost irresistible pleading of a prayer. He stood five feet and ten inches tall, weighed one hundred and eighty pounds, was never sick and never complained; was of fair complexion, with light brown hair, and skin almost as transparent as alabaster, and a voice as rich as the tones of a great pipe-organ; and with a character against which no imputation was ever cast, and upon which no stain was ever seen or looked for. His eyes were blue, his nose Roman, his teeth regular, white and strong; and his presence in his family was like the shelter of a great rock, where no child ever felt or feared an enemy; and around and upon him they played without any thought of not being welcome, and climbed upon him for many years without finding a frown upon his face or a cross word in his mouth.

The Montgomerys

**Reverend
George Washington Montgomery
Charleston, Illinois**

In the month of October, 1851, he was married to Sarah Ann Rankin, then in the 20th year of her age, by the Rev. William Brown, a minister of the Cumberland Presbyterian church; she having been born July 22, 1832, and moved with her parents from Blount Co., Tennessee, to Dade County, in the year 1840. She was a very sprightly, active and most energetic young woman, who had never learned, and has not yet learned, that any possible thing which has not been done may not be done. Nothing that had to be done was to her dishonorable or belittling, and she asked no one to do what she would not do herself. Her hair was dark brown and long and silken and abundant. Her features were classic, and to her form there was nothing to be added. She traced her ancestry with much pride through many generations of the most aristocratic Presbyterian ancestors, in an unbroken chain, to the Scotland of three hundred years ago. Hers was a happy, joyous childhood and young womanhood, where active out-door exercise and especially daring horsemanship in the chase of wild deer and the fleet gray fox, in a still wilder country, with a house full of brothers, was not considered indelicate or unwomanly, but simply a part of the free and uncurbed life of a new and romantic country. She was one of a family of eight children—six sons and two daughters—all of whom lived to be grown, married, and reared families; six of whom are still living, the youngest being nearly seventy years of age, the two youngest being ministers of the gospel in the Presbyterian church and three of them elders.

At the breaking out of the Civil War, the Rev. George W. Montgomery was living and preaching in south-west Missouri, in the very heart of the border-warfare region; and although born and reared in the South he was bitterly opposed to secession and gave to his opposition the whole strength of his character. He did not believe that slavery was right, and he knew that secession was wrong. And without going into the history of a prolonged and exciting and personally dangerous period, it may be stated that after the destruction of most of his property for army and guerilla purposes, he moved with his family to the state of Illinois, where he reared and educated his children, living most of the time at Oakland, in Coles County, but finally in Charleston, in the same County, where, after a long and useful ministry of more than fifty years, loved and venerated by all who knew him, and strong and vigorous in body and mind down to the injury which he received a few months before, and which resulted in. his death, he died on Christmas morning, 1898; and his burial was attended by his eleven grown children, gathered from many states. Sarah Ann Montgomery, his widow, is still in the enjoyment of good health, and spends most of her lime visiting her children, though her home is with her son, Dr. J. T. Montgomery, in Charleston, Illinois, he being her oldest child, and superintendent of the Charleston Sanitarium.

To the Rev. George Washington Montgomery were born the following children:

1. John Theodore, born Oct. 18, 1852 who married Mary Ada Gerard, Oct. 12, 1876. She was born Feb. 1856. They live in Charleston, Illinois, where he enjoys an enviable reputation as a physician and surgeon, and is the father of five children: 1. Sarah Emily Montgomery, born July 4, 1877. 2. Mack Garfield Montgomery, born June 4, 1880. 3., Mary M. Montgomery, born May 2, 1882. 4. John Theodore Montgomery, born April 25, 1887. 5. George Jackson Montgomery, born May 22, 1889.

2. Mack Allen, born Aug. 24, 1854, who after completing his university-course at James Milligan University, and serving for six years as president of Southern Illinois College, moved to the state of Mississippi, where (at Oxford) he entered the State University, took the law course therein, and began the practice of law; and where he has, with the exception of four years, been the United States attorney for the Northern District of Mississippi. He is unmarried. He has rendered valuable service in collecting

data for this family; has visited the old Montgomery Castle and homestead near Ayr, Scotland, where Burns celebrated his love for his "sweet Highland Mary." and has been all over the North of Ireland and through Scotland, where the Montgomerys fought with Bruce and died with his brave Highlanders. And if he had bad time to hunt up family lines he had abundant opportunity, as he has traveled in forty states of the Union and throughout Canada. But at all times he has been so occupied with other matters that he really had no time for outside matters. His first trip abroad was in 1884 as a delegate to the Pan-Presbyterian Alliance at Belfast, Ireland; and he is a delegate to the same Alliance, which meets in England, 1903.

Honorable
Mack Allen Montgomery
Oxford, Mississippi

3. Mary Elizabeth Clementine Montgomery, born June 23, 1856, married to George W. Lippincott, Sept. 4, 1873. He was born June 9, 1848. They have seven children: 1. George W. Lippincott is a business man of fine character and unquestionable integrity, a man of affairs, and lives in Charleston Ill. Their oldest son, Rudolph Peck Lippincott, born Dec. 3, 1874, is a graduate of Washington and Jefferson College, Pennsylvania, and of Alleghany Theological Seminary at Alleghany, Pa.

2. Charles Allen Lippincott, born Oct. 25, 1876, married Carrie Crawford Heintem, Feb. 25, 1899; one child—Elroy Allen Lippincott, burn Aug. 18, 1901.

3. Emily L. Lippincott, born Jan. 15, 1879, married Oct. 12, 1897, Dr. R. H. Craig of Charleston, Ill.; one child—Clotile Craig, born April 14, 1899.

4. Jessie L. Lippincott, born Dec. 26, 1880, married Dec. 25, 1899.____;
one child—Gladys, born Dec. 6, 1900.
   5. Ruth L. Lippincott, born Dec. 25, 1882.
   6. John Theodore Lippincott, born Jan. 24, 1885.
   7. Mary L. Lippincott, born Feb. 18, 1887.

   4. George William Montgomery, born Aug. 30, 1858, Greenfield, Mo., married July 2, 1881, to Nellie E. Mason, of Rockport Ind., who was born at Grandview, Ind., April 22, 1862 He is a graduate of Waynesburg College, Waynesburg, Pa., and of Alleghany Theological Seminary, and pastor of the Presbyterian church at Oakmont, Pa., the leading residence suburban city of Pittsburg, Pa. He has two children: Sarah Elizabeth, born May 19, 1885, at West Union, Pennsylvania, and George Mason, born at McKeesport, Pa., Nov. 10, 1890.

   5. Samuel Thomas, born Nov. 6, 1860, educated in Waynesburg College, graduated from Alleghany Theological Seminary; married to Nettie Gowdy of Enfield, Ill., by whom she had four sons—the oldest George Millage, the next Lowell, deceased; Walter Bindley and Donnell Gowdy. They are located at Buffalo, Pa., where he is pastor of the Presbyterian Church.

   6. Laura May, born March 24, 1863 at Windsor, Ill. married to Prof. Bindley Watkins Gowdy, of Enfield, Ill., at Oakland. Ill., but who has been for a number of years in charge of the city schools, first at Batesville and afterwards at Sardis, both places being County Seats of Panola County, Miss. They have five children: Theodore Allen, born June 9, 1882, at Enfield, Ill.; Deidra Alga Lena, born July 13, 1889, at Enfield, Ill.; Nettie A., born April 17, 1886, at Enfield, Ill.; Dixie A., born May 22, 1889, at Batesville, Miss.; and Laura Bindley, born Oct. 1, 1894 at Batesville, Miss. There are few if any better teachers in the state than Prof. Gowdy.
   Theodore Allen Gowdy was married at Charleston, Ill., Aug. 1, 1901 to Nellie M. Bishop, who was born at Charleston, Ill., Dec. 10, 1881. To them was born John Monroe. Aug. 13, 1902.
   Deidra Alga Lena Gowdy was married Aug. 14, 1902, to William S. Profilet, of Natchez, Miss.

   7. Ulysses Lincoln, born July 22, 1865, at Bethany, Ill., a graduate from Franklin College, Franklin, Ind., and from Alleghany Theological Seminary; married Miss Carrie E. Weise, Nov. 10, 1892 who died March 15, 1900, by whom he has two daughters—Emma Devona, born Jan. 10, 1895, and Carrie

Weise born April 3, 1897. He is pastor of the Presbyterian Church at Thorntown, Indiana.

8. Sarah Lulu, born April 2, 1867, educated in Southern Illinois College; married to Thomas Morgan, editor and author Colfax, Indiana, by whom she has five children, the oldest being Paul Hunter and Ruth; Lucile and Mary.

9. Rose, born April 22, 1869, died Aug. 4, 1869.

10. Donnel Rankin Montgomery, born April 6, 1870, graduated from Franklin College, Indiana, and from Alleghany Theological Seminary; married Miss Sarah Blanche McGill; was consecrated as a missionary by the General Assembly of the Presbyterian Church at St. Louis, Mo., and is stationed at Jackson, Alaska, in charge of the Presbyterian Indian Mission. He has one son about two years old—Robert McGill Montgomery.

11. Carrie M. Montgomery, a twin with Donnel Rankin, born April 6, 1870, educated in the city high school of McKeesport, Pa., and having recently spent more than a year in Alaska is now living in Charleston, Ill., with her sister Mary.

12. Finis Ewing, born March 22, 1877, graduated from the city high schools of Charleston, and from Washington and Jefferson College, where for the past two years he has been captain of their football team, and where he is for the present employed as teacher of English and History in Trinity Hall connected with the college, and is also engaged in the study of law.

From this sketch it will be seen that the Rev. George W. Montgomery was the father of seven sons, all of whom lived to be grown, and each of whom is earnestly engaged in and actively devoting his time to one of the learned professions.

A tradition runs through this family that they are related—not in this country, but in Scotland and Ireland—to General Richard Montgomery of Revolutionary fame; and that name runs through the entire line of all the descendants of Thomas Montgomery, the first ancestor of this family in America, except that of Rev. George W. Montgomery, father of this last family.

And Their Descendants

CHAPTER XVI.
MONTGOMERYS OF NORTH CAROLINA.

On page 11, Series III, Wheeler says that in 1768 the governor called a rendezvous of the state troops to meet at the house of Mr. Montgomery at Salisbury. On page 211, same series, Wheeler says that Robert Montgomery was in the lower house of North Carolina 1785-1790-1-4-5-8-9-1800 and in the senate 1788-1801-2-3-4-5-6-7, a period of sixteen years in all; and that B. J. Montgomery was in the house 1818-19-26-27-28, and in the senate in 1829-31-32; and that G. W. Montgomery was in the senate in 1834-36.

John H. Montgomery was in the North Carolina senate from Montgomery County 1838-40. Moore County joins Montgomery on the east, and it seems that John Montgomery was a joint representative from the two counties 1832-3.

Hon. William Montgomery was long a representative of Orange County, N. C. He was born in Guilford County, on Buffalo. He was by profession a physician. He entered public life as a senator in the General Assembly in 1821, and served with but one intermission until 1834, when he was the next year elected to congress, in which he served with good ability until 1841 when he declined. He died Nov. 27, 1844, aged 53 years, leaving seven children, one of whom, D. A. Montgomery, was a member of the House of Commons in 1850.

OBITUARY OF CAPTAIN CHARLES MONTGOMERY, FIFTH NEW YORK VOLUNTEERS.
(By F. S. M.)

Among the casualties occurring during the recent advance of the army of the Potomac on Hatch's Run, I find the name of Captain Charles S. Montgomery of the 5th New York veterans—a gallant officer and one who had for some time commanded the regiment to which he belonged. This is the second commander that regiment has lost during the present campaign. Captain Montgomery's military career extends through the entire war, and his record was a noble one—enlisting as a private in the celebrated Dury Zouaves, 5th New York Volunteers. In April, 1861, he carried his musket at the battle of Big Bethel, and subsequently became a corporal. In the fall of that year he was promoted to a second lieutenancy, and in that grade served with distinction with his gallant regiment during the Peninsular

Campaign in 1862. He received a first lieutenancy at Harrison Landing, and subsequently a captaincy; and while in command of his company at the disastrous battle of Manassas Plains was wounded and taken prisoner. He was soon after exchanged and rejoined his company after the battle of Antietam. He served in the battles of Fredericksburg and Chancellorsville, and in May, 1863, returned with the 5th regiment New York, at the expiration of its term of service, as senior captain. On the re-organization of the Zouaves as a veteran regiment he returned to the field as captain, and would have been made major had the command reached the maximum number. The regiment went into battle for the first time in this campaign at the battle of Bethesda Church, and up to the present time Captain Montgomery has been constantly in active service. He was killed at the head of his regiment, as its commanding officer, and his loss is deeply felt in the division of which he had so long been a member. Had he lived, speedy promotion awaited him, as his reputation was very high and he had been complimented repeatedly by his superiors for gallant conduct.—G. F. W.

The editor adds: "We had the pleasure of knowing Captain Montgomery whilst with the old 5th New York regiment, and join our regrets with those of his friends over a true gentleman and a brave and meritorious officer."

The above is from a newspaper clipping, but from what paper I do not know.

MONTGOMERYS OF NEWARK, N. J., NEW YORK, OHIO, ILLINOIS, CALIFORNIA and NEW JERSEY.

"Moses Montgomery, with his wife—formerly Martha Gilmore —came to this country 1810 and settled in Brooklyn, New York. They had a family of eight children—five sons and three daughters. They remained in Brooklyn until the family was all married. Three of the sons went west; John, the oldest, going to Queensbury County, Ohio. Robert also settled somewhere in that part of the country. The youngest son, George, settled somewhere in Illinois. The daughters and two sons remained in this part of the country; William going to Massachusetts. My father remained in Brooklyn, where he died about 1874. One of the sisters, Mrs. Jane Marshall, now (1899) lives in Brooklyn. James S. Montgomery, of Logan, Ohio, belongs to this branch of the family.

"Of my own immediate family there are only three left—William Montgomery, of Oakland, Cal., and a sister Harriet, living in Fresno, Cal.

"As I have, by searching the history of my mother's family, established my claim to a Daughter of the American Revolution and been made a member of the Caesarean Chapter here in Newark, N. J., it is unnecessary for me to state that I would take great satisfaction in having my history on my father's side to be quite equal in age and lustre to that of my mother's family. Have you ever heard of the Trinity heirs in connection with the Scotch-Irish branch of your family?" —Mrs. Caroline Montgomery-Thompson.

MONTGOMERYS OF VIRGINIA AND MISSISSIPPI.

Gilbert Montgomery, whose father and grandfather was named John, was born of parents living in East Virginia, in Preston County. He married Dema C. Annon and had four children: Walter T., B. F., Mary Belle and Kimble. The last one is dead.

Walter was born April 26, 1875. His mother died in 1882, when he was placed in the family of Levi and Jane Powling, who did a good part by him. At twelve years old he attended Flemington College, in West Virginia. He advanced rapidly in his studies, and taught school before he was fifteen years old. He taught seven schools and then took up the study of law. He advanced as rapidly in this line as he had in his other studies, and lawyer Hansford introduced him to Judge Hoak for examination. The judge was astonished at his proficiency and complemented him on his splendid work, and admitted him to the bar in 1896. He located at Grafton, the County Seat of Taylor County and married a Miss White of West Virginia. He patiently waited for his first client, whose case he handled so cleverly that it established him in a fine practice. In this case he made no charge, but the client remembered him liberally. Afterward he established a branch office at Tunnelton, W. Va. On account of delicate health he gave up the practice of law and moved to Fruitdale, Ala., and from there to Winchester. Miss., and at present (1902) is engaged in the gardening business.

Judge Hook referred to above, represents the United States in Nova Scotia, by appointment of President McKinley. Walter T. Montgomery has declined accepting offices on account of delicate health.

And Their Descendants

WEST VIRGINIA MONTGOMERYS.

James Montgomery was an officer in the Irish Rebellion, and it is claimed that he was related to General Richard Montgomery. He fled from Ireland when the English had suppressed the Irish, and came to America about 1799 and landed at Philadelphia, Pa., with a wife and two sons, and afterward returned to the old country to recover if possible some of his wealth, and was never heard from again. His widow, a few years afterward, married a man by the name of Lacy, or Tracy, who mistreated the two sons, and they ran away from home and separated. Henry came down the river from Fort Duquesne and was at Point Pleasant the day of the battle with the Indians on account of the execution (murder) of Comstock, whom the Indian chief held as hostage. He went up the Kanawha and settled at Tags Valley, and afterwards moved to Kanawha Falls and was a neighbor of Van Bibber, and owned the ferry. He had three sons: James, Michael and William. The two latter are dead. He also had ten daughters, of whom I have no information. James settled in the Kanawha Valley in 1840, about ten miles below the great falls and twenty-five miles east of Charleston, and owned the ferry at Montgomery's Landing, which was opposite Cannelton, one of the first Cannel coal-oil plants in the world. It was destroyed during the war. Montgomery's Landing was changed to Coal Valley. James Montgomery also owned a fine, large farm there.

In 1873 James Montgomery leased some land, and a mining town sprang up and was called "Coal Valley," being composed of all classes. The town continued to grow, and in 1890 J. C. Montgomery organized the town of Montgomery out of Coal Valley, having the town incorporated and changing the name in honor of the family, which now number about 100, most all of whom live there; he having owned nearly all the land, which he inherited from his father. They are proud of the town and think it the best mining town in the state. They have a city building, six miles of street railway, electric lights, one bank, six saloons, and 25 good stores; two railroads— Pittsburg and Cincinnati; one weekly and two daily boats between Montgomery and Charleston. They have eight churches, a graded public school, and a branch of the West Virginia University, which is a state school and a fine one. They also have a graded colored school. Mr. J. C. Montgomery, who furnished this information, is mayor of the town and expresses a strong desire to know more of the history of the Montgomery family.

MONTGOMERYS OF NORTH CAROLINA, VIRGINIA AND TENNESSEE.

Wheeler says, in series No. 1, page 42, that in 1731 John Montgomery was attorney-general of North Carolina, under George Barrington. So the claim that this John Montgomery was of the Montgomery-Houston family cannot be sustained, as John Montgomery. Sr. of that family did not come to America until 1730, and we do not find that he ever lived in North Carolina, but everything indicates that he was living in Pennsylvania at that time; and the Rev. John. Jr. was not born until 1752. But to what family the Attorney-General Montgomery did belong I am unable to determine.

Later on, in 1775, when North Carolina was preparing for the Revolutionary struggle, we find Hugh and John Montgomery on the Committees of Safety; and they were always present, ready for duty. (See Wheeler's North Carolina, page 370.)

We know nothing more of this John Montgomery, but we have a pretty fair record of Hugh Montgomery. Dr. D. C. Kelly of Nashville, Tenn. (1903), who is a great-grandson of this Col. Hugh Montgomery, Sr., of Salisbury, N. C. says that Hugh was an old man at the beginning of the Revolutionary war, and that he has seen his grave at Salisbury, which is marked. Hugh, Sr., was a large landowner in Virginia and North Carolina. He had several children, but only one son, Hugh, Jr. The names of the daughters were: Jane, who first married Samuel Cowen, of Knoxville, Tenn.; children two: William and Mary Purnell. Later she was married to Col. David Campbell, of Campbell's Station, East Tennessee; children three: Washington and Warren died early in life; Margaret Louisa married in 1833 John Kelly, who lived and died in Wilson County, Tenn. They had only one child—David Campbell Kelly, A. M., M. D., D. D., LL. D., of Nashville, Tenn. He was missionary to China in 1852-53-54-55; is an able minister in the Methodist church. He was a colonel in the Confederate cavalry under General Nathan Bedford Forrest. He married ___.

The other daughters of Col. Hugh Montgomery were Elizabeth, who married a Stewart, and Mary, who married an Ingram, and Martha, who married a Blake.

There are old papers in Dr. Kelly's possession which show that Hugh, Jr., was also addressed as "Col. Hugh Montgomery." Hugh (Sr.) willed to Hugh

(Jr.) and Jane Montgomery land in Virginia. The land willed to Hugh was not transferable, but was to revert to his heirs after his death. However, he sold this land, about 1800, and purchased 5,000 acres for $5,000 near Jacksboro, Tenn., which is about 40 miles south-west of Cumberland Gap.

Hugh, Jr. had seven sons and two daughters—Lemuel, Anthony Newman, Sr., Chesed, Hugh, Rush, Rufus, and Alexander. Dr. Kelly says he was personally acquainted with all of these seven sons except Anthony Newman, who was evidently named for Dr. Anthony Newman of Salisbury, N. C., who married a daughter of Hugh Montgomery, Sr. Anthony Newman of Salisbury, N. C., had a son Daniel Montgomery Newman who was in the Indian wars after the Revolution, and commanded in a battle in Georgia, which secured to him the name of the town of Newman in Georgia, near the site of the battle. He was seen often by Dr. Kelley when he came to Nashville to draw his pension.

Major Lemuel Montgomery, oldest son of Hugh, Jr., was killed at the battle of the Horseshoe, in Alabama, 1814, near where the city of Montgomery now stands. "For him the city of Montgomery was named." His war relics are in the museum at New York.

Only Rufus, Rush and Anthony Newman had children. Rufus lived in Princeton, Ky., 1893. He had a son who at one time was a commercial traveler for a wholesale house in Louisville, Ky. Another one was an engineer on a ship and was seen by his cousin Anthony Newman Montgomery, of Boy, Tenn., in 1888. Thomas, the youngest, was at last accounts farming in Kansas.

The children of Rush Montgomery Sr. were living when last heard from near Chattanooga and Cleveland, Tenn.

Anthony Newman Montgomery, Sr., born near Richmond, Va., 1790, died Nov. 8, 1840, twelve miles from Montgomery, Tenn., had five sons and four daughters: Hugh, Daniel, Lemuel, Rush and Anthony Newman, Jr. The latter is (1901) living at Boy, Tenn., 62 years old. Mrs. Mary E. Bankston, born near Jacksboro, Tenn., July 9, 1836, one of the daughters, is now (1901) living at Ringold, Ga., 64 years old. She compiled the sketch in this book relating to General Richard Montgomery, who fell at Quebec, 1775, and furnished some of the material for this sketch.

MONTGOMERYS OF ADAIR COUNTY, KENTUCKY.

Columbia, Ky., May 4, 1899. H. P. Montgomery. Esq. Dear Sir: The most remote of my ancestors, so far as I can learn, was John Montgomery, who was my great-great-grandfather. My great-grandfather was Francis Montgomery, who moved to what is now Adair County, Ky., from Albemarle County, Virginia, in 1804. He had five sons, whose names were Thomas, Francis, William, Robert and Joel. Francis was my grandfather. My father's name is William B. Montgomery; and, not to lose the name Francis in the family, my name is James Francis. I get this information from my father, Dr. W. B. Montgomery, who is now living in this County and is 78 years of age.

The descendants of my great-uncles, Robert and Joel Montgomery, are many of them now living in this County. As to the other brothers, I have no information as to what became of them. Neither have I any information as to what part of Europe my people came from: but it has always been understood that we are of Scotch-Irish descent. I was once told by my great-uncle, Joel Montgomery, that when his father moved from Virginia he brought with him all of his own household, including sons, daughters, sons-in-law, and slaves— 72 persons.

The Montgomerys of this country have engaged almost exclusively in agricultural pursuits. However, my grandfather was a skilled mechanic, and dabbled some in politics, having been a representative in the legislature several times. My father and one brother are physicians. I represent the only attempt at the law. Some of the collaterals are creditable preachers.

This is about all I can give you about the family. If this is of an interest to you or answers your purpose, or if there is other information that you desire which I can give, I will be glad to hear from yon. If the facts herein stated show any connection between your family and mine, please let me hear from you.

Yours truly,
J. F. MONTGOMERY.

We have known of the Montgomerys in Adair County, Ky., for several years; but this is the first concerning their genealogy that we have obtained. They are a respectable and intelligent family.

Columbia, Ky., Feb. 14, 1903.

D. B. Montgomery:

I received your letter of Feb. 4. The family of Montgomerys that you inquire after, of which the man referred to (S. B. Montgomery, vice-president of the State Saving, Loan and Trust Company, of Quincy, Ill., 1903) is a member, was quite prominent in this country at one time. Nathan Montgomery with a large family settled at Fort St. Aesop, in what is now Lincoln County, in this state. He had a son Nathan who is evidently the grandfather of S. B. Montgomery. This Nathan Montgomery settled in Adair County; had a son Joseph, and Alexander, and Nathan, and one other whose name 1 do not remember. The last named Nathan was half-brother of Joseph and Alexander. He was prominent in the County, lived in this town and was at one time sheriff. None of his family now lives in the County. He has one son, J. B. Montgomery, now living in Louisville, Ky., but I cannot give you his address; but as he is a traveling man and comes to this place occasionally, if you will address him here you will reach him.

The original branch of this family played quite a prominent part in the early settlement of Kentucky and in Indian warfare—especially in fighting and getting captured and killed, as you will learn from an examination of Collins's History of Kentucky. The women married into the Wickliffe, Logan and .Russell families, who were quite prominent. I have no relationship to this family, though we are doubtless of the same stock.

Very respectfully,
J. F. MONTGOMERY.

MONTGOMERYS OF HARDIN COUNTY, KENTUCKY.

Judge James Montgomery, of Elizabethtown, Ky., says:

My great grandfather, William Montgomery, resided in Aughtnacloy, Tyrone County, Ireland, and had three sons; one having gone to sea in 1820 and was never heard from; another remaining in Ireland. My grandfather, William Montgomery, engaged in the Irish rebellion of 1798; was transported, or rather sent over, to the United States through the influence of a cousin or an aunt of his who was either the wife of the Lord Lieutenant or closely related by marriage or blood.

After remaining in Baltimore two years my grandfather came and settled in this place and entered into merchandising. He had only one son—my father, William Withers Montgomery. Our family is quite limited on this side of the water, unless some of the descendants of my great-uncle are on this side.

Hon. A. B. Montgomery, ex-congressman from Kentucky, is a brother of Judge James Montgomery and lives in the same town. He graduated at Georgetown, Ky., taking the first honors in the class of 1859. He also has another brother, Dr. E. R. Montgomery, health officer of Louisville, Ky., and now lives in that city. Also a sister, Mrs. E. M. Bates, who lives in Elizabethtown, Ky.

Judge Montgomery has a son William Slack Montgomery, who has been a lieutenant in the navy for three or four years and was on the Petrel of Manila fame during the fight in Manila Bay.

Judge James Montgomery is a graduate of Center College, at Danville, Ky. He enlisted in the Confederate army in 1861 and followed John Morgan in the Confederate service during the war.

MONTGOMERYS IN SHELBY COUNTY, KENTUCKY.

Taylorsville, Ky., March 20, 1899.

H. P. Montgomery, Georgetown, Ky.

Dear Sir: I take pleasure in giving you all the information in my possession of my father's family. My grandfather, George Montgomery, was of Scotch-Irish descent. He and his brothers Hugh and Green came to this country in the latter part of the 18th century. Hugh and Green finally settled in the state of Indiana.

My grandfather settled near Clay village in Shelby County Ky., where he died in 1836. He raised three sons and one daughter: William, Alexander and John—the latter being my father. The daughter married a man by the name of Ellis.

My father married Sarah Rice, of Clay Village, and lived in that neighborhood until March, 1839, when he moved to Spencer County and died on his farm near Taylorsville the 17th of September, 1845, at the age of

45 years. My two uncles lived all their lives near their birth-place. Alexander died a short time before my father. William died 1881. He raised two sons— W. N. and Joseph. The former now lives at Gaeston, Tenn. The latter died in 1863. He left one son, who now lives in Henry County.

I was born near Clay Village, Shelby County, Ky., Sept. 29, 1832; came to this County with my parents and lived on a farm until Feb. 4, 1850, when I came to Taylorsville and learned the saddler's trade, and finally engaged in that business for myself until December, 1898, when my shop, with eight other house, was burned out.

Yours very truly,
J. R. MONTGOMERY, Sr.

DESCENDANTS OF GENERAL MONTGOMERY, VIRGINIA, MARYLAND, KENTUCKY, TEXAS AND TENNESSEE.

Knoxville, Tenn., June 25. 1898.

H. P. Montgomery, Georgetown, Ky.

Dear Sir: I regret exceedingly that the records my mother gave me have been misplaced so I cannot send the facts to you. My maternal grandfather was Andrew Montgomery. He came from Scotland with three brothers. Andrew and James settled in Westmoreland County, Va. John and Robert settled in Maryland in or near Hagerstown. My mother, Eliza Ann Montgomery, was born in 1809 at Old Ordinary on the banks of the Potomac. She died in 1892, 83 years old. She married John Powers in 1827; had nine children. Two died in infancy. The oldest son was killed in battle, the next by a railroad wreck, the next by disease during the Civil War. One only daughter lives in Brownwood, Texas, two brothers in Augusta, Ky., and one in Knoxville. Tenn. But what you want is to trace this genealogy back to Gen. Richard Montgomery, and I cannot do it, though the descent is lineal and so close that Mother was entitled to a pension and all the proofs were made up when I was a child. Mother's mother was a Miss Hall of England, of noble family—one of the sisters being maid of honor to the queen. But I often think of the Hues—

"Honor and fame from no condition rise.
Act well your part: there all the honor lies."
Yours affectionately, J. PIKE POWERS.

The Montgomerys

MONTGOMERYS IN TENNESSEE.

We find that in 1787 there was a William Montgomery living on Drake's Creek in Tennessee, and the Indians came and shot down his son and scalped him, but did not kill him.

In 1788 the Indians on Drake Creek came again to the house of William Montgomery, the same person whose son was wounded and scalped in 1887, and killed this son and two of his brothers, in daytime, at the spring, one hundred yards from the house.—History of Tennessee, by Haywood, 1823.

Clarksville, Tenn., July 5, 1902.
Mr. D. B. Montgomery, Owensville, Ind.

My Dear Sir and Brother: I hope my communication is not too late for use in the Montgomery History, if you see fit to use it.

My Great-grandfather's name was David Montgomery. He had one son, Thomas, and two daughters, Mary and Susan. Thomas, my grandfather, had five sons: Joseph C., John P., George E., James H., and Newton I.; besides four daughters—Margaret, Nancy, Mary, and Elizabeth. These all married and reared families. Their occupation mostly has been farming and merchandise. A few entered the ministry, legal profession, and medicine.

Newton I. had two sons—E. J., and L. N. The elder died at the age of fourteen years. The latter entered college in 1887 at Lebanon, Tennessee, and graduated from Cumberland University with the degrees of A. B. and B. D., and later took a post graduate course in theology in Union Theological Seminary, New York City. He has served as pastor of the Cumberland Presbyterian church at Punxsutawney, Pa., Jackson Center, Pa., Danville, Ill., and Clarksville, Tennessee.

My great-grandfather, David, and grandfather, Thomas, moved from Virginia to Pennsylvania, and their descendants scattered from there principally over the western states. Sincerely yours.

L. N. MONTGOMERY.

And Their Descendants

MONTGOMERYS OF CLAIBORNE COUNTY, TENNESSEE.

Hugh Montgomery, when a young man, about 1800 came from Kentucky to Tennessee and settled on the old state road leading from Tazewell, Tenn., to Jonesville, Va., 20 miles east of Cumberland Gap. He here built his home, married, lived and died. He had four sons—James, Alexander, Hugh and John; and four daughters—Mary, Bettie, Lucy and Matilda. Hugh, Sr., was impetuous and bold to a fault, but was just and generous. He was very fond of his fine horses. He built and maintained at his own expense a mile track on his farm, which was a place of great resort in those days. He was more than eighty years of age when he died, and still it is said that he had not lost a tooth and did not have a decayed one. I know nothing of any of the children of this Hugh, Sr., except Alexander, who had seven sons—William, Hugh, Thomas, Nathaniel, Henry Clay, George W., and Augustus; and one daughter —Mary Jane. I only know that George W. is a member of the law firm of Montgomery and Arnold, of Tazewell, Tenn.

His father, Alexander Montgomery, prior to the Civil War was a general of the state militia in Tennessee. In that day he became well known in his part of the country. When the Civil War broke out, some of the men who had mustered under him came and told him that they desired him to lead them to battle and tendered him a regiment and said they wanted to march under him as they had done in other days. As it happened they were Confederates, while he was a Union man; therefore he declined to serve them. This was on Monday. On Friday night following, at 11 o'clock, a crowd of eight of them returned for the purpose of hanging him. A fight ensued in which he shot two of them; his sons knocked two others down, and the others fled. Mr. Montgomery received a wound from a chopping ax, from which he never recovered. He left home in the night, on his crutches, and the family never saw him again. He died and was buried in Lexington, Ky.

OHIO MONTGOMERYS.

William Montgomery, who came from Ireland to America in the opening of the nineteenth century (1803), landed in Pennsylvania; then moved to Augusta County, Va., and then to Ohio in 1810. This is a condensed account taken from a very interesting work of 112 pages published in 1897 by Prof.

The Montgomerys

Frank Montgomery of Granville, Ohio; now (1903) in the U. S. signal service, Davenport, Iowa.

William Montgomery, the first ancestor of this large, wealthy, educated and influential family, first married a Miss Wilson. They had one son, John, who was born in Ireland. He married Prudence Channel and settled south of Licking River, in Ohio, and raised a family. When about grown, Samuel, one of his sons, accidentally cut himself with a butcher-knife, from which he died. Late in life John Montgomery and his two sons, Joseph and Isom, sold out and moved to near Brandon, Ohio, where his sons lived for many years. The father died Aug. 27, 1849. The mother died Nov. 9, 1859. One of the daughters of John Montgomery married a Mr. Burgess and moved to Indiana. Isom and his family also moved to Indiana, but we have lost all trace of them.

Joseph Montgomery, one of the sons of John, was born Jan. 18, 1817, died Dec. 25, 1875; children eleven: 1. Samuel, born May 7, 1844. 2. Rolin, born March 31, 1846. 3. Henry B. born Sept, 30, 1818. 4. Amos, born Aug. 2, 1850. 5. John, born Oct. 24, 1852. 6. Albert, born Dec. 26, 1854. 7. Franklin, born Dec. 8, 1856. 8. Squire, born Dec. 8, 1858. 9. Ida V., born March 5, 1861. 10. Elwood, born April 9, 1863. 11. Forest, born Dec. 8, 1865. These were all married and nine of them had families. They were all farmers. William Montgomery, Sr., second married a widow, Mrs., Linn, nee Summerville; children four: 1. Samuel. 2. Margaret. 3. Henry. 4. William.

Samuel Montgomery, second son of William, Sr., became a Methodist preacher at the age of 19 and traveled in Pennsylvania, Maryland and Virginia, and was stationed some time at Baltimore, and spent one year as a missionary in Canada; married Nancy Grimes; no children. He was born May 1, 1785, died Oct. 17, 1867.

Margaret Montgomery, the third child of William Montgomery, Sr., was born in County of Tyrone, Ireland, Oct. 15, 1790; married Joseph Irwin in 1809 and settled in Madison County, Ohio. Mr. Irwin was in the war of 1812. He died in Farmers City, Ill., April 24, 1872. His wife died there April 4, 1856; children eight: Polly Ann, Margaret K., Rebecca J., Samuel W., William, Nancy, Elizabeth C, Fidelia. All these except Samuel and Fidelia married and had families.

Henry Montgomery, the fourth child of William, Sr., born in Ireland in 1791, came to America in 1803: married Mary Grimes, in Augusta County, Va. He died 1870; children ten:

1. Margaret Montgomery born Sept. 17, 1811, married John L. Evans, Nov. 6, 1828; children nine.

2. Wesley G. Montgomery born June 2, 1813, first married Nancy Pinkston Davenport. He graduated from Augusta College, Ky., in 1837; was an influential M. E. minister. Second married Julia Ann Plummer; children four.

3. James S. Montgomery, born in Ohio, April 27, 1815, died March 4. 1896, married Sarah E. Waddell; children four.

4. Catherine Montgomery, born March 28, 1817, married Nathan Conrad in Ohio, Jan. 1840; children eleven.

5. Nancy Montgomery, born Nov. 7, 1818, married James P. Martin, March 15, 1838; children four,

6. Dr. William W. Montgomery, born Dec. 5, 1820, married Catherine Gresham; children four.

7. Sarah Ann Montgomery, born Dec. 4, 1822.

8. John Henry Montgomery, born Sept. 17, 1825, was an enterprising, enthusiastic stockman near Granville, Ohio. "He secured the very best stock with which to start his herd, giving as high as $5,000 for one male, whose mother, a Duchess, sold for $35,000. He first married Margaret Lane; children six: Benjamin, Henry H., Emma, John Wesley, Charles and Frank. The latter was born Oct. 16, 1869; graduated from the Ohio Wesleyan University in 1896, has been principal in the Ohio school for the blind, and is author of the Montgomery and Summerville history, referred to at the beginning of this sketch. He married Alice Edwards, in Ohio, Aug. 24, 1896. He is now, 1903, connected with the U. S. signal service at Davenport, Iowa.

John Henry Montgomery, above, second married Miss Sally Phifer, near London, Ohio: children three: Howard P., Chester Q., and Syrena.

The Montgomerys

9. Milton L. Montgomery, born March 30, 1828, married Matilda J. Fleming Jan. 1, 1852, in Licking County, Ohio. He purchased 300 acres of land two miles south of Perryton, Ohio, and in 1872 built a $4000 brick residence. By economy and industry, which are some of the family traits, he has provided ample means and in his latter days is enjoying the reward of his labors; children three.

10. Samuel Hamilton Montgomery, the youngest child of this large family, was born June 15, 1830. He still lives with his family at the old homestead, to which he has added considerable land. He married Levina Wilson, June 1, 1879; children two: Stanley W., and Edwin Willis.

William Montgomery, the fifth child of William Montgomery. *St.,* born Jan. 4, 1793, died Oct. 4. 1849. At his death he owned several hundred acres of valuable land. He was a religious, enterprising and strictly business man and extensive stock dealer. The worth of his example and influence is seen in the lives of his descendants. He married Margaret Grimes, who was born in Bath County. Va., Jan. 12, 1789 and died in Licking County, Ohio, March 21, 1869. She was the mother of eleven children. You will observe that Samuel, Henry and William Montgomery, brothers, married Nancy, Mary and Margaret Grimes, sisters. The sequel to their marriage proves that the parties to these marital relations did not make a mistake in their selections. William's children were:

1. Samuel Montgomery, born April 22, 1815 was a scientific agriculturist and stock dealer, and was alive in 1897 and about 83 years old. His wife died in 1894, at the age of 80 years. Her name was Sarah Seymore. They were married March 22, 1838; children ten: 1. May Jane. 2. William Clark Montgomery born March 23, 1840; was a soldier in the 76th O. V. I., and served as color-bearer; was in the battles of Ft. Donaldson, Shiloh, Corinth, and Arkansas Post: was on the first boat that went in sight of Vicksburg under General Wood; was one of the 150 volunteers to go to Yazoo City with orders to burn the place, but failed on account of low water in the Yazoo river; went to Jackson with General Grant when he cut off from all communication; was at the great siege of Vicksburg 41 days, and on the day of the great charge was placed on a high point with the colors to signal our general provided the rebels tried to mass their forces in front of us during the charge. At this siege he drank from a pool with three dead horses in it, and was only half a mile from the Pearl River at the time. After the siege

they went up the Mississippi to Memphis and across to Lookout Mountain. He was in the fight above the clouds, and saw the firing after night, which was a grand spectacle; was in the charge at Missionary Ridge, where his regiment captured about four hundred prisoners. Two days later they went to Ringold, Ga., where he lost his right arm four inches below the shoulder and received two wounds in the body while leading a desperate charge. This was Nov. 27, 1863. When discharged he received a gold medal from his regiment bearing the inscription—"For gallantry on the field of battle Nov. 27, 1863." He was married Nov. 29, 1864, the same month he was discharged from the army, to Hannah H. Rodebeck. They live on their farm a mile south of Appleton, Ohio; children three.

The other children of Samuel Montgomery are Adam C., James O., Elizabeth A., Emily C., Margaret A., Louisa, Bruce E. and Henrietta.

Nancy, the second child of William Montgomery, Jr., was born Jan. 19, 1817; married James H. Wilson, Dec. 8, 1836; one child— Jacob Wesley Wilson.

C. W. Montgomery, third child of William, Jr., born Dec. 5, 1818; in 1841 engaged in the mercantile business in Newark, N. J.; then engaged in farming. He married Ellinda Claypool, Aug. 15, 1848; children seven: Thomas W., Levi C., Mary Margaret, Cecili, Charles A., Emma E., Ann L., and Felix S.

Margaret Ann Montgomery, born June 25, 1821, fourth child of William, Jr., and a twin to William Clark Montgomery, married James A. Taylor, Dec. 25, 1841. She died July 7, 1846.

William Clark Montgomery, born June 25, 1821, a twin to Margaret above, and fifth child of Wm. Montgomery, Jr., sold a lot of cattle —70 head at one time—for 2 cents per pound; this being the first cattle sold in Licking County, Ohio, by weight. He married Priscilla Griffith of Pittsburg, Pennsylvania, May 17, 1849; children three.

Henry A. Montgomery, sixth child, born March 24, 1824, has been engaged in mercantile business, meat trade, and farming. He married Mary E. Lemert. He was a lieutenant in 159th regiment O. V. I. Children ten. Edward E. Montgomery, his oldest son, is prominent in the medical profession, being in some way connected with nearly all the medical colleges in Pennsylvania. Alice married James E. Bradfield and lives in

Emporia, Kansas. Henry Clay lives in Decatur, Ill., and has been treasurer of Macon County four years. Ida Margaret married Dr. Albert Chase and lives in Philadelphia, Pa. John A. is a graduate from the Bryant-Stratton business college, of Philadelphia, and is engaged in farming near Decatur, Ill. Thadeus Lemert is engaged in the banking business in____. Nelly Lemert is an artist.

Henry A. Montgomery attributes much of his success in life to his early religious training. He joined the M. E. Church nearly 60 years ago. In reviewing his 73 years of life he can see mistakes, yet in the providence of his Heavenly Father he has been blessed with good health and a fair amount of success in life.

John F., youngest son of William and Margaret Montgomery, was born Dec. 12, 1827; married Mary E. Wickham. April 20, 1854. In 1862 when the state of Ohio was threatened by Morgan's raid, he was one of the band of "squirrel hunters" that responded to the call of Governor Todd for defense. In 1864 he served in company E, 135th regiment O. V. I., through the hundred-day campaign. He died Nov. 12, 1892. Children four.

MONTGOMERYS OF WELLSTON, OHIO.

William Montgomery, of Wellston, Ohio, says: My great-grandfather came from Ireland and settled in Virginia. My grandfather, James Montgomery was born in Virginia. He married Mary Walburn; two children: George and William. William left no children. George was my father; born Feb. 5, 1822, near Fredericksburg, Va. William was born in Meigs County, Jan. 29, 1824. Both are dead. My father left three children: William Montgomery of Wellston, Ohio, George of Columbus, Ohio, and Perry of Berlin Crossroads, Ohio.

My grandfather by a second wife had one son, Harrison, and other children. I have one child—Bessie. I was a soldier in the Federal army, 129th regiment Ohio Vol., Co. F. I now belong to the James Smith G. A. R. post.

MONTGOMERYS OF YOUNGSTOWN, OHIO.

James A. Montgomery, of Youngstown, Ohio, sends the following facts concerning this family:

About the beginning of the Revolutionary War, Robert Montgomery emigrated to America from the North of Ireland. He brought with him his family of fifteen children—thirteen boys and two girls. He settled on Long Island and engaged in farming. Some dispute arose among the sons (of whom, you will observe, there were more than a dozen). Henry, one of the sons, went to Albany, from there to Orange County, and then to Sullivan County where he died in 1835. The family was Presbyterian and produced some Presbyterian ministers.

James A. Montgomery, a son of Henry, born in 1822, is now 77 years old. He says that beyond John, James, Robert and Eli, he does not remember any of his uncles; but he tells of a brother Robert who lived in Brooklyn, N. Y., and was a well-to-do man. A sister, Mrs. Penny, of Mt, Hope, New York; a brother, Stephen, who lived many years in Pittsburg; David and Henry, long since dead. The only living member of the family besides himself is Mrs. John Yard, of Venango County, Pa. James A. says that he has never been ashamed of the name, and of only a few people of the Montgomery family. He also refers to the New York estate referred to in other places.

There are other Montgomerys about Youngstown with whom it seems this family is not connected.

MONTGOMERYS OF WHITEHOUSE, OHIO,

Whitehouse, Ohio, March 20, 1901.

Mr. D. B. Montgomery, Owensville, Ind.

My Dear Sir: I have heard, through the kindness of Thomas H. Montgomery, of Ardrasson post office, West Chester, Pa., that you are contemplating printing a history of the Montgomery family; and as I am very much interested in trying to find my own family record I venture to write to you, hoping you will lend me a little of your valuable time.

I am of the Montgomery family. My grandmother's name was Abigail Montgomery. She was married to Aaron Noble, May 20, 1802. She was born Oct. 13, 1785. The names of her brothers and sisters are as follows: Brothers—John Montgomery, Thomas, Robert, Levi, Calvin, James. Sisters—Sallie Montgomery-Harper, Annie Wright, Marian Brooks.

But I have not obtained her father's name, which I would like so much to have. My grandparents came from Monroe, Mich., to north-western Ohio, and grandmother died at my father's house, near Monclova, Lucas County, Ohio. I would like to learn the whereabouts of any of the families of my grandmother's brothers. I think perhaps you could give me a little information. I would like to read your history. Where can it be purchased? May I hope to hear from you? Enclosed you will find self-addressed envelope. Truthfully yours,

C. H. NOBLE.

MONTGOMERYS OF CLEVELAND, OHIO.

There is a James Montgomery in Cleveland, Ohio, a stationary engineer, who was born June 26, 1864, at a place called Crawford's Bars, in the North of Ireland. His father, grandfather and great-grandfather were natives of Scotland.

MONTGOMERYS OF CINCINNATI, OHIO.

William Montgomery, Jr., was born in Orange County, New York, March 19, 1776. His father was also named William, whose wife was named Mary, maiden name not known. She died when William Montgomery, Jr., was a small boy, and he was brought up by an elective, a Miss Lane. He was the only child. He had a cousin Charles Macneal, and one named William Roland. William Montgomery married Ruth Sweezey, in Orange County, New York, probably about 1799 and immigrated to Cincinnati, Ohio, in 1817. Clark B. Montgomery, an able lawyer of Cincinnati, Ohio, is a son of William Montgomery, Jr., and Mrs. Mary E. Cardwill of New Albany, Ind. is his cousin. They can learn nothing more of their ancestors, though they have diligently sought for information.

The Genealogical Chart by Hiram Davis shows that his ancestry on the maternal side runs back to one Lord James Montgomery of Ireland, and we regret that we do not have positive proof of this statement. It is founded on tradition given by Peggy Montgomery, youngest daughter of John Montgomery, who was a son of Samuel, and whose genealogy is given in connection with that of H. P. Montgomery of Georgetown, Ky. This chart made by Mr. Davis is one of the neatest of its kind that has come to me in my researches for genealogical tables.

MONTGOMERYS OF CARROLTON, ILLINOIS.

H. H. Montgomery, an attorney-at-law (1901), of Carrolton, Ill., was born at Scottsville, Ill.; Joseph Montgomery, his father, near Wheeling, W. Va.; Joseph Montgomery, his grandfather, at Armagh, Ireland, 1777; Wm. Montgomery, great-grandfather, in Ireland, 1745; Joseph, great great-grandfather, Ireland, 1703; and his father, Joseph Montgomery of Ayrshire, in Scotland, 1680.

"This latter, it is said, was a near relative of Sir James Montgomery of Skelmorlie, born 1694, who was a son of Sir Robert of Skelmorlie, born 16__; and on back through Sir Gabriel, the general, who was beheaded in Paris in 1674; Cuthbert, killed at Floden; Alexander, created Lord Montgomery by James II; and further back through Alexander, knighted by Robert Bruce; etc., etc. I am unable to state definitely the connection of my ancestor, Joseph Montgomery (born at Ayrshire) and the Skelmorlie line, but the best history I have makes it so. My chief history information is obtained from a work on the Montgomery pedigree printed in Philadelphia in 1863 and compiled by Thomas Harrison Montgomery. My immediate ancestors are named on last page but one of said work."—H. H. M.

MONTGOMERYS OF PETERSBURG, ILLINOIS.

In an early day three brothers came from Scotland or Ireland— probably Scotland. Two settled in Pennsylvania, of whom we hear nothing more. The other, Humphrey Montgomery, settled in Rockbridge County, Virginia, near Lexington. He served in the Revolutionary War. He had six children—five girls and one boy, Samuel, born 1791, who was left an orphan at an early age. He married Mary Baily, in Virginia, and moved to Adair County, Ky. about 1819, and then to Illinois in 1829. He has a son Samuel, now (1901) living near or in Petersburg, Ill. He is said to be the man who removed the body of Ann Rutledge, the first love of Abraham Lincoln, to a cemetery and erected a monument at his own expense.

The Montgomerys

MONTGOMERYS OF MOUNT VERNON, ILLINOIS.

John Montgomery, a farmer, married Susan McDonald. They came from Ireland to Scotland, and then to "Old Virginia." They were Presbyterians, and left the old country on account of religious persecutions. It is not known exactly at what time they came to America, but probably about 1795, as all their children except the oldest were born in Virginia and the youngest was born in 1800.

They moved from Virginia and settled near Lexington, Ky.; children four:

1. Margaret Montgomery, born in Ireland in 1794, married William Brown.

2. Thomas Montgomery, born in Virginia in 1796, married and moved to Louisville, Ky., and raised a family: 1. William Montgomery, a farmer, moved to Texas and is doing well. 2. John Montgomery. 3. Valentine Montgomery, a farmer, moved to Texas and is in comfortable circumstances. 4. A daughter, who married a Jones, who died and left her a widow with two daughters.

3. Nancy Montgomery, born in Virginia in 1798, daughter of John, Sr., married Sam Howard, in Kentucky.

4. John Montgomery, born Jan. 5, 1800, son of John, Sr., was a miller by trade and a Methodist in church relation. He married Margaret Oler, July 27, 1827. He died in 1873: children three: 1. M. J. Montgomery, born March 13, 1828, married a Vincent and now (1902) lives in Evansville, Ind., 119 Upper Third Street. 2. James T. Montgomery, born Aug. 31, 1830, lived for many years near Boonville, Ind., but now (1903) near or in Mt. Vernon. Ill.: married May A. Honsman, April 3, 1851. She was born June 10, 1831; children eight: 1. Elizabeth J. Montgomery, born Feb. 2, 1852. married Gergerthie Kimnan, Oct. 1868, children six— Richard M., Alvah, Albert, Union, William, Mary; T. F. Montgomery, second child of James T., born May 21, 1856, married Alice P. Manahan Sept. 9, 1877; children nine: Cora B., born Sept. 10, 1878; Maud V. born March 4, 1880; Cretie F. born July 11, 1882; Laura M. born Feb. 14, 1884, died Nov. 6. 1884; Ernest U. born Nov. 6, 1886; James W., born Dec. 2, 1888; Herbert G. born Nov. 20, 1890; Mary S., born March 8, 1893; Edith C. born Dec. 7, 1895. 3. Elvira E. Montgomery, child of James T. Montgomery, born June 21, 1859, married Samuel Perry,

Aug. 1872; children six: 1. Margaret Perry; 2. James; 3. Rosetta; 4. Robert; 5. Ethel; 6. Johnnie. 4. Duran H. Montgomery, child of Jas. T. Montgomery, born Aug. 24, 1861, married Elizabeth Matthews Aug. 1885; children six: 1. May; 2. Union; 3. James A.; 4. Mary; 5. Dennis; 6. Katie. 5. Hester Marie Montgomery, born Sept. 23, 1863, child of James T. Montgomery, married John S. Shehorn, July 7, 1878; children three: 1. Robert Shehorn born Feb. 28, 1881; 2. Francis E., born Feb. 28, 1883; 3. John W., born June 14, 1890. 6. Evaline Montgomery, born May 4, 1866, child of James T. Montgomery, married Joseph M. White, Feb. 1885; children five: 1. Mary E. White; 2. James E.; 3. Carrie; 4. Sylvanus; 5. Lottie M. 7. William P. Montgomery, child of James T. Montgomery, born March 25, 1868, married Victoria Ramsey, March 3, 1889. She died Dec. 8, 1892, aged 27 years; children two: 1. Annie B. Montgomery, died Sept. 18__, aged 2 years, 11 mouths and 12 days; 2. James E. Montgomery, died Aug. 26, 1893, aged one year, five months and 13 days.

William P. Montgomery married a second time Abbie L. Ashlock, Oct. 12, 1897; children two: 1, Edwin L. Montgomery, born Oct. 17, 1899, died Sept. 16, 1900. 2. Everett L. Montgomery, born Oct. 5, 1901.

Minnie N. Montgomery, born May 23, 1870, married Henry Ashlock, Dec. 1887; children four: 1. Wheeler Ashlock; 2. James B.; 3. Hester; 4. Adie.

3. Samuel Montgomery, born probably 1832, brother to James T. Montgomery, married and had a family of six children—one son and five daughters. William, the son, now (1901) lives in Evansville, Ind.

4. Susan Montgomery, born probably 1834, sister to James T. Montgomery married Ben Sealy.

5. Mary J. Montgomery, born probably 1836, sister to James T. Montgomery, married John McCool.

MONTGOMERYS OF FRENCH ORIGIN.

Bishop George Montgomery, of Los Angeles, California, and his cousin, Mary Montgomery of Washington, D. C.

According to our family tradition it is about 200 years since, or about 1700, our ancestors came from France to Maryland. Thomas Francis

Montgomery was born in Charles County, Maryland, June 17, 1791. His mother was of the Ringold family. At the age of seven years he was left an orphan, and was raised by an uncle, James Montgomery. His brothers and sisters died young. In 1812, at 21 years of age, he went in company with a cousin to Nelson County, Kentucky (Bardstown, County Seat), where a number of his Montgomery relatives lived. He married Clotilda Wathen, of Randolph County, Virginia; children ten: Pius, Rebecca, Austin, Margaret, Zachary, Jane, Athanasus, Joseph, Appollania and Raphael. This family was raised on a farm, and most of them remained farmers. Pius Montgomery (No. 1) was the father of Bishop George Montgomery. He married Harriet Warren, of Irish-English-French extraction. The bishop was born in Daviess County. Ky., a few miles from Owensboro, Dec. 30, 1847. He worked on the farm until about 19 years old, attending the district schools. Then he entered Cecilian College, near Elizabethtown, Hardin County, Ky., and remained there for about three years. He then determined to study for the priesthood, and after a year or so went to Charles College, in Maryland, where he remained about five years studying classics, etc. Then he completed the study of philosophy and theology in St. Mary's Seminary, Baltimore, which required about five years. He was ordained a priest Dec. 20, 1879, and immediately moved to California, where he did the work of a priest until April 8, 1894, when he was sent to Los Angeles, California, to become Coadjutor Bishop to Bishop Mara, who resigned in September, 1896, when Mr. Montgomery succeeded him as bishop of the diocese which embraces the southern part of the state of California and covers about 80,000 square miles. This part of the state is not as populous as the center of California, and the Catholic population is small, amounting to about 55,000 souls; about one hundred priests. The bishop says that his people are from an old Catholic family, and as far as he knows have kept the faith pretty well. He further says:

"My work is simply that of a Catholic bishop, trying to keep the faith in those who have it already, and to spread the faith as much as we can among those who have it not. We have a fine climate here in southern California, though I don't know that the road to heaven is any shorter here than elsewhere. I sometimes think it is longer, owing to the fact that the climate is liable to make us contented with what we have."

Zachary Montgomery, the fifth child of Thomas Francis Montgomery and father of Mary Montgomery, of Washington. D. C. was born in 1825; was raised on a farm, and after taking a college course he studied law, and moved to California in 1850 or '51 and engaged in mining for a short time, but soon took up the practice of his profession. He was always a strong Democrat, and in 1861 was a strong Southern sympathizer, declining to take a test oath prepared for the attorneys, and thereby gave up the law whilst that oath was in force.

The ground upon which he refused to take the oath was that it was unconstitutional; and as he had already sworn to support the constitution he could not see that the taking of an unconstitutional oath would help his loyalty. The oath was afterwards decided unconstitutional by the Supreme Court of the state, and when it was expunged from the statutes he resumed the practice of law; in the meantime publishing a paper devoted to parental rights in education.

He served as assistant attorney general of the United States during the first administrate of President Cleveland. At the expiration of his term of office he returned to California and again took up his law practice, in which he was engaged at the time of his death, Sept. 3, 1900 at the age of 75 years.

MONTGOMERY'S OF DENVER, COLORADO.

J. Allen Montgomery earnestly seeks information from F. S. Montgomery, of Shepard, Ohio.

Thomas Montgomery, who came from New York state about 1789 and settled in Lake County, Ohio, and became one of the founders of the First Presbyterian church of Centerville—now Madison. Of his son Benjamin but little is known. His grandson Benjamin had a farm near Painesville, Ohio, and was an expert grafter, making frequent trips into Kentucky for that purpose. He died about 1850. He had a son Dr. Thomas Montgomery, who left Ohio when a boy and was raised in Wisconsin. J. Allen Montgomery of Denver, Col., is his son and is anxious to learn if the tradition is true which says that this Thomas Montgomery of New York was a grandson of an Alexander Montgomery who came to New York from Scotland in the first half of the 18th century and who is said to have married a Jewess.

We presume that reference is here made to the Alexander Montgomery who is supposed to have left a fortune in leased property in New York, referred to in another part of our work, on page___.

MONTGOMERYS IN CANADA.

Edward Montgomery, in Ireland, had two sons—Edward and William.

Edward Montgomery came to Canada from Coleraine, County of Antrim, in North of Ireland, about 1835, and his brother William, who is supposed to have come to New York about the same time and finally settled somewhere in the southeastern states, has not been heard from since.

The second Edward had a son Edward, and he also a son named Edward. Thus the name has been carried down for four generations. This fourth Edward is now (1901) a practicing physician in Winnipeg, Canada and is the first of that branch of the family to adopt a profession. The family has mostly been mechanics, merchants and farmers.

The doctor is a "single-taxer" from the ground up. He has no blood relatives nearer him than Quebec and Boston. He writes a good letter and would like to hear from his relatives who settled somewhere in the southeastern states.

Trinity University, Toronto, Ontario, Dec 3, 1900.

"Prof. Henry Montgomery, M. A., Ph. B., B. S., formerly professor of Geology and Mineralogy in the State University of Utah and North Dakota, and now professor of Natural Science in Trinity University. He is quite an extensive lecturer in his line. He is a graduate of four universities and was on the teaching staff of two American universities for nine years.

"Mr. Montgomery was born in Ontario, Canada. His father's name was George, and was a native of Cavan County, Ireland, and with his wife and one daughter came to Canada some time previous to 1850. The father of Henry Montgomery was George. George Montgomery had a remarkable memory and was well-read, and knew much about the history of his ancestors. He often spoke about Hugh Montgomery, who at the head of a Scottish clan settled upon a large tract of land in the North of Ireland early in the seventeenth century. He had no doubt that this Hugh was his direct ancestor."

This was the Hugh that secured part of the Con O'Neal estate in 1603 of whom a full account is given in the preceding chapters.

It is reasonable to suppose that all the Montgomerys that came to America from Ireland were in some way connected to this Hugh Montgomery.

St. Louis, Mo., January 4, 1901.

Mr. D. B. Montgomery, Owensville, Ind.

Dear Sir: In reply to yours of the 14th ultimo, wherein you mention Clark B. Montgomery of Cincinnati, Ohio, who met me in Paris, France, over four years ago during my official station there, and when I gave him some data of the pedigree of the true Montgomery family laboriously compiled by Mr. Thomas Montgomery of Philadelphia.

I beg now to say that the list I had of my ancestors has been for the present filed in England for certain interests, and I have not a copy of it at my command just now. The origin, history and correct lineal descendants of Gabriel and Roger Montgomery, et al, I have traced, verified and copied at St. Michael, Normandy and other parts of France. I have also acquired the identity of the family with William the Conqueror and his staff officers, one of whom was John Montgomery, who had five sons and who with himself became seized of certain estates at the time of the conquest in Great Britain, he becoming the Earl of Earlington, and his sons in England, Scotland, and Wales also bearing titles and possessing estates. I then traced the true lineage in Great Britain and the United States before and up to the year 1628, when Sir John Montgomery was the fifth colonial governor of the colonies of New York, New Jersey and Delaware, and who died in New York. Subsequent to this I traced the right descendants in various of our states, in Canada and New Brunswick, and again I had recourse to data referring to two of the Irish branch, who settled in Alecanti, Spain, and afterwards came to the United States and held high social standing. It was a sort of labor of love, yet an expensive one.

Mr. Thomas Montgomery's family of Philadelphia and the family in New Orleans, La., are, by all rights, the veritable people of the name.

I will endeavor to get the name of a legal firm in New York that possesses a vast mass of data on this subject, and send it to you. Also a Chicago firm that is exploiting it. In the meantime I am,

Yours truly,

L. M. MONTGOMERY.

The information referred to by Mr. Montgomery which is in possession of the New York and Chicago firms was not received; but the same information to a large extent is found in the history of Thomas H. Montgomery of Philadelphia so often referred to in this work. I do not know positively the purpose for which those legal firms referred to were organized, but there are strong evidences that a part of their business was to investigate the claims made by some Montgomerys and their descendants concerning the vast estate supposed to be in New York and across the ocean.

COLONEL WILLIAM COCKRUM.

On page ___, by mistake, appear some notes concerning Colonel William Cockrum. We here insert what was intended to appear on that page.

Owensville, Ind. Feb, 23, 1901.

Col. William Cockrum, Oakland City. Ind.

Dear Sir:

I find that while the people from whom you probably are descended were by the name of Blair, yet on more mature investigation I find that they not only took the name Cochran from an estate, but also from a family of that name. I find this by reference to Patterson's Parishes and Families of Ayrshire, in Scotland, Vol. 2, pages 507-8.

In note 37, page 163, Montgomery's Manuscript, I find this in reference to Hugh Cochran, who was a lieutenant colonel under Sir James Montgomery and afterwards became a colonel. This was Col. Hugh Cochran, of Ferguslie, near Paisley, who served under Gustavus Adolphus, King of Sweden, and also through all the period of the civil war in Ireland from 1641 to 1652. He was the fourth son of Alexander Blair, who had taken the name of Cochran in compliance with the settlement made by his wife's father, William Cochran, of Castle Cochran, on the borders of Paisley and Lochwinnoch parishes.

You will see by this statement that at that time there was a Cochran family as well as a titled estate of that name. The note continues:

"Hugh Cochran's grandmother was a daughter of Sir Robert Montgomery of Skelmorlie, a titled estate in Scotland. Hugh Cochran had six brothers: First, John who served in Ireland; second, William, who became Earl of Dundonald: third, Alexander, of Auchincrench, also a colonel in the army; fourth, Sir Brice, also a colonel, who served in Ireland and was killed in 1650; fifth, Arthur—or Ochter—a captain; and, sixth, Gavin, a captain, who resided at Craigmuir parish, of Lochwinnoch, and died in 1701.

"Hugh Cochran, mentioned in the text, married a daughter of Hugh Savage, County of Down and by her had the following family: 1. John, of Ferguslie, who married Barbara, daughter of James Hamilton, a merchant of Glasgow, and died without issue prior to 1697; 2. William, who succeeded to Ferguslie at the death of his brother; he married Bertha, daughter of William Blair, of Auchinvale. 3. Grizzle married Robert Miller, Minister of Ochiltree, who was outed in 1662, and died in 1685. 4. Margaret married John Hamilton, of Barr, parish of Lochwinnoch. 5. Eupham married Archibald Stewart, of Newton, in 1668.

"At the funeral, 1663, of the third Viscount Montgomery, afterwards the Earl of Mount Alexander, in Ireland, Lieutenant Col. Cochran is mentioned among the kinsmen of the deceased; but by what family connection or in what degree he was so, the estate is unable to discover. By the act of settlement and explanation, Hugh Cogran—which is the same as "Cochran"—as a 1649 officer obtained his arrears of pay which amounted to the sum of 2,754 lbs., 7s., 11d.

"As the grandmother of Col. Hugh Cochran was a daughter of Sir Robert Montgomery of Skelmorlie, I will here insert some account of his history. You will observe that the grandmother of Hugh Cochran, wife of Sir Robert Montgomery, was the daughter of Sir William Douglass, which adds no little prestige to the genealogical line of your ancestry.

The Montgomerys

"Sir Robert Montgomery of Skelmorlie succeeded his father in 1583-4. He was a man of great courage and came to the estate at a period when the feud between the Montgomerys and Cunninghams was at its highest. This lasted 200 years, and he not only had the wrongs of his chief, but the death of his father and brothers, to avenge. He is said to have set no bounds to his feudal wrath, but indulged in it with such eagerness as to have occasioned much bloodshed of his enemies. For this he was afterwards seized with remorse, and in expiation performed many acts of charity and mortification in his latter days. In 1636 he built the Skelmorlie Aisle of the old church of Lorges, in which is the family vault where he and his wife are buried. It is in this vault that tradition has it the remains of Sir Hugh Montgomery, slain at Otterborne, were found. Sir Robert Montgomery was knighted by James VI, and in 1628 was created baronet by Charles I. He married Margaret, daughter of Sir William Douglass, Lord Drumlarig, the first earl of Queensbury; a lady whose beauty is made the subject of two sonnets by Captain Alexander Montgomery, the author of "The Chery and the Slae"— Sir Robert died in 1651, having engaged the estate for the long period of 67 years. (See History of Montgomery Family by Thomas H. Montgomery of Philadelphia, 1863, pages 138-9.)

There is no question but what there is much more said about the Cochran family in Patterson's Parishes and Families of Ayre in Scotland. I have not seen the book, but it is referred to many times in the two histories I have of the Montgomery family.—D. B. M.

We here give place to an article written by Mr. Alfred Edwards. No. 193, page__. Everybody has probably heard the story of General Taylor's daughter, Knox, running away with Captain Jefferson Davis, contrary to the wish of her parents. For this reason we give this article from one who certainly understands the matter from a true light, and because he is a descendant of Mary Montgomery:

"A PRETTY ROMANCE SPOILED."
Facts about Chatsworth and the marriage of Jefferson Davis to Gen. Taylor's Daughter.

"Editor Courier-Journal: I read with much interest the sketch of Miss Emma Keats Speed in the October number of the Southern Magazine, and felt a certain degree of pride that Chatsworth should have been her birth-place. But I must call the attention of the writer of the article to certain inaccuracies in her reference to Chatsworth.

"Chatsworth has not been the 'manor of the Speeds for two generations.' My father, F. G. Edwards, sold it to Dr. Ewing after the close of the War Between the States in 1866, I think. The Dutchman, to whom those many acres near Louisville were given for meritorious service during the Revolutionary War, was my father's maternal grandfather, Col. Geiger. He, Col. Geiger, gave a large tract of it to his daughter, who married John Edwards, my grandfather, whose mother was Mary Montgomery. My grandfather named the place 'Chatsworth' and commenced the improvement of it. My father was born there in 1806, and at the death of his father he inherited the place. My father married Miss Taylor, the daughter of Mrs. Gibson Taylor, then a widow, in 1830. They continued to improve and beautify Chatsworth until it was regarded even among the beautiful places of the neighborhood, as one of the most beautiful.

"It was from Chatsworth that my father's brother, Samuel Montgomery Edwards, went to fight for the independence of Texas and lost his life at the Alamo.

"In the ante bellum days Chatsworth was a typical Kentucky home. Its doors were always open to all guests, and particularly to the old army officers and their families.

"My parents had eight children born at Chatsworth. My sister, Bettie Edwards, was married to Bernard A. Pratte, of St. Louis, in 1856, at Chatsworth. All the sons, four of us, joined the Confederate army from Chatsworth. Two of the boys—Frederick, at the age of 23, and Zachary, at the age of 18—fell on the field of battle in defense of their principles, and their remains were brought back to Chatsworth and from there placed in Cave Hill cemetery. The Taylor family had no other interest in the place except as the home of my mother, who was the niece of Gen. Zachary Taylor. Two of General Taylor's sisters—Mrs. Allison and Mrs. Gray—died at Chatsworth. Two of his nieces, sisters of my mother, were married there; one to Dr. Randall, U. S. A., the other to Capt. McLaws, U. S. A., and afterwards major-general, Confederate States of America.

"As to the marriage of the Hon. Jefferson Davis, the able and revered president of the Southern Confederacy, to General Taylor's daughter, J. B. C.

has been entirely misinformed. General Taylor's daughter, Knox, was married to Captain Jefferson Davis from my grandmother's house, with her father's (General Taylor's) full consent and in accordance with his expressed wish that the ceremony should be performed at her (my grandmother's) house.

"It seems a pity to spoil such a pretty romance, but no 'faithful old family servant conducted Miss Knox from a second-story window by means of a ladder in order that she might marry Captain Davis.' Any desired or required information regarding the ownership of Chatsworth prior to 1866 can be furnished by children, if there be any living, of our old neighbors and friends, Messrs. William C. Bullitt, William L. Thompson, Maj. Veach, Dr. Norton Gait, and Capt. J. B. Bowls. I beg of you to publish this article, not only in justice to the descendants of my grandsires, but also as a matter of historical fact in the settlement of the neighborhood.

"ALFRED EDWARDS.
"Decatur, Wise Co., Texas, Dec. 1, 1894."

On the 28th of November, 1900, I arrived in Georgetown, Ky., and became the guest of the Honorable Henry P. Montgomery, who has gathered more information concerning the Montgomerys in the South and West than any other person I have met or with whom I have had correspondence. He very generously gave me full access to all this information, much of which has appeared in its proper place under the title—"The History Contributed by H. P. Montgomery, of Georgetown, Ky."

On this same trip I visited Lexington and Mount Sterling. At both of these points several Montgomerys had settled as early as 1788-89-96; but there are now no indications of these old families there.

Mt. Sterling, in Montgomery County—which County was organized in 1796, the same year some of the family from Virginia settled there—was so named for General Richard Montgomery, who fell at Quebec. The town was named for a mound 25 feet high and 125 feet in diameter, which stood out by itself and had been built by the Indians. This mound was torn down about 1864-5, by a Mr. Mitchell, much to the displeasure of the citizens, who wished to retain it, as it had been found by the early settlers. A large brick house was built where the mound once stood, and has been purchased for a Negro public school.

In 1816, says Collins' History, there were trees on the mound as large as those in the forest. In digging it down, many curious things were found—a copper breast-plate, and two white queensware breast-plates, each about the size of a man's hand; a great number of copper and ivory pieces, bracelets of copper, and many human bones.

GENERAL INFORMATION.

There are 26 towns in the United States by the name of Montgomery.

There are eighteen states in which there is a Montgomery County—namely: Arkansas, Indiana, Illinois, Kentucky, Alabama, North Carolina, Texas, Missouri, Virginia, Georgia, Iowa, Kansas, Maryland, Mississippi, Ohio, Tennessee, New Jersey, and Pennsylvania.

So far as I can learn, the most of the counties were named in honor of General Richard Montgomery. Montgomery County in Tennessee is named in honor of Col. John Montgomery, from the Holston country, on the Holston River, in south-west Virginia.

F. S. Montgomery
Shepard, Ohio

GENEALOGY OF F. S. MONTGOMERY.

"Here is all I know of my genealogy: My great-grandfather was John Montgomery, born in 1762 near Irvington, County of Tyrone, Ireland, between Belfast and Londonderry, fourteen miles from the former; married Nancy Brown, came to the United States in 1804, at the time of the whiskey insurrection, together with his wife and six children—namely, Mary, Margaret, Nancy, William and John, together with my grandfather, Anthony M., who was born in 1790. They settled in Armstrong County, Pennsylvania, and my grandfather kept a tavern in the County for many years, near South Bend, where my father, Washington Montgomery, was born in 1829. He had four brothers—John, Absalom, Alexander and Robert, and four sisters, Mary, Jane, Belle and Nancy. John was sheriff of Indiana County, Pennsylvania, and Alex, of Armstrong County, and soon after he retired was succeeded in same office by his brother Absalom's son, Alexander.

"My father went to California in 1849 and settled at Marysville. He was engaged as general manager of the California Stage Co., which operated extensively in the Sacramento valley; and he crossed the plains twice with droves of horses from Ohio and Pennsylvania. He died before he was forty, and I, the only child, was born at Marysville in 1863."

"FRANK S. MONTGOMERY."

Frank S. Montgomery is forty years of age. He was born in 1863 at Marysville, California. He came with his mother, via Panama, to Grinnell, Iowa, in 1868, and since 1878 has resided at Shepard, Franklin County, Ohio, where he has been most of the time engaged in the grocery business. He is vice-president of the Columbus Ice Company, notary public, railroad and express agent, and has been postmaster at Shepard for over twelve years without objection from either of the of the old parties.

Raised a Republican, he became a free trader before he was of age and acted with the Democrat party till 1896; was twice delegate to their state conventions, and several times to their congressional; also member of Franklin County Democratic central committee for three years. In 1895 he was elected treasurer of his township by 144 majority in a vote of about 500, and received every vote cast (about 50) by members of all parties at his home town of Shepard. He has been a member of the Board of Education for six years, and was president of same two years. In 1896 he was a delegate to the Democratic state convention, but left the party when it adopted the single financial plank as its platform, and in the presidential campaign which followed he supported Palmer and Buckner, and made two speeches and held three joint debates in Franklin County. He was a delegate to the state conventions of the National Democratic Party in 1896 and 1897, and the latter year was nominated by them as member of the legislature. While not approving of the present financial system, he regards free silver as of no practical value as a relief to the oppressed, and holds under present conditions monopolies will secure most of the earnings of labor, no matter what form of currency we have or how it is issued. In 1898 he attended the mass convention which formed the Union Reform party, entered into the movement with enthusiasm and became secretary of the Franklin County executive committee; also candidate for County commissioner. He is vice-president of the Columbus Single Tax Association: also of the Columbus Cremation Society.

Mr. Montgomery sends me the following gleanings:

Col. B. Montgomery is President McKinley's executive clerk.

There is a J. W. Montgomery in the pension department. Washington, D. C.

Alexander Montgomery, probably from Virginia, was killed and scalped by Indians in southern Ohio, Sept. 1778, while on an expedition to catch some horses, in company with George Clark and the celebrated General Simon Kenton. Clark escaped, and so did Kenton after a long captivity.

"Greater than all was the mighty house that was formed by the union of Montgomerys and Bellesme—a house holding lands both of Normandy and France, and ranking rather with princes than ordinary nobles."—Encyclopedia Britanica. Vol. 17, page 545. This refers to the Montgomerys of the ninth and tenth centuries.

"General Montgomery Cunningham Meigs, whose mother was a Montgomery, was quartermaster-general of the United States army during the Civil War, and superintended the construction of the dome of the capitol at Washington, D. C.; also the Georgetown aqueduct."

F. S. Montgomery has a copy of T. H. Montgomery's history that at one time was the property of General Montgomery C. Meigs, as he here explains: I quote this from the fly-leaf in T. H. Montgomery's history which was the property of Maj. Gen. Montgomery C. Meigs and is in his writing:

"My mother, 31st in descent from Roger of Normandy, was a daughter of William, born 1752 and died 1831. His first child was born in 1783, Philadelphia. He lived at 178 and 82, two doors west of____, south side, and died there. After my grandmother's death my mother and father, Dr. C.

D. Meigs, were with my grandfather and remained there till they sold the house, between 1832 and 1836, while I was a cadet at West Point. Then they moved into a house on Chestnut Street, above 10th." See T. H. Montgomery's History, pages 91-153.

"CABIN JOHN BRIDGE.

"Largest Single-Arch Masonry Bridge in the World—An Interesting History of This Wonderful Bridge, Erected in War Times.

"Washington, D. C, April, 1901.

"This wonderful work of modern engineering, known as Cabin John bridge, was constructed for use but has become ramous the world over for its beauty. Today its arch, gleaming through the trees of one of the most picturesque spots in America, is an object of the admiration of all visitors to the capital city. No one can be said to have 'seen Washington' who has neglected visiting Cabin John Bridge. In summer, artists bring their easels to the dells and hills in its vicinity and attempt to reproduce this graceful and picturesque structure from every view. Engineers from all parts of the country have made trips to it. Over its beautiful span the carriages of all fashionable and famous Washingtonians bowl; for it is the objective point of those who travel over the conduit road, one of the finest drives in America.

"It stands unique in every way—even in name—an impressive monument to the ingenuity of this progressive age.

"The span or opening at the base of the arch is 220 feet, the rise or height of opening from the base of arch is 57.26 feet, and the height above the bottom of the creek is 100 feet. Its nearest competitor is the Grosvenor Bridge, over the river Dee, at Chester, England, with a span of 200 feet and a rise of 42 feet.

Cabin John Bridge was built as part of the water supply system of Washington, and its object is to carry the pipe nine feet in diameter through which flows the city's water from the Great Falls of the Potomac. It is really not a pipe, for it is a kind of tunnel within the structure of the bridge, which is therefore an aqueduct bridge -that is, a carrier of water. The conduit for the water is just under the roadway of the bridge, which is 450 feet long and 20 feet 4 inches wide. The cost of the bridge was $254,000.

"The water is diverted above the Great Falls of the Potomac river and passes into a conduit which carries it to the city; crossing this bridge and four others. The conduit is about twelve miles long and empties the water into reservoirs, the nearest of which is *about* four miles from the center of the city. For about ten miles of its length the conduit lies under a well-kept and well-graded macadamized road that is one of the favorite drives out of the city,

"Cabin John Bridge derives its name from the creek which it spans, and that in turn was named for a mysterious man who appeared there just before the Revolutionary War. He built a cabin near the creek in which he lived many years and was known by no other name than John, or 'John of the Cabin,' from which the name of the creek was ultimately derived. He lived in his cabin with no companions save his dogs, spending most of his time in hunting. He clothed himself with the skins of wild animals and avoided human society, but was never known to do an unkind act. After many years of this life he disappeared as mysteriously as he had come. His dogs wandered about the cabin for some time and finally deserted it. No trace of 'John of the Cabin' has since been found.

"The construction of the bridge is linked with our national history in an interesting way. It bears on its face an indelible mark of one of the critical periods of our history, which makes it an interesting object for the visitor to Washington. The city's electric car system will carry him directly to it.

"The bridge was designed by General (then Captain) Montgomery C. Meigs, whose mother was a Montgomery, and was begun in 1853. The work continued under him with short intermissions until 1862, when it was nearly finished, it was practically completed in 1863. Until July 1862, the work had been carried on by the Engineers' Department of the army, under the supervision of the secretary of war, and about a year before the work was turned over to the Interior Department a stone had been set into one of the abutments bearing inscription No. 1, which was similar to that often placed on great public works: No. 1—
Washington Aqueduct,
Begun A. D. 1853; President of the U. S., Franklin Pierce;
Secretary of War, Jefferson Davis.

Building A. D. 1861; President of U. S. Abraham Lincoln;
Secretary of War, Simeon Cammeron.

"Soon after the secretary of the interior, the Hon. Caleb B. Smith, took charge of the work, he was informed that the name "Jefferson Davis" appeared on the stone. This was in the early part of the Civil War and feeling ran very high. The secretary immediately ordered the name cut out, which was done by the contractor, so that the stone now appears as in inscription No. 2—

Washington Aqueduct,
Begun A. D. 1853; President of the U. S., Franklin Pierce:
Secretary of War----
Building A. D. 1861; President of IT. S., Abraham Lincoln;
Secretary of War, Simeon Cammeron.

"If it was Secretary Smith's intention to prevent the association of the name of Jefferson Davis with this great structure, he failed utterly; for if the name had been left on it might have been a cause of remark by visitors, but the great majority would soon have forgotten; but now the blank space causes much interested comment on the line that was there, because of the very effort to erase it.

"The bridge bears another inscription, placed there in 1861 by Meigs, as follows:

Union Arch;
Chief Engineer, Capt. Montgomery C. Meigs,
U. S. Corps of Engineers.
Esto Perpetua.

"In spite, however, of his effort to have his great work known as 'Union Arch,' the whole engineering world, as well as everyone in Washington and vicinity, knows it only as the 'Cabin John' Bridge." —The Postmasters U. S. M. Advocate, April, 1901.

Prof. D. H. Montgomery is the author of a United States school history, which is being largely sold by the publishers, Ginn & Co., of Boston, Mass. His address is Cambridge, Mass.

Frank H. Montgomery, M. D., is associated professor of skin, genito-urinary and venereal diseases, at Rush Medical College, Ill., and in connection with Prof. Hyde; has recently published a large medical work on venereal diseases, which is highly spoken of by the medical journals.

"Sir Robert Montgomery, LL. D., born in Ireland, 1809, educated at Foyle College, Londonderry, and in 1828 appointed to the service of the East India Company; in 1853 was appointed judicial commissioner, superintendent of prisons and director-general of police for the province of the Punjaub. For his services in the Indian mutiny and in quelling the disturbances in the Oude, of which he had been made chief commissioner in 1858, he was thanked by Parliament and knighted. From 1859 to 1865 he was lieutenant-governor of the Punjaub. In 1868 he was made a member of the council for India."—International Cyclopedia, page 174.

Ecclesiastical.—Montgomery, Rev. Henry E., D. D., pastor of the Protestant Episcopal Church of the Incarnation, New Jersey City, died Oct. 16, 1874, in his 50th year.

Political.—Montgomery, John G., member of Congress from the 12th district of Pennsylvania, died in Danville, Pa., April 24, 1857; said to have been a victim of the National Hotel disease which caused so much alarm and loss of life just before this date.

Montgomery, William, died at Washington, Pa., April 28, 1870, at the age of 51; born at Canton, Bradford County, 1819; educated at Washington College, studied law, was admitted to the law in 1832 and was a member of Congress in 1856-1860; was the author of the Critenden-Montgomery amendment, which was intended as a sedative measure on the slavery question.

Virginia Convention, Vol. 2, page 366.—There was a James Montgomery, from Washington County, in the Virginia Convention of 1788.
Alexander Montgomery was a Grand Master Mason in Virginia in 1779, and a very prominent man.

I find that in the convention of 1788, Virginia; Walter Crockett was a delegate from Montgomery County. This is probably the man that my father was named for, as he was born in that County in 1784 and named Walter Crockett Montgomery.—D. B. M.

And Their Descendants

Montgomery, James, pioneer, born in Ashtabula County, Ohio, Dec. 22, 1814, died in Linn County, Kan., Dec. 6, 1871. He came with his family in early life to Kentucky and taught, ultimately becoming a Campbellite preacher. Later he devoted himself to farming, but in 1854 went to southern Kansas, where he was one of the earliest settlers. His residence in Linn County was burned by the Missourians in 1856, and this resulted in his taking an active part in the disturbances that followed. The retaliatory visits into Missouri were frequently led by him, and his discretion, courage and acknowledged ability gained for him the confidence and support of the southern counties. His enrolled company included nearly 500 men, all of whom were old residents of the territory and consequently familiar with the peculiar mode of fighting that was followed on the border. Captain Montgomery was one of the acknowledged leaders of the free-state cause during 1857-61. Next to John Brown he was more feared than any other, and a contemporary sketch of the "Kansas Hero," as he was then called, says: "Notwithstanding every incentive to retaliate actuates them to demand blood for blood, yet Montgomery is able to control and direct them. He truly tempers justice with mercy, and he has always protected women and children from harm, and has never shed blood except in conflict or self-defense." In 1857 he represented his County in the Kansas senate, and at other times he was a member of the legislature. At the beginning of the late war he was made colonel of the 10th Kansas Volunteers, but soon afterward was given command of the 1st North Carolina Colored Volunteers. These troops he led on a raid from Hilton Head into Georgia in July, 1863, and at the battle of Olustee, Fla., on the 20th of February, 1864, was one of the few officers that escaped with their lives. Horace Greely says of his regiment and the 54th Massachusetts, "It was admitted that these regiments had saved our little army from being routed." At the close of the war he returned to Kansas and passed the last years of his life at his home in Linn County.—Appleton's Cyclopedia, Vol. 4 page 369. See this same work for —

Montgomery, George Washington, born in Spain, and
Montgomery, George Washington, born in Portland, Maine, 1810.
Montgomery, John, born in North Ireland, 1722.
Montgomery, Martin, born March, 1840.
Montgomery, William, born in Canton, Pa., 1819.
Montgomery, William B., Missionary.
(Included in Thomas H. Montgomery's genealogy, page 3).

"William Reading Montgomery 1801-1871, born in New Jersey, graduated at West Point 1825 and was appointed to the infantry. He served on the western and Canadian border, and through the Florida and Mexican wars. He was brevetted major for gallantry at Palo Alto and Resaca-de-la-Palma. At Malino de Rey he led his regiment after the death of its senior officers, and was dangerously wounded. After further service in Texas and the West he resigned from the army in 1855. On the outbreak of the Rebellion he raised a regiment of volunteers from his native state. For his gallantry at Bull Run he was made a brigadier-general. He was military governor, at various times, of Alexandria, Annapolis and Philadelphia, but resigned his commission from ill health in 1864."

JOHN MONTGOMERY,

Governor of New York was a native of Ayershire, Scotland. He was bred a soldier and was at one period aid to George II. He was a court favorite, governor of the bed-chamber and master of the mint. For several years he was a member of Parliament for Ayershire. In 1727 he was appointed governor of New York and New Jersey, in the place of Burnett, and continued in office from the time of his arrival in April, 1728, to his death at New York, July 1, 1731.

The A. Charter was granted to the city of New Jersey by this John Montgomery, captain-general and governor-in-chief of New York and the province of New Jersey and the territories depending thereon in America, and vice-admiral of the same, under George II., dated Jan. 15, 1730. It extended the Dougan charter and was in force until 1830, a period of one hundred years.

MONTGOMERYS OF AMERICA.

Mrs. Mary S. P. Guild, of North Cambridge, Mass., who published in 1892 a book of genealogies of several families, including some Montgomerys, in a letter to H. P. Montgomery of Georgetown, Ky., written June 17, 1898, says that John Montgomery, who came to America about 1719 and married a Strobridge, had a large family—seven sons and five daughters. One of the sons was named John, who married Margaret Heney, 1771. The names of his children were: Robert, John, Thomas, William, Samuel and Hugh; Margaret, Mary, Jean and Rebecca. The names of the six sons first mentioned are identical with the names of six of the sons of Hugh Montgomery, who is supposed to have settled in Roanoke County, Va., in

1718. Mrs. Guild further says that the Montgomerys in this County are a host, and no attempt, to my knowledge, has ever been made to trace them. Mrs. Guild's genealogy starts out with William Montgomery, who settled in New Jersey in 1701-2, and goes back 27 generations to Roger de Montgomery of Normandy, on about the same line as that given by Fraser, Paterson, Thomas H. Montgomery and others.

SOME EARLY MONTGOMERYS IN THE UNITED STATES.

On pages 176 to 186, MacLean's Highlanders, we find an account of the efforts of Captain Lanchlin Campbell to colonize northern New York—Washington County—with one hundred families on 100,000 acres of land, in 1734; and when he had succeeded in landing 80 families the authorities refused to comply with their part of the contract. Mr. Campbell died of a broken heart. In 1764, descendants by petition secured some of these lands in allotments of from 200, to 600 acres on certain conditions. Among these allotments we find one made to Hugh Montgomery of 200 acres, and one to Alexander Montgomery of 600 acres. These men or their ancestors must have been of the 85 families that came over in 1734.

COLONEL ARCHIBALD MONTGOMERY
IN THE FRENCH AND INDIAN WAR.
(Drawn from MacLean's Highlanders in America.)

"The regiment known as "Montgomery's Highlanders" (77th) took the name from its commander, Archibald Montgomery, son of the earl of Eglinton. Being very popular among the Highlanders, Montgomery very soon raised the requisite body of men who were formed into thirteen companies of one hundred and five, rank and file, each; making in all fourteen hundred and sixty effective men, including sixty-five sergeants and thirty pipers and drummers. The colonel's commission was dated January 4, 1757.

"The regiment embarked at Greenoch for Halifax immediately on its organization. It landed at Halifax June 1857. This regiment was in the expedition against Fort Duquesne, undertaken by Gen. John Forbes.

"In 1759 we find the regiment in New York, under command of General Amherst, who had succeeded Abercrombie as commander-in chief. They were to reduce Ticonderoga and Crown Point, and then effect a junction with Wolf at Quebec.

"At the close of the year 1761, Montgomery's regiment in company with ten other regiments embarked for Barbados, there to join an armament against Martinique and Havana. After the surrender of Havana Montgomery's Highlanders embarked for New York, which they reached Oct. 1762. In the summer of 1763 a detachment of Montgomery's regiment was sent to the relief of Fort Pitt, which was besieged by the Indians. Montgomery's forces suffered severe losses in common with the others in the surprise at Bushy Run.

"Montgomery, with 600 of his own regiment and 600 Royal Americans, was sent to reduce the Cherokees, who were committing cruelties against the settlement. The force embarked at New York in April. Montgomery for a while swept everything before him; and Washington in discussing his campaign said: 'What may be Montgomery's fate in the Cherokee country I cannot readily determine. It seems he has made a prosperous beginning, having penetrated into the heart of the country, and he is now advancing his troops in high health and spirits to the relief of Fort London. But let him be wary; he has a crafty, subtle enemy to deal with that may give him most trouble when he least expects it.'—Spek's Writings of Washington, Vol. 11, page 332; quoted by MacLean in Highlanders of America.

Soon after this Montgomery met with severe losses in an engagement with the Indians and ordered an immediate retreat to New York, and this in the face of the earnest entreaty of the General Assembly not to leave the path of duty in defending the settlers. Leaving four companies of Royal Scots, he sailed for Halifax by way of New York, saying: "I cannot help the people's fears."

"Afterwards, in the House of Commons, he acted as one who thought the Americans factious in peace and feeble in war.

After his return to England he became equery to the queen in 1763, and governor of Dunbartan Castle in 1764. In 1767 he became colonel of the 51st regiment and became an earl. In May, 1772, he became major-general, and in 1777 lieutenant-general. He died a general in the army, Oct. 30, 1796.—Coney Wilson's Orderly Book, page 17.

"COMMODORE JOHN BERRING MONTGOMERY

"Was born Nov. 17, 1794, and married in 1821 Mary, daughter of William Henry, of New York. He entered the United States navy, June 4, 1812, just a fortnight before the declaration of war by Congress against Great Britain, and served throughout that war, being present at the battle on Lake Erie, under Commodore Perry, Sept. 10, 1813. Subsequently he was with Commodore Decatur in the expedition against Algiers. More recently, while stationed on the coast in command of the Portsmouth, the war with Mexico broke out, and in 1846 he took possession for the United States government of the town and harbor of San Francisco. During his stay here he was drawn into a controversy with the British commander on that station in regard to some alleged violations of the blockade, which he conducted with such skill and firmness as eventually to win from the British government a very laudatory notice of the course pursued by him."—T. H. Montgomery History, pages 111-112.

General John Montgomery was born in New Hampshire, 1764 and during the war of 1812 he was brigadier-general of the New Hampshire forces stationed at Portsmouth. He died Feb. 24, 1825. —T. H. Montgomery History, page 153.

COLONEL JOHN MONTGOMERY.

Dr. John T. Graham's article which appeared in the Enterprise of Wytheville, Va., 1895, says that Heitman's Historical Register says Col. John Montgomery commanded a Virginia regiment in the Revolutionary War from 1778 to 1781. He was a remarkable man in that his very presence among the dispirited, home-sick soldiers inspired new life and fresh courage and a readiness to push forward in the campaign. He was with Gen. Ben Logan in Kentucky, and with Gen. George Rogers Clark in his Illinois campaign, and was also in command of a regiment in 1794 against the Creeks and Cherokees, and took part in the decisive battle of Nickagach, Tenn.

Ramsey's Tennessee, page 666, says Montgomery County, in Tennessee, was named in honor of Col. John Montgomery in 1796; also says that he was a native of Virginia. He emigrated early to the West and became a member of the North Carolina legislature and also of the convention of that state which ratified the constitution of the United States. Besides the civil appointments which he filled, he was colonel of the state militia of his County and led more than two hundred of his fellow soldiers in the Nickagach campaign. He was a patriot and hero, and lost his life in giving protection to the frontier. He was killed and scalped by a party of Indians on the 27th of November, 1794. He was living in Tennessee County, Tenn., at this time, which County was divided in 1796 into Montgomery and Robertson counties. So far I have no information as to what family Col. John Montgomery belonged but his troops were raised in the Holston country, Va., at the time he served with Logan and Clark, which indicates that he probably belonged to some of the Holston families.

EARLY TENNESSEE MONTGOMERYS.

William Montgomery was a member of the first legislature of Tennessee, in 1796, from Sumner County.

James Montgomery was a justice of the peace in Washington County, Tenn., appointed by the authorities of North Carolina, 1787.

GENERAL RICHARD MONTGOMERY.

The following account is taken from a letter written by Mrs. Mary E. Bankston, nee Montgomery, of Ringold, Ga., to H. P. Montgomery of Georgetown, Ky., 1901:

Richard Montgomery was born in Ireland in 1737, a descendant of an ancient and honorable family. After receiving a liberal education he entered the army. In his 21st year we find him holding the rank of captain in the 17th British regiment under General Moncton.

He had borne a full share in all the American wars and in the reduction of Canada, and had therefore no common claims to promotion; but although his military abilities were highly distinguished, war and conquest had no other charms to him than as the means of peace to mankind. In 1770 his country was blessed with peace, and he immediately resigned his commission and emigrated to these shores. He selected a delightful spot on the banks of the Hudson River in New York and married a daughter of Judge Livingston of that state and retired from the bustle of a noisy world. He gave full scope to his philosophical spirit and taste for rural elegance. When the unlawful hand of authority was stretched forth, Montgomery was ready to exchange his peaceful groves for the tented field. From that fatal day in which the first American blood was spilled by the hands of the British, and the better genius of the empire turned abhorrent from the strife of death among the children, our hero chose his part. He was appointed a major-general, the second in rank of eight who were chosen by Congress in 1775. His principles of loyalty remained unshaken. Montgomery did not hesitate to accept the commission, praying at the same time that Heaven might speedily reunite us in every land of affliction and interest. He was entrusted jointly with General Schuyler with the expedition against Canada, Nov. 8, 1775, and it was exactly suited to the genius of Montgomery. He understood the blessings of a free government and could display them with captivating eloquence. After capturing Fort Chamblee, St. Johns surrendered to him and the governor of Montreal abandoned that city to his victorious arms. Being joined by Arnold with a body of well-disciplined troops from New England, he laid siege to Quebec on the first of December. He was now on the same plain which had been consecrated by the blood of Wolf. Here Montgomery won his earliest laurels. Owing to the small size of his guns, the bombardment produced no effect and he was compelled to make an attempt to storm the garrison. He passed the first barrier and was about to attack the second, when a fatal shot released his gallant spirit and united him with the glorious command whose fame he emulated.

We have ample testimony in the campaign against Quebec in the year 1775 by John Joseph Henry. He was under the command of Montgomery, and being taken by the enemy had an opportunity of witnessing the honors that were paid to his memory.

Carlton had, in our former wars with the French, been the friend and fellow soldier of Montgomery. Through political opinions they separated, but yet were on friendly terms. To express the high sense entertained by his country of his services, Congress directed that a monument of white marble be erected, with the following inscription, which was executed by Mr. Cassiers of Paris and placed in front of St. Paul's church, in New York:

> This Monument was erected by order of Congress, to transmit to posterity a grateful remembrance of the patriotism, conduct, enterprise and perseverance of Major - General Richard Montgomery, who, after a series of successes amidst

the most discouraging difficulties, fell in an attack on Quebec, Dec. 31. 1775, aged 39 years.

MONTOMERYS OF VIRGINIA.

Lieutenant James Montgomery was in the Revolutionary War in a Virginia regiment, 1778 to 1781; died 1809. It is believed he married a Crockett; had two daughters—Mary, and Elizabeth Crockett Montgomery, the latter born in Wythe County, Va., May 17, 1804; died Aug. 26, 1824, and buried in Princeton, Ky. She married Thomas Jefferson Flourney, who was born in Powhatan County. Va., Jan. 15, 1800; died in Clinton, Iowa, 1882. Their children were:

1. Lafayette Montgomery Flourney born in Powhatan County. Va., Sept. 19, 1820; died in Spokane, Washington, June 1900.
2. David Flourney born in Wythe County, Va., 1822, died 1854.
3. Marcella Elizabeth Flourney born in Wythe County, Va., 1823, in 1895; living with Mrs. James Van Deventer, in Knoxville, Tenn.; never married.

IN THE NAME OF GOD, AMEN: I, James Montgomery, of the County of Wythe, State of Virginia, being advanced in years, frail in body, but of a sound and disposing mind and memory, do make and declare this to be my last will and testament in manner and form following, to-wit:

In the first place, I will that all my just debts be paid, which are but few and none of magnitude, out of those debts due to me, immediately after my decease, by my executor or executors hereafter nominated and appointed, should there not be a sufficiency, so much of my personal estate, such as horses and cattle (negroes particularly excepted) as will be sufficient, sold at a reasonable credit, and the money arising from such sales applied to aforesaid uses. I leave and devise unto my beloved wife, Cynthia Montgomery, the one third part I am in possession of, and hold in jointing with my brother Joseph Montgomery, including the mansion house, together with one-third part of all my other estate, negroes, horses, cattle, hogs, sheep, household, furniture, money, during her natural life; the other two-thirds of my estate I will unto my two daughters, Mary W. Montgomery and Elizabeth C. Montgomery, and their heirs forever, to receive all rents and proceeds arising from aforesaid estate. Again, I leave unto my two daughters aforesaid, after the death of their mother, all and singular my estate, real and personal, of every description whatsoever, unto my two daughters, Mary W. Montgomery and Elizabeth C. Montgomery, and their heirs forever, equally. Again, I will, in case any dispute should arise in the division of my property between themselves or their mother or their husbands or legal representatives, such dispute or disputes shall be settled from time to time by three or four disinterested men appointed by Wythe court. Again I will, should it appear to my executor or executors that hiring my negroes, all but what will be sufficient to till the plantation I live on, the same be hired out, and the money put to interest. Again I will, at such times as it should appear to my executor or executors that the increase of the stock of horses, cattle, hogs, etc., should become burthensome (negroes excepted) sold, and the money put to interest as aforesaid, only reserving what may be sufficient to clothe, educate and bring up my said daughters in a genteel manner. Again, I will and devise, should either of my daughters die without issue, the whole estate to descend to the survivor; incase both should die without issue, the whole to descend to my nephew, James Montgomery, son of my brother Joseph Montgomery, and his heirs and legal representatives forever. Lastly and finally, I do nominate, constitute, appoint, my beloved wife, Cynthia Montgomery, my nephew, Samuel Montgomery, son of my brother John Montgomery, deceased, and Gordon Cloyd and Robert Sproule, my executors to this my last will and testament, revoking all former wills and testaments by me made, and do declare this to be my last will and testament.

IN WITNESS WHEREOF, I have hereunto subscribed my name and affixed my seal, this 12th day of December, 1808.

JAMES MONTGOMERY (Seal).

Thomas Boyd.
Joseph Montgomery,
Heazlet Sproule.
At a Court held for Wythe County, the 10th day of October, 1809.

This is the last will and testament of James Montgomery, deceased; was exhibited in court and proved by oaths of Joseph Montgomery and Heazlet Sproule. subscribing witnesses thereto, and ordered to be recorded; and on the motion of Cynthia Montgomery, the executors named in the said will who entered into bond with Robert Savers, William Foster, Reuben Cosey and Anthony Owens, their sureties, in the sum of ten thousand dollars, with conditions as the law directs, and took the oath required by law; and on the motion of Robert Sproule. one of the executors named in the said will, who entered into bond with Heazlet Sproule, Joseph Montgomery, Samuel Coddell, Francis Foyris and Joseph Spear, his sureties, in the sum of ten thousand dollars, with condition as the law directs, and took the oath required by law.

Probate therefore is granted them.

Teste: JOHN P. MATTHEWS, D. C.

And Their Descendants

CHAPTER XVII.
COLONIAL, FRENCH-AND-INDIAN
AND REVOLUTIONARY SERVICES IN VIRGINIA.

I have made diligent inquiries after these matters, for myself and several other parties, and find that the record concerning the services of the soldiers in the Revolutionary War is very imperfect. A. G. Quisenberry, a genealogical expert, of Washington, D. C., confirms the statement made by Judge H. P. Montgomery on page 54, to the effect that there were 300 or 400 Montgomerys in the Revolutionary War. "It would probably be a tedious and expensive undertaking to get an account of all of them, even if the records were all accessible, and they are not. Searches of the kind you wish will cost you $5.00 a day."

I finally secured the services of Mr. R. A. Brock, ex-secretary of the Southern Historical Society of Richmond. Va. and he is considered one of the best-informed men along this line in the United States. It is questionable if the records of the War Department at Washington, D. C. will give more information on the subject than I obtained from Mr. Brock. I have consulted the records at Washington, through the kindness and with the assistance of the Honorable James A. Hemenway, member of Congress from this district, and will give the information thus obtained in connection with that received from Mr. Brock. There is no question but what there were quite a number of Montgomerys, as well as hundreds of others who were in the Revolutionary War, of whom there is not a line of record concerning this service. The names on record seem to be largely those who went on by proof after the war was over, in obtaining land warrants and pensions.

Besides all this, it is quite a difficult task to bring up the proof that we are the direct descendant of the names we find on record.

Then again, the traditions in our families may not be correct. Some of the older ones took part in the French and Indian War, and the younger ones in the Revolutionary. Nearly all able-bodied men in the United States of those times took some part in one or the other of these wars. Yet we overlook the services in the French and Indian War and are anxious to believe that all our ancestors were in the Revolutionary War.

The tradition in our family is that there were seven brothers in the family to which my great-grandfather belonged, and that all took part in the

Revolutionary War. I firmly believe this is true, but I have not been able to find proof to satisfactorily establish this fact, only in the case of one John Montgomery; his family, I believe, could establish this fact. I find all these names on record— one a colonel, one a captain, one a lieutenant; but there is no tradition in our family that any of these brothers were officers.

Then, again, the residence does not correspond with the known residence of our family at that day. I have written this in order that all those anticipating Revolutionary records will see the difficulties in the way of an investigation of these matters.

We give place to Mr. Brock's letter to us after he had looked up this matter concerning the Montgomerys in the state of Virginia:

Richmond, Va., March 28, 1901.

D. B. Montgomery. Owensville, Ind.

Dear Sir: Enclosed you will find the work of a more comprehensive delineation than I contemplated or you stipulated.

I may state as to the land grants that at first the colonists were practically the servants of the Virginia Company. Later they were allowed grants of 50 acres each, and then grants were made on those brought to the colony as settlers on transports, 50 acres for each. These were transferable and were called "land rights." Later still, grants were made on the payment of the consideration of 10 shilling per one hundred acres. The state of Virginia granted bounty lands for services in the French and Indian Wars and the Revolutionary War. The general government, alter the conclusion of the war, offered to settle all the claims for pay due the soldiers from the several states. These records are in the pension rolls bureau.

G. F. C. AINSWORTH,

Washington, D. C.

Regretting delay in making the report, with which I trust you will be satisfied, I beg to remain yours faithfully,

R. A. BROCK.

The Montgomerys

COLONIAL SERVICES.

Montgomery, Robert, Edward Belson, and other inhabitants in Nanzemond County, Va. (Colonial No. 6, page 678), 850 acres, "for and in behalf of themselves and divers inhabitants residing from Coward's Creek downwards to the said Belson, and from the said Belson to Robert Poole's, by the mill, at the head of Mr. Boxety's Creek; 850 acres of swamp land, and lying in County of Nanzemond, by or near the boundary of said inhabitants and near the Parish lands and the lands of Wm. Staples; April 30, 1679.— Wm. Waylott, Isaac Waylott, Thomas Waylott, Abigail Waylott, San Waylott, Sar. Waylott, John Sawyer, Samuel Lickings, Arod Mills, S. Hetherall, Thomas Alles, Snod Gong, John Hay, Robert Abbott, Sar. Spilman, Thomas Clark, Robert Paters, Sir Henry Checkley. (17 tranport).

Montgomery, Hugh (Colonial No. 7, page 15). 250 acres, in the County of Lower Norfolk, in Elizabeth River Parish, joyning upon Taunder's Creek; 200 acres thereof bounded northerly upon lands of Capt. Thomas Hilcher; east from the Maine River, east on land of Robert Woody; the other 50 acres, joining upon the 200 acres to a point called Sandy Point, formerly granted Lawrence Phillips, and by will given to his son William, who sold to Edward Weilder, who sold to John Wood, and by John Wood given and bequeathed to Hugh Montgomery, Oct. 2, 1689.—Francis Lord Howard.

Montgomery, Alexander (Colonial No. 26, page 5), 450 acres, in consideration of the payment of 45 shillings; in Albemarle County, on both sides of Birch Creek; June 25, 1747.—Wm. Gooch.

James Montgomery, (Colonial No. 33, page 404), 54 acres, consideration 5 shillings, in Augusta County, Nov. 10, 1757.—Robert Dinwiddie.

Montgomery, John (Colonial No. 33, page 484) 2 acres, consideration 5 shillings, in Princess Anne County, in Pagot's Neck and adjoining his land; Aug. 19, 1758. Montgomery, Robert, and Patrick Sharkey (No. 33 page 1045) 85 acres consideration 10 shillings in Augusta County called Sinking Springs; a branch of the Catawba River; July 11, 1761.—Francis Fauquhin.

Montgomery, Thomas (No. 34, page 856), 85 acres, in consideration of two persons: Thomas and Bridget Montgomery; in Albemarle County, on the south side of the branches of Davis's Creek, Feb. 14. 1761.—Francis Fauquhin.

Montgomery, John (Colonial No. 34, page 987), 150 acres, consideration 15 shillings, in Amherst County, on the branches of Buck Creek, near the land of Alexander Montgomery; March 25,1762.— Francis Fauquhin.

Montgomery, John (Colonial No. 35, page 40), 98 acres, consideration of 10 shillings, in Amherst County, on the branches of Rockfish Gap; March 25, 1762.—Francis Fauquhin.

Montgomery, David (Colonial No. 35, page 3621, 270 acres, consideration 30 shillings, in Amherst County, on Davis's Creek, near the land of Col. John Chiswell; Aug. 30, 1763.—Francis Fauquhin.

Montgomery, Matthew (Colonial No. 36, page 768), 172 acres, consideration 20 shillings, in Amherst County, on the side of the mountain and on the south side of Rockfish Gap River, and near land of David Montgomery; Aug. 30, 1763.—Francis Fauquhin.

Montgomery, David (Colonial No. 36, page 818). 22 acres, consideration 5 shillings, in Amherst County, on the Dutch Thoroughfare, near land of Col. Comax: July 26, 1765.—Francis Fauquhin.

Montgomery, John (Colonial No. 37, page 99), 84 acres, consideration 10 shillings, in Amherst County, on the south branches of Rockfish River, near the land of John Kilton and James Montgomery; April 10, 1767.— Francis Fauquhin.

Montgomery, Robert (Colonial No. 37. page 569), 60 acres, consideration 10 shillings, in Amherst County, on the south branch of the South Fork of Davis's Creek, of Rockfish River, near land of Robert Wright; July 10, 1768.—John Blair.

Montgomery, David, Jr. (Colonial No. 38, page 785), 71 acres, consideration 10 shillings, in Amherst County, on the branches of Dutch Creek, near land of Col. Randolph and Wm. Tiller; July 10, 1769.

Montgomery. John (Colonial No. 38, page 794), 30 acres, consideration 5 shillings, in August County, on Ball Pasture River, near land of Wm. Black; July 10, 1769.

Montgomery, James (Colonial No. 40, page 808), 150 acres, consideration 15 shillings, in Botetourt County, on James River, Ritch Patch. Aug. 1, 1772.

Montgomery. James (Colonial No. 42, page 702), 37 acres, consideration 5 shillings, in Botetourt County, at the heart of Roaring Roe, branch of James River; July 5, 1774.

Montgomery, James (Colonial No. 42, page 722), 113 acres consideration 10 shillings, on Patty's Creek, a branch of Cring creek, waters of James River, in Botetourt County, July 5, 1774.

(No grants to the name Montgomery in the Proprietary or Northern Neck Series.)

The following are from a book in the Land Office:

Montgomery, Matthew, for assisting in clearing a road to Kentucky, agreeable to late act of Assembly No. 1215, 300 acres.

Montgomery, John, as a captain in the late war between Great Britain and France (French and Indian War), 1779, No. 1023. 3000 acres.

Montgomery, Jasper, was a soldier in the late war between Great Britain and France (French and Indian War), No. 1031, 50 acres.

Montgomery, William, as a soldier in above war, No. 1034, 50 acres.

Montgomery, Samuel, as a soldier in above war, No. 1039, 50 acres.

Montgomery, John, as a soldier in a company of Rangers, No. 1200, 50 acres.

REVOLUTIONARY WAR.

From the Bounty Land Books, for services in the Revolutionary War:

Montgomery, James, Bounty Land, No. 1, p. 560, 2666 2-3 acres, as a lieutenant in the State Line for three years, May 3, 1784.

Montgomery, John, Bounty Land, No. 1, p. 562, 6000 acres, as a lieutenant colonel in the State Line for three years, May 3, 1784.

Montgomery, Hugh, Bounty Land, No. 2, p. 534, 100 acres, as a private in the Continental Line for three years, Dec. 31, 1806.

Montgomery, John, Bounty Land, No. 2, p. 599, 100 acres, as a private in the Continental Line, Jan. 6, 1808.

From a book of Certificates for Balances of Pay due for services in the Revolutionary War, which as formerly in the Auditor's office of the state of Virginia, but is now in the state library:

Montgomery, James, lieutenant Infantry, delivered Mr. J. Campbell, Dec. 25, 1783, 335 pounds, 12d; State Line, page 15.

Montgomery, John, lieutenant-colonel Infantry, delivered Wm. North, Feb. 25, 1785, 213 pounds, 5d. 6s.: State Line, page 16.

Montgomery, James, Captain State Navy, delivered himself, Nov. 30, 1787, 274 pounds, 3d. 7s.; State Line, page 16.

Montgomery, William, soldier in Infantry, delivered Mr. Broadhead, July 30, 1784, 16s; State Line, page 129.

Montgomery, William, soldier in Infantry, delivered Col. S. Cabee, March 13, 1784, 15 pounds, 9d., 4s.; Cont. Line, page 277.

From a Book of Payments to the State Militia, in State Library:

June 27, 1777—Joseph Montgomery, for taking up a horse belonging to the country, 1 pound 10, 6.

May 31, 1777—Capt. John Montgomery, for pay of his company to this day inclusive, 451 pounds 4, 12.

Oct. 30, 1777—Capt. John Montgomery—for pay for his company to July 23, cont., peer sect., 208 pounds 17, 11.

Nov. 25, 1777—John Montgomery, for pay of sundry persons as spies, 36 pounds, 5, 0.

Feb. 22, 1777—Capt. John Montgomery, for pay of his company in the Kentucky expedition, 1135 pounds, 17, 7.

Nov. 24, 1778—Capt. John Montgomery, pay for his company to Oct. 1778, pay roll, 1518 pounds, 7, 6.

Nov. 28, 1778—Capt. John Montgomery, for provisions, horse hire, etc., 552 pounds 7, 1.

Dec. 15, 1778—Col. John Montgomery, Cloths, etc., to governor of Illinois, 64 pounds 7, 0.

Dec. 16, 1778—Col. John Montgomery, for P. R. Anderson, for his own and the governor of Illinois expenses to Williamsburg, for certificate and receipt, 160 pounds 1, 4.

(The following is from Hening's Statutes at Large of Virginia.)

Montgomery, Alexander (Hening, XIII, page 117), a commissioner for a lottery for the benefit of North Twining, Oct. 1790.

Montgomery, Alexander (Hening, XIII), page 175, a commissioner for a lottery for the benefit of the Amicable Society, Oct. 1790.

Montgomery, Alexander (Hening, XIII, page 316, a) commissioner for a lottery to erect a bleaching mill near Stanton, Va., Oct. 1791.

Montgomery, James (Hening VII, page 199), of Augusta County for service in the French and Indian War, 10 shillings, Sept. 1758.

Montgomery, James, Jr. (Hening, VII, page 199), 10 shillings, Sept. 1758, for services in French and Indian War.

Montgomery, John (Hening. VII, page 191), 7s, Sept. 1758. do.

Montgomery, John (Hening, VII, page 195), 9s, Sept. 1758."

And Their Descendants

Montgomery, John (Hening, VII, page 199), 10s, Sept. 1758."

Montgomery. John (Hening, XI, page 164), trustee for Liberty Hall Academy-now Wallington and Lee University—Rockbridge County. Oct. 1782.

Montgomery, John (Hening, XI, page 335), commissioner to adjust the claims for land to Col. Rogers Clark and his officers, of the Illinois regiment, Oct. 1783.

Montgomery, John (Hening, XIV, page 266), trustee for the town of Hot Baths, Bath County, Oct. 1793.

Montgomery, John (Hening, XIV, page 308), commissioner to collect in Wythe County subscriptions to the Mutual Assurance Society, Nov. 1794.

Montgomery, Joseph (Hening, VII, page 199), Augusta County, for service in the French and Indian War, 10 shillings. Sept. 1758.

Montgomery, Robert (Hening, VII, page 199), Augusta County, for services in the French and Indian War, 10 shillings, Sept. 1758.

Montgomery, Samuel (Hening, VII, page 220), Prince William County, for provisions, 2 shillings, Sent. 1758.

Montgomery, Samuel (Hening, VII. page 199), Augusta County, for service in the French and Indian War, 10 shillings, Sept. 1758.

Montgomery, Thomas (Hening, XII, page 604), trustee for the town of Newport at the north of Grantico Creek, in Prince William County, Oct. 1786.

Montgomery, William (Hening, VII, page 210), Bedford County, for service in the French and Indian War, 5 shillings, Sept. 1758.

Montgomery, William (Hening, XII. page 396), trustee for the town of Stanford, in Lincoln County, Ky., Oct. 1781.

Montgomery, William (Hening, XII, page 456), commissioner to tobacco tax at 23 shillings per hundred, Oct. 1787.

You will observe that Robert had a land grant in Nantgemond County in 1679. Suffolk is the County Seat. That County is in south-eastern Virginia. Hugh had a land grant in Norfolk County in 1689, which joins Nantgemond County: Portsmouth, County Seat. Then Alexander in Albemarle County in 1747; Charlottesville, County Seat. James in Augusta County in 1757; Stanton, County Seat. John in Prince Anne County, 1758; Prince Anne, County Seat. Robert in Augusta County in 1761. Thomas in Albemarle County 1761. John in Amherst County: Amherst, County Seat; 1762: just above Lynchburg. David in Amherst County, 1763. Matthew in Amherst County in 1763. John in Amherst County in 1763. Robert in Amherst County in 1768. David in Amherst County in 1769. John in Augusta and Botetourt counties, west of Lynchburg. 1769; Fincastle, County Seat. James in Botetourt County, 1772; Fincastle, County Seat; also in 1774; also in 1790. Alexander in Augusta County, 1791; Stanton, County Seat. James in Augusta County in 1758. James, Jr., in Augusta County, 1858. John in Rockbridge Co., 1782; also in 1783. John in Bath County in 1793; Warm Springs, County Seat. John also in Wythe County in 1794; Wytheville, County Seat. Joseph in Augusta County in 1758; Stanton, County Seat. Robert in Augusta County, 1758. Samuel in Prince William County; Brentsville, County Seat; south-east of Washington, D. C., 1758. Thomas west of Lynchburg in Campbell County, 1758. William in Bedford County, 1758; Bedford City, County Seat; also in 1787 and in 1791.

The information received through Mr. Hemenway, the congressman referred to, will now be given. The rules of the War Department are such that only one person at a time can call for this kind of information, and can only obtain it on two names. So I asked for information concerning the Revolutionary War record of Samuel and Thomas Montgomery, the two men who settled in south-western Indiana in 1811-1807. Dr. T. J. Montgomery, of Owensville, Ind., asked for information of Hugh and Robert; and J. M. F. Montgomery of Owensville asked in regard to John and Joseph. Here are the replies:

Samuel Montgomery—no information.

Thomas Montgomery served as a lieutenant in Capt. John Martin's company of Clark's Illinois regiment of Virginia state troops, on the late Indian expedition under the command of Brigadier-General George Rogers Clark, Revolutionary War; joined Oct. 22, 1782; discharged Nov. 26, 1782; number of days in service, 36.

Hugh Montgomery served as a private in Captain Arthur Smith's company, 4th Virginia regiment, commanded by Col. Thomas Elliot, in the Revolutionary War. Commencement of pay, April 1, 1777; term of enlistment, two years. His name last appears on the roll for February 1778, with remarks, Discharged Feb. 15.

Robert Montgomery, no information.

Joseph Montgomery, no information.

John Montgomery served as a private in Captain Arthur Smith's company, 4th Virginia regiment, Revolutionary War, August, 1777. Term of enlistment, two years. Discharged Feb. 15, 1778.

The War Department further says: "It is proper to add, however, that the collection of Revolutionary War records in this office is far from complete, and that the absence therefrom of any name is by no means conclusive evidence that the person who bore the name did not serve in the Revolutionary army. It is suggested as a possibility that the desired information may be obtained from the secretary of the Virginia Historical Society, Richmond, Va."

REVOLUTIONARY SOLDIERS.

New York Historical Society,
170 Second Ave.
New York, Sept. 13, 1899.

H. P. Montgomery—

Dear Sir: After an examination of all the material here bearing on the war of the American Revolution, I regret to state that I fail to find the name of Robert Montgomery of Virginia.

On page 285 of Saffelt's records of the Revolutionary War, third edition, 1894. I find the following:

"Humphrey Montgomery, private in Captain Lapsley's company. Colonel Nathaniel Gist's Virginia regiment, 1777."

Possibly this Montgomery may be of the same family as Robert. The state of Virginia issued land grants for services in the Revolution. I suggest that your correspondent communicate with the state authorities; also the Virginia Historical Society.

Very truly yours,
ROBERT H. KELLY.

MONTGOMERYS OF SOUTH CAROLINA, TENNESSEE, MISSOURI AND OTHER STATES.

It is believed that George Montgomery, earl of Eglinton, had three sons—George, Hugh and William. Bancroft gives an account of George Montgomery, afterwards Lord Eglinton, who came to America in 1760 and was active in the Indian war of the South. It is supposed his younger brothers, Hugh and William, came to South Carolina about 1780. In the annals of Newberry, S. C, by O'Neal, 1858, an account is given of Hugh and William Montgomery and Patrick Bradley being fined in the February term of court (1797) for assault and contempt of court; the two former $60 each, the latter $20. This would indicate, from the size of the fine, that they were well connected and rather wealthy. Nothing more is known of this Hugh Montgomery. But William (some say John) had three sons, who came with him to America:

1. John, probably born in 1770, had six sons, whose families settled in South Carolina, Georgia, Florida and Alabama. Thomas, born probably in 1772, left no sons. Robert, the youngest of these three sons, was born about 1774; married Esther Spence. He died 1820, leaving six sons and two daughters: 1. Andrew, who died in infancy. 2. John Montgomery died many years ago. leaving one son, John Calvin Montgomery, who is now (1903), living at Verona, Marshall County, Tenn. Has been twice married; has several sons —Robert, James and Granville. 3. Thomas Montgomery, born Jan. 26, 1808, married Mary Fleming, Nov. 20, 1828; moved to Middle Tennessee, 1844. During the Civil War he was loyal to the Union and had to leave the South, so he journeyed north until he reached Bloomfield, Iowa. Owing to the rigorous climate of that state he could not survive long; he died March 2, 1864, and is buried at Bloomfield, Ia. He was a large land and slave owner in Bedford County, Tenn. He had nine children; the six sons all became prominent men:

And Their Descendants

1. Robert S. Montgomery, born at Newberry, S. C, Nov. 30, 1829; lives at Palmetto, Tenn.; married Susan Dening Bryant, March 13, 1855. She was born Aug. 29, 1831; died April 19, 1881; children eight: 1. Alice E. Montgomery, born July 3, 1856; married J. Frank Tilman, registrar of the U. S. treasury under Cleveland's last administration. She has three boys, aged 23, 8 and 4 years. 2. Mary Montgomery, born Oct. 11, 1858, died June 15, 1864. 3, James D. Montgomery, born Oct. 3, 1860, died March 26, 1862. 4. Thomas A. Montgomery, born July 31, 1863, died Dec. 24, 1890. 5. Lillie Montgomery, born Feb. 15, 1866, married Dr. F. C. Ransom and has one son and two daughters. 6. Dening Montgomery, born March 12, 1871 lives in Washington, D. C.; married and has one son. 7. Gertrude Montgomery, born Oct. 9, 1873, married Ross A. Woods and has one daughter. 8. Robert H. Montgomery, born Jan. 23, 1876, lives in Oswego, Kansas; married—no children.

2. Sarah Elizabeth Montgomery, born Feb. 26, 1833 married Samuel Carpenter, who embarked in the mercantile business 1855 at Palmetto, Tenn., with his brother-in-law, Robert S. Montgomery, above. During the Civil War they had to leave the South also, and with his father and family settled at Bloomfield, Iowa. Peter Carpenter, his father, died in Iowa, as did also his father-in-law. "Thus these two old patriots sleep side by side because of their loyalty to their country and flag." Robert P. Carpenter, of the Deeming investment company, Oklahoma City, Okla., is a son of Elizabeth Montgomery-Carpenter.

3. Mary Jane Montgomery, born May 23, 1835.

4. Joseph T. Montgomery, born Jan. 6, 1838, lives at Yukon, Livingston, County, Tenn.

5. John B. Montgomery, born in Newberry, S. C., Aug. 30, 1840, lives at Springfield. Mo., and is quite a wealthy man; is a retired merchant; married Mary E. Temple, near Farmington, Tenn., March 15, 1866; children seven:

1. Ada B. Montgomery, born at Bedford, Tenn., Nov. 2, 1867; married Charles J. Rose at Oswego, Kansas, Oct. 10, 1888; now living at Springfield, Mo.
2. Mollie H. Montgomery, born at Bedford, Tenn., Aug. 6, 18)9; married Joseph A. O'Day, Sept. 13, 1887, died Aug. 8, 1900, at Marshall, Mo.;

The Montgomerys

children three: 1, Paul, born July 19, 1888. 2, Marie, born Oct. 26, 1890. 3, Ernestine, born April 18, 1893. All these live at Springfield, Mo.

3. Jennie E. Montgomery, born at Bedford, Tenn., May 22. 1871; married Henry Schneider, Aug 16, 1893; children two: 1, Montgomery, born March 26, 1896; 2, Christine, born Oct. 18. 1898.

4. Myrtle J. Montgomery, born at Bedford, Tenn., Feb. 9, 1873; married George A. McGregor, June 27, 1894; she died May 16, 1900 at Oswego, Kansas; children two: 1, Eloise, born Aug. 15, 1895. 2. Allen, born Jan. 30, 1900. They live at Springfield. Mo.

5. Willie B. Montgomery, born at Oswego, Kansas, Feb. -13, 1876, died July 26, 1896.

6. Oliver Montgomery, born 1878, died in infancy.

7. L. Claire Montgomery, born at Oswego, Kansas, July 8, 1879; lives with parents in Springfield, Mo.: single 1903.

6. Thomas S. Montgomery, born March 30, 1843, at Newberry, S. C.; lives at Palmetto, Tenn.; married Maggie L. Hoyle, Sept. 27. 1866; children six: 1. Infant daughter, born July 6. 1867. 2. Flora Esther Montgomery, born Oct. 12, 1869; married Dr. Thomas R. Logan, of Farmington, Tenn., Dec. 27, 1893; no children. 3. Thomas Clarence Montgomery, born Dec. 26, 1871; married Madge Bryant, June 25, 1901. 4. Mary Ethel Montgomery, born May 2, 1875: married Rev. John Royal Harris, of Lewisburg, Tenn., March 16, 1898; died Sept. 18, 1898. 5. Susan Leah Montgomery, born May 15, 1880. 6. Hoyle Fleming Montgomery, born Oct. 25, 1882.

7. William A. Montgomery, born April 1846 lives at Farmington, Tenn.

8. and 9. Margaret and Henry Clay Montgomery, twins, born July 4, 1849.

Robert Montgomery, born about 1810, fourth son of Robert Montgomery, Sr., is now (1903), living at Palmetto, Tenn., at the advanced age of 93 years; children three: 1. Etta Montgomery, married James R. Mount and has four children—three boys and one girl. 2. John O. Montgomery married and has two children. 3. Jane L. Montgomery, married I. T. Wiggs; children seven—one son and six daughters.

Andrew Montgomery, born 1824, the youngest son of Robert Montgomery, Sr., died June 1900, at Carmi, Ill., at the age of 78 years. He was a minister in the United Presbyterian church. His son, Prof. S. A.

Montgomery, was for some years principal of the Grayville. Ill., schools. He died in 1880.

J. Knox Montgomery, the only living son of Rev. Andrew Montgomery, is also a minister in the United Presbyterian church. He is a radical third-party Prohibitionist, and stumped the state of Ohio for governor on that ticket in 1900. Hs home at that time was Cincinnati. Ohio. He had formerly been pastor of a church in Chicago. The last I heard of him he was living in Asheville, N. C. He is a well-known lecturer. Some of his subjects are "Help Somebody," "Cain, Pharaoh, and Company," "The Church that Gets There," etc. I have seen many complimentary notices of his ability as a lecturer. He has three children: 1. John Knox, Jr., now (1901) 7 years old: 2. Don Alonzo, five years old: 3. Son, born May l5, 1900— not yet named, but there is talk of naming him Frank S., for F. S. Montgomery of Shepard, Ohio.

MONTGOMERYS OF SOUTH CAROLINA, MISSISSIPPI AND OTHER STATES.
(By Mrs., Judge G. Q. Hall of Meridian, Miss.)

The earliest knowledge we have of the Montgomerys is of their residence, in County Ayr, Scotland. After the revolutionary times of that country, we next hear of them in the North of Ireland; and it was from old Ireland that they emigrated to America and became the ancestors of the numerous families of that name now scattered all over these United States.

There has come down to us somehow, from somewhere in the dim distance, a tradition that the name originated from a Mount Goma supposed to be in Scotland, but not on the map of this day. The inhabitants of that community were called Mountgomas; and this was perverted into Montgomery.

This sketch is intended to treat of that branch of the family which emigrated to America about 1666—three brothers: William, Hugh and Robert Montgomery. They landed and resided in Virginia, near Jamestown. Their descendants sought "other fields and pastures new." So later we find, in what is known as the old Waxhaw settlement of South Carolina, a family of six brothers— Alexander, Robert, Joseph, Hugh, William and Samuel— sons of a Hugh Montgomery, who to the best of our knowledge is traced as a son of William, the emigrant of 1666.

The Montgomerys

This family had accumulated considerable wealth in South Carolina, for those times, but their estates were devastated by the British and Tories.

Alexander was the first of this family to leave his native state to better his fortune. He first went to Tennessee, then to Mississippi, in 1782, when that state was a Spanish province, and settled in what was known as the Natchez district. Here he prospered and accumulated much wealth, and occupied high positions among his fellow men, as will be seen in Claiborne's History of Mississippi, p. 230.

His first wife was a daughter of Richard King, whom he married in 1797. The issue of that marriage was: 1. Clarissa, who married Judge Whitney of Jefferson County, and who has left numerous descendants. 2. Samuel K. who lived near Natchez; died with Yellow fever in 1848, leaving no descendants. Next was A. B. Franklin who also died with yellow fever in 1823. The next child was Louisiana.

Alexander's second wife was Lydia Swayze. Of this marriage two children reached maturity: Hon. Prosper K., of Jefferson County, who raised a large family and had several sons in the Confederate Army. He was a very bright man and possessed a wonderful memory, but was delicate in health all his life. He was of a very affectionate disposition and truly devoted to his family, and well versed in the history of the Montgomery family. Mrs. J. M. Hickey of Greenville, Miss., a granddaughter of his, promised a sketch of his descendants, but it has not reached me in time to be included in this connection.

The other son of Alexander is and James Jefferson, who was the father of Judge Frank A. Montgomery, now residing at Rosedale, Miss., in his 73rd year. He was a colonel in the Civil War, in 1st Mississippi cavalry, Armstrong's brigade; member of the legislature from 1880 to '96, and one term judge of Fourth Court Circuit District of Mississippi. He was twice sent by his state to Washington, D. C, to urge before Congress the importance of the government looking after the levees of the Mississippi river. He is the author of "Reminiscences of a Mississippian in Peace and War." This is a book of 305 pages, which it will pay any one to purchase and read.

He has an interesting family of nine children: Three sons— Jefferson, Frank and Joseph, all lawyers; six daughters—Martha, the wife of State

Senator E. H. Moore; Harriet, the wife of Dr. John Dulaney: Tillie, Lotie, Fadjie, and Anna.

The Alexander Montgomery heretofore mentioned was followed to Mississippi by four of his brothers—Robert, Joseph, William, and Samuel—but at different periods. Hugh, the remaining brother, settled in Georgia, and his posterity was lost sight of by the rest of the family.

William was the father of W. Pinkney Montgomery, who has numerous descendants, many of whom are settled in the Mississippi Delta, and are men of sterling worth and integrity: also one son, Eugene, of Natchez, Miss. Of the descendants of Robert and Joseph, this writer knows nothing.

Samuel Montgomery, one of the six brothers, was born in South Carolina in 1764. He married Nelly Steen of that state, and three children were born to them: Nelly, Hugh and James. About 1790, Samuel and family moved to Kentucky. This trip was made overland, principally on horseback. It must be remembered that at that day people traveled in companies or caravans, as the country was wild and filled with savages. Many were the skirmishes this company had with the Indians on their tedious trip. Samuel's residence in Kentucky was for about 13 years. Soon after reaching that state he lost his first wife, and thereafter married Margaret Crockett (born 1770), a daughter of Andrew Crockett (born 1747) and Mary McKin (born 1753) of Tennessee. Of this marriage, while still in Kentucky, were born Andrew (1792), Mary (1794), Elizabeth (1796), John (1798), Eli (1800). In 1803, Samuel and family moved to Mississippi, coming down the Mississippi river on a flat-boat. The fourth son, Alexander, by the second marriage, was born on the boat, before they landed at Natchez. After reaching Mississippi three daughters were born: Tennessee (1805), Jane (1807), Sophia (1809).

Samuel purchased a plantation about 15 miles east of Natchez, and only about 9 miles from Washington, then the seat of government of the Territory; the center of culture and refinement. Conflicting land titles attracted many lawyers to this place, and it was the haunt of politicians. It was noted for its wine parties and dinners, not unusually followed by a duel, the code of honor in those days. Samuel prospered in this new and rich country, raised a family of twelve children, and died about 1828. He represented his County in the legislature in 1821-22. The children of Samuel married as follows:

Nelly Steen married a Mr. Crow; several children.

Mary, daughter of the second marriage, married Isaac Briscoe; nine children.

Tennessee married Dr. Penquite; two children.

Jane married William Collins; four children.

Sophia married John Cameron.

Elizabeth married Isaac Selser in 1812. He came from Pennsylvania to Mississippi about 1800.

Elizabeth was a woman of great force of character, possessed a good knowledge of medicine, and as physicians were scarce then in Mississippi she often ministered to her sick neighbors, for sweet charity's sake, as doctor, nurse and general advisor. They resided in Adams County, at what is still known as "Old Selser Town." About 1825 they moved to Hinds County and became quite wealthy, owning over 100 slaves. Selser represented that County in the legislature in 1852. Their children were: Alfred, who died at the age of 12 years; Theresa (born 1815); Agnes Letitia (born 1817); Franklin, died in infancy: Tennessee, died aged 15 years: Eliza, died in infancy; Elizabeth Montgomery (born 1824); Isaac Montgomery (born 1827); Juletta Sophia (horn 1830); Margaret Annie (born 1832); James Montgomery (born 1835).

Theresa Selser married three times—P. Norris. K. Martin, and lastly Dr. D. B. Nailer of Warren County; no children.

Agnes Letitia married Dr. Rossman of N. C.; two children— Rowan and Eugenia. Rowan married Irvine Halsnuth; five children. Eugenia married Chas. B. Allen, a large planter of Warren County; seven children.

Elizabeth M. Selser married Spencer W. Montgomery (1843), no relation: one child, Mary, who married Lieutenant Wm. Noble, of Walker's Texas brigade, in 1865, who died in 1881; Children seven. One died unmarried, and the second, Edward Spencer, was accidentally shot when 17 years old. Third, Elizabeth Montgomery, married a Mr. Oliphant, Fourth, William Frank, Fifth, Mary Virginia, Sixth, Martha Frances, Seventh, Essie Etta.

Dr. Isaac M. Selser was married twice; no children.

Juletta Selser, a beautiful woman, married three times—First, Wesley Rossman of N. C. Second, Col. A. B. Reading, Third, Mr. Waldrip of Mexico. She is now a widow living in Washington state with her only child by the first marriage, Letitia, who married first Mr. Vogt; four children: Albert, Mabel,

And Their Descendants

Frank and Allen. Second marriage to Absalom Stamply; two children—Grace and Rossman.

Margaret Selser married Lytleton Johnson of Brandon; six children: Liela, Frank, Margaret, Effie, Howard and Arthur.

James Montgomery Selser, youngest child of Elizabeth and Isaac, was born on the old plantation—"Poplar Grove," Hinds County: graduated from the University of Mississippi, and made a brave Confederate soldier in Gen. Wirt Adams' cavalry. He was a prosperous planter before the Civil War. In 1857 he married Kate Lindsey, of Jackson, Miss., who still survives him. Their children were: Ida and Lucy, who died in infancy; Aida, who married C.A. Reading; Isaac M., who married Mary Bush: Kate, who married C. W. Grafton; Virginia, who married George W. Stuart first, W. B. Whitehead second; Theresa and James, who died in youth. Elizabeth M. married A. C. Lowry; two children. Frank N., William L. Susie L. and Claude, unmarried, live with their mother in Jackson, Miss.

James Montgomery, son of Samuel and Nelly (Steen) Montgomery, married and moved to Texas and has descendants in that state.

Hugh, the oldest son of Samuel and Nelly, was born in South Carolina, 1785, married Mary Crockett (born 1783), of Tennessee, the youngest sister of his step-mother. He established a home in Jefferson County, Mississippi, seven miles east of Fayette, the County Seat. Here he raised a large family, and died aged 84 years. He was a large planter and slave-holder. He was red-headed, but had only one red-headed child; but quite frequently a red-headed grandchild bobbed up, and to every such he presented a negro. The children of the above Hugh Montgomery were: Telytha, Theresa, Melissa, Jane, Lafayette, Andrew Jackson, Samuel Crockett and Elizabeth.

Telytha married Isaiah Coleman; children —Elias, Green, Christopher, and Lucilla who married first a Cameron, second Ed Guice; and Ann, who married a Whitney.

Theresa, second daughter of Hugh, married Wm. Herter; three children—Sallie, Bettie and Charlie.

Melissa, third daughter, married James Montgomery (no relation); eight children: One daughter married Andrew Rembert, and left two girls—Melissa and Mollie.

Jane, fourth daughter, married Samuel Ratcliff; no children.

Elizabeth died unmarried.

Lafayette, who married Catharine Galbreat, moved to Madison County in 1835 and bought a plantation. He had no children, but raised seven orphans. He was a large planter and slave-holder before the Civil War, and represented his County in the legislature in 1882. He is still living (1903) at the age of 90, on the first homestead he established. His mind is still clear and vigorous, and he is honored and respected by all who know him.

Andrew Jackson, second son of Hugh, born at the old homestead in Jefferson County, Sept. 5, 1816, was educated at Jesuit College, Bardstown, Ky. He moved to Madison County in 1844 and bought a plantation adjoining that of his brother Lafayette, where he raised a family, and died Jan. 23, 1868. He was a prosperous planter and slave-holder. In politics he was a Whig, but after his native state seceded from the Union his sympathies were with the Confederacy, and though in the field only a short time he was in the service of the Confederate states, and sent two sons to the front who came out unharmed.

He married, first, Sarah Ann Cameron. Two sons of this marriage: Daniel Hugh, who married Lena Stuart; two children—Kate and Nola; Dougal Prosper, who married first Jennie Magruder; four children—Emmett, Bruce, Kate, and Hugh, who is married to Willie Stewart—one child, Lena May. Dougal's second wife was Jennie Tompkins; one child, Andrew. The two brothers, Hugh and Dougal, served through the Civil War; the former in 21st Miss, regiment, and the latter in the 4th Miss. Andrew Jackson's second wife was Susan Latham Dixon, born 1832: was raised in Jefferson County, and married in Canton, Miss., in 1851; eight children of this marriage, two dying in youth—Willie and Lucy; Kate married G.Q. Hall of Meridian, Miss., judge of the 10th circuit court district, and owner of the famous Arundel Lithia Springs; two children—William Montgomery of Meridian, a promising young lawyer, who married Isabel Urquhart Harris of Jackson, Miss., and has one child, Francis Urquhart; Ethelbert Barksdale, connected with the New Orleans & Northeastern railroad-unmarried.

Arthur, who married Anna Mann, occupies a high position with the Southern Express Company at Atlanta, Ga.; no children.

Laura, who married Emmett Savage of Canton, Miss., has four children living: Lula, Kate, Herman and Arthur.

Lafayette, prominently connected with the Ill. Central railroad at Jackson, Miss., married first Clara Atkinson; no children living. Second wife, Lutie Smart, of Arkansas; two children—Catharine and Lafayette Hanson.

Andrew Jennings, a planter and merchant, married first Alice Beard; two children—Lafayette and Arthur. Second wife, Evie Smith; one child—Thomas Jones.

Susie Dixon, unmarried, is living in South Carolina.

Samuel Crockett Montgomery, youngest son of Hugh and Mary established a home one mile from his father's old homestead in Jefferson County. He was a captain in the Confederate army: married first Jane Kinison; two sons—Hugh and Samuel: both died without issue. Second wife was Mary Weatherly; six children: Charlie, who married Letha Scott; Rosa, who married first Samuel Ballon, second John Yeizer; Retta, who married McRaven; Kate, who married John Russum; Clem and Russum died unmarried.

Andrew, the fourth child of Samuel and Margaret (Crockett) Montgomery, married Margaret Norris; eight children.

John, the fifth child of Samuel and Margaret, married Sallie Brown: had one child, a daughter.

Eli, the sixth child, married a cousin, Mary Crockett, daughter of Eli Crockett (born 1779), who was a son of Andrew Crockett before mentioned. Of this marriage three children: Matilda, Tulula and Wallace. Matilda married first Malcolm Cameron; one son, John, who was quite prominent in his state; once a popular candidate for governor. Her second husband was S. S. Champion; four children of this marriage, none of whom survive; only one grandchild, a son of her youngest son Sydney, who bears his father's name. Tulula married Joe Lipscome. Wallace, the only son of Eli and Mary Montgomery, is now living in the Mississippi Delta. He was a brave Confederate soldier; married, first, Mary Denson; one son of this marriage, Eli, now living. Wallace married Cora Green in 1864; by this marriage he has two sons—William Alexander, and Robert, prominent business men of Jackson, Miss. Alex., as he is familiarly called, is assistant cashier of The Merchants Bank; married Lillian Smith of Jackson, Miss, great-great-niece of

Jefferson Davis, the Confederate president. They have two children —Lillian Ann and Annie Davis.

These sons of Samuel and Margaret, mentioned, were wealthy planters, and men of sterling worth and integrity.

Alexander, the youngest son—the infant born on the flat-boat— was a lawyer of marked ability, often measuring arms at the bar with the renowned S. S. Prentiss, and many times the victor. He was on the supreme bench of Mississippi in 1831. He lived in Natchez, and in Rodney, and a few years in New Orleans. He died in 1878. His first wife was Margaret Gilbert, by whom be had two daughters. The eldest, Margaret, married Ben Roach and has one daughter living in Houston, Texas—Mrs. Elise Epperson. The youngest daughter married Honel Moss; had two daughters: Margaret, who married Geo. E. Wilkinson of Yazoo, Mary E. who married Geo. S. Dawson, of Yazoo City and has an interesting family of three children; one son bearing the full name of his great grandfather.

Alexander's second wife was the widow Roach, by whom he had no children.

The Montgomerys, being of Scotch-Irish descent, were, generally speaking, Presbyterians in faith—except where they had married into other denominations and followed their wives, religiously. The older set were Whigs in politics, but those of the present generation are generally Democrats, that being the white man's party of the South.

The Montgomerys are considered long-lived people, many of them going beyond man's allotted time—three score and ten years.

MONTGOMERYS OF SOUTH CAROLINA, MISSISSIPPI AND OTHER STATES.

In 1773 there were among the passengers of a certain ship that left Ireland seven Montgomerys—four brothers and three sisters: 1. James; 2. David; 3. Hugh; 4. Charles; 5. Margaret; 6. Jane; 7. Nancy. They landed in Charleston, S. C, a British post, as all the United States was at that time in the possession of the British. Martha Montgomery, another sister, left Ireland in 1775 and came to Wilmington, N. C, and traveled over-land to

Charleston, S. C. Her trip was not on a railroad, as the custom is now, without danger or fatigue, but she spent four weeks on the road—a road that led through thick woods, across un-bridged streams, among uncivilized savages and wild beasts.

Of these brothers, James, David and Hugh married and settled in South Carolina, and died there.

Charles, the other of these brothers, married Margaret Reynolds, an Irish girl who came to this country on the same vessel with him. He wooed her while on the wide, wide ocean, and received her consent to marry him. One year after reaching their adopted land (1774) they were married in Charleston and continued to live in South Carolina until their death. They had twelve children. 1. Sarah; 2. Jane; 3. Charles, born 1781; 4. William, born 1783; 5. James; 6. John; 7. Margaret; 8. David, born 1788; 9. Mary; 10. Nancy; 11. Martha; 12. Hugh, born May 15, 1796.

The above information is as related to E. W. Fulton by David Montgomery, son of Charles Montgomery, 1871.

The older ones of the second generation of this family came over from Fairfield district (or County), in South Carolina, to Oktibbeha County, Miss., between the years 1835 and 1845, and lived near Starkville for many years; and all died there but William, who moved to Hinds County, Miss. The descendants of these families are found in many parts of the South and West, as will be seen in the following account.

Charles Montgomery, Jr., son of Charles, Sr., born probably 1781 (No. 3, Gen. 2), married ___; children nine: 1. James D.; 2. Charles; 3. William T: 4. David F.; 5. John T.; 6. Samuel H.; 7. Mary; 8. Harriett; 9. Nancy.

James D. Montgomery, born March 13, 1809, (No. 1. Gen. 3) moved from Oktibbeha County to Holmes, Miss., and died there Sept. 1851; children seven:
   1. John G. Montgomery (No. 1, Gen. 4). A farmer, who has lived near Dumont, Miss., since 1875, and is in favorable circumstances, and is truly grateful for these blessings, Children seven, all of whom are dead but three. Two died after they were grown, and one of them had a family of seven children.

William P. Montgomery, second son of James D. Montgomery, was killed near Corinth, Miss., in the Civil War, 1862.

Samuel H. Montgomery, third son of James D.

James K. Montgomery, fourth child of James D.

David F. Montgomery, fifth child, died when about ten years old.

Jane Montgomery, sixth child.

Sarah Montgomery, seventh child.

William Montgomery, son of Charles, Sr., born June 16, 1783 (No. 4, Gen. 2), first married and had one daughter. Mary Philippe Montgomery; second, married Rebecca Kincaid; children eight: 1. Alexander K.; 2. Sarah; 3. Spencer W.; 4. Charles W.; 5. Rebecca C; 6. William Franklin; 7. Ann K; 8. Hugh B.

1. Alexander K. Montgomery, born Sept. 5, 1813 (No. 1, Gen. 3), married Elmira Moore, daughter of General Wm. Moore of Tullahoma. Tenn., children six:

1. George W. Montgomery, of Tululah, La., a prosperous farmer and for many years state senator from Madison parish. He was a lieutenant in the Confederate army; married Rosa Treasvant Van Benthuysen, and has one son, George W. Montgomery, Jr., and one daughter, Cornelia Montgomery.

2. Edward C. Montgomery, at present and for many years past one of the appellate judges of that district, and also an ex-state senator. He was a lieutenant in the Confederate army; married Henrietta Miller; children six: Sallie died at the age of 3; Elmina died at 12 years; Callie, Olivia, Alexander, and Edward C. now live at home with the judge.

3. Elizabeth Montgomery married William H. Bush, a lieutenant of Montgomery's Scouts in the Confederate army. Both are dead; left one child, Bettie Bush, who married Dr. George Dorsey, of Vicksburg, Miss.

4. Alexander K. Montgomery, Jr., married Mary Treasvant. Both died near Lamar, La.

5. Olivia Montgomery, of 500 Hellory street, New Orleans, La., married Frank V. Rochester; children four: Robert Robb. John U., Virginia and Frank.

6. Lanson M. Montgomery, of Lamar, La., married Lola____; children, Elmira and Marion.

2. Sarah Montgomery, second child of William, born May 13, 1816 (No. 2, Gen. 3) married Wilmot R. Gibbs of Columbus, S. C, and moved near Edwards, Miss. Their son, William Gibbs was a soldier in the Confederate

army, in the 12th Mississippi regiment, and lost a leg in the battle of The Wilderness, and died soon after the war ended.

Their daughter, Rebecca Gibbs married Dr. G. McD. Brumby now of New Orleans, La. Their children are William, Sallie, Maggie, Robert and Lizzie. The latter married Dr. McMullen and now lives with her mother in New Orleans, La. Maggie married a Mr. Alston and lives at Delhi, La. Sallie married and now lives at Honolulu. The two boys, both physicians, live in Texas.

3. Spencer W. Montgomery, born April 12, 1819 (No. 3, Gen. 3), married Elizabeth Selser. Both are dead, leaving one daughter, Mary R. Noble, of Dallas, Texas, who has seven children: One died unmarried; 2. Edward Spencer, was accidentally shot when 17 year old; 3. Elizabeth, married a Mr. Oliphant; 4. William Frank; 5. Mary Virginia; 6. Martha Francis; 7. Essie Etta

4. Charles W. Montgomery, born Feb. 2, 1822 (No. 4, Gen. 3), married Olivia Feree Moore, also a daughter of General William Moore. Her middle name is for Captain Feree who married her grandmother in one of the forts in Kentucky during the American Revolution, and through whom the daughter and granddaughters and great-granddaughters of Gen. Wm. Moore, a soldier of two wars (Florida and 1812) trace their title to "Daughters of the American Revolution." Charles and Olivia are both dead, and leave sorrowing them only two sons out of eight that were born to them. Archibald Zell and Robert died before they reached their teens; one died in infancy; Lawson Rochester, Charles Kincaid and Joseph Cooper died just as they reached their young manhood—splendid young men, loved by all who knew them. Lawson Rochester, or "Ches," as he was familiarly known among his comrades of the Confederate army, was at 15 years of age recognized as one of the most daring and efficient scouts in the army; a member of his brother William A.'s company of scouts, he would have been next in command to Lieutenant E. O, but he declined the honor.

COLONEL W. A. MONTGOMERY.

One of the most distinguished as well as most useful citizens of Edwards is Col. W. A. Montgomery, whose chivalrous spirit, exalted character and kindly nature win the hearts of all who know him.

The Montgomerys

Col. Wm. A. Montgomery
Edwards, Mississippi

Col. Montgomery was born Oct. 18, 1844, and was at Union College, Murfreesboro, Tenn., when the war commenced. He was ordered home by his father when the state of Mississippi seceded from the Union, and was among the first volunteers from Mississippi, notwithstanding his father's protest on account of his youth. He joined the Raymond Fencibles of the Twelfth Mississippi regiment, and went with that regiment to Virginia for the first year. He was discharged near the end of his first enlistment, and returned to Mississippi and joined the cavalry command of General Wirt Adams.

Young Montgomery made his first military reputation at Fourteen Mile Creek Bridge on May 12, 1863, the day that Gen. Gregg fought the battle of Raymond. Having been sent by Col. Gates, who was then commanding at Edwards, to burn the bridge across Fourteen Mile Creek, to impede Grant's army, and after burning all the bridges below the Dillon bridge on the night of the 11th, he stationed himself, with his detail of about ten men, at the bridge, perhaps one mile from Grant's headquarters, and over which the army was to pass next morning. About midnight, while the bridge was burning, six negro men from the farm of Mr. Thomas Hainan, who lived nearby, came up, and, thinking they were Yankees, proposed to show where their old master was in the woods nearby, with all his movable personal effects. Montgomery sent to the Dillon place, got six axes, and put them all to work; and when Grant's army moved next morning he not only had the bridge destroyed, but had a breastwork of trees on the opposite bank of the creek, where he awaited their approach, giving orders to his men not to fire until they heard his gun. As the stillness of that May morning was broken by the solitary sound of Montgomery's gun, fired into the head of the column at short range, every gun in the small Confederate squad was emptied into the squadron of Federal cavalry. After this repulse the Federals charged again to near where the bridge had stood, to meet another volley from the handful of Confederates; and when the third charge was made to the bridge itself, a Federal horseman in front exclaimed: "My God! The bridge is burned." Soon not less than fifty pieces of artillery and five thousand rifles were ranged upon the hill about half a mile away, and bore with fury upon the spot where Montgomery and his men lay; but they all escaped unhurt during a lull in the firing. This checked Grant's army on that road for the day. General Grant in his official report says that they had quite a spirited engagement at Fourteen Mile Creek, in which they lost 24 men killed and wounded.

At Champion Hill, four days later, Montgomery so attracted the attention of Gen. Wirt Adams that he promoted him to chief of scouts, which position he held until promoted to captain of scouts known as Montgomery's.

Many daring deeds after that made him exceedingly popular with his command. At Champion Hill, Jackson, Clinton, Coleman's Cross Roads, Tinnin Monument, Bear Creek, Mechanicsburg, Decatur, Calhoun Station, Deer Creek, Pritchard's Lane, Goodman, Concord Church, and Gypsy, he was conspicuous for his daring and his skill as an officer.

He surrendered with his company on the 12th of March, 1865, at Joinsville, Ala.

A more daring act, perhaps, than any done in war, and one of lasting benefit to the state, was performed in 1874, during the days of Republican rule. When Ames' negro militia had been organized in Warren County and a fight with the white men seemed inevitable (a fight which would not only have resulted in great loss of life, would in all probability have changed the history of the state), Colonel Montgomery made his way up into the camp of the negroes alone and induced them to disband.

The Montgomerys

He organized and led the body of citizens that first went to Jackson and induced Governor Ames to disarm and disband the negro militia, and even as early as 1870 he was the organizer in Hinds and Warren counties of the "White Camellia"—an order intended to resist the encroachment of the African upon the Anglo-Saxon race.

To Col. Montgomery, as much as to any other leader, is due the overthrow of the Republican Party and restoration of white supremacy.

Colonel Montgomery was appointed colonel of the Second Mississippi regiment in the war with Spain. Since the disbanding of his regiment he has been engaged in the practice of law and is looking after his planting interests.

He is a Knight-Templar, Knight of Honor, Knight of Pythias, Woodsman, and member of the American Legion of Honor. He is a Baptist, and a member of the board of trustees of Mississippi College, and has served in both branches of the legislature. He is now a candidate for Congress in the new Eighth district, with a strong following in all of the counties. If elected he will no doubt be of great service to his country in the halls of Congress as he has been in times of war.—The Raymond Gazette.

He was married to Miss J. Mella Dufree in 1868, and by that marriage had five children. Will and Hugh died in infancy. Patrick Henry, his son, was married in 1893 to Mattie Noblin and had one son, Robert N. Montgomery; his widow surviving him. He died in the prime of his manhood, in Edwards, Miss., May 15, 1901; a man among men, loved, honored and respected by all.

Col. Montgomery's second son, Charles W. was born Sept. 14, 1875, is now living near Tallalulah, La. Olivia, his oldest and only living daughter, married S. S. Champion, of Champion Hill, Miss.. Nov. 11, 1896. He died of yellow fever, Sept. 6, 1897; then a member of the Mississippi legislature. She has one son, Syd. S. Champion.

J. Mella, the first wife of Col. Montgomery, died March 28, 1882. He married, April 16, 1884, Bettie C. Henry, daughter of Capt. B. W. Henry of Edwards, Miss. To this union were born William Alexander Montgomery, Jr., July 29, 1886; Mella, named for his first wife, born July 18, 1888, died Oct. 12, 1889; Wilkins Henry Montgomery, born Feb. 28. 1895.

And Their Descendants

Victor V. Montgomery, the other surviving son of Charles Warren and Olivia Feree Montgomery, and brother of Col. Wm. A. Montgomery, was born July 21, 1861, and now resides on the old homestead near Edwards, Miss. He married Nellie Haynes of Vicksburg, Miss., and has seven children: Victor K., Jr., M. Louise, Joseph C., T. Haynes, Nellie B., and Bettie H. Hattie C. died in 1900.

5. Rebecca C. Montgomery, born March 27, 1825 (No. 5, Gen. 3), married Joseph T. Cooper, of Starkville, Miss. They have one daughter, Annie, who married Joe Beverly; their children are: 1. Lawrence G. Beverly, born March 9, 1878 (Gen. 4). 2. Joseph C. Beverly, born June 14, 1879. 3. Roy R. Beverly, born Nov. 16, 1880. 4. Willie P. Beverly, born March 5, 1887; dead. 5. Mary O. Beverly, born April 14, 1890. 6. Mattie V. Beverly, born March 30, 1891; dead. 7. Floyce R. Beverly, born Sept. 9, 1892. 8. Carrie M. Beverly, born May 1, 1894.

6. William F. Montgomery, born March 28, 1828 (No. 6, Gen. 3), married Miss Kate Douson; had one child, Thomas L. Montgomery, who now resides near Davis Island, below Vicksburg, Miss.

7. Annie E. Montgomery, born July 2, 1831; died early in life.

8. Hugh R. Montgomery, born Feb. 23. 1833 (No. 8, Gen. 3), married Margaret Brumley. They have one daughter, Nettie, who married Dr. Rembout Fremont, of Oak Ridge, La.; children—Lonnie Floy, and others.

David Montgomery (No. 8, Gen. 2, son of Charles, Sr.), born May 16, 1788: children seven:

1. Milton Montgomery, born Oct. 10, 1812 (No. 1, Gen. 3) married Sarah I. Nason in 1830; children three: 1. David M. Montgomery, born April 16, 1841 (Gen. 4), first married Martha Sanders May 4, 1869; one child. Second, married Jennie Bardwell Feb. 11 1875; children four: 1. David M. Montgomery, born Dec. 6, 1871 2. Mattie S. Montgomery born Dec. 18, 1876. 3. William H Montgomery, born March 5, 1878; died Aug. 1, 1878. 4. Brainard B. Montgomery, born Feb. 24, 1881. 5. Roy R. Montgomery, born Sept. 22, 1884; died Feb. 2, 1899.

2. Laura G. Montgomery, child of Milton, born June 20, 1843; married Edwin K. Fulton. Nov. 11, 1863; children three: 1. William M Fulton, born

Aug. 16, 1864. 2. Laura Edwina Fulton, born June 9, 1869. 3. Laura Fulton, born March 20, 1876. The reason two children in this family are named Laura is that the mother died July 20, 1876, soon after the third child was born, and the father wanted a child called Laura. The friends called the other one Edwina.

2. Charles P. Montgomery, son of David, born Aug. 8, 1814 (No. 2, Gen. 3), married Carrie Shivers; children ten:

1. Green Ella Montgomery, born Oct. 1843, married Capt. Wm. Scay. She died Jan. 5, 1866.

2. Jesse S. Montgomery, born Nov. 27, 1845, now a prominent physician of Starkville, Miss.; married Miss Zoe Bard well, Nov. 11, 1859; children two: 1. Hunter Montgomery, born Dec. 6, 1871. 2. Jessie Montgomery, born Oct. 6, 1875; died Aug. 10, 1877.

3. Nena Montgomery, born May 20, 1849, married Edwin K. Fulton, March 17, 1877, whose first wife was Laura G. Montgomery. Mr. Fulton is now a druggist of Gate City, and lives at Woodlawn, both places being near Birmingham, Ala.

4. David H. Montgomery (Munch), born Sept. 6, 1850, married Annie Stinson, May 7, 1874; children five: 1. Eloise Montgomery, twin to Clair, No. 2. Born Feb. 3, 1875; unmarried. 2. Clair Montgomery, born Feb. 3, 1875; died June 6, 1875. 3. Jack P. Montgomery, born July 18, 1877; unmarried.

5. Cora E. Montgomery, born Oct. 17, 1852, fifth child of Chas. P. Montgomery.

6. William H. Montgomery, born March 27, 1854, married Mary Frierson, Dec. 24, 1881. He is in the mercantile business at Starkville, Miss.

7. Charles P. Montgomery, born March 27, 1857 married Hadie Frierson, Sept. 23, 1886; died March 3, 1896.

8. Samuel E. Montgomery, born July 11, 1859 is a prominent merchant of Yazoo City, Miss.; married Sallie Williams July 15, 1881; children five: 1. Carrie M. Montgomery, born April 9, 1888. 2. Glenn Montgomery born Nov. 15, 1893. 3. Lena Montgomery, born Feb. 22. 1895. 4. Edna Montgomery, born Oct. 13, 1898. 5. Julia S. Montgomery, born Sept. 11, 1900.

9. Anna C. (Rosebud) Montgomery born Nov. 5, 1862 married James Balfour, April 8, 1888. They live in Baltimore. Md. Mr. Balfour was born and raised in London, England, and is of the family of Balfour-Burleigh, of Scotland; one child: Catharine Balfour, born Aug. 8, 1894.

10. Patty Montgomery, born Sept 13. 1864: died Feb. 29, 1867.

3. James A. Montgomery, son of David, born Oct. 6, 1816, first married Malone A. E. Jones; second, married Asenath R. Williams, Aug. 31. 1841. He died Dec. 21. 1893: children___: 1. Tommy Montgomery, born April 18, 1843, died in the Confederate army, Oct. 17, 1863.

2. Sunie Asenath Montgomery, born Feb. 22, 1856, married A. M. Maxwell, Sept. 18, 1876, who is professor of bookkeeping in the A. and M. College at Starkville, Miss; children six: 1. James W. Maxwell, born Sept. 3, 1877; unmarried. 2. Juanita Maxwell, born Oct. 12, 1779; died Aug. 8. 1881. 3. Marie B. Maxwell, born March 4, 1882; died Jan. 6, 1883. 4. Claude M. Maxwell, born March 27, 1885: is author of a large part of the genealogy of Charles Montgomery. Sr., who came to South Carolina in 1773. Mr. Maxwell is now in the A. and M. College at Starkville. Miss., as a cadet in that school, and is now only 17 years of age. 5. Anna B. Maxwell, born March 6, 1891. 6. Dorothy G. Maxwell, born Jan. 11, 1899.

4. Lizzie Montgomery, daughter of David and twin to James A., born Oct. 16, 1816: married Wm. H. Glenn, Sept. 20, 1837. She now lives with her daughter, Mrs. Emma Williams, near Starkville, Miss.; children five:

1. Sallie Glenn, born March 21, 1841, was the second wife of Win. B. Montgomery married Aug. 22. 1865; children five: 1. Roy Montgomery, born Oct. 12, 1868. 2. Grace Montgomery, born Dec. 30, 1870. 3. Mabel Montgomery, born April 25, 1873. 4. Walter Montgomery, born June, 13, 1876, died June 28, 1885. 5. Louise Montgomery, born April 20, 1879, died Aug. 10, 1899. They live near Starkville, Miss. William B. Montgomery is one of the most prominent cattle men of the South, having been the first to bring Jersey cattle into that section. A full account of his useful life is given by Miss M. L. Montgomery in this work.

2. Emma Glenn, born May 13, 1843, first married Dr. Nash, Sept. 17, 1851; second married G. Pope Williams, May 2, 1865. They now live near Starkville, Miss.

3. James A. Glenn, born Sept. 6, 1846, married Dora Hogan, Nov. 26. 1875. He is now a prominent farmer of Starkville, Miss.

4. Mary L. Glenn, born Dec. 15, 1850, died June 17, 1852.

5. John T. Montgomery, son of David, born Nov. 29, 1818, married Mary Ann Dunlap, Aug. 1, 1843; is a planter near Lavernia, Texas: children seven:

The Montgomerys

1. John D. Montgomery, born May 28. 1844, died June 10, 1848. 2. Mary Ella Montgomery, born Nov. 26, 1846, married R. E. Carter, Nov. 26, 1875; now living at Abilene, Texas. 3. Henrietta A. Montgomery, born Dec. 6, 1847, died July 21, 1849. 4, William H. Montgomery, born Jan. 22, 1850, graduated at a medical college in Edinburg, Scotland; died May 1, 1882. 5. Glenn Montgomery, born Dec. 1, 1853, died Jan. 10, 1854.

6. Presley Montgomery, born Nov. 11, 1856, married Annie Daniels. Oct. 4, 1888; is a prominent farmer of Lavernia, Texas; children four: 1. John P. Montgomery, born Aug. 6, 1889; died Oct. 25, 1901. 2. Ella E. Montgomery, born May 6, 1891. 3. William H. Montgomery, born Oct. 30, 1892. 4. Ollie Montgomery, born Nov. 22, 1894.

7. Martha E. Montgomery, born Nov. 29, 1858.

6. Emma Montgomery, daughter of David, born Oct. 19, 1825, married James Bardwell. Nov. 3, 1842; children six: 1. Sarah E. Bardwell, born July 29, 1843, died Jan. 4, 1844. 2. David A. Bardwell, born Oct. 16, 1844; now mayor of Starkville. 3. Henry G. Bardwell, born Dec. 23, 1846. 4. Milton Bardwell, born Nov. 19, 1848. 5. Brainard Bardwell, born Nov. 24, 1850. 6. John H. Bardwell, born Aug. 8, 1853, now living at Sweetwater, Texas.

7. Maggie Montgomery, daughter of David, born Dec. 31, 1827, married Cecil Bardwell, March 17, 1846. Children eleven: 1. Issaquena Bardwell, born Jan. 17, 1847, died Sept. 26, 1868. 2., Arthur G. Bardwell, born Aug. 16, 1848. 3. Emma G. Bardwell, born May, 1850; unmarried. 4. Joseph M. Bardwell, born May 1, 1852. 5. James A. Bardwell, born March 15, 1855; unmarried. 6., Elizabeth Bardwell, born Jan. 8, 1858; unmarried. 7. William H. Bardwell, born Feb. 24, 1860; unmarried. 8. Carrie A. Bardwell, born May 29, 1862: 9. Margaret E. Bardwell, born June 2, 1867; unmarried. 10. Cecil C. Bardwell, born Oct. 26, 1869; unmarried. 11. Rosa Bardwell, born Oct. 16, 1872.

Hugh Montgomery, born May 15, 1796, in Fairfield district, S. C, 12th child of Charles Montgomery, Sr., married Isabella Bell, a cousin, who in physical type was the opposite of her husband, being fair with light hair and blue eyes. She was a woman of excellent native sense and strong character, active, energetic, and a great lover of home; children five. The first, Charles, born Dec. 3, 1818, remained only four years to brighten by his presence the family hearthstone—passing away Sept. 27, 1822. Margaret Jane, the second child of Hugh, was born Nov. 8, 1825, and in early womanhood (Dec. 18, 1842) was called to join her brother in the home beyond. Elizabeth, William and Charles Robert completed the family circle.

Hugh Montgomery was a planter among the Mississippi pioneers and located in Octibbeha County, four miles from the beginning of a village called Starkville. He was a quiet, dignified gentleman and pursued his calling with reasonable success. September 2, 1849, he entered the invisible world and was deeply mourned by his wife, who lived to the age of 94 years, and her mission was a large and noble one—in raising a host of nieces, nephews and grandchildren, proving herself thereby a veritable mother in Israel.

Elizabeth Montgomery, third child of Hugh and Isabella Montgomery, born Dec. 3, 1828, was educated at one of the best schools for girls known at that time. She married Nov. 5, 1840, Dr. Brainard Bardwell. She died May 7, 1844. She had two children: First, Elizabeth, who was trained in the best of schools, was an exceptionally loving character: married Lieut. Wm. Bell, and died _____. Second, William Bardwell, her brother, who died at the age of 12 years.

Wm. B. Montgomery born 1830, fourth child of Hugh and Isabella Montgomery, and his brother Charles Robert, received good educational advantages—attending, while still mere boys, school in Tennessee, and afterward college in Due West, S. C. the University of Mississippi, and Princeton, N. J.; the former receiving a diploma at the last place. They both located near Starkville and engaged in agricultural pursuits.

In 1849 William was married to Julia Gillespie, the daughter of Dr. Wm. Gillespie, a prominent planter also. Of this union five children were born: Edwin, Albert, Margery, Julia Alice, and William Robert.

Before and after the Civil War Wm. B. lived at Kushla, Ala., twelve miles from Mobile, and did a prosperous cotton-commission business in the city. In 1864 he lost his wife, and was again married, to Sarah A. Glenn, Aug. 22, 1865; of which union five children were born: Roy, Grace G., Mabel Elizabeth, Walter Bell, and Louise.

Several years after the war, his health in a measure failing, he returned to Starkville and lived on a farm, leading an active, outdoor life. He was much interested in educational work, his children being then in school, and was a little later instrumental in establishing, through his friend, Dr. T. G. Sellers, who became its principal, a female college at Starkville—an institution that for a period of years prospered. In he turned his attention to stock farming and was the first person to introduce Jersey cattle and other grades of fine stock into the South. He also experimented largely in grasses and really changed to a large degree the method of farming in the Gulf States. The most significant thing, in its bearing upon the present and future material advancement of his state and the South, accomplished by the active, fertile brain of this public-spirited man, was his instrumentality in the establishment of a state agricultural and mechanical college, located at Starkville. He was really the founder of the institution by virtue of the constant agitation of the subject through the press of the state, and other means used of ventilating the idea with the legislators and prominent men of the state. This agitation resulted in an act of the legislature in 1881 appropriating money for this purpose. He was appointed one of the commissioners for locating the college, and later, the local trustee of the same, which position he has with faithfulness held through the twenty years of the life of the institution.

He has always stood for a clean, pure government, and in municipal and state affairs has helped to effect needful reforms—among others, that of prohibition of the liquor traffic. His last public work was the formation of a stock company for the establishment of a cotton mill in Starkville, and the buildings for the plant are now in process of erection. Although not robust as formerly, he is still active in public affairs, retaining his position on the A. and M. Board of Trustees, and otherwise manifesting his interest in all that pertains to the progress of his section and state.

In every sense of the word he is a man, the impress of whose character is felt by the people of his own generation and whom many yet to come will have reason to be grateful that his feet rested for a time upon this earth and that his brain planned so well for those yet to follow.

Edwin, son of Julia and W. B. Montgomery was born in 1852. He reached manhood's estate and married Bettie Presley of Camden, Ala. Seven children became members of this household and family circle. Julia Gillespie Montgomery, was born Sept. 18, 1881, and finished her literary education at Due West, S. C, in June, 1901. William Arthur Montgomery, born May 15, 1883, and Tom McMillian, born July 9, 1885, are students at the Agricultural and Mechanical College. Belle Presley, born July 17, 1887. Alice Pope, born Oct. 28, 1892, and two attractive children—Presley and Alberta—who opened their eyes on this great world the same date, Feb. 3, 1895 (twins), and have joyously journeyed together thus far, complete this radius of family influence. Edwin, the father, is engaged in stock farming, with Jersey cattle as a specialty; though for several years before and after his marriage he edited with eminent success the leading agricultural paper of the South—"The Southern Live Stock Journal." which was established by his father.

The Montgomerys

Albert, the second son of William and Julia Montgomery, was born June 17, 1855. He was physically like his mother, with the fairest complexion, eyes tinted with the blue of the sky, and light hair that with years deepened a few shades. In a mere objective sense he was never handsome, but had that rarer, more subtle gift of personal magnetism to a refined degree. In youth he was what might be called a "winsome lad," but with maturity this charm developed into a radiating, all-pervading brightness that, penetrated the most pronounced moroseness of others and illuminated with sunshine every place he entered, including the more abiding ones of home and business.

His mental development was gradual, but the mind itself was of the character that insures growth through thought. He did not take a diploma, but studied at King College, Bristol, Tenn., two years, before the abrupt closing of that avenue of mental culture. He thought of leading a professional life, and for a time read law, but abandoned the plan to enter upon an active and successful commercial career, being born with the instinct of business. His leaning to another life arose from that taste and appreciation of music, oratory and literature that was, unlike many business men, allowed through absorbing interests to become obscured and neglected, but to him was as necessary to the mental and soul life as food to the physical body. Shakespeare, a well-marked copy did not from long disuse gather dust upon its covers, but was to the date of his final illness eagerly devoured, while this mine of thought and expression arose as naturally to his lips as the common phrases of communication to those of others.

He located in New Orleans, La., and engaged in the cattle-commission business, and, considering his limited capital and experience, was in a few years remarkably successful and highly regarded in the financial world. Later he began also to feed cattle for the local and other markets, and in this field, too, was amply rewarded until, in the panic of '93, a reverse of fortune which he bravely bore and from which he was recovering at the time of his death. He was a born financier, the kind of genius that no combination of disastrous circumstances could crush; and men, knowing this, urged upon him the use at a reasonable interest, of thousands of dollars, so that he was wont to say that his adversity had not caused the usual bitterness of spirit, but that the human race was more dignified in his mind than when regarded from the view point of prosperity. He was a cattle feeder, operating largely in New Orleans and at Meridian, Brooksville and Starkville, Miss.; the year of his death the later markets proving that had he lived a fortune would have been realized. In 1883 he was united in marriage to Miss Mary Prowel, a beautiful and cultured young woman of Columbus Miss. Five children came to enlarge the family circle and enrich their hearts and lives: Joseph, born Sept. 25, 1884, who has been a loyal and devoted son to the mother, whom the father left seven years ago, Sept. 24. 1895; is at present a student in the Agricultural and Mechanical College of Mississippi. Marjorie Clifford, the only daughter, was born Aug. 17, 1886, and is a student of the Meridian high school. Albert, the third son was born Dec. 22, 1888, and is also a very promising student of the same school. John Munford and Gillespie, the other children, born respectively Jan. 28, 1890, and July 9, 1895, are healthy specimens of boyhood, and both are in school.

The ill health of his wife caused the family to move to Meridian, Miss., where they had resided a year when the spirit of Albert was claimed, Sept. 24, 1895.

Margery L. Montgomery, the third child of Wm, B., was born June 2, 1857. Her college course was finished at Sullins College, Bristol, Va. After the usual young lady-hood of Southern girls at that time spent in home and social duties, the Temperance Reform as instituted by the W. C. T. U. for a number of years engaged her earnest attention. At the death of her brother Albert, to whom she was united by the tenderest tie, she made her home with his wife in Meridian and endeavored to repay in service to his own the debt of love and loyalty that was due this gentlest and most generous of men and brothers. Following an instinct for journalism, four years ago she purchased a daily newspaper and since that time has engaged in work of that and a similar nature. At present she is staff correspondent of the Meridian Daily Press, the leading daily in the state, and she has been one among the most persevering in furnishing material for this genealogy.

Julia Alice, daughter of W. B. Montgomery, was born June 8, 1862. She finished her education at the Atheaneum, Columbia, Tenn., and in June, 24, 1886, married John Walker Pope, native of Mobile, Ala., but at that time resident of Little Rock. Ark. Mr. Pope was a successful cotton buyer and a highly respected citizen, and died in the midst of his career as a financier, Jan. 17, 1901, leaving three children --- Sarah Glenn Pope, born Aug. 27, 1889; Anne Foote Pope, born Sept. 29, 1893; John Walker Pope, born April 25, 1899. Mrs. Pope is at present residing in Starkville, but for business reasons is contemplating a return to Little Rock.

The Montgomerys

William Robert.

Roy, the son of W. B. and Sarah A. Montgomery, was born Oct. 12, 1868 and at the early age of three years ended his earthly existence, March 11, 1872. He was very bright and attractive, and his removal from the family circle made a sad vacancy.

Grace Glenn, the next child, was born Dec. 30, 1870, and, like a fair and beautiful bud, was at the age of eight months (Aug. 25, 1871) plucked by the Master's hand to bloom in the heavenly garden.

Mabel Elizabeth came April 25, 1873, to fill in a measure the vacancy created by the going of the others, and is now living with her parents in Starkville.

Waiter Bell, the next son was born June 13, 1876, and was in appearance unusually active, while in mind and character his development was one of deep interest to a large circle of relatives and friends, so promising was it; but—alas for the frailty of human hopes!—on the 25th of June, 1886, at 2 o'clock, the day after his sister Alice's marriage, in obedience to a trust committed to him by the manager of the farm, he was, while in the upper story of the barn, struck by lightning—the stroke having come from a perfectly clear sky. A tragic scene followed; the rain poured in torrents on a barn in flames, while the father rescued his boy's dead body from the burning building amidst the distressed cries of his mother and sisters.

Louise, the youngest member of the family, was born April 20, 1879. She was the object of great love and tenderness because of a fall from a rolling chair at the age of three years, causing her to remain practically all through life almost helpless. On Aug. 10, 1899, she was called to a home where suffering is unknown.

Charles Robert, the third son of Hugh and Isabella Montgomery, was born June 16, 1832. As has been stated, he was educated at a common school in Tennessee and later attended college at the University of Mississippi and at Princeton, N. J. In boyhood he was a gay, dashing youth, full of animal spirits and good cheer, which made him a welcome guest in any company. In early manhood, on Sept. 29, 1853, he married Mary Belle McMillan, of Aberdeen, Miss. On Feb. 9, 1855, a little Hugh came to complete this bond of unity, and later the family chain was lengthened by the birth of Mary Belle, Sept. 13, 1856, and John McMillan, 1857. During this period of his life Robert followed planting as a calling, living in the homestead with his widowed mother, but later moved to Starkville and engaged in the mercantile business, though for some years past he has been in the service of the Mississippi and Ohio railway, and possesses the confidence of the company that such faithful and efficient service as he has rendered merits.

In 1857 he lost his wife, and for eleven years lived single, his mother caring for him and training the children. June 13, 1869, he married Miss Catherine Carothers of Starkville, a union that has resulted most happily, and from which eight children have swelled the family circle. Robert Montgomery was made for family life, and in an ideal sense fills the relationship of husband and father, though his influence extends to other spheres, and he holds the respect of people in the state and elsewhere, while in his home town he is universally beloved by all classes and conditions of men.

Hugh Montgomery, the oldest son of Robert and Mary Belle Montgomery, was born Feb. 9, 1855, and grew to manhood, finishing his education at King College, Bristol, Tenn. He was possessed of a fine mind and a gentle disposition; but, being of a retiring nature, the best things he had to offer in the delights of communion were reserved for the inner family life, or the companionship of a few friends. After an illness of three weeks he passed away, in early manhood, in September, 1881, and was deeply mourned by his family and friends.

Mary Belle, the daughter of Mary Belle and Robert, was born Sept. 13, 1856. She attended the schools of Starkville, graduating at the female college there. Since the early years of young womanhood, given to the pleasures and duties of social fife, she has devoted much time to sharing in large measure the family duties, and especially in caring for her younger sisters and brothers, in return receiving the love and appreciation that such unselfishness merits.

John McMillan, the second son, was born Dec. 15, 1857. He spent the closing years of his school life at King College, Tenn., and afterward gave his time to commercial pursuits, though at present he is assisting his uncle on a farm.

The Montgomerys

Evelyn Carothers, the daughter of Robert and Catherine Montgomery, was born Jan. 24, 1871. She finished her education at the Industrial Institute and College, a state institution located at Columbus, Miss., the literary course of which ranks with the best colleges in this country; so that a young woman taking a diploma then, as she did, has a solid foundation upon which to build her future. After her graduation she taught several years, one term in a Sherman (Texas) College, and later at Oxford, Miss. In November, the second day, 1896, she married William Perkins, a professor in the chemical department of the Agricultural and Mechanical College. They reside upon the college campus, and two attractive little girls —Kate Carothers, born Nov. 24, 1898, and Evelyn, born Aug. 7, 1899—complete the happy household.

Martha (or Pattie) Hope, the second child of Robert and Kate Montgomery, was born July 19, 1872, and is a useful and cherished member of the family.

Charles Robert, Jr., eldest son of Robert and Kate Montgomery, was born July 25, 1874, and early drew, by his winsomeness, the hearts of the household, including the largest circle of relatives and friends, to him in close and endearing bonds. As he approached the years of manhood and looked out on the large business and social world, this, kindliness of temper and disposition was retained, reaping for him the legitimate fruit of love and friendship. After a period spent in the Agricultural and Mechanical College, at Starkville, he accepted a position of trust in a mercantile house in Atlanta, Ga., where he rendered acceptable service until called to Chattanooga, Tenn., to a more advantageous position.

As time progressed, in answer to a demand he became identified with that large and respectable class of business men known as "commercial travelers" or "knights of the grip;" a pursuit that he continued to follow with success until the unexpected summons to that "undiscovered country from whose bourn no traveler returns" reached him, July 8, 1900, in Chattanooga, Tenn. The sudden call upon this loved one in the prime of young and buoyant manhood to lay aside the responsibilities of earth to enter upon the larger ones of another sphere was met by his family with deep distress, but also with submission to a Higher Will than theirs.

The next advent into this family was that of Catherine, in 1876, who, as she approached womanhood, attended the Industrial Institute and College at Columbus, Miss., giving special time and attention to music, in which art she became a skillful performer. Following college life she was socially a great favorite, but Dec. 28, 1899, ended in a measure that period of her history because of a union in marriage with Mr. Stewart Weir, a gentleman who filled an important position in the textile department of the Agricultural and Mechanical College at Starkville. November 13, 1900, marked the natal day of Robert Montgomery Weir, son of Catherine and Stewart Weir, whose interesting development was watched with an absorbing interest by fond parents and relatives until, after a brief illness, the shining, heavenly messenger came, June 9, 1902, to gather this opening bud to further unfold its petals in a garden of unfading flowers beyond earth's bounds.

Annie Frierson, the next daughter of Robert and Kate Montgomery, was born Sept. 25, 1878; attended the Industrial Institute and College, and the North Mississippi Presbyterian College at Holly Springs, and is now occupying a place of usefulness in the home and adorning the social circle.

Paul, the next in age, was born Nov. 25, 1880, and is now capably and conscientiously filling the position of operator in Shreveport, La.

Hugh, the next in succession, was born Nov. 16, 1882, to a brief bright existence followed by a sad death from an accidental cause, thus making a corresponding sympathy and grief that the unusual, in life or death, demands of those closely united by blood and association to the one called upon to render a penalty of suffering.

Little Hugh, active, vivacious and beautiful, on a sunny Sabbath morning in April, while the major portion of the family were at service, became the innocent victim of the carelessness of a servant in leaving within easy reach of a child's hands a cup of concentrated lye. He lived for more than a year in more or less comfort, but died at last as a result of the inevitable operation performed by a skillful physician in Nashville, Nov. 16, 1884.

Adelaide came to fill in some measure the vacancy created by the going of little Hugh beyond mortal ken, as well as to make for herself a valued place in this circle of hearts, Jan. 25, 1887. She has now left baby-land well behind and is earnestly applying herself to her studies in the Industrial Institute and College at Columbus, Miss.

The Montgomerys

Margaret, the youngest member of this family, was born Nov. 24, 1888. She is a student of the high school of Starkville; a bright and attractive presence in her father's home with all the wealth of twentieth-century opportunities for a splendid womanly development before her—opportunities of which she will doubtless avail herself.

LAND CLAIMANTS ASTIR.

"The claim of Robert Montgomery, Earl of Eggleston, recently set up making claim to 20,000 acres of land in this country, has set the whole clan of Montgomerys into a lively land scramble. The Earl of Eggleston lives in Scotland. In the dispatches it was recently announced that he was making claim on the United States government for 20,000 acres of land by virtue of a grant from George III to one of his Montgomery ancestors. These land grants of George III were, it is understood, preserved inviolate in the shifting of rights between the governments of this country, and the earl wants his land, or wants the right to locate his grant anywhere in the United States from any other public lands. Of course he does not expect to get the original land granted by George III.

Since the filing of the earl's claim, John M. Smylie of the land office here, who is the agent of the earl in Jackson, has been receiving numerous letters from all parts of the state inquiring as to the rights of the Montgomery heirs. These letters all come signed by some scion of the house of Montgomery, and the writers all claim to be lineal descendants of the Montgomerys of Scotland, and to have rights paramount to Earl Robert. The letters assert that if the government is going to open the doors to the Montgomery claimants, then they want to get into the game and share in the distribution of the land. Mr. Smylie has been designated by the earl of Eggleston as agent for him, to get up evidence from the land records here in support of his claim to the grant. Mr. Smylie has been at work on the case and states that there is no question about the earl's rights in the premises. Mr. Smylie says that many of the Montgomery letters he is receiving make dire threats of swooping down and gobbling the whole United States if their claims are not hearkened to."

The above was clipped from a Memphis, Tenn., paper and sent me by Mrs. Judge G. Q. Hall, of Meridian, Miss., whose maiden name was Montgomery. The agent referred to meet her brother in a Vicksburg hotel and requested an introduction, claiming that he could see in him a strong resemblance to Earl Eggleston, whom he (Smylie) represented. The earl, being informed of this, wrote Mr. Montgomery and sent his picture, which really showed a striking resemblance. The earl also gave Mr. Montgomery a warm invitation to visit him.

VAST MONTGOMERY ESTATE.
(From Pittsburg Leader.)

"Laport, Ind. Feb. 6, 1899."A meeting of the heirs of the Montgomery fortune has been called, to be held in New York, Feb. 8, at which steps will be taken for a thorough legal investigation of the claims of heirs. A. J. Montgomery, of 36 Fremont Street, Alleghany, says that John Montgomery settled in Armstrong County, Pa. in 1804 and that all of the connection now resides in western Pennsylvania. Other Pittsburg Montgomerys have also become interested, and strong proofs of kinship are being developed. The estate now is reputed as aggregating nearly one hundred millions, the New York heirs having unearthed more wealth.

"The meeting of heirs will be held at the office of Mr. Montgomery, a New York attorney, who will be associated with eminent counsel in investigating the affairs of the estate.

"A Leader representative called this forenoon at the Montgomery residence in Alleghany. Mr. Montgomery was not at home, but his wife stated that it was true they were expecting to be included among the heirs to the large Montgomery estate. She said that the estate was located in Ireland and that, although she did not know much of the family history, yet it had always been known here that the family here had wealthy connection in Ireland. Mrs. Montgomery said that her husband's grandfather came to this country from Ireland at the time of the Whiskey Insurrection. A. J. Montgomery, of Alleghany, was born at South Bend, this state, 63 years ago. He is in business at 408 Duquesne Way."

MONTGOMERY FORTUNE.

"My third great-grandfather, James, had a brother John and a brother Alexander and a sister Nancy. I know nothing of any others. Their father's name, I think, was Alexander. He came to this country from County Donegal, Ireland at an early date. He was a cousin to General Richard Montgomery,

The Montgomerys

John and Alexander Montgomery, of Raphael, County Donegal, Ireland. I do not know where Alexander Montgomery first settled, but his children, whom I mention, were in Washington County, Va., in 1765. I am descended from both James and Nancy Montgomery, through the inter-marriage of their children. James served as a lieutenant in the Revolutionary War. His Bible, now 121 years old, is in my possession, but the pages containing the family records had been removed before it fell into my hands. If this is the line you are interested in, I can give you other data. Please give your descent.

E. H. J."

I think this was published in the Louisville Courier-Journal probably about 1898. I do not know who the author is, but I think it is in answer to a question concerning a very large estate supposed to belong to the descendants of one Alexander Montgomery who settled in New York in an early day, as the following will show, which is also a newspaper clipping:

"David Robinson in his will bequeathed to Lifferd Parish, County Donegal, 200 pounds sterling of English money. This was left in the hands of his executors—Archibald Stewart, John Breckenridge, Francis Preston, Alexander Montgomery, and his brother William Robinson, to be given to the minister for charity throughout time. He left to the Hibernian Society in Philadelphia money for the support of emigrants. To his sister, Nancy Montgomery, wife of Captain James Montgomery, he leaves a large legacy.

"James Montgomery's father, Alexander, was cousin to Richard Montgomery of Euchre fame. James belonged to the society of Cincinnati. He left a legacy to Margaret Edmiston, the daughter of Nancy Montgomery and wife of Captain John Edmiston, who was killed at the battle of River Raisin, and whose name is second on the monument at Frankfort, Ky., and for whom Edmiston County was named. John Edmiston was a private in the Revolutionary War under his father, Major William Edmiston, and who was second in command of Virginia troops under Campbell, who behaved so honorably at King's Mountain. John Edmiston was with others, complimented for his gallantry. He left only one son, who died childless. His daughter, Margaret, married William Chandler Pruitt, and their daughter married Richard Spurr of Athens, Fayette County, Ky.

"David Robinson left to his niece, Agnes Preston, wife of Walter Preston and daughter of Nancy Montgomery, a legacy. Walter Preston was father of

John M. Preston of Virginia. To Elizabeth Montgomery, daughter of Nancy and wife of Maj. Alexander Montgomery, he leaves a legacy. His estate in Clark County was called "The. Rye Fields." He owned large tracts in Shelby County, Ky., and Montgomery County, Va. Martha Chandler Pruitt's father was William Chandler of Halifax, Va. Her mother was May Hamlin, who can give their antecedents or those of David Robinson."

MILLIONS.

Montgomery Estate in New York will be claimed by Kentuckians.

"Lebanon, Ky., March 31, "Mrs. William Bricken, who conducts the Bricken hotel in this city, and Mrs. James Adams, also of this city, have just learned through their attorneys that they are direct heirs to the large Montgomery estate located in New York city.

"The estate is estimated to be worth from S30, 000,000 to $50,000,000. This property was owned by Alexander Montgomery, great-grandfather of Mrs. Bricken. When Alexander Montgomery died a search was instituted for his son James, who it seems could not be found, and this delayed the settlement of the estate.

"James Montgomery, who was the grandfather of Mrs. Bricken and the son of Alexander Montgomery, died at this place and was interred here. The parties are very sanguine that they can establish their claim."

IN LINE FOR A FORTUNE.

S. B. Knuckles an Heir to the Montgomery Estate.—Has Figured Out that His Family Tree is Quite Certain his Claim is Regular.

"Fickle fortune seems to be ready to smile again on Mr. Samuel B. Knuckles, the book-keeper at the Hutchinson grocery store. Mr. Knuckles read of the vast fortune left by Alexander Montgomery in New York, and, a branch of his family tree being a Montgomery, he naturally set about to learn if the families were connected. When seen by a reporter for the Herald, Saturday, Mr. Knuckles had figured out his family tree and discussed it at some length with the reporter. He said that if Alexander Montgomery and General Montgomery were brothers he was quite sure that he would come in for a portion of the estate. Of the family Mr. Knuckles said that his great-grandfather, William Scott, was a descendant direct from General Montgomery, who lived at Hagerstown, Maryland, and that William Scott came to Lexington when it was a frontier town and was in the block-house here for several months as a protection from the hostile Indians before moving to his farm. He said that his grandfather Vance married one of Scott's daughters and she gave birth to twin children which she named Montgomery and Alexander Vance, respectively. His grandmother was named Sallie Montgomery Vance, and she was named for Sallie Montgomery, who was a sister to General Montgomery.

"Mr. Knuckles says that he intends to open correspondence with the attorneys who are trying to locate the heirs, and if he learns that General and Alexander Montgomery were brothers he is certainly entitled to some of the estate and will claim it.

"Several years ago Mr. Knuckles fell heir to several hundred dollars through a relative several generations removed, by tracing it up, and he hopes to be as lucky on this occasion; but the amount will be thousands instead of hundreds."

FORTUNE WAITS.

John Lair Said to be Heir to $9,000,000 Property in New York. — Descendants of Alexander Montgomery, Who Leased the Ground for Ninety-nine Years.—He is One of Many.

"John Lair, of 634 East Street, is awaiting with much interest further developments in an investigation that promises to prove him one of the heirs to an estate in New York city, valued at $9,000,000, So far he knows nothing about the circumstances under which the estate is wanting a claimant, nor does he know the exact location or value of the property; but he is daily expecting an agent who is looking for the descendants of Ezekiel Montgomery, of whom Mr. Lair is a grandson. This agent, it appears, has visited a niece of Mr. Lair's in Washington County, Ky., in the course of his investigations, and it is from her that Lair has learned the only definite news of the case. According to her, the agent is coming to Louisville to see Mr. Lair.

"Mrs. Helen S. Crouch is the writer of the letter. According to her presentation of the situation, the estate in question is that of Alexander

Montgomery, who owned land in New York City which he leased to parties for ninety-nine years. This lease has just expired, and no claimant for the property has appeared.

"It appears also that Alexander Montgomery left no issue. He had a brother Ezekiel Montgomery, now deceased, who left children. It is these and their descendants, it appears, that are now being sought. Ezekiel's children were three—Bettie, James and Judy.

"It appears that the Lair family can account for Judy and James, and possibly for Bettie. At any rate, Mr. John Lair is the son of Judy Montgomery, who was married to Hubbard Lair in Kentucky. According to the letter from his niece, Mr. Lair is led to believe that the children of Hubbard Lair are regarded as the direct heirs. Mr. Lair is one of these.

"There are also two living brothers. They are Thomas, who lives near Mackville, Washington County, Ky. and Merritt, who was last heard of at the state insane asylum at Lexington. He lost his mind several years ago, grieving over the death of his wife. He has two children living in Garrard County. Thomas also has children. There were two other brothers, now deceased—William and Andrew. Both left families. One of Andrew's children is Mrs. Crouch, who wrote to Mr. Lair.

"Of James Montgomery, the second child of the deceased Ezekiel Montgomery, not so much is known. It is believed that he had two children—Nat, and a daughter, now Mrs. Coy of Indiana. Whether or not Nat is living is not known by the Lairs.

"A short time before hearing of the estate, Mr. Lair received a letter from a cousin at Columbia, Mo. While she did not bring out anything about claims to an estate, she made inquiries as to the family history, and Mr. Lair believes that she has also been approached in a search for information by someone. This cousin is Mrs. Elizabeth Adams. She appears to be a daughter of Bettie, the other child of Ezekiel Montgomery, whose name after marriage was Mrs. Jack Ashley. Mrs. Adams has a son, and a daughter—Mrs. Brickins, at Lebanon, Ky.

"'I am of course anxious to learn more of this matter,' said Mr. Lair yesterday, 'as all I know about the search for heirs to the New York estate is what is told me by my niece in her letter. She writes that the person who made inquiries of her is coming to Louisville, but I have not yet seen him. If she has been correctly informed as to the family involved, there will be little difficulty for us to prove the descent from Ezekiel Montgomery. If there is really such an estate as is spoken of, I suppose it is one that is about to pass into the hands of the state, and Rome one has devoted himself to saving it to the heirs. Before the present time I have heard nothing of it.' "Mr. Lair removed to Louisville from Washington County, Ky., March 1. He is sixty-five years of age and has several children. He was until recently engaged in farming, and is in moderate circumstances. His father, Hubbard Lair, was a tanner and was born in Lincoln County. He married the daughter of Ezekiel Montgomery, in Washington County."

COMPARISONS OF CLAIMS.

You will notice that Spark's American Biography (see General Richard Montgomery) says General Richard, John and Alexander were brothers. And Mr. Knuckles claims that Alexander was a brother to Richard. Mr. Lair also claims that Alexander left no issue, but claims that he had a brother Ezekiel not mentioned by the other two accounts.

You will also note that Mrs. Brickins of Lebanon, Kentucky, who Mr. Lair admits is also a lineal descendant of Ezekiel, says that Alexander had issue and that she is one of his descendants.

Then, by referring to the will of David Robinson you will see that it is claimed that Alexander, the father of James and great grandfather of Mrs. Brickins, is not a brother but a cousin to General Richard Montgomery. If this be the case, then this Alexander may have had a brother Ezekiel.

And E. H. J., under the head of "Queries," claims that Alexander was a cousin to General Richard Montgomery.

Now turn back and read these accounts again; it will prove a splendid exercise in genealogies.

For the benefit of those who may be inclined to prosecute this matter further, I will say that I have discussed this matter with able legal talent who have given considerable thought to this question, and they give it as their opinion that all means invested in investigating this is not likely to bring back any returns.—D. B. M.

And Their Descendants

APPENDIX.

(This belongs to Judge H. P. Montgomery's genealogical sketch, but was received too late to be included with it.)

SIXTH GENERATION.

Children of James Hervey Montgomery and Malvina Trotter, his wife

1631. Prances Elizabeth Montgomery, born 1828, died 1865: married George Stokely, about 1848.

1632. Wm. T. Montgomery, born 1830, died 1858; married Martha J. Gevorden. 1853.

1633. Margaret P. Montgomery married Lawson Blackaby. 71 and 1634. George Washington Montgomery, born Jan. 17, 1834; married Rachel S. Washburn, Nov. 6, 1856.

1635. Rebecca Montgomery, born 1836, died unmarried.

1636. Miranda Montgomery, born 1838, died in infancy.

SEVENTH GENERATION.

Children of Prances Elizabeth Montgomery (1631) and George Stokely, her husband:

1637. James Stokely.

1638. Frances M. Stokely,

1639. Alexander Stokely, born 1857,

1640. Louvina Stokely, born 1860.

1641. George Stokely, born 1862,

1642. Elizabeth Stokely, born 1864.

Children of Wm. T. Montgomery (1632) and Martha Gevorden, his wife:

1643. John Thomas Montgomery, born March 20, 1854.

1644. Martha Ellen Montgomery, born Nov. 12, 1856.

Children of Margaret P. Montgomery (1633) and Lawson Blackaby, her husband:

1645. Mary Belle Blackaby.

Children of George Washington Montgomery (1634) and Rachel S, Washburn, his wife:

1646. Jesse Francis Montgomery, born Aug. 30, 1857; married Amanda Alice Mercer, March 17, 1881.

1647. Arvenia Jane Montgomery, born June 30, 1860; married John A. Cockriel, May 8, 1879; married, second, Wm. Riley Pres. ton, Feb. 27, 1889.

And Their Descendants

1648. Mary Belle Montgomery, born April 25, 1864; married Wm. L. Wilson, March 4, 1885; died Jan. 31, 1900.

1649. Wm. Byron Montgomery, born Dec. 20, 1867; married Cornelia F. Anderson, Sept. 25, 1889.

Children of Jesse F. Montgomery (1646) and Amanda Alice Mercer, his wife:

1650. Clarence Alton Montgomery, born Aug. 26, 1882.
1651. Ira May Montgomery, born June 3, 1885.
1652. Robert Emmett Montgomery, born Aug. 13, 1889.

Children of Arvenia Jane Montgomery (1647) and John A Cockriel, her husband:

1653. Corda N. Cockriel, born July 14, 1881; married Lee H. Baskam, Sept. 3, 1896.
1654. John Everett Cockriel, born April 29, 1883.

Children of Mary Belle Montgomery (1648) and Wm. L. Wilson, her husband:

1655. Olivia E. Wilson, born June 11. 1886, died July 31, 1886.
1656. Ollie M. Wilson, born July 15, 1887, died Sept. 28, 1887.
1657. Mona H. Wilson, born Sept. 20, 1889.
1658. Arvenia Wilson, born Jan. 17, 1892.
1659. Hardie Wilson, born Oct. 7, 1895.

Children of Wm. Byron Montgomery (1649) and Cornelia F. Anderson, his wife:

1660. Bertie Montgomery died July 16, 1890.
1661. Ray Earle Montgomery, born March 22, 1895.

EIGHTH GENERATION.

Children of Corda N. Cockriel (1653) and Lee H. Baskam, her husband:

1662. Verina L. Baskam, born June 1, 1897, d. Sept. 13, 1897.
1663. Cecil Wayne Baskam, born June 14, 1901.

ISAAC MONTGOMERY, BORN 1823.

Isaac Montgomery, mentioned on page ___, born Feb. 26, 1823 (instead of 1827), near Owensville, Ind., a son of Judge Thomas Montgomery, is not dead, as stated on that page, but is now (March, 1903) still living near

Frankfort, Ill., with his daughter, Louisa Biggs. He made a visit to his old home, Owensville, Ind. a few weeks ago (March 1903) and is over 80 years old. He served in the Civil War in the 15th regiment Ill. Vol. cavalry. He married Elizabeth Armstrong, in Indiana. Aug. 3, 1845 and resided near Owensville, Ind., until about 1847, when he moved to Benton, Franklin County. Ill.; children twelve:

Nos. 1, 2, 3. and 4. All died in infancy. 5. Marion Montgomery, born Dec. 24, 1846, died 1847. 6. Louisa Montgomery, born July 19, 1848. 7. Joseph Montgomery, born Sept. 17, 1850, died 1867. 8. William Pinkney Montgomery, born Feb. 6, 1853. 9. Julian Montgomery, born May 10, 1855, dead. 10. Mary Eliza Montgomery, born July 30, 1858. 11. Henry Armstrong Montgomery, born Feb. 28, 1861. 12. John Martin Montgomery, born Aug. 29, 1871.

Isaac Montgomery second married Ann M. Brashears; no children.

Louisa Montgomery, sixth child of Isaac, first married John McCasland, at Benton, Ill.; children four: Charles, Edgar, Alice and Oscar. Edgar and Oscar are dead. Charles was born Aug. 30, 1867; is a farmer near Ashland. Kansas, and will become treasurer of the County Oct. 1, 1903; married Oct. 16, 1892; children three: 1. Louis L. McCasland, born Oct. 23, 1894. 2. Paul I. McCasland, born June 22, 1896. 3. Hope V. McCasland, born Dec. 20, 1898. Alice McCasland, a sister to Charles, also lives near or in Ashland, Kansas.

Louisa Montgomery second married James Biggs and lives at Frankfort, Ill.; children six.

William Pinkney Montgomery, eighth child of Isaac, lives at DuQuoin, Ill., and is in the U. S. mail service; married, at Benton, Ill., Oct. 17, 1875 to Eva J. Naylor, formerly of Walnut Hill, Ohio. She died Jan. 28, 1896; children three:

1. Augustine B. Montgomery, born April 1, 1877. He served in the Spanish-American War, in Cuba, in Co. C, 6th Ill. Vol. Inf.; married Cora Ragland, at DuQuoin, Ill.; one child—Paul Verne Montgomery, born Nov. 30, 1901. They now reside at Carbondale, Ill., and he is in the employ of the Illinois Central railroad company.

2. Minnie Montgomery, born Feb. 24, 1879 married Ezra Corrall Harris; one child—Gene Statan Harris, born Aug. 23, 1901.

3. Isaac William Montgomery, born Oct. 12, 1885, is now in the high school at DuQuoin, Ill., fitting himself to enter the U. S. naval service at Annapolis, Md.

William Pinkney Montgomery second married Alice Louise Wesmore of DuQuoin, Ill., Oct. 19, 1898.

Mary Eliza, tenth child of Isaac Montgomery, married Simeon Almon, Feb. 15, 1879, and resides near Stewartsville, Ind.; children seven: 1. Robert D. Almon, born Dec. 14, 1879; died Jan. 16, 1880. 2. Fanny E. Almon, born April 23, 1881, died Sept. 27, 1902. 3. Harvey M. Almon, born Sept. 31, 1884. 4. Ruthie M. Almon, born Feb. 13, 1887. 5. Guy A. Almon born Dec. 18, 1888. 6. Nellie L. Almon, born Oct. 8, 1891. 7. Charley M. Almon, born Aug. 8, 1894.

Henry A. Montgomery, eleventh child of Isaac, stock dealer, married at Benton, Ill., Bessie Osborn, June 1, 1882; one child— Ola Montgomery, born 1891. They live in Englewood, Kansas.

John Martin Montgomery, twelfth child of Isaac, married Olive Hart: one child—Hazel Montgomery. He lives at Steelville, Ill,

William Pinkney Montgomery, of DuQuoin, Ill., referred to above, says that Judge Thomas Montgomery, mentioned on page ___, was in the battle of Tippecanoe and that he married Betsy Warrick, Oct. 25, 1797, and had ten children instead of six; and we here give names and dates of birth.

Judge Thomas Montgomery again married, about 1818, Katie Teel, who was then the widow Williams, with two sons—Joseph, who was married five times and died in Atlanta, Ill., and Morgan, who died in Arkansas. By this marriage there were six children, making 16 in all. We here give names and dates of birth of the entire family:

Patsy, born Jan. 13, 1798, Eleanor, born Feb. 3, 1800 married James Roberts, Polly, born Jan. 25, 1802, Moses, born May 1, 1804, Malinda, born Oct. 30, 1806, John, born Oct. 30, 1808, Thomas, born Feb. 3, 1811, Betsy, born March 23, 1813 married Elisha Roberts, Nancy, born March 26, 1815 married Joseph Skelton, Jacob W., born July 17, 1817, Julia, born March 7, 1819, Lucy, born Feb. 1, 1821, Isaac, born Feb. 26, 1823, Henry Clay, born Oct. 13, 1825, Minerva, born Nov. 9, 1827 married Robert Sumner.

Catherine, born April 8, 1832. Of these children there remain living Isaac and Henry Clay.

HUGH MONTGOMERY.

Louisa Montgomery, a daughter or granddaughter of Hugh Montgomery, who was a twin to Houston Montgomery (page ___), married Joseph Garrett. They live near Maumee church, west of Owensville, Ind.; children two: 1. Belva Garrett, born about 1889. 2. Presley Garrett, born about 1895. Mrs. Garrett has a brother Houston Montgomery, and a sister Belle.

SARAH LULU MONTGOMERY.

On page ___, Sarah Lulu Montgomery (No. 8), born April 2, 1867, in Oakland. Ill.; educated in Southern Illinois College; married Thomas M. Morgan, June 7, 1888, who was born in Anderson County, Ky., May 10. 1853. He is an editor and author; lives in Colfax, Ind.; children three: 1. Paul Hunter Morgan, born in Paris, Ill., Dec. 21, 1890. 2. Ruth Morgan, born in Paris, Ill., Jan. 21, 1893. 3. Lucile Morgan, born in Kankakee, Ill. Jan. 21, 1897. 4. Mary Morgan, born in Colfax, Ind. Sept. 7, 1901.

Commodore W. E. F. Montgomery is (1903) in command of the English squadron in the trouble with Venezuela South America.

SUBSCRIBERS' NAMES AND ADDRESSES.

Anderson, Mrs. Mary J..Wessingtown, S. D.
Atkinson, Mrs. Myrtle....................... 360 E. Erie St....................... Chicago, Ill.
Alcorn, J. Grant...Poseyville. Ind.
Armstrong, Warrick... Owensville, Ind.
Armstrong, Pinkney... Owensville, Ind.
Armstrong, Willis... Owensville, Ind.
Armstrong, James.. Owensville, Ind.
Adams, Mrs. Ada.. Princeton, Ind.
Allen, Mrs. C. B.. Greenville, Miss.
Almon, Simeon L..Stewartsville, Ind.

Bohanon, Victor..Bagdad, Ky.
Bledsoe, Mary F... Warsaw. Kentucky

And Their Descendants

Bainum, Miss Hattie B..Carmi, Illinois
Black, George M...Oak Park, Illinois
Benson, Sylvester.. Owensville, Indiana
Barr, Andrew J., Attorney ....Bloomington, Illinois
Brown, Mrs. Mary Jane ....Oklahoma City, Oklahoma
Brumfield, Richard...Haubsradt, Indiana
Barr, John W... Atlanta, Illinois
Bennett, A. W... Princeton, Indiana
Boren, Dr. Samuel W.. Poseyville, Indiana
Bixler, R. B... Cynthiana, Indiana
Bahusen, Mrs. F. W.......... 723 Twentieth Street................. Rock Island, Illinois

Cooper, Mrs. Bessie... Midway, Kentucky
Crouch, Mrs. Myrtle L... Warsaw, Kentucky
Coons, Mrs. Emma................................... St. Joseph, Champaign County, Illinois
Cooper, Callie M...Fowler, Colorado
Crontz, Isabella W............. 711 West Sixth Street..................... Cincinnati, Ohio
Cambron, Mrs. Horace..... 723 Scott Street........................Covington, Kentucky
Carpenter, Mrs. Owen J... Covington, Kentucky
Crawford, Mrs. Margaret.. Princeton, Indiana
Clark, Isaac.. Owensville, Indiana
Carter, Mrs. Ella M... Abilene, Texas
Cobb, Mrs. Jasper..Greensburg, Indiana
Cockrum, Colonel William .... Oakland City, Indiana
Clark, Mrs. Ella.. Spencer, Iowa
Carpenter. R. P.. Oklahoma City, Oklahoma
Carter, R. E.. Abilene, Texas

Dean, Mary A... Milwaukee, Wisconsin
DeVol, Mrs. Jennie M... New Albany, Indiana
Dashiel, Mrs. M. D.. Greensburg, Indiana
Dashiel, Elizabeth...Delaware, Indiana
Darling, Mrs. Rebecca J... Gypsum, Kansas
Dickson, Mrs. Edwin F... Paskin, Wisconsin
Dawson, Mrs. Mary E... Yazoo City, Mississippi
Daugherty, H. C... Poseyville, Indiana
Daugherty, George Ellis... Owensville, Indiana

Evans, Dr. E. F..Youngstown, Ohio
Emerson, J. R.. Fort Branch, Indiana

Eaton, Theodore H.. Detroit, Michigan
Emerson, John W..Owensville, Indiana
Emerson, J. P...Cynthiana, Indiana
Fearnaught, Mrs. Laura.........49 Alabama Street...........Montgomery, Alabama
Files, William..Millshoals, Illinois
Fisher, Helen Montgomery..Huntingburg, Indiana
Frontz, Mrs. Sallie E. M......... Synodical College...............Rogersville, Tennessee
Fisher, Sallie.. Virgil, Kansas
Flourney, Mrs. L. M............. 428 East State Street........... Spokane, Washington

Graves, H. H... Mount Pleasant, Michigan
Griffin, J. W..Warsaw, Kentucky
Gaines, Mrs. H. L... Greensburg, Indiana
Guard, Mrs. Jennetta J... Lawrenceburg, Indiana
Glenn. J. A...Starkville, Mississippi
Gordon, William.. Owensville, Indiana
Hogan, Mrs. Belle F.. Jelico, Tennessee

Hathaway, Mrs. E. T..Denison, Texas
Henegin, Miss Madge W.........W. 524 West 15th Street..........Little Rock, Ark
Helm, Mrs. Elizabeth... Ghent, Kentucky
Heady, Thomas L..Ghent, Kentucky
Helm, Eugene A... Shenando, Iowa
Hollett, Rev. William H. ....Perry, Oklahoma
Harlan, Ollie McCormick ....Greensburg, Indiana
Hayes, Mrs. A. T... Lincoln, Illinois
Hight, Mrs. Cora .... Rural Route No. 3............................ Casey, Illinois
Hollis, Mrs. Sallie ....Princeton, Indiana
Hall, Mrs. G. Q....................... 2914 Eighth Street............. Meridian, Mississippi
Hickey, Mrs. J. M.................... 305 Roland Street............Greenville, Mississippi

Jordan, Mrs. Laura Henigin...Otumwa, Iowa
Johnson, George W.. Owensville, Indiana
Jones, William, Sr.. Owensville, Indiana
Johnson, Levi..Owensville, Indiana
Jones, Mrs. Permelia.. Midland, Illinois
Jones, William, Jr... Owensville, Indiana
Jones, Miss Maria... Owensville, Indiana
Johnson, W. D..Owensville, Indiana

King, Edward P., Jr. .... Atlanta, Georgia
Kinnan, Mrs. Jennie .... Shelby, Nebraska
Knowles, Rev. Wiley .... Madiera, California
Kelly, Dr. D. C. .... The Vanxball .... Nashville, Tennessee

Lewis, Victor .... Windsor, Missouri
Lewis, Mrs. C. E. .... Tyler, Texas
Leighton, Mrs. William .... Diamond Ranch .... Irwin, Idaho
Lindermond. Mrs. Molly A. .... Neal, Kansas
Landrum, Dr. John .... Campobello, South Carolina
Lowery, Elizabeth Montgomery Selser .... Edwards, Mississippi

Montgomery, J. Byron .... Jelico, Tennessee
Montgomery, J. C. .... Centerville, Kentucky
Montgomery, Joseph Ed. .... Warsaw, Kentucky
Montgomery, Hugh .... Warsaw, Kentucky
Montgomery, G. H. .... Warsaw, Kentucky
Montgomery, W. P. .... Montezuma, Indiana
Montgomery, John S. .... Georgetown, Kentucky
Montgomery, J. M. F. .... Owensville, Indiana
Montgomery, Henry .... Duvall, Kentucky
Montgomery, Judge H. P. .... Georgetown, Kentucky
Montgomery, Staiar .... Duvall, Kentucky
Montgomery, William G. .... Birmingham, Alabama
Montgomery, J. F. .... Shelby Street, South Side .... Frankfort, Kentucky
Montgomery, George .... Ghent, Kentucky
Montgomery, S. C. .... Ghent, Kentucky
Montgomery, Curtis .... Ghent, Kentucky
Montgomery, Jesse W. .... Carrolton, Kentucky
Montgomery, Colonel William A. .... Edwards, Mississippi
Montgomery, S. B. .... Quincy, Illinois
Montgomery, Galveston .... Easterday, Kentucky
Montgomery, W. B. .... Caneyville, Kentucky
McCreary, R. E. .... Eagle Station, Kentucky
Martin. J. J. .... Easterday, Kentucky
McDuese, Mrs. Lol. A. .... Warsaw, Kentucky
Montgomery, Dr. T. J. .... Owensville, Indiana
Montgomery, Henry, Sr. .... Atlanta, Illinois
McClure, Permelia .... Gibson City, Illinois

Montgomery, William..Cynthiana, Indiana
Montgomery, Miss Sadie L... Springfield, Illinois
Montgomery. R. H. Oswego...Labett County, Kansas
Montgomery, W. C.. Owensville, Indiana
Montgomery, George W...Tazewell, Tennessee
Montgomery, Samuel N..Cynthiana, Indiana
Montgomery. Dr. Martin A.. Owensville, Indiana
McMurtry, W. H.. Noble, Ill
Mauck, Jacob Warrick..Owensville, Indiana
Montgomery, Hon. Jesse M.. Cynthiana, Indiana
Montgomery, James.. Atlanta, Illinois
Moffett, S. E. ....New York Journal....................... New York, N. Y.
McFadin, F. G... Lexington, Missouri
Montgomery, Warrick... Atlanta, Illinois
Montgomery, Miss Mary E... Neodesha, Kansas
Montgomery, Charles Ed... Fort Smith, Arkansas
Montgomery, L. C.. Winston, North Carolina
Marvel, Mrs. Ella ....Waynesville, Illinois
Montgomery, F. L...Burdette, Missouri
Montgomery, Dr. D. N... Franklin, Oklahoma
Montgomery, James P.. Haubstadt, Indiana
Montgomery, James F. ....Frankfort, Kentucky
Matthews, Mrs. Jason... Lewisburg, West Virginia
Montgomery. J. I... Greensburg, Indiana
Montgomery, R. M. ....Owensville, Indiana
Montgomery, Miss Elsie... Owensville, Indiana
Montgomery, Rev. L. N... Clarksville, Tennessee
McKean, Mrs. Rebecca... Lincoln, Illinois
Montgomery, Mrs. S. A.. Greensburg, Indiana
Montgomery, Aaron... Owensville, Indiana
Montgomery, Mrs. Frank Hugh......5548 Woodlawn Avenue..........Chicago, Ill.
Montgomery, Miss Belle............422 North Franklin................. Greensburg, Ind.
Montgomery, James... Owensville, Indiana
Montgomery, Dr. W. T... Chicago, Illinois
Montgomery, William ....Middletown, Illinois
Montgomery, J. A. ....Birmingham, Alabama
Montgomery. M. A... Oxford, Mississippi
Montgomery, John B...Knoxville, Tennessee
Montgomery, Mrs. M. M.. Meridian, Mississippi

Montgomery, Miss Madge L..Meridian, Mississippi
Montgomery, J. Q.. Vinton, Iowa
Montgomery. V. V... Edwards, Mississippi
Montgomery, John G.. Durant, Mississippi
Montgomery, Frank ....Owensville, Indiana
Montgomery, Juliett... Glenn Summit, Pennsylvania
Montgomery, Joseph H... Birmingham, Alabama
Montgomery, John ....Lavernia, Mississippi
Montgomery, F.S .... Shepard, Ohio
Montgomery, Thomas H... Philadelphia, Pennsylvania
Montgomery, Bishop George... Los Angeles. California
Maxwell, C. F..Starkville, Mississippi
Maddox, Thomas Elmer... Tabor, Illinois
Mauck, Martha...Salubria, Idaho
Montgomery, Walter T.. Winchester, Mississippi
Montgomery, T. E.................... 315 Hunt Street........................ Cincinnati, Ohio
Montgomery, Willis E............................... (Owensville, Ind.) Marcus Hook, Pa
Montgomery, W. A................. 540 Unity Building...................... Chicago, Illinois
Montgomery, Alex.. Reynolds, Illinois
Montgomery. Mrs. R. S... Reynolds, Illinois
Montgomery, William... Centerville, Tennessee
Montgomery, Miss Elizabeth B.. Cadillac, Michigan
Montgomery, J. B... Springfield, Missouri
Montgomery, William A ....Jackson, Mississippi
Montgomery, Thomas S.. Palmetto, Tennessee
Montgomery, R. S. ....Palmetto, Tennessee
Mangrum, T. A....................... Rural Route No. 2.....................Princeton, Indiana
Montgomery, Colonel Frank A...Rosedale, Mississippi
Montgomery, Walter C. Sr... Sebree, Kentucky
Montgomery, L. F... Jackson, Mississippi
Montgomery. W. P... DuQuoin, Illinois
McKinnan, Mrs. F. B...Bloomington, Illinois
Montgomery, Miss Elizabeth J..Owensville, Indiana
McCasland, Charles... Ashland, Kansas
Montgomery, Henry Armstrong ....Englewood, Kansas

Newsom, William..Friendsville, Illinois
Nicholson, Mrs. Clara ....Orleans, Indiana
Neely, I. M. .... 1242 Sherman Avenue................... Evanston, Illinois
Noble, Miss Etta .... Paul's Valley................................Indian Territory

Philips, Mrs. H. N.	Poplar Bluff, Missouri
Powers, Rev. J. Pike	Knoxville, Tennessee
Philips, Samuel L.	Poplar Bluff, Missouri
Preston, Mrs. Arvenia ....602 Wing Avenue	Owensboro, Kentucky
Penn Hist. Society........Gregory B. Keen, Librarian	Philadelphia, Pa.
Pope, Mrs. J. W.	Starkville, Mississippi
Rybolt, Willis	Grant City, Missouri
Round, Mrs. R. A.	Clarinda, Iowa
Robinson, C. V.	Duvall, Kentucky
Roberts, Mrs. Mary	Warsaw, Kentucky
Round, Mrs. A. B......... 432 South Wyoming Street	Butte, Montana
Robinson, Mrs. Jessie Montgomery	Indianapolis, Indiana
Rhodes, Mrs. Alex	Lincoln, Illinois
Redman, Perry	Owensville, Indiana
Robinson, Sylvester B	Owensville, Indiana
Smith, Priscilla	Ghent, Kentucky
Scott, Elizabeth	Ghent, Kentucky
Satchwell, Nannie R.	Gex, Kentucky
Savers, E. B.	Erlanger, Kentucky
Sumner, Richard	Owensville, Indiana
Smith, George W	Owensville, Indiana
Stone, Thomas Jr.	Tolona, Illinois
Simpson. Mrs. Lewra A.	Owensville, Indiana
Smith, William W.	Owensville, Indiana
Sumner, James	Owensville, Indiana
Scott, Capt. S. W.	Elizabethton, Tennessee
Smith, Mrs. Henry W.	Owensville, Indiana
Shultz, Mrs. Nannie E.	Gypsum, Kansas
Stone, Oscar	Owensville, Indiana
Skelton, Thomas	Owensville, Indiana
Skelton, Levi	Owensville, Indiana
Sumner, Mrs. Permelia	Clarion, Iowa
Sloan, Mary E.	Belmont, Illinois
Simpson, Mrs. Jane	Owensville, Indiana
Scudder, Mrs. Mattie	Yeates Center, Kansas
Slaver, Annie W.	Lewisburg, West Virginia
Spilman, John	Chauncey, Illinois
Stewart, Mrs. Elizabeth Montgomery	Rock Island, Illinois

And Their Descendants

Smith, Mrs. C.B. ....Owensville, Indiana
Selser, Mrs. Kate L. .... 123 Griffith Street...................Jackson, Mississippi
Smith, J. Willis.. Owensville, Indiana
Short, Porter F... Owensville, Indiana

Thompson, Miss Jessie... Owensville, Indiana
Taylor, T. U. .... Austin, Texas
Taylor, Miss Margaret..Clare, Pennsylvania
Trible, Samuel N..Fort Branch, Indiana

Woolston, Mrs. G. A..Sugar Lake, Missouri
Wear, Julia E... Springfield, Missouri
Wasson, Elizabeth Montgomery...................................Lewisburg, West Virginia
Welborn, Mrs. Permelia .... Owensville, Indiana
Welborn, Mrs. Nora.. Owensville, Indiana
White, Mrs. Clara Montgomery….. 183 Cass Street.................. Chicago, Illinois
Weady, George H...Ghent, Kentucky
Waters, John... Owensville, Indiana
Weldon, Edward............Carrier Rural Route No 18............. Owensville, Indiana
Yeager, Mrs. Lilly ....Owensville, Indiana
(Supplemental.)
Emerson, Vivian H...Owensville, Indiana

INDEX.

A

Authors consulted -- Page 11
Ancient deed -- 160
Alcorns --200
Alcorn, Katie Montgomery -- 200
Alcorn, Montgomery and Jennie 201
Armstrong, Maria -- 165
Armstrong. William, husband of Emily Smith -- 281
A Pretty Romance Spoiled -- 440
Appendix to H. P. Montgomery's sketch -- 509

B

Better Feeling Among Warring Elements --40

C

Con O'Neil and Hugh Montgomery -- 30
Christian, Samuel, and M. Chappell -- 88
Casey, Colonel William -- 169
Carter, R. E. Abilene, Texas -- 173
Carter, Colonel Champ, of Virginia, Kentucky and Texas -- 174
Churchill, F. D. -- 116
Crockett Family No. 1 -- 329
Crockett Family No. 2 -- 335
Cockrum, Colonel William -- 363,437
Cabin John Bridge -- 446

D

Davis, Joseph M. (233), James B. (235) and Samuel N. (237) -- 91
Dashiell, John W. -- 93
Dean, Silas C. -- 113
Dashiell, Edward N. and Laverne -- 123
Daugherty, James -- 219
Daugherty, Jane and Frank -- 218

And Their Descendants

Descendants of Samuel Montgomery of Virginia, as prepared by Judge H. P. M.:
 1st. 2nd, 3rd and 4th Generations -- 69, 70, 71
 5th Generation -- 71
 6th Generation -- 77
 7th Generation -- 93
 8th Generation -- 124
 9th Generation -- 155

A Key to the Genealogy of Judge H. P. Montgomery:

Take No. 1585, page 157, Davis Montgomery; for his immediate ancestors see No. 1041 on same page, in or near center of page, and we find that his father was Nathaniel C. Montgomery. Now turn back to No. 1041. In the margin, page 132, and we see that the father of Nathan C. Montgomery is Lewis Montgomery No. 378 in the center of page. Now turn back to 378 in margin, page 99 and we find that the father of Lewis Montgomery is John Montgomery No. 98, in the center of the page. Now turn back to 98 in margin, page 80, and we find that John Montgomery No. 98, on page 80, is a son of John, No. 28 on page 79. Now turn to No. 28 in margin, on page 72, and you will see that John No. 28 is a son of Robert Montgomery No. 12, in center of page 72. Now turn to No. 12 in margin of page 71, and you will see that Robert is a son of Samuel Montgomery No. 10, page 71, and that Samuel is a son of Robert No. 4 on same page, and that Robert No. 4 is a son of William No. 1, page 70. You can take any name in this genealogy and follow it out on the same line.

Now reverse this and take William No. 1, page 70, and you will find his children, commencing with Robert No. 4 (see page 71), his children, and No. 10 is Samuel, the known ancestor of this branch. Follow up the entire Fourth Generation, page 71, down to No. 19 and you have his children: the Fifth Generation from No. 19 to No. 69 (on page 74), and you have his grandchildren; the Sixth Generation to No. 275, page 93, and you have his great-grandchildren; then the Seventh Generation from No. 275 to No. 886 (page 124), and you have his great-great-grandchildren; then the Eighth Generation from No. 886 to No. 1544 page 155, and you have his great-great-great-grandchildren; then the Ninth Generation from No. 1544 to

No. 1630 page 159, and you have his great-great-great-great-grandchildren. (See Appendix, page 509.)

E

Edwards, Robert (51) James (52) -- 73
Edwards, John (189) Samuel M. (191) Fredrick G. (190) -- 88
Edwards, John F. (577) Alfred (578) Fredrick (579) Zack T. (580) -- 109
Evans, Edwin F. M. D. -- 111
Emerson. James L. and family -- 188,182
Earl, First of Mt Alexander, Ireland -- 35

F

First Montgomery in America -- 69

G

Genealogical Succession from 912-1865 -- 19
General Remarks by Judge H. P. Montgomery -- 159
Gambrel, Henry, husband of Nancy Montgomery -- 263
General Information -- 443

I

Introduction -- 5
Introduction to Montgomerys in Va., Ky. and Ind. -- 163
Index – 521

J

Jackson, Francis A. (344) -- 97
Jones, Colonel Charles -- 267
Johnson, Levi, husband of Louisa Smith -- 283

K

Knowles, Joseph, No. 12 -- 282
Knowles, Asa and family -- 306, 308
Knowles, John and family -- 319

L

Large Families -- 49
Land Claimants - - 501

M

Montgomery Histories -- 5
Montgomery spelled 44 different ways -- 18
Montgomerys in Ireland -- 27
Montgomery, Rodger De, the 1st, 2nd, 3rd and 4th -- 18
Montgomery, Arnulph -- 20
Montgomery, Hugh and the Scotch emigrants to Ireland --30
Montgomery, Hugh and his lawsuits -- 32
Montgomery, Redhair and Loyalist -- 36
Montgomery, Sir James -- 45
Montgomery, Hon. George -- 46
Montgomery and Percy or Hot Spur -- 47
Montgomery persecuted -- 48
Montgomerys. Educated -- 57
Montgomerys in France --63
Montgomery, James Sproule, Samuel and Com. J. E. -- 74
Montgomery, John (28) Hugh (30) Samuel (34) -- 71
Montgomery, Elizabeth, no information -- 160
Montgomerys in many states -- 160
Montgomery, Nine bold brothers -- 48
Montgomery. 3. Byron (80) W. Graham (82) Galveston (76) and Anderson G. (83) – 79, 80
Montgomery, Hugh (96) G. W. (103) H. P. (105) A. J. (106) -- 79, 80
Montgomery, Arabella, wife of Rev. Samuel Preston -- 79
McCreary, David (368) -- 98
Montgomery, Capt. Richard (139) Bacon (140) John H. (141) -- 85
Montgomery, Hugh Sr. and Samuel Sr. contemporary -- 165
Montgomery, William, ancestor of Mark Twain -- 165
Montgomery, Hugh Sr., of Virginia 149
Montgomery, Samuel, son of Wm and grandson of Hugh Sr., -- 167
Montgomery, Jesse, Sr., and his descendants -- 178
Montgomery. Blind Sam -- 179
Montgomery, John, son of Hugh Sr. -- 181
McKinney, John, or "Wild Cat" -- 181
Mounts, Smith, (born 1770) and family -- 187
Mounts, Mathias -- 187
Mounts, Garrad and family -- 187
Mounts, Montgomery -- 189
Mounts, Smith Jr. and Thomas A. 195
Montgomery, Rachel, and Mounts family -- 187

Montgomery, Samuel Sr., of Va. Ky. and Ind. -- 188
Mauck, Jacob W. -- 199
Montgomery. Origin of name -- 13
Montgomery. Miscellaneous -- 51
Montgomery. Poets -- 57
Montgomery, Robert -- 71
Montgomerys in Revolutionary War --458
Montgomerys in War of 1812 -- 461
Montgomery, Samuel, Sr., of Owensville. Indiana -- 185
Montgomery, Polly, wife of David Swope, of Kentucky -- 186
Montgomery, Rachel, wife of S. Mounts, Sr. Owensville -- 187
Montgomery, Katie, wife of Thos. Alcorn, of Owensville -- 201
Montgomery, Robert. Sr., of Owensville, Indiana -- 205
Montgomery, James, Sr., of Owensville, Indiana -- 206
Montgomery, Benjamin, Sr., of Owensville, Indiana -- 214
Montgomery, Dorcas, wife of T. Stone, Sr., of Owensville -- 220
Montgomery, John. Sr. (Squire) -- 232
Montgomery. Samuel. Jr., of Owensville, Indiana --237
Montgomery, Thomas, Sr. ("Purty Old Tom") -- 245
Montgomery. Hugh, Jr. -- 246
Montgomery, Molly, wife of Mathias Mounts, Owensville -- 246
Montgomery. Judge Joseph, Sr., of Owensville, Indiana -- 253
Montgomery, "Roan Ike," of Owensville, Indiana -- 254
Montgomery, Colonel William, of Owensville, Indiana -- 255
Montgomery, Jefferson, of Owensville, Indiana -- 259
Montgomery, Jane, (wife Capt. Warrick and Dr. Maddox) -- 264
McFadin, John, husband of Betsy Montgomery -- 263
Maddox, Dr. John, 2nd husband of Jane Montgomery-Warrick -- 266
Maddox, Lucy, wife of Samuel Stone -- 265
Meek, Sylvia Jane (538) -- 140
Maddox, Polly, wife of Newton A. Wasson -- 287
Maddox, Thomas, and family -- 289
Montgomery, Judge Isaac, and family -- 292
Montgomery. Judge Thomas, and family -- 296
Montgomery, Dr. George B. -- 293
Montgomery, John R. -- 294
Montgomery, Thomas (born 1806) -- 294
Montgomery, Archilus and Harvey -- 295

Montgomery, Patsy, daughter of "Purty Old Tom" -- 304
Montgomery, Walter Crockett, Sr., Son of "Purty Old Tom" -- 305
Montgomery, Hon. J. W., and family -- 304
Montgomery, "Long armed Joe" and family -- 313
Montgomery, Isaac, and family -- 314
Montgomery, Dr. W. T., of Chicago, Illinois, and family -- 314
Montgomery, John Roberts, and family -- 315
Montgomery, Patsy Barr, and family -- 318
Montgomery, Nellie Knowles and family -- 319
Montgomery, Walter C. (born 1823) and family -- 323
Montgomery, William W., and family -- 324
Montgomery Andrew J., and family -- 325
Montgomery, Elizabeth -- 326
Montgomery, James P. and family --326
Montgomery, Miller -- 327
Montgomerys of Decatur Co., Ind., and "The Old Homestead" -- 345
Montgomerys of Davis County, Indiana -- 359
Montgomerys of Edwardsport, Indiana -- 360
Montgomerys of Seymour, Indiana -- 362
Montgomerys of New Albany, Indiana -- 362
Montgomerys of Gibson and Posey counties, Indiana -- 362
Montgomerys, Early, in the United States-- 362
Montgomerys of Pennsylvania and South Carolina -- 363
Montgomery, Captain John Henry -- 370
Montgomerys. "Boyne Water" family -- 374
Montgomery-Houston family of Pennsylvania and other states -- 385
Montgomerys of Pa., Tenn. Mo., Ill., and other states -- 400
Montgomerys of North Carolina -- 411
Montgomery, Captain Charles, of 5th New York regiment -- 411
Montgomerys of N. J., N. Y., Ohio, Ill., and Calif. --412
Montgomerys of Virginia and Mississippi --413
Montgomerys of West Virginia -- 414
Montgomerys of N. C., Va. and Tenn. -- 415
Montgomerys of Adair County, Ky. -- 417
Montgomerys of Hardin County, Ky. -- 418
Montgomerys of Shelby County, Ky. -- 419
Montgomerys of Va., Md., Ky., Texas and Tenn. -- 420
Montgomerys of Tennessee -- 421
Montgomerys of Claiborne County, Tennessee -- 422
Montgomerys of Ohio -- 423

The Montgomerys

Montgomerys of Illinois -- 430
Montgomerys, French Origin and Bishop George -- 433
Montgomerys of Colorado -- 434
Montgomerys of Canada --435
Montgomery. L. M., Gen. Financial Agent for U. S. Treas. -- 436
Montgomery, F. S. -- 444
Meigs, Montgomery C. -- 445
Montgomery, Prof. D. H. of Cambridge, Mass. -- 449
Montgomery, Frank H., M. D., of Chicago, Ill. -- 449
Montgomery, Henry E. of New Jersey City -- 449
Montgomery, John G., Member of Congress -- 449
Montgomery, William, Member of Congress -- 449
Montgomery, Col. James, Ohio, Kentucky and Kansas -- 450
Montgomerys, Miscellaneous -- 451
Montgomery, William Reading -- 451
Montgomery, Governor John -- 451
Montgomerys, Early in America -- 452
Montgomery, Col. Archibald -- 453
Montgomery, Commodore John Berring -- 454
Montgomery, Col. John -- 455
Montgomerys, Early in Tennessee -- 455
Montgomery, Gen. Richard, killed at Quebec -- 456
Montgomery, Lieut. James of Va., and his will (1808) --458
Montgomerys, Colonial services -- 463
Montgomerys, Revolutionary services -- 466
Montgomerys in French and Indian War -- 463
Montgomerys, Land Grants -- 463
Montgomerys of S. C, Tenn., Mo. and other states -- 471
Montgomerys of S. C. Miss, and other states, by Mrs. Judge G. Q. Hall -- 474
Montgomerys of S. C, Miss. and other states -- 482
Montgomery, Col. Wm. A., Edwards. Miss. -- 485
Montgomery, Hugh and family, of Miss. -- 492
Montgomery, Miss Margery L., Meridian, Miss. -- 496
Montgomery, William B. and family, Starkville, Miss. -- 492
Montgomery, Charles Robert -- 492
Montgomery Estate and supposed Fortune --502
Montgomery, James Hervey --509
Montgomery, Isaac and family, of Owensville, Ind. And Frankfort, Ill. -- 510
Montgomery, Wm. Pinkney --512
Montgomery, Henry Armstrong -- 512

N

Newsom, Harrison, and family -- 199
Neely, Gen. John I., and family -- 291

P

Paden, Jane, Nancy and Frank -- 285
Powers, Rev. J. Pike -- 421

R

Rump Parliament -- 34
Round family -- 113
Roberts, James -- 299

S

Swope family, Henderson, Kentucky -- 185
Stone family, Owensville, Indiana -- 217
Sumner, Robert -- 262
Sayers, James Bruce (607) -- 110
Smith, Warrick, and family -- 284
Skelton, Major James, and descendants -- 296
Skelton, Joseph, and descendants -- 297
Sumner, Richey, Sr., husband of Polly Montgomery -- 261
Sumner, Thomas. Sr., husband of Julia Montgomery -- 301
Subscribers' names --513

T

Titles of honor -- 33
Taylor, Anna Pendleton -- 88
Tippecanoe Heroes – 266

V

Viscount (1, 2, 3,) Montgomery of Ireland -- 32
Viscount (3) Montgomery's will and elegy—Created first earl -- 32
Viscount Montgomery, created second earl --32
Viscount's forces defeated—Vindicates failure and good name --32
4th and 5th Earl Montgomery -- 35

W

Works consulted -- 11
Wood Birch (120), George S. -- 84

Warrick, Captain Jacob -- 264
Warrick, Captain Jacob's descendants -- 265
Wasson, Newton A., and descendants -- 285

For more great books from our past, please visit the Historical Collection at our website. Thank you and have a great day.

WWW.BadgleyPublishingCompany.com

And Their Descendants

Notes

The Montgomerys

Notes

And Their Descendants

Notes

The Montgomerys

Notes

And Their Descendants

Notes

The Montgomerys

Notes

And Their Descendants

Notes

www.ingramcontent.com/pod-product-compliance
Lightning Source LLC
Chambersburg PA
CBHW071641160426
43195CB00012B/1324